D1491929

INTRODUCTION TO COMMUNITY RECREATION

Prepared for the National Recreation Association

GEORGE D. BUTLER

THIRD EDITION

McGRAW-HILL BOOK COMPANY, INC.

New York   Toronto   London   1959

INTRODUCTION TO COMMUNITY RECREATION

II

09358

PREFACE

This volume, like the earlier editions, meets the need for a comprehensive publication describing the nature and significance of community recreation—a rapidly expanding aspect of American life. The term "community recreation" is applied here to recreation programs and services that are provided for the benefit of all the people of a locality. Recreation developments in urban and suburban communities receive major consideration, but in large measure the material is equally pertinent to the village, town, county, or school district. Since local governmental agencies provide a large and increasing proportion of community recreation, this book is devoted primarily to the recreation services of these agencies. Much of the text, however, is applicable to those recreation services of private or voluntary agencies which are made equally available to all the people of a locality.

The striking expansion of community recreation during the past decade and the changes in American life, especially as they affect the recreational use of leisure, made necessary a thorough revision of the text. This edition records significant developments in recreation and related areas since 1949, brings important statistical information up to date, and describes trends in cooperative planning, leadership standards, program features, legislation, organization methods, and other aspects of community recreation. The many illustrations in this edition add to its usefulness.

The book is designed to serve the needs of several groups:

1. *Teachers and students in the expanding number of colleges and universities offering courses in recreation.* Background for further specialized study is given to students preparing for a professional career in recreation. An essential understanding of the field is also presented to students preparing for related professions such as education, social work, and government service.

v

2. *Professional recreation leaders.* Because the book draws heavily on the experience of successful recreation leaders, records local recreation developments, describes methods that have proved effective in conducting recreation activities, and outlines significant trends, standards, and procedures, it has value for all who are engaged in recreation leadership. As the title indicates, however, it is not an administrative manual or a treatise on detailed operating problems but rather an introduction to the entire subject of community recreation.

3. *Members of recreation and park boards.* In view of the responsibility resting upon members of recreation and park boards and commissions for the determination of policies governing the administration and services of their departments, it is essential that these officials be familiar with the nature, significance, and organization of community recreation service. The present volume is designed to provide the information needed for effective service as a board member.

4. *City and school officials and community leaders.* The operation of a recreation department and the provision of a community recreation program involve relationships with many community agencies. The text serves as a reference source for local officials or interested citizens concerned with some aspect of community recreation.

For logical sequence and facility of use, the thirty-four chapters are grouped under seven major divisions. Part One deals with the nature and importance of recreation, the agencies providing recreation—with special reference to recreation as a function of local government—and the history and development of the recreation movement in the United States. Part Two considers the importance of leadership, types of leadership positions, the training and selection of recreation leaders, and the place of volunteers in community recreation. Part Three is devoted to city planning for recreation, the design and equipment of areas, and the planning of special recreation facilities and structures. Part Four reviews the satisfactions achieved through recreation, presents a comprehensive list of recreation activities, considers essential factors in program planning, and describes various methods of organizing and conducting activities. Part Five deals with the factors and problems involved in the operation of basic recreation units, such as playgrounds, buildings and indoor centers, pools, beaches, golf courses, and camps. Part Six describes the major types of recreation activities, such as music, drama, sports, and crafts, and gives examples of the way in which these activities are included in community recreation programs. Part Six also explains recreation services to special groups such as the handicapped and older adults and presents a detailed picture of recreation programs and services in six selected cities. Part Seven deals with major aspects of organization and administration, such as legislation, organization of the recreation department, finance, records, research, public relations, and cooperative relationships.

What value this book may have is due in large measure to the fact that it attempts to represent the best thinking of many leaders in the recreation movement and describes procedures that have proved most successful. It also reflects more than a half century of service to community recreation agencies by the National Recreation Association, with which the author has been associated for forty years. In an attempt to make the text representative and widely applicable, illustrative material has been drawn from communities of various sizes in different parts of the country and with recreation managing authorities of several types.

A word of explanation with reference to a few of the terms used may be helpful to readers: "Community" refers to a clearly designated population unit, normally a political subdivision—a city, town, village, borough, or park or school district; it does not, as is sometimes the case elsewhere, refer to a cluster of neighborhoods. Similarly, the word "city" or "municipality," unless otherwise indicated, applies to any type of local governmental unit, including a county. "Recreation department" is used generically for any local governmental agency providing recreation service, except where a separate recreation department is specifically differentiated from other types of recreation authorities.

Preparation of this volume, which deals with such a wide range of problems, programs, and procedures, was made possible only through the cooperation of many individuals and agencies. Special thanks are due to the recreation authorities who shared their experiences, furnished materials and photographs, or reviewed statements relating to their local situations. Valuable suggestions with reference to revision of the text were received from several members of the National Recreation Association staff. The book owes much of its merit to those who criticized the manuscript of the first edition and whose cooperation was acknowledged therein. Mrs. Gertrude Luquer contributed invaluable assistance in preparing and typing the manuscript.

In expressing thanks one cannot overlook all those whose financial support makes possible the work of the National Recreation Association. Without the aid of these generous contributors the book would not have been written; to them the author is extremely grateful.

Introduction to Community Recreation will have served its purpose if it contributes in some way to a better understanding of the recreation movement, a higher quality of recreation leadership, and a more effective recreation service in communities throughout the land.

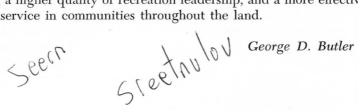

George D. Butler

CONTENTS

ix

Programs — Special Community Events — The Incidental Use of Recreation
Activities

PART FIVE. THE OPERATION OF AREAS AND FACILITIES

The Function of the Playground — City-wide Playground Organization —
The Playground Staff — Program Planning — Playground Programs — Some
Further Important Aspects of Playground Operation

Why Recreation Buildings? — Building and Center Operation — A Few
Suggestions

The Bathing Beach and Swimming Pool — The Golf Course — The Stadium
— The Municipal Camp — Winter Sports Facilities

PART SIX. PROGRAM FEATURES AND SERVICES

Program Characteristics — Playground Activities — Indoor-center Programs —
Special Arts and Crafts Centers — Other Programs

Organization of Games and Sports — Water and Winter Sports — Sports
Programs for Special Groups — Essential Factors in a Successful Program

Drama on the Playgrounds — Drama in the Indoor Centers — City-wide Organizations — Community-wide Services

Children's Activities — Youth and Adult Activities — Opportunities for
Listening to Music — Municipal Music Programs — Community Music Services

Nature Activities for Children — Nature Activities for Community Groups —
Gardening — Outing Activities

Social Recreation — Dancing — Hobbies — Study Groups and Forums — Holiday Celebrations — Community Festivals — Service Activities

Home and Family Recreation — Business and Industry — Churches — Institutions — National and Racial Groups — Special Age Groups — Special Services

PART ONE

RECREATION—ITS NATURE, EXTENT, AND SIGNIFICANCE

The many diverse opinions as to the nature and scope of recreation make it desirable at the start to define it and indicate briefly its essential characteristics. We also consider, in Part One, the reasons why recreation is increasingly important in modern life and how it is related to other community functions. After a review of the numerous types of agencies which in America provide recreation in varied forms, the place of local government among these agencies is treated in some detail. A résumé of the significant steps leading up to the present status of the municipal recreation movement completes this introductory section.

1. WHAT IS RECREATION?

THE WORD "recreation" is heard today everywhere. Yet widely different meanings are attributed to it, and it is applied to a great variety of activities. Because of this diversity in the use of the word, it is desirable at the very beginning of this volume to suggest an answer to the question, What is recreation?

Recreation is commonly referred to as a type of experience, as a specific form of activity, as an attitude or spirit, as an area of rich and abundant living, as off-the-job living, as an expression of the inner nature of man, as the antithesis of work, as an organized movement, as a phase of the total educational process, or as a profession. It has been variously described as refreshment, as diversion, or as the less serious and more passive type of playful activity; but these definitions are inadequate, too general, or too limited in scope. The term is sometimes applied to activities of young people and adults to differentiate those activities from the play of young children. Joseph Lee defined play for children as creation, or the gaining of life, and play for adults as recreation, or the renewal of life. In common usage, however, recreation has a more comprehensive meaning and is not restricted to any particular age group. As Dr. John H. Finley has pointed out, "the word 'recreation' is broad enough to include 'play' in its every expression and also many activities that are usually not thought of as play—music, the drama, the crafts, every free activity and especially creative activity for the enrichment of life." [1]

Activities considered recreation take a great variety of forms. To many people these activities might be fishing, sailing, camping, singing, skating, photography, dancing, or taking part in a play. Nevertheless, one man's recreation may be another man's drudgery; building a boat, for example, can be an ideal form of recreation to one, whereas to another it would be work. Even with the same individual, an activity that affords recreation at one time or under certain conditions does not always yield the satisfaction which makes it recreation. Sometimes a person feels like playing golf or joining a square-dance group; at other times he prefers some other form of activity. Furthermore, recreation takes a multitude of forms

[1] "What Will We Do with Our Time?" *Recreation*, vol. 27, no. 8, p. 367, November, 1933.

3

which have a varying appeal as the age, interests, and desires of the individual change. It comprises activities that are engaged in by a person apart from his fellows as well as others that involve group activity. In some forms recreation consists of active participation; in others, quiet relaxation, listening, or watching. The child playing in the sandbox; the girl keeping house with her dolls, playing hopscotch, or collecting butterflies; the boy making a model airplane or taking a swim; the young couple canoeing in the moonlight; youth hiking, dancing, or producing a play; the family on a picnic, at the theatre, or having an evening of music at home; the older people reading, playing croquet, or collecting first editions—these few examples suggest the wide variety of activities known as recreation. Like education, recreation is for people of every country and of every age.

THEORETICAL EXPLANATIONS

The many theoretical explanations of play and recreation which have been proposed over the years have been thoroughly described in other publications.[2] A brief consideration of some of these theories, however, may indicate the development of the modern concept of recreation and help in understanding its meaning. It will be observed that, whereas these various theories have not proved adequate, their inadequacy has been due to the fact primarily that they were partial and incomplete rather than incorrect. It is of interest to note, too, that most of these theories were based upon, and related to, the play of children rather than the recreation of people of all ages.

The surplus-energy theory—one of the oldest—held that play was the expression of "animal spirits"; that the individual was so charged with muscular energy that he could not keep still. According to the theory, therefore, play is aimless. This, however, is untrue of much observed play activity. It is also obvious that many people engage in recreation in spite of largely depleted physical or mental energy. Their motivations cannot be explained by surplus energy. A partially contrasting theory is the one which viewed play as recuperative activity, required for restoration of physical and mental energies and providing rest and relaxation after work. This theory may be applied to certain forms of adult recreation, but much of the play of children and young people occurs at the peak of their physical and mental energies.

The catharsis theory, somewhat related to the surplus-energy theory, views play as a safety valve for pent-up emotions, such as anger. Although it has some validity, the theory in no sense explains the nature of rec-

[2] See especially Elmer D. Mitchell and Bernard S. Mason, *The Theory of Play,* rev. ed., The Ronald Press Company, New York, 1948.

reation. It is negative, while much of observed play is positive. Furthermore, individuals under the stress of intense emotion tend to be inhibited from play rather than inclined to it.

Karl Gross [3] asserted that play is primarily a preparation for adulthood. It arises in the child as a result of the appearance of certain instincts that impel him to a great variety of activities—running, jumping, fishing, or swimming—essential to meet the demands of later life. Yet childhood is something to be fulfilled for its own sake, not simply a preparation for adulthood. The play experiences of childhood do contribute to the individual's effectiveness in later years, but they cannot adequately be interpreted as merely training for the functions of adult life.

G. Stanley Hall's explanation of play as the result of biological inheritance rests on his unsustained conception of "play as the motor habits and spirit of the past of the race." [4] His theory further contends that the growing child passes through a series of stages which recapitulate the "culture epochs" in the development of the race. It holds that in play the child at certain ages relives the animal, savage, nomad, agricultural, and tribal life stages and rehearses the activities of his ancestors. This explanation assumes the inheritance of acquired characteristics and makes insufficient allowance for the reconditioning of play interests and habits by environment.

Play has also been interpreted as activity called forth by the needs of the growing body. Yet numerous individuals play at tennis, golf, swimming, music, and drama after full organic growth has been attained. The theory obviously can relate only to children and youth; the relaxation theory, on the other hand, is applicable primarily to adults.

The Self-expression Theory. The widely accepted theory of play or recreation as self-expression recognizes the nature of man, his anatomical and physiological structure, his psychological inclination, his feeling of capacity, and his desire for self-expression. It accepts the point of view of Hart that the motive of life is to function and that "joy—real happiness, the thing people are after in all experience—is to act, to do things, to function." [5] The theory further takes into account the fact that the forms of activity through which man achieves this joy are conditioned by his mechanical possibilities of behavior, his physical condition, and his attitudes and habits. Thus play activities are those for which his body structure is well adapted, such as running, climbing, or singing. Man's inclination to activity and the satisfaction he gains from it at a particular time are also influenced by the abundance of his physical energy or the

---

[3] Karl Gross, *The Play of Man*, Appleton-Century-Crofts, Inc., New York, 1901.

[4] G. Stanley Hall, *Adolescence*, Appleton-Century-Crofts, Inc., New York, 1904.

[5] Hornell Hart, *The Science of Social Relations*, Henry Holt and Company, Inc., New York, 1927, p. 15.

nature of his desire for mental or emotional gratification. At one time he may desire strenuous activity, at another relaxation. Under certain conditions he may seek adventure through new experiences; under others he may crave the satisfaction attained through old associations.

According to this theory, recreation is a form of activity, an attempt at self-expression, resulting from man's urge to be active and to use his faculties and equipment to the utmost. It is through recreation that man finds the satisfaction of his desires to achieve, share, create, win approval, and express his personality. The great variety of forms which recreation takes is accounted for by the complexity of man's nature and of his social environment.

While the self-expression theory is somewhat general, it is in line with modern thinking. It is true that man seeks to express himself in work, in religious experience, and in study, as well as in recreation. However, in the first three of these activities, he often seeks rewards outside the activities themselves. In recreation he seeks no outside reward. Thus recreation is activity, self-expression, carried on for its own sake.

The fact that in the past "play" rather than "recreation" received major consideration indicates that recreation has only recently emerged as a recognized aspect of human life. In this book, the word "recreation" is used primarily because it is considered more inclusive and satisfactory than the word "play." The two terms may be used synonymously, however; for if the concept of play as self-expression is accepted as most adequate, then the spirit which characterizes the recreation of adults is much the same as that found in the play of children.

ESSENTIAL CHARACTERISTICS

Although countless, diversified activities are considered recreation, every recreation activity or experience has certain basic characteristics. One is that the person engages in it because he desires and chooses to do so, without compulsion of any type other than an urge from within. Fishing is the most alluring occupation for many a boy on an April morning; at the same time there is nothing his young sister would rather do than play with her dolls. It is this urge to take part in the activity that makes fishing for one and doll play for the other forms of recreation activity. Obviously the range of available opportunities from which to choose influences the degree to which an individual can satisfy his urge for pleasurable activity.

The immediate and direct satisfaction the activity brings to the individual is another characteristic of recreation. Playing in a string ensemble or orchestra brings to the violinist a thrill, a challenge, a sense of group membership, and a satisfaction which he gains in no other way.

The fourteen-year-old boy needs no further inducement to play baseball than the excitement, the challenge, and the fun which he gets from taking part in it. In recreation the individual finds opportunity for self-expression, and from it he derives fun, relaxation, or pleasure. Unless an activity or experience gives a person these satisfactions, it is not recreation for him.

A Matter of Attitudes. The varying nature and intensity of the satisfactions an individual derives from different forms of activity give the activities varying recreation values for him. The specific types of satisfactions are considered in Chapter 14. Because many people gain satisfying experiences from the same kinds of activity, such activities have come to be considered forms of recreation. Yet essentially recreation is the *attitude* which characterizes participation in these activities and which results from the satisfaction they bring to the individual; it is the spirit which finds expression in them and which through them contributes to satisfying, joyous, abundant living.

Dr. James S. Plant, the noted psychiatrist, has pointed out that recreation is "interested in the things which people are doing, rather than in the finished product. . . . It is in the doing of the thing rather than in the final result that we have the real elements of recreation." [6] In other words, an essential characteristic of recreation is that it is an end in itself and has value per se. This characteristic of recreation differentiates it from many other aspects of American life which are evaluated in terms of results.

Dr. Plant has further emphasized the fact that "recreation is an integrating experience for the individual because it catches, strengthens, and projects his own rhythm." In illustrating this he points to the difference between the tool and the machine. The former is an extension of the individual, is subject to his control, and moves on the basis of his own rhythm. The machine, on the other hand, imposes its rhythm on the individual who must adjust himself to its demands. Recreation, then, is more like a tool; it is in tune with nature and therefore is an essential part of living, of direct benefit to the individual. To have value as recreation, activities must be suited to his physical, mental, and emotional needs.

COMMON MISCONCEPTIONS

Because of the widespread popular interest in leisure and recreation, current literature abounds in references to these topics, their nature and significance. All too frequently they carry implications or present points

[6] "Recreation and the Social Integration of the Individual," *Proceedings of the Twenty-second National Recreation Congress*, National Recreation Association, New York, 1937, pp. 58–59.

of view that are believed to be misleading or unfounded, although they contain an element of truth. A few of these misconceptions will be considered briefly.

Leisure and recreation are frequently treated as though they were essentially the same or inseparable. It is true that for most people opportunities for recreation are largely confined to their leisure hours; recreation is therefore primarily a leisure-time activity. Because leisure is a time to relax, to learn, and to cultivate our vital powers, it is increasingly recognized as an important segment of the real business of life. However, unless an individual—or a community—has opportunities to use leisure hours for satisfying, constructive forms of recreation, it can become a liability. Instead of happiness and freedom, leisure brings boredom and dissatisfaction. As David Riesman has said, "Our inventiveness has not found ways of relating masses of men to creative activity or to each other outside of work." [7] Recreation offers a means of helping to achieve this.

The concept that recreation is the antithesis of work is held widely. It is true that for many people the hours of employment are dull, repetitive, boring, or exhausting. Relatively few people today find recreation in their work, but there are individuals whose vocation is so absorbing and satisfying as to make it a form of recreation. The late Thomas A. Edison, for example, gave himself so completely to creative work in his laboratory that he felt no need for recreation outside his working hours. It is not uncommon to find scholars or businessmen engaged in a new enterprise, whose work yields the kind of satisfaction that is commonly associated with recreation. In general, however, recreation takes place during off-the-job periods.

Closely related to the concept of recreation as contrasted with work is the frequently expressed opinion that recreation must be earned by doing useful work. According to this theory, recreation is not a natural or inherently essential part of living or a spirit that can permeate all of life but the use of a sort of recuperative interlude between periods of hard work. Thus it has been said that recreation epitomizes this "whole attitude of conditional joy in which the delights of both work and play are tied together in a tight sequence." As Dr. Alexander Reid Martin says, however, this concept smacks of a "retaliative eye-for-eye and tooth-for-tooth philosophy which leads to a vicious work-play cycle." [8] It certainly fails to recognize the significant nature and purpose of recreation, which cannot be earned and which is rather a God-given blessing.

Many people refuse to believe that recreation is an end in itself—that

[7] "The Suburban Dislocation," *Annals of the American Academy of Political and Social Science,* vol. 314, p. 144, November, 1957.

[8] *A Philosophy of Recreation,* National Recreation Association, New York, 1955, p. 6.

the joy, happiness, and satisfaction which give an experience the quality of recreation are a sufficient justification for it. They hold that recreation is primarily a tool or instrument for improving the mind, developing character, acquiring skills, improving health or physical fitness, increasing workers' productivity or morale, and achieving other desirable ends. Some see recreation as a means of solving or alleviating community problems. True, it has been demonstrated repeatedly that recreation can be a means of achieving these and other desirable individual and social objectives. Every individual knows from his own experience, however, that these are not the primary reasons why he engages in recreation. Fortunately the concepts of recreation as having value per se and because of its by-products are by no means incompatible. In fact, recreation activity is likely to bring greater satisfaction to an individual if it also contributes to his personal growth and to community betterment.

Recreation agencies and professional recreation leaders tend to consider the term "recreation" as applying only to socially acceptable and personally beneficial activities. Gerald Fitzgerald states, for example, that for leisure-time activities to be recreation they "must be morally sound, mentally and physically upbuilding, respectful of the rights of others, voluntarily motivated and provide a sense of pleasure and achievement." [9] Yet everyone does not use his leisure wisely, and many people turn to gambling, vice, and aimless forms of activity for their recreation. There is much evidence to support the statement by Nelson N. Foote: "It seems reasonable to believe that some kinds of recreation are conducive to optimal development of participants; some have little effect; and some are actually harmful." [10] It goes without saying that the many values that have been attributed to recreation apply only to those forms that are beneficial to the individual and to society. Furthermore, these are the only types of recreation that can justifiably be provided by public or community-supported agencies. In this volume only those forms of recreation are considered that have personal and social values. It must be recognized, however, that the public considers as recreation many other types of activity that deserve and receive no place in the community recreation program.

A final misconception of recreation is that unlike education it is essentially without purpose, discipline, or effort. In this respect it is identified primarily with relaxation or inactivity. Yet many forms of recreation involve a high degree of concentration, physical exertion, and mental application. David Riesman, commenting that the child's greatest satis-

[9] Charles E. Doell and Gerald B. Fitzgerald, A Brief History of Parks and Recreation in the United States, The Athletic Institute, Chicago, 1954, p. 127.

[10] "Community Services," Annals of the American Academy of Political and Social Science, vol. 314, p. 51, November, 1957.

faction in play appears to rise from experiences of mastery and control, stated: "Play seems to reside in a margin, often a narrow one, between tasks that are too demanding, and those which are not demanding enough to require the excited concentration of good play." [11] Because young people and adults likewise enjoy doing what they do well—and increasingly better—recreation is inherently associated with personal growth and includes many challenging activities. In fact, recreation has been called a functioning laboratory for the practice and implementation of leisure skills and of much of the content of the school curriculum.

A DEFINITION OF RECREATION

Expressed in terms of activities, recreation, in the author's opinion, may be considered as any activity which is not consciously performed for the sake of any reward beyond itself, which is usually engaged in during leisure, which offers man an outlet for his physical, mental, or creative powers, and in which he engages because of inner desire and not because of outer compulsion. The activity becomes recreation for the individual because it elicits from him a pleasurable and satisfying response. In short, recreation is any form of experience or activity in which an individual engages from choice because of the personal enjoyment and satisfaction which it brings directly to him. This concept emphasizes the personal nature of recreation and indicates why recreation activities are as diversified as the interests of man.

THE RECREATION MOVEMENT

Recreation is not a tangible, static thing but a vital force influencing the lives of people. It is essential to happiness and satisfaction in living. Through recreation the individual grows and develops his powers and personality. As Harry A. Overstreet has expressed it, "The man who plants his garden or plays his violin or swings lustily over the hills or talks ideas with his friends is already, even though in small degree, investing life with the qualities that transform it into the delightful and adventurous experience it ought to be." [12] Therefore it is a matter of public concern that recreation opportunities should be available for all the people. Because conditions in modern life, as outlined in the following chapter, have denied many people outlets for self-expression through recreation, leaders have recognized the resulting danger both to individuals and to society. Out of the realization of this need there arose the recreation movement.

[11] *Child Study*, vol. 31, no. 2, p. 9, 1954.
[12] *A Guide to Civilized Loafing*, W. W. Norton & Company, Inc., New York, 1934, p. 29.

In the words of its leader, Joseph Lee, the purpose is "to liberate the power of expression of people and communities . . . to help the men and women and children of America to find their voice—to set forth in drama, art, and music and in the hundred other forms of play what it is they have all along been trying to say which could not get itself expressed within the confines of their daily work." [13]

Defining the recreation movement, or differentiating it from other fields such as education, is difficult partly because recreation is so closely associated with forms of activity. Recreation and adult education programs, for example, include many activities in common, such as arts and crafts, music, sports, and drama. These activities cannot be classified as belonging exclusively in one field or the other. They have a place in both. Their differences are primarily in the attitudes of the people engaging in them, in the objectives sought, and in the methods by which the activities are conducted. Some of these differences are clear-cut and widely accepted; others are difficult to distinguish and are variously interpreted. The important thing to remember is that the recreation movement represents an attitude or spirit which finds expression in varied forms of activity and which brings a way of rich and joyful living to children, youth, and adults.

[13] Quoted in Augustus D. Zanzig, *Music in American Life,* Oxford University Press, New York, 1932, p. 12.

2. THE IMPORTANCE OF RECREATION

S INCE earliest times recreation, like work, love, and worship, has been a form of human activity. Festivals, dances, games, and music have always been a part of life, although at times they have been looked upon with disapproval by certain groups. During the past few decades, however, recreation in its various forms has expanded to an unprecedented degree. Extensive land and water areas have been set aside for recreation use; facilities for a wide range of recreation activities have been developed; new forms of recreation have been devised; a new profession of recreation leadership has arisen. The significance and values of recreation are being heralded widely in the press, from the pulpit, and by leaders in all walks of life. The desire for recreation opportunities is so widespread and insistent that the American people, even during a depression and a world war, spent several billion dollars annually for them.

Why has man always sought recreation, and why is he demanding it so insistently today? What are the reasons for the remarkable developments in the field of recreation, especially since the beginning of the century? What are the factors which have given rise to the widespread recognition of the need and importance of recreation in modern life? Why are the leaders in many other major fields of human activity turning to recreation for help in the solution of their own problems? In this chapter an attempt is made to suggest an answer to these questions and to point out why recreation is serving an increasingly important function in the life of the individual, the community, and the nation.

RECREATION—A FUNDAMENTAL HUMAN NEED

The preceding chapter made it clear that recreation is a fundamental and universal human need. Among all peoples and in all stages of history, man has found outlets for self-expression and personal development in forms of recreation which have a striking similarity. As Joseph Lee has said, in referring to the different songs, games, art, drama, and literature of the various nations, "The muses that have whispered to us are the same." Recreation is a common heritage of all peoples, although its expression takes varied forms.

12

In all lands, play is the chief occupation of the young child during his waking hours. Through play the child attains growth and experience; it is the major business of life for him. It is nature's way of affording outlets to the great biological urge for activity and the means of acquiring skills needed in later life. At play the child does a variety of interesting things with complete absorption.

As he grows older, other forms of activity make increasing demands on his time, energy, and attention. Nevertheless, as John Dewey has pointed out, the two dominant impulses of youth are toward activity and toward some kind of collective association. Both of these impulses find expression in forms of recreation. In adult life the duties and responsibilities of earning a living, caring for a family, and maintaining a place in human society tend to relegate recreation to a place of minor significance on the margin of life. Too often it is crowded out of people's lives or is present only in harmful or negative forms. Yet the urge for recreation is so fundamental and universal that it will not be suppressed.

Recreation Contributes to Human Happiness. In the last analysis, everyone wishes to be happy. Happiness was recognized by our forefathers as a fundamental and worthy objective for every individual. It can seldom be attained, however, by any one kind of activity. When sought consciously as an end in itself it is most elusive. For happiness is essentially a by-product which can best be achieved in a balanced life, and recreation holds an important place in the balanced life along with work, rest, love, and worship. Life would indeed be incomplete and drab without it. The significance of play to man's well-being was emphasized by Dr. Austin Fox Riggs when he wrote: "The function of play is to balance life in relation to work, to afford a refreshing contrast to responsibility and routine, to keep alive the spirit of adventure and that sense of proportion which prevents taking oneself and one's job too seriously, and thus to avert the premature death of youth and not infrequently the premature death of the man himself." [1]

In spite of the high standard of living in the United States, for large numbers of people much of life is drab, discouraging, harnessed to material things, and devoid of joy or satisfactions. Rabbi Abba Hillel Silver has repeatedly stressed the fact that because this is so there is need for people to create their own inner world where they can truly live during their leisure hours. Among the needs for real living, he cites "beauty, knowledge, and ideals; books, pictures, and music; song, dance, and games; travel, adventure, and romance; friends, companionship, and the exchange of minds." [2] Recreation holds its place of importance in modern

[1] *Play*, Doubleday & Company, Inc., New York, 1935.
[2] Abba Hillel Silver, "Recreation and Living in the Modern World," *Recreation*, vol. 24, no. 10, p. 531, January, 1931.

life because it has afforded and continues to afford opportunities for the attainment of these basic human needs.

Man is the kind of animal that must have adventure, excitement, and romance. The pursuit of happiness, the love of adventure, and the desire for achievement are great motivating forces which, for large numbers of people, are realized most fully in recreation. The sense of achieving and feeling alive is attained by individuals in various ways—while sailing in a heavy breeze, playing football, riding horseback, creating an object of beauty, playing a difficult piece of music on a violin, or watching the sunrise from a mountaintop. The significance of these experiences in sport, in art, and in the processes of beauty is enhanced by the fact that they "give almost as much of satisfaction in memory as at the time." Because it makes such experiences possible for large numbers of people, the recreation movement has been called "the nearest approach to a practical program for carrying into effect and keeping alive a philosophy of happiness."[3]

RECENT CHANGES AFFECTING THE NEED FOR RECREATION

Recreation has always afforded an outlet for self-expression, for release, and for the attainment of satisfaction in life. During the last few decades, however, the marked and rapid changes that have taken place in our social, industrial, economic, and political life have magnified the importance of recreation and have greatly affected the recreation life of the people. Some of these changes and their significance for recreation are presented briefly.

The Growth of Cities. The playground movement in America was a direct result of the development of large cities with crowded, congested neighborhoods in which children had no place to play in safety. As long as the country was largely rural in character, many of the simpler forms of recreation were available to all, even though many rural people had little opportunity for social contacts and fellowship, cultural activities, or even reading. Nevertheless, large open areas enabled children to play near their homes, while the fields, forests, and waters offered adults opportunities for hunting, fishing, and other sports. People knew their neighbors, and the occasions for working and playing together were not infrequent. In their work many gained satisfactions which today must be sought in leisure. The need for special provisions for recreation was consequently less urgent than today, when nearly two-thirds of the population are urban dwellers.

[3] Hugh M. Woodward, "Recreation—A Philosophy of Joyful Living," *Recreation,* vol. 31, no. 10, p. 587, January, 1938.

The growth of cities made streets crowded and unsafe for play; vacant lots were built upon, and the habitual recreation spaces were used for other purposes. Streams and lakes were polluted, forests cut down, and large areas closed to public use. With the complexity of city life neighborliness all but disappeared and living became more artificial and stratified. People became largely dependent upon special agencies to provide opportunities for outdoor recreation. Families moved out of the large cities into the suburbs to seek more open space, often to find in a few

This view of the Garden State Parkway in northern New Jersey illustrates the lack of recreation space in metropolitan areas (Courtesy of Garden State Parkway).

years that their new environment afforded even fewer recreation opportunities than their former city neighborhoods. The rapid spread of population into fringe areas, especially in the metropolitan regions, eliminated many of the recreation places formerly available to city dwellers. The seriousness of the problem is indicated by the fact that the rapidly expanding metropolitan centers now contain about 60 per cent of the country's total population. Man, essentially an outdoor animal, needs recreation spaces, facilities, and leadership to compensate for the loss of natural resources. He also needs, more than before, companionship with his neighbors and with others whose interests are similar to his own. Under conditions of urban living, opportunities for such companionship are found largely through organized recreation. \

Changing Home Conditions. Changes in the home as well as the community have increased the need for recreation. Labor-saving devices such as washing and drying machines, refrigerators, food freezers, electric lights, gas stoves, telephones, and vacuum cleaners, to mention only a few, have revolutionized housekeeping methods. The hours formerly spent in drudgery can now be used for other activities, including recreation. Children who formerly had many chores about the home now find few tasks to perform, and child labor is practically nonexistent. The oil or gas furnace has eliminated the necessity for shoveling coal and carrying out ashes—chores which in turn replaced the task of chopping and carrying in wood.

The rapid increase in the number of multiple-family dwellings has not only eliminated the back yard—the main playground of the small children in many neighborhoods—but also reduced the opportunity for indoor forms of family recreation. The garage has replaced the garden, and the automobile the family horse and buggy. The lack of indoor and outdoor space in many homes makes it necessary for children to seek elsewhere those experiences and values of cooperative and social activity which once they acquired at home. The playground, club, recreation center, and motion-picture theatre owe their popularity in part to changes in home conditions, especially in the cities. The commercial amusement interests have been alert to the opportunities and needs resulting from the lack of facilities for recreation in the modern home.

On the other hand, the importance of providing home and family recreation has been recognized increasingly in housing developments. The recreation room is considered a standard unit in many homes; the home workshop is a center of do-it-yourself activity. Play equipment helps make the back yard attractive for children of preschool age, and the home swimming pool, which affords a recreation center for the entire family, is considered almost as essential as the family automobile in some communities. Watching television, which has replaced radio listening as the chief form of recreation in countless American homes, undoubtedly absorbs more hours of a greater number of people than any other leisure-time activity.

Increase in Leisure. When man worked twelve to fourteen hours a day, six days a week, the problem of the recreational use of leisure, so vital now, was nonexistent. For most people, time for recreation was very short and opportunities were very few. But according to The Twentieth Century Fund,[4] the standard work week in nonagricultural occupations in the United States declined by more than a third—from 69.8 hours in 1850 to 40 hours in 1950. The Fund estimates that there will be continued de-

[4] *America's Needs and Resources*, The Twentieth Century Fund, Inc., New York, 1955, pp. 38–39.

creases to about 36.5 hours in 1960. It also reports a comparable trend in the working time of agricultural workers. The growing tendency to include a provision for vacations with pay in labor contracts has added appreciably to the leisure hours of large numbers of workers. The four-day work week, which has been predicted by leaders of organized labor for the not-distant future, will appreciably affect leisure patterns.

The acquisition by millions of men and women of extensive periods of leisure, which many of them had not been prepared to use intelligently, created a new social problem. Wisely used, this leisure offers promise of becoming a great boon to the individual and to society. On the other hand, it may become a liability if it is dissipated or a menace if it is used for unsocial ends. In this new leisure Joseph Lee saw the most extraordinary opportunity ever granted to a nation and at the same time the heaviest responsibility: "We may employ it in revisiting, in the woods and by the streams and at the playing fields, the ancient sources of our strength and may seek in the pursuit of beauty and of understanding our great inheritance, or we may spend the gift in the frenzied seeking of sensation and in barren pleasures. We may choose the path of life or pass it by." [5]

\ The volume of leisure is further expanded by the tendency for young people to stay in school and college for a longer period and thereby have shorter hours and longer vacation periods than if they were employed. At the other end of the scale, earlier retirement—in many cases, compulsory—is giving the American people more nonworking hours. \

Grave concern has been expressed over the prospects of a misused leisure, and unless local government and citizen groups take steps to prevent it, much of the added leisure will be wastefully if not harmfully used. Commenting on past experiences, Dr. Margaret Mead states that relaxations in the former "relationship between time spent in work and time spent in leisure do often result in boredom, apathy, frantic attempts to fill up the time, too much drinking, promiscuity, gambling, reckless driving, and so forth." [6] Yet there is evidence that people appreciate forms of recreation on a high cultural level and avail themselves of these forms if opportunities are made easily accessible and at a cost within their means. The new leisure presents a direct challenge to each community to provide for the recreation needs of the present and to plan intelligently to meet the increasing demands of the future.

Specialization and Automation in Industry. The changes in working conditions which have come about owing to technological inventions, the development of highly automatic machinery, and specialization of work

[5] Joseph Lee, "Leisure," *Recreation*, vol. 25, no. 2, p. 57, May, 1931.

[6] "Leisure in Contemporary American Culture," *Annals of the American Academy of Political and Social Science*, vol. 313, p. 13, September, 1957.

in both industry and business are well known. Today nearly 99 per cent of the total useful work energy of the country comes from machines.[7] \Although the demands upon the worker's physical and mental powers are less than before, as a rule the nervous tension is greater\ The worker at some repetitive tasks may still be fatigued in body at the end of the day's work, but frequently he is merely bored with the hours of dull monotony. Today most workers are denied the satisfaction which once came from creating an object. What is more, the degree to which they are controlled by the machine or the industrial system tends to develop a sense of inferiority and of nervous tension which is not beneficial to the individual or to society. The current advances in automation indicate that the need to offset this tendency through recreation may be still greater in the years ahead.

Man is not a machine, and his nature is not adapted to long hours of repetitive tasks.\For centuries man has been essentially an outdoor animal whose daily activities have called into play the use of his entire body\ Today the development and maintenance of a well-balanced physique must be attained for a large percentage of our people outside their working hours\ Psychologists have repeatedly claimed that for people whose energies are used mechanically and uncreatively, recreation becomes a matter of absolute necessity\'An additional reason why recreation is so important is the tendency for man to carry over into other phases of life the regimentation and standardization which characterize so much of business and industrial life. Recreation, with its freedom of spirit and action, affords an effective antidote for this unwholesome tendency\

Population Changes. The growth in population since before World War II has been much larger numerically than in any previous period of equal length, and there are indications that the total population of the country may reach 177 million by 1960. For several decades before the forties the proportion of children and young people in our population was declining, whereas the proportion of older adults was increasing. The marked upsurge in births during and since the war years, however, has resulted in a drastic increase in the percentage of children. As a result, an unprecedented demand for playgrounds and recreation programs for children and youth is likely to develop in the years ahead. On the other hand, The Twentieth Century Fund estimates that the number of people sixty-five years of age and over, and the proportion of the total population they constitute—12.3 million, and more than 8 per cent in 1950—will rise over the next two or three decades.[8] If this estimate proves to be substantially correct, the country will face the challenging problem of developing an adequate leisure-time program for older people, since a large

[7] *U.S.A. in New Dimensions,* The Twentieth Century Fund, Inc., New York, 1957.
[8] *America's Needs and Resources,* p. 62.

proportion of this group will be unemployed. Community recreation agencies are already taking steps to make life more pleasant and satisfying for older people.

\ A redistribution of population has also been taking place. Not only have people moved from the country to the city, creating serious recreation problems for the metropolitan areas, but also there has been a general population shift, primarily westward.\ Nearly one out of four reside out-

Creative crafts afford satisfactory and constructive activity for the leisure hours of older adults (Courtesy of Little House, Menlo Park, Calif.).

side their native states. Such large-scale mobility removes people from their accustomed environment, tends to deprive them of the feeling of belonging, and creates a sense of instability that affects both children and adults. \A well-balanced recreation program helps families become adjusted in their new community setting.\

The Rising Economy. The rapid and unprecedented rise in national income and the resulting higher standard of living have materially affected the recreation picture. The average American family, unlike earlier generations, has an income that permits an appreciable expenditure for recreation. Until recent years most individuals and families turned of necessity to simple inexpensive forms of recreation during their limited hours of leisure. The present national economy makes it possible for the American people to spend an increasingly large amount for amusements, travel, hobbies, and sports. The economy has made recreation, as pointed out in Chapter 3, a significant factor in the nation's economic life.

Technological Developments. The products of scientific progress have not only greatly increased the volume of leisure but have markedly influenced its use. The automobile has perhaps affected the recreational life of the American people to a greater extent than any other technological development. A Sunday ride to visit friends or to reach a picnic spot has become a favorite family activity. The construction of hard-surfaced highways resulting from mounting automobile ownership enabled millions of Americans to travel to more distant parks, beaches, and camping and vacation areas and stimulated the public demand for the acquisition and development of additional public parks and private resorts. The striking increase in visitors to state and national parks and forests can be attributed largely to the development of the automobile, which has become the outstanding means of vacation travel.

The airplane has only begun to exert an influence upon recreation, but the motion picture, record player, radio, and television are scientific developments that have revolutionized many of the recreation habits of the American people.

Other Factors. Recent changes have also affected the leisure of the rural population. The development of farm machinery and rural electrification have given the farmer and his family added time for recreation and energy for the enjoyment of their leisure hours. The technological developments previously mentioned have had special significance in rural areas and the automobile has made accessible city recreation resources that were formerly not shared by the rural population. The introduction of music, arts, drama, and sports into the school curriculum has a far-reaching significance for the recreation movement. Each year the schools and colleges are graduating a host of young people who have acquired skill in recreation activities. As a result of their experience, they desire and are demanding opportunity for continued participation in these activities. The change in the United States from an agricultural to an industrial nation, the decline in religious intolerance, advances in methods of communication, new pressures for conformity, the increase in the employment of women and girls, and the rapid expansion of commercial recreation fostered by the development of media for mass propaganda are other factors that have affected the significance of recreation in American life.

RECREATION'S CONTRIBUTION TO OTHER COMMUNITY FORCES

ⅼRecreation is a distinct phase of human activity, characterized by a particular spirit or attitude, which brings direct satisfaction to human beingsⅼ It does not function in a watertight compartment but is closely related to and integrated with other phases of life.ⵏThe value of recreation to the individual and the community is due in part to the contribution which it makes to other major human interests and forces.ⵏ The fact that recreation affords direct benefit to the individual and at the same time serves other constructive purposes explains why it is receiving such widespread recognition as an essential factor in modern life.

Many claims have been made for recreation as a means of reducing delinquency and crime, of building and sustaining physical and mental health, of developing character, of bringing about other desirable results. A word of warning needs to be given, however: So many interrelated forces and factors are present in every neighborhood or community that it is exceedingly difficult to isolate any single one, such as recreation, to estimate its influence or to evaluate the part which it has played in bringing about changes in the situation. For instance, a decrease in the crime rate after the establishment of a recreation center in a neighborhood cannot be attributed to the center except after careful consideration of housing, schools, churches, employment conditions, and many other neighborhood factors.

ⵏThe individual who has a rich recreation life is more likely to be a healthy, well-balanced, law-abiding citizen than the person who is deprived of recreation opportunitiesⵏIt needs to be strongly emphasized, however, that recreation is not primarily a means for attaining some objective such as health, good conduct, or morale, much as it may contribute to these endsⵏ The contributions of recreation to other community forces, important as they are, should be considered by-products.ⵏThe chief value of recreation lies in its power to enrich people's livesⵏ

Recreation and Health. ⵏThe fact that participation in wholesome forms of recreation contributes to the physical well-being of the individual is widely recognized.ⵏ Medical authorities testify that big-muscle activity stimulates growth and is absolutely essential for the growing child, and that athletic games and sports contribute largely to the proper development of the vital organs.ⵏCertain forms of recreation cause increased circulation, greater respiratory activity, better elimination of waste, and improved digestionⵏRecreation which is vigorous, which is carried on in the open air, and which makes use of the fundamental muscles is the best-known means of developing and maintaining healthy organsⵏCertain forms of recreation contribute to emotional stability by affording rest, relaxation, and creative activity. Others give tone to the body by a healthful stimulation of the nerve centers.

\ The value of recreation as a means of developing and maintaining physical health applies also to youth and adults. The building in youth of recreation interests which will carry into adult life has been characterized by Dr. Charles Loomis Dana as an insurance policy against nervous disorders, which when collected in middle age, will reimburse a hundredfold. \

The extent to which recreation contributes to the total fitness of youth was repeatedly emphasized at the President's Conference on Youth Fitness in 1956. This has been further confirmed by Dr. Shane MacCarthy, Executive Director of The President's Council on Youth Fitness, as follows: "We are convinced that no undertaking has a greater opportunity and challenge in achieving fitness goals for youth and adults alike than does recreation." [9]

Many physicians prescribe forms of recreation for their patients, but the effectiveness of the treatment is likely to depend upon the selection of the activity and the attitude of the patient. A study of 1,000 patients in two hospitals, one with a recreation-therapy program under good leadership and the other with no recreation therapy, revealed unexpectedly rapid improvement among patients in the first hospital. The average confinement was reduced by approximately 15 per cent in the institution where recreation therapy was an important part of the management. According to Dr. Joseph B. Wolffe, "Most of the patients have learned through such activities, both directly and indirectly, that they are not hopeless invalids and can return to normal life." [10]

In spite of the widespread and growing use of recreation as a curative factor, its primary contribution to the field of health lies in its value in preventing illness by contributing to healthful, happy living. The importance of recreation to health does not mean that recreation is a part of health or should be considered a phase of health education. The fallacy of considering recreation primarily as a tool for the attainment of health was recognized years ago by Dr. Richard Cabot: "When we give play, recreation, and the other popular arts their proper place beside the fine arts, we shall avoid, then, the popular error which degrades play to a medical instrument." [11]

Recreation and Mental Health. Today in the hospitals of the United States, according to reliable reports, nearly half the beds are occupied by

[9] "Recreation for Fitness," *Recreation,* vol. 50, no. 7, p. 244, September, 1957.

[10] *Recreation, Medicine and the Humanities,* Joseph B. Wolffe, M.D., The University of North Carolina Press, Chapel Hill, N. C., 1957, p. 11.

[11] "The Soul of Play," *The Playground,* vol. 4, no. 9, p. 285, December, 1910.

the mentally ill. Mental illness has been called the nation's number one health problem, and the rapid increase in the number of mental patients is alarming. It has been estimated that out of every twenty children born alive in the United States, one will at some time be hospitalized for a mental illness and one will suffer an emotional disturbance that will interfere with his well-being and general adjustment. Care of those in tax-supported institutions was costing well over $600,000,000 in 1952.[12]

It is therefore significant that national authorities in the field of mental health have asserted that the development of recreation and other resources that serve the leisure-time needs of people are of primary importance in creating a mentally healthful environment. Recreation is also used increasingly in the mental rehabilitation of the individual. People suffering from mental disorders have been found to react quickly to the stimulus of play. Music in particular, recorded in the Old Testament as a soother of troubled spirits, has been used with remarkable success as a therapeutic agent in institutions for mental patients. Crafts and hobbies are likewise valuable, and athletics have proved an effective stabilizing factor. Recreation was widely used in the rehabilitation programs at rest centers and hospitals for service personnel during World War II, and now has an important place in the programs at veterans' and civilian hospitals.

Dr. William C. Menninger of the world-famous Menninger Foundation, in commenting on "very rewarding experiences in the use of recreation as an adjunctive method of treatment," has said: "Recreation has not only played an important part in the treatment program of many mental illnesses but it has been a considerable factor in enabling former patients to remain well. Therefore, psychiatrists believe that recreative activity can also be a valuable preventive of mental and emotional ill health." [13]

Recreation and Character Development. Recreation activity, like many other forms of individual or social action, may be either constructive or destructive. It presents equal opportunities for lying or truthfulness, cheating or honesty, cruelty or kindness, and all the other vices and virtues of life. Many forms of recreation, especially activities of a highly competitive nature, tend to shape the attitudes and conduct of the participants. Recreation not only develops individual qualities, but it strongly influences the growth of social attitudes which affect the individual as a member of his group. In recreation there is repeated opportunity for expression of the ideals of sportsmanship or for violating them. Because this is true, the character of the leadership is of primary significance. Under recreation leaders of integrity and ability, people can be taught

[12] *America's Needs and Resources*, p. 304.

[13] "Recreation and Mental Health," *Recreation*, vol. 42, no. 8, p. 340, November, 1948.

respect for rules, fair play, courage, an ability to subordinate the selfish interests of the individual to the welfare of the group, and a capacity for team play. They also can be given valuable leadership experience.

The civic qualities involving the attitude of the individual toward organized society are also fostered, because forms of recreation—especially team games, drama, and music—require cooperation, loyalty, and team play. Through them children and adults may learn to recognize the rights of others and discover the meaning of freedom through cooperative action.\Recreation has been characterized as a force of tremendous consequence for the personal character and the national culture.\ Yet character development is not an objective specifically sought by persons engaging in recreation activities; it can be a natural by-product of such participation.

Recreation and Crime Prevention. Since participation in wholesome recreation helps to build character, recreation is obviously a potent agent in the prevention of crime and delinquency. Agencies directly concerned with this problem repeatedly turn to recreation as an effective ally. Because recreation activities have a strong appeal for children and youth, delinquency is less likely to flourish in communities where opportunities for wholesome recreation are abundant and attractive than in cities or neighborhoods where adequate facilities are lacking. Children or young people engaged in recreation activities on the playground cannot at the same time be robbing a bank, breaking into a home, or perpetrating some other crime. Furthermore, because the recreation leader helps them develop wholesome interests and furnishes opportunities for pursuing them, the chance that children will become criminals is materially reduced. The boy who "makes" the playground baseball team or who excels in the model-aircraft club and the girl who earns a part in the cast for the drama-guild play or who is a leader in the nature group are finding outlets for the normal desire for recognition, success, and achievement. They have little need to seek such satisfactions in unsocial ways.

Idle time is not an asset to any community. Most delinquent and criminal acts are committed during leisure hours, and a large percentage of these acts are performed in order to get the means for the enjoyment of leisure. Prison wardens testify to the desire of young men and women to do daring things. Many crimes are committed because people want to buy pleasures much less satisfying than forms of recreation which might be provided by the community at little cost. Studies have shown that a majority of children brought into court have lacked adequate provision or direction of leisure-time activities, either at home or in the community. Probation officers, police officials, and prison authorities in large numbers have testified from their experience that much delinquency and crime result from inadequate recreation opportunities. On the other hand, their testimony and juvenile court records offer conclusive evidence of the beneficial effects of wholesome recreation on children and young people.

Confirmed offenders against society need individual treatment before they can be enrolled in the community recreation program, but alert and sympathetic recreation leaders have deterred many a problem boy from a life of crime by taking a personal interest in him and encouraging him to participate in challenging, constructive recreation activities.

America's city children deserve a better playground than this! (Courtesy of New York City Housing Authority).

'The absence of recreation, it must be pointed out again, is not necessarily the cause of delinquency, nor is its presence necessarily the basic cure. Recreation cannot be expected to prevent or eliminate delinquency and crime in a community or neighborhood.' It must be allied with other agencies such as the home, the school, the church, and industry, if this is to be accomplished. Furthermore, it is not the chief function of recreation, any more than of education, to prevent delinquency. Through its positive value in developing wholesome personalities and social human beings, however, recreation helps assure a situation in which antisocial attitudes do not flourish.

The National Conference on Prevention and Control of Delinquency, called in November, 1946, by the Attorney General of the United States, recognized the value of recreation and emphasized its positive aspect. It adopted the principle that recreation is an important part of a living process and recommended that it be "presented to youth positively, with emphasis on his choice in free time and on his dignity as an individual, rather than as a cure-all for his delinquencies." [14] It further recognized that recreation "is one of the effective instruments for the prevention of delinquency. Recreation serves best as a preventive force when opportunities for wholesome recreation are provided for all youth everywhere."

Recreation and Community Solidarity. Many forces in modern life tend to separate people into distinct and often hostile groups, based on differ-

Members of the Aberdeen, S. Dak., community orchestra demonstrate their love of playing together by driving long distances to the weekly rehearsals (Courtesy of American Music Conference).

ences in their economic status, social position, race, creed, nationality, education, or cultural background. The natural outcome of this situation is a growing suspicion, distrust, and dislike of our fellow men and a lack of neighborliness and unity of interest. Recreation affords a common ground where differences may be forgotten in the joy of participation or achievement. Recreation is essentially democratic; interest and skill in sports, drama, or art are shared by all groups and classes. The young man who excels in swimming or basketball is recognized, regardless of his creed or color, by followers of these sports; and the woman who can act

[14] *Summaries of Recommendations for Action*, National Conference on Prevention and Control of Juvenile Delinquency, Washington, 1947, p. 42.

or paint scenery is welcomed by the drama group, without reference to her social position. The banker and the man on relief are found singing in the community chorus or taking part in the activities of the municipal sketch club.

An excellent example of the extent to which recreation activities draw people together from various walks of life is a municipal orchestra in which thirty-five vocations or professions were represented. Its membership included a broker, electrician, physician, boilermaker, housewife, salesman, shoemaker, beauty-parlor operator, manufacturer, barber, and artist—truly a cross section of the community. Among the members of the Clown Club in another city are people with such varied occupations as salesman, stenographer, engineer, housewife, auctioneer, and metalsmith. In many a hiking club the college professor, the factory worker, the salesgirl, and the office clerk tramp over the hills together.

Recreation workers report that gang feuds either have disappeared or have been converted into enthusiastic competitions through participation in organized games and sports. Demonstrations of the crafts, games, and music of other countries presented by national groups have done much to win respect for the foreign-born. There is perhaps no more effective means by which people come to a friendly understanding of each other than by taking part in cooperative recreation activities to which they are devoted. Any force which helps build such an understanding makes for a community solidarity that is greatly needed in the country today.

Recreation and Morale. During normal times and under favorable conditions, man needs inspiration to keep from becoming mentally and emotionally stale. In periods of insecurity, depression, and unusual strain, man is more than ever in need of activity which brings satisfaction and a sense of accomplishment. Dr. George K. Pratt has developed this truth in his book *Morale: The Mental Hygiene of Unemployment,* in which he states: "One of the two convictions essential to a feeling of emotional security is that one can do something really well. . . . It matters little what. Anything in the whole range of human endeavor will suffice— repairing an auto, managing the children, writing poetry, building a house, or mastery of a hobby of some kind: golf, stamp collecting, amateur gardening." [15]

It cannot be doubted that one of the forces making for individual and community morale during the prolonged period of depression was the increased opportunity for recreation afforded by work-relief programs for the unemployed. Recreation agencies have also won high commendation for their service in times of crisis following earthquakes, floods, and other large-scale disasters.

[15] *Morale: The Mental Hygiene of Unemployment,* National Committee for Mental Hygiene, 1933.

Man also needs outlets for draining off pent-up nervous energy. In furnishing opportunities for people to enjoy recreation either as participants or spectators, the community is providing a safety valve.

᾿The value of recreation as a means of building and sustaining morale was convincingly demonstrated during World War II. Comprehensive recreation programs for the men and women in the Armed Forces, leisure-time activities for war workers and their families, and neighborhood and community programs helped sustain morale on the home front. Leaders in government, the Armed Forces, industry, and labor testified to the contribution of recreation services during the war period. As President Roosevelt said, "The recreation services being provided for the Armed Forces, for the workers in war industries, and for the morale of civilian groups are very definitely contributing to our war effort." [16] Recreation agencies in communities near military establishments continue to open their facilities and programs to servicemen and their families. Military leaders repeatedly testify to the morale value of such service.

Recreation and Safety. Safety officials consider that adequate provision for recreation, especially in the form of playgrounds under leadership, supervised swimming, and winter sports centers, contributes definitely to the reduction of accidents. A single instance illustrates the relationship between playgrounds and children's safety. A Middle Western city of 65,000, because of limited funds, closed its playgrounds two weeks before school opened in the fall. Police department records showed that between September 1 and 12 children of playground age were involved in fourteen accidents, all of which occurred while the children were running or playing in the street. The report demonstrated to the local authorities that the increase in accidents was due entirely to their unwise early closing of the playgrounds.

᾿Recreation areas that are properly designed and carefully operated are remarkably safe᾿. A study of playground and playfield accidents during a period of one year in a group of Western cities showed that the ratio of accidents to attendance was only 1.19 to each 100,000 visits. Comparable figures have been reported by other cities.

Drownings rank high in the number of accidental deaths in the United States. Loss of life, however, is negligible in the hundreds of public pools, lakes, and beaches operated under competent management. A typical example is an Eastern city in which the municipal swimming pools had a total attendance of 1,600,000 during the 1957 season without a single serious accident. The hazards presented by unsupervised swimming and the danger of drownings resulting from the current boom in boating emphasize the importance of providing more opportunities for teaching

[16] *Proceedings of the War Recreation Congress, 1942,* National Recreation Association, New York, 1942, p. 9.

and acquiring aquatic skills. Recreation departments also contribute to public safety by providing and supervising ice skating areas, by teaching skills that are essential to safe participation in hazardous recreation activities, and by enforcing safety regulations on public recreation areas.

Recreation and Democracy. Democracy and recreation are alike in spirit, and each tends to promote and strengthen the other. Democracy is committed to giving each individual the opportunity to grow fully, express himself freely, and achieve an abundant life. Recreation, which represents activity freely chosen and which offers the individual opportunity for genuine satisfaction, creative expression, and the development of his powers, helps him attain the objectives of democracy. It contributes to his effectiveness as a citizen in the modern democratic state. Dr. Sherwood Gates has said: "In a society dedicated to the fullest possible growth of all its people, free time and recreation activities have an incomparably important place. . . . The vast and expanding field of free-time activities is and should be, even more than it is now, both the breeding ground and the practicing and proving ground of democracy as a 'way of life.' " [17]

Totalitarian governments have demonstrated the effectiveness with which recreation can be used to build a physically strong people and to develop a loyalty to the state. But in these regimented programs the individual participates as a cog in a machine and not as a free spirit. Yet it is in recreation more than in any other field that free choice counts. Participation in planning recreation programs and in the activities themselves affords experience in the democratic processes and in the give and take of successful group action.

Recreation and Education. In many respects the objectives, methods, and programs of education and recreation are similar, but they are not identical. The fullest development of the individual is sought by both; but recreation affords immediate satisfactions, whereas education aims at a more distant goal. The element of compulsion is present in some aspects of education; it is lacking in recreation experiences. Many activities, such as sports, music, drama, or arts, are common to both programs, but in education they represent areas in which skills, understanding, and appreciation are to be acquired. In the recreation program, however, the activities serve primarily as a means of using and enjoying skills and interests that have already been acquired. Yet educational growth is a part of every satisfying recreation experience.

Each of these major functions can contribute immeasurably to the other. In declaring that the training for the worthy use of leisure was one of the seven objectives of education, the National Education Association implied the importance of recreation and the need to prepare young

[17] From an address before a group of foreign students at the National Recreation Association, June 25, 1956.

people to use it intelligently. The emphasis which the schools place upon training in recreation skills and the variety of recreation experiences they provide prepare children and youth to enjoy participation in recreation activities after they leave school. The schools have thereby created a growing demand that more and more opportunities for recreation be provided by public and private agencies. As John Hutchinson has said, "The early and continuous development of leisure attitudes, habits, skills, and knowledges leads toward developing an educated judgment about recreation." [18]

Because the learning process is involved in many individual and group activities, recreation leaders are recognizing the need to become familiar with educational principles and methods and so bring maximum value to participants in the recreation program. In turn, school authorities are realizing that a recreational setting affords an excellent medium for carrying on the learning process and for achieving educational goals. Recreation therefore plays an increasing role in the school curriculum and in the extracurricular program.

The same activities are commonly included in adult education programs as in recreation; the primary difference is one of objective or emphasis. Self-improvement or the acquisition of new skill or knowledge, often to achieve an economic or social advantage, prompts many people to enroll in adult education classes. The enjoyment or satisfaction to be gained from participation in the same type of activity, on the other hand, explains why other individuals choose to take part in it as a form of recreation.

Recreation and Economy. One of the strongest arguments for municipal appropriations for recreation is that the investment pays dividends in dollars and cents as well as in intangible returns. When it is remembered that a city spends several hundred dollars per year to care for one delinquent, whereas a playground, which may prevent children from becoming delinquents, can be operated at an annual cost of only a few dollars per child served, the economy of providing playgrounds is clear. The saving of a single life justifies many times over the cost of operating a playground or swimming pool. If, as medical authorities state, physical and mental health are dependent upon forms of wholesome recreation activity, the city is wise which spends money for recreation rather than for mending broken minds and bodies resulting from inadequate opportunities for the recreational use of leisure hours.

Leaders in business and industry have long realized that the way in which their employees spend their leisure hours influences effectiveness on the job. Consequently business leaders have been willing to endorse local tax-supported recreation programs. The mayor of an Eastern indus-

[18] "Recreation in the Educational Process," *Annals of the American Academy of Political and Social Science,* vol. 313, p. 53, September, 1957.

trial city attributed an increase of 25 per cent in the recreation department's budget to the fact that the good will of industrial leaders, who are large taxpayers, had been built up for the recreation program. The availability of public recreation facilities and programs for the enjoyment and use of their employees and families has likewise been a high-ranking factor in the location of many industries. On the other hand, more than one city has failed to attract an industry primarily because it lacked adequate recreation opportunities. In a Middle Western metropolis of more than 100,000, a Committee of One Hundred, created to lessen the city's economic dependence upon a single industry, developed a community program which attracted thirty-five new industries within a three-year period. According to the chairman, "We are attracting companies with our new recreational and cultural facilities—two new swimming pools, seven new playgrounds, a storyland zoo, a much enlarged supervised recreation program including a senior citizens' recreation program, and an adult education center."

Real estate men and chambers of commerce are fully aware of the fact that one of the best means of attracting people to a community is by publicizing its parks, playgrounds, bathing beaches, recreation centers, schools, and libraries. Attractive recreation areas used throughout the year by children, young people, and adults are "evidences of a city's greatness quite as impressive as smoking factory chimneys." [19] Studies in a number of cities have indicated that recreation areas and facilities, if well maintained and wisely administered, have caused a marked increase in property values, thereby yielding correspondingly increased municipal income, and have proved a potent factor in maintaining a sound economic condition and a high standard of livability in a neighborhood or community.

It has not been possible in this chapter to treat fully the significance of recreation or to consider all its many and varied relationships. The preceding pages have indicated, however, why recreation has gained a place of importance in modern life and have pointed out several ways in which it contributes to individual and community welfare.

[19] Charles E. Hendry and Margaret T. Svendsen, *Between Spires and Stacks,* Welfare Federation of Cleveland, Ohio, 1936.

3. AGENCIES PROVIDING RECREATION

R<small>ECREATION</small> facilities, activities, and programs are provided by a multitude of agencies, many of which have been created to meet the demand for various types of leisure-time opportunities. Some of these agencies serve only their members; others benefit the entire community. Many are concerned with a single form of recreation, while others offer a wide range of activities. Some agencies exist for the financial profit which accrues from providing the public with recreation; others seek the enrichment of individual and community life. Recreation is the exclusive or primary concern of many agencies, whereas it is merely an incidental activity in the case of others.

⤙ A simple and logical grouping of these agencies can be made under the following headings: (1) governmental—those created and administered by Federal, state, and local governments; (2) voluntary—those supported primarily by private funds, which render community services, are non-exclusive in their membership or extend recreation opportunities to non-members; (3) private agencies, which comprise the innumerable clubs and associations organized primarily for the benefit of their members and in which membership is on a selective basis; (4) commercial agencies, including many business organizations which cater to the public demand for leisure-time activities and which have developed commercial recreation into a billion-dollar industry.

Local governmental recreation agencies share with the other types responsibility for serving the leisure-time needs of the people and must take account of their services in planning a community recreation program. A knowledge of the contribution which these various groups are making in the field of recreation is essential to an understanding of the scope and significance of recreation in American life.

INDIVIDUAL AND HOME RECREATION

† It is well at the start to remember the extent to which recreation activity is initiated and carried on by individuals and family groups. Many forms of recreation are essentially individual activities and are engaged in apart

32

from any recreation agency—for example, walking, nature study, reading, hobbies, creative writing, painting, sculpturing, sketching, gardening, caring for pets, woodworking, and collecting. Automobile riding, hunting, boating, and fishing, which attract millions of participants, also belong in this group. Many of these activities are more enjoyable when engaged in with a group, but some individuals have neither the desire nor the opportunity to share them with others. Participation in many so-called individual activities necessitates a considerable expenditure for equipment, clothing, or materials, but other activities can be enjoyed at little or no expense to the individual.

⅄ In spite of the many aspects of modern living that tend to take people away from their homes, the home is doubtless the nation's chief recreation center. Today's home, with its living and dining areas, family rooms, dens, indoor and outdoor patios, playrooms and workshops, devotes a large percentage of its space to recreational uses. The garden, pets, and the automobile play an important recreation role in the lives of many families. The back yard is still the daily playground of most children under six or eight years of age, and the home is where much of their indoor play activity takes place, whether it is quiet games, reading, playing with dolls or mechanical trains, performing on an instrument, or having a party. Among the many forms of home recreation which appeal to both young and old are watching television, reading, visiting and entertaining, playing cards and other quiet games, caring for the garden, pitching horseshoes in the back yard, singing or playing in family groups, making things in the basement workshop, and sewing for pleasure. Some of these are not available to apartment dwellers, but even in our large cities the home activities of many people occupy more leisure hours than forms of recreation provided by outside agencies. Nevertheless, the limitations of the home are such that many kinds of recreation are possible only as they are provided by the agencies considered briefly in the following pages.

GOVERNMENTAL AGENCIES [1]

Until late in the nineteenth century, Federal, state, and local governments considered recreation primarily a private concern and with few exceptions spent no tax funds for recreation. A striking change in attitude during the last half century, however, has resulted in extensive recreation developments under governmental auspices. Recreation is now considered a major concern of Federal, state, and local governments, which, through a variety of agencies, are contributing to the recreational use of the people's leisure.

[1] Many of the data used in this section were taken from the *1956 Recreation and Park Yearbook*, National Recreation Association, New York, 1956.

The Federal Government. Promotion of the general welfare, listed as one of the purposes of government as established by the Constitution, affords the justification for Federal activity in recreation. The role of the national government in the recreation field has evolved over the years, agency by agency, without reference to any over-all policy or pattern. Today a number of departments and bureaus provide recreation services to the general public, both directly and in cooperation with state governments. Federal recreation functions are of three types: operation of Federally owned properties that contain facilities for public use; provision of funds or advisory services to states and other governmental units on request; conduct of programs and operation of facilities for Federal employees, the Armed Forces, and personnel in Federal hospitals and other institutions. Space does not permit a description of the activities of all Federal agencies providing recreation service, but brief comments on some of the more important ones follow.

The Extension Service. The U.S. Department of Agriculture, through its Extension Service, has long recognized the importance of recreation as a part of its purpose of improving and enriching rural life. This Service, carried on cooperatively with state and county governments, has stressed the importance of recreation and leisure-time programs in small communities and rural areas. It has helped people appraise their recreation needs, organize to meet them, and develop recreation facilities, and has trained leaders to conduct activities for local groups. Through participation in extension programs, rural people enjoy such activities as folk games, dancing, drama, handcrafts, camping, wildlife study, and reading.

Much recreation is afforded through the 4-H clubs, which have some 2,156,000 members. It is one of the main activities in the 4-H club camps throughout the country; in the varied club programs, nature study, arts and crafts, music, and projects in conservation and school-improvement play an important part. The home demonstration agents, a group of Extension Service workers, contribute to better leisure living by assisting communities to plan recreation facilities and develop recreation programs. They help people acquire hobbies and recreation skills, introduce recreation at adult meetings, promote libraries, and conduct vacation camps for rural women. Because rural recreation programs must be conducted primarily by volunteer leaders, the extensive leadership training program of the Service is of major significance.

National Park Service. The National Park Service of the Department of the Interior was created to administer the national parks, which are areas of national scenic, historic, or scientific significance, so they might be preserved for all time and render the maximum benefit and service to the American people. The Service now administers some 175 national, historical, military, and battlefield parks, monuments, and other properties comprising nearly 24 million acres. The attendance at these areas more than doubled in the decade preceding 1955, when it exceeded 50 million. Facilities include tent, cabin, lodge, and hotel accommodations; bridle and hiking trails; boat docks; museums; and picnic facilities. The Service provides in many of the parks an interpretive program with conducted walks and tours, museum exhibits, lectures, and campfire activities. Areas administered by the Service are found in almost every section of the

Half Dome in Yosemite National Park, one of the properties administered by the National Park Service (Courtesy of Southern Pacific Lines).

United States, although the largest number and by far the greatest acreage in national parks lie west of the Mississippi River.

The National Park Service provides, upon request, advisory and consultative assistance to other Federal agencies, the states and their political subdivisions in planning their park and recreation areas and programs. It also cooperates in planning the recreational aspects of water-control projects constructed by the Corps of Engineers and Bureau of Reclamation.

The Service has developed an eight-point program of land acquisition, improvement, protection, and use, designed to give the American people a park system adequate for their enjoyment and inspiration. Known as

"Mission 66," this program is scheduled for completion in 1966, the golden anniversary of the establishment of the Service in 1916.

The Forest Service. Recreation is one of the most important resources on the 180 million widely distributed acres which comprise our national forests. The policy of the Forest Service of the Department of Agriculture has been to develop multiple uses of its areas consistent with the primary purpose of the production of timber and the protection of water flows.

Camping in the Gifford Pinchot National Forest, Washington (Courtesy of U.S. Forest Service).

The recreation objectives of the Forest Service are to provide the facilities and services needed by the people to enjoy the healthful outdoor recreation opportunities available in the national forests and to keep all public-use areas in safe and sanitary condition. Visits at recreation areas and summer homes totaled nearly 46 million in 1955 and represented more than 62 million man-days in the 150 national forests. Camping, picnicking, skiing, swimming, hiking, riding, mountain climbing, hunting, fishing, and other activities appropriate to the forest environment are encouraged. In addition to the facilities built through public funds, many resorts, hotels, organization camps, summer homes, and other structures have been erected by private capital under special-use permits.

The Forest Service has developed a five-year action program for the proper development of recreation facilities on the national forests. Called "Operation Outdoors," the program is geared to accommodate the nation's growing demands for outdoor recreation, and aims at meeting the requirements of 66 million visits by 1962. The Service cooperates with the states in the promotion and recreation planning of state and community forests.

The Bureau of Sports Fisheries and Wildlife. This Department of the Interior bureau assures millions of fishermen and hunters the perpetuation of their favorite sport by its protection of wildlife and propagation of fish. Many of its 264 wildlife refuges comprising more than 17 million acres afford not only havens for game but facilities for boating, camping, picnicking, and nature study. The 1955 attendances at the refuges were 7 million. In addition, a quarter of a million people visited the 105 fish hatcheries operated by the Bureau, from which millions of fingerlings are annually distributed for the stocking of streams throughout the country. A further recreation service is administration of the Federal aid programs for fish and wildlife restoration.

The Bureau of Reclamation. For many years the Bureau of Reclamation in the Department of the Interior has permitted fishing, boating, picnicking, swimming, hiking, and other recreation activities on its reservoir areas. Instead of developing and administering the recreation resources of its areas, however, it has been the policy of the Bureau to transfer them to other appropriate Federal, state, or local governmental agencies. In some cases the Bureau has allowed private individuals or groups to erect cabins or clubhouses and operate limited concession facilities.

Facilities for picnicking are provided at eighty-eight of its 137 areas; for boating, at eighty-six areas; for camping, at sixty-four areas; for swimming, at thirty-three areas, and for organized camping, at twenty-three areas. Boats may be rented at fifty-three areas; cabin sites may be leased at forty-five, and clubhouse sites exist at thirty-four.

A total of 9,596,400 persons visited Reclamation reservoir areas during 1955. A partial measure of the value of public use of the recreation resources created through the Bureau is revealed by a study which indicated an annual expenditure of almost $58,000,000 by out-of-state and local visitors to its areas.

Corps of Engineers, Department of the Army. Recreation and fish and wildlife conservation are collateral uses of many of the reservoir projects of the Corps, the primary purposes of which are flood control and navigation. Recreation facilities for public use make possible the launching and docking of boats, camping, picnicking, and hiking. The majority of these are provided by state, county, or municipal agencies or through private concession arrangements. In 1955 attendances at the Corps of Engineers' projects totaled 62 million.

Department of Health, Education, and Welfare. This Department has a Committee on Recreation, established in 1957, which coordinates the various recreation interests and activities of its constituent units. The Office of Education, for example, provides recreation services to state and local school systems, colleges, universities, and professional organizations. The Children's Bureau of the Social Security Administration has a continuing interest in the health and social significance of recreation opportunities for all children and youth. The Public Health Service assists Federal agencies responsible for recreation areas and facilities in dealing with problems of sanitation and the transmission of communicable diseases.

Other Agencies. The Bureau of Land Management, another Department of the Interior agency, administers 470 million acres of public lands on which recreation is considered a major land use. It makes available all suitable vacant land to public agencies, private groups, or individuals for hunting, camping, fishing, hiking, and similar activities.

The Bureau of Indian Affairs, also in the Department of the Interior, contributes to recreation through the use of Indian reservations for hunting, fishing, and tourist visits. Some Indian reservations have outstanding scenic attractions. The Bureau maintains three museums, and several tribal displays are also open to the general public. The public is allowed to fish and hunt on Indian reservations only with the permission of the local tribes. General tourist travel is not discouraged, since it provides an outlet for the arts and crafts of the Indians and helps to develop interest in and understanding of Indian affairs. However, few vacation and hotel resort accommodations other than camp grounds are available. In general, fishermen and hunters must bring their own tents or other camping equipment.

The Public Housing Administration in the Housing and Home Finance Agency, which is responsible for the administration of the Federally aided low-rent housing program, permits provision of indoor-outdoor community activity space in projects located in neighborhoods with inadequate recreation facilities. The Agency's urban renewal program affords opportunities for cities to acquire recreation areas as they implement plans for neighborhood redevelopment.

Among the responsibilities of the Tennessee Valley Authority are the development and use of the recreation resources of the Tennessee River and its tributaries. By 1956, 262,745 acres of its reservoir land had been made available to other governmental agencies for public access, recreation, and for fish and wildlife purposes. The TVA's program has made possible the construction of boathouses, camp structures, and overnight accommodations that have resulted in a constantly increasing use of the Authority's reservoirs for recreation purposes. Nearly 28 million person-day visits were reported in 1955.

The Bureau of Public Roads in the Department of Commerce contributes to recreation by making national and state parks and forests more accessible and by encouraging the establishment of roadside parks.

The Council on Youth Fitness, appointed by President Eisenhower in 1957, together with its Citizens Advisory Committee on the Physical Fitness of American Youth, is a notable addition to the Federal agencies concerned with recreation. The Council has recognized the important part which recreation plays in the physical and total fitness of youth and the need for expanding and extending existing recreation opportunities.

Passage by Congress in 1958 of the act authorizing appointment of the Outdoor Recreation Resources Review Commission was a significant recognition of the growing importance of recreation in our national life. The Commission is charged with responsibility for (1) conducting a nationwide inventory and evaluation of outdoor recreation resources and opportunities afforded by public and private agencies, (2) determining the amount, kind, quality, and location of such outdoor recreation resources and opportunities as will be required by the year 1976 and the year 2000, and (3) recommending what policies should best be adopted and what programs should be initiated by various agencies to meet such future requirements. The Commission is instructed to present its report and recommendations not later than September 1, 1961. An advisory council of twenty-five members has been appointed to assist the Commission with its task.

Another act of Congress that reflects the widespread interest in the cultural life of the nation was passage of the legislation authorizing a National Cultural Center as a bureau of the Smithsonian Institution. The center, to be constructed through funds raised by voluntary contributions, will be directed by a board of trustees with the cooperation of a national advisory committee.

Among the Federal agencies that provide recreation facilities and activities for their personnel are the Special Services of the Army, Navy, and Air Force; the Bureau of Indian Affairs; the Bureau of Prisons; and the Veterans Administration. Recreation associations have been formed in several departments to sponsor recreation programs for employed personnel.

The Federal Interagency Committee on Recreation. The recreation activities of most of the Federal agencies previously mentioned are coordinated through this committee, composed of representatives designated by their respective agencies. The committee serves as a clearing house for an exchange of information on policies, plans, and activities and for a consideration of common problems. It attempts to determine the place and responsibility of the Federal government in the field of recreation, to discover unmet needs, and to develop plans for achieving cooperative action to meet them.

Many leaders in the recreation movement believe that the Federal government should play a more vital role in the field of recreation. A variety of proposals for accomplishing this have been made. They call for the establishment of a Federal Department of Recreation or a Federal Recreation Commission, for giving official status to the Federal Interagency Committee, or for the creation of a Recreation Bureau in an existing department. It seems certain that, in view of the growing national significance of recreation, the role of the Federal government in this field will receive increasing consideration in the years ahead.

The State Governments. With notable exceptions, state governments showed little concern for providing recreation before World War II. Many states had acquired and developed park systems, in some instances prompted by the availability of emergency funds during the 1930s. Other programs which included recreation were carried on by the extension departments of state universities. Actions taken by state agencies, however, were usually unrelated to any over-all recreation plan or policy. Today practically every state has parks, and many provide some form of recreation service through a variety of agencies.

State forests, parks, game refuges, and other areas total more than 39 million acres. State parks alone, the primary function of which is recreation, numbered over 2,000 in 1955 and had a total area of 2.5 million acres. Many reservoirs, historic sites, and museums serve recreation needs; state forests have a much greater potential than actual recreation use. Attendances in 1955 at state parks alone exceeded 180 million or double the number served ten years earlier. Most frequently reported activities in state parks are picnicking, fishing, camping, swimming, boating, and hiking, with an increasing emphasis upon interpretive services.

The provision of various types of recreation service to local communities is a significant recent development. Supplementing the services rendered for many years by the Department of Agriculture's Federal Extension Service with its training courses, conferences, resource materials, and consultation service are those provided by state education departments and state colleges and universities, a number of which also conduct local recreation surveys. Library departments provide traveling libraries, planning departments furnish consultation service to localities, and health departments regulate community swimming facilities.

The need for coordinating state recreation services has prompted the formation in several states of an interagency committee on recreation which affords a medium for the exchange of information, discussion of common problems, and cooperative planning by interested state authorities. For a number of years recreation commissions in California, North Carolina, and Vermont have rendered a wide variety of services. In a few states youth, education, and welfare agencies have a major concern for recreation at the local level. Persons in state hospitals, prisons, detention homes, children's centers, and other institutions are increasingly served through the provision of leaders, facilities, and programs.

Bird's-eye view of lake and bathhouse, Vogel State Park, Blairsville, Ga.

⋎ **Local Agencies.** Local governmental units—counties, cities, boroughs, townships, villages, school and other special districts—provide a large percentage of the day-by-day year-round recreation service made available by public agencies. Most of their facilities are fairly near the homes of the people they are intended to serve and are therefore used more frequently and intensively than state and Federal areas. The local programs usually include a greater variety of activities than those provided by other governmental agencies. More than 20,000 park and nonschool recreation areas, comprising nearly 750,000 acres, were reported in 1956 by 1,907 counties and municipalities. Although this book is devoted primarily to a consideration of local public recreation agencies and their services, a brief description of their general contribution to recreation in America follows.

༡ *County Agencies.* Taking the country as a whole, the county has played a minor part in the public recreation picture, but in recent years the importance of park and recreation service has been recognized by more and more county authorities. The *1956 Recreation and Park Yearbook* [2] contained reports from 190 counties that provided parks and/or recreation programs. Most county parks are relatively small in comparison with state and national parks, but in general they are more highly developed and receive more intensive use. This is especially true of areas close to or within the boundaries of large cities. Common facilities include picnic centers, tennis courts, bathing beaches, baseball diamonds, swimming pools, winter sports facilities, golf courses, children's playgrounds, and hiking, bridle, and nature trails. The most outstanding county park systems are in counties with metropolitan cities such as Milwaukee, Cleveland, and Chicago, though some county parks serve distinctly rural areas.

County-wide recreation programs under leadership have been undertaken by relatively few counties, but there is a growing tendency to initiate some form of recreation service. Union County, New Jersey, and Los Angeles County, California, furnish outstanding examples of a successful program administered under county auspices. In Westchester County, New York, widely known for its park system, a county recreation commission for many years has conducted a variety of county-wide activities and has assisted communities in the development of their recreation services. Jefferson County, Kentucky, has a typical rural program.

Recently established county programs vary in scope from the promotion of a few seasonal activities to the operation of indoor and outdoor centers and the furnishing of county-wide services under full-time leaders. Responsibility for the program is usually assigned to a recreation board or commission, as authorized under recreation enabling acts in many states. The joint administration or financing of recreation programs by county and local authorities has been achieved in several counties. Cooperation by counties in the program of the Extension Service is widespread.

༡ *Municipal Agencies.* Recreation and park departments furnish a majority of municipal recreation programs, although a considerable number of school authorities perform this function, and in some localities other departments have a place in the recreation picture. In the larger cities there are few recreation interests which cannot find outlets for expression in the services provided by the municipal agencies. Large sections of the population use their facilities and participate in their programs, many of which are available without direct cost to the individuals enjoying them.

Community recreation services of park, school, and recreation departments are similar in many respects, and playground and indoor-center

[2] National Recreation Association, New York, 1956.

activities are essentially the same whether conducted under park, recreation, or school department auspices. Programs are not standardized, but vary according to the interests, desires, resources, and needs of the individual community. The brief description that follows will be supplemented in later chapters.

The recreation services of municipal agencies usually comprise (1) the provision of areas and facilities that are available for informal or organized use; (2) the employment of leadership personnel that organize and conduct outdoor and indoor activities, primarily on properties under public ownership; (3) the promotion and organization of community-wide programs and events, often in cooperation with other agencies; and (4) the provision of materials and advisory services for the benefit of local individuals and organizations.

Municipal park and recreation properties have been developed for a variety of recreation uses and are enjoyed by people of all ages. Activities include picnicking by individuals or groups; boating or canoeing on streams or lakes; swimming, diving, and water sports at pools and beaches; skating, skiing, and tobogganing at ponds, hills, rinks, or specially constructed facilities; hiking along park trails; horseback riding on bridle trails; playing golf, tennis, archery, baseball, handball, or horseshoes; bowling on the green; testing one's skill at trapshooting ranges; dancing in outdoor lighted pavilions; listening to band concerts; observing animal, fish, or plant life at the zoo, aquarium, or botanical garden or along the nature trail; taking part in or listening to plays, pageants, or operettas in an outdoor theatre; and enjoying the beauty of a park landscape. The richness, variety, and value of these activities, most of them carried on out of doors, are obvious.

Typical of the program features made possible by leadership personnel are the conduct of diversified activities at the playground or indoor recreation center; organizing and supervising city-wide athletic programs with teams in baseball, soccer, softball, volleyball, fieldball, football, or ice hockey; organizing choral societies or symphony orchestras where amateur musicians can sing or play for the joy of participation; conducting city-wide learn-to-swim campaigns, gift-making classes, one-act-play tournaments, community holiday celebrations, playdays for industrial women and girls, and municipal tournaments in tennis, horseshoes, archery, fly casting, swimming, and other sports; assisting in the organization of programs for industrial and mercantile workers; sponsoring back-yard playground contests; providing entertainment programs at city institutions; sponsoring hiking, nature, and garden clubs; and organizing groups around various hobby interests such as photography, crafts, or puppetry.

Other special services of municipal agencies are arranging institutes at which individuals may learn the techniques of game leading, play production, or party planning; maintaining a costume library for use in local drama presentations; providing a picnic- or party-equipment loan service; cosponsoring community holiday celebrations or advising individuals and groups in planning and conducting recreation activities. There are comparatively few forms of recreation service or interest that do not fall within the scope of the municipal recreation agency.

✗ THE PUBLIC LIBRARY. The primary function of the library is to provide opportunities for reading—the most common of all recreation activities. The library not only supplies books and magazines for people to read but it offers guidance in the selection of suitable reading material and literature dealing with all forms of hobbies and leisure-time pursuits. It is a community storehouse of avocational information. The library prepares reading lists and exhibits of timely hobbies and recreation activities and its bulletin board carries announcements of cultural and recreation events and opportunities. In many cities storytelling hours are regularly conducted for children at the library; in others storytellers are sent to the playgrounds. Occasionally special craft groups or dramatic activities are a part of the library program.

Library buildings are being equipped with auditoriums and lecture halls which are available to study groups, discussion clubs, and radio-listening groups and for forums, musicales, exhibits of all kinds, lectures, and educational movies. Other special library services are the operation of outdoor libraries in city parks, branch or traveling libraries at city playgrounds, and the libraries-on-wheels which have proved so valuable and popular in rural counties. Some libraries maintain collections of plays and of vocal and instrumental music which are lent to individuals and community groups.

✗ THE MUSEUM. The museum is a building in which are displayed works of art or collections of natural, scientific, literary, or historic interest. In many cities museums are located on public property, although they are commonly administered by a quasi-public agency and financed primarily from private funds. At the art museum, masterpieces in painting, sculpture, and other art forms can be enjoyed by all the people. At the natural-history museum, people learn about life in other lands, observe earlier cultures, and study forms of plant and animal life under varying conditions. Historical museums record the early story of the city, state, or region. The highly popular zoological and botanical gardens belong, in a sense, under this general category; many of them are administered by the municipal recreation agency.

Among the valuable recreation and cultural services the museum authorities render the community are afternoon and evening concerts by outstanding artists; lecture courses for children and adults on travel, science, art, music, and special subjects related to museum projects; workshops for classes and for informal participation in sketching, painting, modeling, crafts, and hobbies; junior nature clubs, collections, hikes, and trips; children's gardens; music appreciation and listening groups; field trips; children's story hours; industrial, craft, and special exhibits, and camera clubs. The use of museum auditoriums, workrooms, and other facilities is occasionally granted to local civic, cultural, nature, and other organizations.

In these ways the museum of today not only is creating a greater appreciation of its own work and program but is also developing interests, abilities, and hobbies which are enriching the lives of an ever-widening group of people.

OTHER MUNICIPAL AGENCIES. As previously stated, there are other city departments that play a part in the city's recreation life. Police departments, for example, have established centers and activities for boys and young men in neighborhoods where recreation facilities are lacking. Water department properties have been developed and made available for golf, picnicking, fishing, hiking, and related activities. Housing authorities have provided outdoor and indoor recreation facilities in many developments. Ways in which other municipal agencies are helping provide recreation opportunities are described in Chapter 34.

VOLUNTARY AGENCIES

Recreation has a prominent place in the programs of most voluntary agencies, which include the YMCA, the YWCA, the Catholic Youth Organization, Jewish community centers, boys' clubs, settlements, Boy Scouts, Girl Scouts, Camp Fire Girls, and many others. These agencies serve varying age groups—children, young people, and adults. They operate largely on a membership basis, but membership is seldom exclusive, and in some cases participation in parts of the program is not restricted to members. The cost of financing the facilities and program is largely met through contributions from individuals or community chests and from membership fees. A number of these agencies which constitute a significant force in leisure-time service are mentioned here.

The Settlement or Neighborhood House. This is a multifunctional agency that serves the social needs including recreation of people living in a given neighborhood—in many cases where living conditions are substandard. The settlement's welfare features, its resident staff, and the various services which comprise its program tend to differentiate the settlement from the recreation center. It serves both individuals and groups—children, young people, and adults.

Since its early days the settlement has emphasized the development of cultural skills. It was a pioneer in the little-theater movement, and many settlement buildings have auditoriums with stages well equipped for dramatic and musical productions. Plays are studied, written, and completely produced by drama-workshop groups. Music is a regular feature of many settlement functions; and in addition, music classes in various instruments, vocal instruction, and group music activities are a part of the program. Gymnasiums are used for a variety of games, gymnastics, and athletic events. Arts and crafts groups, utilizing the special aptitudes and techniques of foreign-born members, produce objects of remarkable beauty. Forums or discussion groups are arranged for the consideration of topics of special interest or significance. Summer camps afford opportunities to engage in woodcraft, nature study, and other outdoor activities seldom otherwise available to the people served by the settlement. The National Federation of Settlements and Neighborhood Centers, with 258 member centers, is the national organization serving such agencies.

Youth Service Organizations. Typical of the agencies in this group are the YMCA, the YWCA, the Catholic Youth Organization, and the Jewish community centers. Although the primary purpose of these organizations is the building of religious life, one of their objectives is the development of interests and skills essential to the enrichment of leisure. Their well-equipped buildings afford facilities for a wide range of recreation activities and social relationships, participation in which is extended to young men and young women. The magnitude of their services is indicated by the fact that in 1956 the YMCA reported 1,820 local associations with a membership of 2,212,618. Among the features of the YMCA program are its Hi-Y organization for high school boys, its activities for industrial workers, and its leadership in the fields of athletics and camping. The YWCA reported work in over 1,800 communities in 1956, and its buildings afford a place for a great variety of social, cultural, and recreation projects. At the end of 1956 there were 348 Jewish community centers and YM-YWHAs, affiliated with the National Jewish Welfare Board, with a total membership of 530,000 in the United States and Canada. These centers contain facilities that make possible a diversified recreation program.

Among the agencies concerned with particular forms of recreation is the American Youth Hostels, which numbers in its membership 9,520 individuals and 154 organizations. It fosters, especially among youth, travel under one's own power—bicycling, hiking, canoeing, skiing, or horseback riding. To this end it furnishes overnight facilities for young people in different parts of the country and conducts trips through the United States and into foreign countries.

Recreation plays an important part in the programs of national organizations serving boys and girls, typical of which are the Boy Scouts, Girl

Scouts, and Camp Fire Girls. These agencies emphasize out-of-door activity and afford opportunity for participation in a wide range of projects, including nature study, games, athletics, community service, camping, and water sports, as well as woodcraft and other craft activities. Their programs appeal strongly to boys and girls and provide a basis for the development of interests that carry over into later life. The expansion of their camping service to include day, week-end, and winter as well as summer camps has enhanced its recreation value.

Boys Clubs of America and Girls Clubs of America represent a group of local agencies that serve the interests of boys and girls, respectively. These agencies differ from the scouting groups in that they have no standardized national program; most of them have a special club building in which their activities are centered, and in many instances they are located in and serve underprivileged neighborhoods. The programs vary according to local interests and facilities, but they are built around informal groups. Their buildings serve as clubhouses where boys or girls can spend a quiet evening reading or playing games with a few friends, where entertainments and social programs are arranged and carried out, and where individuals or clubs engage in a variety of craft, athletic, or cultural activities. Some clubs include in their programs parties, dances, and other social activities for mixed groups, but for the most part participation is restricted to the sex which the club is organized to serve.

PRIVATE AGENCIES

Recreation has a part in the program of innumerable private agencies and organizations. Programs are generally restricted to members; unlike the voluntary agencies, these organizations are not dependent upon community support. A few of the more important agencies in this group are industries, churches, country clubs, service clubs, fraternal organizations, labor unions, women's clubs, outing and athletic clubs, and groups organized to carry on specific recreation activities. Only a few of these agencies, however, can be considered in this chapter.

Business and Industry. Many industries, especially those which employ large numbers of workers or which largely dominate the small communities where they are located, furnish recreation facilities for their employees; in many cases these are open to workers' families and in some instances to the entire community. Similarly, a considerable number of department stores, insurance companies, banks, and other commercial organizations provide recreation facilities and programs. Years ago these recreation services were usually provided exclusively by management and tended to be paternalistic; during the depression years many were discontinued or seriously reduced. A renewed interest on the part of labor and industry in the recreation needs of workers and their families has resulted in a great expansion in the number and scope of programs. Approximately twenty-five thousand companies now provide recreation activities of some nature for their employees, and their estimated 1957 expenditures in support of these programs was in excess of a billion dollars.[3] In most cases management and labor share the responsibility for sponsoring and financing the programs through employee recreation associations. These supplement activities sponsored for employee groups

Lunch-hour concert by the Republic Aviation Corporation employees band at the Farmingdale, N. Y., plant (Courtesy of Republic Aviation Corporation).

by community agencies, which also make their facilities available to employee teams and organizations. Some labor unions provide their own recreation facilities and programs.

Bowling, softball, golf, basketball, outings, dances, and parties are among the activities leading in popularity in plant-sponsored programs. Horseshoes, dramatics, crafts, shooting, fishing, flying, music, and motion pictures are other favorite activities. Lounges, libraries, and facilities for lunch-hour activities are common; well-equipped athletic fields and sports areas are numerous; over one hundred companies own a golf course; and a number provide vacation camps and week-end lodges for their employ-

[3] Don L. Neer, "Industry," *Annals of the American Academy of Political and Social Science,* vol. 313, p. 80, September, 1957.

ees. Travel clubs are multiplying fast in industry and business—about one thousand companies now have them. In many small communities industries commonly provide playgrounds for the children and activities for all members of the family.

 The Hospital. The widespread introduction and use of recreation as a therapeutic factor in hospitals has been a significant development since

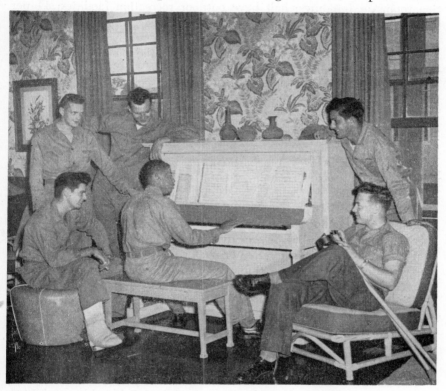

Patients enjoy music in the recreation room at the U. S. Naval Hospital, Camp Pendleton, California (Official United States Navy photograph).

World War II. Recreation has proved its value in the treatment of both the physically and mentally ill. Hospitals making extensive use of recreation include those operated by all levels of government as well as by private agencies. The Veterans Administration and the American Red Cross have played an outstanding role in the movement to employ qualified recreation personnel in Federal hospitals. A survey conducted by the National Recreation Association with the cooperation of several agencies revealed that of 3,500 hospitals responding to a 1957 questionnaire, some 1500 have instituted recreation programs, employing more than five thousand full-time personnel conducting recreation in a medical setting, with approximately thirty-five thousand volunteers involved in these programs. Most frequently reported activities are movies, reading, watching television, and similar passive pursuits. Arts and crafts, social activities, music, active games and sports, and service activities follow in the order named. More than half the 1,500 hospitals reporting have special recreation rooms or buildings; half have outdoor recreation facilities; 11 per cent have swimming pools.

The Church. Most churches encourage their members to participate in wholesome recreation activities, and many of them conduct programs that promote good fellowship among their members and afford a wise use of their leisure time. The church supper and the Sunday-school picnic have long been high spots in the social program of the church, but today offerings are more varied. The dramatic group may present a play, the young people's society a program of folk songs and folk dances, or the church choir an operetta. Frequently such occasions include group singing or games in which everyone participates. In addition, many a church calendar includes dinners, holiday entertainments, athletic leagues, outings, and play nights. Games, music, crafts, and other play activities form an important part of the vacation Bible-school program.

To provide facilities for such varied programs, many churches—not only in large cities but in small communities—have buildings fully equipped for an indoor recreation program. In others the special facilities for recreation are limited to clubrooms, a library, or kitchen. Apparatus for children's play, tennis courts, and other game facilities have been built on many church properties. Recreation activities hold a place of growing importance in the programs of church-sponsored organizations for young people, of which the Luther League, the CYO, and the Mutual Improvement Association are typical. Increasingly representative church teams and groups participate in the municipal recreation program.

Sports Organizations. The tremendous popularity of games and sports, such as golf, tennis, boating, bowling, track and field athletics, fishing, hunting, polo, hiking, and water and winter sports, has resulted in the formation of thousands of clubs or organizations devoted to one or more of these activities. Membership in these groups is exceedingly large—the American Bowling Congress, for example, in 1956 reported 2 million members among the 20 million devotees of the sport—and the acreage of their properties exceeds that of public recreation areas in many communities. Some of these groups, such as yacht clubs, golf clubs, polo clubs, and the more exclusive athletic clubs, are open only to people of considerable wealth or to those who have attained prominence in the particular sport. Many others, however, serve people with moderate incomes. Emphasizing only one or a few types of activity, the clubs appeal to persons who have a deep interest in these particular sports and whose desires for participation or recognition are not fully satisfied by existing public facilities. In addition to the local groups, state and national organizations have been formed for practically every type of competitive game or sport. These organizations set up standard rules for the activity and in many cases promote or conduct state and national tournaments.

Other Clubs. Comparable to the sports organizations are the many clubs which are organized around other activities or interests. Merely to mention a few of them suggests the wide scope of their activity and the variety of their membership: camera, stamp, and hobby clubs, chess and checker clubs, social clubs, dancing clubs, folk-dance groups, players' guilds and little-theater groups, glee clubs, orchestral societies, garden clubs, bridge clubs, discussion groups, civic-improvement associations, marionette clubs, bird clubs, sketch clubs, craft groups, and a host of others. Many of these organizations have a relatively small local membership; but because they are formed around a common interest, they influence the lives of the individual members more than some of the larger agencies with a more varied program. Like the sports organizations, many are served by state and national agencies which promote the particular activity by issuing publications or by sponsoring meetings, exhibits, or competitions on a state or national basis.

No picture of recreation as it affects the people of our country would be complete without reference to the programs of the women's clubs, with their groups devoted to dramatics, music, gardening, art, literature, civics, and current problems. As a rule, the programs of men's community clubs are more restricted in scope, emphasizing civic affairs, social life, and entertainment. Lodges, with their initiations, ritual, social functions, and good fellowship, reach large though decreasing numbers.

Recreation plays an important part in the activities of the many societies comprising the foreign-born. It often outranks discussions of agricultural problems as a means of attracting rural folk to meetings of the farm bureau and the grange. It has a place in the program of the parent-teacher association, the labor union, service organizations, and civic and luncheon clubs, which also frequently sponsor community recreation projects. In college and university life, recreation activities can be seen in intercollegiate and intramural athletic, music, and literary programs; in discussion and special-interest groups; and in dramatic groups, debates, lectures, social functions, proms, and outing clubs. In fact, the private agency that does not carry on some form of recreation is exceptional.

Mention should be made of another group of private organizations which falls between the voluntary agency and the private association. Typical of this group are the opera guild, the symphony society, the historical society, and the private museum. Such agencies extend special privileges to their members but commonly provide recreation opportunities that benefit the entire public.

ʏ COMMERCIAL AGENCIES

The universal urge for recreation, relaxation, and release from the daily routine has been capitalized by commercial agencies which have built up a recreation business totaling several billion dollars per year. This gigantic development testifies to the public demand for recreation and also to the inadequacy of the recreation facilities and opportunities which have been afforded by the agencies mentioned in the preceding pages. Unlike them, the commercial agencies are primarily motivated by profits rather than service. Nevertheless, many of them contribute richly to recreation in America. Although their offerings help to make the American people the world's greatest consumers of passive recreation, some of the most popular forms of commercial recreation involve active participation and strenuous physical activity.

In comparison with the amounts spent for certain commercial sports events, expenditures for other forms of recreation seem insignificant. For example, the "gate" at a world's championship prize fight exceeded 25 million dollars. This, of course, does not include the enormous amount spent for travel, hotels, and other expenses by persons attending it. Commercial agencies account for a large percentage of the nation's annual consumer expenditures for recreation, which have been variously estimated at 11 to 40 billion dollars,[4] depending upon the items included in the term "recreation."

ᚡ **Amusements and Entertainment.** Under this heading may be grouped (1) radio, records, television, and musical instruments; and (2) theatres, night clubs, motion pictures, and amusements. Consumer expenditures for the first group in 1955 exceeded 3 billion dollars; for the second group, 1½ billion dollars.[5] The commercial agencies providing these forms of recreation therefore capture a considerable proportion of the total amount spent for all forms of recreation.

Television has replaced the radio as a most powerful factor in the everyday leisure of the American people. Its various offerings of dance music, classical concerts, sporting events, dramas, news comments, quiz programs, skits, and movies afford unprecedented possibilities for recreation and education. With the possible exception of reading, television is the most widespread form of leisure-time activity—if, indeed, it can be classed as "activity." Because of television's popularity the nature and

---

[4] *America's Needs and Resources,* The Twentieth Century Fund, Inc., New York, 1955, pp. 347–348.

[5] *Survey of Current Business,* U.S. Department of Commerce, July, 1956, p. 21.

quality of the programs broadcast are matters of great public concern. The production, sale, and use of records have also had an amazing growth in recent years.

For many years motion-picture theatres monopolized the amusement field in most cities, but with the development of television their number and income have been appreciably diminished in spite of the large number of drive-in theatres that have been built in the past decade. Even so, movie houses far outnumber theatres used for the production of legitimate drama and opera. The latter, though their quantity is small and their locations are principally in large cities, still make a valuable contribution to the cultural life of America.

In addition to such forms of amusement as the rodeo, circus, and vaudeville, we have the traveling carnival and the amusement park, which have, in some respects, questionable recreation value. The popular desire to dance is capitalized upon by dance halls, dine-and-dance restaurants, cabarets, night clubs, and excursion boats.

Athletics and Sports. Professional sports exhibitions have become a common feature of American life. Public interest in athletics has made profitable the development of professional baseball on a national scale, the growth of professional football and basketball, and the widespread promotion of boxing, ice hockey, and winter sports exhibitions. Horse racing and, more recently, dog racing have a large and enthusiastic following, as do automobile, motorcycle, boat, and bicycle racing. Tennis has joined golf in the field of professional sports. College basketball and track teams, though composed of amateurs, attract capacity crowds at commercial arenas; college football has many characteristics of a professional sport.

But it is not as spectators alone that the American people are being served by commercial recreation agencies. The failure of public agencies to keep pace with the demand for recreation facilities has resulted in their development by commercial interests. Swimming pools, bathing beaches, tennis courts, picnic areas, golf courses, ice and roller-skating rinks, boating facilities, bowling alleys, and billiard parlors under commercial auspices outnumber the public facilities in many cities. The expansion of such facilities in recent years is evidence of the upward trend in participant interest in sport. In fact, the report on excise taxes paid in 1957 clearly shows that Americans are cutting down on passive spectator sports and spending more of their money on active sports participation.[6]

Travel. Travel, including the use of the automobile for pleasure, accounts for by far the largest recreation expenditure of the American people. The American people currently spend more than 25 billion dollars per year for travel at home and abroad (according to the National Asso-

[6] *Athletic Institute Sportscope*, vol. 2, no. 21, p. 1, Chicago, December 2, 1957.

ciation of Travel Organizations), of which amount 18 billion dollars are spent for domestic tourist travel.[7] We are the most mobile people in the world, and an increasing percentage of our recreation expenditures are for holiday and vacation travel. Hotels, motels, dude ranches, private camps and resorts serving tourists and vacationists help make recreation one of the country's largest business undertakings. In several states the income derived from persons seeking recreation represents a top-ranking source of revenue.

Several factors besides increased leisure and rising incomes have contributed to the mounting volume of vacation travel. The expansive highway program has made national and state parks and other recreation areas as well as private resorts readily accessible to the automobile-owning public. All-expense tours at bargain rates, offered by transportation companies, attract vacationists to resorts, winter sports centers, and places of historic interest. Golf courses, swimming pools, and winter and water sports facilities are increasingly provided at vacation centers, where participation activities supplement entertainment programs. Rail and water excursions and cruises conducted by steamboat companies have long been popular. Air conditioning, conventions and conferences, and longer and more widely distributed vacations have also contributed to the mounting volume of travel for recreation.

These activities all provide an income not only for transportation agencies but for the communities which are visited by the travelers and for the companies producing sports apparel and equipment. Increasingly, states are creating special agencies to develop and promote vacation and tourist travel.

THE NEED FOR COOPERATIVE PLANNING

The multiplicity of agencies undertaking some form of recreation activity or serving some recreation interest is largely the result of independent and unrelated attempts to meet specific recreation desires and needs rather than of concerted action to render recreation service according to a carefully devised cooperative plan of action. The rapidity and extent of the changes which have given recreation a place of prominence in American life—some of which were mentioned in the preceding chapter—account in part for the relative lack of coordination among recreation agencies in the past. With the emergence of recreation as a major factor in modern life, however, the need for cooperative planning has become apparent, and notable progress has been made in this direction at various levels of government and by a wide range of private groups.

[7] James L. Bossemeyer, "Travel: American Mobility," *Annals of the Academy of Political and Social Science,* vol. 313, p. 113, September, 1957.

Reference was made earlier in the chapter to the committee which was organized for self-coordination of the work of Federal agencies in the field of recreation. Federal legislation has authorized cooperation between the National Park Service and state and local park and recreation authorities in the acquisition, development, and operation of areas and facilities. In several states interagency committees are studying the states' recreation resources and are suggesting programs of cooperative action. Many state and regional associations of employed recreation workers are actively working to extend and raise the standards of recreation service.

The expansion of recreation areas, facilities, and services at the Federal, state, and local level has given added impetus to the demand for media which will facilitate an exchange of information and assure maximum benefits to the people. Federal authorities that construct dams and thereby create water areas of great potential recreation use are increasingly turning to state and local agencies to develop and operate these recreation resources. The establishment of state recreation services to localities has a direct relationship to local programs and is of concern to local authorities. Plans of national and state park agencies for the development of their properties affect the planning of local recreation areas. It therefore behooves local recreation authorities to encourage and support sound efforts to achieve cooperation between governmental authorities at all levels as well as with private agencies in the community.

The Education-Recreation Council of the National Social Welfare Assembly, composed of representatives of some forty national and Federal agencies interested in phases of the leisure-time problem, serves as a medium for discussing common problems, considering effective methods of joint action, and conducting local studies of agencies serving the people through recreation.

The Federation of National Professional Organizations for Recreation, representing eight professional groups and two consulting member agencies, affords a means for consultation, research, and action on the national level. The joint sponsorship of the National Recreation Congress since 1957 is another example of cooperation between national, state, and local agencies.

Recreation councils, committees of councils of social agencies, and other representative groups have been created in many cities and metropolitan regions to study this problem and to work out ways in which the people can best be provided with recreation. Increasingly, formal agreements or cooperative relationships have been established between local governmental agencies concerned with some aspect of community recreation. Organizations of this type will be considered in a later chapter.

Cooperation, coordination, or centralized control has been achieved also by private recreation groups. Many have established national organizations or federations for the setting of standards, for the promotion of activities or competition on a uniform national basis, or for some other purpose. The Amateur Athletic Union, for example, which includes among its objectives the improvement and promotion of amateur sports, the development of uniform rules, and the supervision of athletic championships, comprises among its membership state and district sports bodies as well as forty allied national organizations promoting various amateur sports programs. The desirability of uniform practices and centralized control has also been recognized by the major commercial recreation interests, notably professional baseball and football and the motion-picture industry.

The many agencies mentioned in this chapter are all contributing in a greater or lesser degree to the enrichment of the leisure time of people. Some of them are serving large numbers without regard to their social, religious, economic, or racial background; others are reaching only limited, homogeneous groups. It is clear that recreation, like education and health, is so vital to the life and welfare of the people that government must assume some responsibility for assuring recreation opportunities for all the people. Private and commercial agencies cannot be expected to meet this universal need. The municipality, therefore, has a place of primary importance in furnishing recreation for all the people and in giving them opportunity to share their common recreation interests in a democratic leisure-time experience. Furthermore, there is much to be gained by cooperative planning and action on the part of all agencies furnishing recreation, public and private, to the end that the greatest opportunities for wholesome and satisfying recreation may be extended to all.

4. RECREATION—A FUNCTION OF LOCAL GOVERNMENT [1]

A CENTURY ago local government was relatively simple and concerned itself with few functions. The complex organization which controls our cities today is the result of the gradual absorption by the municipality of a variety of functions and services. Many of these services were initiated and carried on for a time by private agencies; but as their need and value became recognized, they were gradually taken over by the municipal authorities, who created special agencies to provide and administer them. Education, which before 1850 was largely under private auspices, has been accepted without question as an essential function, justifying not only public financial support and administrative control but compulsory school attendance. About 1880, cities began to recognize that health was a major problem, the solution of which required municipal action. Social welfare, long considered a philanthropic service to be rendered by private agencies, has been taken over by government increasingly since 1900.

THE EXPANSION OF MUNICIPAL SERVICES

To understand fully the manner in which municipalities added to the range and variety of their functions, it is necessary to remember that the local government is not a completely independent unit. It is rather an entity created by the state, and its functions are dependent on legal authority from the state. Fortunately, along with the need for new municipal services, there also developed a liberal attitude toward municipal functions, especially those concerned with human well-being and happiness. The opinion of historian Charles A. Beard, that "nothing human is alien, for in the wide range of its activities, the city summons every power

[1] In this chapter the term "local government" is considered applicable to any local unit of state government such as the county, city, village, borough, or township; or school, park, and recreation districts. The term "municipal recreation" is intended to include services provided by park or school authorities as well as by other local governmental agencies.

of human mind and character," [2] is representative of the broad viewpoint which evolved during the course of the years.

Many local governments, taking advantage of this liberal attitude toward municipal functions, added new services without resorting to special legislation, by invoking the police powers with which they were vested by the state. The police power was utilized because it includes "the right to frame and enforce reasonable measures for the protection of health, life, property, and morals." Furthermore, as A. G. Truxal writes, "modern jurisprudence is giving a more liberal interpretation to this power so that it may include measures adopted to promote the common welfare, convenience, and prosperity." [3]

During a long period recreation was felt to be a matter of no public concern, and the early attempts to provide play opportunities were carried on through private initiative and funds. Like the other municipal services which grew out of "the increasing complexity of civilization and the growing tendency to invoke governmental aid for the satisfaction of wants not previously met, or if felt, met by voluntary action," [4] recreation passed through the stages from private to public support and established itself as one of the functions of local government.

Recreation Is Recognized as a Function of Government. Some of the larger cities first established playgrounds as they did certain other services, under the broad interpretation of the police power granted them by the state. In other cities, existing park or school legislation was deemed sufficient authority for operating playgrounds, or special laws were enacted to provide such authority. As the recreation movement grew in scope, however, and as the demand for such facilities and services increased, there developed a need for specific legislation giving municipalities power to appropriate funds for a comprehensive recreation program. Laws of this type have been passed in a majority of the states. Chapter 28, which considers more fully the legal aspects of recreation, reviews existing legislation of this kind and the extent to which the courts have upheld it by establishing recreation as an essential function of government.

The acceptance of recreation as a reasonable concern of local government has had strong support from leaders in public life and public administration. For example, Dr. Thomas Harrison Reed states in *Municipal Management:* "Public recreation is primarily a function of urban

[2] Charles A. Beard, *American Government in Politics,* The Macmillan Company, New York, 1931, p. 731.

[3] A. G. Truxal, *Outdoor Recreation Legislation and Its Effectiveness,* Columbia University Press, New York, 1929, p. 21.

[4] James Bryce, *American Commonwealth,* The Macmillan Company, New York, 1923, p. 625.

government. . . . Children suffer in mind and body from lack of play. Adult minds, too, fester from lack of occupation in the increasing amount of idle time which unemployment and shortened working hours have brought in their train. It is essential, if we would prevent the breeding of crime and revolution, that opportunity be provided for children's play and for the healthy use of the leisure time of grown people." [5]

REASONS FOR MUNICIPAL RECREATION

In fact, in law, and in public opinion, recreation is recognized today as a suitable and essential function of government. Since most people must spend a large portion of their leisure in the locality where they live or work, the focal point of their recreation is the local community. The participants in a national recreation workshop concluded: "The primary responsibility for recreation is in the local community; and because recreation contributes to the welfare of the people, it is a primary responsibility of local government." [6] Following are some of the reasons why recreation is distinctly a part of the city's job and why the provision of basic community recreation facilities and service is a primary concern of local government.

1. *Municipal recreation affords a large percentage of the people their only opportunity for forms of wholesome recreation.* People of wealth can travel, belong to country clubs, attend the theater and opera, own their own yachts, and secure for themselves many rich and varied recreation opportunities. Those with moderate means can also, to a considerable degree, provide many attractive and satisfying recreation activities for themselves through individual or group effort. For a great many people, however, recreation opportunities are very limited except as facilities, areas, activities, and leadership are provided by governmental or semipublic agencies. Especially in the cities, simple, traditional ways of spending leisure are no longer possible, so that local government has a responsibility for making sure that needed recreation facilities and services are provided. The benefits society gains from participation in recreation will be largely lost if public funds do not make possible recreation programs and services.

2. *Only through government can adequate lands be acquired.* It is not possible for most individuals or private organizations to acquire and develop for recreation the areas necessary for an adequate program. Only through governmental action can the city be supplied with ample and

---

[5] Thomas Harrison Reed, *Municipal Management,* McGraw-Hill Book Company, Inc., New York, 1941, pp. 450–451.

[6] *Recreation for Community Living,* The Athletic Institute, Chicago, 1952, p. 111.

properly located neighborhood playgrounds, parks, and other outdoor areas. Through city planning, subdivision control, eminent domain, transfer of properties between governmental units, acceptance of gifts of land, and ability to issue bonds, the local government has the means for acquiring recreation areas. Thus cities can also secure water-front properties suitable for recreation, large outlying reservations, stream valleys, and areas of scenic interest. Such problems as eliminating the pollution

Orchard Beach is one of several water-front parks to which New York City's millions flock for outdoor recreation (Courtesy of Department of Parks, New York, N. Y.).

of streams, lakes, or beaches in order that they can be used for recreation by the people can be dealt with only by governmental action.

The municipality's essential responsibility in this respect was stressed many years ago by Walter Rauschenbusch, who said: "Public property is the only thing that can beat commercialized amusements. I am for taking the sewage out of our rivers and putting boys and girls into them to swim. . . . I am for stocking the waters inside of the city limits with perch, rock bass, and bullheads. . . . The spirit of adventure is essential to childhood, and nothing but public property creates freedom enough in big cities to invite adventure." [7]

3. *Municipal recreation is democratic and inclusive.* Municipal rec-

[7] *The Playground,* vol. 9, no. 12, p. 468, March, 1916.

reation, unlike that provided by most other agencies, is for all the people. In large measure it is equally available for rich and poor; for people of all ages, racial backgrounds, social status, political opinions, and religious preferences; for boys and girls, men and women. It gives to all the opportunity to engage in activities of their choice. Municipal recreation conforms with the American spirit and way of living.

Since all the people benefit either directly or indirectly, it is fitting that the burden be distributed upon the entire community. There is no more reason why the entire cost of providing recreation for the people should be borne by public-spirited individuals or by a fee-paying public than that the schools should be financed privately or on a basis of self-support. In a democracy the need for recreation facilities and leadership is comparable to the need for public health and education services. The justification for providing such services is equally valid for public recreation as for public education.

4. *Municipal recreation is comparatively inexpensive.* Through a pooling of resources and the provision of services on a county-, district-, or city-wide basis, local government can furnish recreation at a much lower cost than would otherwise be possible. It costs the taxpayers only a few cents every time an individual uses a municipal playground, recreation center, or other facility. Adding a few dollars to each householder's tax pays for day-by-day recreation, indoor and outdoor, for the family for the whole year.

Even with the rapid growth of municipal recreation in recent years, the expenditures for the country are small compared with the amounts spent for other forms of recreation. For example, the 451 million dollars spent in 1956 by local governments for parks, recreation, museums, music, and other related activities, including capital outlays, represents only a fraction of the billions spent for consumer recreation and travel during the year.

5. *The local government gives permanency to recreation.* Private agencies depend for their continuance upon the interest and support of individuals or special groups. The government, on the other hand, is a perpetual agency and can alone assure the continuity of an adequate recreation service. As Supreme Court Justice Burton stated when he was mayor of Cleveland, Ohio, "The children of one family outgrow the recreation problem, but the public's children are there forever." Permanent but subject to the changing needs of the people, the local government stands out as the best-equipped agency for meeting the recreation needs, not only of the present but of the future. Furthermore, many recreation areas acquired and developed by the government are dedicated to public use in perpetuity, whereas private property may be withdrawn from recreation use at any time.

6. *The job is too large for a private agency.* The increase in leisure and the growing need and demand for recreation make the task of providing recreation for all the people too large for any agency except the government. Only by utilizing its powers of acquiring land and raising funds and by taking advantage of the low cost which city-wide, nonprofit service makes possible can a large portion of the public secure the recreation it will demand and which, in the public interest, it should have. Failure to provide that recreation will close such avenues to countless individuals except in forms which commercial interests find it profitable to provide, some of which contribute little or nothing in positive values. Attractive city-wide playground programs under competent leadership would be found in few municipalities if the cost of providing them were left to private agencies. Small-group activities of great citizenship and cultural value, which require expert leadership or special facilities, would be available to comparatively few people except as the municipality provides opportunities for engaging in them.

7. *Recreation plays an important role in the local economy.* The effective development, operation, and maintenance of recreation areas is a potent stabilizer of property values; assessments tend to rise following the acquisition of park lands. The recreation opportunities afforded by a community influence its attractiveness as a location for a new industry or for families seeking a home. The relationship between the maintenance of an adequate recreation program and the city's crime bill has been pointed out repeatedly. Robert Moses, New York City commissioner of parks and a practical realist, has stated the case clearly and emphatically as follows: [8]

No matter how difficult the problem of providing these increased (recreation) facilities may be and afterward maintaining and controlling them, it must be met. It does not matter how conservative a citizen may be or how much he may deprecate the expansion of government facilities into new fields, recreation in cities and municipalities is not a new field and must be recognized as a vital necessity. There is neither justice nor economy nor common sense in dodging this issue. . . .

The demand for all these new facilities in the park system has unquestionably existed. The evidence that these new facilities have improved health, decreased juvenile delinquency and accidents is beyond dispute. I am not referring merely to the claims of exuberant reformers. . . . I have already stated my conviction that the nonrevenue as well as the new self-supporting activities of the Park Department are an actual economy and that they bring about a directly traceable reduction in the cost of policing, crime prevention, operation of accident wards, and health administration. The beneficial effects of park and parkway improvements on adjacent property also needs no proof.

[8] "Who Will Pay the Piper?" *Survey Graphic,* vol. 26, no. 6, June, 1937.

One of the principles of democracy is that unless all the people have a fair opportunity for the good life, the nation as a whole cannot prosper. The public education system is based on the principle that it is essential for *all* the people to be able to read, write, and think. It is admittedly unsafe and contrary to the public interest for part of the population to be without health services; just so, it has been demonstrated that the city cannot afford to have a part of its people deprived of opportunities for wholesome recreation. In fact, it is good economy to spend public funds to provide them.

The Hon. Joseph S. Clark, Jr., when mayor of Philadelphia, expressed a similar opinion before the National Recreation Congress: "I have no doubt that a careful analysis of community costs would demonstrate that the money spent for recreation is paid back many times over in the additional wealth produced by healthier citizens, in the savings in the mental-health field, and the reduced cost of combatting crime."

8. *The people demand it and are willing to be taxed for it.* In the final analysis the services provided by local government are determined primarily by the expressed will of the people and their readiness to pay for them from tax funds. In city after city, by petition and referendum vote, the people have indicated that they consider recreation a needed function of local government. Recognition of this fact has been demonstrated repeatedly in political campaigns and was clearly stated by Mayor Clark as follows: "No elected official could retrace our steps, eliminate recreation as a major function of local government, and expect reelection. Recreation has become a governmental function not from consent, but by the demand of the governed."

GOVERNMENT MUST BE TRUSTED

The argument for a tax-supported recreation program in a democracy such as ours presupposes faith in government and in its ability to render efficient service to all the people. Unless people believe in government and are willing to work to make government something worthy of confidence and support, there is no hope for democracy.

Government, after all, is everyone working together for the common good, and to abandon government is to give up faith in ourselves. To admit that city departments under present conditions cannot successfully carry out the undertakings of the people and truly express their will is fundamental pessimism. It is true that there have been cities in which recreation, like other functions, has been thwarted by the selfishness, lack of vision, or dishonesty of public officials. On the other hand, many of the finest achievements in recreation, as in other fields, have been developed within the government. If recreation for all the people can best be achieved through local government, as suggested in the preceding pages, all who are concerned with recreation should work together for the achievement of high standards in public administration. The results will be measured not merely in terms of greater efficiency but of greater concern by local officials for the welfare of the people.

Strengthening and raising the standards of the public agencies not only is good theory in a government such as ours but is also a wise procedure in view of the growing tendency to expand government services. Public interest demands the development of local governmental agencies that can be trusted with recreation as well as with the education of our children, our health and safety, and similar services. Leaders in many fields are prophesying that present provisions for recreation and education are insignificant in comparison with related programs in the future. If this is true, the building up of a strong, honest, efficient recreation service is a wise and statesmanlike objective.

PUBLIC AGENCIES CANNOT DO THE ENTIRE JOB

The municipality does not attempt to meet all the recreation needs of all the people and can never hope to do so. The interests and needs of any community are too diverse and too extensive to be the sole province of any one agency. Freedom of choice is inherent in recreation, and individuals are best served when there are a number of agencies offering a variety of recreation services from which to choose. The resources of all kinds of recreation agencies will be needed in the years ahead to serve the rapidly increasing leisure-time needs and the growing demand for a great variety of recreation activities.

The questions may be asked, What part of the entire field of recreation constitutes the particular responsibility of the municipality? And what is the relation of municipal recreation to the other agencies providing some form of recreation? The actual role of the municipal recreation agency in a given community will be conditioned by a number of local factors such as its financial status, its standing in the community, local appreciation of the value of recreation and readiness to support a recreation program, the recreation facilities, services and effectiveness of other local agencies, and various community traditions and attitudes. Wide agreement has been reached, however, as to basic functions that can best be performed by the appropriate municipal recreation agency. They are naturally the services which the majority of the public believes to be sufficiently important to the welfare of the community to merit tax support.

The municipality should provide, maintain, and operate for the use of the people a system of major areas and facilities, such as parks, golf courses, water and winter sports facilities, neighborhood playgrounds, recreation buildings, athletic fields, indoor recreation centers, playfields, and reservations. It should also provide leadership for a balanced program of athletics, music, drama, social recreation, crafts, and other activities primarily centered at the public facilities. These two basic functions have been widely recognized by public recreation agencies and have been accepted by many local welfare federations or councils of social agencies.

Other responsibilities that are increasingly accepted are the organization and supervision of a city-wide program of diversified activities, in many cases in cooperation with other agencies, and the provision of a recreation advisory service to all the people and agencies in the community. There are few forms of wholesome recreation that can be carried on in a locality which are not included in the program of one or more municipalities. Suggested criteria for a municipal recreation activity are that it should be constructive, recognized as an acceptable public service, available to all citizens, and reasonable in cost in proportion to the values received; and that participation should not be restricted by political, religious, or other considerations.

The Place of Other Governmental Agencies. Most municipalities cannot provide for their citizens areas of outstanding scenic beauty or extensive properties like the national and state parks and forests which afford opportunities for camping, nature study, boating, and hiking. The provision of such areas which serve the people in a region, state, or the country as a whole is a Federal, state, or county, not a municipal, responsibility. The problem of conserving wildlife and developing large-scale opportunities for hunting and fishing cannot be met primarily through municipal action but is a matter for cooperative action by state and Federal authorities. State agencies are also better qualified than many local authorities to perform such functions as area planning, leadership training, and research.

The Voluntary Agency. The function of the voluntary agencies in the leisure-time field has been the subject of much consideration during recent years. The rapid extension of municipal recreation programs has absorbed many activities which were formerly available primarily through these agencies. Yet it is commonly agreed that even though the local government takes over many of the recreation functions of the voluntary agencies, these agencies will continue to meet definite leisure-time needs. The specific nature of the recreation services which they are best equipped to render varies, just as the personnel, objectives, facilities, and financial resources of these agencies differ from city to city. However, unlike the municipal agency, which must consider the recreation needs of all the people, the voluntary agency usually restricts its primary service to a limited membership group. It is therefore especially fitted to serve the special interests of individuals who desire to engage in forms of recreation with others of a similar religious, social, economic, or racial background. In some cases it is more free than the public agency to experiment, to explore the possibilities of new activities, the value of which has not been demonstrated and for which public funds are not available, and to provide opportunities for the discussion of controversial issues and questions. In some localities, however, it is difficult to distinguish between the program offerings of the public and voluntary agencies.

National leaders of several of these agencies have gone on public record to the effect that support of adequate public recreation programs under competent leadership is a responsibility of their organizations. The YMCA, after a thorough study of the problem of relationships between itself and public recreation agencies, recommended that the YMCA should continue to work for adequate public recreation provisions and cooperate with public recreation authorities.[9] Local councils of social agencies and similar local planning groups have stated their responsibility toward adequate public recreation service and have recognized the need for joint planning and coordination of recreation services.

The Private Agencies. People who can afford membership in exclusive clubs or who desire to join with their friends in restricted recreation groups will continue to enjoy such privileges. It is neither possible nor desirable for the government to replace the many types of private agencies which afford recreation for their members and constituents. On the contrary, one of the outstanding functions of municipal recreation is to stimulate, encourage, and assist the provision of more and better recreation opportunities in homes, churches, industries, clubs, and other private groups. In this way the municipality can render an important and valuable service, make maximum use of its leadership resources, and reach people who may not use public recreation facilities or participate in municipal recreation programs. Private agencies, in turn, frequently give effective aid to the public authorities in organizing and conducting recreation activities. Instances of cooperation with both voluntary and private agencies and of service rendered them by public authorities are recorded in later chapters.

The Commercial Agencies. The only direct relationship between the municipality and the commercial recreation agencies in most cities has been one of regulation. Through a system of licenses, fees, or controls, the city has placed restrictions upon forms of commercial recreation in the interest of public safety, morals, health, or welfare. Responsibility for supervision of commercial agencies is usually placed upon police and licensing authorities; little, if any, attempt has been made to relate or coordinate municipal and commercial recreation services.

[9] Helen E. Davis, *The Y.M.C.A. and Public Recreation, Informal Education, and Leisure-time Programs,* Association Press, New York, 1946, p. 172.

The types of service rendered by the commercial interests do not as a rule duplicate those promoted by the municipal agency, and their objectives are likewise dissimilar. The municipal agency offers activities believed to have the greatest value to the people served; the commercial agency provides the activities that will yield a maximum profit. There is a sound basis for the belief that by establishing high standards and attractive programs within the means of the people the city can render its best service and at the same time help raise the standards of commercial recreation agencies. The municipal recreation program must be equally available to all; the commercial agency, on the other hand, can set up restrictions which give its offerings an added appeal to individuals who are able to afford them. The municipal agency can include in its program only activities that are generally acceptable to the entire community, whereas the commercial agency can offer services that are of questionable value but that assure a large financial return. Recreation is, therefore, likely to continue as a profitable undertaking.

The municipality seldom directly competes with the commercial recreation agency; on the other hand, many recreation departments organize groups that make use of commercial facilities. There have been rare instances where the provision of swimming pools, the conduct of community dances, and other public recreation projects have been opposed by commercial interests. The recreation needs in most cities are so great that if existing commercial activities are reasonably acceptable, the municipal department may well turn its attention to other forms of activity. On the other hand, if these opportunities are unwholesome, inadequate, or too expensive, the city should not be deterred from fulfilling its responsibility to the people by the opposition of the commercial agencies. By establishing cooperative relationships with these agencies, the public recreation authorities can help raise the standards of commercial recreation and thereby assure for their citizens a higher quality of service.

5. THE HISTORY OF MUNICIPAL RECREATION IN THE UNITED STATES

Recreation has played a role of varying importance in the life of all peoples. The earliest known races had their games, dances, music, and ceremonials just as the savage Bushmen today engage in similar activities. Evidences of different forms of recreation have been left by the Chinese, Egyptian, Aztec, Babylonian, and other early civilizations. The Greeks at the height of their achievements held in high esteem games, athletics, and the cultural arts; and during the Dark Ages the ideal of chivalry as well as the institution of minstrelsy, through song and story, helped maintain the play tradition. With the Renaissance a popular interest in the arts and sports was reinforced, growing steadily up to the present time, in spite of attempts of small groups to suppress it. This advance was aided by a number of philosophers and educators who, since the sixteenth century, have advocated recreation as an activity of social and educational value.

New England was settled chiefly by people whose primary concerns were to make a living and build a new home in the wilderness. Consequently, during the colonial period forms of recreation in New England were comparatively few, although quilting and cornhusking parties, apple-gathering bees, and similar occasions provided diversion at the same time they were serving practical ends. Life in other colonies, however, was brightened by a great variety of sports and amusements. Horse racing, dancing, cards, backgammon, bowling, cockfighting, contests of skill and strength, hunting, fishing, and excursions were popular forms of recreation during colonial times and the early part of the nineteenth century. Some of these were limited largely to the well-to-do, although there were occasions when all could take part.

During the early half of the nineteenth century, according to Jesse F. Steiner,[1] popular amusements followed in the main the patterns set during the colonial period and were looked upon with disfavor by many influential leaders. Recreation continued to be chiefly a matter of individual

[1] *Americans at Play*, McGraw-Hill Book Company, Inc., New York, 1933.

concern, although numerous sports clubs were organized, especially among the wealthy. The country was still essentially a pioneer nation in which rural influences played a dominating part, wealth was relatively scarce, and a few enjoyed much leisure. The period therefore gave no indication of the subsequent development of recreation as a major activity and as an organized service of local government.

SUMMARY OF SIGNIFICANT EVENTS IN THE RECREATION MOVEMENT

The history of municipal recreation in the United States, like that of other movements of social significance, cannot be told fully in terms of a series of specific events which mark distinct stages or periods of evolution. The recreation movement was the result of a combination of ideas, experiments, and developments. Some of them were closely related to each other in time, place, and influence; others seem to have had little connection with preceding, current, or subsequent happenings. Events now regarded as significant had only a remote relationship with other events immediately preceding them, yet they all contributed to the growth of the recreation movement. For this reason the following chart, which points out some of the significant happenings, serves as a guidepost in tracing the history of this uniquely American movement.

1820–1840 Opening of outdoor gymnasiums at several schools and universities.
1853 Purchase of land for Central Park in New York City.
1866 Vacation school started in Old First Church of Boston.
1872 Brookline, Massachusetts, purchased land for two playgrounds.
1885 The first sand garden conducted in Boston.
1889 The Charlesbank Outdoor Gymnasium for men and boys opened in Boston.
1892 A model playground established at Hull House, Chicago.
1898 School buildings in New York City opened as evening recreation centers.
1898 The New England Association of Park Superintendents (now the American Institute of Park Executives) organized.
1903 5 million dollars voted for creation of small parks by South Park Commission in Chicago.
1904 Board of Playground Commissioners appointed in Los Angeles.
1905 Opening of ten South Park centers in Chicago.
1906 The Playground Association of America organized in Washington, D. C.
1907 Opening of social and civic centers in Rochester schools.
1907 First "play" congress held in Chicago.
1909 First normal course in play published.

1911 Playground Association of America changed its name to Playground and Recreation Association of America.

1917 PRAA organized program for servicemen for the War Department, later known as War Camp Community Service.

1924 Conference on Outdoor Recreation called by President Coolidge.

1926 National Recreation School organized.

1928 The National Conference on State Parks organized.

1930 White House Conference on Child Health and Protection called by President Hoover.

1930 Title of Playground and Recreation Association of America changed to National Recreation Association.

1931–1932 Dr. L. P. Jacks's lecture tour of United States.

1932 First International Recreation Congress in Los Angeles.

1933 Federal government established first nationwide emergency works program, including expansion of recreation facilities and services.

1938 The Society of Recreation Workers of America (now the American Recreation Society) organized.

1938 The American Association for Health and Physical Education, a department of the National Education Association, became the American Association for Health, Physical Education, and Recreation.

1941 United Service Organizations established for war recreation service. Federal Security Agency war recreation program started.

1945 North Carolina established a State Recreation Commission.

1946 Federal Interagency Committee on Recreation formed.

1954 The Federation of National Professional Organizations for Recreation organized.

1956 The President's Conference on Youth Fitness called by President Eisenhower.

1956 The First Cooperative Community Recreation Exchange Project sponsored by the State Department.

1956 The International Recreation Association established.

1958 The Outdoor Recreation Resources Review Commission Act became law.

1958 The National Cultural Center of the Performing Arts Act became law.

EARLY DEVELOPMENTS

↳The event generally accepted as distinctly marking the beginning of the recreation movement in this country was the opening of the sand garden in Boston in 1885. However, events which took place before this date influenced the recreation life of the people and focused attention upon the value of a public recreation program. The opening of outdoor gymnasiums at several schools and universities between 1820 and 1840, largely the result of German influence, served to bring formal gymnastics and physical education to the attention of the people in this country. The experience of English schools and universities influenced the introduction of games and athletics into school and college life soon after the middle of the century. The many athletic and sporting clubs organized during this period likewise affected the development of recreation as a distinct movement.

Sand play appeals as strongly to children today as when the sand gardens were opened in Boston in 1885 (Courtesy of Board of Park Commissioners, Wichita, Kans.).

The purchase of a large tract of land by New York City in 1853, later developed and known as Central Park, was of great significance. This is believed to be the first municipal park in the United States to be established as a result of a "conscious effort of a democratic body to meet a proven need." [2] Horseback riding, boating, skating, walking, and picnicking were provided for in Central Park, and a special section was developed for the play of young children. Many cities followed New York's example and acquired large parks during the latter half of the century, but for years parks were considered primarily for rest and contemplation and not for recreation activity.

[2] Frederick Law Olmsted, Jr., and Theodora Kimball, *Central Park—as a Work of Art and as a Great Municipal Enterprise*, G. P. Putnam's Sons, New York, 1928.

The opening of the first vacation school on record in the Old First Church in Boston in 1866 was another important event which preceded the beginning of the recreation movement. Twenty years later, Newark made such schools a part of the city school system. Singing, manual work, and nature study—typical play activities—had an important place in the program of these schools.

Arising as the recreation movement did, out of a great social need, it is not surprising that social workers played a great part in launching the projects which were the forerunners of the recreation movement as we know it today. As was shown in Chapter 2, the social problems attendant upon the growth of cities and the industrialization of the country focused attention upon the need for wholesome recreation opportunities for the people. Bad housing conditions resulting from the growth of tenement slum areas, the great influx of immigrants, the rising tide of juvenile delinquency, the increase in factories accompanied by the evils of child labor and unsanitary and unsafe working conditions, and the spread of commercialized amusements which were often associated with vice all helped to create a condition which made the provision of wholesome recreation a necessity.

Play Centers in Boston. The year 1885 is memorable in playground history because of the outdoor play center for children established in Boston in that year and its influence on later playground developments. In 1885 a large sand pile was placed in the yard of the Children's Mission on Parmenter Street in Boston through the efforts of the Massachusetts Emergency and Hygiene Association. Each day an average of fifteen children attended this first Boston playground, which was open three days a week for six weeks during July and August. The children dug in the sand, sang songs, and marched about under the guidance of a woman who lived in the neighborhood.

This successful experiment was continued in succeeding years, and by 1887 ten centers had been opened. It was not until 1893 that a supervisor and trained kindergartners were used to conduct the play activities. During the first years the sand piles were in mission yards, but by 1894 all the sand gardens—or playgrounds, as they came to be called—were on school property. Operating funds were provided by the Massachusetts Emergency and Hygiene Association until 1899, when the city council appropriated $3,000 toward meeting their cost. In this same year three of the twenty-one centers were designated as playgrounds for boys between twelve and fifteen years of age and were equipped with a limited amount of gymnastic apparatus. The Boston School Committee in 1901 took over the operation of several playgrounds, although the association continued to conduct activities at many areas. Much of the credit for the success of this first playground effort belongs to Miss Ellen M. Tower, for many years chairman of the playground committee of the Massachusetts Emergency and Hygiene Association.

Since the experience in Boston had a direct influence upon the opening of playgrounds in other cities and gave definite direction to the development of the entire movement, it is worthwhile reviewing the stages which marked the evolution of the Boston experiment:

1. Started as a private project, it was later taken over and operated as a public responsibility.
2. Financed in the beginning through private philanthropy, support from public funds was later secured.
3. The playgrounds were originally on private property but were gradually transferred to public areas.
4. The playgrounds were at first under volunteer leaders, but soon matrons were employed, and subsequently kindergartners and other trained workers were used as play leaders.
5. The first centers were merely sand piles for little children, but apparatus and areas for older boys were later provided.

The experiment in Boston proved to be a forecast of the course the recreation movement was to follow. Each of these developments—from private to public management, financial support, and areas; from untrained to trained leaders; from young children to boys and girls of all ages—has been characteristic of the growth of the movement throughout the country.

The Movement Spreads to Other Cities. The success of the Boston sand gardens prompted similar efforts elsewhere, and at least ten other cities had established playgrounds before the end of the century. In practically every instance the initiative and funds were provided by philanthropic individuals or social agencies. A playground was opened in New York in 1889. In 1892, as we have seen, a model playground was opened in connection with Hull House in Chicago. It provided, in addition to sandboxes, apparatus and areas for playing handball and indoor baseball. Because the playground was larger and had more varied facilities it served older children than the earlier sand gardens. In 1893 two summer kindergarten playgrounds, one of them in a schoolyard, were established in Philadelphia, and the following year sand gardens were started in Providence. Other cities which made a beginning in playgrounds before 1900 were Pittsburgh, Brooklyn, Baltimore, Milwaukee, Cleveland, Minneapolis, and Denver. As in Boston, these playgrounds, although started and financed by private initiative, were taken over by city or school authorities after their value had been demonstrated. In New York City in 1899, ten years after the first playground was opened in that city, the New York school board conducted thirty-one school play centers.

Cities Acquire Recreation Areas. The close of the nineteenth century saw an awakening on the part of city officials to the importance of acquiring and developing special areas for recreation use. As early as 1871 the voters of the town of Brookline, Massachusetts, authorized the purchase of land "for public commons or playgrounds." Two properties were acquired, but nothing was done to develop them. In 1876 Washington Park in Chicago was opened as a recreation park, but it was not used for this purpose until ten years later, when two tennis courts were built in

The combination gymnasium frame was a distinguishing feature of the playgrounds built early in the century.

it. By 1892 over one hundred cities were known to have acquired parks, but few of these areas were used for active recreation.

In 1889 the Boston Park Department converted a 10-acre tract along the Charles River in a congested neighborhood into an open-air gymnasium for boys and men. Two years later a section was provided for women and girls. This area, known as the Charlesbank Outdoor Gymnasium, established a pattern which had a widespread influence. It was fenced, landscaped, and equipped with swings, ladders, seesaws, a sand garden and a ⅕-mile running track. Wading, bathing, and rowing facilities were also provided, and supervisors were appointed to conduct the program.

Other cities also acquired public playgrounds, largely because of the insistence of social workers and influential citizens. In New York City a tract of 2⅞ acres, covered with five- and six-story tenements, was purchased in 1897 at a cost of $1,800,000. After a determined effort led by Jacob A. Riis, this area, now known as Seward Park, was developed as a demonstration playground and opened in 1899 as a neighborhood playground. In addition to apparatus, wading pool, and game spaces, a gymnasium with baths was constructed, and seats were provided for spectators. The success of this experiment induced the Park Department to provide similar equipment and facilities in other parks in congested sections of the city.

By 1900, four play parks were in operation in Louisville, Kentucky, and in 1901 a special park commission opened four municipal playgrounds in Chicago. Franklin Field in Boston, purchased in 1894, was an early and outstanding example of the large athletic field. The first recreation pier was opened in New York City in 1897.

Chicago's Neighborhood Recreation Parks. Chicago, through its South Park playgrounds and centers, influenced the development of playgrounds and recreation in the United States more than any other city, with the possible exception of Boston. In 1903, a 5-million-dollar bond issue was voted for the acquisition and development of small recreation parks in the crowded neighborhoods of south Chicago. The creation of these parks, ten of which were opened in 1905, was called by Theodore Roosevelt "the most notable civic achievement of any American city." They established a new standard in park and playground building. Heretofore facilities were mostly out of doors, used only a few months of each year, designed primarily for athletics and other physical activities, and not related closely to the needs of the people in the neighborhoods they served. Chicago's South Park areas, on the other hand, were designed to serve persons of all ages and with varied interests throughout the entire year. They afforded both indoor and outdoor facilities available for a wide range of recreation uses and were intended to supplement the meager facilities for happy, wholesome living, which many of the neighborhoods afforded.

These parks varied from 7 to 300 acres in size; and although large portions were used for active recreation, a high degree of landscape beauty was attained through effective planting. Field houses provided indoor facilities including an assembly hall with stage and dressing rooms, gymnasiums for men and women, shower and locker rooms, refectory, clubrooms, and a branch of the public library. The cost of some of these buildings exceeded a quarter of a million dollars. The outdoor plants were equally elaborate, including fully equipped children's playgrounds and separate outdoor gymnasiums for men and women—with equipment and game courts, fields for a variety of games and sports, bandstands, and outdoor swimming pools. Trained leaders under a general director of field houses and playgrounds made possible a wise use of these plants.

The widespread favorable publicity which these parks received, especially at the first playground convention in Chicago in 1907, held under the auspices of the Playground Association of America, was a powerful influence in extending the recreational use of parks in other cities. It also contributed to the growing concept of the indoor recreation center for young people and adults. The South Park example was soon followed by the West Chicago and Lincoln Park Commissioners; and when these three park boards, with seventeen other small districts, were consolidated into the present Chicago Park District in 1934, the city possessed 137 parks with eighty-five field houses equipped for recreation use.

A Playground Board. The appointment of a Board of Playground Commissioners in Los Angeles in September, 1904, was a significant event, showing that a city recognized play and recreation as having sufficient importance to justify the creation of a special department to take charge of these functions. This step, like many of the others previously mentioned, resulted from the initiative of several local organizations. The first playground was opened in 1905, and a superintendent of recreation was employed by the board. Several playgrounds were acquired; and although most of them were under 10 acres, they were equipped with diversified outdoor facilities and with clubhouses, including an assembly hall, clubroom, kitchen, and quarters for the director. Like the Chicago centers, they served all ages and were open under leadership the year round. These were among the first tax-supported playgrounds not on park or school property. During the decade following 1905, several cities appointed playground or recreation boards and acquired recreation areas that were equipped with a variety of indoor and outdoor facilities.

School Buildings Are Opened for Recreation. Paralleling the development of the municipal recreation centers was the tendency to use school buildings for community recreation. Many school plants contained an auditorium, gymnasium, swimming pool, library, and special rooms which were suitable for recreation purposes but which were generally idle during the evenings, week ends, and in vacation periods. The economy of opening these facilities to the public rather than spending money to duplicate them in special recreation buildings soon became apparent. Many states prior to 1900 had passed laws permitting school buildings to be used as civic or social centers. As early as 1898, schools were opened under leadership for evening recreation in New York City as a continuation of the summer playground program; and by 1907, twenty-six schools were being used as evening recreation centers. The movement received nationwide attention when in 1907 a school extension committee was organized in Rochester. An appropriation of $5,000 was made for a demonstration of school centers, and a supervisor was employed to direct the program under the auspices of the school board. The name "social and civic centers," which was adopted, suggests the attempt to encourage better citizenship through a democratic method of operation. Although only moderately successful, the experiment stimulated the wider use of the school plant in other cities. The gradual introduction into school buildings of features which serve both school and community recreation use was later fostered by the National Community Center Association. In 1911, Wisconsin passed legislation authorizing school authorities to levy a 0.2 mill tax for recreation purposes. Milwaukee took advantage of this law in establishing its widely known playground and community center program.

THE PLAYGROUND ASSOCIATION OF AMERICA IS ORGANIZED

As interest in playgrounds spread, leaders in cities with unusual playground developments were deluged with requests for advice and information. It was natural, therefore, that they should come together to discuss ways in which help could be given to other communities. A small group, including such prophetic spirits as Jane Addams, Henry S. Curtis, and Luther H. Gulick, met in Washington, D. C., in April, 1906, and for three days considered the nation's play needs, particularly those of the children in the large cities. During the course of these meetings—one of them held at the White House—the group decided to organize a national body. The purpose of the Playground Association of America, as stated in its constitution, was "to collect and distribute knowledge of and promote interest in playgrounds throughout the country, to seek to further the establishment of playgrounds and athletic fields in all communities and directed play in connection with the schools." President Theodore Roosevelt gave his hearty endorsement to the new association, which launched the recreation movement on a nationwide basis, and he was elected honorary president. Other officers of the association were Jacob Riis, honorary vice-president; Dr. Luther H. Gulick, president; and Dr. Henry S. Curtis, secretary.

↗ No single event has had greater significance for the recreation movement than this Washington meeting. Previously the drive for playgrounds had received no concerted guidance or support; formation of the Playground Association of America, which received invaluable help from the Russell Sage Foundation, gave it new impetus and competent national leadership. A monthly magazine, the *Playground,* was started; field workers were employed who went from city to city, meeting with committees and public officials, exchanging experiences, and assisting in the establishment of playgrounds and recreation programs; a central clearinghouse for information was established; publications were issued; and annual play congresses were organized. Among the early activities of the association was the preparation of a normal course in play, which was widely used by schools and colleges in the training of play leaders.

In 1910 Joseph Lee, who has been called the philosopher of the movement for creative recreation, was elected president of the association, a position in which he served with practical wisdom, social insight, loyalty, and generosity until his death in 1937. The name of the organization was changed in 1911 to Playground and Recreation Association of America. This change indicated the enlarging scope of the movement, which was then concerned not only with children's playgrounds but with providing recreation facilities and programs for young people and adults. Years later the name was again changed to the National Recreation Association, its present name.

A testimony as to the association's influence upon the recreation movement was voiced as follows by the recreation commission in a large Western city:

The National Recreation Association is to playground departments what the Federal Reserve is to member banks—a sustaining influence, a source of information, and an able representative on matters of national import. The association, serving as the clearinghouse for the recreation movement in America, has been the means for focusing the attention of the nation upon the need for and the importance of public recreation. It has worked to determine needs, to plan adequate programs, train leaders, and raise standards of service and leadership. It has put its resources behind private and governmental agencies interested in recreation and has served as a unifying force for all who are working through recreation to make life in America a rich, joyous experience.

The National Recreation Association has done more than any other organization to make America conscious of the importance of wholesome recreation.

This statement, typical of many received on the occasion of its fiftieth anniversary, will be questioned by very few.

DEVELOPMENTS, 1910 TO 1932

⸸ One indication of the association's accomplishments is the marked increase in the number of cities which established playgrounds in the years immediately after it was founded. During the six years prior to 1906, twenty-six cities had established playgrounds, or an average of four cities a year. In the next six years a total of 158 cities started playgrounds, or an average of twenty-six cities a year. The association's emphasis upon the responsibility of the municipality to provide playgrounds and recreation centers helped to bring a general acceptance of the idea of public support.

⸰ In the years preceding World War I, the scope of the recreation movement was gradually enlarged. As its value was demonstrated, recreation came to be accepted as serving a universal need and not merely a need of congested or underprivileged communities. From the idea of a program at playgrounds and centers emerged the concept of recreation service for the entire community. More emphasis was laid upon music, drama, arts, and civic activities. Neighborhood groups were organized to help plan and conduct the program; city-wide projects such as holiday celebrations, pageants, and festivals were carried out. Comprehensive recreation surveys disclosed facts concerning existing opportunities for recreation, unmet recreation needs, delinquency, accidents, street play, and other related subjects. They helped focus public attention upon the need for city-wide recreation systems and provided information which was useful in organizing municipal recreation programs.

Influence of World War I. The trend toward city-wide recreation systems affording opportunities for everyone in the community received a further impetus after War Camp Community Service was organized by the Playground and Recreation Association of America at the request of the War Department. The task of this service was to mobilize the recreation resources of communities near the military camps and to provide wholesome recreation activities for the men in uniform as a relief from the daily camp routine. These activities also demonstrated the value of a recreation program under competent leadership, not only for servicemen but for civilians as well. In order to conserve the values created in war-camp communities and to extend this type of program to other cities, a national organization known as Community Service was established in 1919. With its assistance, recreation programs, financed through community effort, were established in a large number of cities.

Although the recreation service conducted by War Camp Community Service ended with the closing of the army camps, and the local Community Service programs were gradually taken over by municipal recreation agencies, these two nationwide efforts exerted a great influence upon the recreation movement. Servicemen who had become accustomed to out-of-door life and sports and who had enjoyed the recreation programs provided in the war camps desired the same opportunities in their home communities. The people who saw during the war what community singing, pageants, athletic meets, and neighborhood parties could mean in community life insisted that means be devised for continuing them. Influential citizen groups and committees had come to realize the value of volunteer recreation service and the satisfaction obtained from it. Social, civic, and religious agencies had acquired common interest in community recreation and a sense of responsibility for providing it. Many communities for the first time had observed the vital contribution made by a worker who gave his full time to planning the effective utilization of the community's recreation resources. The rapid expansion of the municipal movement in the 1920s, with its enriched programs and enlarged public support, was due in large measure to these wartime experiences.

Community Houses Are Erected. A widespread construction of community houses occurred during the years following the war because of the emphasis upon neighborhood and community recreation and the stimulus of a nationwide campaign for the erection of buildings as war memorials. In most cases, these buildings were financed through private funds, were managed by boards of directors, contained meeting rooms for local organizations and an assembly hall for community gatherings, and provided recreation facilities for the use of individuals and groups. In a few instances a trained recreation director was employed, but as a rule the leadership was furnished by the groups using the building. Many of the community houses erected in small towns and rural communities served as centers for their social and cultural life and consisted merely of an assembly hall with platform or stage and perhaps a kitchen. Other buildings contained elaborate recreation facilities. In several cities the war memorial took the form of a municipal auditorium with limited recreation facilities.

The Importance of Leisure Is Recognized. As early as 1912 the Playground and Recreation Association of America had issued pamphlets discussing the relation of recreation and leisure. In 1918 the National Education Association focused attention upon leisure as a major community problem by declaring that the training for the worthy use of leisure was one of the seven objectives of education. It was not until the late 1920s, however, that the important place of recreation in the rapidly increasing leisure time of the people was widely heralded in books, magazine articles, and the daily press. The tour of Dr. L. P. Jacks, noted English educator, who from 1931 to 1932 visited cities from coast to coast under the auspices of the National Recreation Association, interpreting the significance of recreation and leisure, did much to call attention to this problem. Nationwide publicity resulted from the three-day hearings arranged by the New York Leisure Time Committee of the National Recovery Administration in 1933, during the course of which such outstanding figures as Newton D. Baker, Alfred E. Smith, and Nicholas Murray Butler testified to the need of public planning for the recreational use of leisure.

"No phase of American life is more interesting than the rising tide of recreation during the 1920s," said Jesse F. Steiner in 1937, who added that during this period "play for the first time took its place alongside of work and was recognized as one of the major interests of life." [3] This decade was characterized by a growing appreciation of the importance of leisure and a marked expansion in public recreation services. The rapid increase in community recreation areas and facilities reflected the acceptance of recreation as an essential factor in city planning. Recreation programs were greatly enlarged in scope and in the number of participants as recreation budgets increased. Leadership training was emphasized, and the production of recreation literature increased markedly. State legislation authorized municipalities to establish and to maintain recreation systems, and many cities created a special department to handle the expanding recreation programs. The Conference on Outdoor Recreation called by President Coolidge in 1924 helped focus national attention on the importance of municipal recreation and other phases of outdoor leisure-time activity.

Areas and Facilities. During the 1920s the number and variety of recreation facilities increased by leaps and bounds. Playgrounds, golf courses, swimming pools, bathing beaches, picnic areas, winter sports facilities, and game fields were constructed in unprecedented numbers. Municipal park acreage, especially during the latter half of the decade, expanded more than in any other period of equal length, due partly to the fact that many cities acquired parks outside the city limits. Several county park systems providing a variety of recreation facilities were established. The growth in recreation areas accentuated the important relationship between recreation planning and other features of the city plan. The practice of dedicating space for recreation in real estate developments, actively stimulated by William E. Harmon, the Harmon Foundation, and the National Recreation Association, resulted in the dedication of recreation areas in hundreds of subdivisions. Many notable recreation areas and parks were also acquired by gift during the 1920s.

Programs. The decade is also significant as a period of expanding programs. Music, drama, arts and crafts, and nature activities received increasing emphasis. More recreation opportunities were provided for older girls and women, and more adequate consideration was given to recreation needs of minority groups. Picnic and party-loan services, the organization of activities for workers in stores and industries, and the extension of recreation service to public institutions and to shut-ins were new types of services which found their place in the recreation department program. Guidance to parents in providing back-yard play facilities and in the promotion of play in the home was included in the service of many recreation departments.

Leadership. With the expansion of recreation facilities and programs,

[3] *Research Memorandum on Recreation in the Depression,* Social Science Research Council, Washington, 1937, p. 38.

the need for trained, competent leadership became increasingly apparent. The number of employed recreation leaders, according to the *Recreation Yearbook*,[4] increased from 10,218 in 1920 to 22,920 in 1929. Greater emphasis was laid upon the provision of training courses for both paid and volunteer leaders. The growing recognition of recreation leadership as an emerging profession and the difficulty in securing properly trained personnel led to the establishment of the National Recreation School in New York City in 1926. This one-year graduate course helped 300 persons prepare for executive leadership in the recreation field. Institutes conducted by workers of the National Recreation Association under the auspices of the Extension Service of the U.S. Department of Agriculture afforded training opportunities to thousands of rural community leaders.

Expenditures. The growth in facilities, programs, and leaders obviously resulted from greater expenditures for municipal recreation service. According to the official recreation yearbooks, expenditures for organized community recreation service rose from $7,199,430 in 1920 to $33,539,806 in 1929. Reports of the Bureau of the Census show that municipal expenditures for all types of municipal recreation service including parks, museums, and public celebrations also increased to a remarkable degree during this period. Recreation was one of the few functions of local government that accounted for a larger percentage of total municipal expenditures in 1929 than it did ten years before.

Research. To meet the needs of the recreation profession and to serve more adequately the growing movement, many research projects were undertaken during this period. Nationwide studies of organized camps, municipal and county parks, music in American life, and leisure and the public schools were made by the National Recreation Association and were followed by the publication of comprehensive reports. Publications on music, crafts, drama, and social recreation swelled the rapidly increasing library of recreation literature. Committees of recreation executives, after a thoughtful pooling of experiences and opinions, issued authoritative reports on widely different subjects. President Hoover's Committee on Social Trends issued comprehensive reports based on nationwide surveys in the field of recreation and the cultural arts. Local recreation survey reports afforded a basis for local planning and action and also contributed valuable data on many aspects of recreation.

RECREATION IN THE DEPRESSION

The Depression and the unemployment which accompanied it inevitably had their effect upon the recreation movement. An added burden was thrown upon public facilities and leadership as people without work

[4] National Recreation Association, New York, 1930.

or with limited funds turned from more expensive forms of recreation to the public playgrounds, recreation centers, beaches, and picnic areas. The unprecedented attendance at indoor and outdoor recreation centers created new demands for additional leadership, facilities, and services and for the adaptation of existing facilities to more diversified and continuous uses. The rapid expansion in municipal sports programs provided opportunities for increasing numbers of participants and spectators. Instead of expanding their budgets, however, cities were obliged to cut their appropriations for recreation because of the financial crisis. As a result, in several cities the leadership staff was reduced to a point where it was unable to operate the playgrounds and centers. Realizing the seriousness of the situation, citizens offered to serve as volunteer leaders during the period of stress so that recreation services could be maintained without interruption and, after a period of training, they took the places of the paid workers. In 1932 and 1933 especially, playgrounds and indoor centers were operated in many cities primarily by volunteer leaders working under a limited paid staff.

Early in the Depression some of the larger cities established special centers for the unemployed, and programs for the families of persons out of work were also provided in a number of smaller communities. On the whole, however, the unemployed were encouraged to take part in the recreation activities provided for the entire community. Many playgrounds and centers were kept open for longer periods than before in order to serve the unemployed, and the tremendous increase in attendance at municipal recreation areas was due in no small measure to their use by this group.

The Depression caused an increase in home activities such as listening to the radio, reading, gardening, and hobbies,[5] whereas activities carried on outside the home involving considerable expense or elaborate equipment were engaged in by fewer people. The value of sporting goods produced in this country, for example, declined 57 per cent from 1929 to 1933. Local recreation authorities did their utmost to provide the greatest possible service with the curtailed funds at their disposal, but the recreation needs of the people would have been largely unmet were it not for the financial resources made available by emergency agencies.

The Use of Emergency Funds for Recreation. Early in the Depression cities used persons on relief to work on projects for the improvement of recreation areas, and in a few states comprehensive recreation leadership programs were worked out by the relief authorities. The object of these programs was to provide employment for white-collar workers as recreation leaders and to furnish recreation opportunities especially for the

[5] See *The Leisure Hours of 5,000 People,* a report of a survey conducted by the National Recreation Association, New York, 1934.

unemployed and their families. These earlier efforts pointed the way to the subsequent Federal projects carried on by the Civil Works Administration, the Federal Emergency Relief Administration, and the Works Progress Administration, which supplanted them, and by the National Youth Administration. The Federal recreation projects were of two types: (1) those involving the construction and development of recreation areas and facilities and (2) those providing leadership for recreation activities.

Through the use of local, state, and Federal relief funds, communities throughout the United States improved existing parks, playgrounds, and school sites and developed them for recreation uses. In addition, hundreds of athletic fields, swimming pools, tennis courts, golf courses, and winter sports facilities were constructed. Relief workers serving as leaders enabled recreation agencies to maintain programs which otherwise would have been curtailed; workers also made it possible for agencies to operate their enlarged facilities. Leaders trained in music, crafts, drama, art, dancing, or other activities introduced or extended activities in these particular fields. Therefore, even though municipal recreation budgets were reduced during the Depression, emergency leadership made possible expansion of the program in many cities and enabled other communities to secure the benefits of a recreation program for the first time.

Trends, 1930 to 1940. Few cities dismissed their recreation executive or eliminated their program during the Depression; in fact, recreation budgets were soon fully or partly restored to pre-Depression levels in many cities. The need for greater citizen interest and a more generous public support, in order that the enlarged program might be continued and the new facilities maintained and operated adequately, led to the widespread formation of advisory councils or lay committees. Increased municipal revenues, resulting from greater employment and production due to the country's preparedness program, greatly accelerated the recovery of municipal recreation budgets and programs at the end of the decade.

Adults took a more active part in municipal recreation programs than ever before; many of the new facilities were primarily for adult use. Large numbers of school buildings were opened for community recreation use for the first time. The value of recreation in sustaining morale and in affording joyous, constructive, healthful use of leisure time was more widely demonstrated and more generally appreciated than ever before. Municipal recreation leaders, having observed the public response to such activities as winter sports, roller skating, bicycling, and camping promoted on a commercial basis, expanded their facilities to afford more opportunities for the public to enjoy these activities. Music, nature, crafts, and drama activities were introduced more widely, and greater emphasis was placed upon co-recreation for youth. Universities and colleges became deeply interested in recreation and considered the desirability of establishing courses to prepare individuals for recreation leadership. The organization of the Society of Recreation Workers of America, now known as the American Recreation Society, by full-time workers in the recreation field indicated that recreation leadership was approaching the status of a profession.

RECREATION AND WORLD WAR II

World War II caused inevitable adjustments in recreation programs and new developments to meet wartime needs. Large numbers of recreation leaders entered the Armed Forces or war agencies, leaving a heavy burden on few or inexperienced workers. In-service training programs were expanded, and volunteer helpers were enrolled and trained in large numbers. Recreation budgets were increased, and tax-supported programs were inaugurated in many cities.

The war period saw many adjustments in program emphasis. Athletic programs were curtailed because of the limited number of available young men or because of the shortened leisure hours of workers. Victory gardens, learn-to-swim campaigns, and salvage drives were widely introduced. Gas and tire rationing and other restrictions on travel increased the load on neighborhood recreation facilities and services. The growing demand by youth for better recreation opportunities, coupled with an alarming increase in juvenile delinquency, caused teen-age centers to spring up all over the country.

Communities near military installations organized committees to mobilize local recreation resources for the use of visiting service personnel. Recreation departments put all suitable facilities at the disposal of units of the Armed Forces stationed nearby and organized special programs for them and their families. Immediately upon the passage of the Selective Service Act, the National Recreation Association inaugurated a special field service to assist localities near training camps. The Recreation Division of the Office of Community War Services of the Federal Security Agency was created in 1941 to assist with leadership and funds, and the United Service Organizations (USO), representing six national organizations, was formed to furnish recreation programs and operate clubs for men and women in the Armed Forces. Local programs included sports, information centers, lounge and checking service, dances, home hospitality, dramatics, church services and socials, sailing and fishing parties, sports carnivals, holiday festivals, and reduced rates for commercial recreation.

Abnormal wartime living conditions made recreation especially important in war production centers. A rapid expansion in plant recreation facilities and in the employment of recreation directors in industry resulted. Recreation departments extended their facilities and services to local industries and welcomed workers and their families into their programs. Centers for preschool children and afterschool play programs were provided for children of working mothers, and recreation buildings were kept open from early morning till late at night to serve night-shift workers.

Long-range plans for the acquisition of recreation areas and the construction of needed recreation facilities were developed in many cities in cooperation with city planning agencies. These plans were designed to afford a basis for postwar public works programs and to meet the demand for greatly expanded recreation facilities.

The effects of World War II upon local recreation were even more striking than those following World War I. Large numbers of servicemen and -women for the first time had an opportunity to enjoy extensive recreation facilities and diversified recreation programs. Furthermore, every community in the country felt the effects of home-front recreation activities during the war. The *Recreation Yearbook* for 1946 [6] revealed great forward strides since 1941, the last prewar year, and a greater volume of service than ever before recorded. A renaissance of the movement for living war memorials, initiated after World War I, also took place. The widespread acceptance by communities of the idea of living war memorials prompted the planning and subsequent construction of many memorials in the form of recreation buildings, playgrounds, parks, athletic fields, swimming pools, band shells, and forests.

RECREATION IN THE ATOMIC AGE

Significant developments in the recreation field have occurred since the end of World War II. Some were the result of wartime conditions; others have come about from a variety of causes. Several of these developments are likely to continue, perhaps in accelerated form in the years ahead. Later chapters describe in greater detail some of the major trends in the past decade.

Expanded Facilities and Service. Following the end of the war, steps were taken to carry out deferred plans for new recreation facilities and the rehabilitation of recreation properties neglected during the war years. The Korean War, however, caused a continuing shortage of critical building materials and a further postponement of needed construction. The unprecedented expansion of recreation facilities since the war ended has added appreciably to the country's recreation resources. Swimming pool

[6] National Recreation Association, New York, 19 .

construction has had an exceptional boom, but recreation buildings, sports facilities, artificial ice-skating rinks, and boating facilities, in particular, have multiplied. New types of playground equipment, designed to stimulate creative and imaginative play, have been developed. The growing tendency to install lights at outdoor recreation areas has greatly extended their periods of use and has enabled a larger number of people to benefit from them.

Present-day playground equipment stimulates imaginative play (Courtesy of Board of Recreation Commissioners, East Orange, N. J.).

The past decade has seen a great increase in insistent public demand for municipal recreation services, due partly to the influence of wartime recreation activities for service personnel and war workers and partly to the growing desire for recreation opportunities. A readiness on the part of local authorities to accept responsibility for meeting this demand resulted in the establishment of seasonal and year-round recreation programs in hundreds of localities. This growth was indicated by the *1956 Recreation and Park Yearbook* [7] which recorded some form of park or recreation service in 2,754 localities, 2,164 of which provided a recreation program

[7] National Recreation Association, New York, 1956.

under paid leadership. The unprecedented local expenditures for recreation service in 1955 further reflected the growth of the recreation movement as well as the prosperous state of the nation's economy.

The expansion of state participation in the recreation field, mentioned in Chapter 3, has been a striking postwar trend. Although only California and Vermont have followed the example of North Carolina, which established a recreation commission in 1945, many states have assigned recreation responsibilities to other agencies and have established interagency committees. Nearly every state has one or more parks, and a majority offer some form of advisory recreation service to their political subdivisions. State agencies promise to exert an increasing influence upon community recreation programs.

Program Emphases. Several trends in recreation programs and service are:

Greater consideration of the recreation needs of older adults

Growing concern for the needs of the physically and mentally handicapped

Added provision of areas, facilities, and leadership to meet the growing demand for swimming, boating, fishing, and other aquatic activities

Increasing participation by family groups, especially in picnicking and outing activities

Growing interest in camping, nature study, and conservation

Nationwide promotion of competitive sports programs for junior boys

Continuing desire by youth for opportunities to engage in activities with their own age group

Recognition of the need to offset the emphasis upon competitive programs by providing outlets for cooperative activities

Growing awareness of the need for greater stress upon activities that contribute to physical fitness for children and young people

Cooperative Action. The need to deal with increasingly pressing and complex problems has resulted in many examples of cooperative action. The series of workshops financed by The Athletic Institute has brought together outstanding leaders in various recreation agencies and has resulted in the production of reports of exceptional value. Increasingly, state and regional conferences and workshops are conducted under the joint sponsorship of several groups. The Federation of National Professional Organizations for Recreation, formed in 1954, now provides a clearinghouse for the growing number of national groups of professional recreation workers. In 1957 for the first time the National Recreation Congress was jointly sponsored by the National Recreation Association and several other agencies. The advisory committees appointed by the National Recreation Association have extended to hundreds of individuals concerned with various aspects of recreation an opportunity to share in projects beneficial to the entire recreation field. The Conference for National Cooperation in Aquatics and the Council for the Advancement of Hospital Recreation are examples of joint effort by national organizations to promote a specific phase of recreation.

Cooperation between school and municipal authorities in the acquisition, development, operation, and use of properties designed for both school and community recreation use has been achieved in many cities.

The National Advisory Council of the National Recreation Association meets in New York to consider recreation topics of national interest.

The principle of community use of school properties for recreation has become widely accepted, but until the last few years the concept of cooperative planning of such properties had been adopted in exceedingly few localities.

Leadership Trends. Recreation leadership positions involving full-time, year-round employment have been created in unprecedented numbers, especially in hospitals and in the Armed Forces.

Opportunities to secure an education designed to prepare one for recreation leadership have also expanded, as undergraduate recreation curricula and advanced courses on the graduate level have been established in colleges and universities. In-service training programs in the form of institutes and workshops for executives and other personnel have increased in number and effectiveness. In spite of these, a shortage of trained competent personnel exceeding that of any previous period exists because the openings in public departments, hospitals, military establishments, and other agencies far exceed the number of individuals completing their recreation training.

Volunteers have always played an important role in recreation but in recent years their service has been more widely used and more highly appreciated. The expanded junior sports programs have been made possible in large measure by the services of unpaid leaders. Expansion of many program features has resulted from volunteer assistance. The recognition by the National Recreation Association of individuals or organizations that have made conspicuous contributions to recreation in their communities—a feature of National Recreation Month—has focused public attention upon the degree to which the success of recreation programs depends upon unpaid leadership.

Outstanding Problems. Authorities and the public have awakened to the fact that they are faced with a serious problem of retaining their present recreation areas and of securing adequate recreation space to meet future needs. In most localities, acquisition of land for recreation has not kept pace with population increase, so shortages are greater than before. Competition for open space resulting from the marked industrial expansion and urban growth has removed much suitable land from potential recreation use and made more difficult and costly the acquisition of needed areas; it has also caused increasing and often successful attempts to divert recreation lands to nonconforming uses. Encroachments resulting from highway developments have been most serious, and park and recreation authorities are concerned over the prospect of further losses of needed park land as the current unprecedented Federal highway program is developed. The need for prompt action to acquire suitable land for recreation has stimulated the preparation and implementation of city-wide recreation plans.

The rapid expansion of housing, industrial and commercial developments outside city boundaries, in most cases in unincorporated areas, has created a cluster of recreation problems, which call for new forms of organization and for cooperation on the part of residents of the central city and the fringe areas. Many proposals have been made, some of which necessitate city-county consolidation or cooperation, involving methods of providing recreation areas, facilities, and services to metropolitan or fringe areas on an equable basis. A satisfactory solution of this urgent problem, however, lies in the future.

The Supreme Court decisions affecting integration have exerted marked and divergent influences upon local recreation services, especially in the South. In some instances, recreation facilities have been made available to all in the community, regardless of color; in other localities steps have been taken to dispose of recreation areas rather than to integrate their use. Some communities have abandoned plans for new facilities; others have provided new facilities, especially in neighborhoods with Negro residents. This problem still awaits a satisfactory solution.

Other Developments. The tendency for local recreation and park services to be united under a single department or agency has gained impetus in recent years, and in some states the combined park and recreation department is the prevailing form of managing authority. Consolidations of existing park and recreation departments have been comparatively few, but recreation and park functions have been combined in the creation of many new agencies.

Recreation has received more favorable and widespread attention than ever before. Partly because of its economic significance, but also because of its inherent value, recreation has been the topic of countless articles in top-ranking magazines with national circulation. Many television programs have centered about a recreation interest or activity. The promotion of National Recreation Month, endorsed through proclamations by governors and mayors and publicized through special programs in the localities, has focused public attention upon recreation as never before. The emphasis on recreation at such significant meetings as the President's Conference on Youth Fitness and the Symposium on Open Space, sponsored by *Fortune* and *Architectural Forum,* has accentuated its significance before influential groups.

In the atomic age, when the nations of the world have become neighbors, geographically if not always spiritually, international interest in recreation is natural. Recent years have seen a remarkable development of recreation in several nations and significant steps toward cooperation in the promotion of recreation around the world. Establishment of the International Recreation Service by the National Recreation Association, followed by extensive visits to many lands, culminated in the creation of the International Recreation Association in 1956. Cooperative exchange programs sponsored by the State Department have brought to America representatives of many foreign countries to study and observe recreation developments here. Americans in increasing numbers have visited other countries to become familiar with recreation developments abroad and to share experiences with their recreation leaders.

As the preceding paragraphs make clear, the recreation movement is not static; it has no stereotyped pattern or standard program. Over the years it has evolved and expanded to meet the increasing, ever-changing needs of the people. Even though rapid gains in recreation have been made since the war, opportunities for wholesome recreation are far from universal. The future holds both a challenge and an opportunity for providing rich and satisfying living for the people. Government—especially local government—will continue to play an important part in the provision of this essential service.

PART TWO

LEADERSHIP

Leadership, more than areas and facilities, activities and programs—important as they are—determines the success of municipal recreation service. In a field where human relationships and values are so important, it is absolutely essential to have creative, intelligent, trained leaders. Part Two is concerned with the nature, objectives, and methods of recreation leadership and with the general and special qualifications for various positions in the recreation department. Other aspects of the subject receiving consideration are preliminary and in-service training and methods of selecting and maintaining a leadership staff. Because volunteer leadership plays an important part in municipal recreation programs, a chapter is devoted to the problems involved in the use of volunteers and to the significance of citizen groups in the recreation field.

6. RECREATION LEADERSHIP

"There is no substitute for qualified leadership, and any compromise in this matter is false economy. The best leadership possible is none too good to guide and serve the leisure-time interests of the American people."[1] This statement by Joseph Prendergast reflects the opinion of all who are familiar with the recreation movement and recognize its potential contribution to the welfare of America. A study of the development of community recreation makes it clear that the greatest advances have been made and the outstanding achievements have been attained under competent and devoted leaders. On the other hand, programs have failed and facilities have received little use in communities where leadership was considered unimportant or where unqualified personnel were employed as recreation leaders. The greatest need of the recreation movement, in community, state, and nation, is for personnel who can give it intelligent and effective guidance in order that opportunities for the recreational use of leisure may be expanded and enriched in the years ahead.

The concept of leadership in recreation has undergone a drastic change in the past half century, as indicated in Chapter 5. In the early days of the movement the primary consideration was to provide interesting activities for small groups of young children. Recreation leadership today takes many forms, involves widely different functions, and has varied objectives. Leaders in different positions deal with children, young people, and adults; they help organize and conduct programs comprising a wide variety of activities; they administer many types of indoor and outdoor facilities, and they have relationships with recreation boards and committees, public authorities, community organizations, and the general public. The significance of recreation leadership has become increasingly recognized and it is gaining acceptance as a profession.

[1] Joseph Prendergast, *Personnel Standards in Community Recreation Leadership*, National Recreation Association, New York, 1957, Foreword.

LEADERSHIP OBJECTIVES AND FUNCTIONS

Estimates indicate that some ten thousand men and women are employed for recreation leadership on a full-time, year-round basis by public authorities and an equal number by voluntary agencies. Several times this number serve on a part-time or seasonal basis. The impact of these leaders upon the public—in many cases upon children and young people primarily—makes it highly important that their objectives be consistent with our democratic way of life.

This principle was stated clearly by Sherwood Gates, director of the Office of Community Services, United States Air Force, in addressing a group of recreation leaders from several foreign countries: "In a democracy the central objective of all conscientious, devoted leadership—whether that leadership be in the home, the school, the church, or in the area of recreation—is to promote the fullest possible growth of the individual as a free, responsible, happy and full-statured personality." [2] In the light of this objective he proposes that "only those who are completely dedicated to the purposes and convictions and processes of democracy have a rightful, continuing place of leadership in the recreation movement of a free country." He challenges recreation leaders to the task of "elevating the level and widening the range of recreational literacy; of enriching the leisure-time tastes, interests, and habits of the people."

Lawrence K. Frank has urged that we must develop the kinds of leadership in our group activities that are "appropriate to a free society and to the goals we are seeking." [3] There is general agreement among recreation leaders that the essential objectives of recreation leadership are to guide and serve the leisure-time interests of all the people—not to dictate them; to enlarge and deepen interests so that they will be more satisfying; to provide organization and instruction in recreation activities where desired; to furnish opportunities for self-expression through recreation so that the hours of leisure will make for joyous living.

In achieving these objectives, recreation leaders perform a variety of functions, of which the following are typical:

1. Guide and encourage individuals to acquire new interests and to gain greater satisfaction from participation in familiar activities
2. Help to organize recreation groups and to assure successful group operation
3. Attempt to expand and equalize recreation opportunities

[2] July 25, 1956, at the National Recreation Association office in New York.

[3] Lawrence K. Frank, *How to be a Modern Leader,* Association Press, New York, 1954, p. 11.

4. Teach people to acquire new or more advanced skills
5. Provide and maintain places in which individuals and groups may engage in activities
6. Assure safe and healthful conditions and practices
7. Furnish equipment and supplies essential for the enjoyment of many types of recreation

The preceding objectives can be achieved, and the functions listed performed satisfactorily, only by trained, sympathetic leaders.

PLAY LEADERSHIP FOR CHILDREN

In view of the status of play at the beginning of this century, it is not surprising that the question, Why teach a child to play? was frequently asked. Even civic leaders and parents who readily recognized the need for providing playgrounds in crowded cities felt that leaders were unnecessary. Play is natural, they asserted; children don't have to be taught to play. Today most people realize that while the impulse to play is natural, the forms of play are not. A child is born with the ability to talk, but the words he uses are taught him by his mother, his father, and his companions. It is the same with play. A baby does not inherit his finger plays and nursery rhymes, nor is a boy born with the knowledge or skill which enables him to play baseball. A boy learns to play the game from his father, his older brothers, or his companions on the playground. Even a little girl's doll play is an imitation of her mother's activity. Play has always been taught.

Parents, sisters, brothers, and companions still teach children to play, either by offering an example for them to imitate or by actually instructing them. The recreation leader, in supplementing the teaching of parents and companions, gives a deeper significance to the child's play life by bringing to it a wider experience and trained understanding. This is especially true today because the conditions which made playgrounds and recreation centers a necessity have also made the recreation leader indispensable.

As cities became congested, children's play opportunities grew more restricted. With the disappearance of the wide fields and streams went the child's chance to roam adventurously with his playmates, to climb trees, to fish, and to swim. The street with its limits and hazardous play resources became his playground. As houses became smaller and the farm was replaced by the back yard—and for many children by the crowded city tenement with no place to play indoors or out—the opportunity to play games, build things, and have pets and gardens was lost to many children.

Play without Guidance. The impulse to play was too strong, however, to be short-circuited by a change of living conditions. But if the environment frustrated its free expression, play activities were likely to be destructive rather than constructive. Juvenile-court records are full of cases of misdirected play, the right expression of which would have meant much to the boy or girl involved and to society.

The public playground was designed to remedy the situation. Playgrounds took children off the streets and gave them a place where they

Under competent leadership the game of dodge ball is fun and develops alertness of mind and body (Courtesy of Los Angeles City Board of Education).

could play freely and without interference from objecting neighbors. They were the city's answer to the question, Where shall we play? But without leadership playgrounds were no guarantee against rowdyism and unsocial conduct. In fact, playgrounds presented more difficulties to the child than the open fields where he roamed with his friends. On the city playground a child must learn to adjust his activities to the limitations of space and equipment and to share the facilities with large numbers of other children. He must take turns using the swings or playing on the ball diamond, and he must acquire the ability to cooperate with children he has never seen before. Children need help to cope with such complex problems. They do not have the necessary self-discipline, social experience, or maturity of judgment to appraise each situation properly, or the ability to deal with it satisfactorily. An adult leader is needed to see that rowdies do not monopolize the playground, that the shy, retiring child has a chance to play, and that little children have a place in which to play safely while the older boys are engaged in vigorous activities.

Playground Leadership. Leadership on the playground assures much more than the maintenance of discipline and order. Park guards can look after the equipment, and policemen, who represent organized force and authority to the child, can enforce good behavior; but this discipline has only negative value. It lacks the vital, positive influence on the growing child which a competent leader brings to the playground. Unlike the policeman or guard who acts only when some disciplinary problem arises, the leader is in constant association with the children. He keeps the child happily engaged in activities which interest him deeply and conducts the activities in such a way that occasions for dispute are minimized. When fights do occur—and they sometimes do—the leader helps the combatants settle their difficulties and reach a solution through understanding. He seeks to enlist the children's active cooperation in curbing an undesirable activity for an understandable and worthy end. In this way children learn self-control and restraint in their social relationships; they learn the value of discipline by experiencing the good it brings them, not by resisting its restraints.

Leadership and Character. Character building is not the primary purpose of leadership, but the playground under competent leadership is an excellent place for a child to learn proper conduct. The social situations a child meets there closely resemble those he must cope with in later life. The child comes into free association with other children as individuals and in groups. He is not compelled to attend or to participate in the program. If he does choose to participate, however, and the playground is under the guidance of a good leader, the child learns to give and take with others, to win graciously, and to accept defeat without complaint. The rules that govern the child's conduct are chiefly the rules of the game and the rules of social living; the child may have a share in preparing and in enforcing them. The leader remains in the background and exercises direct control only when it is necessary. Consequently, the children learn by firsthand experience how to get along with others, and the play experiences afford valuable lessons in social conduct.

Under the guidance of a capable recreation leader the child has the opportunity to develop desirable character traits, individual as well as social. Since the playground is essentially free from compulsion, the child makes his own decisions and experiences the results, good or bad, that come directly from these decisions. He has the opportunity to initiate and lead activities, and through actual practice he acquires judgment, self-reliance, and the ability to handle responsibilities. The same results are achieved not only at the playground but wherever groups of children engage in recreation activities under competent leaders.

Leadership Methods and Values. Recreation leaders know that a happy childhood is essential to a child's normal growth and personal development, that self-discipline and proper conduct are natural results of a situation in which a child engages in activities of absorbing interest under wise guidance. The chief purpose of leadership, therefore, is to fill the child's play hours with challenging, creative, enjoyable activities which foster the free expression of his play interests and to conduct these activities in such a way that every child is assured of a happy and richly satisfying playtime. To the extent that the leader succeeds in achieving this objective, he is contributing to the children's happiness and personal development.

The recreation leader provides not merely the opportunity for children to play the games, to sing the songs, and to make the things they want, but the infectious enthusiasm which gives a zest to the activities. He gives direct guidance where it is needed to take care of particular difficulties or to make participation more enjoyable. The leader sees that the necessary equipment, playing space, and materials are provided for the activities in which the children have a definite interest. In planning and conducting the program, he seeks to assist the children in achieving self-expression, physical fitness, personality, and character development. He takes into account the children's individual interests and abilities; he preserves initiative by allowing ample opportunity for self-directed activities; and he takes into consideration each child's need for recognition and for experiencing success. He fosters the children's creative planning ability and encourages exploration in new fields of activity. By getting acquainted with all the children he tries to discover interests which are not immediately apparent. He pays special attention to the needs of the timid and awkward child. He introduces new activities so the children will have a greater range of choices than they would have if left entirely to themselves. By helping them develop skills, he increases the satisfaction and enjoyment which they gain from taking part in the activities.

Leadership Teaches Skills. The importance of teaching skills and providing a variety of play opportunities is sometimes overlooked by people who do not understand the nature and purpose of leadership. The acquisition of skill is a prerequisite to satisfactory participation in many forms of recreation. To a degree, skill is acquired by trial and error, but trained leaders can save individuals costly and discouraging experimentation. People enjoy most the activities which they perform well, and they tend to avoid those in which they have little skill. By arousing in children a desire for self-improvement and by helping them to learn better ways of playing old games and the best ways of performing new activities, the leader increases the satisfaction and fun which they derive from participation. In addition he helps overcome the reluctance of many children as well as adults to take part in activities which they do not perform well and prepares them for a richer recreation experience in later life.

Variety is essential in a child's play life for the fullest development of his interests and personality. Children tend to get into mischief because

Helping children acquire recreation skills is a major leadership function (Courtesy of Long Beach, Calif., Recreation Commission).

they are bored with playing the same old games and are at a loss to know what to do. "The world is so full of a number of things, I'm sure we should all be as happy as kings," said Robert Louis Stevenson when he was writing for children. Playtime is the time to play games of all kinds, to explore the world of fairies and make-believe and adventure in stories, to become acquainted with the world of song, to build things, to produce plays and learn about drama and the stage, to dance, to discover nature and the world of growing things. Leadership makes possible a variety of such experiences.

Children learn best when they are free from compulsion and motivated from within. Because the child is most free and most himself when at play, the lessons of the playground and recreation center are quickly learned and long remembered. Suggestion and imitation are powerful influences in determining children's behavior; and because in the play group the child sees others playing happily, he has the desire and incentive to join them. On the playground the child has the opportunity to experiment with many different activities and to discover the interests which for him have the greatest value. The discovery and development of latent skills and potential interests are among the primary functions of the recreation leader.

The real test of recreation leadership is the extent to which the activities engaged in and the attitudes taught at the center are carried over into the child's play life at home and in the neighborhood. The influence of the leader is also indicated by the degree to which interests fostered by him persist in later life and afford rich leisure-time resources. In teaching skills and acquainting children with a variety of activities, the leader awakens and encourages interests which may last a lifetime and make the difference between richness and drabness in adult living.

Leadership and Freedom. The objection has sometimes been made that recreation leaders encroach on a child's freedom, destroying the spontaneity of his play and initiative. This argument reveals a failure to understand the nature of freedom and of leadership. Freedom is inherent in a play situation, where a child can come and go as he chooses. But at a playground or indoor center under competent leadership he is more free to play his own games and to follow his own inclinations than on a playground monopolized by older children or dominated by bullies. Under leadership he learns control, but most of his restraints are inherent in the activities themselves or are established by the play group. If he wants to play, he must recognize the rights of his comrades and abide by the rules.

The leader creates an environment in which it is easy for children to express their play interests and to function as individuals and social beings. Far from destroying freedom, leadership increases the only freedom which matters—freedom with control based on understanding, willing acceptance, and cooperation.

Quality Leadership Essential. To accomplish the purposes and attain the objectives described in the preceding pages, it is obvious that trained leaders of intelligence and high moral caliber are necessary. What children play and how they respond to group situations on the playground are often the direct result of the leader's own enthusiasms and of his personal attitudes and conduct. Certainly children cannot be expected to develop desirable character traits on the playground unless the leaders themselves possess and demonstrate such qualities in their varied daily relationships.

The recreation leader, because of his prowess in one or more recreation activities and by the circumstances of his position, is a natural object of hero worship. Children are therefore kindly disposed toward him, and the whole association between the leader and the children is a happy one. It is natural for them to like him; and liking easily becomes admiration, which in turn leads to imitation. Since the leader through his position exerts such a profound influence on the children, only the best and highest quality of leadership is acceptable.

The idea that leadership is necessary is not mere theory. Boys and girls have demonstrated repeatedly that they value it highly. The history of playgrounds at which no leadership has been provided has been universally disappointing, and the experience has been little better where incompetent persons were employed as leaders. Children have shown that they want more than just a place in which to play; they want leadership that can make the place interesting and exciting with challenging activities.

Recreation leadership is just as important in rural as in urban communities because the need for variety in play and for acquiring recreation skills is universal. Most rural children have ample space and materials for play and a rich and potentially stimulating environment. But they need leadership to help them make the most of these resources and to provide opportunities for them to play happily with other children of the same age.

LEADERSHIP FOR YOUTH AND ADULTS

Many communities fail to realize that modern city living has created the need for recreation leadership for youth and adults as well as for children. The argument is frequently raised that young people and adults should have the maturity to look after their own recreation. This shortsighted viewpoint completely overlooks the fact that youth and adults are restricted in their recreation opportunities by the conditions of urban living just as much as the children are. Admittedly many adults have the maturity to choose and the ability to direct their own activities. But they cannot play in a baseball league unless they have access to a diamond; they cannot play tennis if there are no courts; they cannot swim if there are no pools or bathing beaches; nor can they play in a community orchestra unless someone takes the initiative to organize one and to provide a meeting place.

Leadership is necessary to provide recreation opportunities. The young people and adults who need recreation most can seldom secure the facilities for themselves. Leadership is necessary to bring together people of similar tastes, for in a modern city people often do not know other individuals who are interested in the same activities. Leadership also furnishes young people and adults the opportunity and experience of conducting their own activities and provides instruction in these activities when it is needed. Most adults today have fewer recreation interests than children because in their early years they were denied opportunities to play and to develop recreation skills. Countless individuals will never experience the joy of participating in recreation activities except as leadership extended to adult groups makes such participation possible.

Volunteer leadership plays an important role in adult recreation groups, but paid leaders are considered essential by many organizations providing recreation service for adults. Private athletic clubs employ directors and instructors in various sports. Country clubs have their managers, golf pros, riding masters, and tennis instructors. Sketch clubs have their art teachers, and dramatic groups their coaches and directors. The majority of people, however, do not belong to such organizations and cannot afford them. But where communities have made recreation leadership available, adults have demonstrated by their enthusiastic participation in the program that they want not only the type of leadership which provides facilities but the leadership which organizes activities and furnishes instruction when it is needed.

The number of older boys and men playing baseball, softball, and other team games has grown by leaps and bounds in cities where athletic directors have been employed to organize and promote teams, leagues, and contests. The attendance at city golf courses and tennis courts has shown a marked increase in cities where the recreation authorities have conducted golf and tennis schools. People who did not know how to play were eager to learn when offered the opportunity; others were anxious to improve their skills. In one city hundreds of adults who had formerly taken no part in the recreation program joined a newly organized drama group after a trained director was added to the department staff. Comparable results experienced in the case of other types of activity have demonstrated the essential role of leadership in bringing to large numbers of people the opportunity to engage in satisfying recreation activities.

Leadership Methods. People who question the value and need of providing recreation leadership for youth and adult groups ignore the fact that every such group involves leadership either from within or from the outside. This leadership may be represented by one individual, or it may be exerted by the cooperative action of certain members, but no group can operate without it. The chief function of professional recreation leadership for young people and adults is to draw out, strengthen, and put into action the leadership capacities inherent in the members of the group. It is "helping the group learn to decide and act for itself more efficiently," [4] and it establishes a dynamic relationship in the group by encouraging each member to share in a creative group process.

[4] Malcolm Knowles and Hulda Knowles, *How to Develop Better Leaders*, Association Press, New York, 1955, p. 12.

Many a recreation leader gradually withdraws from continuous direct leadership of an adult group after an activity has been started and the group has learned to carry on successfully under its own leadership. It is in this respect that the functions of leaders of adult groups differ most from those of the playground leaders. Since, in general, adults are more disciplined than children, are more experienced in group relationships, and have more defined, though fewer, recreation interests, they can take greater responsibility for determining and directing their own activities. They can assume a larger measure of self-government and self-organization, and the paid recreation leader does not need to give so continuous or direct guidance as is necessary in dealing with children's groups. Young people often select and direct their own activities, but skillful leadership is required to inspire them to seek perfection. In many instances the most valuable service which the paid leader can render is to advise and assist people in forming their own recreation groups and in establishing their own standards and procedures. The trained worker helps lay leaders acquire the skills and techniques which are essential to effective self-leadership within these groups. He establishes a climate in which maximum values from recreation experience are achieved.

Group leadership of youth and adults is involved in the organization and promotion of athletic leagues, orchestras, drama groups, social and hiking clubs, hobby groups, community-wide events, and a great variety of program features. Its functioning is perhaps best demonstrated by the recreation center leader who, like the playground leader, comes into direct relationship with individuals and groups of diversified interests. He must be able to help the participants discover interests, introduce variety when it is needed, and furnish instruction where it seems advisable. But the recreation center leader often remains in the background and encourages members of the group to accept leadership roles. He assists individuals in getting together with others who have a similar interest, and he helps groups in organizing their activities and getting their programs under way, after which he withdraws except for occasional contacts and help with specific problems. He offers suggestions but keeps responsibility for decisions within the group. Thus in the active sharing of ideas the participants acquire the experience of functioning as a group and increase their skill in managing their own activities. This experience, especially in recreation activities, is available to large numbers of young people and adults only as leadership is provided by the recreation department.

Sometimes individuals want specific instruction in recreation activities but are not interested in joining a highly organized group. They want to learn to dance, to play a musical instrument, to make jewelry or some other type of handcraft. Here the leader's primary function is to give instruction, but he also has an opportunity to develop a feeling of fellowship among the members of the class and to make its meeting a pleasant social experience. Furthermore, by introducing the class to related, diversified activities the leader is often able to arouse the members' interest in other parts of the program and to broaden their field of recreation activity.

So far the discussion has dealt only with the leadership of group activities for children, young people, and adults. Other types of leadership are required for the successful operation of a well-rounded community recreation program. Activities such as picnicking, horseback riding, bathing, tennis, and golf are largely self-directed and are engaged in by individuals rather than groups, but the provision of the necessary facilities requires a certain form of leadership. Effective operation of these facilities calls for a close and friendly relationship between the persons using them and the officials in immediate charge of them.

EXECUTIVE AND SUPERVISORY LEADERSHIP

The preceding pages have dealt primarily with aspects of leadership that are involved in direct relationships between leaders and the individuals and groups they serve. Many leadership functions, however, are performed by workers who have little personal contact with the people who benefit from their service. These functions may be the administration of a system of recreation areas and facilities; the planning and supervision of a city-wide recreation program; the recruiting and effective use of a competent staff; the development and maintenance of a system of attendance, personnel, service, and financial records; the securing and disbursement of funds; and the establishment of cooperative relationships with municipal and school authorities, local organizations, and the public. Such functions are typical and are primarily the responsibility of the superintendent of recreation and the general and special supervisors; but to a lesser degree they are shared with other members of the leadership staff. The center director, for example, performs executive and supervisory duties when he plans the center program, manages his staff, supervises the operation and maintenance of his center, and oversees the work of his paid and volunteer leaders.

Some of the most useful functions of recreation leadership are concerned with relationships apart from the department's properties, staff, and program. The good executive works closely and continuously with his board or advisory committee, city council, or city manager, in order that they may understand clearly the functions, problems, services, and needs of his department and thus be prepared to act intelligently when decisions affecting it must be made. He seeks to establish and maintain cooperative relationships with the heads of other departments, with voluntary agencies, and with local organizations that are in a position to help with the work of his department or that his department might serve. He takes advantage of every opportunity to acquire new areas or facilities, to capitalize upon every significant event that demonstrates the importance or value of recreation, and to enlist understanding and support for the recreation program. More important, he develops plans and programs of action based upon a study of conditions and needs. A measure of the effectiveness of his leadership is the degree to which his enthusiasm and zeal for the advancement of recreation are shared by the members of his board, commission, or committee. These lay groups can and often do perform some leadership functions more effectively than professional workers. The duties, responsibilities, and relationships of paid and volunteer leaders are considered in detail in later chapters.

In view of the present-day competition for open land, for the tax dollar, for competent personnel, and for people's time and interest, it is obvious that the recreation needs of the public will be adequately served only as qualified recreation leadership is made available. Therefore communities which value recreation and expect a fair return on their investment in areas and facilities cannot afford to stint on providing competent leaders. They must insist on the kind of dynamic leadership that vitalizes and energizes the whole recreation life of the community.

7. RECREATION DEPARTMENT PERSONNEL

THE RECREATION department, like every other organization or municipal agency, can function effectively only if it has a competent, loyal staff. The need for such a staff is particularly apparent in the recreation department because most of its workers have a direct personal relationship with the individuals and groups who use the department's facilities and participate in its program. To plan and conduct the various activities and services comprising the comprehensive program, described in later chapters, and to operate and maintain its many areas and facilities, personnel of diversified qualifications, training, experience, and ability is required. Different positions call for varying degrees of ability as executive, supervisor, director, manager, group leader, and teacher. In addition to the leadership personnel, maintenance workers keep the recreation plant in good condition; clerical assistants handle the department records; and many other types of employees serve in varying capacities.

Each worker in the recreation department has an important place to fill, but of special significance are workers employed to perform the leadership functions which are peculiar to the recreation department and which differentiate such service from work carried on in other governmental agencies. They are the workers who comprise the group which has become recognized as a new and distinct profession. This chapter considers the types of leadership positions in municipal recreation, the duties performed, and some of the essential qualifications for workers in each of these positions.

GENERAL QUALIFICATIONS FOR ALL LEADERS

"The leader must be an individual of well-rounded personality and upright character, with power to influence character and personality in both children and adults." In these words Joseph Lee points out two basic qualifications without which the recreation leader cannot be successful and recognizes the influence which the leader continually exerts in his relations with individuals and groups.

The requirements for recreation leadership positions increasingly call for greater knowledge, technical ability, skills, and educational background, but experience has taught that these qualifications are of limited value to the recreation leader unless he has the proper attitudes, interests, and personal qualities. No person who does not have personal integrity, a sound educational background, and potentialities for growth and development should be accepted, even for the least responsible position, in a profession where dealing with people is the prime concern. Unless a person lives joyously and creatively, he is not likely to help others find satisfaction in recreation activities under his leadership.

Educational Requirements. The educational standards required for employment have taken on greater significance as the requirements for recreation service have become higher and as recreation leadership has sought a place among the professions. At present, graduation from a college or university of recognized standing with a bachelor's degree based on a major in recreation leadership, including supervised field work, is considered as a minimum basic qualification for employment in practically all leadership positions in the recreation department. Graduate study is recommended for persons planning to serve in an executive capacity because it is an essential requirement for an executive position.

To encourage young people to enter the recreation field and to give them opportunities for leadership experience under guidance, preprofessional positions are created for which graduation from college is not required. Completion of two years of college with a major in recreation is recommended for the student recreation leader, and completion of two years of high school for the junior recreation assistant. Persons serving in these positions are considered trainees, not professional leaders.

Educational qualifications are sometimes waived in the case of individuals who, because of some specific skill or special ability, are able to serve as instructor or specialist in a particular phase of the program. Although such individuals can perform useful service under supervision, they cannot meet the basic educational requirement for classification as a recreation leader. Membership in the recreation profession must be reserved for those who have the necessary personal qualities and the best possible educational preparation.

Personal Requirements. The essential personal qualifications for service as a recreation leader are difficult to define and measure, but they form the foundation of successful leadership. Every person considering recreation as a field of work would do well to rate himself in the light of the qualities listed as follows:

Sterling character and personal and professional integrity
Faith in people and belief in the worth and dignity of every human being
Personal realization of the joy of life and of the art of living

Good sense of humor

Sense of service above personal ambition

Concern with the growth of individuals through creative expression

Appreciation of leadership as an art

Belief in democracy in recreation, as in government

A pleasing, friendly personality

Organizing ability

Productive energy and contagious enthusiasm

Ability to get along with people—to accept others' opinions and personalities

Good physical and mental health

Important as all these qualities are, if one of them—character—is lacking, an individual should seek some other field of work, because without it he will never become a truly successful recreation leader.

TYPES OF LEADERSHIP POSITIONS

In spite of widely different local conditions and variety in the types and titles of recreation positions throughout the United States, cities increasingly tend to adopt a standard nomenclature. This is due in no small measure to the influence of a series of reports issued by committees appointed by the National Recreation Association. Many of the statements in this chapter are based upon or adapted from the latest of these reports [1] prepared for the association.

The following is a brief description of the titles generally used and of the major responsibilities usually assigned to the representative positions:

1. Executive

   a. Superintendent of recreation: Chief executive officer in charge of a recreation department or division and its personnel; responsible for planning, promoting, and administering a comprehensive recreation service for all the community.

   b. Superintendent of recreation and parks: Chief executive officer in charge of a recreation and parks department and its personnel; responsible for the administration of a comprehensive recreation program for the entire community and for the administrative management of the public parks, playgrounds, and other recreation facilities. (In communities utilizing a combined recreation and park department, the superintendent of recreation heads the recreation division within this department.)

[1] *Personnel Standards in Community Recreation Leadership,* National Recreation Association, National Advisory Committee on Recruitment, Training, and Placement of Recreation Personnel, New York, 1957.

   c. Assistant superintendent of recreation: Executive officer responsible for administration, planning, organization, and supervision of the recreation program as general assistant to the superintendent of recreation; acts for the superintendent in his absence.

2. Supervisor

   a. Recreation supervisor (general): Supervisor responsible either for all recreation services for a district or a large subordinate geographic area of the community, or for all services or facilities of a similar type.

   b. Recreation supervisor (special activity): Supervisor responsible for the planning, promotion, development, and supervision of a specialized activity phase of recreation as a community-wide program (e.g., music, athletics and sports, arts and crafts).

3. Center director

   a. Recreation center director: Responsible for the direction of a comprehensive program for a single recreation center which may include a recreation building or indoor center, playground, playfield, camp or day camp, or combination of any of these.

   b. Assistant recreation center director: Responsible for personal direction of assigned portions of the recreation program for a recreation center, and serves for the recreation director in his absence.

4. Leader [2]

   a. Recreation leader (general): Under close supervision, is responsible for the promotion, organization, and personal leadership of a variety of recreation activities at an indoor and/or outdoor recreation center and for related work in the community.

   b. Recreation leader (special activity): Under close supervision, is responsible for the organization, development, and personal leadership of one recreation activity or several closely related activities at one or more recreation centers.

5. Trainee: The trainee positions prepare young people for professional recreation leadership; they should not be considered substitutes for professional positions.

   a. Recreation intern: Responsible for various administrative, supervisory, and leadership functions in a rotated work program under

---

[2] "Recreation leader" is used both as the title of a basic leadership position and as the generic term for all who practice the profession of recreation leadership. Educators and groups within the profession have advocated the adoption of a single word such as "recreator" or "recreationist," but these have not received sufficient acceptance to justify their general use.

supervision of the superintendent. This is a professional internship for graduates of recreation curricula.

b. Student recreation leader: Under close supervision of a full-time staff member, responsible for the promotion, organization, and personal leadership of a variety of recreation activities in a field-work program supervised by agency and college.

c. Junior recreation assistant: Under continuous supervision, assists recreation leaders to conduct games, special events, and other activities. Oversees free-play activities and does routine tasks in both leadership and nonleadership work.

A leader has the undivided attention of her singing group (Courtesy of St. John and St. Joseph Home, Utica, N. Y.).

It is clear that many recreation departments do not employ all the types of workers mentioned in the preceding list. With the growing diversification in recreation programs and the expansion of recreation facilities, however, cities are finding it necessary to employ more and more workers who are particularly equipped to assume responsibility for special features and services. A superintendent of recreation is needed as executive director in every recreation department; in large cities he requires the services of an assistant superintendent. In cities where there are more playgrounds and centers than can be supervised effectively by the superintendent and his assistant, one or more general supervisors are needed. Many departments today employ special supervisors to promote and direct certain phases of the program such as athletics, music, and drama, at least on a part-time or seasonal basis. Some of the larger systems have several such workers. Every city needs directors to operate its playgrounds and indoor centers, as well as leaders to conduct a wide variety of activities. Few cities have an intern, but young people are being increasingly employed as student leaders and junior assistants.

DUTIES AND SPECIAL QUALIFICATIONS

In the light of experience, recommended standards have been adopted for the various positions. These standards set forth the duties, special qualifications, education, and experience considered necessary for satisfactory service. The first three of these essentials do not vary, as a rule, according to the size of the city in which the service is to be rendered. However, the minimum experience requirements, in the case of the executive and supervisory positions, differ for cities of varying populations. In general, the larger the community, the broader the program and the more complex the executive and supervisory problems; greater experience is therefore considered essential in handling them. The standards are not to be applied rigidly to given positions, but they do set forth normal minimum requirements which should be met by persons seeking employment in recreation. To qualify for a position, a person who fails to meet the standard in any respect should have a compensatory qualification.

The following pages contain brief statements outlining the essential duties of workers in the various leadership positions and a few of the basic qualifications for effective service. As previously indicated, college graduation or its equivalent is considered a requirement for all the positions, except where otherwise indicated. The duties and qualifications recommended are described in detail in the report of the National Advisory Committee on Recruitment, Training, and Placement of Recreation Personnel.

Superintendent of Recreation. As chief executive officer in charge of a recreation department or division and its personnel, the superintendent carries out the policies of the recreation board or other recreation authority and serves as technical advisor to the authority as well as recreation consultant for the community. His executive responsibilities may be grouped under the following headings: administration, areas and facilities, planning and research, program, staff, finance, public and community relations, and records and reports. The relative demand which these duties make upon the superintendent's time varies with the size and type of the community and of the recreation system. In the large city, responsibility for performing some of these duties is delegated to subordinates. In the small community, the executive must assume some of the duties normally assigned to persons in subordinate positions. The duties of the superintendent of recreation are described in greater detail in Chapter 30.

Among the special qualifications for this position are a thorough knowledge of the theory and philosophy of recreation; an understanding of community recreation problems; ability to organize, administer, and operate recreation areas and facilities and a comprehensive community recreation program; skill in selecting, training, and supervising a staff; a capacity for cooperative action and decision making; and skill in the techniques of management and in interpreting recreation through speech and writing. A master's degree in recreation or in a related field is a minimum educational qualification. Proven successful experience of from one to six years in a supervisory or executive position in recreation, depending upon the size of the city, is also recommended.

Superintendent of Recreation and Parks. This worker, as the executive responsible for both parks and recreation services, has much the same duties and requires the same qualifications as the superintendent of recreation. In addition, he has greater responsibility for area and facility acquisition and planning, for the operation and maintenance of properties, and for cooperating actively with agencies concerned with city planning, conservation, parks, and related problems. He must also understand the design, construction, and maintenance of parks, be able to superintend a program involving these functions, and to supervise personnel such as landscape architects, engineers, foresters, and horticulturists in the planning and care of parks and recreation properties. Because his duties are more complex than those of the superintendent of recreation, a longer period of successful experience is required—from two to seven years.

Assistant Superintendent of Recreation. This worker serves as the general deputy or assistant to the superintendent of recreation and, under his supervision, helps the superintendent perform any of the duties assigned to him. He needs the same personal and special qualifications, including experience. Graduate education is not considered essential for this position, but the committee recommends that a year's graduate study in designated areas be allowed as a substitute for a full year of experience.

Recreation Supervisor (General). Typical titles in this classification are district recreation supervisor, supervisor of playgrounds and centers, and supervisor of special facilities. As officer responsible for the total program in a district or for a particular type of city-wide facilities, the general supervisor acts as a deputy to the superintendent of recreation in the promotion and administration of a comprehensive district or community-wide recreation program. He exercises responsible judgment in performing his duties, and reports to and receives guidance from the superintendent.

His duties likewise cover the various aspects of planning and administering a recreation program and relate to areas and facilities, staff training and relationships, supervision of activities and centers, public and community relations, budgets and records, study of special problems, etc. Special qualifications are generally comparable, though somewhat less demanding, than for the superintendent. From one to five years of related successful experience in recreation is considered a minimum requirement, although a master's degree in recreation may substitute for one year of required qualifying experience.

Recreation Supervisor (Special Activity). This category applies to persons who are responsible for a specialized phase of recreation on a community-wide basis, such as athletics and sports, drama, puppetry and storytelling, arts and crafts, music, dance, nature, and camping; or programs for a special age group, like older adults. A supervisor may be responsible for two types of related activities. His duties are primarily those of planning, initiating, organizing, and supervising a city-wide program of activities related to his specialty. In doing this he utilizes the personal and material resources at his command and cooperates with workers inside and outside the department in assuring the maximum interest, participation, and benefit from his part of the program. Qualifications for the position are less broad but quite similar to those of the general supervisor. He must have professional skill in the planning, organization, and leadership of the special activity and in relating it to other phases of the recreation program. From one to five years' experience are recommended, although completion of a master's degree is considered in lieu of one year of qualifying experience.

Recreation Center Director. This title encompasses the wide variety of positions which involve primarily the responsibility for the operation of a recreation building, indoor center, playground, playfield, or camp. The titles of playground director and camp director are typical of those applied under this general category. The director is in full charge of the center, subject to policies and regulations established by his superiors, and directs its total operation. In doing so he plans and administers the program, supervises the personnel assigned to the center, oversees the maintenance, promotes good relationships, assures the proper handling of funds and supplies, and performs other essential duties. (For a more detailed statement of his duties see Chapters 17 and 18.) Special qualifications include personal skills in the leadership of activities used at the center, ability to organize and direct a comprehensive program and to utilize the skills of center personnel, a knowledge of the philosophy of recreation and its application to individuals and groups, and ability to administer the operation of a center. If a position involves the supervision of full-time recreation leaders at a large center, a master's degree in recreation or one year's successful full-time experience in recreation leadership is recommended.

The special responsibilities associated with the management of a camp involve duties and requirements that can be performed or met only by persons who have had special camping education and experience. In general, however, standards for the camp director are similar to those for the directors of other centers.

Boys and girls learn to ski at the Tacoma ski school sponsored by the Metropolitan Park District and the *Tacoma News Tribune* (Courtesy Tacoma, Wash., Metropolitan Park District).

Assistant Recreation Center Director. Under the supervision of the director, this worker conducts portions of the program, aids in the administration of the center by performing whatever duties may be assigned to him, and acts in the director's absence. In view of his limited responsibility, he is not required to have as much ability in organization and management as the director. One half year of graduate study in recreation leadership is considered a substitute for six months of full-time experience.

Recreation Leader (General). Under close supervision, the leader performs a variety of duties, usually at an indoor or outdoor center. He conducts activities, organizes and advises clubs and groups, promotes and directs special events, supervises facilities and equipment, and assists his superiors with assigned tasks. He requires personal leadership skills, competence in organizing and conducting activities, and the ability to deal readily with individuals and groups. No previous experience is required other than the supervised field work performed as part of his preparation as an undergraduate recreation major.

Recreation Leader (Special Activity). Unlike the general leader who is called on to help with many phases of the program, the special activity leader under close supervision is responsible for the organization, development, and personal leadership of one activity or of several closely related activities. Program activities in which such leaders are employed include athletics and sports, arts and crafts, drama, music, dance, social recreation, nature, and camping. These are the same types of activity for which special activity supervisors are employed. This recreation leader organizes and leads groups in his specialty, trains volunteer leaders, plans and conducts special events, and helps relate his activity to the total center or community recreation program. The qualifications for this position are similar to those of the general recreation leader, except that specialized skill and education in the area of specialization are essential.

Trainee. Positions in this category are those designed to offer young people opportunities for appropriate experience in recreation leadership. They supplement rather than replace the professional leadership staff, and use of trainee leaders is recommended only in departments which have achieved reasonably high leadership standards. The three trainee positions are recreation intern, student recreation leader, and junior recreation assistant. The first two of these are open primarily to persons who are actually preparing for professional service in the recreation field. The position of junior recreation assistant serves a dual purpose: It frees professional leaders from routine tasks and affords an opportunity for the assistant to gain practical experience in recreation. Completion of sophomore year in high school and attendance at a preseason training institute are recommended minimum qualifications for this position.

Other Workers. As mentioned earlier in the chapter there are other types of workers in the recreation department. Some of them, like the manager of a golf course or stadium and the lifeguard at a beach or swimming pool may perform leadership functions. Others, like the cashier at the golf course or bathing center, greenskeeper, maintenance foreman, mechanic, gardener, janitor, camp cook, and clerical personnel, do not serve in a leadership capacity. The nature of the tasks performed by many of these workers requires that they meet and deal with the public; in some cases they have frequent relationships with children. For this reason character, personality, and ability to deal with people in a courteous, friendly, but efficient manner are important. In most of these positions it is not necessary or practical to demand the same educational and personal qualifications as in leadership positions, but training, skills, experience, and personality traits which make for success in them must be considered in employing personnel for these nonprofessional tasks. Workers in non-leadership positions comprise a majority of the personnel in departments that provide both organized recreation and traditional park services, which, as mentioned in Chapter 5, are becoming numerous.

CONDITIONS VERSUS STANDARDS

The preceding general and special qualifications for leadership personnel in the recreation department represent standards which have been developed by the recreation profession. They have been generally approved by recreation authorities and have been incorporated in varying degrees in locally adopted personnel standards. Although some local recreation departments fall short of meeting them, there is a growing appreciation of the importance of desirable personal and educational qualifications for recreation leadership personnel. In spite of unsatisfactory conditions in some cities, a steady advance toward higher standards and toward the acceptance of the standards recognized in the profession is being achieved. This has been facilitated by the adoption in many localities of job classifications, descriptions, and qualifications. More adequate training opportunities, more honest and intelligent methods of selecting workers, and greater assurance of security and promotion for persons who render satisfactory service are contributing to this end. Some of these factors affecting recreation leadership will be considered in the chapters that follow.

OTHER PROFESSIONAL LEADERSHIP POSITIONS

Even though this chapter deals primarily with positions in the public recreation department, brief mention will be made of employment opportunities open to professional recreation leaders in several other agencies. Some of these have established personnel standards that are uniformly applied throughout the agency; others have not. In general, the qualifications are similar to those for comparable positions in public recreation. Unquestionably, the positions open to the qualified recreation leader are increasing in range and variety.

The American National Red Cross, for example, seeks qualified young women to serve men and women in the Armed Forces in the position of recreation worker in military hospitals. Persons must be college graduates and available for assignment in the United States or overseas. Some recreation positions involve the operation of clubmobiles in Korea; others are at recreation centers overseas or in the States, where leaders plan leisure-time activities for servicemen and their families and develop a better understanding between the local community and the American serviceman.

The Armed Forces also seek qualified leaders. The Army Special Services recreation and service-club program requires recreation supervisors and leaders as well as directors of crafts, sports, and entertainment. Women only are employed as recreation leaders and supervisors in the service clubs, but both men and women are eligible for positions as director of a special activity. Qualifications include a minimum age of twenty-three or twenty-four years, a college degree, and for most positions one or more years of professional experience. Two years of service are required in the majority of overseas commands.

The Air Force is convinced that wholesome recreation is a fundamental part of the American way of life and is determined to provide recreation opportunities for its personnel and their families located near air bases. It therefore employs qualified recreation personnel, primarily for three types of positions. The recreation manager has responsibilities somewhat comparable to those of a superintendent of recreation and must therefore have similar qualifications and experience. The other positions—club director and youth activities director—are classified at a lower grade, but call for personnel and qualifications similar to those associated with these types of service.

Hospital recreation is another new and rapidly expanding career area for professional recreation leadership. Much of its growth has taken place since the end of World War II. Recreation leaders are employed in Federal hospitals under the auspices of the Veterans Administration and the U.S. Public Health Service, in state mental hospital systems and to a lesser degree in private, voluntary, municipal, and county hospitals. Positions include the hospital recreation director, recreation leader, and recreation aide. Recreation personnel are a part of the hospital team and provide a wide variety of recreation activities for the patients. The Council for the Advancement of Hospital Recreation has developed standards for the education of hospital recreation specialists. College graduation with a recreation major is a basic requirement for hospital recreation service.

Industrial and business firms, voluntary agencies, and the other organizations mentioned in Chapter 3 similarly seek qualified leadership. It is therefore evident that the individual with the personal and professional qualifications for recreation leadership will find a wide range of opportunity for satisfying service.

8. EDUCATION FOR
RECREATION LEADERSHIP

REMARKABLE progress has been made in the development of formal academic education for recreation leadership since the end of World War II. Recreation leadership obviously could not take its place among the professions unless high standards of education were established and adequate means of furnishing preparation for effective service were made available. Opportunities and methods designed to prepare persons for employment as recreation leaders are largely provided by colleges and universities. In-service training after employment, intended to make leaders more effective in their work, is likewise essential. Both approaches are considered in the pages that follow.

PRELIMINARY TRAINING

As pointed out in Chapter 7, standards adopted by the profession make college graduation or its educational equivalent a basic requirement for all professional recreation positions, and recreation agencies are more and more accepting these standards. Until recent years few educational institutions showed concern for the preparation of men and women for recreation service, and training opportunities were comparatively few. Courses offered in schools of education and social work afforded valuable basic preparation, and the art, music, physical education, and other divisions provided instruction in subjects useful to the recreation worker. Little consideration was given, however, to the problems involved in the operation and administration of the municipal recreation department or any other type of recreation agency or service. The outstanding exception was the National Recreation School, a one-year graduate course, established in 1926 by the National Recreation Association. After nine years this course was temporarily suspended, when, owing to the Depression, difficulty was experienced in placing graduates in suitable executive or supervisory recreation positions.

120

The increase in people's leisure, the expansion in recreation programs, and the growing demand for qualified recreation leadership caused educational institutions to face seriously the need to train workers for this field. The establishment of a suitable program of professional education for the recreation field required the cooperation and collaboration of educational institutions and the groups who represented the profession (and who therefore were most familiar with the needs of the field). The development of standards for various recreation positions and the delineation of leadership roles by the profession were also prerequisites to the planning of a sound recreation curriculum. The problems involved in providing professional education for recreation were discussed by university and recreation leaders at several national conferences devoted to this subject and at many National Recreation Congress sessions.

By 1958, some seventy-five colleges and universities had established recreation curricula, and thirty-five were granting advanced degrees in recreation. Some sections of the country had inadequate recreation education opportunities; others had too many. A growing tendency for a team approach to the problem and an increasing readiness on the part of educational institutions and the profession to cooperate in achieving a satisfactory solution give promise of more acceptable programs of recreation education in the years ahead.

Among the questions faced in considering the preparation of recreation leaders are the positions for which persons are to be trained, the qualifications of institutions that are to provide the training, the nature of the courses that should be offered, the methods to be employed, the length of the training period, and the probable demand for leaders.

COURSES IN COLLEGES AND UNIVERSITIES

Opinions differ as to the best method by which universities or colleges can organize a recreation education program. Some would place it under an existing department; others would create a special department to administer it; others would appoint a coordinating committee to plan and direct the program. The first method subordinates recreation to another field, and the faculty is not always selected primarily because of its ability in the field of recreation. The second method is sound in principle but generally impracticable under present conditions because of the relatively small enrollment in the curriculum. The third method—appointing a coordinating committee—helps assure consideration of the problem from many points of view. It enables the divisions and departments which have an interest in recreation education to share in planning the program and to contribute to it. In planning a recreation education program, faculty competence and cooperation and a proper organization of the curriculum are of greater importance than the form of administration under which the program is set up.

The Conference on Professional Preparation of Recreation Personnel [1] in 1956 made recommendations with reference to personnel, faculty, and facilities essential to an institution offering a recreation curriculum. It proposed that in addition to qualified experienced personnel drawn from other departments there should be a director who should "devote full time to development, conduct, promotion and evaluation of the recreation curriculum." The institution should also provide properties needed for a variety of indoor and outdoor recreation activities, adequate library facilities for study and research, and field-work opportunities.

The Undergraduate Curriculum. Opinions also differ as to the specific subjects which should be included in a recreation curriculum, but there is wide agreement that persons preparing for professional recreation leadership should have a sound foundation in the form of a liberal, cultural education. This means that the student should be required to take a variety of courses in the humanities, social sciences, natural sciences, and communicative arts. The consensus of the 1956 conference was that approximately 50 per cent of the content of the undergraduate program should be devoted to broad cultural education, 25 per cent to specialized professional preparation, and 25 per cent to related areas of competency. In the first group are such subjects as sociology, psychology and mental hygiene, history, philosophy, the cultural arts, physiology, anthropology, and government—especially courses which help the student gain an understanding of man as an individual and as a social being.

The second group, the specialized professional part of the program, falls into several fairly distinct categories, none of which can be neglected. Throughout this part, leadership techniques, methods of dealing with people, and familiarity with recreation materials should be constantly emphasized and related to actual leadership experiences. Major aspects of professional preparation of the recreation leader are:

1. An understanding of recreation, its nature, development, and significance in our civilization; also a knowledge of the nature and scope of the recreation movement.

2. Familiarity with the various program areas and personal skills in at least two of them. The student should gain the ability to organize activities such as arts and crafts, games and sports, social recreation, dramatics, music, dance, outdoor recreation, hobbies, and other special events.

[1] Some of the statements in this chapter are based upon recommendations in the report of this conference, entitled *Professional Preparation of Recreation Personnel,* published by the American Association for Health, Physical Education, and Recreation, Washington, 1957.

3. An understanding of methods and procedures needed to organize and administer a recreation program. The student should gain knowledge of such procedures and topics as:

a. Conduct of an indoor or outdoor center or a city-wide system of centers.
b. Planning, organization, and supervision of a program.
c. Selection, use, and supervision of a staff.
d. Design, equipment, and maintenance of areas and facilities.
e. Preparation of a budget and administration of recreation facilities.
f. Record keeping and the preparation of reports.
g. Public relations media and techniques.
h. Evaluation of areas, programs, and services.
i. Departmental organization—functions, duties, relationships.
j. Legal aspects—powers and liabilities.
k. Intergovernmental and interagency relationships.

4. Directed field experience is an essential part of education and should extend throughout most of the four years. It adds immeasurably to the value of the periods spent in the classroom. At first it consists primarily of observation, participation in activities, consultation, or volunteer service. Much value can be secured from extracurricular activities in such fields as athletics, music, dramatics, and debating, either as an active participant or in a managerial capacity. As the student gains in knowledge and skill, he accepts increasing responsibility. The final stage is that of internship, in which the student spends specified periods on the job as a recreation staff member but under the supervision of the agency and the institution. Summer or schooltime employment as a leader in camp, club, recreation building, or playground affords practical training which enables the student more quickly to assume a position of responsibility upon completion of his course.

The third segment of the undergraduate program recommended by the Conference on Professional Preparation of Recreation Personnel—the 25 per cent devoted to related areas of competency—includes education, business administration, public relations, health and safety, and group processes.

The basic four-year curriculum outlined above leaves little opportunity for specialization, which should be kept at a minimum. If leaders are being trained primarily for the rural field, for service in industries or institutions, or with group work agencies, the courses must be oriented to the special needs of these groups. A few institutions are giving major emphasis in their recreation curriculum to preparation for a special field of recreation service, but specialization in recreation on the undergraduate level is not generally advisable.

Graduate Education. More and more, people seeking recreation positions of an executive or supervisory nature are continuing their studies on the graduate level, frequently after a period of employment in leadership positions. Much consideration has been given to the objectives, nature, and content of graduate education for recreation. John Hutchinson has listed the following five major purposes: [2] (1) To conduct research, (2) to apply research, (3) to develop scholarly leaders, (4) to develop the ability to communicate, (5) to specialize in a particular area.

Norman P. Miller has also stated: "Primarily, the objectives of graduate education focus on the competencies required for higher-level-leadership positions in administration, supervision, training, research, and in special areas of concentration." [3] He adds that graduate study presupposes competence on the part of the student, developed through undergraduate education and actual recreation experience, and that it should build upon this background.

Educators and professional leaders agree that graduate study in recreation should include consideration of the following:

1. General education areas such as the history and philosophy of American culture, human growth, and the working of social forces.
2. The principles and methods of research and evaluation.
3. The relationship of recreation in its various forms to political, social, economic, and cultural aspects of the American scene.
4. Concepts and methods of administration, with special emphasis upon the application to recreation of such aspects as community organization, finance, legislation, physical and social planning, personnel, and public relations.

Some of the preceding topics are treated in an introductory manner on the undergradaute level but receive more advanced or comprehensive study in the graduate curriculum. Areas of specialization such as municipal recreation, hospital recreation, industrial recreation, or camping and outdoor education are considered more appropriate for graduate than undergraduate study. A specialized graduate recreation curriculum can be effective only in institutions which have schools or departments offering the necessary courses and which are able to provide opportunity for appropriate field experiences.

Nonprofessional Courses. Colleges and universities are making a unique contribution to the recreation movement by offering nonprofessional courses which are available to the entire student body. Such courses

[2] "Purpose of Graduate Education for Recreation," *Recreation*, vol. 49, no. 3, p. 134, March, 1956.

[3] "Professional Education," *Annals of the American Academy of Political and Social Science*, vol. 313, p. 41, September, 1957.

represent a segment of a liberal education and give the student an appreciation of the ways by which recreation can contribute to the enrichment of leisure. Two types of courses serve this end: (1) those dealing with the significance of recreation and leisure in modern life and (2) others offering opportunity for participation in crafts, social recreation, sports, drama, music, and related activities. Such courses help students interpret the significance of student leisure-time activities, introduce them to activities which promise genuine enjoyment and satisfaction in their own leisure hours, and equip them to serve as volunteer recreation leaders. Suggestions on the content of such courses are offered in Chapter 10.

Of equal importance to courses is the fact that the institution which provides a rich campus life enables the students to gain an appreciation of the value of the wholesome use of leisure time. Such experiences help to equip students for effective service in the promotion and support of recreation programs in their home communities.

THE INCREASING DEMAND FOR TRAINED LEADERS

The readiness of colleges and other institutions to establish recreation curricula was presumably based upon the expectation that there would be a marked increase in employment opportunities in the recreation field. The demand for trained leaders for the wartime recreation programs far exceeded the supply, and the number of openings in full-time and part-time recreation positions with governmental, voluntary, and private agencies increased notably during the next decade. In community recreation alone the total number of reported leaders increased from 25,000 in 1930 to some 78,000 in 1955. Of these leaders the number employed full time the year round was 2,660 in 1930; 3,559 in 1940; 6,784 in 1950; and 8,387 in 1955. The number of full-time and of part-time leaders therefore more than tripled in the twenty-five-year period, and the present demand exceeds the available supply of qualified workers. The increase in full-time recreation positions in hospitals, the armed services, and industry was even more striking during this period, and the demand from such agencies is still growing, thus further accentuating the shortage of competent leaders.

Estimates vary as to the extent of the probable future demand for professional leadership personnel, but the indications are that the present shortage will continue. In fact, unless recruitment for the field receives greater impetus, the demand for workers may still further outstrip the supply. Many recreation leaders are deeply concerned as to the sources for future personnel. A study sponsored by the National Recreation Association in 1958 showed that the number of college and university graduates in recreation totaled only 683 in 1958 compared with 692 in 1951.[4] Of this number 448 received bachelor's degrees, 206 master's degrees, 11 director's degrees, and 18 doctorates. The men outnumbered the women more than three to two. A larger enrollment in recreation courses is imperative if present needs, to say nothing of future demands, are to be met. The sixty-one institutions reporting in the 1958 study had a total current enrollment of 2,298 recreation majors, whereas they were prepared to train 3,678 students without expanding their faculty or facilities.

Only an aggressive and successful campaign to recruit young men and women for service in the field can justify some of the institutions now offering recreation education in continuing their curriculum. Yet there is wide agreement that it is desirable for many institutions in different parts of the country to offer education on the undergraduate level designed to prepare large numbers of persons for recreation leadership positions.

Because only a small percentage of the positions in recreation work are of an executive or supervisory nature, however, and because preparation for these positions should be on the graduate level, enrollments in graduate courses must be limited and students selected with the greatest care. It is desirable that graduate students be drawn as far as possible from men and women who have had experience in the field of recreation and who have shown the capacity for positions of greater responsibility. Since a graduate course requires a highly specialized, experienced faculty it seems probable that under present conditions a few institutions, properly located and adequately staffed, could provide the education needed for executive and supervisory personnel.

IN-SERVICE TRAINING

For many years, because of the limited training opportunities afforded by colleges and universities, a large percentage of the men and women who engaged in recreation work undertook their tasks without adequate preparation for the duties and responsibilities placed upon them. Many of these workers had a general cultural education or were trained for other fields such as teaching, physical education, music, social work, religious education, or drama. Much of the knowledge of recreation activities, organization, facilities, and leadership which these workers acquired was gained after employment through in-service training. Even though most workers now employed have had special recreation education, no recreation department can afford to neglect its training program, and the need for in-service training will continue, regardless of how

[4] See "1958 Recreation Graduates Increase," *Recreation*, vol. 51, no. 6, p. 257, September, 1958.

adequately institutions may prepare recreation workers in the future. The field is so wide in scope and changes so rapidly that workers must continue to study, observe, and keep abreast of new developments in recreation and related fields.

The comprehensive in-service training program is not only continuous but includes all workers in the department. It is in no sense considered a substitute for professional education, but it is a means of encouraging growth in knowledge and effectiveness. Among the methods commonly used by recreation departments to accomplish in-service training are institutes, conferences, staff meetings, supervised reading, workers' committees, group study and discussion, observation trips, active participation in professional organizations, and demonstrations.

Preseason Institutes. Most recreation departments conduct one or more leadership training institutes each year. Perhaps the most common type is the institute for summer playground leaders, which is held just before the opening of the playground season. All summer workers and applicants for positions are required to attend, although experienced workers are sometimes excused from parts of the course. The program generally includes inspirational addresses on the value of playgrounds; discussions of program planning; lectures on safety, first aid, and care of supplies; practice, demonstrations, and group participation in playground activities; workshop classes in handcrafts and other special subjects; and interpretation of the objectives, relationships, techniques, rules, procedures, schedules, and assignments to be in effect during the playground season.

Leaders from other local agencies, recreation officials from different cities, or training specialists from state or national agencies are sometimes brought in to present special subjects. In cities with a year-round staff the responsibility for planning the institute is assigned largely to these workers, who also have an important part in the actual conduct of the sessions. Much the same procedure is followed in preparing workers for the indoor-center season. A growing tendency is for a central city to invite neighboring communities to send their workers to its institute or for several localities in a given region to sponsor a joint training program and thus make it possible to enlist a better faculty and offer a richer program than any of the individual communities could provide.

General Recreation Courses. A number of recreation departments, sometimes in cooperation with other local agencies, conduct courses for the purpose of providing general supplementary training for their workers. These courses afford a means of considering basic recreation problems and of interpreting the significance of recreation. Topics presented vary from city to city, depending upon local interests and needs, but typical subjects are cooperation among recreation agencies, municipal responsibility for recreation, group organization, problems related to competitive athletics, mental health, operation of centers, behavior problems of children, or family recreation. Like the preseason institutes, these courses include both lectures and participation in activities and afford opportunity for group discussion. A number of short courses have drawn leaders from a considerable area or region. State and national agencies have conducted many local training courses, varying in content and scope, for the benefit of community recreation leaders. Training institutes of various types are also sponsored and conducted by colleges and universities, who similarly furnish instructors and lecturers for courses under other sponsorship.

Institutes in Special Activities. The institute dealing with some special phase of activity such as music, drama, social recreation, nature, or crafts, and conducted by a specialist in this particular activity, is a third type of course. In cases where it is conducted by a person from outside the city, representing a college, a state or national agency, or the National Recreation Association, it is usually intensive in nature; otherwise it commonly extends over a longer period, with weekly sessions. Music and drama institutes frequently terminate in a production by the student group.

Such institutes afford an excellent means by which staff workers can increase their own skills and learn not only the techniques of group leadership in specific activities but also effective methods of organizing special projects. Furthermore the institutes give opportunity for training and enlisting volunteer leaders in the activity.

Training for Other Employees. Some department workers perform routine tasks which require little or no special skill; but it has become increasingly apparent that every employee should share in an in-service training program. More and more park departments are conducting training schools in which all employees take part, either as students or instructors. The schools cover a wide variety of subjects but commonly include departmental organization, policies and regulations, the use and care of equipment, maintenance methods, public relations, safety and accident prevention, and staff relationships. Participation in such programs has resulted in a better understanding of the purposes and policies of the department, the solution of perplexing problems, the discovery of unsuspected talents and weaknesses, notable gains in efficiency, and development of an *esprit de corps*.

An In-service Training Program. The nature and variety of training media are illustrated by the program of the Fort Wayne, Indiana, Board of Park Commissioners in 1957. Camp counselors met for three days prior to the camp season, and during the summer weekly in-service meetings were held. Junior and senior camp leaders and counselors-in-training also met throughout the year. All playground leaders were brought together for three days before the summer playgrounds opened and weekly throughout the season. Indoor-center procedures were reviewed with the fall and winter staff in early October, and special sessions were held later for craft leaders and basketball coaches. Personnel assigned to the skating rinks met with the safety director for instruction prior to the ice-skating season. An indoctrination meeting was held for swimming pool personnel with a representative of the American National Red Cross, and teaching procedures were reviewed before the start of the learn-to-swim campaign. Park foremen and all recreation division personnel received first-aid and safety instruction, and safety was a topic in the in-service training program of all park division personnel.

Education for Lay Leaders. In many communities institutes are designed to give lay leaders an understanding of the recreation movement and the importance of the local recreation program. An attempt is made to enlist the attendance of city authorities, members of recreation boards and committees, volunteers in the recreation department, and lay leaders in local agencies concerned with recreation, such as churches and industries. Sessions are few in number and are devoted to talks and discussions on such topics as organization of recreation services, local recreation needs, interagency relationships, and special recreation problems. Participation in this type of institute, whether as student or instructor, affords excellent training for members of the recreation department staff. Programs designed to prepare volunteers for service as activity leaders are described in Chapter 10.

Staff Meetings. The staff meeting is a widely used and effective means of in-service training. In cities with a year-round program, staff meetings are held at least once a month, but during the summer playground season workers are called together each week. As a rule all leaders are obliged to attend staff meetings, which serve the following purposes: to inform the staff about department rules, regulations, policies, and plans; to afford instruction in specific recreation activities and projects; to plan city-wide and other special events; to confer on staff relationships; to hear reports on special problems submitted by staff members; to discuss community events affecting recreation; and to consider methods of self-improvement. Outstanding leaders on various phases of recreation sometimes address the group.

Members of the department staff increasingly share in the responsibility for planning and conducting staff meetings. Individual workers are assigned topics which are presented before the group; others are called upon to provide instruction in special activities and projects. Committees of workers are appointed to study special problems and to lead discussions at staff meetings. Such methods stimulate study and research, furnish training in public speaking, and keep workers in touch with new developments in the recreation field. The staff meeting, if wisely planned and conducted, affords a splendid opportunity for raising standards of work in the department and for developing a spirit of cooperation among the members of the staff.

Conferences. Opportunities for exchanging ideas among workers in different cities and of learning about new methods of conducting recreation work are stimulating to workers. Progressive recreation departments therefore encourage their workers to attend national, state, and district conferences where recreation is discussed. The most outstanding of these gatherings is the National Recreation Congress, which is held annually

Members of the municipal recreation staff in Cleveland, Ohio, addressed by Anne Livingston of the National Recreation Association.

and is attended by hundreds of recreation leaders and representatives of related fields. At the congress, workers gain inspiration from addresses by outstanding speakers; participate in discussions of techniques, trends, and problems at the many section meetings; observe exhibits and displays of recreation products and local recreation service; take part in informal sessions devoted to demonstrations and to participation in social recreation, music, and other activities; observe local facilities and activities; and, most valuable of all, exchange ideas through informal conferences and meetings with individuals confronted by the same kind of professional problems.

Workers also benefit by attending the district conferences sponsored by the National Recreation Association each year in various sections of the country and meetings of state and regional societies of recreation and/or park workers. Increasingly short-term workshops organized on a state or regional basis are devoted to specific topics such as design and maintenance, swimming pools, or administrative problems. Institutes or workshops for administrators have also been held in connection with the National Recreation Congress and district conferences. Local, district, or national meetings of groups primarily concerned with such fields as physical education, parks, camping, athletics, or group work afford recreation leaders valuable opportunities for extending their knowledge. Recreation workers are encouraged to take part in local conferences arranged by city-wide groups for discussions of problems touching the field.

Other Training Methods. Directed reading is used in some cities as a means of in-service training. Workers' attention is called to publications of unusual value and interest. Workers are encouraged to devote time regularly to professional reading, and books on recreation are made available through the department, city, or municipal reference library. Local departments subscribe to magazines like *Recreation,* for use by members of the staff. New publications dealing with specific aspects of recreation are made required reading by staff workers directly concerned with the topic and are reviewed at staff meetings. Proficiency in communication is fostered by providing opportunities for workers to speak before local organizations, participate in conference programs, and take part in radio and television productions, as well as by encouraging them to prepare articles for magazines and periodicals.

Supervision provided by the department staff is perhaps the most effective means of in-service training. Through visits to centers, meetings with junior workers, and demonstrations and guidance in the development of projects, supervisors and executives help workers acquire skills and understanding. Alert executives call their workers' attention to local events such as exhibits, demonstrations, and music, dance, or athletic programs from which they might gain useful suggestions. Some cities pay the tuition for workers who take correspondence or other training courses that would be helpful in their work; employees are permitted to take time off to attend the courses.

The value of apprenticeships in the field of local government is widely recognized, and a beginning has been made in the use of apprentices in recreation departments. For several years the National Recreation Association financed apprentices in local recreation departments in the belief that the training, experience, and guidance which they received during their apprenticeship better equipped them for effective service in positions of responsibility. In 1956 the association instituted an internship program under which graduates of professional recreation curricula are serving for a period of one year in city recreation departments or in state mental hospitals. In selecting locations for training, criteria included a wide geographic basis, ability to pay the intern, and readiness to establish a good training situation with provision for adequate supervision. Designed to bridge the gap between education and experience, the plan affords a means of preparing carefully selected interns for responsible positions in the recreation field. The possibilities which an exchange of personnel offers for the growth of workers and the benefit of programs have only begun to be appreciated in the recreation field.

Professional organizations of recreation workers also serve as media for gaining knowledge and experience. Recreation authorities as well as an increasing number of workers recognize that serving as an officer or committee member of a state or national organization can widen an individual's outlook and acquaintance and can contribute to his personal and professional growth. Monthly or occasional meetings of state or district leaders enable a worker to share and exchange experiences, to discuss common problems, and to observe recreation areas, facilities, and activities. Through such experiences recreation leaders gain a sense of belonging to a professional fellowship.

9. SELECTING AND MAINTAINING THE LEADERSHIP STAFF

RECREATION authorities have no more important task than the selection and effective use of their leadership personnel. In the competitive market for intelligent, capable workers, they must attract young men and women to recreation as a desirable field of service. To do this they must create positions which provide challenging, constructive work, opportunities for advancement, reasonable compensation, and satisfactory working conditions. Increasingly, recreation departments are instituting effective personnel policies and procedures in order to attract and retain the qualified workers essential to the success of their operations.

ESSENTIAL PERSONNEL FACTORS

Conditions and factors which affect the ability of recreation authorities to select and retain competent leaders include the following:

1. Interpretation of employment opportunities
2. Installation of a classification plan for recreation positions
3. Adoption of satisfactory procedures for the selection of workers
4. Ability to pay salaries commensurate with the preparation and responsibilities involved
5. Opportunities for full-time, year-round employment
6. Assurance of security for satisfactory workers
7. A definite policy governing advancement
8. Assurance of good working conditions and fringe benefits
9. Adequate provisions for retirement

The ability of recreation authorities to influence or control these factors varies widely from city to city. In some cases they have the power to fix conditions relative to the selection and retention of their workers; in others these conditions are largely determined by different officials. Some personnel policies are fixed by the recreation authorities and apply only to their own workers; other policies are established by the municipal

133

authorities and apply to all employees of the city. Noteworthy progress is being made toward the attainment of satisfactory conditions relating to employment as they affect recreation workers. Among the agencies that have contributed to this end are the American Recreation Society, the National Recreation Association, and the various state organizations of professional recreation workers.

RECRUITMENT

The possibilities for professional service which the recreation field offers must be interpreted more widely and effectively in order that persons with the proper qualifications may consider recreation leadership as their lifework. Many recreation leaders believe that the need to recruit qualified and promising young people for professional leadership is the most urgent problem facing the recreation movement. As mentioned in Chapter 8, college graduates with a recreation major represent only a fraction of the number needed to fill the demands which have been estimated at some three thousand per year. Enrollments do not begin to tax the available resources for recreation education. A current campaign to stimulate recruitment, conducted by national, state, and local recreation agencies, is making use of a variety of methods, such as:

1. Providing guidance counselors in secondary schools with literature describing the advantages and opportunities in the field of recreation. Literature of this type is available from the National Recreation Association and the American Association for Health, Physical Education, and Recreation.
2. Giving talks at career days in high schools.
3. Enlisting the cooperation of all professional recreation leaders in seeking to interest promising young people to prepare for the profession. (Several state and national committees are promoting such action.)
4. Establishing accredited high school courses in leadership training, with supervised leadership experience.
5. Publishing articles emphasizing the satisfactions to be gained by service in recreation.
6. Creating more challenging jobs such as junior assistant, especially during the summer months.
7. Securing additional funds for scholarships and fellowships for students preparing for recreation service ($40,000 per year was available and specifically earmarked for recreation students for scholarships, fellowships, and assistantships in 1958).
8. Interpreting to the public the importance of recreation and the necessity for employing qualified, adequately paid workers.

Efforts to encourage young people to enter the recreation field through one or more of these procedures have produced gratifying results in a number of cities. Results were particularly rewarding in localities that have established credit courses in recreation leadership for high school juniors and seniors and that have provided supervised employment opportunities for students who demonstrate leadership ability.

A CLASSIFICATION PLAN

A classification plan helps the recreation department administer its personnel matters in an equitable and efficient manner. Position classification "is a system of identifying and describing the different kinds of work in an organization and then grouping similar positions together under common job titles. . . ." [1] Job descriptions, known as class specifications, indicate the duties, responsibilities, and qualifications of the positions in each class.

J. J. Donovan of the Civil Service Assembly has listed the typical major parts of a written class specification, as follows: [2]

1. A standard job title
2. A general statement of the duties of the job and where it fits in the organization's structure
3. Supervision received and supervision exercised
4. Typical duties
5. Job qualifications

The standards for recreation leadership referred to in Chapter 7 are designed to afford a guide for the classification of recreation positions in a locality. Where a sound classification is in effect, the recreation authorities have a basis for recruiting, setting pay rates, organizing the staff, budgeting personal services, promotions, and evaluating job performance. In order to work, the plan must be realistic; the qualifications should screen out incompetent personnel and attract suitable applicants.

SELECTING WORKERS

Because recreation authorities are responsible for the quality and quantity of the service rendered by their workers, they must have freedom to choose the best qualified personnel available. Regardless of the specific

[1] Kenneth Byers, M. Robert Montilla, and Elmer V. Williams, *Elements of Position Classification in Local Government*, Civil Service Assembly, Chicago, 1955, p. 1.

[2] "The What and Why of Job Analysis," *Recreation*, vol. 48, no. 10, p. 491, December, 1955.

method used, workers employed for recreation leadership, as well as for other services in the recreation department, should be selected on the basis of merit. Political pressure and personal favoritism have no place in the selection process. As recreation leadership has gained professional status, personnel standards have won wide acceptance; and as municipal, school, and recreation authorities have established classification plans for recreation positions, more satisfactory selection procedures have been developed. Increasingly, recreation authorities have been given greater freedom to seek competent personnel from outside the locality.

Responsibility for selecting recreation department personnel is fixed by state or local legislative action and varies from state to state and city to city. It is usually assigned to the recreation authority itself, a central personnel agency, a civil service commission, or the city manager or mayor. In recreation departments with an official policy-making board, the board generally appoints its executive without the approval of any other individual or group; a majority of such boards also have the authority to employ all full-time workers, usually on recommendation of the executive. In most recreation departments with an advisory board or no board, workers are hired by the city manager, mayor, or council committee, in many instances after approval by the city council or another authority. The superintendent in some recreation departments without a policy-making board is authorized to hire and fire subordinate workers; executives under this type of board usually require its approval before taking such action.

The chief function of the central personnel agency or civil service body is to establish and administer a classification plan which includes the testing of applicants for recreation positions and the preparation of lists of personnel eligible for appointment. Close cooperation between the recreation department and the personnel agency is essential to produce the best results.

Sources of Workers. Attracting qualified applicants for recreation positions is an important aspect of the selection process. The most effective means of accomplishing this differ with the type of position and with the size of the city. In a large city with a highly organized departmental staff, the executive and supervisory positions may be filled by the promotion of workers who have demonstrated ability and capacity for larger responsibilities. On the other hand, suitable candidates are not always available in the locality, so the recreation authorities canvass the best available personnel in comparable positions in other cities and attempt to induce these workers to apply. Competent workers can usually be secured locally for the positions of minor responsibility, especially in a large city, but recently graduated recreation majors are commonly sought as applicants. Recreation departments rarely need to seek outside applicants for seasonal or part-time jobs.

Public announcements in the local press and notices in state and national publications serving the recreation field are means of informing prospective applicants about open positions. Valuable assistance in recruiting candidates is rendered by the Recreation Personnel Service of the National Recreation Association, which maintains a roster of recreation personnel and a free service to individuals and agencies. State recreation associations and colleges and universities offering professional recreation education can also suggest suitable candidates. An effective means of attracting good prospects, screening unpromising ones, and reducing correspondence is the distribution of a statement giving full information concerning the opening. It contains facts individuals wish to know so as to determine whether they are interested in the particular position. The statement should contain not only information about the job itself but something about the recreation department—its budget, facilities, personnel, program, and legal status; and about the community—its government, physical features, economic status, housing conditions, living costs, schools, and religious and cultural institutions.

Part-time Workers. Because their periods of employment and remuneration are comparatively limited, part-time or seasonal workers are usually recruited from the city employing them. Schoolteachers and supervisors of physical education, music, crafts, and science are employed in large numbers for summer playground leadership. School, college, and university faculties and students who are specializing in recreation furnish much of the leadership personnel employed at summer camps, swimming centers, and playgrounds.

Teachers of physical education, manual arts, and other subjects are employed one or more evenings a week to conduct groups or classes at indoor recreation centers in many cities. Persons with a strong hobby interest and teaching ability have proven effective leaders. A professional musician may be employed to train the orchestra, a dressmaker to conduct the sewing classes, a craftsman to assist the group making jewelry, and an artist to instruct the sketch club. Many women who before their marriage were recreation workers or teachers are glad to accept such part-time employment. Departments in cities with colleges or universities offering recreation education make effective use of students who are assigned to them for their supervised field experience.

Salaries. The comparatively low salary scale for recreation personnel that has prevailed in most cities has been a deterrent to the employment of competent workers. Until recreation departments offer salaries and working conditions that compare favorably with those available to school personnel and workers in other fields of public service that require comparable education and experience, they cannot compete successfully for qualified workers. Adoption of a sound classification plan helps justify a compensation scale commensurate with the duties and qualifications established for the recreation positions. Salaries of personnel in top executive positions in many cities have been raised to a satisfactory level, but those of workers in subordinate jobs are generally inadequate to attract workers with the qualities that will enable them to advance into positions of greater responsibility. In general, boards of education that administer recreation departments which employ full-time recreation leaders have a higher salary scale for these workers than recreation departments under other types of managing authorities.

Certification and Registration. Certification or licensing as a prerequisite to employment in recreation exists in a few states; such certification affects only recreation workers paid from school funds or employed by school authorities. Under this method only persons who have been certified by a central state body are eligible for local employment in recreation leadership positions. Many recreation executives believe that certification of all recreation leaders is desirable, but that it would be satisfactory only if it were administered by a body controlled by the recreation profession. Such a body would have the authority to establish classifications for recreation positions, set standard requirements for them, fix fees, conduct necessary examinations, and issue certificates for each major classification. Persons licensed by this body would provide a reservoir of personnel from which positions might be filled after further examination by the employing agency.

As a step toward official certification of recreation personnel, several state recreation societies have established a voluntary registration plan for full-time leaders. Its purposes are to demonstrate the feasibility of a legal certification of the recreation profession, to identify professional leaders in the field, to recognize the essential qualifications for recreation leadership, and to provide a roster of qualified workers for the benefit of communities seeking to employ recreation leaders. Some states have adopted a recommendation of the Personnel Practices Committee of the American Recreation Society—that in the beginning only one classification be established. North Carolina, however, issues four types of certificates: (1) administrative, (2) supervisor and specialist, (3) provisional, and (4) apprentice. A state committee is appointed to administer the plan. A "blanketing-in period" is usually established, during which a recreation leader employed full time in the state when the plan is put into effect may receive an appropriate certificate without examination. Procedures are adopted whereby other leaders may qualify for certificates after examination by the state committee. For the benefit of workers who move from one state to another, several state recreation societies have mutually agreed to recognize the status of certified leaders coming from the other states.

Examinations. Some form of a testing procedure is essential in selecting workers under a merit system. A complete examination consists of several parts:

1. An evaluation of the applicant's education and experience, on the basis of a verified application blank and work record
2. A test of personal qualifications and fitness for the position, determined by an oral examination designed to reveal the applicant's probable success on the job
3. Tests of professional or technical competence revealed by a written examination or a performance test, or both
4. A medical examination and in some cases a demonstration of physical fitness in terms of performance

The probationary period following employment may also be considered a phase of the testing process.

All candidates for positions should be required to meet minimum standards of education and experience and submit evidence of good character and citizenship before they are permitted to take the examination. The relative importance of the various parts of the examination as well as the nature and content of the tests vary according to the type of position. The oral examination is considered highly significant in the case of executive and supervisory positions because the worker's personality and ability to sell himself to his superiors, subordinates, and the general public determine his success to a large degree. The oral examination is also important in selecting subordinate workers who have the qualities and capacity for promotion to more responsible tasks. The performance test, on the other hand, is seldom used in selecting an executive, but rates high in the examination of applicants for the position of swimming instructor, craft specialist, or special activity supervisor. A physical examination may be necessary for a sports leader but not for a general supervisor. The written examination is naturally composed of questions relating to the problems, techniques, and procedures with which the worker should be familiar in performing his job. The validity of the examination process depends upon the soundness of the tests, the manner in which they are conducted, and the ability and integrity of the testing officials.

In cities with a personnel agency such as civil service, the agency is responsible for the preparation, conduct, and grading of the examinations. It works in close harmony with the recreation department, however, and in some cases experienced recreation workers from outside the department are employed to assist with or administer some of the tests. In other cities, the recreation authorities employ much the same procedure as civil service in selecting their workers. Less comprehensive examinations are usually given persons applying for part-time and seasonal positions.

APPOINTMENTS

Under civil service, lists of qualified personnel eligible for appointment on the basis of a satisfactory rating in the complete examination are prepared by the civil service authorities. The recreation department is required to make its appointments from the names on this list, preferably in the order of their test scores. Under any merit system the individuals who have made the most creditable showing in the examination receive the appointment. Whether civil service is in effect or not, experience has shown that a probationary period of at least six months is highly desirable for all appointees; many authorities believe a two-year period is necessary in the case of the more responsible positions. The probationary period enables the department to observe the worker's attitudes, the quality of his work, and his suitability for the position. During this period he should be helped in becoming effective in his job. Probation is considered an essential phase of the examination process during which the department determines whether the worker passes or fails and therefore does or does not qualify for the job. It is desirable for the superintendent of recreation to report regularly on his work to the civil service commission and to the recreation authorities. He should recommend that the worker be dropped if he has not demonstrated his fitness for the position, because civil service regulations make it difficult to discharge workers after final appointment, except for serious offenses. If at the end of the probationary period the worker has demonstrated his fitness for the position, his appointment becomes permanent.

Performance Evaluation. The continuous evaluation of the workers on his staff is one of the most important tasks of the recreation executive. A sound, well-administered program of staff evaluation is an effective management tool which has as its primary purpose the improvement of performance, service, and ability of the workers. Because the quality of leadership determines the success of the recreation program, and its leadership staff is the greatest asset of the recreation department, any procedure that makes for more effective workers deserves a high priority. In practice, a rating system also provides a basis for salary increases, transfers, and promotions, lets the worker know how satisfactorily he is performing his duties, and encourages self-improvement. Performance report forms listing factors to be evaluated are used in many recreation departments.

It is commonly agreed that ratings ought to be made periodically throughout the year, that several competent individuals—including the worker's immediate superior—should have a part in the rating process, that as far as possible ratings should have a uniform basis, that workers should be rated on specific, objective qualities or factors, and that rating systems ought to facilitate checking individual scores. A worker's record should be analyzed and reviewed with him at least once a year; outstanding work should be given special commendation and failures accounted for. Workers should be made to feel that rating is designed to help them raise their professional status.

Self-evaluation by recreation leaders, including seasonal workers, is encouraged in some departments that do not use formal official performance reporting. Check lists covering a wide range of personal characteristics and job functions have been devised. They help the worker detect his own strengths and weaknesses and thereby encourage him to improve if he seeks to advance his professional status.

Advancement. Promotion of workers within the department is desirable whenever possible because it helps to attract capable people to the service and maintain worker morale. Recreation cannot become a career service, however, if advancement is based upon length of service alone. Promotion must be on merit as demonstrated through service records, proven effectiveness, and examinations. Definite periodic salary increases for satisfactory service and additional amounts for exceptional work offer an incentive to continue with the department. Examinations for positions in higher classifications are sometimes restricted to persons already employed and giving satisfactory service in subordinate positions. Supplementary education secured by employed workers is sometimes taken into account in making promotions, but such training deserves credit only as it is reflected in increased effectiveness on the job.

Recreation executives have a responsibility for the professional growth and advancement of all subordinate workers. If opportunities are not available locally, executives should help workers to secure more responsible positions in other communities.

FRINGE BENEFITS AND WORKING CONDITIONS

The salary does not represent the only measurable compensation a worker receives for his services. In considering the advantages in a position, an applicant takes into account the fringe benefits such as vacations with pay, sick leave, time off for professional study, overtime pay, pensions, medical and health services, group insurance, retirement plan, food and lodging. Workers in executive and supervisory positions are commonly granted the use of an automobile or are given an allowance to compensate for the expense of using their own automobile on the job. Recreation workers employed full time the year round are also entitled to the various benefits provided by state or Federal legislation such as social security, workmen's compensation, and unemployment payments.

Part-time and seasonal employees are not entitled to all of these basic and fringe benefits.

The hours of service which workers in subordinate positions are expected to spend on the job are usually limited and clearly specified. Recreation leaders in executive and supervisory positions, however, have traditionally devoted long hours to the work of the department—far in excess of the normal working day or week. The fact that many leaders must work evenings, Saturdays, and vacation periods, when most other people are enjoying leisure hours, deters persons who do not have a high sense of service from seeking or continuing employment in the recreation field. Favorable working conditions foster morale and encourage dedicated workers to give their best to the department.

10. VOLUNTEER SERVICE IN THE RECREATION DEPARTMENT

VOLUNTEER service has played an important role in the development of community recreation. As pointed out in Chapter 5, many present-day public recreation departments grew out of the work of the voluntary playground or recreation associations which sprang up in the 1890s or later. As municipalities took over the programs, leaders in these associations were commonly appointed to serve on recreation commissions, advisory boards, or committees. Each year thousands of other individuals contributed time and service to municipal recreation agencies. During World War II the volunteer really came into his own. It was demonstrated that volunteers will work long and hard when they feel they are needed and when they are given interesting work along with training that increases their confidence in their own abilities.

Volunteers in recreation are also needed today to meet the increasing demand for wholesome leisure-time activities. Many communities aware of the importance of enriching and expanding their recreation program can afford to do so only if the services of volunteers are made available. According to the *1956 Recreation and Park Yearbook* [1] nearly 165,000 persons contributed their services to recreation agencies in 1955 in addition to the thousands of children who served as junior leaders or aides. Approximately 100,000 of these volunteers served as activity leaders in 1,244 communities; the others served as board members or helped in some other capacity than activity leadership in 1,311 localities. The men outnumbered the women by a considerable margin in both groups.

Public recreation agencies will not be able to employ from tax funds the personnel needed to provide all the recreation which the people are certain to demand in the years ahead. Volunteers will be needed in still larger numbers to make effective use of the new recreation areas and facilities that are being developed throughout the nation and to supplement the services of the limited number of professional leaders. Fortunately for the movement, the expanding amount of leisure affords a

[1] National Recreation Association, New York, 1956.

143

reservoir of free time which recreation agencies can tap for volunteer service. Because the ability of the recreation department to provide needed services depends more and more upon its use of unpaid personnel, the enlistment of volunteers has become an important function of the paid leadership staff.

The situation presents a challenge to those men and women who are willing to serve their communities by securing training that will help them give effective volunteer recreation service. It also challenges public recreation departments and other recreation agencies with the need for a richer recreation program. Since the recruiting, training, and guidance of volunteers is so essential to effective recreation service, the extent to which a recreation department performs these functions is an indication of the caliber of its leadership. Some of the major problems and methods in the use of volunteers are considered in this chapter.

TYPES OF VOLUNTEER SERVICE

The many different ways in which volunteers serve recreation departments may be grouped according to the following types:

Administrative, Promotional, or Advisory. Lay service of this type generally involves membership on boards, councils, or committees. Typical groups composed of volunteers are official recreation boards or commissions, advisory recreation boards or committees, city-wide or neighborhood recreation councils, or committees assigned a specific task such as conducting a referendum campaign, supervising a recreation survey, or determining the need for a recreation building.

Activity or Group Leadership. This involves organizing, guiding, or instructing people—for example, advising a hobby club, conducting nature hikes, or teaching a craft class. Playground storytellers, tennis instructors, social recreation leaders, or persons who assume responsibility for organizing and conducting a bowling tournament, softball league, or doll show render this type of service.

Nonleadership Help with Program Projects. Officiating at athletic games or contests, serving as a judge at special events, or helping in the preparation of a playground pageant are examples of such service. Many individuals perform at department entertainments, usher, help with the scenery or lighting equipment at dramatic productions, furnish transportation for playground groups on special occasions, or help maintain discipline.

Clerical or Maintenance. Registering children at playgrounds, checking attendance at indoor centers, and typing or mimeographing bulletins are a few clerical services. Marking game courts, maintaining ball diamonds, painting equipment, serving as janitor at an evening center, and repairing toys and game materials are ways in which volunteers help the tax dollar go further.

Miscellaneous Services. A few examples are advice rendered by a lawyer or architect, the creation of a poster by an artist, taking pictures of recreation events, the preparation of publicity material, lecturing at a training institute, or reading to shut-ins. The types of volunteer service which the alert recreation worker can enlist are limitless.

Volunteer leaders make possible the NORD junior baseball program that attracts over 5,000 youngsters each summer (Courtesy of New Orleans, La., Recreation Department).

It is clear that persons of widely different training, experience, interest, and ability can find opportunities for service with a recreation agency, and that the resourceful recreation executive can use volunteers effectively in a great variety of activities. Portland, Oregon, affords an outstanding example of the use of volunteers. A report of the city's recreation division indicated the amazing number of more than 14,000 volunteers. Nearly 1,700 helped with baseball; 575 with junior Olympics and swimming; 2,217 with other phases of the sports program; 485 as chaperones, movie operators, and game leaders; 3,085, not including performers, blended their talents to bring into production the various music, drama, art, and dance programs and festivals. In fact, volunteers contributed to the rising attendance and success of nearly every phase of the recreation program.

Junior Leaders. Volunteer service is not restricted to adults; boys and girls display a desire and capacity for leadership and service which express themselves in various ways, especially on the playground. Children are helpful in telling stories to younger children, guarding at wading pools, assisting with first aid, preparing publications, giving instruction in simple crafts, caring for supplies and equipment, carrying responsibilities in athletic organizations, and instructing younger children in the use of apparatus. Safety patrols, junior police, junior leaders' corps, playground town governments, and junior towns give opportunity for voluntary leadership by boys and girls and also provide valuable leadership training.

Services of Organizations. Local organizations or groups interested in leisure-time activities, as well as individuals, also render valuable assistance. The cooperation of an organization has frequently made possible the starting of a new program feature such as a drama or nature club, the development of new facilities, or an increase in the department's budget. Local organizations have donated playgrounds, swimming pools, or other recreation facilities to the city; have met the expense of operating camps; or have provided leaders for specific program features such as storytelling, a nature museum, or an indoor center. The recreation council, on which local agencies interested in recreation have representation, is a means of stimulating volunteer service and securing support for the recreation program. This form of organization, which has proven a great asset to many recreation departments, will be discussed later in the chapter.

VALUES IN VOLUNTEER SERVICE

The examples just cited clearly indicate that the active interest of unpaid lay men and women is vital to the larger success of the movement. There are so many tasks to be done that, were it not for volunteers, much work would remain unaccomplished. Among the chief advantages of volunteer service to the recreation department are the following:

1. Volunteers bring a fresh point of view and an enthusiasm valuable to both the professional staff and the participants in the program.
2. By performing specific functions or helping with details, the volunteer frees part of the professional worker's time and makes it possible for him to render more effective service.

3. Volunteer service utilizes the skill, intelligence, enthusiasm, and support of persons interested in the development of a particular part of the program such as nature study, chess, or puppetry and thereby makes possible a richer, more varied program.
4. The fact that people are willing to serve the department gladly without compensation gives the employed staff a renewed sense of the value of the work.
5. The trained volunteer, through his work on committees and in the conduct of activities, can make easier the acceptance of high performance standards.
6. Persons serving as volunteers gain a knowledge and appreciation of the objectives and values of recreation that enable them to become intelligent and enthusiastic interpreters and supporters of the work of the recreation agency.

The effectiveness of volunteers in action was illustrated by the experience in Richmond, Virginia, where nearly five thousand served ten hours or more in the local recreation department during 1956. The city council approved practically all the department's requests for budget increases for 1957 and five times as much money for capital improvements as during the preceding seven years. According to the director, the efforts of the volunteers were responsible: "Without the interpretation and enthusiastic and informed interest of these citizens, this department would have been confined to a *status quo* budget."

As another superintendent of recreation has pointed out: "Volunteers of wealth and prestige have the power to safeguard, interpret, and promote any program for public good to which they may care to commit themselves." Realizing the truth of this statement, forward-looking recreation authorities are enlisting the interest and support of prominent men and women in their communities.

Difficulties in the Use of Volunteers. It must not be taken for granted that because volunteers can and do render valuable service, no difficulties are experienced in using them. In fact, some recreation workers do not use volunteers extensively because they believe that it requires more time to secure, train, and supervise them than it does to do the work themselves. Others, because of unfortunate experiences with volunteers, are unwilling to make further use of them. It is important to recognize some of the difficulties experienced with volunteer service.

Except in rare instances, the volunteer's recreation interest is a secondary one which is likely to be sidetracked by others. It is more difficult to hold to strict account persons who are giving their services rather than selling them. Unless volunteers are dependable, tardiness and absenteeism tend to be more frequent. Volunteers do not always have free time at the hours or periods they are needed. The different basis upon which volunteers and paid workers serve has sometimes given rise to problems in their relationships. Programs dependent upon lay leaders have less assurance of being completed or maintained continuously than when paid workers are used. If the social status of the volunteer and the people served differs greatly, a lack of sympathetic understanding and confidence may result unless the volunteer is a person of very good judgment. Some persons willing to serve have had little or no specific training for the job; others, who have had highly specialized training in some form of recreation, do not understand leadership principles and methods or share the ideals and standards of the department. Occasionally persons feel that after a period of volunteer service they should be employed. Experience has shown, however, that these difficulties can be surmounted if they are anticipated and if steps are taken to minimize them.

Securing the Best Results. The following are conditions which experience has shown to be conducive to successful and satisfying work on the part of volunteers:

1. When they feel there is a genuine need for the work they are asked to do.
2. When the assigned tasks are definite, written, and adjusted to their abilities.
3. When they see the relationship of their task to the objectives and functions of the department.
4. When they are made to feel an important part of the team.
5. When department personnel devote the necessary time to train and supervise them.
6. When they are not kept waiting long for assignments.
7. When the paid workers are cooperative and helpful and do not expect the volunteers to do the work for which they themselves are paid.
8. When their associates are sociable and congenial.
9. When reasonable attention is paid to the proper maintenance of the places in which they are asked to work.
10. When there is progression in service. Volunteers expect no money reward, but they appreciate promotion in responsibility.
11. When appropriate recognition is given for satisfactory service.

PROCEDURES IN DEVELOPING VOLUNTEER SERVICE

The effective use of volunteers obviously requires careful planning and administration on the part of the authorities in order that the maximum benefits may be secured. The principal procedures in the development and use of volunteer service are recruiting, training, assigning, supervising, and evaluating the workers. The following discussion of these factors relates primarily to volunteer service involving activity or group leadership or assistance with program projects. Much of it applies also to clerical, maintenance, and other nonleadership service. For the most part administrative or advisory service involving membership on boards, committees, or councils presents special problems and procedures which will be considered separately.

Recruiting. The recruiting of volunteers requires time, studied effort, and in some cases expert salesmanship on the part of the board, executive, or staff. In recruiting, recreation authorities keep in mind the general qualifications desirable in all volunteers and the particular requirements called for by the work to be done. Among the qualities considered essential in all individuals to be used by the recreation department, regardless of the type of service to be performed, are:

1. Character and high standard of personal conduct
2. Dependability
3. Conscientious workmanlike approach to tasks
4. Acceptance of the department's methods, policies, and philosophy
5. Readiness to undergo essential training
6. Willingness to accept and benefit from supervision, suggestions, and criticism
7. Ability and willingness to carry projects through to completion
8. Emotional stability

Additional qualifications for activity leadership specifically are a knowledge of activities, a certain amount of personal skill in them, and ability to organize, teach, and deal with groups.

While the volunteer who comes to an organization equipped with skill, education, experience, and a sympathetic attitude finds readiest acceptance, this does not mean that the inexperienced youngster or adult whose only apparent asset is a desire to serve is useless. The recreation department has so many types of tasks covering so wide a range of responsibilities that there is certain to be a place where every intelligent and earnest volunteer can serve effectively.

Sources of Volunteers. In view of the great variety of tasks performed by volunteers, these workers are recruited from widely different sources. People who can be enlisted to help with leadership projects include former recreation employees, teachers, hobbyists of all kinds, experts in activities such as swimming, tennis, or bird lore, and young people who have been trained in leadership methods and have enjoyed their experience as participants in various forms of recreation. Often willing to help are adults and young people who have benefited from the department's program, parents of playground children, retired men and women, and young women with leisure. Older boys and girls taking part in playground or center activities can frequently be enlisted for some form of volunteer service.

If technical ability or special skills are required for a job, the sources of volunteers are thereby limited. A leader for an orchestra or choral group is sought among persons who are actively engaged in music or who have had experience in this field. For help in conducting a track meet or water sports carnival, the recreation department turns to those who have been members of college track or swimming teams or to athletic organizations promoting these sports. The ranks of the archery enthusiasts usually include a person who is ready to furnish instruction or take charge of a tournament in this sport. If a group of playground children need transportation to a swimming pool or museum, the best source of volunteers may be the parents of the playground children.

When help with a specific project is needed, recreation authorities turn to local organizations which might be expected to have an interest in the project. The American Legion is asked to help conduct the Fourth of July celebration, the parent-teacher association to sponsor a back-yard playground contest, or one of the service clubs to help finance an overnight camp. A little-theatre group may provide volunteer leadership for a children's drama club, the local garden group for a community garden project, or the women's club for a girls' activity. The resourceful recreation executive can usually find an organization which will assist with a worthwhile project which requires volunteer service or support. Later chapters, especially Chapters 27 and 34, contain numerous references to successful activities sponsored by or carried on with the help of local organizations.

Enlistment Methods. Experience has indicated that it is usually necessary to ask people to help; rarely do they volunteer on their own initiative. The most successful means of enlisting volunteers are personal contacts with individuals who have special interests or hobbies and appeals to organizations known to be interested in recreation. Talks to parent-teacher associations, church groups, or men's and women's clubs are generally more effective than newspaper, radio, and television appeals or other public announcements, which sometimes produce applicants that lack proper qualifications. Persons participating in recreation institutes or taking part in the recreation program are especially good prospects as program volunteers. Students enrolled in university, college, and high school recreation courses are an important source of volunteer leaders and aides in many cities. Recreation departments also utilize volunteer service bureaus, which have been established in large cities, usually by councils of social agencies.

Motives in Volunteer Service. In looking for volunteers and in appealing to individuals for help, the recreation executive must keep in mind the motives that impel a person to serve. A desire to be of service in the community doubtless underlies most volunteer service in recreation. In every community there are individuals who consider part of the fun of living to consist of neighborliness, generous helpfulness, and everyday human kindness; they are genuinely fired with a sense of the human need for recreation and wish to have a part in meeting it. However, this dominant impulse is often combined with other more or less selfish motives, which may or may not interfere with an individual's usefulness as a volunteer leader. Some see in recreation service an opportunity to secure recognition, prestige, and possibly some business advantage. Others who enjoy participation in group activity find leadership of a recreation group a satisfying social experience. In fact, with the great increase in leisure, such volunteer service is itself becoming a distinct form of recreation activity. When individuals offer their services, the recreation executive must therefore attempt to discover their reason for doing so.

Training. The importance of adequate training for recreation leadership, pointed out in the preceding chapter, applies also to volunteers, especially those who serve as group or activity leaders. In selecting helpers the executive naturally seeks to enlist individuals who by training and experience are best qualified to perform the work to be done. Nevertheless, every volunteer leader requires some training by the recreation department, regardless of the skill and experience which he brings to his work.

The department obviously cannot train an individual to be an orchestra conductor, a crafts instructor, or a naturalist. On the other hand, a person who has had special training in the field of music, crafts, or nature, needs to become familiar with the aims and ideals of the department, the objectives to be sought in the activity, the general procedure to be followed, the principles of recreation leadership, and the specific duties he is expected to perform. He needs to know the nature of his relationships with and his responsibilities to the members of the group to be served and to the employed workers. Persons who are to serve the department in other ways than through leadership or program projects also need similar instruction. As with the paid workers, training does not consist merely of preliminary preparation for a job. It is a process which is continued throughout the period of service by means of staff meetings, conferences, advice from supervisors, directed reading, and observation of the work of others.

Institutes. Recreation departments which use volunteers extensively conduct special institutes for them or permit them to share some of the training opportunities arranged for paid workers. In one city, a ten-session course was held for young married women who were eager to help with the summer playground program. An institute in another city was designed to train women as volunteer storytellers at the summer playgrounds. An annual feature of the training program in a third city is an institute designed primarily for men and women leaders of adult groups, covering such topics as social recreation, hobbies, handcraft, progressive-game parties, music, and drama. Some volunteer institutes are primarily to train leaders for service with other agencies or recreation groups. These institutes enable the recreation department to extend its

Volunteers attending leadership training institute in Boise, Idaho, learn action songs taught by Mildred Scanlon of the National Recreation Association (Courtesy of the *Idaho Statesman* and Boise, Idaho, Recreation Department).

influence far beyond its own facilities and program, and are a means of assisting community groups to expand and enrich their own recreation activities.[2]

College Training for Volunteers. Many of the most useful volunteers in recreation departments are drawn from the ranks of college students and graduates. Their educational background, usually supplemented by specialized training and participation in forms of recreation activity, has fitted them particularly for service in the recreation field. The growing importance of recreation in modern life, the desirability of exposing stu-

[2] In 1958 the National Recreation Association published a booklet by Edith L. Ball, *Developing Volunteers for Service in Recreation Programs,* containing suggested outlines for courses for volunteers.

dents to a variety of leisure-time activities, and the increasing opportunities for volunteer service which the recreation field affords have caused college authorities to establish nonprofessional courses in this field. Graduates who have taken such courses and who have participated in recreation activities are unusually well fitted for volunteer service in the recreation field.

Nonprofessional courses are not intended to develop experts in any particular form of recreation, but they are built largely around the practice and demonstration of social recreation, music, crafts, nature, drama, and other activities. Program planning, recreation objectives, leadership methods, and the responsibilities and qualifications of volunteers are also discussed. Such courses interpret the significance of leisure, the importance of recreation in modern life, and the relationship of the recreation department to other community agencies. Observation of representative programs and visits to recreation centers enable students to test the knowledge acquired through their classroom work and supplementary reading.

Assignment of Duties. Assignments must be made with a full realization of the requirements of the work to be done and the abilities of the persons available for service. If volunteers have been recruited with care and have completed satisfactorily a period of training, the recreation executive has a sufficient knowledge of their aptitudes and abilities to enable him to assign them successfully. If he has a definite idea as to the task to be performed before he asks a volunteer to undertake it, assignment presents no problem. Since people like doing what they do well, the skills and interests of the volunteers must be taken into account in making work assignments. It is important that the volunteer understand the place and time at which the service is to be performed, the duration of the assignment, the nature of the duties to be carried on, the individual to whom he should report, the assistance he is to receive, the type of records he must keep, or the materials he should provide or that will be provided for his use.

It is desirable to limit the task to a definite period such as a month or a season because volunteers like to have the satisfaction of completing a job they have undertaken. Helpers can usually be recruited more easily for a specific period; also, in case a volunteer is not rendering satisfactory service, it is easier to end the arrangement than if no definite date is set for terminating it. This problem does not arise in cases where the service involves work merely on a particular day or at a specific occasion. In order to have a complete and accurate record of volunteers for current and future reference, the department keeps on file a card for each individual, on which are entered personal data, a record of the type and amount of work done, and an appraisal of its quality.

A few recreation departments ask persons accepting assignments for activity or group leadership to fill out and sign a formal contract covering the nature and duration of their service. Service agreements are useful primarily in cases where an individual is expected to report for duty at a specified time over a considerable period. Among other things, the signer agrees to abide by departmental policies and regulations, perform the duties assigned to him, and send a substitute if prevented from keeping an appointment for service. The use of a formal agreement tends to weed out the well-intentioned individual who has not considered the obligation involved in undertaking service as a group or activity leader.

Supervision and Evaluation. Experience has shown that volunteer service is likely to be successful to the degree that a competent paid staff supervises and guides the work of the volunteers. It has been truly said that successful development in leisure-time activities through volunteer leadership depends upon the existence of an adequate number of paid and trained leaders of organizing ability and inspirational power, who provide dynamic power and sound guidance. A capable playground director can use volunteers to good advantage, and an experienced center director can likewise help volunteer leaders conduct a successful club or activity program. Rarely, however, can unpaid leaders assume full responsibility for directing an indoor or outdoor center. They need to have the suggestions, advice, and inspiration which the paid worker can give and the assurance that he is at hand to help them with difficult problems. The executive and his assistants have a responsibility to the public to keep in close touch with the work of volunteers in order to assure the proper conduct of the activities and to protect and maintain the standards of the department.

The success of a volunteer is evaluated by the executive, his supervisors, and the other paid workers who have an opportunity to observe him and his achievements. An activity leader may be judged primarily by the attitude, attendance, and accomplishments of his group. Other factors to be considered are his relationships with other paid and volunteer leaders, his punctuality, his sense of responsibility for carrying out assignments, and his attitude toward the department and its work. Much can be learned by the executive or supervisor through discussions with the volunteers and self-evaluation of their own work. Recreation departments are anxious to secure renewed offers of service from individuals whose work has been satisfactory; but kind though firm action is necessary to discontinue service which does not contribute to the department's effectiveness.

Recreation volunteers share with all other people the desire that their work be appreciated, and the recreation departments that are most successful in enlisting and maintaining volunteers are fully aware of this fact. The amount and type of service rendered naturally influence the form of recognition, but some departments send a thank-you letter to everyone who has assisted in some way and list the names of individuals and agencies in the newspapers and annual report. Certificates are given persons who have served in a continuing leadership capacity, and junior leaders receive a felt emblem or other tangible symbolic award.

CITIZEN GROUPS

As stated early in this chapter, many committees, councils, associations, and other citizen groups are lending effective support to local recreation departments. Such organizations are particularly useful in cities where the department is not administered by a recreation board or other lay group because they make possible citizen participation in recreation planning. They supplement the program of the recreation department or serve it in an advisory capacity. Committees are often formed to study local recreation problems and needs and to recommend a plan of action. Advisory committees are especially useful in exploring the possibilities of expanding the department's program and in guiding the development of special activities. Several examples of the service rendered by such groups are cited in Chapters 27 and 34.

The Recreation Board. No form of volunteer service has made a more valuable or influential contribution to the recreation movement than membership on a recreation board or commission. In selecting persons for such service, the appointing authorities naturally turn to civic or community leaders of unusual ability who have demonstrated a sincere interest in recreation and a willingness to work for its advancement. Desirable qualifications for board membership include a genuine wish to serve the city, integrity of purpose, an open mind, an enthusiasm for and belief in the work of the department, keenness of judgment, ability to make some special contribution to the work, willingness to devote time to it, and a readiness to give loyal support to the department staff and its program. In cities where board members have been selected with care, they have rendered inestimable service. Unlike the other citizen groups mentioned in this chapter, this board is an official part of the local government and is charged with the responsibility for administering the recreation department. Its duties, procedures, and relationships will be considered in Chapter 30.

The Recreation Council. The recreation council, one of the most useful and common of citizen groups, is usually created at the suggestion of the recreation authorities or of community groups such as a council of social agencies. It is composed of representatives of organizations concerned with recreation and influential citizens selected because of their interest in some phase of recreation. The functions of a council are primarily to educate the public to the importance of community recreation, arouse interest in specific projects, and serve as a nucleus of organized favorable opinion in support of the recreation department. The council can be an effective instrument, especially if the executive is alert to suggest specific ways in which it can serve and projects which it can support. A few of the activities of recreation councils are:

1. Educating the public to the value and need of adequate recreation
2. Keeping in close, continuous touch with local recreation needs and problems and advising the recreation authorities on methods of solving them
3. Addressing meetings of civic clubs, women's organizations, and other groups
4. Visiting activities and facilities conducted by local recreation agencies
5. Sponsoring or conducting community-wide or holiday programs involving the cooperation of many organizations
6. Interesting potential donors of land or money for recreation purposes
7. Making or sponsoring surveys of recreation needs and services of the city and presenting recommendations for desirable action
8. Raising money for specific recreation projects
9. Initiating recreation projects involving cooperative action on the part of local agencies
10. Supporting recreation budget requests before the city authorities

In addition to the city-wide recreation councils, similar neighborhood councils have been formed at individual playgrounds or indoor centers. They represent, as a rule, neighborhood agencies and the people using the playground or center. The objective is to further recreation interests in the neighborhood and support the center program.

PART THREE

AREAS AND FACILITIES

Recreation authorities can serve large numbers of people only if there is a well-balanced system of suitable areas, properly located, developed, and equipped, where recreation activities and programs can be carried on. Part Three treats the importance of city planning for recreation, the types of areas needed for a municipal recreation program, and some of the problems encountered in securing such properties. Areas have only a limited recreation value until they are designed and equipped for specific recreation uses. Essential principles and methods of developing different types of properties and of constructing recreation facilities and buildings are discussed briefly in this part.

11. CITY PLANNING FOR RECREATION

IN ORDER to provide an adequate recreation program, a city must have sufficient land and water areas of satisfactory size, properly distributed and developed to serve a variety of recreation functions. Many urban areas have a serious problem because they lack a well-balanced system of recreation properties. Land, which was once the cheapest thing in the world, but today in congested centers of population is scarce, costly, and in great demand, is indispensable to a well-balanced community recreation program. The relation of recreation areas to the city plan, the essential requirements of an adequate system of publicly owned recreation spaces, and the methods of acquiring such areas are subjects of primary importance to the recreation movement.

THE VALUE OF PLANNING

American cities have been wasteful of their natural resources. Water fronts are lined with ramshackle structures, streams are polluted, woodlands are destroyed, ravines are used for dumping grounds, and roadsides are disfigured. Frequently the most beautiful sections of our cities and the sites which offer the greatest opportunity for civic development are turned over to uses which not only fail to take advantage of the beauty of these areas but actually destroy it. Neighborhoods are fully built up with no space set aside for the recreation of the people who are to live in them. However, cities with intelligent, aggressive leadership have taken steps to correct their mistakes. Outstanding examples of such action are the reclaiming and rehabilitation of the lake fronts in Chicago and Milwaukee and the remarkable progress which New York City has made toward restoring to the people's use many of the natural advantages which its water frontage offers for various forms of recreation.

Studies of the effect of recreation areas upon the value of property in the neighborhood have shown that properly located and well-designed recreation areas have so raised property values in the vicinity as to more than offset their original cost. The monetary value of parks developed in accordance with a master plan has been repeatedly demonstrated.

159

Testimony to this effect is included in the report of the Postwar Planning and Housing Committee of the New York Association of Real Estate Boards as follows: "A master plan for parks and recreation areas is not a dream; it is absolutely necessary to promote sound, stable real estate values. In the future, realtors and building promoters who crowd as many houses in a given area as possible and provide no play space will

The reclamation and development for recreation of Chicago's lake front represent a significant civic achievement (Courtesy of Chicago Park District).

be unable to sell their houses at a profit, because the public will demand parks and recreation areas near their homes." [1]

All Communities Need Planning. The advantages of planning are not restricted to the larger cities. Many suburban communities, towns, and even rural areas are more drab and devoid of opportunities for joyous, satisfying living than the cities. In an address before the National Appraisers Forum, John E. Burton, director of research of the New York State Mortgage Commission, pointed out how unsupervised suburban

[1] The *New York Herald Tribune,* November 28, 1937.

developments degenerate into dreary shanty towns and concluded, "All this might have been prevented by proper supervision providing recreation centers, playgrounds, swimming pools, the foci of community life." [2] One of the urgent problems today in improving living conditions in both large and small communities is to make the people aware of the profound values of recreation facilities in civic life. Walter H. Blucher, long a leader in the field of city planning, has warned: "It is time we awakened to the fact that recreation is essential to the well being of the people and

This "playground" in a large city, like many others built early in the twentieth century, provided little space for free or organized play.

of the community, and if we do not acquire park and recreation land now, there will be none left to acquire in the future." [3]

Only an awakened and insistent public opinion can demand that governmental agencies take immediate steps to secure adequate and suitable areas to care for present and future recreation needs in our towns and villages as well as in the large population centers.

RECREATION AS A FACTOR IN CITY PLANNING

Before 1900 little thought was given to the acquisition of public open spaces according to a city-wide plan, but with the growth of the city-

[2] June 1, 1944.
[3] *Recreation*, vol. 50, no. 6, p. 197, June, 1957.

planning movement after the turn of the century, cities began to study their park and recreation needs and to prepare plans for meeting them. An early example of such plans, and one of the first attempts to set up recreation space standards, was proposed at the organization meeting of the Playground Association of America in 1906 and later adopted by the Board of Education of the District of Columbia. It sought to provide 30 square feet of school playground for each child enrolled, an outdoor playground of not less than 2 acres for each school district, and an athletic field for each of the four sections of the city of Washington.

The subsequent expansion in municipal recreation areas and the increasing demand for the development of recreation facilities were factors in emphasizing the importance of city planning for recreation and in developing suitable standards. As early as 1923, the noted city planner George Ford urged recreation authorities to help formulate standards which could be used as a guide by his profession. Today recreation spaces are a major factor to be considered in the city plan along with zoning, streets, public utilities, and building sites. The properties required for parks and recreation areas are included in the master plan for the long-range physical development of the city. A scheme for the acquisition of recreation areas is likely to prove sound and effective only as it is intelligently integrated with other aspects of the city plan.

Important to the recreation movement is the fact that city planning concerns itself not only with physical development but also with the enrichment of life in our cities. According to one city planner, its object is "to discover and prepare the road to human happiness." Recreation agencies welcome the recognition by city planners of their responsibility in the field of recreation and look to them as effective allies in the attainment of an adequate system of suitable areas. City planning can help bring to realization in our cities the priceless benefits—rest, sunshine, fresh air, nature, and recreation activities—which permanently dedicated open space yields to the people.

City Planning Affects Recreation Planning. The growth of most American cities has been characterized by a lack of planning, but city officials now exercise a considerable degree of control over present and future development through zoning, subdivision regulation, and a program of public improvements. Future recreation-space requirements of cities and neighborhoods can therefore be estimated more accurately than before. In view of the high cost of land and improvements, recreation authorities have no excuse for ignoring the city plan when acquiring new areas. Additions to the recreation system should be made in conformance to the recommendations of the local city plan or should be related to them. Zoning, for example, affects recreation needs because the open-space requirements of a neighborhood zoned for apartments differ from those of neighborhoods restricted to single-family dwellings. In considering future needs, land for playgrounds will be required in areas zoned for residential development but not in areas zoned for manufacturing. In business districts, small landscape parks are more needed than areas for active recreation use.

Proposed major highways, transportation systems, large-scale housing projects, and other public improvements affect materially the requirements for recreation areas in the vicinity of such contemplated developments. The plans of school authorities for the acquisition of school sites have a vital relation to the need for other publicly owned neighborhood recreation areas. In fact, cooperation among planning, school, and recreation authorities has repeatedly resulted in economical and functional grouping of indoor and outdoor recreation facilities. Just as recreation authorities must be guided by the city plan, planning authorities require the advice and experience of recreation workers in determining the recreation needs of the people and the types of areas which enable these needs and desires to be satisfied.

PLANNING FOR RECREATION

Effective integration of recreation areas in the city plan, or indeed any sound plan for the acquisition and development of recreation space, must be based upon accepted objectives, principles, and standards: definite objectives to be achieved by the system, basic principles essential to attain the objectives, and specific standards for implementing the principles.

The chief objective sought in recreation, and which a system of areas is designed to help realize, has been called "the enrichment of living through the constructive use of leisure and the expression of normal human interest in art, dance, drama, music, sports, nature, the world of the mind, and social activities." [4] However expressed, the purpose underlying a local recreation system is the enrichment of individual and community life through the beauty and recreation opportunities which the development of such areas makes possible.

Planning Principles. Broad objectives have little significance until they are supplemented by principles that afford a basis for planning and action. Since the function of recreation areas is to serve recreation needs, the principles that underlie a recreation program (see Chapter 14) naturally have a direct bearing upon the planning of a well-balanced system of

[4] *Guide for Planning Recreation Parks in California,* California Committee on Planning for Recreation, Park Areas, and Facilities, Sacramento, 1956, p. 22.

recreation areas. Such a system is achieved when it is designed to meet the following criteria:

1. Make possible recreation opportunities for all, regardless of age, color, race, creed, or economic status
2. Provide areas and facilities that make possible a great variety of recreation activities that serve a wide range of recreation interests
3. Include areas that differ widely in size, location, natural features, and potential development, and that consequently serve different recreation uses
4. In so far as possible, provide an equable distribution of areas in each major section of the city
5. Provide a multiple-use area as near as possible to the center of every residential neighborhood, preferably at or adjoining the elementary school, so as to afford opportunities for recreation day by day and during brief periods of leisure
6. Provide at a greater distance from the homes of the people other areas that require more space and develop them for recreation activities that require longer periods of use
7. Take into account existing outlying recreation areas and facilities that serve the people of the locality and, where advisable, include additional extra-urban areas primarily for week-end and holiday use
8. Be based upon a thorough study and appraisal of existing local recreation resources and needs, conducted with the full cooperation of citizens, municipal, school, and planning authorities, and other interested agencies

AREA TYPES AND STANDARDS

Because of divergent conditions and resources in different cities and neighborhoods, as well as varied recreation interests, habits, and desires of people, present-day recreation systems comprise many different types of properties developed for a variety of uses. Experience has demonstrated that several of these types are essential to a well-balanced recreation system; others are less common but make possible valuable recreation services. Space, location, and development standards, as well as names for several types of areas, have been proposed by various groups.[5] Standards promoted by the National Recreation Association have been widely adopted in localities; subsequent proposals by other groups call for greater amounts of recreation space and emphasize the value of integrating recreation areas and school sites. The functions, size, and location of several

[5] This applies especially to neighborhood and community areas. The terms "playground" and "playfield" used here have been most widely adopted by planning and recreation authorities.

important types of areas will be considered briefly here. Their layout, equipment, and special features will be treated in the next two chapters.

The Play Lot or Block Playground. Play lots are small areas intended for the use of children of preschool age. They serve as a substitute for the back yard and are rarely provided by the municipality except in large-scale housing projects or underprivileged neighborhoods where back-yard play opportunities are not available. A space from 2,000 to 5,000 square feet is considered adequate. The play lot is usually located in the interior of a large city block or near the center of one or more units of a multiple-family housing development. Small children should be able to reach a play lot without crossing a busy street.

The Neighborhood Playground. This area is primarily intended to provide opportunities for children, especially between the ages of six and fourteen, inclusive, to take part in a variety of constructive and enjoyable play activities. It also provides limited facilities for the recreation of young people and adults, and a small section is set aside for the exclusive use of the preschool group. The size varies according to the present or estimated future population in the neighborhood to be served, but it is usually between 4 and 8 acres. A smaller area is seldom satisfactory; if a playground larger than 10 acres is required, two smaller areas will usually give more effective service. For most cities, a reasonable standard for total neighborhood playground space is 1 acre for each 800 of the total population.

A central site in each neighborhood is preferable, for the playground is an important part of the neighborhood's center of community activities. Location at or adjoining an elementary school site is practicable, economical, and assures its maximum use, for the playground then serves school groups during and after school hours and community groups at other times. There is a growing tendency, therefore, to combine the neighborhood school and playground. The combined site is sometimes called a neighborhood park-school; it requires at least a 10-acre site.

In high-density neighborhoods, the most effective radius is ¼ mile or less; under the most favorable neighborhood conditions there should be a playground within ½ mile of every home. The location of playgrounds along heavily trafficked streets, railroads, or other natural or man-made barriers is to be avoided, because children should be able to reach a playground without being exposed to special hazards.

The Community Playfield. This area provides varied forms of recreation for young people and adults, although a section is usually developed as a children's playground. A playfield serves an area comprising about four neighborhoods. At least 15 to 20 acres are required; larger sites are sometimes developed as playfield-parks. A reasonable standard for total playfield space in a city is, as with playgrounds, 1 acre for each 800 of total population. There should be a playfield within ½ to 1 mile of every home, the distance depending upon population density and ease of access.

Many of the facilities provided by a playfield are used for activities in the curriculum of the junior and senior high school. It is usually desirable that the playfield be a part of or adjoin a high school site. Because this arrangement facilitates dual maximum use, it has been widely adopted. In some cities the combined high school–playfield site is called a community park-school.

The Large Park. This area is intended, in part, to provide the city dweller with an opportunity to get away from the noise and rush of city traffic and to enjoy contact with nature; but its primary purpose is to provide a pleasant environment for engaging in a variety of recreation activities. There is a current tendency to devote a greater percentage of most parks to active recreation uses.

The desired park effect can seldom be achieved on less than 100 acres, whereas suitable areas of more than 300 acres are rarely available within the city limits. Each city needs a major park, and it has been suggested that large cities provide one for every 50,000 inhabitants. There is an advantage in selecting an area the shape of which is related to the pattern of the city and interferes least with normal traffic flow.

The Reservation. The reservation is a large tract of land which is kept primarily in its natural state, although sections of it are made available for such activities as hiking, camping, picnicking, nature study, and winter sports. Most municipal areas of this type are located either near the boundaries of the city or outside its limits. Many cities have acquired reservations, but most of them rely upon Federal, state, or county authorities to provide them. The reservation is usually 1,000 acres or more in extent, although smaller properties sometimes serve the purpose.

Special Recreation Areas. Areas that primarily serve a particular active recreation use contain facilities such as the golf course, camp, bathing beach, swimming pool, athletic field, and stadium. Sometimes these facilities are established in the areas previously discussed, but cities increasingly tend to acquire special properties for them.

The space requirements of these recreation areas vary widely. A nine-hole golf course requires 50 acres or more; an eighteen-hole course, a minimum of 100 acres—usually 120 acres or more. The bathing beach may comprise a small tract of land along a river, lake, or ocean; on the other hand, it may extend along a mile or more of water frontage. One acre may suffice for a small neighborhood swimming pool, but several acres are required for a major swimming center, especially since a parking space for automobiles is generally needed on the site. The athletic field or stadium is a special type of center intended primarily for highly organized games and sports. At least 6 acres are required for an athletic field, and 20 acres or more may be needed for a large stadium with extensive parking facilities. A minimum desirable site for a municipal camp is 20 acres; some camps occupy sites of several hundred acres. Day camping can be successful on only a few acres, but access to a large area is desirable.

Definite location standards for special recreation areas are not practicable. The golf course—requiring a large acreage, preferably with an uneven topography and some woodland—must be located where suitable land is available at reasonable cost. People will travel farther to play golf than to engage in some other forms of sport. The location of the bathing beach is determined by the availability of property with suitable natural features. The athletic field or stadium is often established at a high school site or on a special area that is readily accessible by various forms of transportation. The organized camp, for which a degree of isolation and seclusion is desirable, is almost always located outside the city limits, although many day camps are located within the city limits, generally in large park areas.

The Neighborhood Park. This area is primarily a landscape park with trees, shrubbery, and lawn and is intended to provide an attractive neighborhood setting and a place for quiet, informal recreation. In some instances facilities are installed for the use of young children or older adults, but the park serves chiefly as a restful breathing spot in a business district or congested residential neighborhood or as a setting for a civic center. Uneven terrain such as ravines or steep, wooded slopes not suitable for building purposes may serve admirably as neighborhood parks.

Proposed standards for the neighborhood park vary widely, but requirements for this type of area are far greater in residential neighborhoods of high density. The American Public Health Association has proposed 2 acres of park per 1,000 persons in neighborhoods with a multiple-family development, as contrasted with $7/10$ of an acre per 1,000 in neighborhoods with one- or two-family dwellings. The neighborhood park is seldom less than 2 acres, and in some cases it is as large as 50. The growing tendency to include it as a unit in a combined neighborhood park-school-playground has eliminated the need for a separate park in many neighborhoods.

The Parkway. The parkway is essentially an elongated park with a road running through it, the use of which is restricted to pleasure traffic. As in the case of other park properties, abutting-property owners have no rights of light, air, or access. Many parkways afford a connection between the center of a city and one or more outlying park areas; others serve as a circumferential highway connecting several large units of a park system. Stream valleys often lend themselves to parkway development. Portions of a parkway are sometimes devoted to playgrounds, picnic centers, or other recreation uses. The parkway is rarely found in the smaller cities, although it holds a place of growing importance in metropolitan, county, and regional park systems.

Other Types of Recreation Properties. In this group are squares, plazas, and the areas acquired as sites for museums, zoological gardens, botanical gardens, nurseries, bird sanctuaries, community gardens, outlooks, nature trails, and other special purposes. The location and size of these different areas vary widely, and in some cases are not subject to definite standards.

HOW MUCH SPACE FOR RECREATION?

It has been shown that a well-balanced system of recreation areas consists of many types of properties and that their location can best be determined in relation to the city plan. But the question arises, How much permanent open recreation space is needed in a city in order to make possible a comprehensive, well-balanced recreation program? Clearly the needs are affected by density of population, economic status, available private and commercial facilities, recreation opportunities in the surrounding region, climatic conditions, and other factors. Hence no formula for determining the precise amount of publicly owned park and recreation space needed for such a program can be applied uniformly in all cities.

Attempts have been made to determine the amount of recreation space needed in terms of a certain percentage of the city's total area. It has repeatedly been proposed that at least one-tenth of its area should be devoted to parks and other recreation uses. A standard of this type is not satisfactory, however, unless it provides a varying percentage dependent upon the density of population. It is obvious that a city with a high density will need a larger proportion of its total area for recreation than a city which is sparsely settled. Present—or estimated future—population is a sounder basis for determining recreation standards because recreation areas are provided to serve people.

Experience has demonstrated that in general any city seeking to furnish a well-balanced recreation program for its people will need at least 1 acre of permanent, publicly owned open space for each 100 of the population. This ratio applies only to park and recreation areas within or immediately adjoining the city and not to properties at a distance from the city. In the future, cities will undoubtedly have higher requirements; and most municipalities of less than 10,000 population today need more than 1 acre of recreation area per hundred. The National Park Service has suggested that communities of less than 2,500 population provide an acre of park for each forty to fifty people. Various proposals have been made that *in addition* to the parks within and adjoining the city limits, there should be for each 1,000 people in a region, 10, 20, or more acres of park lands in such properties as stream-valley parks and parkways and large scenic recreation and forest parks. Most of these, however, would be under county, state, or other authorities, rather than municipal properties. The growing demand for recreation areas indicates that present standards should be considered as minimum requirements which may well be supplemented by additional acreage in anticipation of future needs.

A Well-balanced System Essential. Acreage alone, essential as it is, does not assure a well-balanced municipal recreation system. The recreation needs of all the people can rarely be met satisfactorily by a single large property, even though it affords 1 acre for each 100 or less of the population. The needs can never be met by small properties alone, because many popular forms of recreation can be carried on only in a large area. The best results are attained when there is a proper relationship in number, type, and location among the types of areas mentioned earlier in the chapter.

Various suggestions have been offered as to the percentage of a city's recreation area, which should be in different types of properties; but no rigid formula can be prescribed for use in all cities. Widely differing local conditions affect the requirements and composition of a municipal recreation system. Playgrounds and playfields, however, are needed in all residential neighborhoods, and their space requirements can be determined with some degree of accuracy; thus it is possible to estimate the percentage of open space they require. A city which has an acre of playground and an additional acre of playfield for each 800 of its population—standards suggested earlier in the chapter—and which has 1 acre of open space for each 100 will have one-fourth of its open space in these two types of areas. In addition, the city will probably have athletic fields, golf courses, bathing beaches, and other areas used for various forms of active recreation. It is gradually becoming recognized that at least half of a city's total park and recreation acreage should be developed for active uses.

To What Extent Have the Standards Been Attained? The standards that have been suggested for a city's recreation area are not ideal or theoretical objectives; they are practically attainable. A study of municipal parks in 1940 [6] revealed that 370 cities of varying sizes, or about one-fourth of those reporting, had acquired more than 1 acre of park for each 100 of the population. Most of these cities also had playgrounds on school property. It is true that some of the largest park properties owned by a number of these cities are outside the city limits, but for the most part they are fairly accessible.

[6] George D. Butler, *Municipal and County Parks in the United States,* National Recreation Association, New York, 1940.

A later study based on park acreage reported by each of 189 cities during the years 1930, 1940, 1950, and 1955 revealed that the same number of cities—49—had achieved the standard in 1955 as in 1940.[7] Since 1940, however, population has increased faster than park acreage in most of these cities. Between 1940 and 1950, park acreage per capita decreased in 108 cities and increased in only 79. A still smaller number made a relative gain between 1950 and 1955. The fact remains that in a majority of cities recreation space is far below the widely accepted standard and is not expanding at as rapid a rate as the population. There are still hundreds of communities that do not own a single acre of park.

Deficiency in Playgrounds and Playfields. Available figures indicate that American cities have been more successful in acquiring park acreage than in developing well-balanced recreation systems. Cities tend to be most deficient in the number and acreage of playgrounds and playfields, especially in substandard neighborhoods where the need for them is greatest. Many cities have paid more attention to acquiring large outlying properties than to the purchase of high-cost land in built-up neighborhoods. Some cities, on the other hand, have a playground within ¼ mile of the homes of the majority of their children and within ½ mile of practically all of them. Others are taking steps to correct their deficiencies in accordance with recommendations based upon surveys of current and long-term needs.

The movement for large-scale public housing, involving as it did the planning of new neighborhoods and the rebuilding of slum areas, offered an exceptional opportunity for the acquisition of adequate neighborhood recreation space. Cooperative planning by recreation, city planning, and housing authorities resulted in the acquisition and improvement of recreation areas in many neighborhoods. Public housing authorities provided such areas in some of the neighborhoods they created, but other municipal agencies frequently shared with them the responsibility and cost of providing, improving, and operating them. The current Federal program of aid to municipalities in the planning and redevelopment of substandard neighborhoods and communities affords an incentive and opportunity for setting aside adequate space for recreation.

CITY RECREATION AREAS AND SCHOOL SITES

Earlier in the chapter it was pointed out that in general the best location for the neighborhood playground is at or adjoining the elementary school; and for the playfield, at or adjoining the high school site. The problem of providing neighborhood and community areas for active

[7] "Park Acreage and Population, 1930–1955," *Recreation*, vol. 50, no. 6, p. 228, June, 1957.

recreation would be drastically reduced if all schools attained nationally adopted school-site standards. The National Council on Schoolhouse Construction, which includes many state school authorities, advocates that the *minimum* site for an elementary school should comprise 5 acres plus 1 acre for each 100 of the ultimate enrollment. For the junior high school it recommends 20 acres plus 1 acre per 100 of ultimate enrollment; and for the senior high school, 30 acres plus 1 acre per 100. The council emphasizes the fact that these are minimum standards and encourages

The modern, well-designed school playground makes possible a variety of recreation activities (Courtesy of Long Beach, Calif., School Department).

the acquisition of larger sites wherever possible. A large percentage of these school sites would normally be developed in a manner that would enable them to be used for recreation by school and community groups.

For many years there was little coordination in the location and development of school and municipal recreation areas. Because schools were under the jurisdiction of a separate governmental unit in many states, schools were not included in the city plan. A distinction also existed between the legal status of parks and of school property. A park was a plot of land which could be used only for recreation, and in some states it could not be disposed of or used for any other purpose, except by court or legislative action. It is true that in recent years encroachments on park property have increased, especially as a result of accelerated highway-construction programs, and valuable recreation areas have been diverted to nonconforming uses. In a number of cases, however, the integrity of park land has been sustained in court decisions, and in other instances the principle has been established that where park property has been taken for another public use, sufficient compensation shall be paid to enable the property to be replaced by the purchase of other land.

The school ground, unlike the park, was essentially a building site which could be built upon or disposed of at the will of the local school board. It was often restricted to use by school groups during or after school hours and therefore did not always serve as a public recreation area; high school fields were frequently withheld from community use to protect playing surfaces for interscholastic competition. Such restrictions are infrequent today, and school authorities generally consider school property as a community resource, to be used by the people whenever it is not required for school purposes. Consequently school grounds and buildings are made available for activities sponsored by recreation departments and other community groups.

In view of this dual function of school properties—the school program and community recreation—and because most substantial community recreation programs on school property are conducted by municipal recreation departments, the principle of cooperative planning is gaining wide support. Since school and municipal authorities require, in the same neighborhoods or communities, areas of comparable size and with much the same facilities; since they serve the same people, although during different time periods; and since they have essentially the same basis of financial support, the advantages of cooperative planning are obvious. The examples of such planning and action in the past decade represent a forward step in city planning for recreation—a procedure that has been long recommended by the National Recreation Association and more recently by such groups as the National Facilities Conference and the California Committee on Planning for Recreation, Park Areas, and Facilities.

Cooperation has taken a variety of forms. Formal agreements endorsing the general principle of cooperation in the acquisition, improvement, and use of properties have been reached by school and city authorities in several cities; in others they have related only to specific properties. Officially appointed coordinating committees in some cities review all proposals for new areas and facilities and recommend to the respective authorities procedures that will bring maximum benefit to all. Other methods for facilitating cooperative action are informal arrangements whereby school and recreation-area plans are reviewed regularly and in their early stages by recreation or school personnel; joint employment of a landscape architect by the two departments; and agreements for leasing school properties to the park or recreation department for development and maintenance.

Cooperative arrangements cover such factors as land purchase and ownership, the preparation of site and building plans, development programs, operating procedures, maintenance, and uses. They set forth the specific responsibility which the school and the city authorities accept for sharing costs and their respective rights in the use of the property. The scope and nature of these agreements vary widely, depending upon local conditions and relationships, but they help assure more functional facilities and a saving in capital and annual costs. In such cooperative action, especially if carried out in conformity with an effective city plan, lies the hope that cities may be able to acquire adequate neighborhood and community recreation areas.

METHODS OF ACQUIRING LAND FOR RECREATION

A city plan for recreation, to be effective, must include recommendations for implementing the plan through the acquisition of needed recreation areas. Among the various ways by which land can be acquired for recreation use, the most widely used are purchase, gift, and transfer. A city requiring additional land for recreation will do well to consider carefully the possibilities of the various available methods.

Purchase. The most common method of acquiring areas is by direct purchase after negotiation between the owner and the governmental agency desiring the property. In case satisfactory terms of purchase cannot be arranged, condemnation proceedings may be resorted to, but they are avoided wherever possible as they are likely to be long, tedious, and expensive. In rare instances recreation areas have been acquired through excess purchase,[8] but the constitutionality of this method is open to question in many states. A special assessment plan, under which benefited property owners meet at least part of the cost, has been used to finance the purchase of neighborhood playgrounds and parks in several cities and for the acquisition of parkways. Under city-planning legislation in certain states, a city may reserve for purchase, within a stipulated period, areas designated for recreation on subdivision plots submitted for approval. In rare instances areas have been purchased with the understanding that they will be paid for from revenues secured from their use.

Gifts. Gifts of land for recreation purposes have played a large part in the development of many municipal park and recreation systems. A study of 3,158 donated parks and playgrounds in nearly one thousand communities indicated that their combined area equaled nearly one-third

[8] This is a procedure whereby more land is acquired than is needed for the public purpose; the balance is disposed of by subsequent sale.

of the total municipal park acreage in the country at the time the study was made.[9] Many gifts of land and money for the purchase of recreation areas have been subsequently reported. Land is usually given in fee simple and deeded directly to the municipality; a provision in the deed that if the land is not used for recreation it shall revert to the donor or his heirs helps assure its use for recreation in perpetuity. Experience has shown that although gifts of land should be encouraged by city authorities, it is wise to accept only areas which are adaptable for recreation, free from narrow use restrictions, and suitable in location, size, and topography.

Dedication. Some city authorities require the owner of land being subdivided for residential use to set aside one or more areas and dedicate them in perpetuity for recreation. Many subdividers have followed this practice voluntarily because it has demonstrated its practical value. They continue to hold title to these areas, deed them to an organization of property owners, or give them outright to the city. Many dedicated areas have proven unsuitable for recreation because of their substandard size, location, or topography. A number of cities have therefore adopted a policy of requiring subdividers to contribute money instead of land; the funds are used to purchase needed recreation areas in accordance with a city-wide plan. The legality of such action, however, has been questioned in more than one state.

Transfer. Many properties which were originally acquired by a governmental agency for some purpose other than recreation were later no longer needed for the original purpose and were transferred to the city park or recreation agency. State and county lands have been turned over to cities for recreation purposes, but much more numerous are the cases where land under the jurisdiction of some other city department has been transferred to a park or recreation commission. Abandoned city reservoirs, institution sites, cemeteries, commons, and water-front properties have been added to city park systems.

Sanitary–land-fill operations are creating land for recreation in dozens of cities. Reclamation through hydraulic or sanitary fill has been the means of transforming marshes, swamps, and dilapidated water fronts from unsightly, unhealthful areas into attractive recreation properties serving a useful purpose. Numerous tax-delinquent properties have also been turned over to city recreation authorities to be developed for recreation use or to be exchanged for other more suitable areas.

The importance of long-range planning to assure the acquisition and reservation of open space in what has been termed "our explosively expanding metropolitan areas" was repeatedly stressed at the 1957 sym-

[9] *Donated Parks and Play Areas in the United States,* National Recreation Association, New York, 1929.

posium on "The New Highways: Challenge to the Metropolitan Region." It was pointed out that for the masses of our people cities are no longer agreeable places in which to live. Authorities must act to make life livable and attractive by providing more open space for recreation. Early action in accordance with a sound city plan is essential if our communities are to achieve a status worthy of the nation's wealth, leisure, and culture. The purchase by governmental agencies of development rights, whereby owners of open land are compensated for withholding them from development, offers promise as a tool for the conservation of open spaces for recreation and other uses.

12. THE DESIGN AND EQUIPMENT
OF RECREATION AREAS

THE USEFULNESS of a city's recreation areas depends not alone upon their size and location but upon the way in which they are designed, developed, equipped, maintained, and operated for recreation use. Most of the activities that comprise the municipal recreation program are possible only when fields, courts, buildings, facilities, and equipment are provided. The extent to which a city's recreation system furnishes such features determines largely the nature and scope of its recreation service.[1]

The problem of developing a system of recreation areas is relatively simple if ample funds are available for acquiring suitable areas in accordance with a city plan, for employing competent personnel to prepare development plans, and for carrying them to completion. In most communities, however, limited funds and substandard areas necessitate resourcefulness on the part of the recreation authorities in order to assure maximum use of the properties available. They must utilize fully the possibilities offered by the areas under their control and recognize the potentialities for recreation of other properties which might be acquired by the city. In the hands of competent authorities a vacant lot, a city dump, or an abandoned farm may be transformed into a children's playground, an athletic field, or a golf course, respectively.

A recreation leader with imagination can accomplish much with limited space and facilities, whereas the finest equipment will not assure a successful program under poor leadership. On the other hand, a well-balanced program is not possible without suitable areas and facilities. For example, sustained interest in such games as tennis, handball, or bowling depends primarily upon conveniently located, properly constructed, and well-maintained courts. Many playgrounds fail to attract teen-age boys because they are too small to provide a baseball or even a softball diamond. Others offer only a sports program because they lack suitable indoor or outdoor facilities for dramatics, arts and crafts, and other activities. Water sports, winter sports, camping, golf, and picnicking

[1] For a comprehensive volume dealing with this subject, see George D. Butler, *Recreation Areas—Their Design and Equipment,* rev. ed., The Ronald Press Company, New York, 1958.

are possible for large numbers of people only if necessary facilities are provided through public funds. During much of the year recreation opportunities are very limited unless buildings are made available for indoor activities.

TYPES OF OUTDOOR RECREATION FACILITIES

Recreation areas contain a great variety of outdoor facilities which serve men and women, young people, and children. Some are used the year round; others during a single season. Many afford opportunities for highly organized, competitive sports; others provide recreation for individuals or family groups. They differ widely in the activities made possible; in their construction and operation cost, space requirements, location; in the number of persons served; and in the amount of leadership or supervision required. These factors are important in evaluating the service they render. The following list includes most of the important and commonly provided outdoor facilities: [2]

Game Courts and Fields

Badminton courts
Baseball diamonds
Basketball courts
Boccie courts
Bowling greens and alleys
Clock-golf courts
Cricket fields
Croquet courts
Curling rinks
Football fields
Giant checkers courts
Handball courts
Hockey fields
Horseshoe courts

Ice-hockey rinks
Marbles rings
Paddle-tennis courts
Polo fields
Quoits courts
Roque courts
Shuffleboard courts
Soccer fields
Softball diamonds
Speed-ball fields
Tennis courts
Tetherball courts
Touch-football areas
Volleyball courts

Sports Areas and Facilities

Archery ranges
Artificial ice rinks
Athletic fields
Batting cages
Bicycle tracks
Bridle trails
Casting pools
Coasting areas
Drag strips
Golf courses
Golf driving ranges
Ice-skating tracks and areas
Jumping pits

Marinas
Pistol ranges
Putting greens
Rifle ranges
Roller-skating tracks
Running tracks
Ski jumps
Skiing areas
Sled slides
Toboggan slides
Trapshooting ranges
Vaulting pits
Yacht harbors

[2] For a list of recreation building types and of indoor facilities, see Chap. 13.

Structures

Bandstands and shells
Bleachers
Boat docks and ramps
Council rings
Dance pavilions
Diving pools
Fishing piers
Grandstands
Outdoor theaters

Pavilions
Recreation piers
Shelters, open
Shower baths
Spray pools
Stadiums
Stages
Swimming pools
Wading pools

Equipment

Amplification equipment
Backstops for baseball, basketball,
and softball
Barbecue pits
Benches
Bicycle racks
Block-building platforms
Box hockey
Bulletin boards
Drinking fountains
Fences
Fireplaces
Flagpoles

Mobile service units
Motion-picture screens, portable
Night-lighting equipment
Picnic facilities—benches, tables,
ovens
Playground apparatus
Playground showers
Playhouses, portable
Sand courts and boxes
Score boards
Signs
Tables for games and crafts
Table-tennis tables

Special Areas

Arboretums
Bathing beaches
Camps
Concert areas
Day camps
Farm plots
Gardens
Hiking trails

Model-airplane fields
Model-yacht ponds
Multiple-use paved areas
Nature trails
Parking fields
Picnic areas
Playgrounds for children
Tourist camps

PRINCIPLES IN PLANNING RECREATION AREAS

Each recreation area presents a distinct problem in landscape design, requiring individual analysis and treatment. The effectiveness and appearance of the area depend in large measure upon the understanding, skill, and imagination of the planner. Naturally the problem of design varies with the type of area being planned, but full advantage should be taken of the peculiar characteristics of the site, such as uneven topography or existing trees, streams, and other natural features that contribute to its beauty. In planning an athletic field, however, other considerations are paramount, and the plan must evolve around certain essential sports facilities such as the football or baseball field and running track, which are highly standardized in their space requirements and development. The desired facilities, their area requirements, arrangement, and use demand primary consideration in planning properties intended for active recreation, but interest and beauty are essential ingredients in the design of every recreation area.

Planning Objectives. Regardless of the type of recreation area, certain factors to be considered and objectives to be sought in planning it are:

Effective Use of the Entire Area. Since public recreation areas are seldom larger than necessary, every part of the property should have a definite function and contribute to either its utility or beauty or both. The maximum possibilities for the multiple use of areas should be realized where desirable.

Location and Arrangement of the Areas and Facilities. Major or primary features are planned first; minor or incidental features receive secondary consideration.

Adequate Space for the Facilities. To assure safety and satisfactory play, ample space must be allowed for equipment, game courts, and playing fields. In areas used for picnicking and camping, considerable space is desirable for privacy.

Ease of Supervision or Operation. Some recreation facilities require constant supervision; others, little. This fact is important in designing an area.

Accessibility. Sections serving small children are located near the entrance or on the side nearest the children's homes. Ease of access is less important in the case of most units used by adults.

Utilization of Natural Features. A natural slope may be used to advantage for an outdoor theater or for winter sports, a grove of trees for a picnic area or music shell, and a large, level, open area for an athletic field.

Safety. On the playground, safety may be secured by careful arrangement of apparatus and game courts; on the large park or reservation, by a proper location of roads and paths in relation to major features.

Economy in Construction. Through careful planning expensive operations like grading and drainage may be reduced to a minimum, multiple use of facilities may be secured, and plumbing, surfacing, and other costs may be kept low.

Economy in Maintenance. Maintenance costs often bear a direct relation to construction costs; a small addition to the latter through the use of better materials may result in a considerable saving in maintenance. Careful planning simplifies such duties as grass cutting, hedge trimming, cleaning of pools and buildings, and the care of game courts. Areas such as bowling greens require much maintenance and so should not be constructed unless adequate means of maintenance are assured.

Conveniences for People Using Area. Frequently an otherwise satisfactory area fails to provide adequately for the comfort and the convenience of the people using it. Toilet facilities, drinking fountains, seating accommodations, and parking space are essential service features. In the case of some large areas, roads leading to recreation facilities are needed.

Appearance. Every recreation area should present a pleasing appearance from within and without, even though little space can be made available for plantings. This is achieved through proper architectural and landscape design.

Achieving These Objectives. These objectives are attained by a variety of methods, the importance of which varies with different types of properties. The problem of determining the most essential areas and facilities is comparatively simple in the case of the small playground but complex when a plan for a large park is under consideration. Accessibility is less important in selecting the site for a golf clubhouse than it is in locating a shelter house to serve children on a neighborhood playground. Other factors that influence design are the size and shape of the area, its topography, the type of neighborhood, needs to be served, special recreation interests of the people, funds available for development and maintenance, and probable amount and type of leadership. The effective solution of a particular problem demands, on the part of the designer, an understanding of the recreation needs and interests to be met by the area; a knowledge of the facilities which can meet these needs; their requirements as to space, location, and construction; and the ability to arrange these features upon the area in such a way as to produce an effective and attractive plan.

ESSENTIAL FACTORS IN DEVELOPING RECREATION AREAS

Certain procedures and operations are essential to the proper development of every recreation area. A few of them are described briefly in the following paragraphs.

Survey and Plan. It is unwise to start work on an area until a general plan has been prepared and approved by the proper authorities. To assure the best results the plan should be prepared by a competent recreation planner or landscape architect experienced in the design of recreation areas. Personnel who are to be responsible for the operation and maintenance of the area should participate in the planning process. The general plan indicates the location of the various features on the site and affords a basis for orderly development in case the work cannot be completed at one time. Before preparing the plan, the designer needs to know the boundaries of the area, the topography, the location and size of trees and other natural features, the location and size of the sewers and water mains, and the soil, water, and drainage conditions.

Grading and Drainage. Uneven properties may serve admirably for golf courses and camp sites, but comparatively level areas are needed for playgrounds, playfields, and athletic fields. It is frequently necessary to grade parts of an area in order to provide level spaces for such games as

The small children's section in this municipal playground provides unusual and attractive play equipment (Courtesy of Oakland, Calif., Recreation Commission).

tennis, handball, baseball, and football; but because grading is expensive, it should be reduced to a minimum. On large properties, grading is usually limited to sections developed for roads, parking areas, building sites, and other special features.

The purpose of drainage is to remove excess surface and ground water which would otherwise interfere with the recreational use of an area. Excess surface water is usually carried off by inlets and catch basins which are connected with a storm sewer or nearby stream. Ground water, on the other hand, is collected and removed by tile drains laid under the surface of the area. The use of underground drainage systems is most common in the construction of athletic fields and special game areas such as tennis courts and bowling greens.

Surfacing. Different forms of recreation activity require different kinds of surfaces, and a great variety of surfacing materials is used in the development of a recreation system. Tanbark, sand, and sawdust provide a suitable cushion under climbing types of playground apparatus. Turf is the best surface for small children's areas, the golf course, the bowling green, and the croquet court, and for such games as football and baseball. On the other hand, courts requiring an accurate bounce and subjected to intensive use, such as handball and tennis, usually have a surface of concrete, clay, or bituminous material. In large parks and reservations, only paths, roads, and areas of intensive use receive special surface treatment. Authorities have experimented widely with various surfacing materials including rubber for intensively used play areas, but a satisfactory solution has not yet been discovered. Excellent results have been secured from the use of cork asphalt on the children's playground, but the expense of this material is comparatively high.

Lighting. The installation of lights at recreation areas has become widespread, for it prolongs the hours of use and increases greatly the number of persons served. Areas are lighted not only for general play but for court and field games and for activities such as swimming and winter sports. Installation of equipment of the proper type, height, and location is essential for successful results, and it is therefore highly advisable to secure the advice of experienced illuminating engineers. The use of steel poles and underground wires increases the cost but is desirable from the standpoint of appearance.

Paths, Roads, Parking. On small, intensively used properties, paths assist people in reaching directly and easily the various facilities and special features and also help prevent interference with play activities. In larger outlying areas they may contribute directly to such forms of recreation as walking, hiking, bicycling or horseback riding; they lead to or through areas of special beauty or scenic interest or afford access to centers of activity. With the exception of service drives, roads have no place in the smaller recreation areas. In most larger properties, however, roads are needed to make the various sections accessible. Parking spaces for automobiles must be provided in connection with playfields, athletic fields, swimming pools, picnic centers, camps, zoos, and other features which attract or serve large numbers of people.

Fencing. It is generally agreed that the neighborhood playground should be fenced for safety, effective operation, and the protection of neighboring property. Along thoroughfares, it is desirable that fences be set at least 10 feet inside the property line to permit a planting area outside the fence. The athletic field and stadium site are almost always enclosed in order to facilitate control and the collection of admission fees. A fence is essential around the outdoor swimming pool in order to restrict access to the pool to bathers alone. Tennis requires a fence for satisfactory play, and low fences are often erected on the playground around facilities such as the wading pool and game courts in order to protect planted areas or to separate various sections of the area. There are few recreation areas where some form of fencing is not necessary or desirable. Care needs to be taken in the location of gates, exits, and entrances.

Water. Water contributes to both the appearance and usefulness of recreation areas. It enhances the beauty of the landscape, can be stocked for fishing, affords a habitat for waterfowl, and makes possible bathing, boating, and other aquatic sports. In addition to water surfaces it serves many essential functions. Drinking fountains, sprinkling systems for the running track, athletic field, and planted areas, service rooms in field houses and other structures, swimming and wading pools, all require a large quantity of pure water. Water mains and pipes should be installed when the area is being developed.

Beauty. Beauty, whether derived from existing natural features or resulting from human planning, should be a major objective in the design of every recreation area. It has always been considered an essential feature of the neighborhood park, the large park, and the reservation, but has often been sadly neglected on such areas as the playground and athletic field. No matter how small an area may be or how intensively used, it is possible to provide pleasing landscape effects and at the same time secure maximum use. This is achieved primarily through the wise selection, location, and maintenance of plant materials likely to thrive in the location, climate, soil, and conditions to which they are subjected. Large, uneven properties afford greater possibilities for more interesting and varied developments. Plant materials, however, are not the only features that contribute beauty, attractiveness, and interest to a recreation area. Every building, structure, or piece of equipment can be so designed, constructed, and maintained as to add to the appearance of the property of which it is a part.

EQUIPMENT AND GAME FACILITIES

Before considering the design and equipment of typical recreation areas, it may be well to point out some of the features which are commonly found on these areas, especially on the playground and playfield. They include apparatus, facilities for games and sports, seating facilities, the wading pool, and other types of equipment.

Playground Apparatus. Apparatus has an important place on the playground and is also used at the playfield, the bathing beach, and the picnic center. Children enjoy using it. It contributes to physical development, cares for many children, and provides a much-needed opportunity for such age-old activities as climbing, swinging, balancing, and hanging by the hands and feet. Less space is devoted to apparatus on the playground today than a generation or two ago, when large amounts of equipment of various types were installed. Increasingly, authorities tended

Novel and standard types of children's play equipment as well as game courts and playing fields for adults make the Metropolitan Beach playfield popular with all age groups (Courtesy of Huron-Clinton Metropolitan Authority, Detroit, Mich.).

to favor a few types that had proven to be safe and popular, such as the swing, slide, sandbox, horizontal ladder, horizontal bar, seesaw, and a variety of climbing devices. Modifications of some of these types have made them more attractive in appearance and more popular with the children. Color is also more widely used and has achieved the same results.

Significant developments have occurred, primarily during the past decade, in response to a demand for equipment that would arouse and sustain children's interest to a greater degree than the standard types and that would encourage imaginative and creative play. One consisted of the installation on children's areas of discarded airplanes, fire engines, trucks, locomotives, and boats, in and on which children can play to their heart's content. Equipment has been built and installed on many areas to simulate ships, automobiles, and similar features. Playgrounds have also been developed around a special theme. In Philadelphia a play lot simulates a seaport, equipped with a concrete ship which doubles as a sandbox, a wharf, and a climbing and sliding device in the form of a giant porpoise. Another area, equipped with a unique log stockade and a corral with wooden horses, provides a Wild West setting. Montebello, California, has a 20-acre "Playshore" park in which all features are in keeping with the theme of sea life and the seashore. Its seventeen units of uniquely designed equipment include a sea serpent, lighthouse, submarine, whale, crow's-nest, starfish, pirates' ship, and wading pool, and provide a wonderland for preteen children.

Another change has been the development of forms that give a new look and a novel appeal to the playground. Play sculptures, built of reinforced concrete, cast stone, Fiberglas, or other materials, take many shapes and forms such as fish, animals, caves, playhouses, or free-form structures. Another group consists of a network of plastic-coated cables, strips of spring steel, and concrete structures. Cinder-block walls in varied patterns, pipe tunnels, play pyramids, and platforms of concrete were devised by the New York City Housing Authority and have been installed widely. A playground in Monterey, California, opened late in 1956, is an outstanding example of an attempt to provide a unique and challenging play area for children. Among its features, many of them built of colorful plastic-covered material, are an umbrella tree, a balancing bridge, a giant swing, and a structure which could be a space ship, bird, or fish.

These recent experiments in the use of new materials and types of equipment are being studied with keen interest. They may not replace some of the long-standard features such as the swing, slide, and sandbox, but they assure more attractive and challenging playgrounds in the years ahead.

The Wading Pool. The wading pool is perhaps the most popular feature of the playground during the summer months; it is also commonly installed as a unit of the modern swimming center. It is seldom possible to use a stream for wading because of pollution of the water; most pools are therefore built of cement and are filled from the city water system. When not used for wading, pools may serve as basins for sailing model boats. Some are also used, when empty, for games, roller skating, and, in the winter, ice skating.

Wading pools vary in size, shape, and depth, depending upon the location and the requirements of the area. In planning and constructing a pool, special attention is given to drainage, water supply, outlet controls, and the surrounding area. As a rule, the maximum depth does not exceed 15 inches, and the deep area is at or near the center. On some playgrounds, pools are constructed with a depth of water of 24 or even 36 inches, but such pools are for all practical purposes children's swimming pools. They should be enclosed by a fence, and the same measures should be taken to assure safety and sanitation as at a swimming pool.

Many cities have constructed shallow basins equipped with sprays as a substitute for the wading pool. Although less expensive to build and simpler to maintain, spray pools provide limited opportunities for enjoyment as compared with the wading pool.

Areas and Facilities for Games and Sports. Fields and facilities for games and sports are provided in practically all recreation areas except small landscaped parks. They occupy a large percentage of most playfields, athletic fields, and playgrounds. Their importance is due to the strong appeal which games and sports have for people of all ages and of both sexes. Old as well as young enjoy horseshoes, lawn bowling, croquet, and shuffleboard. Young men find a keen interest in handball and football, young women and girls in field hockey and fieldball. Tennis, softball, and volleyball are played by men and women, boys and girls.

The requirements of these games and sports in the way of space, surfacing, and equipment vary widely. Mention has already been made of the different types of surfacing needed for different games. Only when a suitable surface for play is provided can people thoroughly enjoy most games or attain a high degree of skill in them. Orientation is also important because unless courts or fields are properly laid out, the sun is likely to interfere with some of the players. Most of the play is lengthwise of the court in such games as tennis, volleyball, archery, and horseshoes; therefore these courts are laid with the long axis in a general north and south direction. Since football is usually played in the fall, it is best for the field to lie northwest and southeast. There is no ideal orientation for baseball, but many favor placing the home plate in the southwest or northwest corner; others prefer a north or south position.

Permanent equipment is essential for most games. It generally consists of (1) items essential to the game itself, such as tennis nets and posts, goal posts for soccer and football, horseshoe stakes, and basketball goals, and (2) items incidental but necessary to playing the game in a satisfactory manner, such as baseball backstops and tennis-court enclosures. The proper development of a recreation field requires a knowledge of the essential materials, dimensions, location, and installation of this equipment.

Limited space in most public recreation areas generally necessitates use of the same area for different games at different seasons of the year or even during the same season. Careful planning makes it possible for baseball and football fields to overlap and the same space to serve for field hockey and softball, avoiding the use of skinned diamonds for other activities whenever possible. Increasingly, paved multiple-use areas are being built for paddle tennis, volleyball, and other court games. To get the maximum service from an area, removable standards or goals are used whenever possible, and permanent fixtures are erected where they will not interfere with areas required for play.

Official dimensions have been adopted for many game areas; courts or fields of varying dimensions may be used for others. Games like shuffleboard and roque require very little space outside the actual game courts, whereas tennis and baseball necessitate considerable space outside the boundaries of the court or field. The tables shown on pages 188 to 190, adapted from *Recreation Areas—Their Design and Equipment*,[3] indicate the court dimensions, the approximate space needed for the activity, and the number of players served in most of the common games.

Facilities for Track and Field Events. The running track, jumping pits, and other facilities for field events are essential features of the athletic field and are also found in many large parks and playfields, especially at or adjoining high school sites. Playgrounds are rarely equipped with a running track, although a straightaway for use in the dashes and a jumping pit serve a useful purpose. A ¼-mile track with an end radius between 100 and 125 feet is recommended for general use. The track is measured 12 inches from the inner edge of the curb; it should be level throughout its perimeter, but a slight grade toward the curb is recommended. Opinions differ as to the best methods of track construction, and a study of the construction of satisfactory tracks in the region is recommended to any city that is planning to build one.

Field events—the running broad and high jumps, pole vault, hammer throw, shot put, javelin throw—are usually carried on within the track enclosure. Runways, pits, and areas for these events are arranged so as to minimize the danger of injury to participants, enable spectators to see, and interfere as little as possible with the use of the field for other sports.

Seating Facilities. Seating facilities, which contribute greatly to the comfort and convenience of people using recreation areas, vary in size and type from benches placed alongside the tennis court or wading pool to the stadium seating thousands of people. On the playground, benches are provided for mothers in the small children's section, near the game courts, in the older adults' area, and at the other suitable locations. Knockdown bleachers are set up near the softball diamond and additional temporary bleachers are erected when a circus, playday, or other special event is to be held. On the playfield and large park, benches are needed,

[3] George D. Butler, *Recreation Areas—Their Design and Equipment*, rev. ed., The Ronald Press Company, New York, 1958, pp. 96–97.

Table 1. Space Requirements for Games and Sports (Youth and Adults)

Name	Dimensions of game areas, ft.	Use dimensions, ft.	Space required, sq. ft.	Number of players
Archery	90–300 long	50 × 175 (min.)	8,750	2 or more
		50 × 400 (max.)	20,000	
Badminton	17 × 44 (singles)	25 × 60	1,500	2
	20 × 44 (doubles)	30 × 60	1,800	4
Baseball	90-ft. diamond	350 × 350 (average with hooded backstop)	122,500	18
		400 × 400 (without)	160,000	
Basketball	50 × 94	60 × 100 (average)	6,000	10–12
Basketball (adol. boys)	50 × 84	60 × 90	5,400	10
Basketball (adol. girls)	35 × 70	45 × 80	3,600	12
Boccie	10 × 60	20 × 80	1,600	2–4
Bowling on the green	14 × 100 (1 lane)	130 × 130	16,900	32–64
Bowling (alley)	3½ × 62	10 × 100	1,000	2 or more
Checkers (giant)	12 ft. sq. (min.)	20 × 20 or more	400	2
Clock golf	20–30-ft. diameter	40 × 40 (min.)	1,600	2–8
Cricket	Wickets 66 ft. apart	420 × 420	176,400	22
Croquet	30 × 60	40 × 75	3,000	2–8
Croquet (modern)	41 × 85	50 × 95	4,750	2–8
Curling	14 × 138	25 × 160	4,000	2 or more
Deck tennis	14 × 40 (singles)	20 × 50	1,000	2
	17 × 40 (doubles)	26 × 50	1,300	4
Fieldball	180 × 300 (max.)	200 × 320 (average)	64,000	22
Field hockey	150 × 270 (min.)	210 × 330 (average)	69,300	22
	180 × 300 (max.)			
Football	160 × 360	190 × 420	79,800	22
Goal-hi	50–60-ft. diameter	65 × 65 (min.)	4,225	2 or more
Handball	20 × 34	32 × 44	1,408	2 or 4

Hand tennis	16 × 40	25 × 60	1,500	2 or 4
Horseshoes (men)	Stakes 40 ft. apart	12 × 52 (or more)	624	2 or 4
Horseshoes (women)	Stakes 30–40 ft. apart	12 × 42 (or more)	504	2 or 4
Ice hockey	60 × 165 (min.) 110 × 250 (max.) 85 × 200 (recommended)	100 × 220 (average)	22,000	12
Lacrosse (men)	180 × 330 (min.) 210 × 330 (max.)	225 × 360 (average)	81,000	24
Lacrosse (women)	Goals 270–330 ft. apart No definite boundaries	240 × 360 (average)	86,400	24
Paddle tennis	20 × 44 (doubles)	35 × 70	2,450	4
Polo	600 × 960 (max.)	600 × 960	576,000	8
Quoits	Stakes 30 ft. apart Stakes 54 ft. apart	12 × 44 25 × 80	528 2,000	2 or 4
Roque	30 × 60	40 × 70	2,800	2 or 4
Shuffleboard	6 × 52	10 × 60	600	2 or 4
Six-man football	120 × 300	180 × 360	64,800	12
Soccer (men)	195 × 330 (min.) 225 × 360 (max.)	225 × 360 (average)	81,000	22
Soccer (women)	120 × 240 (min.) 180 × 300 (min.)	200 × 320 (average)	64,000	22
Softball (men)	60-ft. diamond	275 × 275 (min.)	75,625	18
Softball (women)	60-ft. diamond	250 × 250 (min.)	62,500	18
Speed ball (men)	160 × 360 (max.)	200 × 420	84,000	22
Speed ball (women)	180 × 300	220 × 350	77,000	22
Table tennis	5 × 9	12 × 20	240	2 or 4
Tennis	27 × 78 (singles) 36 × 78 (doubles)	50 × 120 60 × 120	6,000 7,200	2 4
Tetherball	Circle 6-ft. diameter	20 × 20	400	2
Touch football	160 × 360	190 × 420	79,800	18–22
Volleyball	30 × 60	45 × 80	3,600	12–16

Table 2. Space Requirements for Games and Sports (Children)

Name	Dimensions of game areas, ft.	Use dimensions, ft.	Space required, sq. ft.	Number of players
Archery	60–150 ft. long	50 × 135 (min.)	6,750	2 or more
	Targets 15 ft. apart	50 × 235 (max.)	11,750	
Baseball	75-ft. diamond	250 × 250	62,500	18
	82-ft. diamond			
Basketball	40 × 60	50 × 70	3,500	10
Box hockey	4 × 10	15 × 20	300	2
Field hockey	120 × 200 (max.)	150 × 250 (max.)	37,500	22
Hopscotch	5 × 12½	10 × 20	200	2 or 4
Horseshoes	Stakes 25 ft. apart	12 × 40	480	2 or 4
Marbles	10-ft. diameter	18 × 18	324	2–6
Soccer	100 × 200	125 × 240	30,000	22
Softball	45-ft. diamond	175 × 175 (average)	30,625	18
Speedball	120 × 220	150 × 260	39,000	22
Team dodge ball:				
Boys	Circle 40-ft. diameter	60 × 60	3,600	20
Girls	Circle 35-ft. diameter	50 × 50	2,500	20
Touch football	120 × 240	140 × 280	39,200	18–22
Volleyball	25 × 50	40 × 70	2,800	12–16

especially near the game courts used by adults and in the picnic area. Bleachers, preferably of the knockdown or movable type, are erected for the convenience of spectators at ball games and other special events. Seating facilities are also needed at outdoor areas where concerts, motion pictures, or dramatic productions are presented.

At the athletic field or stadium the seating of spectators is a major consideration, and permanent structures are erected for this purpose. Toilet, shower, locker, and storage rooms are often provided under such structures. Other things being equal, the main seating facilities should be on the west side of the field so that afternoon sun will not shine in the spectators' eyes. In the neighborhood parks and at points of scenic interest in the large park or reservation, benches are frequently provided for the comfort of people who come to enjoy the beauty of the area.

Other Equipment. Tables and benches are needed in connection with craft activities, for quiet games enjoyed by children and adults, and also for use at picnic centers. Other valuable playground features are a platform for folk dancing and block building, a bicycle rack, bulletin boards, drinking fountains, receptacles for waste materials, boxes for storing supplies and equipment, and a flagpole with an American flag. A fireplace and council ring on the playground or playfield serve playground, family, or scouting groups. Other types of equipment will be mentioned in later sections.

THE DESIGN AND EQUIPMENT OF SPECIFIC TYPES OF AREAS

A few significant characteristics of the design, equipment, and general development of the chief types of recreation areas are described briefly in the following pages.

The Play Lot. The play lot in many instances is a separate area; in others, it is a section of the neighborhood playground, set aside for the use of preschool children. Desirable features are a row of shade trees around the borders and a central grass plot, play equipment placed under the trees, and possibly a wide concrete walk separating the apparatus area from the grass plot, to be used for tricycles, scooters, and other wheeled toys, as well as for baby carriages. The equipment includes sandboxes, blocks, sand tools, playhouses, a low drinking fountain, a small shallow wading or spray pool, and a few pieces of apparatus such as chair swings, low slides and climbing devices, and sculptured units. Benches and tables for mothers, an open shelter for baby carriages and for use in case of sudden showers, a flagpole, and a birdbath are desirable features. Safety requires that the play lot be surrounded by a low hedge or fence.

The Neighborhood Playground. No standardized pattern of playground design is desirable or practicable, but the divisions suggested here provide for the essential playground activities and services for different age groups, especially children of elementary school age. In some areas it is necessary to combine or eliminate one or more of the divisions. These should be so planned and located as to facilitate circulation, simplify supervision, and enable the activities to be engaged in with a maximum of enjoyment. The following divisions are suggested:

Small Area for the Exclusive Use of Children of Preschool Age. In crowded neighborhoods this section is essential; in better residential areas it may not be needed. Its layout and equipment correspond to those previously suggested for the play lot. Proximity to the entrance and to the shelter house is desirable.

Apparatus Area for Older Children (primarily for six- to eleven-year-olds). As a rule it is preferable to have the apparatus for this age group concentrated in one section rather than scattered over the playground. A single set usually serves the needs of both boys and girls. The selection and location of the apparatus units and the provision of ample safety zones require special care. If near the shelter house, this section is readily accessible and easily supervised.

Area for Free Play and Low Organized Games. Children six to eleven years of age require an open space for free play and a great variety of running, circle, and low organized games. The section set aside for these activities is frequently near the apparatus area which is used by children of the same age.

Multiple-use Paved Area. The growing practice of using playgrounds the year round makes this an important area. Usually rectangular, it is marked off for court games and equipped with removable goals and net posts. It can also be used for roller skating, dancing, and general play and —if curbed—for ice skating. A good location for this area is between the sections used by younger children and the area for field games, preferably next to the boundary fence which serves as a backstop.

Area for Field Games. This area meets the needs of older boys, teen-age girls, and young adults for vigorous sports and athletic activities such as softball, soccer, touch football, and—if the area is large enough—baseball and football. (See Table 1, earlier in the chapter, for space requirements.) Badminton, croquet, clock golf, horseshoes, box hockey, goal-hi, tether tennis, and similar activities can be pursued along the sides and in the corners of the area. Since both sexes use the area, it should be large enough to accommodate boys and girls at the same time and should be laid out in a manner that makes this possible. Where the area is small, facilities should be scheduled for use by both groups on an equitable basis.

Shelter House and Wading Pool. The shelter house is an essential unit, and its location is important, since it serves as the center of control and also the chief architectural feature of the playground. A location fairly near the main entrance makes it accessible from the various divisions and lends itself to an attractive landscape development. However, the building should not be so near the street that it invites use as a public comfort station. Often the wading pool is constructed near the shelter house—an economical and effective arrangement.

The Parade Grounds in Minneapolis serves as a center for the city's municipal sports program (Courtesy of Minneapolis Park Board).

Shaded Area for Handcraft and Quiet Activities. Crafts, storytelling, music, drama, table games, and other quiet activities can be carried on inside the playground building. For some activities, however, a shaded outdoor area is preferable, equipped with tables and benches, a small stage or platform, and spaces for marbles, hopscotch, and other quiet games. A quiet corner of the playground adjoining the small children's area is a good location for this section.

Area for Older People. Little space is needed on the playground to serve older adults. A small, secluded area should be set aside for this age group, away from the noisy wading pool, apparatus, and low-organized-game areas, and near the courts for such games as shuffleboard, horseshoes, *boccie,* and roque. It should be shaded and generously provided with comfortable benches and tables for quiet games.

Landscape Area. Landscaping is important on all playgrounds, and space for it should always be provided. Common locations for landscaping are between the boundary fence and abutting sidewalks, around the playground shelter, and in areas set aside for quiet activities.

Parking and Service. Although most people who use a playground walk to it, a few parking spaces are generally needed. Access must be provided to the playground building, especially if it is used the year round. Little space is needed for the service drive if the building is located near the street.

Although no definite space requirements can be prescribed for the various divisions of the neighborhood playground, the following table suggests minimum and average amounts which might well be allotted to each. Where available, more space can be used to advantage for field games and for the landscape area. It will be noted that from 4.5 to 7.5 acres are required for the amounts suggested. If a playground is to have a swimming pool, as provided in congested neighborhoods in a number of cities, at least one additional acre will be required.

Table 3. Space Requirements for Playground Divisions

Playground division	Suggested space in sq. ft.	
	Minimum	Average
Area for children of preschool age	6,000	10,000
Apparatus area	5,000	8,000
Free-play and low-organized-game area	10,000	25,000
Multiple-use paved area	20,000	30,000
Area for field games	120,000	180,000
Shaded area for crafts and quiet activities	6,000	10,000
Shelter house and wading pool area	10,000	16,000
Area for older adults	3,000	5,000
Landscape area	10,000	30,000
Parking and service area	5,000	10,000
Total	195,000 (4.5 acres)	324,000 (7.5 acres)

The Playfield. The design of the playfield is even less subject to standardization than that of the playground, but a few guiding principles are considered important. A section of the playfield comprising not more than 3 acres is usually developed as a playground for children. This is placed along the side which is most accessible from the children's homes so they will not have to cross sections of the field used for baseball and other adult activities. Separate sections consisting of large, comparatively level open areas are devoted primarily to field sports for men and women. The men's section contains fields for baseball, football, soccer, and softball; the section for women and older girls is devoted largely to games such as softball, soccer, field hockey, and volleyball. Areas are also set aside for game courts and lawn games.

The swimming pool is a common playfield feature. The bathhouse is sometimes planned as the service building for the entire area or is incorporated in a well-equipped recreation building, which enables the playfield to serve as a year-round, indoor-outdoor center. The pool and building are often placed near the street so people can reach them easily without crossing other sections. Features like an outdoor theatre, bandstand, and fireplaces, tables, and benches for neighborhood picnics are best located in a section removed from the noisy, intensively used areas. Paths separate the various sections and lead people directly to the main features. If a part of the playfield is wooded and rugged, it can be developed as a landscape park. A parking area is a necessity.

In general, a site of 18 to 32 acres is needed to provide the units comprising a well-developed playfield. Experience has indicated that the space requirements of various sections of the playfield are likely to be met if the area is distributed as follows:

Table 4. Space Requirements for Playfield Divisions

Playfield division	Suggested acreage
Area for children's playground	2–3
Area for game courts	1–2
Field for men's sports	5–8
Field for women and girls	3–4
Area for lawn games	1–2
Swimming pool and building	1–2
Area for special features	2–4
Landscape area	2–5
Parking area	1–2
Total	18–32

The Large Park. In designing this type of property, two major objectives are sought. The planner seeks first to utilize the natural features and advantages of the site in order to secure interesting and varied landscape effects through the effective use of woodland, open lawn, meadow, and valley. Vistas are created, sequestered sections are provided, and access to vantage points is afforded through the effective location of paths, roads, and hiking and bridle trails. Besides, the designer takes advantage of the opportunities which the area affords for various forms of recreation that are appropriate in such a setting. Sections are developed for picnicking, games, and sports. Boating and bathing facilities are provided at water areas, which may also serve for skating in the winter. Park slopes are used for toboganning, coasting, and skiing. Space is set aside near the entrance for parking automobiles, which are used by large numbers of people in reaching these areas. Comfort stations or shelters are provided at places where people congregate in the largest numbers. A zoological garden, waterfowl sanctuary, outdoor theater, botanical garden, nature trail, and nature museum are common features, and a section is sometimes developed for a day camp or golf course.

The Reservation. In developing the reservation an attempt is made to keep it as nearly as possible in its natural state. Improvements and facilities are therefore segregated and introduced in such a way as not to interfere with the naturalistic condition of the remainder of the site. Water areas are utilized for fishing and water sports or are set aside as sanctuaries for waterfowl, and camps and picnic centers are established at suitable locations. These facilities are made accessible by automobile roads, but large sections can be reached only by bridle and hiking trails. Reservations are increasingly used for winter sports and nature activities.

The Neighborhood Park. The wide range in the size and topography of these areas necessitates varied methods of development. Some are distinctly formal in design; others, especially where there are interesting natural features, are treated in an informal, naturalistic manner. Much space is devoted to trees, shrubs, turf, and other plants. A fountain, pool, band shell, statue, and ornamental flagpole are common features, but in some neighborhood parks, paths for pedestrians and benches where people can sit and enjoy the beauty of the park are the only facilities provided. Occasionally pools are used for sailing toy boats, small sections are developed for little children's play, and shuffleboard, croquet, or other courts are provided for older people. These facilities add greatly to the usefulness of the parks and, when properly designed and located, do not detract from their beauty or interfere with their primary function.

Principles in the design of several types of special recreation areas are presented in the next chapter.

13. PLANNING SPECIAL AREAS AND STRUCTURES

IT IS impossible in this volume to discuss the design and construction of all the facilities and special areas listed at the beginning of Chapter 12. However, a few of them, serving large numbers of people and commonly provided by recreation authorities, will be described briefly. The many types of buildings which are essential to a community recreation program also are considered in this chapter.

SPECIAL RECREATION AREAS

There is an increasing tendency for cities to acquire and develop special-use areas for a camp, golf course, bathing beach, or stadium, although facilities for golf, swimming, camping, and major sports events are sometimes included among the features of the playfield, large park, or reservation. In either case, the design, construction, and equipment of these properties are influenced by certain definite use requirements.

The Bathing Beach. Comparatively few cities are so fortunate as to have water-front property that is suitable for development as a bathing beach. The ideal bathing beach combines deep water for experienced swimmers, ample shallow water for beginners, and a wide expanse of sand area for sun bathing. Its slope is gradual and free from obstructions or holes, and its sand surface extends into the water beyond the wadable area. In selecting a site for a beach, especially along a river, care must be taken to make sure that the water is pure and free from swift currents. Jetties or groins are required at some ocean beaches to prevent the sand from being washed away or to help build up the beach. Fences are erected at some beaches to facilitate control and to restrict bathing to supervised, safe areas.

The bathhouse is a necessary feature. It varies from a simple structure with toilets and spaces for storing personal belongings to one affording locker, shower, checking, toilet, bathing-suit, first-aid, refreshment, and office facilities. All these rooms are needed at an extensive beach attract-

197

ing large numbers of people from a considerable distance; less ample facilities serve if many people come to the beach dressed for bathing. Ready access to the water from the building is desirable, but the building should not encroach upon the sand beach. Facilities for volleyball, horseshoes, handball, and shuffleboard and an area for informal games, conveniently located so as not to interfere with bathers, add greatly to the popularity of a beach. A picnic area with tables, benches, and fireplaces is also a popular feature. The space needed for the parking of automobiles is determined primarily by the capacity of the beach.

Safety equipment is a factor of first importance; different types are required at lake, river, and ocean beaches. Towers for lifeguards on the beach, lifeboats, surfboards, ring and torpedo-can buoys with ropes, first-aid supplies, water fins, inhalator, and megaphone are in common use. For nonswimmers a portion of the water area is often marked off or is enclosed on three sides by lines of rope supported by floats secured in place at the corners. The area to be used by swimmers is also plainly indicated. A float with diving boards or platform is generally provided and is anchored in at least 10 feet of water.

The Golf Course. Best results are usually secured when land is acquired and developed primarily for golf. Uneven but not rugged topography, some woodland, a soil such as sandy loam, and good drainage are desirable characteristics of a site. The golf course presents an exceptional opportunity for harmonizing landscape beauty and active play. Expert advice is needed in solving the peculiar problems which arise in the planning and construction of a golf course. It is necessary to decide at the start whether the course is to be built for the expert, the average golfer, or the "dub." Some public courses are too difficult for the average golfer, with the result that play is slowed up and satisfactory golf is possible for only a few. Courses are made interesting through variation in the length of holes, in the width of fairways, the introduction of hazards, and the utilization of varied topography and natural tree growth. Provision of water holes, dog-leg fairways, traps, and hazards makes the course more difficult.

Important factors in golf course design and construction include the location and length of the holes, orientation of fairways, construction of tees and greens, provision of traps and hazards, drainage, seeding and fertilizing, installation of a watering system, and the location and construction of the clubhouse, entrance road, and parking area. The clubhouse is placed near the first and the last greens where people start and finish play and, like the parking area, is usually close to the entrance. Wherever possible, roads bordering or passing through the course should be eliminated. When facilities such as tennis courts, practice greens, croquet courts, and a playground for children are provided, preferably near the clubhouse, the golf course serves as a family recreation center. In the Northern states, where little golf is played during the winter months, the course is used for coasting, skiing, and tobogganing, and the clubhouse serves as a warming house and indoor recreation center.

Short golf courses with holes that average 30 to 100 yards or more each are growing in popularity. They have grass fairways, sand traps, and regulation putting greens, and can be used for all except wood shots. In addition to the course itself, a water system, fencing, building, parking area, and maintenance and play equipment are needed. These courses, which help stimulate interest in the game of golf and in the acquisition of golf skills, can be built on as little as 3 acres, although a site of 10 acres or more makes possible a more satisfactory layout.

The Camp. In planning an organized camp for boys, girls, or family groups, an attempt is made to conserve the natural beauty of the site and to create an environment in contrast to artificial city conditions. This is achieved through the use of native materials and through the selection of a site large enough to permit a considerable degree of isolation for the camp. Most municipal camps are therefore located in a large park or forest area or in a special site, usually at some distance from the city.

Many buildings are needed in the camp—among them cabins, floored tents or other sleeping quarters, recreation hall or lodge, dining hall, administration building, boathouse, toilets, infirmary, washhouse, barn or stable, storage and pump house, craft building, and nature museum. Topography influences the layout of the camp, although other factors are more important. The sleeping quarters are usually grouped in one or more units, the administration building is centrally located, and the kitchen is at a distance from both sleeping quarters and toilet buildings. Special care is taken to protect the water supply and to prevent the pollution of water used for drinking, washing, or water sports.

Most camps have access to a lake or stream where a bathing beach is developed and facilities for boating such as a dock and boathouse are constructed; otherwise a swimming pool is needed. A council ring, camp-fire circle, or outdoor amphitheater affords a center for evening activities, and the camp museum and nature trail serve the nature interests of the campers. These facilities are much more important to the camp program than game courts or a sports field, although these, too, are usually provided. Most municipal camps were designed primarily for summer use, but more and more they are being used throughout the year.

The Day Camp. Many cities have set aside sections of their parks or reservations to serve as day camps, where groups of children are given an opportunity to enjoy a limited camping experience. Areas of a varied and rugged character with interesting natural features are well suited to such use. Day-camp sites need to be readily accessible from the homes of the campers, yet large enough to afford a degree of isolation for them. The few essential facilities are outdoor cooking places, a supply of good drinking water, shade, a building with toilets, storage space, and room or shelter in case of sudden showers. A level area for games, tables and benches, council ring, nature trail, birdbaths, feeding station, and other aids to nature study are desirable features.

The Athletic Field or Stadium. This area, primarily an enclosed center for major games and sports, varies from a field with bleachers seating a few hundred people to a stadium accommodating thousands. Its chief characteristics are one or more large open spaces including a running track and major sports areas, permanent seating facilities for spectators, a field house—unless lockers, toilets, showers, and storage spaces are provided under the stands or in a nearby school building—parking spaces for automobiles, and a fence or wall around the entire area. The layout of the athletic field is determined by the activities to be carried on and the number of spectators to be accommodated. If the field is to be used primarily for football and track, as is often the case, the problem of layout is comparatively simple, for the football field can be laid out within the track, and the same area can be used for both sports. On the other hand, because baseball cannot be played to the best advantage on a field designed for football and track, a separate diamond and bleachers are often provided for this sport. Otherwise, the diamond must be laid out within the track enclosure, which also affords the location for facilities used in the field events. Orientation is highly important from the point of view of both participants and spectators.

The efficient handling of crowds at athletic events requires that entrances be properly located, that paths, ramps, stairways, and aisles be of ample width, that sections of the stands be clearly marked, and that the parking area be convenient to the stands, large enough to serve the field adequately, and located so as to minimize the traffic problem. In recent years there has been a definite trend toward lighting athletic fields and stadiums to permit their use at night for games and sports and for other community events. Another tendency has been for cities to build a stadium for a single sport, such as baseball or softball, and install lights for night play. Some athletic fields are still used primarily for exhibition games, but more and more of them are being used for a variety of activities.

The Swimming Pool. Most outdoor pools are in playgrounds, playfields, or large parks; some occupy special sites developed as swimming centers, and in recent years a number of cities have built them at or adjoining school sites. Great care in the planning and construction of the swimming pool is essential because of the varied and complex problems involved and also because if it is not built properly, the health and safety of the bathers are endangered. The problems confronted in pool construction relate to location, size, cost, and shape of the pool; thickness and reinforcement of pool walls and bottom; and drainage, water supply, waterproofing, heating, circulation, filtration and purification equipment, lighting, and bathhouse design and construction. Authorities responsible for the development of a swimming pool should never proceed with the project until they have secured the advice of a competent engineer experienced in pool construction and have consulted their state health department.

The popularity of swimming is demonstrated at the well-designed Gage Park pool (Courtesy of Topeka, Kans., Recreation Commission).

Swimming pools vary in size from the small neighborhood pool to the Olympic-type swimming center accommodating hundreds of people at one time. There are also many types and shapes of pools. The neighborhood pool is usually a single rectangular unit with water varying from 2½ to 5 feet in depth. The fan-shape pool is well adapted to the needs of the small community, if the narrow end is deep enough for diving and the opposite end is of wadable depth. Many rectangular pools are still being built, but modified forms such as the L and T types are increasingly popular, partly due to the fact that they provide a separate unit for divers. A number of rectangular pools have been built, 150 feet or more long, with shallow sections at each end and a deep section for diving across the center of the pool. Several cities have built pools consisting of two or three distinct units: one used for general swimming, another for diving, and a third for children or nonswimmers. A multiple pool of this type has many advantages where the volume of use justifies its construction.

A few principles in planning and constructing the swimming pool follow:

The slope of the bottom should be gradual wherever the depth is 5 feet or less.

As much of the pool as practicable should be wadable. Depths should be clearly marked, and the height of diving boards should be related to the depth of water under them.

The dimensions of the pool should be such as to facilitate its use for competitive events.

Essential parts are overflow troughs, properly sloped wide decks around the pool, recessed or removable steps or ladders, and water inlets and outlets adequate in size and located so as to assure proper circulation. Filters must be installed to clean the water, as well as a chlorinator or other device to disinfect it. Other items of equipment are pumps, heater, strainers, and cleaning equipment.

Pools should be surrounded by a fence which serves as a safety measure and makes the pools accessible to bathers only; bleachers for spectators may be erected outside the pool enclosure.

Special equipment used at pools includes diving boards and towers, floats, first-aid kits, lane markers, starting blocks, lifeguard chairs, vacuum cleaner, water-testing set, and lifesaving equipment. Many pools are equipped with underwater lights as well as floodlights, which illuminate the entire pool area. Game courts, playground apparatus, and large turf or sand areas for sun bathing are sometimes provided; the last named should be separated from the pool by a fence to compel users to pass through a shower before reentering the water. Some of the larger pools are equipped and used for a variety of games and play activities outside the swimming season; others serve as ice-skating rinks during the winter.

The bathhouse, a necessary feature, is located close to the pool, preferably near the shallow end. When the pool is located on a playfield, the bathhouse can be included in the field house or other recreation building. Except at small neighborhood pools, bathhouse facilities include locker, shower, dressing, checking, and toilet rooms, as well as an office, laundry, and first-aid room. They are arranged so as to simplify the circulation of bathers and facilitate supervision. Units in some bathhouses are designed to serve as club, meeting, or activity rooms during the winter months.

Boating Facilities. Boating is perhaps America's fastest-growing sport, and communities with opportunities for boating have a recreation asset of great value. Boating facilities vary according to the nature and extent of available water areas, which determine the types of boats used and their docking and storage requirements. At a small lake or stream where rowboats and canoes only are used, the facilities may consist of a landing dock, a boathouse for canoe storage, and a mooring place for the rowboats. Adjoining large water areas more elaborate marinas are developed. Piers, protected boat basins with walks affording access to the berthing

The Bahia Mar, one of the world's largest municipal marinas, is equipped to serve every type of pleasure craft (Courtesy of Fort Lauderdale, Fla., Department of Recreation and Parks).

places, floats, shipways, and hoists and ramps for removing boats from the water afford accommodations for owners of motorboats, passenger launches, and sailing craft. Mooring posts are provided for sailboats, whereas slips and berthing spaces are used by motor craft. In case of large or exposed water areas it is sometimes necessary to construct a breakwater or sea wall to afford protection for the boat basin.

Boathouses afford such widely used facilities as storage racks or lockers for small craft, repair shop, dining room, clubroom for modelboat builders, dressing rooms and showers, and storage room for outboard motors, paddles, oars, and other equipment.

Winter Sports Facilities. Recreation areas afford many facilities for winter sports. Where conditions are favorable, tennis courts, pools, and fields are turned into skating rinks; park hills are set aside for coasting and skiing; toboggan slides and ski jumps are erected on golf courses and reservations; and ponds kept clear of snow serve as skating and ice-hockey centers. The use of these facilities is, of course, dependent upon the weather, and disappointments are numerous. However, where climatic conditions permit winter sports, the effort to provide the necessary facilities yields large returns in healthful, enjoyable outdoor activity.

Slow-moving streams and ponds make the most satisfactory skating areas; but where they are lacking, rinks may be formed by either flooding or spraying. Flooding has proved successful on large areas such as baseball and football fields and on general play areas with a concave surface, when soil conditions are such as to prevent the water from seeping away. Building an ice surface on the ground by spraying is often more satisfactory on small, unpaved areas. Both methods have been used on tennis courts and other paved areas. Several cities have experimented with a white plastic or vinyl film as lining material for an ice rink. It retains water and retards melting of ice but is hard to apply and easily cut by skates. Natural and man-made rinks require continuous and careful maintenance in order to assure good skating conditions. A section of the ice area is often set aside for ice hockey, a popular winter sport which requires a rink approximately 100 by 220 feet.

Uncertain and variable weather conditions have produced unsatisfactory skating conditions in most cities and have not justified the expense of preparing rinks for winter use. As a means of assuring a continuous skating season of four months or more, and in response to public demand for skating facilities, many cities are constructing rinks with artificial ice.

An artificial rink consists of a floor or area sprayed or flooded and frozen for skating plus the refrigeration equipment essential to produce and maintain the ice. Three types of artificial rinks are in common use. The floor of one type is composed of a reinforced-concrete floating slab in which has been installed a system of pipes through which the freezing solution circulates; another type consists of an area in which the pipes have been imbedded in sand, crushed stone, or similar material. The third type, known as the "roll-up" or "take-up" rink, consists of some form of plastic pipe laid on supports and set on a thin layer of sand over a turf, soil, or paved surface. Ammonia or a brine solution is used as a refrigerant, and the refrigeration unit is connected with the pipes in the rink floor through header or feeder pipes. A building is needed to house the refrigeration machinery, unless it is mounted on a trailer truck, and to afford a shelter for skaters. Determination of the type, size, arrangement, and location of the equipment and the piping system involves a variety of local factors and requires the advice of an experienced refrigeration engineer.

Where other coasting facilities are lacking, small sled slides with platforms about 10 feet above the ground are sometimes erected on playgrounds for children's use. A few cities have built hills or mounds to provide coasting. Toboggan slides constructed of sections of wooden troughs or of snow are built cn natural slopes. In constructing a slide, care must be taken that the trough is not too wide, that the sections are strongly built and fitted together carefully, that the sides are of sufficient height, that curves are avoided, and that there is a long, level outrun, free from obstructions. A northerly slope is desirable. In cities where winter sports are an important part of the program, ski jumps have been provided, but their use is restricted to expert jumpers. Warming shelters with checking facilities are commonly provided at winter sports centers for the comfort and convenience of the people using them.

Picnic Centers. Picnicking has become one of America's most popular outdoor recreation activities, so most cities provide picnic areas and facilities. There are two types of picnic centers: (1) those designed for use by large organized groups and (2) areas intended primarily for families or other small groups. The same center may provide both types, but better results are likely to be attained if the two sections are developed as separate units. Desirable features of any picnic center are a wooded area, preferably bordering a stream or lake, a location distant from sections used for other purposes, an attractive setting, and easy access from an automobile road.

The picnic center for large groups is equipped with several fireplaces, one or more large ovens where quantities of food may be prepared at one time, or a barbecue pit. Numerous picnic tables and benches, preferably the combination type, are grouped near the fireplaces or ovens. Containers for rubbish, drinking fountains, and one or more faucets for drawing water are also provided. Toilets for both sexes are located at a distance from the other facilities. A refreshment stand where fuel, food, and picnic supplies can be secured and equipment rented is a useful feature at a group picnic center, and some type of shelter is necessary. It may consist of an open structure affording protection in case of sudden rains, or it may include toilet rooms, a stove, a caretaker's room, and other features. An open field for sports and for children's games makes possible activities which are commonly included in the picnic program, and a few types of playground apparatus appeal to the children.

Most families and other small picnic groups like seclusion, so it is customary for the facilities provided for them to be more widely distributed. Small, simply constructed fireplaces or open grates are most satisfactory; tables and benches are desirable; toilets, water supply, and shelter are essential at most such centers. Large game areas are not needed, but a few horseshoe, volleyball, and deck-tennis courts are popular features.

Because picnic centers often cover a considerable area, it is helpful if each unit has a name or number and if well-placed signs indicate the location of the various facilities. Maps posted at strategic locations are also useful. Central parking spaces are set aside near large-group areas

The music pavilion in Fairmount Park provides the setting for the widely known Robin Hood Dell concert series (Courtesy of Philadelphia Department of Recreation).

and at some family centers. Individual picnic units are sometimes built along a park road, in which case space for parking an automobile is provided near each unit.

The Outdoor Theatre. The need for a suitable place in which to hold outdoor plays, pageants, concerts, and meetings can be met by the construction of an outdoor theatre or band shell. The simplest type of theatre consists merely of a quiet corner of the playground, bordered by a fence or a hedge. A section of the turf serves as a stage, and curtains are temporarily erected for dressing rooms and wings. On some playgrounds, small, naturalistic theatres have been developed; at others, platforms have been erected on which plays are presented or the theatre is built in combination with the playground shelter house. Few playground theatres provide permanent seating facilities.

Most municipal outdoor theatres are designed in a naturalistic manner to conform to the character of their setting. A natural slope affords a desirable location for the amphitheatre, especially if it is distant or well screened from noisy streets or recreation areas. Unless there is a natural wooded background, trees and shrubs are planted along the rear and on the wings of the stage for the sake of appearance and to serve as a sounding board, or walls are erected for this purpose. Good acoustical properties are essential, although in a large theatre amplifying equipment is needed. Suitable entrances must be provided to the stage, which at most theatres is of turf. Grassy slopes, sodded terraces, walls in the form of steps or terraces, or permanent or removable benches serve as seats for spectators. Wide aisles and ample level space at the rear are necessary to facilitate circulation and the seating of large numbers of people in a short time. Other desirable features are dressing rooms for participants, amplifying equipment, orchestra pit, lighting equipment, and water basin between the stage and audience. Fountains or water curtains with colored lights are installed at some more elaborate theatres. In a few cities theatres have been constructed, formal in design, like the Greek Theatre in Griffith Park, Los Angeles. A parking area for automobiles is essential, located where noises do not reach the theatre.

In localities where a structure for concerts and other musical productions is the primary need, a band shell best serves the purpose. Many types are in use, but expert opinion indicates that a shell with a vertical rear wall and an inclined ceiling with a flat surface affords excellent acoustical qualities and is simple and economical to construct. The outdoor theatre and the band shell have been combined in a few cities, as in the Zoological Park in Toledo, Ohio.

Other Facilities. The preceding pages indicate only a few of the diversified facilities which enable people to find outlets for their desire to engage in various forms of outdoor activities. Several other recreation provisions can merely be mentioned. Bridle, riding, and nature trails lure riders and hikers from congested sections of recreation areas; hurling, cricket, *boccie,* and pelota courts enable foreign-born groups to play familiar games; hunters and fishermen develop their skill at trapshooting ranges and fly-casting pools in anticipation of the open season for their respective sports. Gardeners and nature lovers find enjoyment and enduring interest and satisfaction in the rose garden, conservatory, or botanical garden. The zoo has a universal appeal to young and old alike. Through the development of their properties for such uses, recreation authorities make a great contribution to the richness of people's lives. In many communities, however, only a beginning has been made in utilizing the possibilities afforded by existing areas.

FACILITIES FOR INDOOR RECREATION

Many popular forms of recreation can be carried on most successfully indoors. Furthermore, only a limited number of outdoor activities are possible for large numbers of people during several months of the year. Suitable buildings must therefore be provided if people are to have an opportunity to engage in recreation activities throughout the year. They are also essential to the satisfactory use of many outdoor facilities.

Buildings of many types have been erected by municipal recreation authorities. Most recreation areas have some kind of structure, varying from the simple open park shelter to the elaborate building which serves as a center for the recreational life of a community or neighborhood. Some recreation buildings occupy sites acquired especially for the purpose; others are located on areas which also provide outdoor facilities.

School buildings provide the basic facilities for indoor recreation and are operated as indoor recreation centers in hundreds of communities. In fact, most schools built in recent years have been designed to serve a dual purpose—the school program and community recreation—and contain facilities that serve a variety of recreation uses. Many municipal auditoriums, libraries, and other public buildings not primarily intended for recreation have one or more rooms equipped for community recreation use.

Types of Recreation Buildings. Buildings used primarily or exclusively for recreation may be classified into three groups according to their primary functions, as follows:

1. Multiple-use buildings which have diversified facilities and are used for many types of activities
2. Buildings designed primarily for a single type of activity although they may be adapted for other uses
3. Buildings designed primarily to provide service facilities in connection with the recreational use of areas, although they may have one or more rooms used for recreation activities.

In the following list, buildings provided by recreation authorities are classified according to three groups:

Multiple-use Buildings

Amphitheatre	Camp lodge	Playhouse
Arena	Clubhouse	Recreation building
Arts center	Community house	Teen center

Single-use Buildings

Aquarium	Dance pavilion	Observatory
Art museum	Historical museum	Planetarium
Band shell	Ice hockey rink	Swimming pool
Conservatory	Natural-history museum	Theatre
Crafts center	Nature museum	Zoo

Service Buildings

Administration building	Field house [1]	Picnic shelter
Bathhouse	Golf course buildings	Playground shelter
Boathouse	Overlook shelter	Restaurant
Comfort station	Overnight cabin	Stables

A fourth type, which is not a recreation building but which is necessary in a recreation system, includes such structures as the office, garage, blacksmith shop, greenhouse, carpenter shop, and storage warehouse. These are essentially service buildings, but they are used by department personnel rather than the general public. Mention has already been made of buildings such as the school, city hall, and municipal auditorium, which are not used primarily for recreation but in which recreation activities are sometimes carried on.

Facilities in Recreation Buildings. A survey of the recreation facilities provided in the buildings previously listed would show that almost every type of recreation interest which can be met indoors is served in one or more of these buildings. Some of the facilities, like the gymnasium, clubroom, or auditorium, serve a wide variety of uses; others, like the rifle range, squash court, or bowling alley, can be used for only one activity. The list which follows comprises the rooms and special features more or less commonly provided in recreation buildings:

Archery range	Gymnasium	Office
Art gallery	Handball court	Pistol or rifle range
Auditorium	Indoor swimming pool	Pool and billiards room
Banquet hall	Indoor tennis court	Reading room
Bowling alleys	Heater room	Roller-skating rink
Card room	Janitor's room	Rooms for boxing,
Checkroom	Kitchen	wrestling, etc.
Clubroom	Lecture hall	Rooms for special crafts
Craft room	Library	"Roughhouse" room
Dance hall	Lobby	Running track
Darkroom	Locker room	Shower room
Dining room	Lounge	Snack bar
Drama workshop	Machine shop	Social hall
Dressing room	Meeting rooms for clubs	Stage with equipment
Exhibition room	and hobby groups	Storage room
First-aid and	Motion-picture booth and	Table-game room
physical examination	projector	Team room
room	Music room	Teen center
Game room	Nature museum	Television room

[1] In some cities this term is applied to a multiple-use recreation building.

PLANNING THE RECREATION BUILDING

There are no standard recreation buildings. Each one is planned to meet the requirements of the particular location, and afford the facilities required by the neighborhood, community, or recreation area it is to serve. If a special site is to be acquired for a building, location is a most important factor; on the other hand, if the building is to be erected on an existing recreation area, the problem is primarily one of relating its location to that of other features on the area. The economical and successful operation of a building depends to a great extent upon proper planning. Best results are obtained when the plan is prepared by a competent architect experienced in the design and use of recreation buildings, in cooperation with the local recreation authorities who are familiar with the requirements to be met and the problems encountered in operating and maintaining a building.

Essential factors to be considered before a building is planned are:

The specific activities which it is intended to make possible

The number of people who need to be accommodated in these activities at one time

The extent to which multiple use can be made of various rooms

The needs of children, women and girls, youth, older adults, and other special groups

The amount and types of leadership and maintenance service likely to be provided

The length of season the building will be in use

The desirability of closing off parts of the building during certain periods

The relation of the rooms to outdoor facilities and to their use by outside groups

The amount of money available for construction and operation

The possibility of later expansion

The problem of acoustics—important but frequently neglected

Local building regulations and limitations of the site

The collaboration of an experienced architect and capable recreation personnel helps prevent costly mistakes and assures a building which is attractive, in good taste, suitable for its location, and likely to function efficiently.

Essential Planning Objectives. Several objectives which apply to all types of buildings, although relatively more important in the case of the larger, more elaborate ones, are optimum functional use, ease of supervision and circulation, flexibility of use, and minimum upkeep and operating budget. When these objectives are realized by proper planning, maximum use of the building is secured, and the problems of the supervisory and maintenance staff are reduced to a minimum.

Constructing the auditorium as a unit with separate entrances and exits is usually advisable. Placing the director's office where it overlooks access to as many rooms as possible facilitates control. Corridors should be reduced to a minimum, but adequate space should be allowed to assure easy circulation. Flexibility of use is achieved when facilities such as the pool and the gymnasium are located so that men can use one while women are using the other. Multiple use is facilitated by providing ample storage facilities so that clubrooms and meeting rooms can be made available to many groups rather than assigned to the exclusive use of a single organization. A wise selection of building materials and careful planning of construction details enable yearly repairs, maintenance costs, and janitor service to be reduced to a minimum. Unneeded space in rooms and corridors means greater original cost and added insurance, daily janitor service, increased cost of heating and lighting, and periodic painting. Inadequate space, on the other hand, hampers the program.

Important Construction Details. The selection of materials for the exterior of the building is determined primarily by local conditions—the site, type of building, style preferences, and available funds. Many of the rooms and indoor facilities, on the other hand, have fairly specific though widely different material requirements. Experience has indicated that best results are achieved when floors, walls, windows, and fixtures in various rooms are built of certain materials. Care must therefore be taken in preparing specifications for each unit in a recreation building.

The size of rooms must also be determined on the basis of their proposed uses. Experience has taught that a gymnasium will not prove satisfactory if its floor is less than 50 by 80 feet and its height less than 20 feet; a larger floor space and a height of 22 feet are desirable. If spectators are to be accommodated on fold-up bleachers, a floor at least 65 by 90 feet is recommended. At one time relegated to the basement, the gymnasium and swimming pool are now placed where an abundance of light and air is available. If funds and space are limited, folding bleachers are better than permanent seating facilities. A separate gymnasium and auditorium are preferable; but if a single room is to be used for both, an elevated stage is needed at one end. The minimum desirable stage dimensions for dramatic productions are as follows: width 40 feet, depth 20 feet, height at least 3 feet above the proscenium opening, which should be not less than 12 by 24 feet. Stage design involves not only the stage itself but also the location of the lights, entrances, dressing rooms, and doors for bringing in and taking out the scenery. The control of lights in an auditorium from several points, such as the main entrance, stage, and motion-picture booth, is essential.

The indoor pool, which is a valuable feature of any recreation building or school, comprises a separate unit in some buildings; in any case, it presents special design and construction problems. A recent tendency is to build larger pools—at least 75 feet long and from 35 to 42 feet wide, with ample deck space around the pool. Most indoor pools are rectangular in shape and equipped with diving boards, which require from 10 to 12 feet of water. A number of so-called indoor-outdoor pools have been built

The architecture of the Chinese recreation center is appropriate for its neighborhood setting (Courtesy of San Francisco Recreation and Park Department).

in recent years, in an attempt to make the indoor pool more attractive and popular during the summer months and thereby assure greater year-round use. The rooms enclosing these pools have one or more sides that can be removed or opened up in warm weather, thereby tying the pool into the adjoining outdoor area. These facilities are essentially indoor pools, however, and because of their high construction cost there is a question whether the same money would yield a greater return if applied to separate indoor and outdoor pools.

The importance of providing large, conveniently located storage rooms in every recreation building cannot be emphasized too strongly, especially where the same facilities are to be used for different activities. Removable chairs are commonly used, since they can be piled on rubber-tired trucks and stored under the stage when the auditorium is used for games, for dancing, or for social recreation. Special care needs to be taken in the arrangement of the toilet, locker, and shower rooms for the two sexes. The installation of a public-address system is an effective aid in supervising the building. When a building also serves people using outdoor facilities, separate convenient entrances to the shower and toilet rooms are often provided for them.

GENERAL RECREATION BUILDINGS

Many recreation buildings, as previously stated, provide diversified facilities and are used for a wide range of activities. This type of building is found in many towns and smaller cities, where it is known as a community house and serves as a center for the indoor recreational life of the community. Other examples are the multiple-use recreation buildings located on playfields in many cities.

The facilities provided in this type of building, although all of them are seldom found in a single building, are:

A social hall which can be used for dances, parties, dinners, or entertainments

An auditorium equipped with stage and motion-picture projector, used for concerts, community sings, dramatic productions, lectures, movies, and debates

A gymnasium with removable or folding bleachers, used for gym classes, basketball, volleyball, wrestling, dancing, stunts, and exhibitions

Locker, shower, and toilet rooms for people using the gymnasium

Meeting rooms for clubs, organizations, and music and other groups

Workshops for handcrafts, arts, dramatics, and hobbies

Game rooms with facilities for table games, ping-pong, billiards, or bowling

Kitchen and serving pantry

Library and reading room—also used for storytelling

Lobby and lounge

Indoor swimming pool with spectators' gallery

Service features such as office, heater, and fuel rooms, storage, janitor's room, and general toilet rooms

The number and kinds of facilities required in a new building depend upon existing facilities, local interests and needs, available funds, and the number of people to be served. In neighborhoods or communities where large numbers are likely to use the building daily, several rooms are provided in which different activities can be carried on at the same time. In a small community fewer rooms are needed, but they are planned for several uses. Some buildings have a separate gymnasium and an auditorium as well as a social hall; occasionally two gymnasiums are provided, one for men and one for women. Other buildings, however, have only one large room equipped to serve as gymnasium, auditorium, and social hall and one or two smaller rooms which are used as club, craft, meeting, and game rooms.

In many communities or neighborhoods where the schools contain facilities such as gymnasiums and auditoriums available for community use, recreation authorities do not duplicate these costly features but erect buildings of the clubhouse type. These contain a large multiple-purpose room and several smaller rooms which serve the varied interests of groups that cannot be accommodated readily in the school centers.

Two Typical Recreation Buildings. The community house at Dalton, Massachusetts, an example of the community type of recreation building, is situated on a site of 1½ acres near the center of this town of some 6,000 people. Across the front of the first floor are the rooms available for general use, including a social hall, men's clubroom, ladies' parlor, offices, two clubrooms which may be combined, and rooms for the Red Cross and American Legion. To the rear is a well-equipped gymnasium with permanent and knockdown bleachers and a portable stage equipped with curtain, drops, and lights. In the basement is a swimming pool 20 by 60 feet, with adjoining rooms and lockers for men and for women. On the same floor are four bowling alleys, a clubroom, and pool tables. This building affords excellent opportunities for indoor recreation to the people of this small community.

Midland, Michigan, in its community center, has one of the finest and most fully equipped recreation buildings in the country. Opened in 1955, the building cost $1,500,000 and provides a varied indoor recreation program for the 21,000 people of the city. A gymnasium 64 by 102 feet, a small exercise gymnasium, a pool 30 by 75 feet, a firearms range, four handball courts, and a squash court serve the needs of the sports-minded. Other units include a teen-age center, the Pioneer Room for retired adults, the Mirror Room for parties and receptions, a dining hall with kitchen accommodating 200 people, two arts and crafts rooms, photographic facilities, a snack bar, and nine conference and meeting rooms. An outdoor terrace is designed for seasonal outdoor activities, and a lobby and foyer invite informal use. A covered walkway 130 feet long affords protection to persons leaving or entering automobiles during inclement weather, and the 7-acre site also provides a parking area for 300 cars. Midland's new building replaced a center that had been operated successfully for thirty-six years.

SPECIAL RECREATION BUILDINGS

Most recreation buildings, like the ones previously described, serve many uses, but several cities have erected structures designed for experimentation and participation in one specific form of recreation activity. Typical of such buildings are the community drama center, the crafts workshop, the sports building, the swimming pool, and the nature museum. In some instances these buildings serve as city-wide centers where people who have developed interest or skill in the particular activity in their neighborhood centers can participate more intensively or on a more advanced basis. Such centers may attract fewer individuals than a general recreation building, but they foster a continuing, progressive, and absorbing interest in the special fields to which they are dedicated. For this reason they are likely to play an increasingly important role in recreation programs of the future.

The planning and construction of special-use buildings necessitate a careful study of their particular requirements. It is easier to work out a satisfactory plan for a building to be used for one activity, however, than for a multiple-use building. For example, in designing a theatre to be used exclusively for the presentation of dramatic productions, the units are so arranged and the materials selected to best suit the particular purpose. Seats are placed to the greatest advantage for viewing productions. The special requirements of the stage with respect to space, equipment, lighting, and facilities for erecting and moving scenery receive primary consideration. Dressing, work-, and storage rooms essential to carrying on a comprehensive drama program are important features in the building plan. These units cannot be arranged so effectively or provided so completely in a building where the auditorium must also serve as a gymnasium and social hall.

Two Special Recreation Buildings. The Josephine D. Randall Junior Museum, operated by the San Francisco Recreation and Park Department, is an example of a building dedicated to a special, though diversified use. The museum "seeks to help young people realize the beauties of nature, the important facts of history, and the achievements of man; to illustrate the principles of science; and to provide opportunities for creative education through various activities or hobbies." This modern three-level building of brick, glass, and stucco occupies a 14-acre site near the geographic center of the city. It contains workshops and clubrooms for nature study, a ceramics shop, lapidary room, model room, weaving room, woodworking and metal shops, photographic laboratory, printing room, miniature zoo, and a 240-seat theatre equipped to project sound movies and colored slides. The museum affords a center for constructive and enjoyable activities, many of them conducted on a club basis, for children and young people throughout the city.

Palo Alto, California, is one of the few American cities that has a municipal community playhouse, a gift of one of its residents. The playhouse serves as a completely furnished center for artistic and cultural activities, and is used for music and dance recitals, dramatic productions, musical programs, lectures, and forums. The auditorium seats 418 people, and the stage, fully equipped with up-to-date devices, is larger than that of many commercial theatres. Other facilities include a two-story workshop, rehearsal hall, dressing rooms, property and costume rooms, greenroom, offices, rest rooms, checkroom, and foyer which is designed to serve also as an art gallery. Citizens of Palo Alto and surrounding communities are finding in this building a center where they may spend their leisure hours in enjoyable relaxation or in creative participation. It is a major influence in the recreation and cultural life of the community.

SERVICE BUILDINGS

These structures afford the facilities necessary to accommodate the people making use of recreation areas such as swimming pools, golf courses, and boating areas. They commonly contain dressing, locker, toilet, and shower rooms for both sexes, and rooms for checking or storing sports and maintenance equipment, a shelter, lobby or lounge, refectory, and repair shop. Without service buildings outdoor recreation areas could not accommodate the large numbers of people who use them.

Many such buildings contain, in addition to their service features, rooms in which recreation activities are carried on. Dressing rooms in bathhouses at municipal pools are used for group activities during seasons when the pool is closed. One large bathhouse has a room 60 by 100 feet in which basketball and volleyball courts are laid out, and a portable stage at one end enables it to serve as an auditorium seating 1,000 people. Clubhouses at golf courses contain rooms which are used for dances, banquets, parties, and other social functions. A clubroom for model-yacht enthusiasts is provided by a Western city at one of the boathouses; another boathouse has facilities for picnic groups in case inclement weather prevents the use of the nearby fireplaces and barbecue pit. Most playground shelter houses have a room in which club meetings, crafts, and other activities can be carried on.

INDOOR RECREATION CENTERS

Indoor recreation activity is by no means restricted to buildings constructed exclusively for such use. Recreation departments conduct activities in many buildings intended primarily for some other purpose, such as schools, churches, industrial plants, institutions, settlements, apartment houses, and municipal buildings. The facilities vary from elaborate school plants including gymnasiums, auditorium, swimming pool, library, workshops, and special-activity rooms to a storytelling room in a library or a city-hall basement in which bowling alleys have been installed.

Reference was made in Chapter 11 to the growing tendency of school and city recreation authorities to cooperate in the acquisition and planning of properties designed for school and community recreation use. Many recreation facilities in school buildings are not needed for full-time use by the school program. To permit them to be idle during long periods or to duplicate them in separate buildings is economically wasteful and unjustifiable. This is especially true of facilities like the gymnasium, auditorium, and manual-arts room, which involve high construction and maintenance costs. At slight additional expense, school buildings can be planned so as to facilitate community use. Because modern schools contain many rooms designed or adaptable for recreation and because community use is widely recognized as a function of such buildings, a large percentage of the indoor activities in most community recreation programs is carried on in school buildings.

The American Association of School Administrators and the National Recreation Association have jointly issued the following suggestions for carrying out basic principles in planning school buildings for community as well as school use. Some of them are equally applicable to other buildings designed for recreation use by community groups.

1. Provide one or more community rooms to serve as lounges or places where young people or adults can drop in outside school hours under proper sponsorship or supervision. Attractive, well-lighted, and well-ventilated ground-floor rooms prove most satisfactory.
2. Provide special cupboards for storing equipment, tools, and materials used for community groups in art rooms, craft shops, and other rooms where such duplicate storage space is necessary for convenient use.
3. Provide separate lockers for community use in locker rooms serving the gymnasium, swimming pool, or outdoor recreation areas.
4. Control heating and lighting for parts of the school used by community groups to reduce heating and lighting costs.
5. Provide for closing off corridors and hallways where necessary to control community use after school hours and to prevent excessive custodial service cost for this purpose.
6. In elementary schools and in junior high schools to be used by younger children, provide a playroom that opens on the playground, which is large enough for a variety of activities and contains cupboards for storing play materials.

7. Provide toilets and drinking fountains that are easily accessible from the playground and that, with the playroom, can be shut off from the rest of the building.
8. Provide an entrance to the section containing community facilities that is easily reached from the street and well lighted at night.
9. There is an advantage in floodlighting play areas so that there can be a maximum of twilight and evening use.
10. Cafeterias can be used to greater advantage if there is a small stage to encourage wider utilization of a space which is normally used too little.
11. Plan all facilities with a view to multiple use. Many of the facilities designed primarily for school purposes will be usable for community purposes; very few of the facilities designed for community use will not be usable for the school program.

ADAPTING OLD BUILDINGS FOR RECREATION USE

The steadily increasing demand for more indoor recreation facilities has resulted in the utilization for recreation of many buildings originally planned for some other use. In one city, a two-story bakery was transformed into a recreation center. An old three-story medical-school building in another city was turned into a fully equipped center with large meeting room, library, clubrooms, handball courts, and music, card, and game rooms. A building once an armory now houses a large gymnasium and reading, club-, and game rooms. An old county jail with its 13-acre site has been handed over to a recreation commission and adapted as an indoor and outdoor recreation center. Garages, stores, skating rinks, lodge halls, churches, and abandoned school buildings have been reconditioned and utilized for recreation purposes.

Often the adaptation of old buildings presents serious problems, but ingenuity, imagination, and effort have accomplished remarkable results. Windows and lights have been screened where there was a room large enough for games like basketball and volleyball or suitable for a "roughhouse" room for strenuous low organized games. Unpromising rooms have been made attractive for club meetings, crafts, quiet games, and reading, by whitewashing the walls, installing suitable lights, and hanging bright-colored curtains. Many teen centers have been established in old buildings that were transformed into inviting centers through the efforts of the young people themselves. In adapting old buildings, care must be taken to make sure they are structurally sound, conform with building-code requirements, and are provided with adequate stairways and fire escapes. In more than one city, the successful operation of a remodeled building has demonstrated the value of an indoor program and has paved the way for the acquisition of a new center.

A SUGGESTION

In conclusion, the more knowledge the recreation worker has of the design and equipment of recreation areas and facilities, indoor and outdoor, the better able he will be to secure the maximum returns from the available properties in his charge. Furthermore, he will be in a position to give intelligent guidance to any projects involving the development and expansion of the city's recreation areas and facilities. He must remember, however, that many problems require technical advice which can best be secured from the architect, engineer, and landscape architect And he must not forget that there is much excellent literature available which can help him in the solution of his design and equipment problems.

PART FOUR

ACTIVITIES AND PROGRAM PLANNING

Activities are the medium through which individuals satisfy their recreation desires and interests. The recreation department performs its chief service by employing a staff who, utilizing areas and facilities, plan, organize, supervise, and conduct a program of attractive activities. In addition, it assists people in the use of their leisure time and stimulates individuals and groups to develop recreation interests and to provide their own programs. Recreation leaders therefore need to know the activities commonly considered recreation, the satisfactions they afford, and the conditions under which they may be best introduced in the program. They must be familiar with the factors that influence the planning of a recreation program, such as the age, sex, and skill of people, the type of community and its economic status, the size of the group, and the amount of leisure time available. Because of the diversity of recreation activities, different methods must be used in initiating, conducting, and guiding various parts of the program. The significance of these activities and some of the problems and procedures involved in their use in community recreation programs are considered in Part Four.

14. RECREATION ACTIVITIES

RECREATION activities cover the whole field of human interests. The forms of recreation vary as widely as the interests of a single individual throughout his lifetime and are as diverse as the differences between people. Beginning with the play of babyhood, up through the active games and sports of youth, to the quiet pastimes of old age, the variety of recreation activities in which an individual engages is almost limitless. Yet this diversity of an individual's interests is small in comparison with the difference in the recreation interests of the people of a neighborhood or city.

All forms of recreation, however, have one characteristic: They each provide a gratifying outlet for some basic urge or need. Each form represents a medium through which personality achieves satisfying expression and which contributes to human happiness. This explains the close relationship between the essential satisfactions which people seek in recreation activities and methods of personality growth and development. Just as the individual personality expresses itself through the exercise of its physical, social, mental, and creative powers, so recreation activities in their varied forms bring physical, social, mental, and creative satisfactions to the individual engaging in them.

Recreation activities are frequently grouped according to these major types of personality expression, but such a grouping is not entirely satisfactory. In an activity like a modern dance, originated and executed by a group, the individual participants may find expression not only physically and socially but mentally and creatively as well. A classification of activities under such headings as physical, dramatic, rhythmic, or social is convenient and useful for the recreation leader, especially in planning programs; but in considering recreation activities from the point of view of the individual participant, an entirely different approach is desirable.

SATISFACTIONS ARE THE FUNDAMENTAL TEST

The satisfactions which people seek and find in various forms of recreation activity afford such an approach. Among these satisfactions which large numbers of people attain through forms of recreation are fellowship, the opportunity to create, adventure, a sense of achievement, the enjoyment of one's physical powers, the use of one's mental powers, emotional stimulation, beauty, relaxation, and opportunity for service. Because some individuals find that certain activities yield one or more of these satisfactions, the activities become recreation. The same activities are not recreation for others who gain no satisfaction from taking part in them. In planning programs, the recreation worker must therefore consider not only the types of activity but the motives which induce people to engage in them.

No hard and fast grouping of activities under the various types of satisfactions is possible or essential. In the first place, different people seek and find different kinds of pleasurable responses from the same activity. One person may sing in a chorus primarily for the sociability which it affords, another because it furnishes an outlet for using and developing his skill as a singer, and a third for the emotional satisfaction which comes to him while singing with a group. Furthermore, a single form of activity may yield several types of satisfaction to the same individual. The recreation value of an activity for a particular person depends upon the way in which he is affected by it and upon the richness of the experience which it brings to him.

The use of the term "higher recreations," which is sometimes applied to certain forms of activity such as the cultural arts, implies that activities differ in value. Yet the connotation is not always justified. Swimming, square dancing, or mountain climbing may have more meaning and offer more satisfying outlets of expression for a certain individual at a particular time than the so-called higher recreations. No specific forms of recreation have an exclusive right to this title; but certain activities which serve a wide range of basic human needs and afford great possibilities for rich and satisfying experience have gained for themselves a high rank in recreation values. Thus an activity in which an individual can create, achieve, and find beauty, fellowship, and relaxation is more likely to have enduring value than one which yields only one or two types of satisfaction. The relationship between senses and satisfactions is indicated by Harry A. Overstreet in his statement, "The more senses we lend to an experience, the more vivid and rich it becomes." [1]

SATISFACTIONS AS A BASIS FOR CLASSIFYING ACTIVITIES

The preceding statements make it clear that activities cannot be divided into groups according to the satisfactions which people seek from them in the same manner as they are classified according to types, such

[1] *A Guide to Civilized Loafing*, W. W. Norton & Company, Inc., New York, 1934.

as music, drama, arts and crafts, and games and sports. The recreation leader must be familiar with the activities which are commonly grouped under these headings, but it is still more important that he know in what ways they satisfy the fundamental desires of people.

The following pages point out some of the satisfactions which people seek through recreation and indicate how different forms of recreation activity contribute to human happiness by supplying these satisfactions. A comprehensive list of the activities commonly considered recreation, grouped under the type headings by which these activities are frequently and readily identified, is presented at the close of the chapter.

The Joy of Creation. Civilization affords a striking illustration of the potency and universality of man's urge to create. His desire and capacity for creative craftsmanship are two precious possessions which have persisted "through the ages like a rainbow thread." The child building a castle in the sand, primitive man shaping and carving his canoe, and the artist painting on his canvas are all giving expression to this desire. The effectiveness of creative ability as a means of self-expression is pointed out by Howard Braucher in the following quotation: [2]

Culture is not a matter of words and sounds alone. The hands may speak also—may convey messages, may reveal thoughts and emotions too deep and too sacred for careless, easily uttered words.

Working with wood and clay and marble, fashioning images of dreams and emotions, . . . man becomes articulate, reveals himself even to himself, lives in another world, understands himself better, whence he has come, whither he is moving, adds another dimension to his world.

The most common forms of recreation activity in which this urge finds expression are the arts and crafts. There is such a wide variety of them that every individual, regardless of age, sex, education, occupation, or skill, can find a suitable medium. The materials available for these activities are limitless. Among the most common are wood, clay, plastic, metals, oils, cloth, and paper. The desire to create brings together young and old in the photography club, gives model-aircraft building its strong appeal to young men long after they have lost their interest in many other activities, and attracts women to the needlework groups where clothing is designed and made or to the weaving class where original patterns are worked into rugs or blankets. Among children the creative urge finds expression in making mud pies, weaving baskets, and constructing realistic animals for the circus parade.

Important as arts and crafts are among the creative activities, there are other ways in which creative needs find expression. Some people compose music, others write poetry or develop characters in a story or

[2] "Make," *Recreation*, vol. 29, no. 11, p. 525, February, 1936.

play. In a sense the dancer, the actor, and the director of a dramatic production create the personality of the characters portrayed. The true gardener joins forces with the Creator in bringing into being a place of beauty.

Of special significance to recreation workers is the extent to which a creative program can be related to and integrated with a variety of activities. The making of bows and arrows, model boats, kites, or push-mobiles, for example, leads up to the actual use of the objects made. Important features of the drama program, in which the creative interest predominates, are the making of puppets, scenery, costumes, and stage equipment. In the field of nature are the building of birdhouses, the mounting of exhibits, and the construction of nature trails. A part of the music program often consists of making the instruments. Trips to museums, industries, and other centers of interest afford opportunities to observe the results of others' creative activity. These few illustrations make clear the important part which the desire for self-expression through creation plays in the recreation life of people. In fact, the degree to which the creative spirit is present in any activity determines to a large extent whether it is a dull or a vital experience.

Fellowship. Man is essentially a gregarious being. No human desire is perhaps more fully met through recreation or is achieved in as many forms as the desire for fellowship. Because most forms of recreation are essentially group activities or may be carried on by individuals with others, they minister directly to man's need for companionship, social relationships, and cooperative activity. The importance which young and old attach to social activities is illustrated by the widespread desire of youth for centers of their own and the enthusiastic response of older adults to the programs afforded by "golden age" clubs.

Activities which usually meet this particular need are community gatherings, parties, social dancing, dinners, and outings of various types. Such widely differing activities as a birthday party in the home, a holiday celebration in a large recreation center, or a chamber of commerce clambake all belong within this group. Fellowship plays a part in team games, athletic contests, group singing, and clubs of all types. It is basic in such a simple but widespread activity as conversation. Canoeing, hiking, camping, and many other activities are enriched when they are done in the company of others with similar interests. Frequently a discussion group is held together as much by the sociability of its members as by the topics discussed. Part of the value of membership in an orchestra, chorus, nature club, crafts group, or baseball team is derived from the fact that these groups make cooperative activity possible.

Failures in the recreation program are often caused by the fact that the element of sociability has been lacking. The primary satisfactions which an individual gains from most forms of recreation activity are enhanced by the sociability, stimulation, and mutual helpfulness that result from group participation. The strong and widespread desire for fellowship is recognized by introducing regular or occasional social activities in the programs of groups primarily formed for some other purpose.

The Vermont country-dance festival is one of the popular activities sponsored by the state recreation department (Courtesy of Vermont Board of Recreation).

Adventure—The Desire for New Experience. Children are living question marks, and the persisting desire on the part of man to extend his knowledge and to gain new experiences makes for continued growth and progress. The spirit of adventure affords, at least in part, the incentive that prompts men to undertake such challenging tasks as climbing the Himalayas or exploring outer space. Many forms of recreation owe their appeal to the fact that they contribute to this universal human desire. This is especially true of nature activities, which afford unlimited opportunities for exploring the wonders of the world about us. Man's curiosity and his desire for new experience go far in explaining the tremendous popularity of travel. The drawing power of the zoo is different only in degree from that which induces man to track the animals in their native habitat, and the excitement which attends the nature lover's search for new birds, flowers, or marine life is not essentially different from the thrill of hunting big game.

Sailing, camping, mountain climbing, and photography alike open avenues of adventure to large numbers of people. Just as truly, though perhaps to a lesser degree, the musician finds it in playing a new composition for the first time, the craftsman in working in a new medium, or the actor in learning a new part. The recent but expanding field of recreation through service offers limitless opportunities for pioneering and adventurous experience. The widespread appeal of many popular story and pictorial magazines and of the motion picture may be accounted for in part by the fact that they afford opportunities for new, though vicarious, experiences to large numbers of people, many of whom do not have the courage, opportunity, or ability to seek their own adventure.

The elements of variety, adventure, and surprise are important in planning and conducting children's play activities. Programs which are stereotyped, unchanged from day to day, unrelated to the varying interests of boys and girls, have little appeal. The bleak, unattractive playground, lacking in interest or beauty, fails to attract and hold children partly because it offers no opportunities for adventure. The popularity of the new forms of equipment that stimulate exciting, creative play experiences illustrates children's response to a different environment. The imaginative leader who introduces new games, initiates novel, challenging activities, and encourages the children to adapt them and to work out new play forms and projects is building a continuing interest in the program. Similarly with adults, the occasional introduction of a surprise feature, the undertaking of an experimental project, or the sponsoring of an untried activity yields an added element of satisfaction.

Sense of Achievement. Man craves some area in life where he can excel and feel a sense of achievement. Because most people fail to get this satisfaction in their work, they seek it in recreation. They can achieve it in some form if they can only be helped to find the right medium. Satisfaction of the need is commonly associated with competitive activities, especially games and sports, but it is possible—and frequent—in almost any form of recreation activity. Most people attain it by raising their own standard of performance rather than by surpassing others in competition. Only a favored few can achieve outstanding success, but everyone can gain the satisfaction which results from making progress and increasing his skill in some activity.

This desire for achievement accounts in part for the widespread interest in games and sports. The boy willingly spends time and energy and undergoes strict training in order to make the school team. An individual feels a sense of accomplishment when he has mastered a difficult music score or dance step, found a long-sought specimen for his nature collection, solved a difficult problem in designing the scenery for a play, completed a satisfactory job of leadership service, or even solved a knotty crossword puzzle.

Part of the fascination of many recreation activities is the opportunity they offer for the utilization of existing skills and their challenge to greater attainment. Interest in an activity often dies when it no longer affords opportunity for further progress or presents a challenge to the participant. Much of the value of team games, choral groups, debating, and other group activities lies in the fact that the collective achievements are shared by the individual members, some of whom may have no means of gaining individual success. Satisfactions resulting from achievement are comparatively lacking in the appeal of such activities as social recreation and reading. Some spectator activities provide it vicariously to a limited degree.

There is a close relationship between the satisfactions of achievement in recreation activities and the recognition or prestige which these activities bring to individuals. In seeking recognition through recreation, an individual is most likely to select an activity in which he has the greatest likelihood of achieving success or of excelling the performance of others. However, when he chooses an activity primarily because it promises prestige, the experience may lose much of its significance as recreation.

Physical Well-being. Physical activity is a fundamental function of life. The play of the child is characterized by continuous bodily activity; and as he grows older, he continues to gain satisfaction from the spontaneous use of his growing physical powers. Running, jumping, throwing, climbing, or wrestling are engaged in for the pure joy of it. Later, team games and individual sports give the sense of well-being which comes from the full use of the body, although part of the satisfaction in these activities, as previously mentioned, is derived from the fellowship which accompanies them and from the opportunities for achievement which they provide. Through adult life such activities as skating, swimming, or hiking bring joy and a sense of well-being to the individual primarily because they afford satisfying outlets for his physical energy. Certain forms of the dance also bring a sense of coordination, balance, and control of the body and its movements.

The expenditure of physical energy plays a secondary though important role in many other forms of recreation. Social recreation programs are enlivened by periods of active games, and much of the fun of camping, picnicking, and nature hiking lies in the exertion which these activities entail. Many people because of chronic fatigue or laziness do not enjoy strenuous physical exercise. They seek recreation which is essentially passive in nature and in which this element of satisfaction is entirely lacking. Some, after a hard day's work, normally choose recreation that demands little physical exertion, whereas others seek activities which furnish outlets for their physical energy. There is something about a basketball and a mountain, to cite widely different examples, that arouses an irresistible urge to activity on the part of certain individuals; the energetic response to this urge is a factor in its satisfaction. Other activities, such as playing certain musical instruments, make strenuous demands on the physical stamina of the participants; this may detract from the enjoyment rather than contribute to it.

In cooperation with school and other community groups, recreation authorities must provide the organization, leadership, and facilities that will afford opportunity for all boys and girls to (1) acquire basic skills in a limited number of games and sports, (2) experience the satisfaction that results from participation in these activities, (3) take part in a varied, progressive, and challenging sports program throughout the year.

Use of Mental Powers. Because of the common association of mental effort and work, the relationship of recreation to the exercise of one's mental powers may not be immediately apparent. Yet man engages in many forms of recreation primarily *because* they afford a stimulation to mental activity. This point is important in understanding such activities as forums, debating, discussion-group meetings, chess, nature study, music appreciation, and creative writing. In fact, there are few forms of recreation with lasting or growing appeal that do not call for a considerable degree of intelligence and mental effort. Interest in an activity is likely to lag when it no longer makes demands upon the mental powers of the participant.

A few examples will illustrate the important place of mental alertness in activities in which some other factor is usually considered more important: playing bridge—frequently classed as a form of social recreation but essentially a mental activity; sailing a boat requires careful study of the boat and its equipment, wind, waves, charts, and weather, as well as constant alertness in observing conditions along the course; the actor studies not only his lines but also the character he is portraying; collecting, whether it be stamps, books, or fossils, involves much reading and careful research; making or performing good music is a matter of intelligence as well as of spirit and technique. Most games call for keen judgment and mental alertness, and the challenge of volunteer service as a club leader lies partly in the resourcefulness required to keep ahead of the group. Because the interplay of minds is stimulating and revealing, many of the so-called mental activities are most successful when carried on within a group.

True, there are widely popular forms of recreation such as reading the pulp magazines, certain types of conversation, and watching particular television programs in which this appeal is entirely lacking. Nevertheless, the challenge that many other types of recreation activity afford to the mental powers of the participant accounts for their extensive and enduring appeal.

Boys sail their "sabots" in Alamitos Bay (Courtesy of Long Beach, Calif., Recreation Commission).

Emotional Experience. The significant part which emotional response plays in giving to activities the character of recreation makes it a factor of fundamental importance. Unless participation in an activity brings a favorable emotional response to the individual, it is not likely to become for him a form of recreation. The emotional satisfactions which are sought and achieved through recreation are as varied in quality and scope as humanity itself. In so far as they are wholesome, inspiring, or rich in association, they make a contribution of the utmost importance. On the other hand, the danger of some forms of commercial recreation lies in the fact that they have a strong appeal which is directed toward the individual's baser emotions.

The thrill of tobogganing, the mass hysteria at the championship fight, the suspense of the reader as he approaches the climax of the novel or the solution of the detective mystery, illustrate how in certain forms of activity emotion plays a large or predominating part. Emotional satisfactions are shared by participants and spectators alike, though in different ways and intensities. The tense excitement of the ninth-inning rally thrills the crowd in the stands as well as the players, the soul-stirring majesty of the symphony is felt by both musicians and listeners, and the emotion with which the actor plays his part or the warmth with which important issues are threshed out in the forum is shared by the audience. The strong appeal to the emotions which characterizes many of the offerings of the motion-picture theaters, dance halls, and sex and adventure magazines explains much of their widespread popularity.

There are other forms of recreation in which the element of emotion is less important but in which the emotional experience may be heightened by the recreation leader. For instance, a simple game like horseshoes or jacks may arouse considerable feeling if a tournament is organized. Public performances or demonstrations by music, drama, or hobby groups may be the means of stimulating added enthusiasm on the part of the members. The emotional appeal of a party, beach picnic, or moonlight sail is greatly enhanced when it is conducted as a co-recreational project and is present to a greater or less degree in all activities engaged in jointly by young men and young women.

Enjoyment of Beauty. The universal love of beauty, like the craving for emotional experience, underlies many forms of recreation activity. Man seeks not only to create beauty but to experience it in its various forms. The love of beauty is closely associated with the desire to create, a desire which finds its highest fulfillment in objects of beauty. Beauty of landscape, scenery of unusual grandeur, gardens, works of art, poetry, stage designs, and outstanding architecture are among the most commonly understood mediums through which man's yearning for beauty finds gratification. They are not, however, the only means at his disposal. The grace and rhythm of the athlete, the dancer, and the skater; the sheer beauty of certain musical passages; the possibilities afforded by collecting articles of unusual line, form, color, and texture; and the still greater satisfaction which comes from shaping objects or ideas with one's own hand or mind are merely illustrative of the ways in which recreation activities are characterized by the beautiful. The lure of travel and the drawing power of the large park and forest areas are due in great measure to the opportunities which they afford for seeing and enjoying places of unusual beauty. The satisfaction of this love of beauty is one of the primary functions of the art museum and the botanical garden.

It was because he saw these endless possibilities which recreation affords that Lorado Taft, the American sculptor, had a passion to help people "find recreation in the love and study of beauty." The failure of many recreation agencies to appreciate and serve this universal human desire accounts in part for the fact that their programs have not elicited a more favorable response from the public. The motion-picture theater, on the other hand, has been alert to satisfy this desire by bringing to the people pictures portraying natural scenery of supreme beauty; handsome, well-dressed actors; buildings, gardens, and home interiors of quality and luxury; and other objects of beauty which the world of tangible reality denies to most people.

Sense of Service. Service is seldom considered as contributing to recreation because it is commonly associated with self-sacrifice, moral duty, and a sense of obligation, all of which run counter to the essential nature of recreation. Yet service activities afford outlets for the benevolent impulses of people, and the satisfaction which results from serving our fellow men brings service within the sphere of recreation.

People have discovered that membership on a recreation board or playground committee, helping with a community chest drive, or leadership of a boys' club, junior choral group, or playground team brings returns in satisfaction comparable to those resulting from participation in the more common forms of recreation activity. One can secure just as great joy and satisfaction watching the development of a group of children in a club under his guidance as he can watching the unfolding of the flowers in his garden. Other satisfactions which result from participation in service activities are the sharing of special interests and skills and the fellowship which results from leading or working together with a group. There is no lack of mental stimulation or adventure for those who wholeheartedly engage in such activities. The genuine desire of children to help is illustrated by the junior leadership and service groups found on many playgrounds. Experience has shown that the enthusiasm of the volunteer helping a group in his own hobby often exceeds that of a paid leader.

Relaxation. Relaxation is what many people who approach their leisure hours fatigued in body, mind, or spirit most desire from their recreation. Like the other satisfactions previously considered, relaxation is achieved by different people through different forms of recreation. For some, an evening spent with a good book affords the ideal antidote for a hectic day. Others find relaxation in listening to the radio, attending the movies or theatre, listening to a concert, or taking a brisk hike with an agreeable companion. Individuals whose work taxes their mental rather than their physical energy may relax in a game of volleyball, tennis, or bowling. Gardening, caring for pets, conversation, the enjoyment of nature, a social game, or just loafing are ways in which this desired end is attained by large numbers of people. Children rarely seek relaxation; it has a minor place among the satisfactions desired by young people, but it is a factor of primary importance in the recreation life of adults. The significance of the various forms of recreation activity cannot be fully appreciated except as their possibilities for relaxation are understood.

RECREATION PRINCIPLES

The recreation leader must know not only what people seek and find in various forms of recreation activity but also the kinds of recreation that are most popular and best meet the needs of large numbers of people. Some forms of recreation are so fundamental and have such a wide appeal that they are immediately recognized as deserving a place in every recreation program. The National Recreation Association has prepared a statement entitled "Nineteen Recreation Principles," which sets forth the fundamental needs of individuals in terms of specific recreation activities. This statement, based upon the association's long experience and approved by hundreds of leaders in American life, affords a foundation for the building of a recreation program for the individual or the community. The major desires and interests of individuals outlined in the preceding pages can be fulfilled when the following principles are practiced:

1. Every child needs to be exposed to the growth-giving activities that have brought satisfaction through the ages—to climbing, chasing, tumbling; to tramping, swimming, dancing, skating, ball games; to singing, playing musical instruments, dramatizing; to making things with his hands, to working with sticks and stones and sand and water, to building and modeling; to caring for pets; to gardening, to nature; to trying simple scientific experiments; to learning team play, group activity and adventure, comradeship in doing things with others.

2. Every child needs to discover which activities give him personal satisfaction. In these activities he should be helped to develop the essential skills. Several of these activities should be of such a nature that he can keep them up in adult life.

3. Every person should have certain forms of recreation which require little space and which can be fitted into small fragments of time.

4. Every person needs to know well a certain limited number of indoor and outdoor games which he himself likes so that there will never be an occasion when he cannot think of anything to do.

5. Every person should be helped to form the habit of finding pleasure in reading.

6. Most people should know at least a few songs with good music so that they may sing when they feel like it.

7. Every person should be helped to learn how to make something of beauty in line, form, color, sound, or graceful use of his own body. At least he should find pleasure in what others do in painting, woodworking, sculpture, photography, if he cannot himself use these forms of expression.

8. Every person should be helped to form habits of being active, of breathing deeply in the sunlit outdoor air. Man thrives best in the sunlight. Since

living, not business, is the end of life, our cities should be planned for living as well as for business and industry. Sunlight, air, open spaces, parks, playgrounds in abundance, are essentials to any living that is to give permanent satisfaction.

9. Every person should be encouraged to find one or more hobbies.

10. It is of the greatest importance that every person be exposed to rhythm because without rhythm man is incomplete.

11. About one year in every ten of a person's life is spent in eating. It is of fundamental importance that this one-tenth be so lit up by play of mind upon mind that eating shall not be a hurried chore but an opportunity for comradeship and for growth for the whole person. Eating should be a social occasion, in the home something of a ceremony.

12. Rest, repose, reflection, contemplation, are in themselves forms of recreation and ought never to be crowded out by more active play.

13. Those recreation activities are most important which most completely command the individual so that he loses himself in them and gives all that he has and is to them.

14. Ultimate satisfaction in recreation comes only through one's own achievement, of some kind.

15. The form of one's recreation as an adult, often though not always, should be such as to use in part powers unused in the rest of one's life.

16. A person is successful in his recreation life in so far as the forms of activity he chooses create a play spirit, a humor, which to some extent pervades all his working hours, helping him to find enjoyment constantly in the little events of life.

17. The happy play of childhood is essential to normal growth. Normal persons are most likely to grow from the children who have played well and happily. They more easily continue normal as they keep up childhood habits of play.

18. Participation as a citizen in the cooperative building of a better way of life in which all may share is one of the most permanently satisfying forms of recreation.

The final principle is of a totally different nature and indicates the community action needed in order to create the conditions under which people may be helped to achieve the satisfactions listed in the other principles.

A CLASSIFIED LIST OF RECREATION ACTIVITIES

Recreation activities may be classified in many ways. They are commonly grouped according to types, such as games and sports, crafts, or nature activities. Or they are classified by the age or sex of the persons participating, by space requirements, skill, cost, seasons, members taking part, or forms of organization. Indoor activities are segregated from outdoor; individual activities from those in which formal or informal groups participate. Few recreation activities lend themselves to classification under exclusive categories. Therefore, although these groupings are useful to the recreation leader, their limitations as well as their values must be recognized.

There is considerable value, however, in listing the many forms of activity which are considered recreation and in grouping them according to general headings such as music, drama, and athletics. Such a list indicates the diversity and extent of the activities encompassed within the field of recreation, and is useful to the recreation worker in planning programs

Archery skills learned in childhood can be carried over into adult life (Courtesy of Leonia, N. J., Recreation Commission).

and considering the forms of recreation which might appeal to a particular community or group. The following pages are therefore devoted to a list of the more or less common types of recreation. Certain characteristics shared by the activities under each type afford the basis for grouping, although many activities are of such varied nature that they might be classified under two or more types.

In studying the list which follows, one should bear in mind that some of the activities are primarily for children, others are for youth or adults, while many appeal to people of all ages; some are essentially for men and boys, others for women and girls, and still others for mixed groups of different ages. Large spaces and elaborate equipment are necessary for some activities; some may be carried on in the home. Solitude is essential for the fullest enjoyment of certain pursuits; others yield their greatest satisfaction when engaged in by a group. Some activities have an almost universal appeal, whereas others are enjoyed by comparatively few. In contrast to activities engaged in informally are those requiring a high degree of organization. Some are competitive in nature; others are not. Some require active participation for fullest enjoyment; others give equal satisfaction to the spectator and the participant.

It is clear that a list of activities, helpful as it is, does not alone provide a sufficient basis for planning a recreation program. In addition to being familiar with the range of activities, their forms and adaptations, and understanding how the activities serve fundamental interests and needs, a person must have a knowledge of the facilities which they require and the conditions and forms of organization under which the activities are likely to prove successful.

Active Games and Sports

Low organized games

Bull in the ring	Hide-and-seek	Relays
Cat and mouse	Hill dill	Snow games
Club snatch	Poison	Tag games
Fox and geese	Prisoner's base	Three deep
Hare and hounds		

Individual and dual games and activities

Athletic tests	Golf	Quoits
Badminton	Golf croquet	Ring tennis
Baseball pitching	Handball	Roque
Billiards	Hand tennis	Shuffleboard
Boccie	Hopscotch	Smash
Bowling on the green	Horseshoe golf	Squash
Box hockey	Horseshoes	Stilt walking
Clock golf	Indoor bowling	Table tennis
Code ball	Jacks	Tennis
Croquet	Marbles	Tetherball
Curling	O'Leary	Top spinning
Dart baseball	Paddle tennis	

Gymnastics and stunts

Apparatus work	Gymnastic marching	Rope jumping
Bag punching	Lariat throwing	Trampoline
Baton twirling	Pyramid building	Tumbling
Calisthenics		

Group or team games

Baseball	Captain ball	Football
Basketball	Cricket	Goal-hi
Bat ball	Dodge ball	Hit-pin baseball
Bicycle polo	End ball	Ice hockey
Broom hockey	Fieldball	Kickball
Cage ball	Field hockey	Lacrosse

Active Games and Sports (Cont'd)

Long ball	Shinny	Touch football
Netball	Soccer	Tug of war
Newcomb	Soccer baseball	Volleyball
Polo	Softball	Water polo
Roller-skate hockey	Speed ball	

Sports

Aquaplaning	Figure skating	Rifle shooting
Archery	Fly casting	Roller skating
Aviation	Glider soaring	Sailing
Bicycle riding	Horseback riding	Skiing
Boating	Horsemanship	Skijoring
Bobsledding	Hot-rod racing	Ski jumping
Boxing	Ice boating	Skin and scuba diving
Canoeing	Ice sailing	Snowshoeing
Coasting	Ice skating	Swimming
Crew racing	Kite flying	Synchronized swimming
Cross-country running	Lifesaving	Tobogganing
Diving	Model-airplane flying	Track events
Dogsledding	Model-boat sailing	Trapshooting
Fencing	Motorboating	Water skiing
Field events	Motorcycling	Wrestling
Jumping	Parachute jumping	Yachting
Pole vaulting	Pistol shooting	
Discus throwing		

Social Activities

Banquets	Old-home weeks	Pencil-and-paper games
Barbecues	Parties	Playing house
Barn dances	Barn warming	Pot-luck suppers
Basket suppers	Beach and pool	Scavenger hunts
Candy pulls	Birthday	Social dancing
Card games	Block	Square dancing
Bridge	College	Straw rides
Canasta	Costume	Table games
Hearts	Hard times	Anagrams
Pinochle	Holiday	Backgammon
Pit	Christmas	Caroms
Clambakes	Halloween	Checkers
Conversation	New Year's	Chess
Corn roasts	St. Patrick's	Crokinole
Dating	Twelfth night	Dominoes
Entertaining	Valentine	Monopoly
Family or club reunions	Washington's birthday	Parchesi
Father-and-son dinners	Masquerade	Scrabble
Fun nights	Progressive contest	Treasure hunts
Get-acquainted stunts	Progressive games	Visiting
Lodge and club meetings	Quilting	Wiener roasts
Marshmallow roasts	Sailing	
Mother-and-daughter dinners		

Music

Vocal

A cappella choirs
Action songs
Choruses
Christmas caroling

Community singing
Glee clubs
Informal singing groups
Mothers' choruses

Opera groups
Quartets
Singing games
Whistling groups

Instrumental

Accordion
Bands
Bugle corps
Chamber-music groups
Fife-and-drum corps

Harmonica bands
Instrumental choruses
Kazoo bands
Mandolin and guitar
    groups
Ocarina choirs

Rhythm bands
Saxophone ensembles
String quartets or
    ensembles
Symphony orchestras
Ukulele orchestras

Performances

Band concerts
Cantatas
Glee-club concerts
Incidental music at
    pageants, festivals, etc.
Music competitions

Music festivals
Old fiddlers' contests
Operas
Operettas
Oratorios

Orchestral concerts
Original-song contests
Radio or
    television concerts
Record concerts

Miscellaneous

Composing music
Listening groups

Making musical instruments
Music-appreciation courses

Music-study clubs
Music weeks

Arts and Crafts

Basketry
Beadcraft
Block printing
Bookbinding
Cabinetmaking
Cardboard construction
Carving—soap,
    wood, bone
Cementcraft
Ceramics
Cookery
Drawing
Dyeing and coloring
Embossing
Embroidery
Etching
Fabric decoration
Finger painting
Furniture refinishing
Home decoration

Jewelry making
Knitting
Leathercraft
Making recreation
    equipment
Map making
Mechanics
Metalcraft
Millinery
Modeling
Model-aircraft
    construction
Mosaic crafts
Needlework
Painting
Papercraft
Paper folding and cutting
Photography
Plastic crafts

Poster making
Pottery
Printing
Quilting
Radio
Reed- and raffiawork
Rugmaking
Sandcraft
Scrapbook making
Sculpture
Sewing
Ship-model building
Sketching
Snow sculpture
Stagecraft
Tincraft
Toy making
Visiting art museums
Weaving
Woodworking

Drama

Carnivals
Charades
Costume design
Doll fashion shows
Dramatic stunts
Fairs
Fashion shows
Feast of lanterns
Festivals
Follies
Impersonations
Informal dramatizations
Marionettes
Mask making
Masquerades
Mimetic exercises

Minstrel shows
Mock trials
Movie making
Movie shows
Musical dramas
  and comedies
One-act plays
Pageants
Pantomimes
Parades
Peep shows
Play-exchange circuit
Play reading
Play tournaments
Playwriting
Playwriting contests

Puppetry
Radio dramas
Scenery making
Shadowgraphs
Song impersonations
Stagecraft
Stage lighting
Story dramatization
Story plays
Storytelling
Television and radio
  productions
Three-act plays
Traveling theater
Vaudeville acts
Water pageants
Workshop

Dancing

Acrobatic
Ballet
Classic
Clog

Eurythmics
Folk
Gymnastic
Interpretive

Modern
Social
Square
Tap

Nature and Outing Activities

Astronomy
Auto riding for pleasure
Bee culture
Bird walks
Camping
  Auto
  Day
  Family
  Group
  Overnight
Caring for home grounds
Caring for pets
Dog-obedience classes
Excursions or trips
  Art galleries
  Industrial plants
  Museums
  Parks
  Places of historic interest
  Places of scenic interest
  Public buildings
Exploration
Fishing

Flower arrangement
Fruit raising
Gardening
  Flower
  Indoor
  Miniature
  Vegetable
Hiking
Hunting
Log rolling
Making nature trails
Microscope study
Mountain climbing
Nature games
Nature hikes
Nature museum projects
Nature study, collection,
  and identification
  Animals
  Birds
  Flowers
  Fossils
  Insects

Marine life
Minerals
Mosses
Reptiles
Trees
Nature tours
Nature treasure hunts
Orienteering
Pet shows
Picnicking
Pigeon clubs
Plant-exchange days
Raising poultry
Sand play
Snow tracking
Travel
Traveling garden
Wading
Zoos
  Traveling zoo or
    barnyard
  Visiting zoo
  Playground zoo

Literary, Language, and Related Activities

Book clubs
Charm school
Creative writing
Debates
Diction
Discussion clubs
Foreign-language
    study groups
Fortune telling
Forums
Guessing games

Lectures
Listening to radio
Magic
Mathemagic
Mental games
Paper-and-pencil games
Poetry groups
Public speaking
Puzzles
    Crossword
    Jigsaw

Reading
Reading aloud
Reciting
Riddles
Spelling bees
Storytelling
Study groups
Television programs
Tricks
Verse-speaking choir
Writing letters

Collecting

Antiques
Armor
Autographs
Bookplates
Books
    Almanacs
    Autographed books
    Cookbooks
    Dime novels
    Early printings
    First editions
    Manuscripts
    Specific authors
    Specific subjects
Bottles

Butterflies
Buttons
China
Clocks
Coins
Dolls
Etchings
Firearms
Fossils
Furniture
Glassware
Indian arrowheads
Lamps
Match covers
Medals

Miniatures
Music instruments
Paintings
Pictures
Post cards
Pottery
Sea shells
Ship models
Silver
Stamps
Tapestries
Toys
Weapons
Woodcuts

Service Activities

Group leadership in settlement, boys' club, recreation building, playground, or youth
    center
Membership on park, school, or recreation board
Service as scoutmaster or troop committeeman
Service as assistant at playground or recreation center
Coaching or managing junior teams in baseball or basketball
Directing glee club, orchestra, dramatic group
Helping conduct a hobby, craft, or nature project
Assistance in organizing a holiday celebration or a campaign for civic improvement
Assistance with publicity, money raising, or public relations program of a recreation
    or other agency
Teaching a Sunday-school class
Serving on a city council or other municipal agency
Transporting aged or handicapped to recreation centers
Assisting with the recreation program at a hospital, correctional institution, or home
    for the aged

The preceding lists, though far from complete, indicate the wide diversity of activities that bring people direct satisfaction and that merit consideration in the development of a comprehensive community recreation program.

15. PROGRAM-PLANNING PRINCIPLES AND METHODS

THE COMMUNITY recreation program is the term applied to the total experiences of individuals and groups resulting from community action in providing areas, facilities, leadership, and funds. These experiences represent a wide range of activities, planned and spontaneous, organized and informal, supervised and undirected. The activities comprising the recreation program are designed to meet the fundamental human needs described in the preceding chapter and to contribute to a satisfying, abundant life. In order to achieve this, however, programs must be planned with a knowledge of human needs and of the methods by which they can be served effectively. Participants at a recreation workshop concluded: "The objective of program planning is to provide those experiences that will bring to the participant the most satisfying values and that in addition will have desirable social effects. It should be kept in mind that in many cases the planning process itself has recreation values." [1]

THE COMMUNITY RECREATION PROGRAM

Local governments, as previously pointed out, cannot provide all these experiences, but the municipality has a responsibility for furnishing the base of leadership, facilities, and services upon and around which others will develop their own programs and activities. This does not mean that community recreation programs should be standardized, for widely differing conditions—urban or rural, climatic, racial, social, and economic—make variations in such programs necessary and desirable.

The basic requirements of a community recreation program were defined briefly by Joseph Lee in the following words: [2]

A community program for recreation must include the discovery of potential interests, talents, and skills, training and education in the creative use of leisure,

[1] *Recreation for Community Living*, The Athletic Institute, Chicago, 1952, p. 139.
[2] "Certain Basic Assumptions Underlying the Work of the National Recreation Association," *Recreation*, vol. 28, no. 7, p. 313, October, 1934.

and a wide variety of opportunities to serve the multitudinous interests—physical, social, musical, dramatic, nature, etc.—of different individuals.

Government, the collective agency of the people, is responsible for fostering and administering such a rich program of leisure-time opportunity.

Cities are increasingly building their programs upon the principle of extending to the greatest possible number of people in all parts of the city the most desirable and the most varied activities which it is practical to originate and sponsor. In spite of the fact that communities, like individuals, differ in their recreation interests and needs, it is nevertheless possible to set forth certain essential characteristics of a community recreation program. They apply particularly to the program of the recreation department; some relate to the program of any recreation agency.

Criteria for a Community Recreation Program. The following may be considered essential criteria for an adequate recreation program regardless of the size or type of community. They are based upon the principle that all such programs should minister to individual and social needs, afford outlets for creative expression, and contribute to a fuller life for all the people. They take into account the activities which everyone needs and which have a universal appeal, as well as individual differences in recreation tastes and interest. These criteria have been widely accepted by recreation authorities.

Every community recreation program should:

1. *Provide equality of opportunity for all.* This democratic principle applies particularly in the field of recreation. For example, as far as possible *all* neighborhoods, not just a favored few, should have adequate playgrounds. Facilities and programs should be sufficiently broad and well distributed to enable all the people to be served.

2. *Serve all ages.* It should provide for children of all ages, young people and adults, including the aged. Facilities for adults should not be expanded if children's play needs are thereby neglected; and in meeting the demand for youth programs, the older people's needs should not be overlooked.

3. *Provide equally for both sexes.* Activities for men and boys still receive a lion's share of consideration in many cities. Men and boys and women and girls are entitled to equal opportunities in the recreation program.

4. *Provide opportunities for co-recreation.* Many activities can be enjoyed most fully when engaged in together by people of both sexes. The program should provide many opportunities for participation in appropriate co-recreational activities. They are especially important in programs for youth and older adults.

5. *Encourage family recreation.* Many forms of recreation tend to divide or separate the family. Opportunities should be provided for the family to play together, either as a separate unit or with other family groups, in the home and at outside areas and facilities.

6. *Provide a wide range of individual choices in different types of activities.* The program should not be devoted primarily to a single type of activity such as athletic games and sports, to the neglect of other interests, but should include games, music, arts and crafts, nature, drama, social recreation, and other activities.

7. *Include relaxing as well as active forms of recreation.* There are times when people do not desire strenuous activity. Some people find their greatest satisfaction in quiet or passive recreation. Programs should provide not only for vigorous participation but for the enjoyment that comes from watching, listening, or contemplation.

8. *Offer possibilities for varying degrees of skill and ability.* Some measure of success is necessary if the activity is to afford satisfaction and contribute to the individual's personality development. The person of average skill and the "dub" must be provided for as well as the very proficient, since the former are more numerous and need greater encouragement.

9. *Provide activities of a progressive nature.* Few people keep a long-continuing interest in activities unless they afford challenging goals or objectives. Organization of music, drama, or craft groups, for example, which function on different levels of skill or ability offer incentives for individuals to advance to higher achievement.

10. *Carry over the leisure-time skills and interests developed in the schools.* The recreation program should make it possible and easy for young people who in school have played on athletic teams or taken part in other extracurricular activities to join groups in which their interests and abilities may continue to find satisfactory expression.

11. *Include activities that will persist at the adult level.* So many activities can be carried on into adult life that they should have an important part in community recreation programs. In the field of sports, for example, swimming, tennis, and volleyball satisfy this criterion, whereas track events and football do not.

12. *Continue throughout the year.* People need recreation twelve months of the year, and a responsibility rests upon the city to provide a year-round program. Activities are especially needed during seasons when other recreation opportunities are limited.

13. *Provide activities for different periods of free time.* Noon hours, after-school periods, week ends, holidays, twilight hours, recess periods, vacations, all afford opportunity for recreation. Unless these periods are utilized, the needs of many people are likely to be neglected and valuable

opportunities for service lost. The recreation needs of people who work nights or who have unusual free-time periods must not be overlooked.

14. *Represent cooperative planning.* This is exceedingly important if recreation is to function in a democratic setting. Program participants and the public should share with the professional staff and the governing bodies in developing the program. Only when this is done does the program truly reflect the desires of the people it is intended to serve.

15. *Encourage individuals and groups to provide their own activities.* The recreation program should encourage people to use initiative in developing their own program ideas. By stimulating interests and developing self-leadership, individuals can be helped to provide recreation for themselves and the groups to which they belong.

16. *Be related to other local programs.* Cooperative planning with other organizations providing recreation assures maximum use of available resources and enriches the total recreation opportunities in the community. It also prevents duplication or overlapping in recreation services.

17. *Furnish outlets for satisfying group activity.* Through the recreation program people should have opportunities to achieve a sense of belonging, to develop social qualities, and to experience the fellowship which results from participating membership in a group.

18. *Recognize the different tastes and interests of the individual.* Important as group activity is, the needs and personal development of the individual should receive primary consideration. As the well-known recreation leader Ott Romney has said, programs must "shun assembly-line methods, mechanized processes, wholesale production, and specialization in sedatives."

19. *Provide outlets for creative expression.* Although it is important that large numbers of people be served in activities in which the creative factor has little significance, the needs of the small group who desire outlets for their creative ability should not be neglected.

20. *Serve the specific interests and needs of the people in different neighborhoods.* The racial, economic, and cultural backgrounds of people affect their recreation interests and needs. Consequently neighborhood programs, as well as activities for individuals, need to be diversified and adapted to conditions in the various parts of the city.

21. *Provide for the ill and handicapped.* Special consideration should be given to the needs of the ill and handicapped who normally are unable to participate in the regular activities unless these activities are adapted for them.

22. *Afford opportunities for developing good citizenship.* The program should include activities in which team play is featured rather than individual achievement, cooperation stressed rather than competition, and opportunity afforded for leadership and service. Through the program,

people should learn by experience the values of cooperative effort in service to the community.

23. *Utilize fully all existing properties.* Indoor and outdoor recreation facilities which are idle or restricted to one or two activities when they are capable of serving many uses represent an economic loss as well as a failure to realize full service potentialities. The program should be planned so facilities can yield the maximum returns in enjoyable activity for the largest number of people.

Physical handicaps do not prevent these boys from enjoying fishing, the popular American sport (Courtesy of Recreation Center for the Handicapped, San Francisco).

24. *Make possible the wisest use of available resources.* Unwise or extravagant expenditures for special services for a limited number deprive the majority of essential, greatly needed recreation opportunities. In spending money for leadership, facilities, supplies, or other purposes, the best interest of the largest number of people should be considered.

25. *Place recreation opportunities within the financial abilities of all the people.* Facilities and activities can render maximum service only if they are free or available on payment of fees or charges which a large part of the population can afford. Many essential services must be free and easily accessible to all.

26. *Conform to recognized program standards.* Many national organizations have adopted standards setting forth desirable procedures for the conduct of certain activities, for participation in various events, for organizing competition, and for personal conduct. The program should reflect the adoption of such appropriate standards or their modification to conform to sound local recreation policy.

27. *Assure safe and healthful conditions for recreation activity.* The contribution which recreation can make to healthful living is realized only when precautions are taken to protect the health and safety of participants and spectators. Safeguards are of primary importance in program features such as swimming, boating, camping, and in strenuous competitive sports, particularly when engaged in by junior boys and women and girls.

28. *Be subject to continuous evaluation.* Only those phases of the program that afford satisfactions to the participants, serve basic needs, and produce a response that justifies their cost should be continued. Authorities, staff, and participants should share in a periodic evaluation of the program. Flexibility is essential. Both short-term and long-range planning are necessary, but programs should be subject to revision as experience proves change to be desirable.

IMPORTANT FACTORS IN PROGRAM PLANNING

Program planning involves the setting up of a comprehensive, city-wide plan of recreation service; the selection of activities in the individual neighborhoods, playgrounds, and centers; and preparations for conducting single events such as a swimming meet or a community-wide music project. Several factors play a large part in determining the success or failure of program planning. The significance of these factors and the principles which experience has proved practical in dealing with them are briefly presented here. Detailed suggestions for the application of these principles will be found in later chapters.

Interest. Recreation programs must be built around the desires and interests of the people to be served. Many interests of children are so universal that activities such as sand or water play, or play with pets or toys, have a fundamental appeal. The interests of young people and adults are more diverse; but even so, certain activities are widely popular. Games and sports, for example, are greatly desired by most young men; social dancing is enjoyed by large numbers of people; a community Christmas celebration appeals to old and young; and swimming is popular among people of all ages. In view of the wide variation in individual tastes and interests, however, a diversity of activities must be provided if the program is to serve a large percentage of the community. Studies of the recreation interests and desires of children, youth, and adults provide data which are of great value in program planning, but a knowledge of neighborhood conditions is essential in planning the program for a particular recreation center, especially if adults are to be served. The use of check lists on which people may indicate their choice of activities is a helpful means of determining recreation interests. Neighborhood leaders can often advise as to projects which are most desired or which would bring the greatest response from the people.

Common interests afford a sound basis for organizing recreation groups. After discovering what people would like to do, the recreation department helps those with similar interests to form groups which engage in the activities of their choice. Children are eager for any new recreation experience, but most adults are attracted to the program only when the first approach is through an activity they already know and enjoy. Starting with this activity, the skillful leader can expand and enrich the individual's recreation life by creating opportunities for him to engage in other forms of activity which yield a pleasurable experience. In this way new interests are revealed and developed. Programs sometimes fail because the leaders stress activities which reflect their own interests and experience rather than those of the people to be served. To be inspiring and helpful to the group the leader must obviously be interested in the activity he is conducting, but the interest of the group and not that of the leader should determine the activities to be carried on.

Age. The variation in recreation interests at different ages is another planning factor. The young child's favorite activities lose their appeal as he grows older and develops new desires and interests. Some activities have a brief interest span; others persist throughout life. Sports and activities involving strenuous physical exertion have an important part in the play life of children and youth. On the other hand, recreational reading, club activities, hobbies, social service, and gardening are more representative adult leisure-time activities.

Recognition of the differences in play interests at different age levels as recorded by thoughtful observers of children's play activities is fundamental in successful program planning. The playground program which attracts and holds the interest of large numbers of boys and girls of varying ages is one which provides activities that strongly appeal to various age groups. The length of play periods and the conditions of play, as well as the activities themselves, must be adapted to the ages of the players. Differences in the function and methods of recreation leadership in dealing with various age groups were pointed out in Chapter 6.

Planning recreation for children and youth is comparatively easy because they have so many vital common interests at the various age levels. Planning for adults is more difficult because the individual's response to recreation is influenced largely by the activities he engaged in before he was eighteen and because many adults have had only a limited experience in recreation activities. Nevertheless people can and do acquire new skills and interests after reaching maturity. Age differences are less significant among adults than children, although most people like to play with persons of their own age because endurance, skill, and understanding are likely to be similar in the same age group, especially in the case of active games and sports. A person skilled in dramatics, crafts, or nature, however, may be an acceptable member of a group composed of persons interested in one of these activities, even though he is much older or younger than a majority of the members.

Sex. Differences in the two sexes influence their interest and participation in many forms of recreation, although boys and girls under ten years of age are much alike in their ability and interests, and it is generally believed desirable for them to play together. After puberty is reached, however, boys usually excel in games and sports to a degree which makes competition between the sexes unsatisfactory. Programs for older girls feature activities in which form and skill are emphasized rather than strength and speed. Competition between older boys and girls in games involving bodily contact is avoided, but normal relationships of the two sexes are encouraged through participation in dramatics, music, handcraft, social dancing, and outing activities and in such games as tennis, bowling, volleyball, or badminton.

After maturity there is a tendency for men and women to engage in common activities, although differences in the interests of the sexes are still apparent. Games and sports play a more important role in recreation programs for men, whereas social and cultural activities have a larger place in women's programs. Men enjoy crafts utilizing wood or metal, whereas needlework and interior decorating appeal more strongly to women. On the whole, however, individual skills, habits, tastes, and interests exert a greater influence than sex in determining the activities in which adults take part.

Place. The places required for different forms of recreation vary from the quiet corner in which one reads a book to the extensive properties needed for hunting, horseback riding, or mountain climbing. Effective program planning involves a knowledge of the space requirements of various activities and a familiarity with those which may be introduced successfully in available indoor and outdoor spaces. Play lots do not make possible a program which appeals to the twelve- to fourteen-year-old boys, although they may be adequate for younger children. The popularity of such games as softball and paddle tennis has been partly due to the fact that they require less space than baseball and tennis—activities which could not be provided on many playgrounds. Recreation programs are therefore limited not only by the space available but by the type of recreation possible in the given area.

In a gymnasium where the ceiling is low, where projecting walls create a hazard, and where shower and locker facilities are lacking or inadequate, a basketball tournament is conducted under a severe handicap. A play night is highly successful in the large clubroom or auditorium with attractive furnishings and a congenial atmosphere, but it is a failure

The skill required in lawn bowling accounts in part for its appeal to older adults (Courtesy of Department of Parks, New York, N. Y.).

when held in a drab and badly ventilated gymnasium. The easy chairs, flowers, piano, and fireplace in the community house lobby present a more hospitable appearance and create a more friendly atmosphere than the entrance hall of many a school center. More people attend a band concert, play, or sports demonstration if seating facilities are provided than if they are obliged to stand throughout the program. When events designed to attract only a small number of people are held in a large auditorium, the psychological effect is likely to be worse than when overcrowding occurs. These few illustrations indicate the importance of place and space in planning recreation programs.

Skill. Successful planning involves the selection or adaptation of activities to the skill or ability of the people who are to take part in them. In starting a choral group of untrained singers it is unwise to introduce the same types of music as in a group composed of experienced musicians. People are likely to be discouraged if they undertake craft projects which are too difficult for them. Matching the beginner and the expert in tennis, golf, or handball brings satisfaction to neither player. Activities must be provided which call for varying degrees of skill in order that all who are interested may find a level at which they can participate successfully. As individuals acquire greater skill, they can join groups engaging in the activity at a more advanced level. Careful classifications of participants in activities involving competition is especially important.

The successful recreation program lays special emphasis upon activities like coasting, hiking, community singing, and bathing in which large numbers may take part and in which no special skill is required. It also utilizes the possibilities of the ski jump, *a cappella* choir, and diving pool, which serve a limited group with special skills. The desire of people to improve existing skills and to acquire new ones is satisfied by the provision of instructors in such widely different activities as golf and puppetry, folk dancing and ceramics, baseball and debating. The teaching of fundamental skills involved in the individual and highly organized team games contributes to succesful participation in these activities.

Time. The significance of time in program planning is demonstrated by the well-balanced program in which activities follow in a reasonable progressive sequence without overcrowding of schedules or long periods of inactivity. Special events are arranged from time to time to provide occasions toward which groups may direct their efforts and demonstrate their achievements. Full advantage is taken of brief seasons when water and winter sports may be carried on and of the opportunities which holidays and special days offer for developing novel and attractive features.

The dates for opening the season at the golf course, the indoor center, or the municipal camp are determined only after careful study of local conditions. In some neighborhoods playgrounds or centers need to be open for a longer season or more hours each day than in others. Some activities have a brief interest span, whereas others can be carried on indefinitely. The recreation worker needs to know how much time is required for developing an activity to a point where it may be carried on successfully. He does not attempt to organize a symphony orchestra in a short, summer playground season, although he might develop one as a feature of the longer indoor-center program. In arranging league schedules, games must be played often enough to sustain the players' interest and to permit completion of a satisfactory schedule within a reasonable period, but overcrowding must be avoided and time allowed for postponed games.

The time factor is especially important in arranging meetings and events. In an industrial community where people work near their homes, evening affairs may be scheduled at 7:30, but in a suburban community with many commuters it is difficult to start programs before 8:30. The working and living conditions and habits of the groups served must also be considered in selecting the time of day and day of the week for regular program features and for special events. Failure to realize that activities must begin and end on time has resulted in the failure of many otherwise excellent programs.

Timeliness in program planning is also taken into account by alert recreation workers who capitalize on widespread public interest in an event of unusual importance. An international competition such as the Olympics, the arrival of a circus, the launching of a satellite, or an event of local or national significance may prove an incentive for developing some new phase of the recreation program or lend added interest to existing activities.

Size of the Group. Program planning involves a knowledge of the numbers of people who are needed to carry on different activities in a satisfactory manner. A few stamp or chess enthusiasts may form a highly successful club, but a community chorus or a play festival cannot be carried on unless a considerable number of people wish to take part. The size of the group is also a factor in scheduling the use of indoor or outdoor facilities, since a large organization or meeting will require an auditorium, whereas a small group may be accommodated in a clubroom. The use of large picnic-center units is sometimes restricted to church, lodge, industrial, or other groups. If a certain number of people express a desire to engage in an activity, some recreation departments will furnish a leader and a regular meeting place.

The interests of the largest possible number of people deserve primary consideration, and emphasis is laid on activities and events which have a wide appeal and benefit many. Still, the interests of relatively small groups must not be overlooked. If a genuine and enduring curiosity about nature can be aroused in even a small number of children through a nature club, or if a limited group can be given a satisfying, creative experience through a craft class, the resulting benefit justifies the expense and effort involved. Nevertheless, a community playday in which large numbers can take part has, in all probability, more value than a city-wide track and field meet in which only the best athletes participate.

The size of the group frequently influences the method of conducting an activity. A volleyball league may be organized on a large city playground, but in a small neighborhood it may be possible to have only one team of a particular age group, in which case games must be arranged with outside teams.

Type of Organization. The purpose of organization in recreation is to provide a setting and procedure which enable the recreation program to yield the maximum benefit and enjoyment. Some activities, such as reading, listening to the radio, card playing, or creative writing, require no special organization or promotion. Others, like gardening or hiking, are

Boys in craft class make shingle boats to be entered in competition (Courtesy of Department of Parks and Recreation, Los Angeles County).

primarily self-operating, yet through organization their recreation possibilities are greatly enlarged. When the recreation department helps hiking enthusiasts form a club, the activity takes on a new element of sociability; and when it organizes a horseshoe league or tournament, the game acquires an added incentive in the form of friendly rivalry. The skillful leader knows how to use organization as a means of bringing out these added values without causing the individual to lose any of the satisfaction which he gained from participation in the activity on an informal basis.

Many recreation activities are most successful when carried on by highly organized groups. Baseball yields the greatest satisfaction to most individuals when they play on a team enrolled in a league and competing on a regular schedule. An orchestra is likely to succeed only if its membership is restricted to persons who have suitable qualifications and who are willing to attend rehearsals regularly. Other group activities such as dances, parties, and fun nights do not require formal group organization. Many interests are best served through the organization of clubs, either around a specific activity such as bird study or puppetry or around a common age, neighborhood, or other interest.

The planning and conducting of special performances, exhibitions, or community celebrations, especially if they involve cooperation between different groups, require another type of organization. The drama group prepares zestfully for and eagerly awaits its public productions, the music group its concerts, the arts and crafts group its exhibits, and the sports group its carnival. The playground circus and festival require long and careful preparations, but they afford opportunities for demonstrating many of the regular playground activities. The Christmas celebration, an occasion for combining the interests of many groups, similarly requires a high degree of organization.

Type of Community. Nationality, race, occupation, education, economic status, and standard of living are factors which must be known in planning a recreation program for the people of a city or neighborhood. A program which appeals to a cultured, well-to-do community may fail in an industrial town with a high percentage of underprivileged foreign-born. Differences are less marked among children than adults, but a knowledge of home conditions is essential even in the planning of playground programs. Factory workers often want and require different forms of recreation from office workers. A program designed for a Junior League may not meet the needs of a group of girls in industry. Lighted tennis courts are of limited value in a low-income neighborhood unless equipment is provided and no charge is made for their use. Some foreign-born adults are reluctant to go outside their immediate neighborhood for recreation, so programs must be provided near their homes. On the other hand, in neighborhoods where most families own automobiles, people will drive a considerable distance to take part in group activity. Many city dwellers like to be entertained, but in rural communities people would rather create their own forms of recreation than to have talent brought in from the city.

Communities or neighborhoods with many foreign-born can feature in their recreation program arts, crafts, games, music, and folk dances which are related to the former life of the people. Rhythmic activities are stressed in planning for Negro groups; debating, dramatics, and club activity appeal strongly to Jewish people; competitive athletics are popular with the Italians; and singing with the Welsh. Special aptitudes of national and racial groups are particularly valuable in initiating recreation programs for them, although an attempt should be made to broaden the interests of these groups and to draw them increasingly into community-wide activities.

Purpose. The primary purpose of recreation program planning—to help individuals gain the greatest satisfaction, joy, and benefit from their leisure time—is achieved in many different ways. The recreation worker must organize, conduct, or promote activities in ways that contribute to the attainment of this objective. The same form of recreation, however, may serve different ends. For example, a band concert may be designed to give a large audience the enjoyment of listening to a professional band or to culminate a long period of effort by an amateur music group which has gained its greatest value from playing together. Arts, crafts, and nature activities not only furnish immediate satisfactions, but contribute richly to one's life over a long period. Holiday celebrations develop community solidarity and enthusiasm in addition to yielding direct satisfaction to the individuals taking part. Demonstrations of recreation activities give pleasure to the participants but may also be arranged to interest others in the activities demonstrated or to convince the community of their value. Many activities offer possibilities for achieving secondary as well as primary objectives; however, recreation leaders must be alert to prevent recreation from being exploited for unjustifiable or questionable ends.

Leadership and Funds Available. Workers should have certain qualifications for the job, but the particular skills and abilities of the available leaders naturally influence the type of program. A worker specially trained in music, for example, is likely to develop music activities to a greater extent than nature study or athletics. Employment of a leadership staff with a sound recreation education and practical experience assures a well-rounded program; the specialized skills and interests of the individual workers make it possible to offer a wide diversity of activities. The fact that competent leaders discover the capacities and skills of people in the community and enlist them for volunteer service further emphasizes the significance of leadership as a factor in program planning.

The available funds often determine whether or not a particular project can be carried out; the unit costs of different activities must also be considered in program planning. The number of people a particular activity will serve, the extent to which it may lead to continuing self-activity, its contribution to participants and the community in happiness, safety, health, or civic value, and its possibilities of becoming self-sustaining must be considered in relation to its cost. Activities must not be appraised, however, in dollar terms alone. In attempting to secure the maximum benefit from the funds available, it is necessary to determine the activities to be carried on, the centers to be operated, the length of the season, the leadership to be provided, the fees to be charged, if any, and other factors. Wise planning also recognizes that certain types of programs which appeal to influential groups in the community may serve as foundation for increased financial support.

Other Local Recreation Programs. Since recreation budgets are never adequate for all recreation needs, consideration must be given, in planning the municipal program, to the recreation services of other community agencies. Recreation needs are so great that full use of the total resources of all agencies, governmental and nongovernmental, is essential. The problem in all communities is one of inadequacy of total resources. Hence, effective, continuing, cooperative planning and operating relationships must be developed, so that each agency can make its most effective contribution without duplication of services. The division of responsibility for cooperative planning depends upon local considerations, for no standard blueprint is applicable everywhere. Encouraging progress is being made in the acceptance of the basic principle of unselfish, wholehearted cooperation on the part of local recreation agencies.

A FEW PLANNING SUGGESTIONS

Thus far consideration has been given to the essential principles underlying the planning of community recreation programs and to the factors which influence planning. This chapter ends with a few comments on the problems and difficulties encountered in the practical application of these principles, as well as a brief statement on the responsibility for program planning in the recreation department.

Responsibility for Program Planning. The general planning of the municipal recreation program is one of the major responsibilities of the recreation executive, although final approval rests with the authorities to whom he is responsible, whether a recreation board, school board, city manager, or other official. Planning the program is a cooperative undertaking in which board members as well as the entire professional staff should share. Supervisors submit for approval a tentative program for their respective divisions. Workers at the individual playgrounds and centers contribute valuable suggestions because they are close to the people and therefore are familiar with the desires and needs of the neighborhoods they serve.

Giving the people of a community or neighborhood a share in planning programs intended for their benefit is a desirable democratic procedure; it is also a means of assuring their participation in the activities. Playground and indoor center committees are an effective means of achieving these ends. Committee members assist the employed staff in determining the interests and desires of the people in the neighborhood and in selecting the projects to be undertaken.

It should perhaps be pointed out that determination of the specific activities and projects to be included in the program is only one step in the planning process. It is the essential prerequisite, however, to the assignment of personnel, the fixing of work schedules, the distribution of budgeted funds, and the development of areas and facilities. All these steps are functions of the executive, after approval by the authorities.

Administering the Program. After the department's general program for the year has been prepared by the executive and approved by the managing authority, it becomes the basic plan which the leadership staff is responsible for carrying out. No essential features can be changed without proper approval, although considerable flexibility in selecting and conducting the activities is essential in order to allow for varying neighborhood conditions or for unexpected developments. The workers must be thoroughly instructed as to the program, the methods to be followed in carrying it out, and the conditions under which variations are authorized. The degree of freedom allowed workers within the general limits of the program adopted depends largely upon their competence and experience and upon the amount of general supervision available. Personal observation, regular reports, and the visits of supervisors are means used by the executive to keep him informed on the results obtained at each center and to assure the proper conduct of the program.

A Definite Progressive Plan. The word "planning" implies looking toward the future. Every progressive recreation department is considering plans not merely for the current year but for the years ahead. It is anticipating the future needs of the community and is taking steps to secure additional areas and facilities, is building up public support for an enlarged program, and is interpreting the significance of new recreation developments. Because the work of the department is largely dependent upon governmental funds for its support, plans must be related to the city's financial resources. They must have flexibility in order that they may be readily revised to meet changing conditions and unexpected needs. In view of the steady increase in leisure time and the rapid growth of understanding of recreation values, no city is justified in failing to give serious thought both to present-day needs and to the probable demands for expanded programs and services in the years ahead.

Extremes to Be Avoided. Two shortcomings characterize many community recreation programs. Frequently programs comprise only a narrow range of recreation interests and lack a varied, rich, creative, challenging quality. Usually they provide outdoor activities at the summer playgrounds and a limited number of indoor-center projects, but the cultural arts, nature, hobbies, services to special groups, and community-wide features are largely or entirely neglected. Such programs obviously fail to meet the criteria for a good community recreation program suggested early in this chapter, and they indicate a lack of imagination, initiative, or understanding on the part of the recreation authorities, executive, and staff.

A less common tendency is to schedule more events and to start more projects than can possibly be carried to a successful conclusion. When this is done, parts of the program suffer and some activities are doomed to failure. The result is disappointment, loss of interest, and a setback to the work as a whole. Desirable as it is that the program offer a great variety of recreation opportunities, it is unwise to initiate activities and organize groups unless there is sufficient leadership, time, and interest to ensure the likelihood of their success.

Types of Programs. Planning a municipal recreation program, as has been indicated, is not a simple problem. The program itself has many aspects, each of which involves special procedures. One phase of the program is the scheduling of the major city-wide events in which the department as a whole participates and which are often arranged on a month-by-month basis. The planning of events to be carried on by each of the major divisions is another problem. The athletic division, for example, determines the various leagues that are to be formed, prepares a detailed schedule for each team in each league in each sport, determines the tournaments, special events, and championships to be held, and selects the dates, places, and officials for each. Separate programs must be prepared for the playgrounds and indoor centers, indicating the dates of opening and closing, the special events to be carried on, and daily, weekly, or seasonal schedules. Each club or organization served by the department's staff and facilities prepares its own program more or less subject to the department's approval. If there are swimming pools, golf courses, or other such facilities, definite schedules must be drawn up covering their season, hours of operation, and special events.

Program planning is clearly a most important phase of the recreation department's work. Knowledge of the criteria and factors discussed in this chapter and of the special requirements of various activities and groups is necessary to successful planning. Obviously no specific rules can be laid down for the preparation of all types of programs, but the chapters that follow indicate some of the ways in which the planning principles can be put into effect.

16. ORGANIZING AND CONDUCTING RECREATION ACTIVITIES

IN THE organization and conduct of activities the recreation leader reveals his knowledge of the activities, his understanding of program-planning principles, his ability to apply them in the situation confronting him, and his competence and aptitude for working with individuals and groups. The diversified content of the recreation program necessitates the use of widely different methods of initiating and carrying on the various activities. In starting a recreation program in a locality, the leader must also apply the principles and procedures of community organization as they relate to recreation. Before describing how specific recreation activities are started and carried on, a few essentials in establishing a program will be considered briefly.

STARTING A PROGRAM

Every community recreation program owes its origin and development to the initiative of an energetic citizen or group of interested community leaders. The initial objective may be a summer playground program under leadership, establishment of a youth center, or the construction of a swimming pool. Subsequently the scope of the program is expanded, additional facilities are acquired, and finally there arises a public demand for recreation opportunities under continuous leadership throughout the year. Most year-round programs have evolved gradually; seldom does a community that has not provided some form of seasonal recreation service establish a recreation department with full-time leadership.

In initiating a community recreation program, a desirable first step is a meeting to which all local organizations are asked to send representatives and all interested citizens are invited. At such a meeting the importance of recreation is indicated, obvious local needs are pointed out, the achievement of other comparable communities in furnishing recreation is reported, and the desirability of local action is discussed. If interest justifies it, a representative committee is appointed to make a study of local

259

recreation resources, conditions, and needs and to submit to a subsequent meeting a report of its findings and recommendations for action. In preparing its report the committee investigates the legislative authority under which a public recreation program can be developed and financed and the type of managing authority under which such a program can best be administered. It estimates the amount of money required to launch the program and studies the city's ability to provide the needed funds. The assistance of a recreation consultant is often enlisted in the conduct of the study and the preparation of the report.

The recommendations of the committee are submitted and discussed at a public meeting; and if they receive general approval, they are widely publicized and submitted to the appropriate local authorities with a request that suitable action be taken to put them into effect. Such action usually involves the passage of a local ordinance or resolution creating a recreation department, authorizing the appointment of an official recreation board or commission, appropriating funds for its work, assigning recreation areas and facilities, employing a superintendent of recreation and other personnel, and initiating a community recreation program.

Guiding Principles. One of the first steps to be taken by an agency or department responsible for developing a recreation program, whether for a single season or an entire year, is to determine what activities and special projects should be carried on. Responsibility for their recommendation rests primarily with the recreation executive. Local conditions and requirements alone afford the basis for selecting them, and they differ for every city, but there are a few principles which serve as guides.

1. The program should start with the activities that have been carried on before in the city and that have proved successful. Activities with which the people are familiar and which have proved popular in the locality serve as a nucleus around which to build the program. They assure participation in and support of these program features.

2. The program should be expanded in fields of universal or well-known interest. Observation and experience have demonstrated that children will respond to familiar playground activities, that young men want to play softball or baseball, that young people are eager to dance, that family groups enjoy picnicking, that swimming is a very popular activity. Well-planned and well-conducted programs run no risk of failure when built upon such activities.

3. The recreation activities provided by local organizations should be considered in planning the program. Duplication of service should be avoided, but in some instances activities restricted to a small number of people or limited to a portion of the city can be made generally available. The department may be asked to take over certain projects which for-

merly were sponsored by volunteers; in other cases it may offer its cooperation in conducting them.

4. New activities should be organized as the special interests or desires of the people are discovered and as new needs develop. In working with people the recreation leaders make it a point to find out what they want to do, encourage them to make their wishes known, and use every opportunity to draw out suggestions for new projects. Thus the growth of the program expresses the evolving desires and expanding interests of the people.

5. When the executive has had an opportunity to study the community, its resources, people, and needs, he should attempt consciously to develop new activities which will enrich the life of the community. Experience has shown that large numbers of people desire to participate in a particular activity only after they have had an opportunity to observe it or to experience the joy and satisfaction which it can bring them. The agency should therefore gradually introduce into the program activities for which there may be no immediate popular demand but which are likely to be successful once their value has been demonstrated.

Considerable time is required for the worker to know his community, gain its confidence, and establish a well-balanced program of recreation activities. An adequate year-round recreation program is rarely possible unless a trained man or woman gives full time to thinking, planning, and working toward this end. In building the program the executive will seek and be guided by the advice of local leaders, of the people participating in the program, and of the community at large. He will, of course, be restricted by factors more or less beyond his control, such as limitations of his budget, the areas and facilities at his disposal, and the qualifications of his workers.

Although the general planning of the program is primarily a responsibility of the executive, the work of forming the participating groups, of furnishing direct leadership and guidance, and of caring for the details involved in carrying on the activities rests largely upon the rank and file of the recreation staff, with the active cooperation of volunteers.

WHY METHODS DIFFER

A few illustrations indicate why organization methods vary. A glee club may be started with a small group at a single center, but a community Fourth of July celebration involves a city-wide organization in which many groups cooperate and a large number of individuals take part. Teaching a game on the playground is a relatively simple process compared with the promotion of the same game on a city-wide basis or the organization of a municipal athletic association. Different methods are used in developing a miniature garden project for shut-ins and in building a nature trail. The techniques which make a charm school a successful girls' club project do not necessarily apply in setting up a sports program for girls in industry.

Even on a single playground the storytelling hour, the folk-dancing period, the safety club, and the closing festival present widely differing problems of organization. Swimming centers and band concerts are designed to serve large numbers of people, while the playground team and the club at the indoor center are small-group projects. Preparation for an opera or a community pageant extends over a period of weeks or even months; other events require little advance planning. Some involve a high degree of organization, whereas others are more or less self-operating. In club programs, personal relationships and individual guidance by the leader play an important role, while in mass activities they are less important factors. These few illustrations indicate why the recreation department requires a staff with diversified training, resourcefulness, and ability. Detailed description of methods used in conducting various phases of the recreation program are described in the pages that follow.

CONDUCTING ACTIVITIES ON THE PLAYGROUND

The playground is a most important feature of the municipal recreation system, and although it serves primarily a limited age group—from six to fifteen years—its operation calls for a variety of organization methods and leadership techniques. Even though the program must conform to a general city-wide pattern, every playground worker has a certain freedom to determine the particular activities to be encouraged on his playground, the degree to which they are organized, and the manner in which they are conducted. Successful playground leadership requires an understanding of child psychology, children's play interests, and the techniques of organizing activities. In addition, the leader must recognize the limitations which the peculiar conditions found on his playground place upon him in conducting a program.

Conditions Affecting Playground Operation. In the first place, attendance is entirely voluntary; if the boy and girl do not enjoy the activities presented or dislike the way in which they are carried on, they do not attend. Child interest is at the heart of all successful playground activity, for unless the program appeals to the children, it is doomed to failure. Attendance is seldom regular or continuous, especially during the summer months, when family outings and vacations interrupt the playground schedule. Because playground programs must compete with a great variety of other attractions and distractions, organization must be comparatively informal and groups more or less flexible. Eligibility requirements must be less strict for playground teams than they are in school or indoor-center leagues, and a more generous use of substitutes must be permitted; otherwise teams would find it impossible to meet league schedules.

The playground worker carries a greater responsibility than the leader of many other groups. He must consider the happiness and safety of a large number of boys and girls of different ages taking part in a variety of activities and scattered about a large outdoor area equipped with many types of facilities. In a situation of this kind the leader cannot give his undivided attention to a single group except for short periods because he must keep an eye on the other children and supervise the use of other facilities. He must develop skill in starting one group after another in different activities and in giving intermittent leadership or supervision to these groups as need arises. Some forms of activity, such as tumbling or crafts, can be carried on successfully only if a leader gives them continuous supervision; others, like apparatus or sand play, require little guidance.

Children are not likely to attend regularly or spend many hours on the playground unless the program has variety and includes projects which sustain interest over a long period. Scheduling specific activities at a fairly definite hour encourages children who are interested in that activity to come at that time. Yet, because many children drop in at the playground at different times of the day and for varying intervals, the program must be flexible enough so these children can fit into it readily. It must be made easy for children attracted to the playground by curiosity to be drawn into group activity; otherwise they will not return. Children come to the playground bursting with energy, and the leader must find suitable outlets for it. Because of the space limitations at most playgrounds, skillful planning is required to assure all groups a fair opportunity to engage in strenuous activity without jeopardizing the safety or enjoyment of the others.

Weather, too, is very important. Few playgrounds have ample indoor facilities for accommodating large groups, and in some cases the program must stop entirely whenever it rains. In planning for special events and in arranging schedules, the possibility of rain makes it necessary to allow ample time for preparations and for playing postponed games. The leader is often obliged to make quick substitutions in the announced program when weather conditions make such action necessary or advisable. This applies not only to rainy days but to periods when excessive heat makes it wise to postpone events calling for strenuous physical activity.

These limiting factors should be kept in mind in reading the following statements describing some of the methods used in conducting forms of playground activity. For a detailed discussion of playground operation, see Chapter 17.

Typical Playground Activities. Many activities such as apparatus, sand-box, or wading pool play are informal, individual, unorganized, and more or less continuous. They require, however, general supervision on the part of the leader in order to assure safety and fair opportunity for all the children. These free-play activities can be made more interesting or purposeful if the leader teaches stunts on the apparatus, helps plan sand-modeling projects, or organizes a wading pool carnival. Doll play requires no special organization, but it is likely to take on added significance if a group of children undertake a dollhouse-building project or form a group to make dresses for their dolls.

Team games for the older boys and girls are played informally by pick-up teams or unorganized groups, but they are usually conducted on an organized basis, with the participants classified to assure fair, keen competition. Teams in the various sports compete in inter- or intraplayground or city-wide leagues. Crafts are usually carried on through informal, unrestricted groups which meet at regularly scheduled periods, although they are also engaged in by individual members of these groups at other times. Interest in a particular activity such as nature study or chess is stimulated or perpetuated through the organization of a club with officers, although participation is rarely limited to club members. Active games like paddle tennis and horseshoes, and quiet games like checkers and crokinole, are played more or less continuously; but occasional instruction periods and ladder, king's, and ranking tournaments encourage participation and the improvement of the players' skill.

Unlike the activities mentioned in the preceding paragraphs, most of which are carried on throughout the season, special events arranged from time to time afford the highlights of the playground program. Some, such as the wiener roast, the treasure hunt, and the playground picnic, are unrelated to the regular playground activities. Others, like the circus, closing festival, folk-dance demonstration, and hobby show, afford an opportunity for demonstrating the results accomplished through the playground program. Another type of special event is the musical festival, playground dance, or father-and-son party, in which the parents of the children and neighborhood groups have an opportunity to participate.

Organization Methods. The extent of preparation, kinds of organization, and leadership techniques used in conducting a few of the regular and special playground activities will be considered in the pages which follow.

TEAMS AND LEAGUES. Owing to the popularity of team games and individual sports, facilities for these activities receive considerable use even though no special form of organization is provided. Participation in team games is more interesting, satisfactory, and sustained over longer periods, however, when play is organized on a team and league basis. If at a playground the attendance and interest in a game are sufficient to enable several teams to be formed into an intramural league, the game can be made largely self-operating. An occasional game with an outside team or a baseball playday affords an interesting variation in the league program. At the end of the season a short series of games is arranged between the winning teams on the individual playgrounds for the purpose of determining the city playground championship. Unless at least four teams of fairly equal ability can be organized in a particular sport, it is usually not practicable to form such a league, but one or more teams can be organized and entered in a district league.

INFORMAL GROUP ACTIVITIES. Competition provides the chief incentive for team games and individual sports, but is relatively unimportant in many other activities. Folk dancing, tumbling, finger painting, and crafts such as beadwork or soap carving are typical of activities usually carried on with informal groups. When interest in a particular activity is discovered or expressed, the director forms a group and encourages boys or girls to join it. He finds a suitable place on the playground for conducting it, secures the necessary equipment or supplies, and sets aside definite periods for the activity. He either arranges for a member of the playground staff to meet with the group or enlists the services of a volunteer leader, who helps the group set up definite goals to be accomplished or specific activities to be carried on.

The activities are conducted in an informal manner so that new children can join the group from day to day or week to week just as they would a low organized game. Under such conditions it is impossible to expect as high a standard of achievement from all members of the group as is attained in a small, restricted class, but on the summer playground regular attendance throughout the season, which formal group organization requires, is impossible for many children. Furthermore, boys and girls feel more free to attend meetings of informal groups and to try out the activities which are being conducted than they do to join formal classes. Usually one or more occasions such as a craft exhibit, folk-dance exhibition, or tumbling demonstration are arranged during the season. Participation in these special events is usually restricted to members who have attained a certain degree of skill or who are willing to rehearse regularly in preparation for them.

PLAYGROUND CLUBS. Nature study, puppetry, and gardening are activities which are often organized on a club basis. When a leader finds that several children have a great interest in nature, for example, he knows that this will take on added significance for the individual children if it is shared in a nature club. He also knows that the organization of the club will tend to arouse the curiosity of other children. So a nature club is formed, officers are elected, and tentative plans are considered for the season's activities. These plans must be elastic, but the program becomes more purposeful when it is decided that the club will conduct nature hikes, make collections, label the trees on the playground, conduct a pet show, or sponsor a birdhouse-building contest. The playground leader attends the regular meetings of the club and supervises its various activities. He also encourages the members to continue their study of nature between meetings and away from the playground. Enlistment of a qualified volunteer to serve as club adviser helps assure its success.

Interest is the primary qualification for membership in playground clubs, and as a rule all playground children are free to participate in most of their activities.

THE CIRCUS OR FESTIVAL. Outstanding examples of the special events which are arranged from time to time are a circus or a festival to provide the climax to the playground season. Sometimes this is a city-wide event, but there is a growing tendency for each playground to conduct its own closing program. This type of feature involves cooperative planning on the part of the leaders and many playground groups; and since a period of careful preparation is required, plans must be made weeks in advance. Preparations involve the planning of the program and the selection and training of the participating groups. Additional steps include the preparing of posters and other announcements; providing the necessary equipment, costumes, and properties; securing a permit for a parade; and arranging for seating facilities, lights, ushers, programs, and police protection. A city-wide event necessitates a rather complex organization because playgrounds must be assigned their part in the program, transportation has to be provided, and arrangements must be made to care for large numbers of children at the place where the event is held.

Responsibility for the circus preparations is often shared by a committee of playground children, with subcommittees made responsible for specific features. Posters announcing the event are prepared by the arts group, animals for the parade constructed in a handcraft class, and costumes made in a sewing group. Tumbling and acrobatic stunts, folk dances, dramatic skits, music, and other features demonstrate regular playground activities. Because the circus affects so many children and includes so many events, there is some danger that it will be permitted to dominate the regular play activities, that undue emphasis will be laid upon circus preparations, and that children will be urged to participate in circus projects when they prefer to take part in other activities. These undesirable results can be avoided by intelligent advance planning.

Few features in the recreation program furnish greater enjoyment to participants and spectators alike than does the closing special event of the playground. It enables many children to take part, and they enjoy the opportunity which the occasion affords for dressing up and performing before their parents and friends. The circus or play festival is an effective and integrating project which serves as a culmination of the normal summer activities and gives the public a review of the playground program. Many adults enjoy assisting the leaders and children in staging events of this kind. For these reasons it is essential to make plans carefully, check all details thoroughly, and conduct the circus in a manner which brings satisfaction to participants and spectators alike and credit to the playground authorities.

Themes of closing festivals or other special events successfully carried out include "The United Nations," "Wings of the World," "Hobo-Gypsy Day," "All-American Pageant," "Indian Summer," "Days of '49," and a "Mother Goose Party."

CONDUCTING INDOOR ACTIVITIES

The methods of organizing and conducting activities in the recreation building or indoor center differ in many respects from those used on the playground. Many of the individuals using the center are young people and adults, whereas the playground is attended primarily by children. Many adults have definite recreation interests, but they do not make them known so readily as children do. They tend to be less willing to mingle with strangers, to try out new activities, and to join recreation groups. Because the playground is an open, out-of-door area visible to all who pass by, affording opportunities for informal recreation, there is a greater tendency to drop in at the playground than to visit the indoor center. Activities in the latter tend to be more highly specialized because the indoor-center season is longer, and it is therefore possible to organize more elaborate projects and more specialized groups, which can prove successful only if carried on over a considerable period.

Many adults come to a center after a hard day's work feeling somewhat fatigued and desiring relaxation, whereas most children come to the playground to engage in strenuous play activities. The weather is a less important factor in center programs, inasmuch as the activities are carried on indoors. Because adults are commonly charged a fee for indoor activities, attendance is generally more regular at the indoor center than at the playground, where most activities are free. Another difference affecting program planning at indoor centers is the fact that many of the leaders are part-time workers responsible only for a specific phase of the program, whereas most playground workers, at least during the summer months, give full time to the program. Some of these differences between conditions on the playground and at the indoor center help to explain the differences in organization methods.

Types of Center Activities. One method of classifying indoor-center activities is to group them according to the way in which they are organized and carried on. Informal, continuous, self-directing activities are provided in the rooms devoted to reading, quiet games, table tennis, or watching television. Drama, chess, nature study, or hobbies are conducted on a club basis, although some clubs have a wide range of interests. Class organization is used for activities involving instruction such as tap dancing, millinery, public speaking, or certain kinds of crafts.

Fathers and sons prepare for the fishing season in this fly-casting class (Courtesy of Board of Park Commissioners, Wichita, Kans.).

Athletics are carried on by teams organized in the center or formed outside but permitted to use the center's facilities. The center program also includes activities to which the entire neighborhood is invited, such as holiday celebrations, parties, social dances, and demonstrations. Methods of organizing a few of these activities will be considered briefly. A detailed discussion of indoor-center operation is found in Chapter 18.

Informal Activities. Organization of informal activities consists primarily of providing the facilities and equipment, of maintaining a hospitable and attractive atmosphere, and of assuring to all who visit the center a cordial welcome and a pleasurable recreation experience. Through the game room, reading room, or lobby, many individuals get their first impression of the center. If they enjoy their experience and meet congenial people, they are likely to return and ultimately to participate in other features of the center program. The director therefore encourages visitors to use the equipment, provides instruction in its use when necessary, helps the newcomers to make the acquaintance of others and to join in activities with them, finds out their interests, and encourages them to join congenial groups and to take part in center activities.

Clubs. Clubs play an important role in the center program. They differ from many other center groups in that they usually have officers and a constitution, keep attendance records, charge dues, and set up qualifications for membership. Most center clubs meet weekly, and a suitable room is assigned for their exclusive use during these meeting periods. Some clubs devote themselves to a particular interest which provides the basis for the organization; others consist of neighborhood groups who just want to do things together and to belong to some group. Different leadership methods are used in organizing and conducting these two types of clubs.

THE SPECIAL-INTEREST CLUB. The special-interest club is often started by the center director because several people have expressed a desire for a particular activity, whether it be bird study, model aircraft, science, or photography. Sometimes a special program or lecture at the center or an event of local or national significance gives rise to a desire to form a club to study a particular subject or to engage in an activity. Before the club is organized, announcements are posted conspicuously in the center and are made at meetings of center groups and at neighborhood gatherings. Recruits are enlisted from those taking part in the informal activities or belonging to the general-interest groups. When a club is being organized, it is customary for a member of the center staff to be assigned as leader or counselor, depending upon the type of group and the age of its members.

The degree of organization desirable varies with the size of the group, its primary purpose, and the ages and abilities of its members. Formal organization procedure is less important in the special-interest club than in the club formed around a natural neighborhood group. Details are worked out by the group in consultation with the leader, subject to modification as the club develops. The success of the club program depends in large measure upon the extent to which it reflects the genuine interests and desires of the members and affords them opportunity for active participation in the particular activity around which interest centers. A leader skilled in this particular field is necessary; in an adult club he may be chosen from within the group. A fairly definite program with specific objectives can often be worked out for this type of club.

THE GENERAL-INTEREST CLUB. The club formed around some natural motivation or group consciousness usually has a different origin from the special-interest club. The group is often formed outside the center by the members themselves, and its first contact with the center director is when it seeks the use of center facilities. On the other hand, the suggestion that a group of boys, girls, or young people in the neighborhood form a club and make use of the center may originate with the director or with individuals taking part in the center program. In any case a leader is assigned to assist the group in developing its club organization and membership and to help the members plan and carry on a program based upon their common interests. Young people like this type of club; adults are more likely to join a group formed to engage in a specific activity.

The club members are usually brought together by common factors of age, national background, class, or neighborhood, and they are held together by a strong sense of group interest and loyalty. They are anxious to do things together; the particular activity in which they engage is of secondary importance. Unlike the special-activity club—where the chief interest of the members centers about a specific activity, whether it is bowling, debating, checkers, or boat building—the desires of its members often must be discovered or stimulated by the club leader. Skilled leadership is required in selecting activities which will enlist the continuing interest of club members and in developing projects which afford progressively satisfying participation.

The objectives in organizing such a club are to preserve the natural group relationships and to afford opportunities for the individual members to participate in constructive, joyous recreation activities with the group. The club leader has a real responsibility, however, not only for maintaining the group but also for guiding its members into activities outside the club which may have special value for them. A boy who shows a special aptitude for music is therefore encouraged to join one of the music groups, and a girl who has unusual artistic ability is helped to find an opportunity for developing it. In some instances it may even be advisable to suggest that an individual drop out of the club entirely if it is clear that he will gain more from some other activity or group. The club leader needs to recognize the limitations of the small, exclusive club and to bring its members into contact with a variety of personalities, interests, and group activities afforded by the center. One means of accomplishing this is by arranging events in which a number of clubs cooperate, such as a father-and-son dinner.

Community Nights. In marked contrast to the indoor center's clubs and classes, composed of comparatively small groups, are the events conducted for the entire community. In many centers a social recreation evening is held regularly every week or two for the persons attending the center and also for the people of the neighborhood. Some community nights take the form of a music festival, Christmas pageant, hobby show, or gymnasium demonstration presented by center groups; others, such as a dance or play night, are designed to secure participation by all who attend. Some programs include both features. The special events are usually arranged by center groups such as drama clubs, athletic teams, or music organizations; sometimes they are sponsored by an interclub or center council. The preparation for these events is a factor in planning the programs of the individual clubs and affords occasions for cooperation between the various center groups. If properly planned and well conducted, these features serve to inform the neighborhood about the center and to enlist recruits for the center activities.

In planning and publicizing these special programs as well as the regular community-night features such as dances and parties, the most effective means of informing the residents of a particular neighborhood are utilized. In selecting the best time for holding the programs, other neighborhood events and the habits of the people are considered. Besides preparing an attractive, well-presented program, the director must make sure that people receive a cordial welcome, that facilities are provided for checking wraps, that the room where the event is held has a suitable temperature and adequate seating facilities, that the program starts and stops at a reasonable hour, and that the people are given some opportunity to participate. In some neighborhoods where parents cannot attend these programs unless they bring their young children, a leader conducts play activities for the children in another room while the community programs are being carried on in the auditorium or gymnasium.

ORGANIZING COMMUNITY SPORTS PROGRAMS

In most cities sports attract a larger number of individuals of all ages and of both sexes than any other type of recreation activity. They require special areas and facilities, include widely differing types of activities, and involve many forms of competition. The organization of the sports program is therefore an important and complicated procedure. It must provide for the varying ages and skills of the players, furnish opportunity for those who wish to participate informally and those who desire highly organized competition, assure the maximum use of areas and facilities, take into account not only the programs at the individual centers and areas but the promotion of city-wide activities, and include individual and group sports as well as team games. Much has been written on the problems involved in organizing and conducting athletic games and sports, so only two aspects of sports organization will be mentioned here —city-wide organization and the promotion of individual sports. Several municipal sports programs are described in Chapter 21.

Adult City-wide League Organization. In initiating a city-wide organization in a particular team game, a meeting is usually called by the recreation department to which all interested groups and all existing teams are invited to send representatives. At the meeting the advisability of organizing one or more leagues is discussed; and if the interest warrants, plans are made for the setting up of such leagues on a basis which will assure keen interest and satisfactory play. Teams may be classified according to a common factor such as industries, churches, clubs, or neighborhoods, or they may be grouped on the basis of skill. League organization involves the creation of a more or less formal association, council, or committee to assume responsibility for working out the many details and for conducting the leagues. Such a group is comprised largely of representatives of the various teams, with a member of the department staff serving as secretary and adviser.

Details for which this body is responsible include the grouping of teams into leagues, adoption of rules governing eligibility and other conditions of play, determination of the length of the playing season, arrangement of team schedules, provision for the filing and consideration of protests, selection of capable officials, fixing and collection of entry fees, disposition of funds, and the conduct of a postseason interleague championship series. Since a large degree of democratic control within the leagues is desirable, major responsibility for determining their policies and administering their activities rests with the team representatives. However, since the leagues are a part of the municipal recreation program and use the recreation department's facilities, it is necessary that their actions be subject to its approval. Some recreation departments have taken the initiative, also, in the development of a city-wide sports body, usually a federation of the city-wide organizations in various forms of sport.

Responsibility for initiating athletic leagues and for guiding them throughout their season of play is assigned to a particular member of the recreation department staff, usually the supervisor of athletics. He calls together the team representatives at the beginning of the season, helps them form their organization, and meets with the league committees and officers as they make plans and determine policies. He advises the group as to the department's policies, puts into effect the plans adopted by the group, and assigns the use of fields, courts, or indoor facilities to the various teams at specified times throughout the season. One of his important functions is to arrange training courses for league officials where such action seems necessary. He encourages widespread participation in the sport and assures all interested teams an opportunity to enroll in a league and share the use of the department's facilities.

Individual Sports. One of the most effective methods of stimulating public interest in a particular sport such as badminton, shuffleboard, or skiing is through the organization of a city-wide club or association which undertakes to promote the activity. The recreation department cooperates by helping form the organization, encouraging groups at the public centers to be represented in it, clearing schedules and policies, placing its facilities at the association's disposal for championship and other tournaments, and utilizing new ideas for instruction in and conduct of the activity. A city-wide group of this type can frequently revive a sport, the popularity of which has waned due to lack of adequate promotion. As an example, canoeing in the lakes of a New Jersey county park system was given a new and expanding interest through the formation of canoe clubs which organized regattas and conducted water carnivals.

The recreation department also encourages and facilitates participation in individual sports through the development of centers devoted to a particular activity. A centrally located, well-lighted battery of tennis or horseshoe courts, for example, attracts players from all over the city, is used for important local and intercity matches, and stimulates interest in the sport. Classes, or "clinics," are formed for group instruction in golf, tennis, archery, or some other sport, either free or at a nominal charge. Such classes are welcomed by people who have been deterred from playing a game because of their lack of skill. The rental of equipment such as golf clubs by the recreation department has encouraged many to try the game who otherwise would have hesitated to do so because they lacked the equipment.

Hiking. This differs from most forms of sport in that the element of competition is very small and it requires no special equipment, expense, or skill on the part of the participant. Most municipal hiking clubs are recruited from all parts of the city and are composed of both men and women. Unlike most of the activities previously described, hiking is not dependent upon facilities provided by the recreation department, although it sometimes makes use of them. It is one of the few outdoor activities that can be engaged in the year round. A few aspects of its organization are illustrated by the experience of local hiking clubs.

One of the best known municipal hiking groups is the Minnehikers, affiliated with the Minneapolis Park Board. It was organized in 1920, when a group of park officials and others interested in the out-of-doors began a series of Sunday afternoon hikes, each of which included some part of the city park system. Out of this small beginning grew the club. As the demand for more hikes increased, several Sunday hikes a month were held, and Wednesday night hikes were added to the schedule. Hikes are now conducted throughout the year, and the club program is varied with skating and sleigh-ride parties, canoe trips, week-end outings, yearly two-week vacation trips, dances, and other social occasions. At first all programs were arranged and led by a representative of the park board, but gradually a share of the responsibility for planning and conducting them was turned over to the members of the group, and finally a committee was appointed to take charge of the schedule. The club has grown in membership and in the scope of its activities so that now it has

Learning and fun are by-products of a nature hike in Myakka State Park (Courtesy of Florida Park Service).

a board of directors and several standing and special committees. The member of the park board staff who is responsible for working with the hiking group serves as executive secretary of the club board.

There are several reasons for the success of municipal hiking clubs. Although they are organized on a democratic basis and the planning is in the hands of the club members, continuous leadership and guidance are provided by a worker on the recreation department staff. The department office usually serves as the club's headquarters. The activity is inexpensive, membership fees are low, and even in the case of the special outings costs are kept at a minimum. Social events and the publication of a club yearbook help to maintain interest and encourage sociability between hikes. The fact that most hikes average only about six miles makes it possible for all who are interested to take part; occasionally more strenuous outings are arranged for members who prefer them. There is a tendency for a hiking club to remain at about the same size because when it becomes much larger than forty it becomes unwieldy and cannot be accommodated in a single bus or served meals quickly. The hiking club is an excellent example of the type of organization which crosses neighborhood, age, and natural group lines and which draws together people with an enthusiastic interest in a simple form of recreation.

SPECIAL COMMUNITY EVENTS

Most recreation department activities are carried on more or less regularly throughout a season or the entire year. Just as feature events are scheduled from time to time at the playgrounds and centers, however, special programs are also arranged which serve the entire city. Some of these are organized entirely by the recreation department; others are projects in which many agencies cooperate. Because these activities present unusual problems of organization and the methods of conducting them are different from others mentioned in this chapter, a few are described briefly.

The Halloween Celebration. Typical of the projects which attract large numbers of people is the community-wide Halloween celebration. In the small communities it may be organized as a single unit; in larger cities the celebration is conducted on a neighborhood or district basis. Features commonly include a parade in costume for boys and girls of all ages, with appropriate prizes for costumes of various types; a huge bonfire, which may provide the incentive for a clean-up campaign; stunts; and singing around the bonfire. Following the parade the participants may assemble in a large auditorium for motion pictures, games, music, and refreshments. Some communities confine their festivities to indoor activities and provide separate programs for different age groups. Such a celebration furnishes the thrills and excitement which the children desire and consumes the energy which otherwise might be spent in destruction of property. It is at once a joy for the participants, a spectacle for the assembly, and a civic asset. Its success requires effective advance publicity, a wisely selected route for the parade, adequate policing, careful planning of the events following the parade, preparation for providing and serving refreshments, and competent leadership. Most important of all, the entire celebration must be carried on in a spirit of hilarity appropriate to the holiday.

Christmas Caroling. In several cities the recreation department organizes and conducts a community Christmas caroling campaign. Preparations for a caroling program bring into play the active cooperation of large numbers of people. For this reason it is often jointly undertaken by a group of community agencies, even though the recreation department assumes major responsibility for the project. The care required in preparing adequately for such an event is apparent from the following steps which need to be taken: enlisting the participation of vocal groups, especially church choirs, or forming groups in the various community

All set for the annual Halloween parade (Courtesy of Greensburg, Pa., Recreation Board).

agencies or neighborhoods; securing leaders and meeting places for rehearsals; dividing the city into districts and assigning choral groups to districts; listing by districts the names and addresses of shut-ins and institutions; selecting carols to be learned and sung; providing music and song sheets; furnishing transportation for caroling groups; arranging for publicity and preparing costumes for the carolers. Paid workers with the recreation department and other agencies usually carry the major responsibility for the campaign, but many of the tasks are performed by volunteers.

Nationality Programs. The racial and cultural heritages of the various nationalities represented in American life have contributed to community recreation programs and have been integrated in our American culture. The simple folk dances, songs, and games of other countries have long been a feature of playground activities and closing festivals. Many communities hold folk festivals or fairs for adults, frequently in connection with citizenship ceremonies such as those held on I Am an American Day. These range from simple programs of national songs and dances to more extensive plans which also include exhibits of national arts, crafts, costumes, and other treasures and the serving of special national foods. The cooperation of nationality groups is enlisted in planning and conducting the events. Through this type of program the recreation department can draw out hidden talents, develop public respect for the various racial groups, enlist participation on the part of many who otherwise have no share in the recreation program, encourage foreign-born groups to perpetuate their native recreation heritage, and afford entertainment to large numbers of spectators.

THE INCIDENTAL USE OF RECREATION ACTIVITIES

Thus far in this chapter it has been assumed that the activities described were organized to meet a major interest of the individuals taking part in them. Thus baseball leagues are arranged for the baseball teams; archery is organized for the archery enthusiasts; the hiking club affords recreation to persons interested in hiking. Most of the recreation department's activities are organized to serve directly the particular interests of individuals and groups. At the same time, the recreation leader needs to appreciate the ways in which simple recreation forms may contribute to activities of a totally different type.

For example, music may be introduced in an indoor center, apart from the special music groups and projects. Gymnasium activities such as mass gymnastics, marching, or dancing are enlivened by the use of a piano or by singing on the part of the participants. Community singing and solo or group numbers between the acts of a play tend to bind the audience together and to make the intervals pass quickly and pleasantly. Singing at dinners or club meetings and radio concerts in craft or quiet game rooms are other examples of the informal use of music to enrich recreation activities. The skillful leader is continually alert to take advantage of such opportunities. The incidental use of such activities in the program is sometimes more successful than introduction of the activities on an organized basis. Group singing may be more spontaneous and enjoyable on a boat ride, on a hike, or around a campfire than in a scheduled meeting where the group is brought together for a period of singing. Informal occasions may prove the means of arousing interest in activities of a more formal type.

The few illustrations presented in this chapter suggest the variety of problems faced by recreation departments in organizing and conducting different phases of the recreation program and describe organization methods which have proved successful. Additional detailed information on the organization of many types of recreation activity will be presented in later chapters.

PART FIVE

THE OPERATION OF AREAS
AND FACILITIES

Leadership, areas and facilities, and activities are the principal elements of the municipal recreation program. The program in most cities consists largely of activities furnished at playgrounds, recreation buildings, indoor centers, golf courses, bathing beaches, swimming pools, and other facilities operated by personnel of the recreation department. The operation of these properties involves consideration of many factors and gives rise to many problems, the solution of which requires the use of divergent methods and procedures. Part Five deals briefly with some of these factors and problems and with methods of dealing with them.

The programs at these areas and facilities, especially the playgrounds and recreation buildings, comprise a great variety of activities. Only brief mention can be made of them in the three chapters which follow. Detailed descriptions of many of these activities are contained in Part Six, which deals with special program features and city-wide services.

17. THE OPERATION OF PLAYGROUNDS

The NEIGHBORHOOD playground, as indicated in Chapter 11, is the type of area designed to afford a wide range of enjoyable and desirable activities for children of elementary school age and limited activities for preschool children, youth, adults, and families living in the neighborhood. It was noted that from 4 to 8 acres are required for a playground which provides a wading pool, small children's area, shelter house, apparatus area, small section for older adults, some landscaping, section for outdoor crafts, drama, and quiet games, and space for low organized games, team games, and such games as tennis, handball, and horseshoes. A playground is needed in every neighborhood, and a location at or adjoining the elementary school site is generally desirable. The operation of playgrounds is a major feature of most community recreation programs.

THE FUNCTION OF THE PLAYGROUND

The ideal playground is a place where children have a chance to enjoy themselves completely, where they may take part in many activities which appeal to them and which, for the most part, cannot be carried on elsewhere. It affords not only fun but safety—an important factor in modern city life. On the playground children build up healthy bodies and physical vigor by spending hours in the air and sunlight in varied forms of active play. Good habits and attitudes are developed under the guidance of able leaders, and sportsmanship and cooperation are put into practice through participation in team games. Well-equipped, ample, and properly located playgrounds under competent leadership encourage wholesome, constructive activity and thereby tend to reduce juvenile delinquency. They also afford centers for family play and neighborhood events.

It must be admitted that many playgrounds contribute little in fun, safety, health, and character because they fail to meet conditions which are essential if a playground is to yield definite and lasting satisfactions. A few of the characteristics of the ideal playground are:

1. It is large enough to afford opportunities for all the children in the neighborhood to engage in their favorite play activities.

2. It is attractive and well designed and affords a pleasant setting for play.
3. Boys and girls can let off steam there and play without repression.
4. Children of every age and girls as well as boys are given equal consideration.
5. A variety of skills is developed, and children with all degrees of ability have a chance to play.
6. Varied interests are considered—music, dramatics, crafts, nature, athletics.
7. It gives an opportunity for making new acquaintances.
8. There is always something interesting for all to do.
9. Fair play is the rule; all have equal opportunity.
10. Safety and healthful participation are assured.
11. Children are given opportunities for service and training in leadership.
12. Family play and neighborhood gatherings are encouraged.
13. Older adults can enjoy limited forms of recreation without interference.

The playground "should intensify the natural functions of play, offering the richest possible experiences of sensation, creation, socialization, physical development, aesthetics." [1] The purpose of playground administration is to make sure that it fulfills these functions for the benefit of every child, including the physically handicapped, to bring into reality the possibilities which the playground affords for fun, health, growth, and good citizenship. It further aims to make the playground a vital recreation center for the entire neighborhood.

CITY-WIDE PLAYGROUND ORGANIZATION

Organization of a city-wide playground system or program involves many procedures such as selecting the playgrounds at which programs are to be conducted under leadership; fixing the length of season, hours per day, and days per week when leadership is to be provided at each; determining the personnel required and selecting and assigning the staff; providing equipment, supplies, and play materials; arranging for the maintenance of the grounds and buildings; and developing a general program and a plan for administering and supervising it. Uniform methods cannot be used in all localities or for all types of playgrounds, but the local plan of organization must be worked out in such a way as to secure the maximum service and benefits from the areas, facilities, personnel, and funds available.

[1] Nelson Van Judah and Robert N. Marona, "What Should a Playground Be?" unpublished master's thesis, Pratt Institute, New York, 1957.

Selection of Playgrounds. In selecting the playgrounds at which programs are to be provided, an attempt is made to serve each section of the city. Neighborhoods in greatest need of a program merit primary consideration. Normally the larger, well-equipped playgrounds are selected first, but small, inadequate areas are sometimes used in order that play opportunities may be provided within walking distance of the younger children. In some neighborhoods it is necessary to operate two playgrounds, one of which may be suitable only for small children's play, the other affording facilities used only by older children.

Among the questions to be answered in determining the number of playgrounds to be conducted are the following: Is it better to open a few large playgrounds with a staff which will enable a well-balanced program to be provided at each or to open many playgrounds even though the program provided will be limited? Is it better to open a few playgrounds during a long season or to open more playgrounds and reduce the period of operation? Is it desirable to operate some playgrounds for only one or two sessions per day in order that other playgrounds, in neighborhoods where the need is greater, may have a longer daily program? Local conditions alone can provide the answers.

Length of Season. Most playgrounds are conducted during the summer, when children have the greatest amount of free time. In many cities playgrounds are conducted under leadership only during the summer months. In others they are also open under leadership for several weeks during the spring and fall, but in most large cities programs are conducted throughout the year. Year-round operation is especially desirable where weather conditions permit outdoor play during most of the year, where recreation opportunities in the homes or other neighborhood agencies are lacking, and where the playground affords suitable indoor facilities. The length of the summer season is influenced by that of the school vacation; in general, the playgrounds open on a full schedule soon after the schools close and remain open until the end of the vacation.

Playground Hours. The hours during which playgrounds are open under leadership vary from season to season. During the school year the playgrounds are usually open only during the afternoon; but if they are part of a combined indoor-outdoor center, leadership is sometimes provided both afternoon and evening, especially if outdoor facilities are lighted for evening use. Leadership is occasionally provided on nonschool grounds in the morning, when activities are conducted for very young children or people beyond school age. During the summer months many playgrounds are conducted morning, afternoon, and evening, although in some southern cities activities are not promoted during the hot afternoon period.

The playground hours vary not only from season to season but from one playground to another. In some neighborhoods the needs of the children can be met adequately if the playground is open only a few hours a day. In congested, substandard neighborhoods, however, there is usually need for playgrounds to be open continuously from early morning until late in the evening. Occasionally, owing to the fact that many families seek recreation elsewhere, playgrounds are closed or operated with a limited staff on Saturdays. Regular programs are carried on in few cities on Sundays, although most playgrounds are open for informal play.

THE PLAYGROUND STAFF

Because leadership is the most important factor in successful playground operation, the selection of the staff is a major responsibility of the recreation authorities. Workers who have a share in the playground program are the recreation superintendent, special-activity supervisors, playground directors and assistants, and general- and special-activity leaders. The personnel required for a playground system also includes office and maintenance workers, and in a large city one or more general supervisors are needed.

The duties and qualifications of persons serving in the leadership positions listed above and methods of selecting and training them were pointed out in preceding chapters. In most cities the playground staff consists largely of persons employed for the summer months only or on a part-time basis during the school year, but increasingly cities employ personnel on a full-time, year-round basis who combine service on the playground with other departmental duties.

Requirements of a Small City. Every playground system requires some degree of supervision in addition to the leadership assigned to the individual grounds. The superintendent of recreation provides this if there is a year-round recreation program; otherwise a supervisor of playgrounds is employed on a seasonal basis. He recruits, organizes, and trains the playground staff, maps out a general program, and oversees the work at all the playgrounds. In the small city the only other essential leaders are the playground directors and their various assistants. As a rule, however, one or more special-activity supervisors or leaders are employed, sometimes on a part-time basis, to help with particular phases of the program. Unless arrangements are made for the upkeep of the playgrounds by another department, maintenance workers must be employed. An office worker is usually needed, at least part of the time, to serve as supply clerk and keep the playground records.

The Staff in a Larger City. Since the executive in a community with many playgrounds is unable to supervise personally the work at all centers, the city is divided into geographical districts, and a general supervisor is assigned to each. He usually serves ten or more playgrounds and visits them frequently to observe the work being done, to ensure compliance with department policies, to arrange interplayground and city-wide projects, and to help the directors with their programs, special problems, and reports.

Picture books and stories fascinate the very young in Central Park, New York, as everywhere (Courtesy of the New York Public Library).

One or more supervisors of special activities such as arts and crafts, nature, music, or drama are also employed, the number depending upon the kinds of activity to be featured and the ability and experience of the workers in the system. If, for example, a nature program is to be promoted and if the playground leaders know little about nature activities, a nature supervisor is essential. To serve the increasing popular interest in the acquisition of recreation skills, the playground staff often includes one or more special-activity leaders, such as a tennis instructor or a teacher of some particular form of craft or music activity, who organize and instruct groups on the different playgrounds. In addition to the leadership staff, maintenance personnel are required as well as clerical workers to care for playground supplies, reports, and office records.

The Staff on the Individual Playground. It is desirable that each playground have a director with full responsibility for the area and its operation. This position is generally open to both men and women; if the director is a man, the assistant director is a women, and vice versa. At least two leaders should be on duty at all times. A playground that meets space and facility standards requires a larger staff if more than a minimum program is desired. Where three workers are employed, it is possible to arrange their schedules so that two of them are on the playground during each morning, afternoon, and evening session. The training, experience, and abilities of workers are taken into consideration in making assignments. Thus, if the man is experienced in conducting games and athletics, an attempt is made to assign to the same ground other leaders who are skilled in arts, crafts, drama, or other forms of activity. Since the more competent, experienced directors are usually assigned to the larger playgrounds which require more workers, assistants and recreation leaders have an opportunity to secure valuable training by working under their direction. In addition to the special skills, aptitudes, and personalities of workers, the characteristics and requirements of different neighborhoods are taken into account in making assignments in order to assure a maximum degree of success.

No hard and fast rule can be applied to the division of work on a playground, but usually the man conducts most of the activities for the older boys, and the woman works with the small children and the older girls. Special activities such as nature, drama, or crafts are cared for by the individual worker who is best qualified to conduct them, and feature events are jointly planned and conducted by all the workers. Responsibilities are fairly divided and determined by the director, who takes into account the qualifications of each worker. Time schedules of the workers are arranged so that either the director or the assistant director is present at the playground during all periods.

Junior Leaders. Children constantly practice leadership on the playground, and capable playground workers are alert to the opportunities for developing qualities of leadership and for directing them into proper channels. Few playgrounds have an adequate staff; and where junior leaders are used, part of the workers' time is released for other service. At the same time boys and girls secure valuable training and experience through performing duties, making decisions, exercising judgment and control, and leading other children in play activities.

Types of Junior Service. Children assist with the playground activities in a variety of ways. An older boy helps in coaching or managing a team; a girl who is skillful in some form of crafts conducts the activity for a group of younger girls; a child who has a special interest in storytelling or nature conducts the storytelling hour or leads a nature club. More common types of junior service are collecting game materials, guarding children in the wading pool, marking game courts, or taking the attendance.

Service is usually rendered informally by children whose desire to help has been recognized and used by the playground leader; but junior organizations such as a safety patrol, junior police, or junior leaders' club are sometimes organized. Such formal groups require expert handling; otherwise, they may require too much of the workers' time, limit service opportunities to only a few children, benefit those children who need them least, and interfere with the members' own play life. Under wise leadership these groups render valuable playground service, provide excellent leadership training, encourage self-government, and win an important place in the playground program.

PROGRAM PLANNING

In outlining the general playground program for a city, the executive includes the activities and events that have demonstrated their popularity and that promise to bring the maximum value and enjoyment to the greatest number. He keeps in mind the abilities and qualifications of his workers, the amount and type of supervision to be provided, and the funds and facilities available. With the assistance of the staff he develops a general plan for the entire playground system, including intraplayground, interplayground, and city-wide activities. This provides a framework upon which the individual playground programs are built, each of which is adapted to meet the special interests and needs of the neighborhood served.

Instructions governing programs and program planning issued to all workers at the beginning of the playground season indicate the objectives to be sought by the program and general methods of attaining them. They point out the types of activities which directors are expected to carry on regularly from day to day or from week to week. They list a number of special events, tournaments, and activities which are to be conducted at all playgrounds or from which the directors may select the ones best suited to their individual grounds. They indicate the times when the special-activity supervisors and leaders are to visit the playgrounds, the special features to be arranged by every playground—such as a weekly community program or a closing festival—and the interplayground or city-wide events. These instructions enable the directors of the individual playgrounds to plan their programs in such a way that they conform with the general pattern followed by all the playgrounds of the city, even though they are adapted to meet the needs of the individual neighborhoods.

Advance Planning Essential. At first glance the idea of a program prepared in advance might seem out of place on the playground, to which people come voluntarily to do only what they want to do. Yet only by planning can the playground's facilities be fully utilized, the varied play interests be served, and the leadership staff render the maximum service. The fullest use of popular facilities such as softball diamonds is secured only if they are set aside for the use of teams or informal groups during definite periods. Without a program, interests like nature or music are likely to be neglected. Children look forward eagerly to special events such as a picnic or festival, but unless arrangements are made well in advance, the leaders are swamped with last-minute preparations—with the result that the children do not get as much fun out of the occasions as they should.

As he interprets and supervises the program, the executive urges each leader to use his resourcefulness in adapting old forms of play and in devising new ones. He insists that the worker provide a variety of activities to meet the needs of all the children but does not require the same projects to be carried on at all playgrounds. He expects that program schedules will be adjusted when desirable. A playground group is not required to stop its activity the moment an assigned period has been completed. If the nature period is scheduled for Wednesday afternoon but on Tuesday a rare bird is seen or a locust emerges from its shell, the wise leader considers the children's nature interest more important than the prearranged program. Through supervisors' reports, staff meetings, and weekly playground reports, the executive supplements his own observations as to how the program is progressing. Questionnaires submitted to the playground workers at the close of the season yield practical suggestions which prove useful in planning the program for the following year.

Factors Affecting Planning. Uniform playground programs or play projects cannot be developed at all units of a playground system even if this were advisable. Many activities which are possible on a 5-acre playground cannot be considered on a small schoolyard. The playground with three or more workers offers greater possibilities for a varied program than one with a single worker. Several of the general planning factors mentioned in Chapter 15 affect the operation of the individual playground and influence the type of program.

The Leaders. If only one worker is present on a playground which serves children of a wide range of ages, he gives most of his time to general supervision of the area. He suggests activities, helps start games, and assures safety and fair opportunity for all; but he cannot spend much time in working with small groups. When two leaders are present, however, one can conduct special events or instruct groups engaged in such activities as arts and crafts or nature while the other gives general supervision to the playground. When three or more leaders are available, a richer and more diversified program is possible. The qualifications of the workers also influence the type of program because leaders tend to emphasize those activities with which they are most familiar. When special-activity supervisors or leaders visit a playground regularly, they can develop major projects which otherwise would not be possible.

Learning to play together on a grassy city playground (Courtesy of Los Angeles Department of Recreation and Parks).

The Playgrounds. Small playgrounds afford few opportunities for team games which appeal strongly to the boys over twelve, but they may meet admirably the interests of the younger children. Large playgrounds, on the other hand, if properly developed, make possible a varied program and attract the older boys and girls. Unless reasonably adequate facilities for activities like drama, music, and arts and crafts are available on a playground, it is difficult to carry on such projects successfully. A playground with limited facilities also gives children who attend it a handicap when participating in interplayground or city-wide activities. Where space and equipment are inadequate, the leaders need greater resourcefulness in adapting games and in discovering activities which can be carried on satisfactorily.

The Children. Playground programs are built around the interests of children—are child-centered and not activity-centered. Leaders justifiably stress activities which have a wide appeal and in which a large number of children can be served, but the special interests of the individual child must not be neglected. Small-group activities requiring considerable guidance are conspicuous in the program where adequate and competent leadership is available.

The ages of the children attending a playground affect not only the activities provided but the length of the play periods, for the younger children have a shorter interest span. Fewer children of preschool age attend playgrounds in neighborhoods with single-family houses than in high-density areas. The economic status of the neighborhood may also influence the playground program. In high-income residential neighborhoods, activities involving the purchase of expensive materials or individual equipment may be feasible, but in the poorer sections children cannot afford to take part in such activities. Trips or outings are a regular playground feature in some communities, but owing to their cost they are not practicable in others.

A Few Planning Methods. Certain principles and methods described in an earlier chapter have been found useful in planning programs of all kinds, but a few of them are especially applicable to playgrounds.

Variety of Play Interests. The successful playground leader realizes that children like variety, that they have widely different interest spans, that all children do not like the same activities, that some forms of play have a much wider appeal than others, and that strenuous and quiet activities should be interspersed in the program. Variety is essential in order to attract a large number of different children and to sustain their interest after they come to the playground. Experienced leaders do not start more major projects than they believe can be carried through successfully, but those selected include several types of activities and furnish outlets for a variety of play interests.

Various Organization Methods. One effective device for introducing variety into the program is to utilize different methods of organizing activities. Thus children's desire to increase their skill in a game like jacks, shuffleboard, or paddle tennis can be stimulated by organizing tournaments in which participants are classified according to age, ability, or sex. Competition between mixed teams or teams composed of brothers and sisters arouses unusual interest; groups with a common interest are helped to organize clubs or teams, and apparatus play is stimulated through the teaching of stunts. Playground leaders make the program more purposeful by relating activities to a definite objective or event. A pushmobile or kite contest affords an incentive for boys to make pushmobiles or kites and thus provides a valuable craft project during the weeks preceding the event. Activities that require little preparation appeal to young children, but older boys and girls will spend weeks getting ready for a special event.

In planning and conducting the program, a balance is sought between individual and group projects, competitive and cooperative activities, free and organized play, informal sports and tournaments, clubs and open groups, pick-up games and league play, routine and special feature events.

Interrelating Activities. The most absorbing and valuable playground projects involve the cooperation of different groups and bring together diversified play interests. Many playground activities are admittedly unrelated to one another. For example, handball played by fifteen-year-old boys has no relation to apparatus play or the little tots' story hour. Birdhouse construction, however, is not only related to the study of nature but involves craft and service interests. Play production offers opportunity for creative writing, acting, the study of speech, designing costumes, scenery, and posters, and constructing scenery, properties, and lighting equipment. Program features such as the festival or playday not only have value to the many children who participate but encourage mutual understanding and cooperation on the part of the workers on the individual playground.

PLAYGROUND PROGRAMS

There are three general types of playground programs—daily, weekly, and seasonal—each of which is described in the following pages. Special consideration is given to summer activities, since this is the season when most playgrounds are in operation, but the same principles generally apply in the planning of programs for other seasons.

The Daily Program. The playground day is divided into periods set aside for different kinds of activities for the various age groups for both boys and girls. By following the same general schedule day after day, children learn the times when the activities of special interest to them are carried on. The opening period in the morning is usually one of preparation and informal activity. The midmorning hours are well suited to strenuous activities. The periods before and after lunch are usually devoted to relatively quiet forms of play and to group activities such as crafts and drama. Tournaments, special events, and league games are often scheduled in the middle of the afternoon. The early evening hours are among the busiest, and events are frequently planned in which young people and adults participate.

Classes, clubs, and other groups meeting regularly are scheduled at the hour when most members can be present. At least two and frequently more activities are being carried on at all times; while one worker is with

Table 5. Suggested Daily Summer Playground Program

	Children under 8	Children 8 to 11	Boys and girls over 11
9:00–9:30	Flag raising, getting out equipment, inspecting apparatus and grounds, marking courts, posting announcements		
9:30–9:45	Greeting children, distributing game supplies, organizing groups for morning play		
9:45–10:30	Group games * Apparatus play Sandbox play	Low organized game * Apparatus play	Group and team games * Practice for contests and tournaments
10:30–10:45	No scheduled activity; free play, attendance taken, team games continued		
10:45–11:15	Storytelling * Block building Wading pool play	Handcraft * Tumbling * Quiet games Nature activities *	Folk dancing (girls)* Tumbling * Handcraft * Nature activities *
11:15–11:45	Quiet games Wading pool play	Wading pool play	
11:45–12:00	Call in equipment, clean up grounds		
12:00–1:30	No scheduled activity—one leader present; occasional picnics or wiener roasts, quiet games		
1:30–2:00	Sandbox play Free-play activities Quiet games	Apparatus play Music * Quiet games Storytelling *	Music * Individual games and athletic stunts Sports clinics *
2:00–2:30	Storytelling and story acting * Apparatus play	Preparation for special events * Wading pool play	Practice for league games Preparation for special events * Meetings of clubs and committees *
2:30–2:45	No scheduled activity; free play, attendance taken, preparation for special events and contests		

Table 5. Suggested Daily Summer Playground Program (Continued)

	Children under 8	Children 8 to 11	Boys and girls over 11
2:45–4:15	Singing games Taking part in or watching special events Wading pool play	Contests, tournaments, or special features * Handcraft * Watching league games Wading pool play	Special features, contests, tournaments, or outings * League games Handcraft *
4:15–5:15	Sandbox play Quiet games Apparatus play	Group games * Dramatics * Quiet games Completion of special features * Meetings of clubs and committees Preparation for community night events *	
5:15–5:30	Collecting game materials and playground supplies, checkup on playground		
5:30–6:30	No scheduled activity—one leader present; playground used by young people or adults for team games and informal play		
6:30–8:30	Free play on apparatus and self-organized games Watching special events Quiet games		Informal individual and team games * ("twilight" leagues for young people and adults, special neighborhood programs and demonstrations)

* Activities to which a leader gives more or less continuous supervision.

a group requiring continuous attention, the other is helping with less formal activities. Brief intervals between periods encourage informal play, give leaders an opportunity to prepare for scheduled activities, and avoid crowding of the program. Activity periods for small children are short; craft classes and team games, on the other hand, require considerably more time for satisfactory participation. Some activities such as apparatus or sandbox play may be carried on continuously throughout the day.

A standardized daily playground program is neither feasible nor desirable owing to the varying factors and conditions that have been discussed previously. Table 5, however, illustrates a typical daily playground schedule. It has been set up for a playground at which three leaders are employed—one man and two women, with two workers on duty during each morning, afternoon, and evening session. In cases where two or more activities to which the leaders give direct and continuous supervision are scheduled in a given period, not all the activities are conducted each day. Thus at 9:45 on Monday, Wednesday, and Friday, a worker may conduct group and team games for the boys and girls over eleven; on other days he conducts low organized games for the younger group at this hour. The number of activities that can be carried on successfully depends partly upon the extent to which volunteer leaders are available, either to conduct specific activities or to give general supervision to the playground. The age classification indicated in the schedule, like the program itself, is merely suggestive. Groups formed in such activities as music, drama, and nature commonly include children from eight years of age upward, and children from the two younger groups often join in the same activities.

The Weekly Program. The diversity of interests and activities on the playground makes it impossible with a limited staff to conduct all activities each day. A weekly schedule is therefore needed to supplement the daily program. It indicates the days on which periods will be devoted to crafts, drama, nature, and other activities which require fairly continuous guidance and are usually scheduled two or three times a week. It notes the time when safety or leaders' clubs will meet and when tournaments or special events will be held. There is an advantage in scheduling the special weekly events on the same day each week, and it is common practice to hold all community evening programs on a certain day of the week so people will tend to reserve that time for them. Adjustments in the daily schedule are needed for the weekly staff meeting, the occasional playground outing, and interplayground activities; but in preparing the weekly schedule an attempt is made to fit the activities as closely as possible into the regular daily program.

The suggested weekly program in Table 6 illustrates the scheduling of activities which are not conducted each day and most of which require fairly continuous supervision. This weekly program is closely related to the suggested daily program in Table 5.

The Summer Program. A third type of program deals with the special events that stand out as the highlights of the summer season. These vary with local traditions, interests, and resources, but they often include such events as a water sports day, pageant, hobby exhibit, track and field meet, circus, or festival. Some are related to day-by-day activities and focus attention upon them; others may take the form of an outing or trip to a major-league baseball game. The well-planned summer program furnishes objectives for the regular activities, includes events which ap-

Table 6. Suggested Weekly Summer Playground Program with Three Workers (Two Women and One Man)

	Monday	Tuesday	Wednesday	Thursday	Friday	Saturday
9:45–10:30	Staff meeting 9–10:15	Group games Team games (boys)	Low organized games Team games (girls)	Same as Tuesday	Same as Wednesday	Team games (boys)
10:45–11:45	Handcraft Storytelling	Tumbling Folk dancing	Handcraft Nature activities	Tumbling Folk dancing	Handcraft Storytelling	Nature activities
12:00–1:30		Cookout		Cookout		
1:30–2:30	Club and committee meetings	Music Sports clinics	Storytelling Playground hike	Music Sports clinics	Preparation for feature event	
2:45–4:15	Tournaments and contests	Handcraft League games	Trip to swimming pool or inter-playground event	Handcraft League games		
4:15–5:15	Dramatics Group games	Preparation for special events	Group games	Dramatics Preparation for community night	Special weekly feature event	
6:30–8:30	Twilight-league games	Special events	Twilight-league games	Community night (biweekly)	Twilight-league games	

peal to all ages, and distributes these events throughout the summer in such a way as to prevent overcrowding of the schedule and permit adequate preparation for them.

Occasionally a special theme is selected for the program, which is carried throughout the entire playground season. Programs have been built, for example, around the American Indian or the colonial period, with games, crafts, ceremonials, dances, plays, and other activities related to the particular subject. One city chose the theme "Pan-America," and each playground represented an American country or a section of the United States; another city selected "The United Nations" as its theme, and a different member nation was featured each week on all the playgrounds.

In preparing for the summer, some playground authorities, besides outlining special events to be carried out during the season, select a theme or special designation for each week, suggest the special activities to be carried on, and outline the projects which should be initiated each week in preparation for future events. Such a program helps to focus attention upon desired objectives, secure balance in the program, and assure adequate preparation for special events.

Programs for Other Seasons. The same general principles apply in planning playground programs for other seasons, but in actual practice the problems differ from those during the summer months. While school is in session, most of the children served by playgrounds are busy until midafternoon, and outdoor activities are limited largely to a two- or three-hour session daily. Because children have been in school most of the day, and because climatic conditions are usually suitable for them, vigorous activities play a large part in the programs carried on in the fall, winter, and spring. Events which require long periods of preparation are less satisfactory than intraplayground leagues, contests, tournaments, hiking, low organized games, and seasonal activities such as marbles, skating, and snow games. Programs are frequently hindered by inclement weather, especially where suitable indoor facilities are lacking. Playgrounds operated in connection with buildings or indoor centers usually serve many young people and adults during the evening hours.

SOME FURTHER IMPORTANT ASPECTS OF PLAYGROUND OPERATION

The suitable development of areas, the selection, training, and assignment of a competent staff, and the planning and conduct of a program of interesting activities are primary requisites for a successful playground program. Other factors must be taken into account, however, and many policies and procedures must be adopted in order to assure satisfactory results. A few of them are mentioned briefly.

Safety. Safety is a basic consideration in playground operation, and the well-managed playground is a safe place for children to play. This does not mean that all opportunity for adventure has been eliminated, but continual care is exercised to prevent accidents on play areas where large numbers of children are taking part in a variety of activities. The following are some of the most effective means of assuring safety on the playground:

1. Lay out the playground wisely, with proper locations for the various sections and features, with adequate space for each, with fences, en-

Children learn and practice safety rules on this school playground.

trances, and paths so placed as to reduce hazards. If these conditions do not obtain, the playground needs to be redesigned.
2. Install only equipment and apparatus that is well constructed and safe for the children. High apparatus and deep wading pools are not desirable on the playground because of the hazards arising from their use.
3. Assure proper utilization of the apparatus by teaching correct methods of use and insisting that they be followed. Prohibit all misuse of equipment.
4. Inspect regularly and thoroughly all apparatus and equipment and withdraw it from use immediately when it gives evidence of needing repairs.

5. Prepare and enforce simple rules for game areas. Restrict the playing of games such as horseshoes or the batting of balls to areas set aside for them.
6. Eliminate all hazards such as exposed pipes, unprotected window wells, and poor surfacing, especially under the apparatus.
7. Be vigilant in enforcing safety rules and in preventing dangerous practices, and enlist the cooperation of the children, perhaps through the organization of a junior safety corps.

Playground authorities also have a responsibility for safeguarding and promoting health and for eliminating conditions which might undermine it. To this end they check carefully the condition of the water in the wading pool, maintain buildings and grounds in a sanitary condition, supervise participation in games involving extreme exertion, and are on the watch to prevent children with evidence of infections or contagious diseases from taking part in the playground program.

Playground Accidents. No matter how carefully they are guarded against, accidents are bound to occur, and playground workers must be prepared to act promptly and intelligently whenever there is an accident. Absolutely essential are:

1. A first-aid kit, easily accessible and adequate for all ordinary situations. It should be available at all times, and supplies should be replenished regularly and used only for first-aid purposes.
2. A knowledge of first-aid methods on the part of all playground workers. Often the playground is in charge of a single worker, and he must know what action to take and how to perform it.
3. A knowledge of the procedure to be followed in the case of serious accidents. Local practices differ, but each worker must receive explicit instructions as to what to do in case of an accident requiring more than first-aid treatment. Failure to know and act promptly and to submit accident reports may prove serious.

Problems of Conduct. On the playground all are permitted the greatest possible freedom in the use of facilities and in the choice of activities, provided such freedom does not interfere with the best interests of the entire group. Discipline is essential on the playground, but the need for enforcing it is least evident when there is the greatest amount of interesting activity. Among children who attend the playground regularly, it is seldom necessary to do more than call attention to their misconduct or infraction of a rule. Occasionally they must be denied for brief periods the privilege of using certain facilities or of taking part in an activity, but disciplinary cases requiring severe penalties are rare. On the other hand, in problem neighborhoods rowdies sometimes come to the playground to disrupt the program and to destroy property. In such cases exceptional tact and firmness on the part of the director are needed, and prompt, decisive action is essential if trouble is to be averted.

The playground worker who understands the nature of children and gives them a sense of reality in the program is not likely to have great difficulty in handling them. Proper conduct is encouraged by having a few concise rules and enforcing them, by anticipating trouble before it gets under way, by encouraging self-government, by dealing fairly, by investigating before punishing, and by making few threats and promises. Penalties vary with the nature and seriousness of the offense and, if possible, are linked up with it. Suspension or expulsion is used only as a last resort after consultation with the supervisor or superintendent. Close cooperation between the playground workers, parents, and the neighborhood police helps to reduce the problem of discipline on the playground.

Supplies. Supplies of many kinds are needed on every playground. Game courts and fields, playground buildings, and other features can be used to advantage only as suitable materials and supplies are available. Crafts, drama, nature, social, and most other playground activities cannot be carried on successfully without them. The requirements of a playground vary according to its size, attendance, facilities, and the program to be carried on. Essential supplies are provided by the authorities, but children often bring additional materials to the playground. Care in the use and conservation of supplies is a responsibility of playground workers.

The following are the types of supplies commonly used:

Game Supplies. These include handballs, horseshoes and stakes, softballs, bats and bases, volleyballs and nets, play balls, soccer balls, rainy-day materials, and paddle-tennis outfits. As a rule, children provide their own tennis racquets. If the playground includes a baseball diamond or running track, additional supplies are needed. Quiet-game materials such as beanbags, pegboards and pegs, ring toss, checkers, caroms, and chess are of great value and can be made by the children as a craft project. Materials used in conducting social games and parties are needed at playgrounds having buildings serving as indoor centers.

Craft Supplies. These consist primarily of tools and equipment such as hammer and nails, knives, scissors, pliers, files, sandpaper, paste, crayons, and paints and crafts materials such as clay, cloth, wood, leather, magazines, and yarn. Materials supplied by the department are often supplemented by those brought by the children or obtained by the leaders from neighborhood stores or local factories.

Accessories. Many types of supplies are needed for the music, nature, or drama program. A phonograph and records are useful for folk dancing. Equipment is also needed for the office. Every playground needs a flag, bulletin board, drinking fountain, repair kit, and first-aid kit; many need a bicycle rack.

The Playground Library. A set of publications on playground operation and activities is a part of the essential equipment of the director's office. Books containing rules for games, publications on program features, manuals and other instructions issued by the department office, and standard publications on playground work have a place in the playground library.

Adults enjoy a game of chess in a city park (Courtesy of Department of Parks, New York, N. Y.).

General Supplies. Necessary maintenance supplies include materials for marking courts, dust binders, sawdust, grease, and janitor's supplies. Office forms and other materials are also needed.

Tools. Regardless of the system used for maintaining playgrounds, at least a few tools are required at every area.

Maintenance. The playground represents a considerable public investment, and playground authorities have a responsibility for keeping it in the best possible condition. Otherwise it cannot render maximum service and is likely to become a neighborhood liability. Continuous care and proper use of the grounds and buildings minimize the amount of major maintenance work that must be done.

On large, well-equipped playgrounds with recreation buildings used the year round, a worker is employed full time as caretaker and janitor.

Since most playgrounds do not require the services of a caretaker more than a few hours daily, a single worker sometimes cares for two or more areas. In several cities a specially trained traveling crew maintains several playgrounds. It eliminates the need for a worker and a complete set of maintenance equipment at each area and performs duties which the individual caretaker could not perform. A certain amount of cleaning, marking, and other tasks must be performed regularly each day, but most maintenance can await the periodic visits of the traveling crew. Among the usual maintenance duties are keeping a satisfactory surface, cleaning the building and grounds, caring for plants, marking game courts, cutting grass and hedges, cleaning and changing water in the wading pool, keeping sandboxes clean, inspecting apparatus, bringing in and setting up equipment, keeping tools and equipment in good condition, and making minor repairs.

These activities have a definite relationship to the playground program. Game courts and fields which are marked accurately and distinctly not only look well but facilitate the teaching of obedience to the rules of the game. Safe and satisfactory play is impossible on apparatus that needs repair or on a poorly surfaced court or field. A thoroughly cleaned wading pool makes for safe, healthful, and enjoyable play. Supplies and game materials last longer and give better service when children are taught to use them properly, when they are stored carefully while not in use, and when they are repaired promptly. The attitude of the playground workers toward the appearance and condition of the playground goes far in determining the degree to which the children and the entire neighborhood take pride in it. Enlistment of the cooperation of the children, sometimes through the organization of junior service groups, has been found helpful in developing a respect for playground property and preventing damage to it.

Regulating the Use of the Playground. Spontaneous free play should be encouraged on the playground, and there should be a minimum of suppression and regulation. A few simple rules, however, are usually needed, setting forth the conditions under which the playgrounds can be used. The adoption and enforcement of such rules prevent undesirable uses, facilitate control, help protect local authorities in case of accidents, and assure to all equal, convenient, safe, and satisfactory use of the areas and facilities. In cities where the demand for buildings, tennis courts, and ball diamonds exceeds the supply, rules are needed governing the conditions and periods of play, permits, making of reservations, collection of fees, or restrictions as to the people who can use the facilities.

Records and Reports. The primary job of playground workers is to conduct and promote play programs. Hence they should be asked to keep only records which have real value and require little time. In most cities a weekly report is required of each director, and some departments also require their workers to prepare a report for the playground at the end of the year or season. Unusual events, relationships, successes, and failures are recorded in it as well as attendance, activities of various types, volunteer service, club projects, and suggestions for the future. Such a report is valuable as a historical record and is exceedingly helpful to a director assigned to the playground for the first time. The subject of records and reports, including a discussion of attendance taking on the playground, is treated more fully in Chapter 32.

Other Aspects of Playground Operation. Among the many other problems that arise in playground operation are budgets and the handling of playground funds. Policies must be adopted with reference to fees and charges. Effective methods must be used to inform the public about the services available at the playgrounds. Awards play an important role on the playgrounds in many cities, and their use can give rise to many problems. Interplayground and city-wide projects necessitate consideration of factors not present in programs on the individual playground. Trips by groups to points at a distance from the playground call for precautions to assure children's health and safety. Regulations are needed governing rainy-day procedure, the type of costume to be worn by workers on duty, relationships with neighborhood agencies, the opening and closing of the playground, the promotion of activities by outside groups, and many other points. Workers must be informed as to the liability they and the department may incur in case of accidents on the playground. Some of these problems are considered later in this volume, but for a detailed treatment of these and related subjects, readers are referred to *Playgrounds: Their Administration and Operation.*[2]

[2] George D. Butler (ed.), *Playgrounds: Their Administration and Operation,* rev. ed., The Ronald Press Company, New York, 1950.

18. THE OPERATION OF RECREATION BUILDINGS AND INDOOR CENTERS

Recreation buildings and indoor centers play an important part in the service of the recreation department because they make possible certain indoor activities; and in most cities a continuous, year-round program cannot be carried on without them. The different types of buildings and the great variety of facilities provided in them were listed in Chapter 13. Because the general recreation building and the school recreation center are most important and most numerous, major consideration will be given to the problems involved in operating them.

Operation of a building or center involves the selection, organization, and supervision of a staff; expenditure of funds for operation and maintenance; planning and conducting a program; scheduling activities; determining the conditions under which facilities may be used; and establishing relationships with the people in the city or neighborhood. Local conditions and the facilities provided at the building naturally affect both the plan of operation and the program carried on in the case of the general recreation building and the school center.

WHY RECREATION BUILDINGS?

For many years few multiple-use recreation buildings were built except in the large cities because of the high construction and operating costs and the rather widespread opinion that indoor recreation needs could be served by facilities in school buildings. The increasing demand for year-round recreation programs since the end of World War II, however, has resulted in the construction of hundreds of recreation buildings of all types in large and small cities. The 1956 Recreation and Park Yearbook [1] recorded a total of 4,097 such buildings in which programs were conducted under leadership, located in more than 1,000 communities. Of these buildings, 1,254 were large, with a gymnasium or auditorium or both. Attendances during 1955 at 2,553 buildings totaled 110,000,000 or an average of 43,000 each.

[1] National Recreation Association, New York, 1956.

As previously indicated, school buildings are widely used as community recreation resources, and marked progress is being made in cooperative planning between school and city authorities, to the end that schools are designed for such use. In most cities school buildings are made available to the recreation authorities for their programs, and in some communities the schools contain the only publicly owned indoor recreation facilities. A total of 8,334 indoor school centers in 1,162 communities were reported in 1955, with attendances exceeding 66,000,000 or an average of 12,336 per center reporting.

Since the modern school contains many excellent recreation facilities, the question is frequently raised as to why a community should incur the expense of constructing and maintaining a separate recreation building. The need for separate buildings and the types of facilities to be provided in them are increasingly influenced by the development of the modern school plant with its gymnasiums, auditorium, workshops, music room, stage, library, art room, and other features admirably equipped for recreation. To duplicate these facilities in separate buildings and at the same time to permit the schools to be unused outside of school hours would be an unjustifiable economic waste. Rarely, however, can the school serve the total need for indoor facilities unless a wing is set aside exclusively or primarily for community use. Rooms suitable for recreation are needed for school activities during school hours and are reserved afternoons, and in some cases evenings, for the use of school groups engaged in extracurricular activities, inter- and intraschool athletics, socials, dances, music, or drama productions. Even where school authorities are sympathetic toward community use, school events have a priority and community use is usually restricted to a limited schedule—in some cases to a tentative one.

In many communities, buildings are therefore needed where activities can be scheduled during the morning and afternoon hours, especially for women and older adults, and where the facilities can be fully utilized by recreation groups. Such buildings commonly contain a lounge, a reading room, and game room where an individual can drop in for a brief period to chat with friends, read a magazine, or play a game—rooms that create the informal social atmosphere of a neighborhood clubhouse and that are not available in most school buildings. The tendency is to rely upon the use of schools for activities requiring major facilities such as the gymnasium or auditorium. In communities where suitable school facilities are lacking or in congested city neighborhoods where they are inadequate to serve recreation needs, more elaborate buildings must be provided by the city authorities. The demand for such facilities is increasingly apparent in cities where a considerable percentage of the child population is enrolled in parochial or other private schools.

BUILDING AND CENTER OPERATION

Where the recreation building is a major feature of a playground, play-field, or other recreation area, and where the school is on a site used for community recreation, the outdoor and indoor facilities are usually administered as a single unit. The general plan of over-all playground organization described in Chapter 17 therefore applies to the indoor centers as well. However, there is less uniformity in the methods used to supervise the operation of buildings and centers because, unlike playgrounds, they are seldom as widely or evenly distributed throughout a city. Special-use buildings such as the museum, craft shop, or theatre are usually administered more or less independently of other centers, although they serve many individuals and groups whose interest in the special activity was stimulated at the neighborhood centers.

Administration. Most recreation buildings are administered by municipal recreation authorities, although some privately owned buildings, often designated as community houses, are controlled by a board of trustees or a private membership organization. There is a growing tendency to relate the operation of the community house or other privately owned building to the recreation department. Coordination of its activities with those of other local centers is effected through the appointment of the recreation executive as community house director; in other cases the director is given responsibility for supervision of the playgrounds and other public facilities.

In a majority of the school buildings operated as indoor recreation centers, the recreation program is administered by a municipal recreation agency. Centers in a few of the large cities and in many small communities, however, are conducted by the school authorities through a department of recreation, adult education, or physical education. In the final analysis, the local school board is responsible for the school properties and therefore for the manner and conditions under which they are used as recreation centers. When these are conducted by a nonschool agency, specific agreements must be reached with the school authorities covering the conditions of operation and use. The agency must establish and maintain cooperative and satisfactory working relationships, not only with the school board, but with the school superintendent and the instructional and custodial staff serving in the school buildings used as centers. For many years the community use of schools was hindered by the real or imagined difficulties resulting from the conduct of a program on school property by nonschool agencies. The remarkable degree to which school authorities cooperate with recreation departments conducting school centers was revealed in a study of center operation in 105 cities.[2]

Advisory recreation councils have been organized in many cities to assist recreation authorities in planning building and center programs and in interpreting them to the people of the neighborhood or community. Members are selected because of their interest and influence and commonly include the clergy, businessmen, members of labor unions, veterans' organizations and women's clubs, and persons active in the center program. They serve as individuals rather than representatives of an organization. Most councils have a formal organization, meet regularly, and work closely with the paid staff. They render valuable service by determining needs, interpreting the program and policies of the center, investigating criticisms, conducting studies, recruiting volunteers, enlisting cooperation, raising funds, and helping in other ways. The effectiveness of an advisory council depends on the quality of its membership and on the resourcefulness of the professional staff in suggesting challenging and useful tasks for it to undertake.

The Staff. Leadership is as vital an element in determining the success of the recreation building or indoor center as of the playground. The leadership requirements of a building vary according to its facilities and the program to be carried on, but every building, like every center, needs a director. He is responsible for the operation of the building and usually has charge of the playground or playfield on which it is located. Regardless of the auspices under which a school center is conducted, the school principal has full authority over his building and grounds at all times, and the center director must work closely with him. Other members of the leadership staff are an assistant director and special-activity leaders who assist with program features such as sports, music, dancing, drama, or crafts. Employment of school personnel such as the manual training or home economics teacher, the physical education instructor, or the music supervisor to conduct activities that involve the use of schoolrooms or equipment for which they are responsible tends to be mutually satisfactory. It is the function of the leadership staff to help people attracted to the building gain the maximum benefit and enjoyment from participation in its activities and use of its facilities.

At most recreation buildings and at some indoor centers the director and at least one assistant are employed on a full-time, year-round basis. In such cases trained personnel can be secured who devote their entire time to the center, become acquainted with the neighborhood, and establish relationships with the individuals and groups using the center. Employment of full-time, year-round workers makes possible a continu-

[2] *The Use of School Buildings for Recreation*, National Recreation Association, New York, 1950.

ous, coordinated indoor and outdoor program closely related to neighborhood interests and needs. Unless the staff is built around one or more such workers, the potentialities of the building as a genuine center of neighborhood life are not likely to be realized. Full-time leaders are rarely employed at school centers except in a few large cities.

In addition to the leadership staff, one or more janitors or caretakers and a full-time secretary or office clerk are usually required. Part-time assistants are employed for checking, taking tickets, helping in the locker room or for various other duties. No consideration of the school-center staff can fail to take into account the janitor or custodian, whose attitude commonly reflects the point of view of the school board and principal. Recreation executives have repeatedly been brought face to face with the fact that the smooth, harmonious, and effective operation of a school-center program depends in no small measure upon the cooperation of the janitorial staff. Center directors who insist upon proper care in the use of school property and recognize the responsibility of janitors for its protection and maintenance find that their difficulties on this score are minimized. Needless to say, the janitor should be compensated for added duties resulting from the operation of the center.

Hours of Operation. Most recreation buildings are open morning, afternoon, and evening, except Sundays, throughout the year. Increasingly, buildings are being used seven days a week. The hours depend somewhat upon the nature of the facilities, the type of neighborhood, and the available funds and personnel. The greatest activity is in the late afternoon and evening, but because of the growing participation of women and older adults in the recreation program, buildings are often opened for morning use, usually with a limited staff. Morning activities for children of preschool age are conducted in some cities.

School centers for the most part are conducted during the evening, although some are also used during the late afternoon and on Saturday morning. Some centers are open five or six evenings a week; others only one or two. The evening periods are usually from two to four hours in length, although they vary from city to city; and sometimes when a special event such as a dance is held, the center is kept open later than usual. As a rule, the center season extends from early in the fall until well into the spring, although many of the classes or special activities are scheduled for an eight- to ten-week period. When the center is operated in connection with an outdoor recreation area, or the program extends throughout the year, activities may be carried on continuously from mid-afternoon throughout the evening. Because of its use by regular school groups the school center obviously cannot be made available for as long a period daily as the building used exclusively for recreation purposes.

Use of Facilities. Careful organization is essential to assure maximum use of the building facilities, satisfactory conduct of the various program features, and equal opportunity to all who desire to participate in them. To this end, gymnasium periods are divided between basketball teams organized in leagues playing on a carefully worked-out schedule and informal groups who meet for low organized games, gymnasium classes, or individual sports. Club and social rooms are allotted for definite periods to classes in arts, crafts, or dancing; to clubs formed by individuals interested in such activities as gardening, radio, stamps, or chess; and to

Few indoor activities exceed arts and crafts in their appeal to young and old alike (Courtesy of the Denver, Colo., Recreation Department).

neighborhood groups formed into general-interest clubs. Table-game rooms and reading rooms are usually open at all times and without restriction as to age or sex, although children are sometimes excluded during the evening. If the building contains an auditorium with stage, it is used not only by drama and music groups but also for community affairs such as entertainments, motion-picture shows, lectures, or dances. A clubroom or assembly hall is sometimes made available at stated times for meetings of organizations like the American Legion or Red Cross.

In preparing a schedule for the use of the building facilities, an attempt is made to serve varied interests, to prevent any particular group from securing special privileges, and to give equal consideration to young and old, boys and girls, men and women. Only in exceptional cases should exclusive use of a room be granted to a club or organization, although a room may be set aside for use as a teen center. Periods are made of sufficient length to assure satisfactory participation in the particular activity; for example, strenuous activities such as handball require less time than craft projects. Except in substandard neighborhoods or on special occasions, evening activities for children are scheduled only on Friday or Saturday in most cities. It is advantageous to assign a gymnasium and related facilities such as showers and locker rooms to men's and women's groups on different evenings rather than to alternate the sexes at successive periods on the same evening. This procedure simplifies supervision and permits more effective assignment of leaders.

The dual use of school facilities gives rise to problems that are not generally encountered in the recreation building. When desks are moved from a classroom to make space for center activities, they must be replaced before school opens the following morning. The tables, chairs, and equipment used for these activities must be safely stored until they are next needed, when they must be brought out and set up again. The use of a drama or craft workshop or art rooms by adult groups raises problems as to the care and use of tools and equipment, the storage of materials, and the protection of articles in process of construction. Additional locker and storage facilities are usually needed in a school where the gymnasium is to be used by evening groups. Unless a building has been designed for dual use, difficulty in conducting activities and in providing and caring for equipment is encountered in using it as a recreation center. As indicated elsewhere, these problems are not insurmountable, and the public interest demands that school buildings be used as fully as practicable for community recreation.

The type of community use of buildings and centers considered in this chapter is that in which a program is regularly carried on under leadership of a recreation agency serving all the people. However, schools and recreation buildings are used in other ways. For example, in some communities, organizations such as a scout troop, orchestra, or women's club are permitted to use rooms for their regular meetings; in others, independent teams or groups use the gymnasium for their weekly games. Some authorities grant organizations free use of auditoriums for lectures, concerts, and other events which are open to the public without a charge. The practice of renting school facilities to organizations for regular or special functions is common. Most recreation buildings, however, are scheduled so fully for activities organized or sponsored by the recreation department that their facilities are seldom available for use by outside groups.

Finance. The expense of operating city-owned recreation buildings is met primarily through funds provided in the recreation department budget. At some buildings all activities are free; at others a fee is charged for admission to special events, for enrollment in a class, or for the use of a facility such as a swimming pool or bowling alley. On the whole, however, the buildings are open for use by the public without charge. Since recreation authorities do not need to rely on income from admission charges or rental fees, they are free to plan the program and operate the building so as to serve the best interests of the people rather than to yield the maximum revenue. In some buildings, as we have noted, facilities or rooms are rented to organizations at nominal rates when they are not needed for departmental use.

Items in the operating budget of a recreation building are salaries and wages of leadership, clerical and maintenance personnel, fuel, light, water, recreation and office supplies, telephone, insurance, janitorial supplies, repairs, and miscellaneous expenses. The largest expenditure item, salaries and wages for leadership, sometimes represents as much as one-half the total current building budget, which for some buildings equals between 10 and 15 per cent of the construction cost.

School centers operated by school authorities, like other parts of the school program, are financed primarily through budget appropriations. School funds usually cover heat, light, janitor service, and leadership. In some cities a special mill tax authorized by state legislation is levied by the school board for recreation. Two or three states grant subsidies to local school authorities for specified recreation activities. Many center activities are free to all, but nominal charges are commonly made for enrollment in classes requiring special leadership or equipment to defray the cost of this special service.

Costs of school centers not conducted by the school authorities are met in various ways. In many cities where the recreation department conducting the centers provides the program leadership and meets other expenses incidental to the program, the school budget carries the cost of heat, light, and supplementary janitor service; in others, the schools provide heat and light only. In the few cities where the schools meet none of the expense of center operation, the department conducting the centers is charged for the use of the building and must include in its budget an item for school rentals as well as for leadership and other necessary services. Increasingly, cooperative plans include an agreement as to the responsibility for meeting or sharing operation and maintenance costs resulting from the use of schools for community recreation.

The Program. The activities carried on in a building or center depend primarily upon its facilities and the resourcefulness of the leaders in putting them to varied recreation uses. Needless to say, they must be related to the interests and desires of the people living in the neighborhood or community. Games and sports receive major emphasis in a building where a gymnasium is the chief feature, although the building can serve many other types of activities. Social, cultural, and club activities predominate in smaller buildings. A great variety of indoor activities is possible in buildings with ample and diversified facilities and competent leadership.

Programs are built around several general types of activities which involve different organization methods and require varied facilities. Use of the rooms set aside for reading, table games, low organized games, and billiards does not involve enrollment in a group or formal participation. Many activities are carried on through clubs, classes, or selective groups.

Children are intrigued by a backstage visit to a marionette theatre (Courtesy of Department of Parks, New York, N. Y.).

Choral or instrumental music, dramatics, and arts and crafts are usually conducted as group projects with regularly scheduled meetings and with special instruction or leadership. Most social clubs, married couples' clubs, chess, or photography clubs are self-operated membership groups which meet regularly. Parties, dances, concerts, and dinners are scheduled from time to time and are occasionally open to the entire neighborhood. In some centers intracenter leagues and informal use of the gymnasium receive more emphasis than intercenter sports competition. A swimming pool schedule provides periods for instruction, special aquatic activities, and recreational swimming. The methods commonly used in organizing and conducting several typical indoor activities were discussed in some detail in Chapter 16. The following pages describe typical programs in several buildings and centers; other indoor program features are described in subsequent chapters.

Typical Building Activities. The Cone Recreation Center in Greensboro, North Carolina, contains exceptional facilities including a swimming pool, game rooms, bowling alley, ballroom, gymnasium, rooms for drama and arts and crafts, clubrooms, kitchens, and teen-age room. The variety of activities available at the center is attractively outlined in a folder issued by the Greensboro Parks and Recreation Commission:

The green light flashes daily for games of all kinds: handball, billiards, bowling, volleyball, television, swimming, teen-age activities, basketball, and just plain fun. . . .

Adults get the "go" sign with: ballroom dance instruction—variations of the fox trot, waltz, rhumba, conga, and tango—courses in interior decorating, camera club, American Red Cross water safety courses, aquatic club, Greensboro Swimming Association.

Athletic goings on: boys' and girls' basketball, women's basketball, midget basketball, men's basketball, swimming, high school swimming team practices.

We go at a gallop with: young folks clubs (one each for boys and girls 8 to 12), children's swimming, social dance instruction, children's game room, Thursday night teens club (teens 13 to 20 who have charge of the Teen-Age Room), Sans Souci Girls Club (a social and service organization), teen-age bridge instruction, sports and games instruction and tournaments.

A Recreation Building Program. The Bureau of Parks and Public Recreation of Portland, Oregon, operates several recreation buildings and conducts programs in many school buildings. The Knott Street Center, an old two-story building with basement, originally built as a school, is an example of how a building can be remodeled for community recreation use. Classrooms have been converted into rooms for club meetings, television, pool tables, music, table tennis, and other activities, and the old-fashioned domestic science room serves as a kitchen. The full-time leadership staff consists of two men and two women; a boxing instructor and a maintenance crew of three men are also employed on a full-time basis at the center.

The 1958 spring program, which follows, includes an unusual variety of music activities because the center houses the city's rapidly expanding music program. Feature activities such as teen dances, a mothers' chorus, family nights, drama productions, and holiday programs supplement the regularly scheduled activities. Also carried daily, Monday through Friday, are boxing from noon to 8 P.M. in the boxing gym; sports for adults (seventeen years and over) from 2 to 4 P.M. in the gym; pool and ping-pong from 2 to 10 P.M. in the pool room and game room, respectively; crafts for girls from 3:30 to 5:30 P.M. in the small-fry room, and table

Table 7. Weekly Program of the Knott Street Center, Portland, Oregon

Day	Time	Activity	Place
Monday	10:00–12:00	Preschool (2–4 years)	Small-fry room
	12:00–4:00	Golden-age Club	Auditorium
	3:45–5:00	Tumbling (boys)	Junior gym
	7:00–9:45	Sport skills (boys, high school)	Gym
		Record dance	Social room
Tuesday	10:00–12:00	Preschool (2–4 years)	Small-fry room
	2:00–3:00	Conditioning class (women)	Gym or social room
	3:00–4:00	Tumbling (girls, 6–8 years)	Junior gym
	3:45–5:00	Crafts (boys, 7 years and over)	Crafts basement
		Softball sport skills (boys, grade school)	Gym
	4:00–5:00	Tumbling (girls, 8–10 years)	Junior gym
	6:00–7:00	Recorder (beginning)	Music room
	7:00–8:00	Guitar (beginning) Violin (parent-child)	Music room
	8:00–9:00	Violin (beginning and intermediate) Viola (beginning and intermediate) Recorder (intermediate)	Music room
	9:00–9:45	Record dance	Social room
	9:00–10:00	Sports (adult)	Gym

**Table 7. Weekly Program of the Knott Street Center,
Portland, Oregon (Continued)**

Day	Time	Activity	Place
Wednesday	10:00–12:00	Preschool (2–4 years)	Small-fry room
	12:00–4:00	Golden-age Club	Auditorium
	3:30–5:00	Sewing (girls, 8–11 years)	Small-fry room
	3:45–5:00	Tumbling (boys)	Junior gym
	6:30–7:30	Harmony and counterpoint	Music room
	7:00–9:45	Record dance	Social room
	7:30–8:30	Recorder (advanced)	Music room
	8:00–9:00	Sport skills	Gym
	8:30–9:30	Madrigal-reading chorus	Music room
	9:00–10:00	Basketball practice (adults)	Gym
Thursday	10:00–12:00	Preschool (2–4 years) Mothers' Homemaking Club	Small-fry room
	2:00–3:00	Conditioning class (women)	Gym or social room
	2:00–3:30	Crafts (adults)	Small-fry room
	3:45–5:00	Crafts (boys, 7 years and over)	Crafts basement
	6:00–7:00	Guitar (intermediate)	Music room

Table 7. Weekly Program of the Knott Street Center, Portland, Oregon (Continued)

Day	Time	Activity	Place
	7:00–8:00	Violin technique (advanced)	Music room
	7:00–9:45	Sport skills (boys, high school)	Gym
		Record dance	Social room
	8:00–9:30	String orchestra	Music room
Friday	12:00–4:00	Golden-age Club	Auditorium
	3:30–5:30	Special crafts	Small-fry room
	4:00–6:30	Sport skills (intermediate)	Gym
	6:00–7:00	Harmony and counterpoint	Music room
	7:00–8:00	Sport skills	Gym
		Recorder (beginning)	Music room
	8:00–9:00	Folk-song chorus	Music room
	8:00–10:45	Dance (teen-agers, 13–18 years)	Music room
Saturday	10:00–	Violin (grade school)	Music room
		Music for children	
	11:00–	All-city choir (boys)	Music room
	2:30–	Guitar (advanced)	Music room
	4:00–	Guitar (beginning, children)	Music room
	5:00–	Harmony and counterpoint	Music room

Table 8. Weekly Spring Schedule for the Dixwell Neighborhood Program, New Haven, Connecticut

Room	Monday	Tuesday	Wednesday	Thursday	Friday
Fourth, fifth, and sixth grades (3:30–5:30)					
Craft room	Woodwork 4th grade	Cooking	Woodwork 5th grade	Sewing 4th grade	Ceramics
Auditorium		Tap class	Modern dancing	Ballet class	Social dance class
Social hall	Tigers Club	Tiny Tots Club	Tigers Club	Tiny Tots Club	Tigers Club
Library	Musical instruction	Girl Scouts	Glee Club		
Classrooms	Junior Council	Brownies		Girl Scouts	Harmonica Club
Gym	Minor sports (girls)	Minor sports (boys)	Minor sports (girls)	Minor sports (boys)	
Seniors and adults (7:00–9:30)					
Gym	Recreation (adult and senior girls)	Minor sports (senior boys)	Recreation (adults, coed)	Minor sports (senior boys)	
Craft room		Ceramics (boys and girls)		Domestic repair	
Auditorium	Golf instruction	Mambo band	Mambo band	Dramatics	
Classrooms	Cub Scouts	Bridge Club	Boy Scouts		Special events
Library				Musical instruction	
Lounge				Women's Club	
Cafeteria		Dressmaking		Dressmaking	

games from 3:30 to 5:30 and 7 to 9:45 P.M. in the game room. A television room is in use daily from 4:30 to 5:30 and 6:30 to 9:30 P.M.

Dixwell Neighborhood Program, New Haven, Connecticut. This program, conducted primarily in the Winchester School, a building in an underprivileged neighborhood, is unusual in that it is under the Redevelopment Agency of the City of New Haven, Connecticut. The total operating cost is met from a city appropriation, and the only fees are for some craft materials. A community coordinator, program director, and secretary, assisted by a corps of part-time paid and volunteer leaders and instructors, administer the program under the guidance of an advisory committee and

Table 9. Social-center Activities, Milwaukee, Wisconsin
(B = boys, G = girls, M = men, W = women)

Activity	Age group		
	Grade school	Teen-agers	Adults
Arts and crafts	Art, handcraft, needlecraft	All adult activities (same classes)	Art and sketching, ceramics, lapidary work, leathercraft, metalcraft, millinery (W), needlecraft (W), sewing (W), tailoring (W), weaving, woodwork
Dancing	Creative rhythms; folk, social, and tap dancing	Modern dancing and all adult activities	Ballet; folk, round, social, and square dancing
Drama	Drama clubs	All adult activities	Drama clubs, Milwaukee Players, Milwaukee Light Opera Company
Lectures, demonstrations, and entertainments	Children's theatre, motion pictures	Athletic contests; music and drama presentations; music, drama, and art lectures	Great-books lectures, lectures on women's points of view (W), and all teen-ager activities

Table 9. Social-center Activities, Milwaukee, Wisconsin (Continued)
(B = boys, G = girls, M = men, W = women)

Activity	Age group		
	Grade school	Teen-agers	Adults
Miscellaneous instruction classes		Health (teen-agers and parents), photography	Cake decorating (W), citizenship, drivers' clinic, English, first aid, home nursing, home repairs, landscaping (M), parliamentary procedure, party foods and favors (W), and all teen-ager activities
Music	Choruses	All adult activities	Bands, choruses
Social recreation	Clubs, story hour	Social clubs, dances, recreation lounges, athletic clubs (B)	Square-dance socials; folk-group, golden-age, and social clubs
Sports and games	Basketball (B), golf (instruction), indoor baseball (B), low organized games, tumbling (instruction)	Archery, badminton (G), basketball, billiards (B), bridge (instruction), boxing (B, instruction), chess (B), dart ball (B), fly tying (instruction), golf (instruction), indoor baseball (G), sports clinics, table games, table tennis, volleyball (G), weight lifting (B), wrestling (B, instruction)	Archery, basketball, billiards (M), bridge (instruction), boxing (M), chess, dart ball (M), fly tying (instruction), golf (instruction), gymnasium (instruction), indoor baseball (W), sports clinics, table tennis, volleyball, weight lifting (M), wrestling (M)

with the help of a consultants group. The 1958 spring program is outlined in Table 8. Additional activities, not conducted in the Winchester School, are junior boys' sports in another school gymnasium, boys' and women's bowling groups, and a rifle club.

Activities in Milwaukee, Wisconsin. The school centers in Milwaukee are conducted by the board of education through its department of municipal recreation. Its program, presented in Table 9, illustrates the great diversity of leisure-time interests served by one of the country's outstanding recreation departments. The indicated activities were offered during the 1958 indoor season at the city's thirty-eight afternoon and thirty-one evening social centers.

School Building Activities. The diversified program that can be carried on in the various units of a school building is illustrated by the list that follows, which records the activities in the Central Avenue School Center in Newark, New Jersey:

Auditorium

Dramatic presentations	Band concerts	Dance-band rehearsals
Community singing	Safety programs	Minstrel singing
Symphony orchestra rehearsals	Choral-group rehearsals	Church choir festivals
Forums and lectures	Motion pictures	Recitals

Large Gymnasium

Exhibitions and demonstrations	Special holiday dances	Gymnastics
Leagues in all indoor sports	Reducing classes	Roller skating
Club activity programs	Game tournaments	Sports clinics

Small Gymnasium

Fencing	Fife and drum corps	Calisthenics
Social dancing	Scout program	Parties
Square dancing	Boxing	

Kindergarten Room

Dance parties and socials	Lectures to small groups	Bridge games
Dance-band rehearsals	Tap-dancing groups	Checkroom
Social-dancing classes	Toy bands	Choral-group rehearsals
Social-club meetings		

Domestic Arts Rooms

Sewing	Arts and crafts classes	Preparation for party
Millinery	Nutrition classes	refreshments
Glove making	Cooking groups	

Library

Conferences	Music appreciation	Chess and checker club
Club meetings	Book club	PTA meetings
Reading		

Classrooms

Club meetings	Dressing rooms	Civic-group meetings
Checkrooms	Literary-club meetings	Hobby groups

Industrial Arts Room

Household mechanics	Woodcraft	Hobby crafts
Fix-it classes	Metalcraft	

Medical Room

Home-nursing instruction	First-aid classes	Hygiene classes

Special Events. Regular meetings of the many groups that come to an indoor center to engage in activities of their own choice and to enjoy the sociability of others with similar interests constitute the bulk of the indoor-center program. The program, however, includes a number of feature events, some in the nature of demonstrations, others utilizing the interest in a holiday or special season. The following list of the feature activities at a Newark center illustrates the nature of such events:

Dedication of Christmas tree	Church choir festival
Playground springtime revue	Senior chorus concert
Negro History Week program	Joint council meeting
Symphony orchestra concert	Mothers' Club rally
Negro Health Week program	Youth Week program
Sewing Club fashion show	Annual club plays
Junior-chorus operetta	Holiday festivals

Riverside Recreation Center, Greenville, Pennsylvania. The building in Greenville differs from most of those described in this book in that it has characteristics of a community house and is operated by a recreation association. It is borough-owned, however, and several board members are borough or school officials. The borough maintains the building and pays for light, heat, and water; the school district pays salaries for professional workers; and the community chest contributes to the cost of supplies, incidentals, and janitorial and secretarial services. The center, built for the USO, is located on property adjoining a borough park. Its facilities include an auditorium-gymnasium, with stage and dressing rooms, two meeting rooms, and a lobby with fireplace, shuffleboards, table-tennis tables, and television. One of the rooms is used by the schools for a community day-care training school.

Activities comprising the 1957–1958 winter program included basketball and sports for adults and for boys and girls from the fourth grade through high school, bowling for boys, girls, and housewives, baton twirling, an airplane club for boys, ceramics for children and adults, a golden-age club, a rifle club for boys twelve years and up, senior teen dances, and square dances conducted as family nights. A total of 705 activity sessions, meetings, or classes conducted under supervision attracted a total attendance of 31,812 in 1957. In addition to the program, the building provides a center for meetings and social activities of civic, fraternal, labor, church, political, professional, and rural organizations. In 1957 the building was used 365 times for such events, with a total attendance of 18,714.

Practicing for the pocket-billiard tournament (Courtesy of Danforth Center, Rochester, N. Y.).

A FEW SUGGESTIONS

Many other aspects of building and center operation merit careful study, but only a few can be mentioned briefly here.

1. A brightly lighted entrance to the building helps advertise the center, serves as a welcome, and reduces discipline problems.
2. Making visitors welcome is an important function of the doorman, host, or director. An attractive lobby helps to create a favorable impression.
3. Registration of regular attendants creates a sense of belonging to the center, facilitates record keeping, and reduces problems of discipline.
4. A room for checking wraps encourages a person to prolong his visit to the center, facilitates control, and improves the appearance of the center.

5. Attractive posters and program schedules, newspaper announcements, and talks to neighborhood groups help build center attendance and interest.
6. Carefully kept attendance and cost records facilitate the evaluation of services and costs, and are an aid in future planning.
7. Payment of activity and use fees in advance helps assure continued participation in an activity.
8. A feeling of pride in the center is developed when proper conduct, dress, and care of rooms are recognized as essential by persons using the center and by the neighborhood.
9. The interest and support of city and school authorities are fostered through regular reports and invitations to attend special events. In one city a tour of the centers was arranged, and news photographers took pictures of officials taking part in the activities.
10. Occasional events in which the various center groups participate help develop a feeling of solidarity and foster social relationships in the center and neighborhood.

19. THE OPERATION OF RECREATION FACILITIES

THE MANY types of areas and facilities comprising a modern municipal recreation system were described in Chapters 11 and 12. The effectiveness of the service which they render depends upon the manner in which they are administered as well as upon their design, development, and equipment. Some of the factors that must be considered in the operation of recreation buildings and centers also apply to special recreation facilities, but the successful operation of these facilities calls for a knowledge of the problems peculiar to them and effective operation methods. The fullest utilization of recreation facilities and their maximum service to the public are assured only when they are administered by qualified personnel familiar with leadership methods and operating techniques.

Major objectives in the operation of recreation facilities are to extend their use to the greatest possible number of people, to assure equal opportunity to all, to maintain the facilities in the best possible condition, and to make their use safe, convenient, pleasant, and satisfying. To achieve these objectives, recreation authorities adopt general policies relating to the facilities and regulations governing their use by the public, and employ a competent staff. Leadership principles and methods have long been applied to the municipal camp program, but they have been considered less important in the operation of most other facilities. Progressive recreation authorities now utilize recreation leadership at the golf course, swimming pool, bathing beach, and athletic field. Promotion of a varied, interesting program of activities is considered just as important as facility maintenance.

THE BATHING BEACH AND SWIMMING POOL

Swimming is not only popular with people of all ages but also an ideal form of recreation for the family and mixed groups, an all-round type of exercise, and an excellent means of social activity. Among municipal recreation facilities, only playgrounds have as high an annual attendance as pools and beaches. In a single year more than 200 million visits have

323

been recorded at the public swimming centers for which attendance was reported.

The problems of operating the bathing beach and the swimming pool are similar in many respects, but the methods employed at the beach have little in common with those used at an indoor pool. Three factors that require major attention at all types of swimming centers are (1) the purity of the water, (2) the safety of the bathers, and (3) the promotion of swimming and other aquatic activities. To assure these conditions, a trained and competent staff is needed at the beach or pool whenever it is open for use.

The Staff. The manager has full authority and responsibility for the operation of the beach or pool. One or more lifeguards are on duty during all bathing hours, the number required varying with the size of the beach or pool, the depth of the water, the number of people served, and the duties assigned to each. An attendant stationed at each shower room or pool entrance inspects the bathers and ensures their taking a thorough cleansing bath before entering the swimming pool. Additional workers are a cashier, suit attendants, and a caretaker. At many pools a worker performs two functions; for example, the manager may also serve as engineer. The lifeguards provide instruction at most pools; otherwise leaders are assigned to conduct classes. Generally speaking, the minimum staff at a beach or outdoor pool includes a manager, a cashier, two lifeguards, a man and a woman attendant, and a caretaker. At large centers, as many as twenty workers may be needed. Employees should be capable swimmers and competent in lifesaving methods. To assure adequate preparation of workers, special schools or training institutes are held in many cities prior to the swimming season.

Sanitation. Recreation authorities have a serious obligation to the public for maintaining a high standard of cleanliness at pools and beaches. Purification and recirculation systems are installed at artificial pools to assure a sanitary condition of the water, but they require careful and continuous supervision. In most states the sanitary control of pools and beaches rests with the public health authorities, and local health departments render valuable assistance in testing the water and checking the purification methods and equipment. Recently constructed pools have equipment that completely recirculates the water every six or eight hours. At bathing beaches it is seldom feasible to treat or control the water supply and thereby assure its purity, but in all pools daily tests of the water are essential. Care is also taken to assure the sanitary condition of bathhouses, dressing rooms, toilet facilities, suits, and towels. Before entering a pool, persons are generally required to take a cleansing bath, using warm water and soap. Persons with open wounds or with evidence of communicable or skin diseases are not permitted to enter.

Safety. Constant vigilance is required on the part of the lifeguards to prevent accidents and to render prompt assistance to bathers who need it. Safety rules posted at the beach or pool indicate the water areas which may be used, the conditions of use, and the practices which are not permitted. Running and playing games on the pool deck and horseplay in the water and around the pool are prohibited. Diving boards and the deep section of the pool require special attention. At the beach, the frontage in which swimming is permitted must be designated, and areas with rip tides, piers, or other obstructions are clearly marked as dangerous. Food is banned from the pool area in many cities, though picnic facilities are commonly provided at beaches. The use of glass containers should be barred at swimming centers.

Rules must be strictly enforced, lifesaving and first-aid equipment must be constantly available and in good condition, and workers must be instructed as to the procedure to be followed in case of serious accidents. At some ocean beaches, lifesaving methods include the use of fast patrol boats, two-way radios in the lifeguard ambulance, and high-speed rescue cars. Junior lifeguard corps have been organized in several cities. The efficiency of the accident-prevention and rescue work of municipal lifeguards is illustrated in the case of the municipal beaches in a Western city, which in one summer had 6,364,691 visitors without a single drowning. Other cities have a perfect record over a period of years.

The Program. The chief activities at municipal pools and beaches are (1) general swimming and diving, (2) swimming and diving instruction, (3) competitive swimming and diving, (4) lifesaving instruction, (5) water games and stunts, (6) synchronized swimming, and (7) feature events such as carnivals, pageants, or playdays. Periods are set aside for handicapped groups in some cities; also for members of scuba groups. The popularity of the pool or beach depends partly upon the promotional and leadership ability of the manager and his assistants. Learn-to-swim campaigns, the formation of swimming clubs, the use of progressive aquatic tests, and the organization of meets and special events are effective methods of developing more widespread interest and participation in the water sports program. The outdoor swimming season extends for about three months in most parts of the country.

General Swimming. Most people come to the outdoor pool or beach to engage in informal swimming, diving, and sun bathing and to enjoy the relaxation and invigoration which come from participation in these activities. The sociability which swimming and informal water sports afford attracts more people than competitive activity. Care must therefore be taken not to schedule too many special events which interfere with general swimming periods. In the multiple-unit pools the largest unit is usually used for general swimming as a co-recreational activity. Most indoor pools are used primarily for swimming instruction or for general swimming by organized groups, usually of one sex. Increasingly, however, mixed swimming for young people and adults is encouraged where proper dressing and shower arrangements can be provided.

Swimming Instruction. People cannot fully enjoy the water unless they know how to swim well. Swimming instruction is therefore a valuable feature of the program at most municipal pools and beaches. Tens of thousands of children are taught to swim each summer, and others are helped to attain greater proficiency in swimming, diving, lifesaving, and water sports. Definite periods are set aside for instruction, demonstration, and practice. Many cities encourage boys and girls to improve their skill in the water through the use of graded tests developed locally or Red Cross swimming and lifesaving events. Swimming classes are usually free to children, although a nominal charge is made for adult instruction in some cities.

Competition. Swimming and diving are also conducted on a competitive basis, and teams formed at the playgrounds or swimming centers compete regularly in interplayground or interpool contests. Occasional swimming meets provide an incentive for enrollment in the instruction classes or for improving one's proficiency in the water. A city-wide tournament is commonly held at the end of the season to determine the champions in the various events.

Games and Stunts. The potentialities of pools and beaches as places where water games and stunts can be enjoyed, especially by children and young people, have seldom been realized. Shallow-water areas can be used for such team games as volleyball and water baseball; deeper areas, for relays, races, and stunts, many of which give children greater skill and confidence in the water. Water polo attracts the men who seek strenuous competitive activity. Synchronized swimming, which appeals to participants and spectators alike, is gaining wide popularity, especially with young women and girls.

Feature Events. Much variety in the program can be achieved through aquatic carnivals, including water games, stunts, and special events; pageants in which large numbers of people take part; a water circus; exhibitions of swimming and diving; and lifesaving contests. At beaches, general swimming is often permitted while a part of the beach is reserved for special events, but pools are closed to public use during these programs. Events featuring canoes, rowboats, sailboats, and distance swims are possible at ocean, lake, or river beaches. Boats are excluded, however, from the areas used by bathers.

At bathing beaches, and to a lesser extent at swimming pools, there is a growing tendency to provide facilities for games such as badminton, volleyball, table tennis, paddle tennis, and shuffleboard, which have increased attendance and have proved very popular. Refreshment facilities are provided at most beaches; at some, beach chairs and umbrellas are rented, and areas are set aside for picnicking.

Costs. Most cities charge admission to their swimming pools, and fees for services rendered at bathing beaches are also fairly common. The fee usually covers services such as the checking of clothes and valuables,

The food-bar terrace and service structures are important features at Metropolitan Beach, serving the Detroit region (Courtesy of Huron-Clinton Metropolitan Authority, Detroit, Mich.)

provision of soap, and use of the beach or pool. An additional amount is charged for suit and towel, if provided. The usual fee is between 25 and 50 cents for adults and 10 to 20 cents for children. Some cities have an intermediate rate for youth; others charge a higher fee on week ends. Morning sessions are set aside as free swimming periods for children at most pools. Few cities attempt to make a profit on their swimming facilities, but pool income meets a large part of the operating cost, and receipts exceed expenditures at some pools. Operating costs vary widely because pools are so different in size, type, and facilities, but at a majority of public outdoor pools they are between $6,000 and $12,000 per season.

THE GOLF COURSE

The remarkable growth of municipal golf has been due in part to the promotion of the game on a national basis. The insistent demand by golfers for additional facilities and the possibility that these would prove self-sustaining have resulted in some cities in a more adequate provision for golf than for children's play or other types of recreation service. The golf course has become an important feature of the recreation system in many cities, and its operation presents special problems.

The Staff. The golf course, like the beach or pool, is usually in charge of a manager who in many cities is employed on a twelve-month basis. In practice, the functions and duties of the manager vary, but many officials believe that he should be given entire responsibility for the maintenance and operation of the course and clubhouse. Other workers commonly employed include a professional, a course superintendent responsible for maintenance, greenskeeper, starter, caddiemaster, janitor, locker-room attendants, rangers, cashier, refectory clerks, cook, and maintenance crew. The number and duties of the different types of workers vary widely, depending upon the intensity of play, the facilities and services afforded at the clubhouse, and the general plan of operation. At many courses two or more functions are cared for by a single individual, as, for example, the professional and manager or the starter and caddiemaster. The average number of employees at an eighteen-hole course during the active playing season varies from ten to twenty.

In many cities play continues the year round, although in some Northern cities the season is only about eight months. As a rule, a few workers are employed on a year-round basis, and others are used only during the busy summer season. The maintenance staff at the municipal golf course is exceedingly important because only through the employment of a sufficient number of competent workers can a course which receives intensive use be kept in a satisfactory playing condition. The starter also has a key role since, as the National Golf Foundation points out, "Nothing breaks down good public relations any faster than a slipshod first tee operation." [1]

Controlling the Play. Only a limited number of persons can use a golf course at one time, so methods must be devised to assure to all who desire to play a fair opportunity to use the course. Some municipal courses operate on a first-come-first-served basis. People desiring to play wait their turn if there are others ahead of them waiting for a chance to tee off. Unless there are four individuals waiting who can be started off together,

---

[1] *Municipal Golf Course Organizing and Operating Guide,* National Golf Foundation, Chicago, undated, p. 61.

foursomes are given the preference. In other cities a dual system of assigning periods of golf is in use, especially over week ends. Half of the starting periods may be reserved in advance, the alternate periods being kept free for persons who have not made reservations. The reservation system is convenient for golfers because they do not have to wait in line for a chance to play, and it relieves congestion at the first tee. At courses where special privileges or reduced rates are granted to holders of season tickets or to local residents, registration cards, sometimes containing the holder's photograph, are issued and used for identification purposes. According to the National Golf Foundation, "Today most golf course operations use a fairly standard starter sheet. This sheet is usually large enough so that four names can be placed opposite a starting time. Collection of the fee is also usually a part of the operation. The purpose of the present-day starter sheet is to place thereon all the pertinent information which the starter needs and the auditing system requires to give a clear view of the operation." [2]

As a rule foursomes are run off every five minutes, which means that forty-eight people can leave the first tee each hour. Rangers employed at busy courses regulate the play, settle difficulties, protect the course, and encourage players to observe the common courtesies associated with the sport.

Costs. Perhaps no other municipal sport has offered greater promise of being self-supporting than golf. In constructing their courses most cities have assumed that income would equal operating costs and, in a few instances, that the cost of acquiring the land and building the course could be met from the profits. A 1954 study of seventy-nine municipal eighteen-hole courses [3] showed that the average annual operating cost varied from $19,653 in cities under 10,000 to $36,917 in cities of 500,000 and over. Comparable figures for average income were $22,855 and $48,054. Data for thirty-two nine-hole courses showed an average annual operating cost varying from $7,873 in cities under 10,000 to $20,477 in cities of 500,000 and over, with comparable income figures of $9,654 and $30,540, respectively. Most courses have proved self-supporting. Weekday rates are usually lower than over the week end, when play is heaviest; annual or seasonal fees are used in some cities for the benefit of golfers who play regularly. At a few courses an additional fee is charged for making reservations and accommodating nonresident golfers.

Promoting an Interest in Golf. The success of golf is measured in some cities by the receipts at the courses; but the game, like other parts of the recreation program, should be considered an activity to be made available

[2] *Ibid.,* p. 62.

[3] *Average Income and Operating Costs of Municipal Golf Courses,* National Golf Foundation, Chicago, undated.

at a minimum cost to the greatest number of people. Several departments stimulate interest in the game through offering lessons to beginners, organizing classes, promoting golf in high schools and business concerns, renting equipment at a low fee, and fixing low rates for school pupils. Family golf is also encouraged. Golf clubs and associations at municipal courses have proved a means of sustaining a year-round interest in golf, of elevating standards of play, and of enforcing the rules. Exhibitions, demonstrations, and tournaments are arranged from time to time, but they should not be so frequent as to interfere seriously with play by the general public. Interest in the game has been stimulated in some cities by special events such as father-and-son, professional-and-caddie, or intercity caddie tournaments.

Other Activities at the Golf Course. The desirability of encouraging family recreation and the demand for the maximum year-round use of all public recreation facilities have prompted many authorities to introduce at the golf course activities which appeal to all members of the family and which are carried on throughout the year. To this end, play facilities and programs are provided for children whose parents are playing golf. Archery, tennis, bowling, and other game courts have been constructed near the clubhouse, and courses are used for tobogganing, coasting, skating, and skiing during the winter months. Practice greens and fairways have been laid out near the start of some courses so that persons waiting to play may have an opportunity to improve their game. Golf clubhouses with their dance floors, informal clubrooms, and attractive dining facilities are used by community groups for social events, especially during the winter months. Under competent leadership, the golf course is becoming a genuine recreation center rather than an area used exclusively for a highly specialized activity by a small percentage of the residents of a community.

THE STADIUM

Stadiums are specialized structures seating anywhere from a few thousand to one hundred thousand people. In proportion to their cost, some large stadiums contribute little to the recreation life of the cities in which they are located; others are operated in such a manner as to make them valuable recreation assets. Experience has demonstrated the truth of the statement that it is not easy to justify such an expensive project as a municipal stadium unless it is built and managed with the general recreation needs of the community in mind. The most useful and successful stadiums are those which have been erected to meet a definite community need rather than as a means of attracting major sporting events to the city. A few cities in recent years have built stadiums primarily as a means of attracting a major-league baseball club. Some of the largest stadiums are administered by special commissions; others are controlled by the recreation authorities.

Operating Factors. The problems and policies of stadium operation differ with the type of structure and the major function it is expected to fulfill. The stadium seating 25,000 people and upward, for example, is rarely required for events organized and conducted by the local recreation authorities. It is used primarily for college football games, professional baseball, sporting and other events promoted by municipal agencies, private organizations, and commercial interests. Rental of the stadium for such uses produces revenue which helps meet the cost of its maintenance and operation. The preference in rentals is given to the group that promises the greatest revenue and consequently the largest number of spectators. Local groups benefit more, however, when the authorities in making reservations give priority to the recreation department, city schools, and local colleges rather than to outside groups, even though outside groups guarantee greater attendance and larger gate receipts. Because the stadium, unlike most recreation facilities, is fenced and is primarily for the accommodation of spectators at special events, an admission fee is usually charged.

A definite policy governing rentals and rental fees must be adopted by the stadium authority. At the large stadium, rental fees vary according to the type of organization or use. Some events require the installation of special equipment or the assignment of an unusual number of personnel; others may cause damage to the playing field. Some authorities have a sliding scale of rental fees; others require a percentage of the gate receipts. Rentals at one large stadium, for example, represent a certain amount per paid admission for professional baseball, a flat rate for professional football and a much lower one for high school football, a flat rate plus a percentage of fees for a rodeo and boxing matches, and no rental for an Easter sunrise service or spring music festival. Formal contracts are customary, covering the conditions and restrictions of use of the stadium.

The operation of a large stadium involves the handling of crowds, public relations, the control of motor and pedestrian traffic, and the recruiting and training of a corps of workers to serve as ticket sellers and takers, guards, ushers, and parking-field attendants. All these problems are faced to a lesser degree at the smaller stadiums. The large stadium has a manager whose chief function is booking attractions and supervising operations; but the small stadium, usually located on a general recreation area, is administered by the director of the area, although special events may be scheduled through the central office of the department. A competent maintenance crew is needed to keep the grounds in condition and to make quick change-overs between events; the crew must be supplemented before and after events at which large crowds are accommodated.

Soldier Field, Chicago. Soldier Field, under the management of the Chicago Park District, is one of the most successful of the large municipal stadiums. Its normal seating capacity is 85,000, but as many as 110,000 have attended a football game in it. The policy established by the Chicago Park Commission has been:

. . . to permit the use of Soldier Field for any sort of civic, sports, musical, or other form of entertainment or event which does not entail its use as a forum for propaganda on political or economic subjects of a controversial nature. Organizations using this institution are charged a fee either on a percentage basis of the gate receipts or on a rental basis in addition to a guarantee of all expenses incurred by the Chicago Park District in the preparation of the field before the event and the restoration of the grounds to the proper condition following the event.

Attractions at Soldier Field have included such widely different events as Easter sunrise service, I Am an American Day, the Ringling Brothers circus, religious assemblies, industrial shows, military reviews, rodeos, automobile races, professional boxing, polo games, track and field meets, dog shows, Fourth of July celebrations, Chicagoland Music Festival, all-star, college, and professional football games, Victory Garden Roundup, and open- and square-dance demonstrations. In spite of the fact that the stadium is well designed and efficiently managed, the total attendance at all events during the year represents only a few times its capacity. Likewise the Municipal Stadium in Baltimore, administered by the department of recreation and parks, in 1955 received only sixteen uses with less than 200,000 attendances, except for professional baseball games and football games, which attracted well over 1,000,000.

Smaller Stadiums. A stadium seating 10,000 to 15,000 people is adequate for the normal needs of most cities, and a smaller one may be ample. If properly designed it can be used for a variety of recreation activities such as city-wide championship games in various sports, major track and field meets, pageants, festivals, playground demonstrations, special music events, opera, civic meetings, and mass gatherings. Toboggan slides have been erected at stadiums in some cities, enabling the area to serve as a winter sports center. Under competent leadership a well-rounded municipal recreation program is likely to include a sufficient number of special outdoor events to assure a fairly continuous diversified use of such a stadium during many months of the year. When not required for use by the recreation authorities, it can be rented to organizations for suitable purposes; such use, however, should be secondary.

Rancho Cienega Stadium, Los Angeles. This stadium seating 6,000, operated by the recreation and parks commission, is fenced so that crowds can be controlled and admission conveniently charged. The policy adopted for its operation was designed not only to protect the department's program but to avoid competition with commercially managed stadiums in the city. The following excerpts from the regulations governing the stadium's use, adopted when it was opened, indicate the basis on which the stadium is operated, along with a few important operation details:

The main purpose of the stadium is to provide a place for recreation activities that are an outgrowth of the city-wide program conducted by the department and which require accommodations for a large number of spectators or unusual control of spectators. . . . The stadium is not intended primarily as a place for the raising of revenue or for the accommodation of professional and semiprofessional events from which profit is made. . . . The recreation program of the department taxes the capacity of the stadium, consuming all available periods. . . . Contests are confined primarily to Saturday afternoons and Sundays. High school contests, however, are held usually on Friday afternoons. . . . Practice of teams in various sports is curtailed and is the exception rather than the rule in order to preserve the grass for the week ends. . . . Interdistrict school contests, contests of parochial schools and of private schools are considered suitable for the stadium. . . . Generally speaking and for all department activities, admission is without reserved seats. . . . Applications for special uses of the stadium outside of the department's regular program are considered on their individual merit and permits are granted on satisfactory terms only by action in each case of the board of commissioners. Such outside uses are governed by a standard form of contract. . . . The standard of maintenance and condition of facilities is a little higher than that which applies to playgrounds generally. . . . When and if any nondepartment events are held, the management of the spectators is under control of the department, but the cost thereof including ushers is borne by the lessee. The lessee also pays a reasonable charge for clean-up. . . . Concession rights are reserved by the commission, but no concession for more than a single event is granted until use of the stadium indicates the advisability of such concession. . . . The director of the Rancho Cienega Playground acts as manager or director of the stadium and reports to the superintendent of recreation.

THE MUNICIPAL CAMP

Camping affords an unexcelled opportunity for adventure, discovery, developing social relationships, appreciating nature, and a change from routine activities and the urban environment. There is a growing belief among leaders in the fields of education and recreation that all citizens, young and old, should have the benefit of a camping experience. The greatest development of organized municipal camping has taken place on the Pacific Coast, where several cities have established camps, many of them in national forest areas. With the pronounced trend toward the acquisition of state and regional parks, the camping movement has received greater attention. Many communities provide some of the values of camping experience through the operation of overnight or day camps which involve little expense. Exceptional opportunities for municipal camping are afforded in Oglebay Park, a large outlying area owned by the city of Wheeling, West Virginia. They include camping facilities serving individual guests, a center where large groups can be accommodated, a conference camp unit consisting of farm cottages grouped about a main building, and family cabins which can be rented by the week. The operation of the various types of camps naturally involves different personnel, regulations, rates, and services.

The Organized Municipal Camp. In this type of camp [4] the recreation agency, besides providing the facilities, feeds the campers, conducts a program of activities, and in some instances furnishes transportation to and from the camp. In practically every instance these camps are at a considerable distance from the city; one such camp is 335 miles away. Reservations, which are made in advance at the department office, are usually on a weekly basis, but campers may stay for more than one week. One- and two-week outings are featured at some of the family camps. A few camps accommodate families; others are for boys or girls. A nominal fee is charged, which helps considerably in meeting the expense of operation, but arrangements are sometimes made for children without funds to attend the camp. A few municipal camps are for underprivileged or undernourished children selected by the social agencies of the city, although most camps are open to everyone. As a rule, camps are operated during the summer months only, although they are increasingly available for week-end or vacation use during other seasons; in a few cases they serve as centers for winter sports.

Staff. Every camp is in charge of a manager who has full responsibility for its operation and who acts as host. In many instances his wife serves as camp hostess. The recreation program at the camp is conducted by a director, and in some camps a naturalist and activity leaders are also employed. A most important member of the staff is the cook, who has one or more assistants in addition to dishwashers and kitchen helpers. Other employees are a dining-room manager, waitresses, office clerk, general utility man, lifeguard, nurse, and one or more caretakers. These are seasonal workers with the exception of the caretaker, who is often employed to care for the camp throughout the year. If a city operates several camps, a general supervisor is needed; and since many camps are used continuously, this person is usually a year-round worker.

Programs. Programs are planned to take advantage of the camp environ-

[4] A description of the vacation camps conducted by the Oakland Recreation Department, a pioneer in this field, will be found in Chap. 27.

ment and afford a change from the activities regularly engaged in at home. Swimming, boating, and fishing are popular camp activities, and nature hikes are conducted regularly by the naturalist, who also helps campers in nature study and in making nature collections. Horseback riding, picnics, overnight hikes, moonlight rides, and pack-train trips into the mountains are featured, especially at the Western camps. Courts are provided for tennis, badminton, horseshoes, archery, and a variety of sports. Social activities, dances, and parties are arranged from time to

Campers furnish the entertainment at San Francisco's Silver Tree Day Camp (Courtesy of San Francisco Recreation and Park Department).

time. The center of interest in the evening is the campfire, where amateur theatricals, impromptu musical numbers, storytelling, stunts, community singing, and frankfurter and marshmallow roasts round out the camp day.

Some camp programs have been criticized on the grounds they are too highly organized, that too many activities are crowded into the day, and that the campers do not have an opportunity for sufficient rest and relaxation. Municipal camp programs are rarely open to this criticism. They provide varied, attractive activities, many of which utilize the special advantages afforded by the camp environment; but they are informal in nature, and campers are free to choose the activities in which they desire to take part. As one camp folder states, the sole duty of the campers is "to make the most of their time in the enjoyment of their vacation." The camp staff helps them to achieve this objective.

Protection of the Campers. Recreation authorities have a greater responsibility in operating a camp than they do in conducting a center located near the homes of the people served. In the summer camp, which is usually many miles from the city in which the campers live, the people must be cared for twenty-four hours a day for periods of a week or more. A nurse and access to medical service are essential in every camp, and special precautions must be taken to protect the health and safety of all the campers. For example, individuals are generally required to submit health certificates before they are permitted to register; people who handle the food must also meet standards of good health; a supply of pure water for drinking purposes and for swimming must be assured. Provision has to be made for the proper disposal of waste, and continuous care taken to assure the sanitary condition of the entire camp site. Regulations governing boating, swimming, and other activities should be designed to assure safe and enjoyable vacations for all.

Overnight Camps. The overnight short-term camp makes it possible for boys and girls who are unable to attend camps for a longer period to experience some of the joys of camping. Several cities have established camping centers where groups of boys or girls are accommodated during a twenty-four-hour period, usually in an outlying park. Various methods are used to reach camp—hiking, trolley or bus lines, private cars, or chartered buses. Children arrive in camp in the early afternoon and leave after lunch the following day. It is generally desirable for the camp to supply the food, with the children paying a moderate fee to defray the cost; preparation of one or more meals is a part of the camp experience. In certain cities the camp is conducted continuously throughout the summer, with groups from the individual playgrounds attending the camp, in some cases once a week.

The staff at a camp which has been operated successfully for several years consists of a director, a caretaker, a cook, and a lifeguard. Programs are designed to give the children a good time—an experience which they will remember with pleasure. Hikes, nature activities, swimming, boating, campfire programs, and games appropriate to the camp setting are featured. Consideration of others, self-reliance, and cooperative activity are by-products of the overnight camp, as well as of the other types.

Day Camps. The day camp has had a more rapid growth than any other type of camp operated by municipal recreation authorities. It affords much of the appeal and joy of camping without the expense and responsibility involved in providing overnight accommodations for the campers. Most day camps are conducted in large parks, although some have been established on neighborhood areas. A site that can be closed to the public while used as a day camp is highly desirable. Day camps are usually accessible by bus or streetcar, but in some instances chartered buses bring the children from playgrounds, settlements, private agencies, or schools to spend the day at camp. Milk is generally furnished by the camp agency; lunch, too, is sometimes provided at a small charge. In addition to the director and one or more assistants, the staff may well include a naturalist and a nurse.

Day-camp programs are designed to take fullest advantage of the opportunities offered by the camp site and to satisfy the child's craving for adventure. They supplement, not duplicate, the usual playground activities. Nature collections are made, weather signs are noted, campfire methods are taught, treasure hunts are held, nature games are played, and Indian crafts, dances, and ceremonials are enjoyed. For many city children, wading in the brook, running on the grass, and climbing trees are new and thrilling experiences. As a rule, the camp day closes in the late afternoon, but an evening campfire program affords a fitting climax to the day's activities and is a feature at a number of camps.

WINTER SPORTS FACILITIES

As a result of the remarkable growth of public interest in winter sports, facilities for skating, tobogganing, skiing, and other outdoor winter activities have become common features of the municipal recreation system in parts of the country where such activities are possible. Winter sports afford healthful and stimulating activity to large numbers of people at a relatively low cost.

The Skating Rink. Natural, quiet, shallow-water areas make excellent skating rinks. Care must be taken to prevent people from skating on the ice until it is sufficiently thick to assure safety; and if the water is deep, lifesaving equipment must be conspicuously provided nearby in case of emergencies. Except in neighborhoods with natural water areas, rinks must be constructed as described in Chapter 13. The preparation of areas for skating requires advance planning, since equipment must be ready and workers informed as to methods of constructing the rinks so that no time is lost when cold weather arrives. As a rule, rinks are sprayed or flooded at night when the temperature is lowest, and the maintenance work is done after the rink is closed in the evening. Proper and continuous care of the ice is essential to secure the maximum number of skating days and satisfactory ice conditions. Because of the shortness of the season it is desirable to light the facilities to permit evening use.

A worker is generally assigned to each skating rink to maintain order, care for the ice, and have general supervision of the rink while it is in use. One or more additional workers may be employed for a few hours each day after the rink closes to scrape, clean, and resurface it for the following day. In one city three-man crews clean and flood several rinks each night. In case a building near the rink is used as a warming shelter and has facilities for checking skates, a worker is generally needed to care for it. There is much to be said in favor of employing a recreation leader to take charge of a large rink; for in addition to serving as a general supervisor, he can help children learn to skate, organize hockey teams, and promote a program of special events.

Construction of the Farwell Rink in Detroit. This artificial ice-skating center includes an oval skating track, hockey rink, and general skating area (Courtesy of Detroit, Mich., Department of Parks and Recreation).

On ponds and most natural skating areas there is ample space for a variety of ice activities. A section approximately 100 by 220 feet can be set aside for ice hockey and another for figure skating, while the rest of the area is used for general skating. If competitive skating is popular, a track may be marked off, possibly around the hockey rink. Space is limited, however, at most man-made rinks, whether of natural or artificial ice, and consequently the rinks must serve as multiple-use areas. Periods for general skating predominate, but at designated times the areas are set aside for specialized activities.

The operation of artificial rinks involves different problems and procedures. Once the rink is prepared for winter use it continues in operation for several months. Special events can be arranged with reasonable assurance that the condition of the ice will permit them to be held. The greater volume of use of artificial rinks and the care of the refrigeration equipment necessitate a larger staff. In spite of the popularity of these municipal rinks and the fact that an admission charge is usually made, the cost of operation often far exceeds the income.

The Toboggan Slide. Tobogganing is a thrilling sport which requires a well-constructed, carefully operated slide and at least two workers to operate and keep it in good condition. One worker is the starter at the top of the slide, who sees that persons are properly seated and that the toboggan does not start down the slide until the preceding group is clear of it. The other worker, usually stationed near the bottom, is the signal man, who indicates when the toboggan may start down the slide and who prevents persons from crossing the course. There is seldom a charge for the use of a toboggan slide if a group has its own toboggan; if toboggans are rented, as is often the case, a worker is needed to care for them.

Coasting. The great popularity of coasting among children has caused recreation authorities to utilize for this sport golf courses, park hillsides free from obstructions, and other large areas with natural slopes. These areas, as well as the low sled slides erected on playgrounds, require some supervision, but their operation and maintenance are relatively easy. In spite of traffic hazards, the street is still the most popular sliding place; and where other suitable areas are not available, recreation authorities set aside certain streets for coasting. With the cooperation of the police, barriers are placed at these streets during the periods when coasting is permitted and supervised. Access is not denied to vehicles, but traffic is reduced to a minimum. Police are stationed at some coasting streets; usually, however, the streets are supervised by the recreation department, which is also responsible for placing barricades at the top and bottom of the hills and for filling, cleaning, and lighting the lanterns placed on the barricades. In one city, information as to the condition of the coasting hills is furnished the newspapers and telephoned daily to each of the schools.

More detailed information on the operation of the facilities discussed in this chapter and on other facilities such as tennis courts and ball diamonds may be found in the publications listed in the bibliography at the end of the book.

PART SIX

PROGRAM FEATURES AND SERVICES

One method of analyzing the service rendered by the recreation department is to consider, as was done in the previous section, the programs carried on at the various units in the recreation system—the playground, recreation building, or golf course. Another method is to appraise the department's program in respect to various forms of recreation—music, athletics, nature, crafts, and so forth. The following chapters deal with the contribution which the recreation department is making in several of these major forms, at its centers or on a city-wide basis, to groups participating in its own programs or to other community agencies. The chapters in Part Six describe the specific activities carried on and the many different methods used in conducting them. Because of its significance, the service to homes, industries, hospitals, the handicapped, and other special groups is recorded in a separate chapter. Part Six concludes with a description of the recreation facilities, activities, and services of six representative recreation departments.

20. ARTS AND CRAFTS

D R. L. P. JACKS, the noted English educator, has said, "Recreation includes all the beautiful skills, crafts, and hobbies that human beings can practice, on and up to the finest arts." Few other activities yield as direct, immediate, and lasting satisfactions to the individual as arts and crafts. Seeing an object take shape in one's own hands or transforming an idea into tangible form gives a person a satisfying sense of achievement. Through arts and crafts people may develop skills and hobbies which they can enjoy in their homes throughout their entire lives. They can make objects of usefulness and beauty, find outlets for their creative abilities, and relieve many of the nervous tensions of present-day living. "The field of arts and crafts represents one of the many outlets for human expression and serves as a form of release for the universally inherent desire to create . . . however, no arts and crafts activity can remain static, but must provide continuously a chain reaction to new and increasingly significant fields of expression for the individual." [1]

Fortunately, many kinds of craft activity are closely related to other forms of recreation, such as music, drama, games, and nature. It is not surprising, therefore, that arts and crafts have an important place in the program of the recreation department. Some of the specific ways in which the possibilities of these activities are being realized on the playgrounds, in the centers, and through community-wide activities are described briefly in the pages which follow.

PROGRAM CHARACTERISTICS

Municipal recreation programs vary widely in the nature, scope, and quality of their arts and crafts activities. Recreation authorities realize more and more, however, the potential value of these activities and the necessity of high standards in conducting them. Projects are selected according to the abilities, interests, and capacities of the members of the group; individuals are encouraged to create their own designs rather than to follow patterns worked out by others. A spirit of informality characterizes most groups, the members of which are free to select the

[1] *The Recreation Program*, The Athletic Institute, Chicago, 1954, p. 17.

particular project to which they wish to devote their efforts. In an indoor center one may find a ceramics class in which the members are making a wide variety of objects or a workshop group in which men and women are building model sailboats, desk lamps, or fine furniture.

Development of an appreciation and recognition of beauty should be an objective of the arts and crafts program, but the usefulness and value of well-designed objects are also emphasized. The use of simple hand tools is encouraged; the need for implements may itself furnish the basis for a craft project. Utilization of local materials is fostered, often for reasons of economy but also because using resources in the community offers the possibility of developing local folk arts and crafts. Honeysuckle, where abundant, may be widely used for basketry; sea shells, pine cones, and other native materials likewise serve a variety of craft projects.

More and more, recreation departments employ skilled craftsmen to serve as instructors, who, under the guidance of trained recreation leaders, help both children and adults attain greater skills and secure more satisfaction from their participation in the arts and crafts program. They recognize increasingly the fundamental standards considered indispensable in conducting such a program by the arts and crafts committee of The Athletic Institute's recreation program workshop: integrity, quality of performance, preservation of individuality, respect for property, and safety.

PLAYGROUND ACTIVITIES

Since the early days of the playground movement, arts and crafts in various forms have had a place in the program. The term "industrial work," first applied to these activities, suggests their restricted, practical, and formal nature. Today, however, playground crafts are almost limitless in variety, using widely different media and producing an equally varied list of objects. The character of the workmanship, the specific types of projects, and the time required for completing them vary according to the age and skill of the individual children; many crafts appeal to both boys and girls. At most summer playgrounds, due to the short season and the fluctuating attendance because of vacations, arts and crafts are conducted in a relatively informal manner.

The range of arts and crafts programs is illustrated by the list of playground activities in which weekly instruction has been provided in Greensboro, North Carolina. They include carving of wood and colored plaster of Paris; modeling sawdust, clay, excelsior, and papier-mâché; making shell earrings and pins; finger painting on glass, paper, and wood; making things of leather and plastics; weaving potholders and rugs with looper clips; textile painting including stenciling; potato prints and spatter prints; carving and hammering metal trays and pins; and constructing marionettes from wooden blocks. In addition, each playground competes in the annual sandcraft contest by building a sandbox display. On one occasion, structures featured included an Independence Day scene, an ideal community playlot, a drive-in theater, Alcatraz, and a boxing bout in Madison Square Garden, all constructed with sand, materials native to the playground, and objects made in the craft classes.

Relating Crafts to Other Activities. Many craft projects are related to other phases of the program or to special events in which the objects made are either displayed or utilized. Spatter printing and the construction of feeding stations and ant houses combine both the craft and nature interest. Flower and leaf arrangements and prints furnish motifs for art projects. The program posters, costumes, properties, and stage equipment needed for simple plays or an elaborate playground pageant are made by arts or crafts groups. Music and crafts are related through the construction of tom-toms, tambourines, snare drums, pipes of Pan, shepherd's pipes, and simple stringed instruments used in music activities. Puppetry combines both the craft and drama interests. The announcement of a pushmobile derby is an incentive for boys to construct all kinds of vehicles, just as the opportunity to test kites and model boats in a contest gives added zest to these constructive activities. The design and decoration of floats for a parade stimulate resourcefulness and encourage expert workmanship.

The ways in which crafts can be related to special weeks on the playground have been graphically demonstrated by the Milwaukee Department of Municipal Recreation. For example, during Pet-show Week, daily craft activities consist of carving soap animals, plaster casting of animals, and making badges for the winners, animal felt novelties, wooden garden ornaments, and stuffed animals. For Flower-show Week, suggested activities are the decoration of flower containers, flower arranging, preparing awards, and making wild-flower scrapbooks, flower labels, ornaments, and identification tags. Similarly, crafts can be integrated with other playground features throughout the season.

Indian Crafts in Louisville, Kentucky. Occasionally a recreation department builds its summer playground program around a particular theme such as colonial or Indian life; and when this is done, crafts, like other activities, are directly related to this theme. In Louisville, a playground contest based on Indian themes furnished the incentive for many craft projects some of which are described as follows: [2]

Tepees were fashioned from burlap bags sewn together, brown wrapping paper, and old sheets painted in approved Indian style and color. Macaroni,

[2] "On the Summer Playgrounds of 1934," *Recreation*, vol. 29, no. 3, p. 147, June, 1935.

painted and broken into short lengths and then strung, made necklaces. Melon seeds colored with crepe-paper dye, and bits of colored magazine advertisements rolled into cylinders also made effective beads, while polished tin provided material for jewelry making. War bonnets and other headdresses were made from crepe paper, feathers, and painted tag board. Twisted strands of black crepe paper and old stockings became long, realistic braids of hair of the Indian maidens. Moccasins were created from old tennis slippers and sneakers painted with appropriate designs. Tin cans filled with pebbles served for rattles.

The properties used in this Indian ceremonial were made by the playground children (Courtesy of Chicago Park District).

The "boom-boom" of the Indian drums came from wooden cheese boxes and large lard cans covered with stretched canvas and decorated with mystic symbols. A local pottery furnished slightly chipped jars and bowls at give-away prices, and four-hour enamel was used to give them a permanent decoration. Snowshoes were woven from willows gathered near the Ohio River, which also furnished shells for other projects. Burlap bags, expertly cut and decorated, supplied the basis for most of the costumes, and so well done was the work that these costumes belied their humble origin. One playground made a beautiful canoe of light wood and strips of paper mounted on a coaster wagon which supplied the necessary power for the canoe to glide majestically on its way.

This brief account indicates the great variety of interesting activities undertaken in preparing for a playground contest and suggests the infinite possibilities which the playground program offers to the resourceful recreation leader. Similar experiences in many other cities in preparing for the playground circus, festival, pageant, or other feature event could be recorded.

Craft activities are usually carried on within or on the porch of the playground building, although benches and tables are set up out of doors, preferably in the shade. Tools and supplies are provided as part of the equipment of every playground, their amount and types varying with the funds available, the number of children to be served, and the projects to be undertaken. Because of limited funds, inexpensive and salvaged materials are widely used in some cities.

A craftmobile has greatly increased participation in and enthusiasm for the craft program in St. Cloud, Minnesota. The mobile consists of a brightly colored house trailer containing a section with machines and electrical devices, a workbench area, and storage lockers for supplies and equipment. Long collapsible tables are also stored in the trailer. The craft specialist makes the rounds of the city's seven playgrounds with the mobile on a regular schedule. Its use has made possible a greater variety of activities, economy in the utilization of supplies, and wide public awareness of the craft program.

INDOOR-CENTER PROGRAMS

Because indoor centers are open for a longer season than most playgrounds and serve primarily young people and adults, a more highly specialized arts and crafts program is possible. Many people attend a center to take part in a specific activity, and special instructors conduct classes or serve groups interested in arts and crafts. Most of these groups are informal in organization and are open to all who wish to enroll. Other groups that have developed a continuing interest in a particular activity —often one which involves progressively higher degrees of skill—have been organized on a formal club basis, sometimes with definite membership requirements. Examples are model-boat and -aircraft building, photography, ceramics, sketching, or quilting. The range of arts and crafts included in a comprehensive indoor-center program is indicated by the list of such activities in the Milwaukee centers, appearing in Chapter 18, as well as the activities listed in Chapter 27.

The seriousness with which boys voluntarily undertake difficult craft projects is recorded in a report [3] of the Chicago Park District. The members of the model-airplane clubs, it is pointed out, "must cultivate patience

[3] *Annual Report,* Chicago Park District, 1937.

and application. Their workmanship is unbelievably delicate. They make completed planes weighing less than half an ounce." Other boys' groups talk overseas with fellow enthusiasts abroad by means of short-wave radio sets which they have engineered and put together. In one of the park shops, boys fabricated vest-pocket engines from solid blocks of steel, operated by an eye dropperful of gasoline, to drive their miniature powered planes. A score of junior yachting clubs built passenger dinghies of solid mahogany, accurate to within one-quarter of an inch. The rocket

Basketmaking class at the Washington Recreation Center (Courtesy of Waterloo, Iowa, Recreation Commission).

club organized by the Fairlawn, New Jersey, Recreation Department illustrates how alert authorities are providing the expert leadership required to enable a group of boys to pursue safely a new and challenging interest. In all these activities boys meet and overcome difficult and challenging problems.

Indoor Facilities. Many recreation buildings have well-equipped craft rooms such as a woodworking shop, a weaving room, or a ceramics studio. Such facilities make possible a highly specialized crafts program, facilitate the storing of tools and materials, and enable the rooms to be reserved for individual or group use. A few recreation buildings contain a room set aside for art instruction or for the exhibition of paintings and other art objects. Many arts and crafts programs, however, are handicapped by the fact that they must share the use of facilities with other activities. At many school centers sewing, leathercraft, clay modeling, art classes, and other crafts which require no fixed equipment are carried on in classrooms, but an increasing number of manual training and domestic science rooms are opened in the evening for such activities as sewing or cooking classes and woodworking, metalcraft, or hobby groups. The employment of day-school instructors to take charge of the evening activities in these rooms minimizes the problems resulting from their dual use. In a number of instances arts and crafts groups, as a service project, have undertaken to make center facilities more attractive.

Typical Programs. The variety of opportunities for creative arts and crafts offered at indoor centers is illustrated by the activities available to the people of Hutchinson, Kansas, and Waterloo, Iowa. Fall and winter activities offered by the Hutchinson Recreation Commission have included the following, many of them with separate classes for beginners and for advanced students:

Aluminum etching	Millinery
Ceramics—creative, molds	Model-airplane construction
Charcoal sketching	Painting—oil, water color
Copper enameling and tooling	Photography, photo tinting,
Crocheting	darkroom technique
Embroidery	Puppetry
Children's crafts	Rug weaving
Knitting	Sculpture
Lapidary work	Textile and Dresden china painting
Leathercraft	Construction of wood fiber flowers

All classes are open to men and women of all ages on payment of a modest fee and are held weekly, either afternoons or evenings, in most cases for eight sessions. Necessary materials are available at the center at cost. Each year a general crafts clinic is held for a period of several weeks, designed to teach persons who are to serve as instructors in vacation Bible schools, scout troops, YMCA camps, and related groups.

The indoor program provided by the Waterloo Recreation Commission similarly comprises a variety of craft activities serving a wide range of interests and includes the following classes for adults:

Archery-equipment construction	Hatmaking
Basketry	Interior decorating
Ceramics	Knitting
Chair caning	Leathercraft
Christmas-card painting	Oil painting
Copper enameling	Pottery making
Costume-jewelry making	Upholstering
Flower arranging	Water-color painting and drawing
Fly tying	Weaving
Fur repairing	Woodworking

An open-house and registration day at the center early in the fall is the occasion for demonstrations of many of the activities scheduled. Classes are open to men and women of all ages, are limited in size to assure maximum benefits, carry a nominal fee, and in most cases comprise eight weekly sessions. Special classes for children afford the opportunity to develop skills in painting, clay modeling, drawing, and woodworking. Art and photography exhibits are arranged from time to time, and several one-day workshops for youth leaders offer instruction in crafts related to various holidays. Facilities at the center are used by such groups as the Camera Club, Hatmaking Club, Color Camera Club, and Weavers' Guild.

SPECIAL ARTS AND CRAFTS CENTERS

Many arts and crafts activities carried on at the playground or indoor center are more or less related to other parts of the program, but several cities have special centers for arts and crafts. Some of these centers are used primarily for advanced groups that have acquired elementary skills at the neighborhood centers; others provide the place where most of the arts and crafts activities, primarily for adults, are carried on. Many offer instruction in specialized activities that are not available elsewhere in the community. A director is in charge, supplemented by a staff of special instructors.

"Art for fun" is the keynote of the adult Arts and Crafts Center operated by the recreation department in St. Petersburg, Florida. Hundreds of men and women, many of them elderly, are gaining satisfaction and sociability every week in fifty different class groups. Its success is indicated by the fact that the center has been moved to larger quarters three times since it was established in 1952. The classes are taught advanced techniques in loom weaving, woodworking, basketry, ceramics, art in metal, enamel on copper, leathercraft, puppets and marionettes, and dollmaking. Members of classes in the art groups—painting in oils and water colors, pastel drawing, and sculpturing—find colorful and fascinating subjects in the nearby boats, docks, and waterfront activities. The Weavers' Guild, consisting of elderly ladies, has the use of a room with forty looms.

Each person registering at the center pays a membership fee of one dollar per year. Courses are offered on a four-week basis, two classes per week, at a nominal charge plus the cost of materials. The center is open morning, afternoon, and evening, Monday through Friday. Income from class fees is divided; part goes to the instructor and part to the department to cover cost of operation, maintenance, and equipment. The instructors who supplement department staff members and who have numbered as many as thirty-two at the height of the season, are required to have teaching ability as well as training and experience in their field of arts and crafts. Many of them are retired; all have a keen interest in their craft and in the people they are teaching.

The Westchester Workshop, established in 1930 and operated by the Westchester County, New York, Recreation Commission, serves as the center of creative arts for the entire county. Operated in the County Cen-

The play-school program introduces young children to the elements of art (Courtesy of Willamalane Park and Recreation District, Springfield, Ore.).

ter, the workshop offers opportunities for participation in a variety of activities—morning, afternoon, and evening throughout the year. Among the many courses offered to adults are flower arranging, furniture refinishing, motion-picture photography, silk-screen decoration, slip-cover and drapery making, and landscape, still-life, and portrait painting. A Junior Workshop for boys and girls eight to sixteen is open on Saturday mornings, and courses offered include woodwork, puppetry, jewelry making and metalcraft, pottery, and painting.

More than 1,000 adults and 150 boys and girls attend some seventy workshop classes each year. The staff also conducts a training course in recreational crafts for local leaders throughout the county, arts and crafts sessions and swap shops in local communities, and a lecture demonstration of craft projects for recreation leaders in county institutions. In many ways the center is contributing to an appreciation of creative activities on the part of the people in the county.

OTHER PROGRAMS

Supplementing the activities regularly carried on at the playgrounds and centers, the recreation department fosters an interest in arts and crafts in many ways, some of them conducted on a community-wide basis.

Arts and Crafts Exhibits. The arts and crafts exhibit is an annual feature in many cities. Exhibits of the articles made at the playgrounds or centers are sometimes shown in the neighborhood stores, but more often the exhibition is city-wide and housed in a centrally located building with suitable display facilities. Greater interest is stimulated when displays are accompanied by demonstrations of arts and crafts activities by playground and center groups. In one large city where the exhibit was on display for an entire week, several booths were devoted to such demonstrations. In one booth labeled "For the Home," leathercraft, metalcraft, rug hooking, loom and raffia weaving, pottery, and other crafts were demonstrated on succeeding days. In the "To Wear" booth, weaving, sewing, crocheting, knitting, and jewelry making were demonstrated. In the workshop, groups constructed model airplanes and yachts, games, musical instruments, and archery tackle, while model airplanes were flown in the hall. Puppetry shows were held, as well as group musical and dramatic performances.

Such exhibits and demonstrations are exceedingly valuable in interpreting to the public this phase of the department's program. They afford an occasion for informing people as to the time, place, and nature of the various clubs and classes and for recruiting new members. They furnish a special incentive to the individuals in the arts and crafts groups to put forth their best efforts and an opportunity for them to show their friends and the public objects which in varying degrees express their own personality. Closely related to the crafts exhibits are the exhibitions of photographs, which are arranged by photography clubs; or the hobby shows, an annual event in some cities.

A Community Art Program. The Oglebay Institute in Wheeling, West Virginia, serves a tri-state area with an art program and exhibitions in a city that does not support an art gallery. It functions both as a gallery and an art institute. At Oglebay Park a summer gallery offers one-man shows, changed weekly, with Sunday demonstrations. Annual events are a regional artists' show, a spring exhibition for children, a "bohemian" art show in an old downtown market, and winter exhibitions in the city's largest hotel. The summer exhibition series furnishes inspiration for a tremendous demand for the winter classes for children and for adults. During the winter at least two weekly art programs are presented before community groups through the media of television and illustrated lectures. Built around the theme "Art in Everyday Life," the programs are designed to make art understandable and to awaken the public to the importance of aesthetic satisfaction. Art instruction is also a feature of the summer day-camp program.

21. ATHLETICS, GAMES, AND SPORTS

The widespread public interest in athletics, games, and sports is an outstanding characteristic of American life. These activities play a larger part in most community recreation programs and attract more people than any other form of recreation. Participation by large numbers of people rather than by a few highly skilled players is encouraged, and attention is given to the development of programs for all ages and both sexes.

The contribution of athletics, games, and sports to the well-being of American youth is widely recognized, and the importance of giving all children and youth an opportunity to engage in them was repeatedly emphasized at the President's Conference on Fitness of American Youth, held in June, 1956, at Annapolis, Maryland. Principles underlying the provision of such activities for boys and girls have been stated as follows by the Educational Policies Commission of the National Education Association: [1]

All children and youth should have opportunities to develop skill in a variety of athletic activities. Young children need chances to play games that involve few rules and small numbers of players. For children in the upper elementary grades there should be limited experiences in team games suited to their needs, interests, and stage of development. As they progress through school, boys and girls become more interested in the more highly organized individual, dual, and team sports.

There should be dual sports and team sports, easy sports and hard ones, indoor and outdoor, common games and unusual ones, some for boys alone, some for girls alone, and some for boys and girls together. There should be activities suitable for children with physical handicaps, some for small and delicate children, some to test the mettle of the larger and stronger ones.

No other agency is doing so much as the recreation department to implement these principles and to promote and provide games and sports for children, young people, and adults. On the playgrounds boys and girls are helped to develop interests and skills and to acquire experience

[1] *School Athletics: Problems and Policies,* National Education Association, Educational Policies Commission, Washington, 1954.

354

in sportsmanship and competition. Similar opportunities are provided for all ages at the recreation buildings and indoor centers. The recreation department furnishes ball fields primarily for league play; swimming pools and skating rinks where individuals may engage in informal, self-directed activity; and facilities such as courts for tennis, handball, horseshoes, and badminton. By lighting these areas and facilities it has greatly extended periods of play. It encourages advancement in skill through the organization of contests and tournaments in these activities, and offers individual or group instruction in fundamental game skills. Through the organization of teams and leagues in baseball, volleyball, soccer, and other games, it affords opportunity for large numbers of individuals to play regularly with others of similar ability, whether they are "dubs" or players of high rank. It helps people interested in a particular sport to find means of enjoying it and of enlisting others in the activity. It cooperates with local, state, or national bodies in the promotion of special events, some of which involve intercity competition.

The nature and content of the sports program in a locality naturally vary according to the community's size, local interests, facilities, traditions, climate, type of organization, and other factors. Complete figures are not available as to the number of localities that conduct various activities and the number of individuals that participate in them. The *1956 Recreation and Park Yearbook*,[2] however, affords a fairly accurate picture of the extent to which various games and sports are included in community recreation programs. It also records how many different participants in each activity were reported by the limited number of local authorities that keep registration figures or close estimates. Table 10, following, indicates the number of departments reporting that they organized, supervised, conducted, or promoted each of thirty-two activities, and the average number of different people taking part in each. In many cases the participation figures are estimates, and they do not include the people who occasionally take part in the activity on an informal basis. Nevertheless the table indicates the relative emphasis on the various activities in local recreation programs and the average number of persons per community taking part in each.

ORGANIZATION OF GAMES AND SPORTS

There is no standard pattern of municipal sports organization, but similar procedures are followed in most communities. The program promoted by the recreation department usually has two principal parts: (1) The activities organized and conducted by the playground and indoor-center staff in much the same manner as the other phases of the program.

[2] National Recreation Association, New York, 1956.

The activities are designed primarily for the children, youth, and adults living in the neighborhood. (2) The city-wide activities, usually developed by a division of municipal sports under a special supervisor. Certain activities such as basketball and softball may be included in both sections of the program, but they are organized and conducted on a somewhat different basis.

Table 10. Games and Sports in Local Recreation Programs, 1955

Activity	Number of Localities Reporting	Average Number of Participants
Baseball	1,733	657
Softball	1,661	903
Swimming	1,454	5,174
Basketball	1,408	705
Horseshoes	1,383	342
Tennis	1,344	133
Volleyball	1,261	277
Table tennis	1,130	616
Badminton	973	187
Shuffleboard	799	342
Ice skating	748	3,336
Croquet	744	137
Track and field sports	740	472
Paddle tennis	679	396
Archery	678	197
Touch football	664	348
Athletic tests	607	528
Tetherball	607	518
Golf	546	2,016
Tumbling and gymnastics	433	228
Soccer	321	340
Synchronized swimming	301	556
Regulation football	300	390
Boxing	278	127
Handball	266	368
Indoor bowling	260	229
Boating	251	1,017
Skiing	217	463
Ice hockey	189	248
Tobogganing	136	736
Six-man football	105	216
Lawn bowling	100	514

Playground Programs. On the playground, children take part in a variety of running, circle, and low organized games and relays; in team games such as softball and volleyball, organized on a league basis; in round-robin, perpetual, and elimination tournaments in a wide range of activities; and in playdays, junior Olympics, track and field meets, and sports days that are highlights of the summer sports season. Children are classified, usually by age, for participation in the activities, and appropriate co-recreational events are included in the program. Winners of events at the individual playgrounds compete for district and city-wide championships. However, the joy of participation, the development of sportsmanship, and the acquisition of game skills—rather than the winning of championships—are major objectives.

A *Typical Program.* The variety of activities included in a playground program is illustrated by the summer events scheduled in Leonia, New Jersey, a community of 8,000. All the activities except baseball and softball take place at a central playground. In the list that follows, an asterisk marks those activities in which tournaments are conducted.

Archery	Punching bag
Baseball *	Shuffleboard *
Baseball clinic	Smash
Basketball	Softball *
Baton twirling	Stickball *
Bounce ball *	Table tennis *
Box hockey *	Tennis *
Circle games	Tennis clinic
Handball *	Tetherball *
Hopscotch *	Touch football
Horseshoes *	Tumbling classes
Miscellaneous	Volleyball *
skill games *	Wrestling classes
Paddle tennis *	

Other special activities are a father-and-son softball game, state playground championships, a foul-shooting contest, a father-and-daughter softball game, and a football contest. Outings include trips to a major-league baseball game and to a lake where swimming and boating may be enjoyed. Occasionally a ball game or contest is arranged with a playground group from a neighboring community. This type of program serves boys and girls of different ages with interest in a variety of sports.

Indoor-center Activities. Games and sports are conducted at recreation buildings and indoor centers in much the same way as at the playgrounds. They are organized or supervised by the center staff, and primarily serve groups that attend the center regularly. Owing to the lack of gymnasiums in most cities, however, facilities in recreation buildings are also needed for the city-wide program. Consequently in many buildings and centers, periods are designated for the use of teams or groups organized by the supervisor of municipal sports. The types of games and sports conducted indoors are indicated by the programs appearing in Chapter 18.

City-wide Programs. Supplementing the activities at the playgrounds and indoor centers is the program organized and promoted on a city-wide basis. It comprises not only teams and leagues formed among clubs, industries, churches, and other groups for competition in team games but also players organized to participate in a variety of individual or dual sports representing all segments of the community. Since most of the activities take place on public properties such as playfields, sports cen-

Mercury vapor lamps installed at this softball field extend its service to players and spectators alike (Courtesy of Burbank, Calif., Park and Recreation Department).

ters, or facilities in large parks, the assignment of courts, fields, and facilities to affiliated groups for specific periods is a major responsibility of the sports supervisor. Methods of organizing city-wide leagues and individual sports were described in Chapter 16. Additional suggestions for city-wide sports organization follow.

Organizing Players in a Particular Sport. The common method of administering a city-wide program in a particular game or sport is through an association representing the leagues, teams, and individuals participating in the activity. The groups interested in baseball, for example, form a baseball association which, in cooperation with the recreation department, groups the teams for competitive league play and adopts rules and regulations for the conduct of the game on an organized basis. In the same way, a municipal tennis association fosters the game of tennis, develops rules and policies, and arranges and conducts tournaments. These organizations are designed to permit a democratic control by the teams, clubs, and individuals primarily interested in the respective sports. Policies and methods must conform to basic principles laid down by the recreation department, which is responsible for the areas and facilities used and for the general conduct of the program, but the rules are largely determined by the member groups. The magnitude of the sports organization in many cities would make it impossible, even though it were desirable, for the department staff to arrange the many details involved in league organization, schedule making, officiating, handling protests, and conducting tournaments. Valuable assistance in taking care of such matters is rendered by the officers and committees of the sports associations.

The Municipal Athletic Association. The necessity of setting up a separate organization for each major sport is eliminated in some cities by the formation of a municipal athletic association. All groups interested in sports and taking part in the municipal sports program may hold membership in the association and share in the responsibility for its operation. Subject to the general approval of the recreation department, the association administers the entire city-wide sports program and serves as the spokesman for all participating groups. Committees are commonly appointed to administer specific forms of sport in much the same manner as the city-wide organization in a single sport. The association affords much the same values as this type of organization; in addition, it brings together individuals and groups interested in a variety of sports and helps foster and promote ideals and standards in the conduct of all amateur athletic activities. By establishing unified eligibility rules and registration methods for all sports, the association helps avoid confusion and misunderstanding; and by creating a uniform procedure for the handling of protests and appeals, the problem of dealing with disputes is simplified.

The association has proved to be an effective means of coordinating activities in the field of sports and of eliminating the difficulties often encountered in cities with many local sports-governing bodies and a wide variation in their standards and practices. A representative of the recreation department, usually the supervisor of municipal athletics, serves as executive officer for the association, thereby assuring a close relationship with the municipal authorities. The sports program in Minneapolis, described in Chapter 27, is administered by a city-wide municipal athletic association.

A Typical Program. The list of activities promoted during the year on a city-wide basis by the Omaha, Nebraska, Park and Recreation Commission illustrates the nature and scope of such a program. City-wide leagues, some of them for boys, girls, men, and women, are conducted in softball, baseball, basketball, soccer, bowling, wrestling, and swimming. Tournaments for various classes are held in tennis, basketball, table tennis, wrestling, swimming, bait casting, archery, and pistol shooting. Annual clinics or schools in tennis, baseball, bowling, wrestling, and swimming are conducted prior to the playing season. Organizations such as the Omaha Tennis, Softball, and Wrestling Associations, the Municipal Baseball Association, and the Men's and Women's Bowling Associations cooperate with the commission in its sports program. Several junior and senior pistol and archery clubs use the commission's indoor range. Other activities, in addition to playground sports, include golf, rifle shooting, tennis, weight lifting, and track.

WATER AND WINTER SPORTS

The rapidly growing public interest in these seasonal activities, pointed out in preceding chapters, justifies special consideration of water and winter sports programs. These are commonly promoted by the department's sports division, although responsibility for the water sports program is sometimes assigned to a division of aquatics or of pools and beaches. In most of the country the season for these activities is comparatively short, and unlike much of the athletic program conducted on a city-wide basis, water and winter sports are restricted largely to a few special centers.

The Aquatic Program in Long Beach, California. This city is outstanding in its program of aquatics, largely because of its excellent water areas and facilities, which include several miles of salt-water frontage in addition to its indoor and outdoor pools. Swimming, diving, and lifesaving are taught at three beach areas and four high school pools, where many thousands swim. Weekly swimming meets culminate in the annual all-city swimming championships. Diving championships and lifesaving meets are other city-wide events. The 150 boys and girls of the Leeway Sailing Club and the adult members of the Senior Sabot Fleet experience the thrills and learn the skills of sailing through races and regattas. In the Tackle Buster clubs junior fishermen learn how to make and use tackle and go on fishing excursions. Youngsters construct, sail, and race their model boats at facilities furnished by the recreation commission. The Marine Stadium, the scene of motor boating and water skiing, attracts speedboat drivers from all over the nation, and the Municipal Marina affords a center for both motor boating and yachting enthusiasts. The program is designed to assure enjoyment and safety to the people while in, on, and near the water.

Aquatic Training. A large percentage of those who patronize municipal pools and beaches are primarily interested in informal recreational swimming, but an increasing number of people desire to become proficient in aquatic activities. Training programs therefore are no longer confined to teaching swimming or offering instruction in lifesaving. The Topeka, Kansas, Recreation Commission conducts a program including classes in synchronized and competitive swimming, water safety, and staff training. Classes are conducted from November through May on Saturdays according to the following schedule:

Class	Time
Intermediate synchronized	9:00–10:30 A.M.
Advanced synchronized	10:30–12:00 M.
Beginners synchronized	2:00– 3:00 P.M.
Senior competitive	3:00– 4:30 P.M.
Junior competitive	4:30– 6:00 P.M.

Staff- and instructor-training classes begin in March and terminate in time for a five-night water-safety instructors' course taught by a representative of the American Red Cross. Success of the program is evidenced by the waiting list for all classes and increased use of the municipal pools during the summer months.

Skin and Scuba Diving. These underwater activities hold a high rank among America's fastest growing sports, and recreation departments with access to water areas are beginning to realize that they deserve a place in the aquatics program. The Department of Parks and Recreation in Los Angeles County, California, has played a leading role in the promotion of skin and scuba diving. It pioneered public instruction in the sport in 1954, when classes were conducted for adults and late teen-agers. The department now offers instruction to junior skin divers—boys and girls from ten to fourteen years of age—at county pools. It also certifies underwater instructors who complete an extensive sixty-hour course and conducts monthly seminars for this group. The department with the assistance of a technical advisory committee has issued a comprehensive manual, *Underwater Recreation*, and a training film in color, both of which have been widely distributed and have proved useful to other agencies in initiating and conducting underwater programs.

Winter Sports Activities. Snow and ice sports afford thrilling and healthful features in the winter athletic program. Common activities are skiing, skating, coasting, tobogganing, ice hockey, and snow and ice games, which are carried on chiefly at the large parks and in the neighborhood recreation areas. The highlight of the season is the city-wide winter carnival, in which a variety of special features is introduced. Where facilities are available and conditions favorable, the program includes skate sailing, skijoring, snowshoeing, curling, slalom racing, cross-country skiing, dog racing, winter camping, and other activities. To a greater degree than many other athletic activities, winter sports appeal to people of a wide range of ages and attract many family groups. In general, the expense of providing them is comparatively low; on the other hand, unfavorable weather conditions often interfere with carefully prepared programs or necessitate their postponement.

Training young Americans for safe participation in skin diving, a rapidly growing sport (Courtesy of Department of Parks and Recreation, Los Angeles County).

A Typical Winter Sports Program. The residents of Grand Forks, North Dakota, take full advantage of their long winter season. Hockey is a favorite sport at five lighted hockey pens for juniors, maintained by the park board. Each fall, leagues are organized in four age divisions up through seventeen years. League play starts following a knockout tournament during the Christmas holidays, and is opened officially with a series of clinics conducted by a hockey supervisor. Special events include an annual hockey roundup and an annual series with Winnipeg, Manitoba, teams.

The city's outdoor ice rinks with their lights and music attract young and old. Classes in figure skating and in downhill skiing, open to all ages,

Table 11. Daily Schedule for Sports-fitness Camp, Portland, Oregon
(Monday through Thursday)

Time	Age group	Activity
	Girls	
9:00–9:10	All	Flag raising
9:10–9:30	All	Rhythmical group calisthenics
9:30–10:00	1	Gymnastics and posture training
	2	Track and field, softball
	3	Soccer, volleyball
10:00–10:35	1	Track and field, lead-up games
	2	Gymnastics and posture training
	3	Softball, tennis
10:40–11:45	1	Selected games and introduction to sports
	2	Volleyball, tennis
	3	Gymnastics and posture training
11:45–12:00	All	Beginning, intermediate, and advanced swimming
	Boys	
2:00–2:10	All	Flag raising
2:15–2:30	All	Rhythmical group calisthenics
2:30–3:05	1	Gymnastics and posture training
	2	Track and field, soccer
	3	Wrestling, volleyball
3:10–3:45	1	Soccer, touch football
	2	Gymnastics and posture training
	3	Track and field, soccer
3:50–4:25	1	Track and field, volleyball
	2	Touch football, tennis
	3	Gymnastics and posture training
4:30–5:15	All	Beginning, intermediate, and advanced swimming

participation rather than upon the development of star athletes or teams. The widespread introduction of games and sports in school and college programs has given large numbers of girls and young women an interest and skill in these activities, which can be continued through the recreation department program after they leave school.

Such team games as volleyball, basketball, and softball are highly popular with women and girls, but the interest in them is primarily among the younger groups. Individual activities like archery, badminton, bowling, tennis, golf, and swimming have gained in popularity. These activities do not tax the player's stamina so much as some of the team games, and their appeal continues into later life. They can be played by two or more individuals and have co-recreational value because men and women can play them together. Gymnasium classes in which weight reducing replaces recreation as the major objective are a popular feature of the women's program in a number of cities. Games and sports are widely organized and conducted for women, as they are for men, on a city-wide basis, with league schedules and championship tournaments. Enrollment is often arranged through the industries and commercial organizations where the girls and women are employed.

ESSENTIAL FACTORS IN A SUCCESSFUL PROGRAM

The organization and operation of a successful municipal sports program involve consideration of many factors, several of which have already been mentioned. One of these is the selection, training, and assignment of officials; without capable officials no sports program can prosper. Another is the provision of satisfactory accommodations for spectators, who thereby share the enjoyment and benefits of the program. The health and safety of participants must be assured through various means. The development of the spirit and attitude of good sportsmanship is one of the chief objectives of a publicly sponsored sports program. A system of awards must be developed that bears a relationship to achievement and avoids offering an inducement for people to take part in an activity or event. Reference has been made repeatedly to the importance of offering instruction in sports skills. The informal use of game facilities and unorganized participation in sports activities are encouraged as representing as valuable a contribution to the recreational life of the people as the highly organized sports program. These and many other topics are treated in detail in *Community Sports and Athletics* prepared by George D. Butler for the National Recreation Association.[4]

[4] George D. Butler, *Community Sports and Athletics*, National Recreation Association, The Ronald Press Company, New York, 1949.

22. DRAMA

Drama, like music and dancing, has always belonged to the people. As Barrett Clark reminded a National Recreation Congress group, the plays of all primitive peoples arise out of a superabundance of the joy of life. In commenting on the extraordinary interest manifested in dramatics in this country, he pointed out that it is "not a fad; it is no more than a natural and inevitable development of a deeply rooted instinct almost as old as man himself. It can no more go out of style than blue eyes or an autumn sunset." One of the functions of the recreation department is to afford opportunities for children, young people, and adults to enjoy various forms of drama as participants or spectators. The department's drama activities, like other phases of its program, are not confined to its playgrounds and indoor centers but include diversified services to groups throughout the community.

DRAMA ON THE PLAYGROUNDS

Simple, spontaneous forms of drama such as play with dolls, dressing up, playing store or house, or acting out stories are a fundamental part of children's play life which find expression on the playground. Provision of toys, costumes, accessories, and a playhouse encourages imaginative play. Storytelling is a program feature at most playgrounds, and the story hour furnishes the incentive for many drama activities. A traveling storyteller who makes the rounds of the playgrounds each week is employed in several cities. In some cases she selects a weekly theme, wears a costume related to the tales she plans to tell, and climaxes the hour with an appropriate dance.

Storytelling is used as a steppingstone to play acting, as in Norfolk, Virginia, where the drama supervisor has conducted informal plays on the playgrounds: [1]

She ingeniously presents fairy-tale plays outdoors by merely hanging quilts and blankets between trees for a stage, using old clothes and crepe paper for costumes; then by simply telling a fairy tale, she puts on an entertaining pro-

[1] Yolanda Grant, "Storytelling Plus," *Recreation*, vol. 49, no. 4, p. 156, April, 1956.

duction. No actual script is followed. With lines from favorite stories as a guide, she lets the children use their own imaginations and spontaneous enthusiasm. Through her inspiration and direction the play leaders on all of the areas have begun to put on their own once-upon-a-time dramas.

Drama activities of a more formal nature include puppetry and the production of one-act plays. The latter involve plays with lines that must be memorized and rehearsals in which the play is prepared for production before an audience. Plays have been produced successfully at areas where the stage consisted merely of cretonne hung on the playground fence to serve as backdrop and with portable screens used for wings. In one city the screen frames, constructed as a handcraft project, were made with grooves to permit the insertion of panels of composition board. These panels can be decorated and changed easily as the scenes in the plays presented may require. Audiences are sometimes called upon to imagine there is a curtain while the scenery is being changed before their eyes. Many simple, attractive playground theatres have been constructed with background and wings of growing trees and shrubbery, and in a few cities elaborately equipped outdoor theatres affording seats for a large number of spectators serve as centers for children's playground drama activities.

Other playground activities are easily correlated with drama, and contribute to its success. For the storytelling hour, stories are selected which relate to the play being presented; a singing group or rhythm band may furnish incidental music, and occasionally dancing groups take part in the production. Costumes and properties are made during the handcraft period, miniature stages are constructed, and posters and invitations are prepared. All these activities add to the effectiveness of the plays and make possible greater unity and interest in the entire playground program.

Special Programs. In larger cities with specialized drama leadership and more adequate facilities, a greater variety of projects is possible. The drama activities regularly carried on at the individual playgrounds are supplemented by special programs at centers where play production and related activities receive major emphasis. One city has designated several well-distributed playgrounds as matinee centers, at each of which weekly programs are presented by boys and girls from various playgrounds of the district. Each playground has an opportunity to present at least one performance during the summer. The programs include not only one-act plays but children's choruses, instrumental and dancing groups, and participation by the audience in community singing. The popularity of these matinees is evidenced by the fact that the attendance exceeds that of any other activity at the grounds where they are presented. In some cities where plays are presented at summer playgrounds, the season closes with a tournament or festival in which children's drama groups from all the playgrounds participate. As many as 1,000 children from sixteen playgrounds have taken part in the event in one city where a children's drama tournament has long been an annual feature.

Programs about different national backgrounds, affording opportunity for developing a variety of drama activities, have been the feature of the summer playground season in a number of cities. Folk tales are told and dramatized, and songs are acted out in native costumes. Characters representing the various nations are portrayed in puppet shows, pantomimes, shadowgraphs, and one-act plays at the various playgrounds. Such programs give children experience in creative and formal drama and also a better understanding of life and people in other lands.

Hand puppetry and the marionette theatre have become popular playground features. Stage, puppets, and costumes are made by the children, who write the plays which are presented and construct and operate the theatre. Remarkable skill and ingenuity have been developed in making and using marionettes—activities which appeal especially to the older boys and girls. In some cities marionette theatres constructed and operated by playground groups travel from playground to playground. In this way many children have an opportunity to see the plays which have been worked out on the different grounds, and the troupes gain added experience.

The Cain Park Playshop in Cleveland Heights, Ohio, is an outstanding example of a municipally operated center for creative activities, in which drama holds a conspicuous place. A visit to the playshop reveals children receiving instruction from expert and understanding leaders. One group of youngsters may be working out in their own words a scene from a story which the leader is reading to them in installments; a new scene is added each day as the story is continued. Another group backstage of the small amphitheatre may be painting scenery or fitting costumes for the afternoon's play. Groups on the lawn may be making puppets or rehearsing a radio script one of them has written. Facilities include a miniature theatre suitable for either puppet or live shows, with backstage dressing rooms and workshop space and a combination radio shack and ticket booth. Classes, however, are held outdoors on the grass, which is the best place for a summertime creative playshop.

The Pageant. The pageant is the culmination of the playground season for groups interested in drama; it frequently is also the major event in the entire playground program. The production of a pageant affords opportunity for many playground groups to participate, because music, dancing, and games usually share a place with drama in the pageant program. The costumes, properties, and stage sets can be made by playground children with the help of leaders, parents, or volunteers.

Mother Goose stories and fairy tales are popular themes, and in many a city the pageant has been built around the story of Cinderella, the Old Woman Who Lived in a Shoe, Snow White, Alice in Wonderland, Hansel and Gretel, or the Pied Piper. Historical pageants also have a strong appeal, particularly if they are related to local history; and where the entire playground program is related to an idea such as Indian or colonial life, this also affords the subject for the closing pageant. Play itself can

These pleasant robots were participants in a space-ship playground pageant (Courtesy of Austin, Tex., Recreation Department).

furnish the theme, enabling playground groups to demonstrate present forms of play and to depict the sports, music, dances, and games of other peoples and other times. Interest in space travel has suggested pageant themes appropriate to the space age. Austin, Texas, developed its pageant around a great silver space ship, named for a character in a local television show and operated by a crew from one of the centers. The cast of 250 children from seventeen playgrounds included birdlike creatures from Uranus, men from Mars, round men and triangle ladies from Pluto, weird black and white visitors from Mercury, and wiggly creatures from

Neptune. Each group presented a special act in the form of a military routine or ballet, tumbling, tap, square, or modern dance, accompanied by lighting and sound effects.

Pageants of this type enlist the participation of large numbers and also demonstrate to the large audiences which usually attend them the significance of the playground program. Sometimes the pageant is a city-wide project with all the playgrounds taking part, but there is a tendency,

This traveling marionette theatre makes the rounds of Topeka's playgrounds (Courtesy of Topeka, Kans., Recreation Commission).

especially in the larger cities, for each playground, or group of playgrounds in a district, to present its own pageant. Such a plan enables more children to take part and eliminates some of the difficulties of a city-wide production, such as transportation and rehearsals.

Traveling Theatres. Theatres on wheels, commonly known as "show wagons," have been built by many recreation departments, primarily for use during the summer months. They make it possible for children's plays, talent shows, marionette performances, and other drama productions to be presented in neighborhoods and at centers throughout the city. Various methods are used in selecting the performing groups and in arranging schedules for the show wagon. In some cities, each playground has an opportunity to develop a show and to present it at several areas; in others, plays are rehearsed and prepared for production by groups at designated centers. The show wagon in one city is a part of a summer theatre, and the casts are selected from boys and girls enrolled in it. One city's show wagon serves one evening each week as a stand for a dance band that plays for street dances at playground locations throughout the city. It serves as a stage for talent shows on a different playground each Friday evening. A specialist arrives at a playground on Monday and spends the week organizing, costuming, and directing the Friday program. The following week he moves on to another playground.

The show wagon has proved an effective medium for stimulating children's interest in drama. After a season of operating one, a recreation superintendent commented that for the first time the dramatics program rivaled the athletic program in publicity and general interest. The traveling theatre with its gay colors, novel decorations, and identification with the recreation department, makes the people of all neighborhoods aware of the recreation program and proves an excellent and favorable public relations medium. Important considerations in designing a show wagon are its portability, sturdiness, attractiveness, and multiple use. Special care must be taken to assure satisfactory sound, lighting, and stage equipment.

DRAMA IN THE INDOOR CENTERS

Unlike playground drama, which is primarily for children, drama in the indoor center serves large numbers of young people and adults as well. Men and women of various ages use the center's facilities for play production, occasionally under the guidance of an expert director but frequently under leadership drawn from their own groups. Classes are conducted in such subjects as stagecraft, play reading, casting, diction, lighting, and directing. Indoor-center activity in the field of drama is limited largely to members of participating groups, although from time to time public performances are arranged. In some cities where drama clubs have been organized at several centers, an exchange of plays is arranged between them, thus giving groups an opportunity to present their plays several times and to observe the work done by other drama organizations.

In Kansas City, Missouri, the recreation division provides classes in creative dramatics, puppet clubs including marionettes and fist puppets, teen-age dramatic clubs, and storytelling hours in all its indoor centers. An entertainment series is also arranged for the centers by its music, dance, and drama sections. Objectives are to provide good family-type entertainment, encourage more participation in the activities, set high standards for center programs, and enable people to appear in the shows presented throughout the city. Monthly programs include a variety show, a Christmas play, a professional-type fist-puppet production, a Gilbert and Sullivan operetta, and a Children's Theatre production. Most of these shows are presented in the round. A Children's Theatre trouping unit that gives performances in many elementary schools and a Golden Age theatre group are sponsored by the recreation division. Its drama section also conducts after-school programs, including puppetry and creative and informal dramatics; produces an outdoor Nativity pageant, and sponsors a city-wide annual drama festival in celebration of International Theatre Month.

Play Tournaments. The one-act play contest or tournament, a common feature of the drama program, affords a special incentive and objective for center groups and other local drama organizations. In most tournaments entries are limited to amateur troupes, each of which presents a one-act play. Usually four plays are presented each evening, and participation is limited to sixteen groups. In this way the preliminaries extend over a period of four evenings, and the winner in each of the evening programs competes in the finals, thus enabling the tournament to be completed within a week. Each play is judged according to a number of factors such as presentation, acting, diction, and choice of play. In one city, groups are classified into junior high school, senior high school, and adult divisions, and winners are selected in each division. Great care needs to be taken to make sure that all participating groups receive fair consideration and equal opportunity and understand fully the rules and regulations governing the tournament.

Many leaders believe that a play festival in which the element of competition is eliminated and at which no awards are made offers the benefits and avoids the disadvantages of a tournament. Drama festivals have replaced tournaments in several cities. The contest or festival, in addition to affording opportunities for public performances and an incentive for attaining a high standard of production, can serve as an educational medium. An outstanding drama authority is usually engaged as a critic and adviser; each evening he meets with the groups presenting plays, criticizes their productions, and for the benefit of the audience gives a brief résumé of the evening's presentations at the close of each program.

CITY-WIDE ORGANIZATIONS

Little-theatre organizations with city-wide membership have been established under the sponsorship of the recreation department, although they are not necessarily related to other parts of its drama program. The primary purpose is to give those with a vital interest in the theatre an opportunity to enjoy dramatics under trained supervision and to produce and see a variety of plays and other forms of drama, some of which are rarely presented on the professional stage. Primarily for amateurs, they frequently include in their membership persons who have had professional drama experience.

The program of these organizations is not limited to play production, but features classes in diction, playwriting, scenic design, creative movement, and make-up. The workshop is an important feature. In one city the program of the community players organized under the recreation

A teen-age group before the footlights (Courtesy of St. Louis Department of Parks and Recreation).

department includes two major productions each year, four monthly theatre nights, eight workshop nights, weekly radio plays over the local radio station, and weekly lectures on acting. An annual playwriting contest, a drama tournament, and a civic Christmas pageant are among the activities of another similar group, the major productions of which combine the allied arts of the theatre—music, dancing, and drama.

Little-theatre groups vary in the methods by which they are organized, directed, and financed and in the type of facilities at their disposal. They are usually administered by a board of directors and officers elected by the membership. Funds are secured through membership dues, sponsors' contributions, and the sale of single-production and season tickets. The recreation department sometimes shares the expense or pays the salary of the director, provides clerical help, and furnishes rooms for rehearsals, tryouts, the building of scenery, the storage of costumes, and the major productions.

The Milwaukee Players. An example of a successful drama group sponsored by a recreation department is the Milwaukee Players, organized in 1931 with eleven members selected as the outstanding actors in the city's social centers. The following year the School of Drama was founded. Any Milwaukee resident who has reached eighteen years or has been graduated from high school is eligible to enter the school. Admittance, however, is gained only through being cast in a Milwaukee Players' production; once cast, the individual becomes a student apprentice, but not a member of the players. Membership is conditional upon successful completion of the courses in the school. The school faculty consists of the supervisor of drama and music in the department of municipal recreation, plus two assistants, who are specialists in music and the dance, respectively.

The program of the school reflects the director's belief that "theatre isn't only acting; it is all art combined and disciplined to effect as perfect a creation as is humanly possible." [2] Courses are given at two social centers each week from mid-September to mid-June and cover voice, diction, bodily movement, and action. Supplementary instruction is offered in the allied theatrical arts of make-up, fencing, and the reading of dramatic literature. All apprentices must also devote a certain amount of time to working on sets, props, costumes, ushering, ticket selling, and ticket taking. Workshop productions are rehearsed under the direction of experienced members. It usually takes an individual about one year to accumulate the required number of credits, according to a point system, for membership in the players. Experience has demonstrated that only through this basic and thorough concentration upon the arts in the School of Drama has it been possible for the Milwaukee Players to produce the great classics of the theatre.

Philadelphia's Playhouse in the Park. The widespread interest in summer theatres in the region prompted the commissioners of Fairmount Park in Philadelphia to build a park theatre. It took the form of an oval tent composed of strips of colored canvas, seating approximately one thousand, and equipped with lights and sound equipment. An experienced producer was engaged to handle the productions, and a new play was offered each week. Many actors appeared in more than one play, but the leads were changed weekly. Plays selected were in good taste, suitable for in-the-round production, and largely drawing-room dramas inter-

[2] Robert G. Pitman, "Milwaukee Trains Its Players," *Recreation*, vol. 46A, no. 5, p. 306, October, 1953.

spersed with broader comedies. Attendances during the first summer totaled 75,000. The playhouse proved so popular that it was converted into a permanent hard-top structure.

COMMUNITY-WIDE SERVICES

Recreation departments, especially those with full-time drama supervisors, provide additional special services to groups participating in their drama program and to other individuals and agencies interested in drama. These range from assisting with the selection of a play to assuming full responsibility for the production and staging of a pageant. Some departments maintain a play library from which local groups may borrow plays for study or use in productions. Other departments conduct courses which are open to representatives of drama groups and to individuals responsible for drama activity in churches, clubs, and other local agencies. The courses afford practical training in play production and other drama forms, often culminating in the presentation of plays by the members.

Costume and Service Bureau. The costume bureau, a feature of the drama service of many departments, varies from a collection of costumes kept in the department office or storeroom to a special building equipped for the manufacture, storage, and collection of costumes. Costume buildings are furnished with ironing boards, wash tubs, cupboards for storing costumes of all types, gas plates, sewing machines, and various facilities for making, dyeing, and washing the costumes. Storage space is also provided for properties, lighting equipment, scenery, curtains, and other accessories which are also loaned by the department. In one city, masks, jewelry, and miscellaneous materials used in plays are also available; in another, stage-lighting equipment is constructed and loaned to drama groups. Several departments loan Santa Claus costumes to organizations during the Christmas season.

The costume service is provided in some cities exclusively for groups affiliated with the department for use in connection with playground and center plays, community pageants, festivals, and other special events. In others, local community groups may avail themselves of the service, sometimes at a nominal charge. The wardrobe service of one recreation department in a single year supplied nine center drama clubs with 1,889 costumes, furnished nearly 11,000 costumes for use in public school programs, and provided more than 2,000 to private schools, churches, clubs, and individuals. In this city, costumes, stage properties, and equipment are also furnished, and a large number of wigs have been made for use in dramatic productions.

Other Activities. Other drama activities, which can only be mentioned, are the promotion of play-writing contests, the organization and production of city-wide holiday pageants, the sponsoring of professional artists, and the arrangement of a series of matinees for children. In one city such a series is promoted by the recreation department in a downtown theatre, with weekly performances during the school season. Radio and television programs, in which drama plays an important part, are presented by an increasing number of recreation departments. They not only provide entertainment features on the air but afford opportunities for playground and center groups to perform for the benefit of a large public and incidentally inform the public concerning activities in the department's program.

23. MUSIC

"There is no country today where so many people are listening to music, practising the art, and engaging in music composition." This statement, made in 1938 on the basis of a study of music in America, is just as true two decades later when the twelve hundred community orchestras functioning in the United States surpass any previous record, when membership in school bands, orchestras, and choral groups runs into the hundreds of thousands, and when attendances at concerts exceed those at professional baseball games. Although in most cities only a beginning has been made in the utilization and development of the community's music resources, many recreation departments give music an important place in their programs. They recognize that it has a universal appeal, that more and more of the population are seeking recreation through it, that people can engage in music activity in many forms and on various levels, and that music can contribute richly to other forms of recreation. The municipal recreation program is in a position to furnish opportunities for large numbers of people to enjoy a rich music experience.

Music activities sponsored or conducted by recreation departments vary widely in type, in the numbers and ages of the people participating, in purpose, and in value. In considering the department's music services, its activities may be grouped as follows: (1) conducting music activities for children, which supplement instruction in the schools, and relating them to other phases of the recreation program; (2) organizing groups of young people and adults, thus enabling them to participate in various music activities; (3) affording opportunities for people to listen to and enjoy music provided by others; (4) cooperating with other agencies in organizing and conducting community-wide activities, such as festivals or caroling projects, and bringing together leaders of existing music groups; (5) serving individuals and community groups through training institutes, music instruction, and the provision of music leaders; (6) providing community music groups with auditoriums, concert halls, and clubrooms for concerts, rehearsals, meetings, and related activities.

378

CHILDREN'S ACTIVITIES

Music instruction in the schools makes a valuable contribution to music in American life by arousing children's interest in music and by developing skills which enrich the child's life outside the school and in later life. Much music instruction, however, is formal in character and unrelated to the child's own desires and interests. The music program of the recreation department supplements that of the schools in two ways: It gives children an opportunity to use interests and skills developed in school, and it also provides attractive music activities in which children freely choose to participate. During the long vacation periods these activities are the only outlet for musical expression available to a large number of boys and girls.

The activities provided by one recreation department illustrate this phase of the music program. Toy and rhythm bands are organized for the small children, who are taught the fundamental rhythms through the use of cymbals, tambourines, drums, sticks, and triangles. As they grow older and progress, the children become interested in and join one of the harmonica bands. For the more advanced students a city harmonica band has been formed. Experience in these activities stimulates many boys and girls to study orchestral and other standard instruments.

Several recreation departments, realizing the value of relating their children's music program to that in the schools, have employed school music supervisors to take charge of the music activities at playgrounds and indoor centers. This arrangement resulted in the enrollment of 540 boys and girls in fourteen different bands and orchestras at one city's summer playgrounds. These groups enjoyed the experience of presenting concerts throughout the season, closing with a final program in which they all participated. In another city, where three part-time music directors were employed to help with the summer playground program, activities consisted of rhythm orchestras, children's chorus, glee clubs, group and community singing, singing games, and folk dancing.

Typical Playground Activities. Music activities on the playground are usually informal in nature, except where specialists are employed to organize vocal or instrumental groups and to offer instruction in music activities. Rhythms, singing games, and recorded accompaniments for various types of dancing are common. Leaders who lack expertness in music can effectively conduct community singing or rhythm bands. Instrumental groups add to the effectiveness of informal drama presentations and are essential elements in a circus, pageant, or festival. In one city, where the summer program centered about the theme of early American life, a glee club for boys and girls was organized at each playground. A music week was scheduled in August, when each playground gave a concert in which Appalachian ballads, Southern melodies, sea chanteys, and folk songs of the surrounding countryside were featured. In another city where each playground had its own original song, a "songaree" was held at which the songs were presented by playground groups, some of which wore a distinctive costume. Singing on the playgrounds became a popular activity in a city where a leader used an Autoharp.

Youngsters rehearse on their kazoos for a radio performance (Courtesy of Torrington, Conn., Recreation Department).

The tremendous interest that can be developed in the playing of a simple musical instrument is illustrated by the experience of Torrington, Connecticut, where at the suggestion of the recreation department the owner of the local radio station offered to distribute 5,000 kazoos through the station, local merchants, and the ten playgrounds. A kazoo band was formed at each of the playgrounds early in the summer season. They later performed over the local radio station and the best was designated as the city kazoo band. The entire town became kazoo-conscious, and several men's clubs formed their own bands. The windup of the playground season was a program in a local park, consisting of an amateur talent show followed by a concert led by the best playground kazoo band and a similar men's band. Several thousand people took part.

The possibilities of playground music were demonstrated in a large Western city in which the recreation department employed a supervisor of music. She first made a survey to determine what activities were practicable and best suited to the interests and needs of the children. Within a few years there were sixteen groups of small children who met regularly for singing, twelve toy symphonies, five harmonica bands, several small orchestras, and a city-wide boys' choir, which has sung during several opera seasons.

In cities with a large foreign population, neighborhood bands, orchestras, and choral groups have been formed to take advantage of the special skills and interests. Typical of such groups is a tamboura orchestra composed of young Croatian musicians, which has represented its playground on many occasions. The possibilities of making musical instruments on the playground were mentioned in the section relating to the arts and crafts program. A few playground groups have been formed for the presentation of light operas, but projects of this type are rarely attempted except at playgrounds conducted the year round.

Music in the Indoor Centers. The music interests of children are also served at indoor centers, where the longer season permits the introduction of more ambitious projects. In a small Illinois city the initial effort to develop music activities for children was a series of tryouts at each of the centers during the first two weeks of the season. Children were permitted to try various band and orchestral instruments to determine their fitness or aptitude for a definite type. Small instrumental classes were subsequently formed at each center; and as the groups advanced in skill and began making public appearances, interest and participation increased and orchestras were organized. The study of new music and the thrill of playing with a group stimulated membership in the orchestras. When the desire to play more ambitious music was expressed by children of unusual ability, a recreation department orchestra was organized. Its members included a number of children who began their music career in groups organized by the department. Biweekly instruction was also given to beginners who looked forward to membership in an orchestra, and children of kindergarten and primary age were organized into rhythm and melody bands.

YOUTH AND ADULT ACTIVITIES

In order that interest in music be sustained in later years and that boys and girls continue to use their music skills, recreation departments afford music opportunities for young people and adults. The program, especially at the indoor centers, includes such features as choruses, glee clubs, orchestras, small instrumental and vocal groups, opera clubs, music-appreciation groups, and community singing. Occasionally one of the center's instrumental groups furnishes accompaniments for the weekly sings and may be invited to take part in programs at the center.

A nationally known community-music authority, after a visit to the

Wilmington children take advantage of free lessons—a phase of the city's summer music program (Courtesy of Recreation Promotion and Service, Wilmington, Del.).

school centers in Milwaukee, reported enthusiastically on the music groups which he observed, as follows:

We saw young people's opera groups practicing the *Nautical Knot;* an Italian young people's group practicing *Lucia;* two fretted-instrument organizations, one Hawaiian and elementary, the other mostly German and just about perfect; a barn-dance group entertained us; a splendid adult women's chorus sang for us; a colored band played; a Jewish women's group sang its Old World pieces for us. Twelve hundred people are participating in the public recreation music programs.

In the same city, a number of other flourishing music groups had their beginnings in the social centers.

Instrumental Groups. Instrumental groups organized and conducted by recreation departments vary from harmonica bands to symphony orchestras. The Bloomfield, New Jersey, Recreation Department, for example, sponsors a symphony orchestra, a mandolin orchestra, and a civic band;

the Westchester County, New York, Recreation Commission through its music division conducts a county band, a dance band, a "pops" band, and an accordion band. These groups afford their members the joy of playing together and contribute to special events at the centers and in the community. Playing under the guidance of competent directors, they acquire immense satisfaction through progress in musical ability and appreciation. Members of most orchestras represent many nationalities and occupations and a wide range of ages. Instrumental groups are occasionally formed from individuals of a particular nationality or background. Typical of such groups are a Czechoslovakian tamboura club, which plays folk music on native instruments, and a band composed of veterans of circus or local community bands.

Several recreation departments sponsor a civic orchestra, which they have organized. Most members are amateurs, and the membership usually includes both men and women. Some civic orchestras perform throughout the year, presenting summer concerts in the parks as well as concerts during the indoor season. The members of one women's symphony orchestra, sponsored by a recreation department, were organized into small instrumental groups, including a violin choir of twenty, a flute choir of ten, and a trumpet ensemble. Such groups appeal strongly to the younger members of the orchestra, many of whom are high school students, and there is a great demand for their services. Requests for appearances at dinners, meetings, and entertainments are handled by the department, which arranges for transportation, compensation, and other details.

In some cities, recent high school graduates are encouraged to continue their interest in orchestral music through the organization of orchestras recruited from former members of high school orchestras. Instrumental teachers in the high schools are paid to take charge of these groups, thus assuring leadership accustomed to deal with young people and familiar with the school music program. The success of these so-called alumni groups is partly due to the fact that their members are approximately the same age and enjoy being and playing together, and that social activities are arranged in connection with the meetings.

Choral Groups. Civic choruses and glee clubs as well as singing groups organized on a neighborhood or center basis are important units in many municipal music programs. Alumni choruses in several cities afford opportunities for young people to continue singing after they leave school. Among the widely different vocal groups organized at recreation centers are glee clubs formed among mothers of playground children, groups of young men who meet regularly to sing together, madrigal groups of high school students, and men's and women's choruses developed among Negro groups. Male quartet singing has attained high popularity in many cities. Groups regularly meet for the enjoyment of singing together, and competitions among quartets and barbershop contests usually attract enthusiastic audiences.

One recreation department has sponsored four choruses: a civic chorus, composed of 300 men and women, and the other three, alumni groups of young people. Supplementing the weekly rehearsals for operas, concerts, and other programs, dances and social get-togethers have helped in maintaining a unity among them and in recruiting new singers. The caliber of music sung by such choral groups is usually high; occasionally they join with orchestral groups in producing programs of city-wide interest, as in one city where the civic chorus, with the cooperation of the women's symphony orchestra, presented Handel's *Messiah*. The organization of music festivals, holiday programs, and special musical events enables the instrumental and choral groups to produce music that brings satisfaction to the participants and enjoyment to large numbers of listeners.

Community Sings. Outdoor community sings have proved successful in a number of cities; in some cases they are arranged as a feature of motion-picture programs or of concerts by instrumental groups. Sings have been highly successful in Roanoke, Virginia, where they are held in neighborhood parks. Old favorites, folk tunes, popular song hits, and hymns are sung under the direction of an experienced volunteer leader with piano accompaniment. Singing is interspersed with entertainment furnished by youngsters from the playgrounds; following the sings, movies are shown. A stage about 30 feet square and benches to seat elderly people are set up in the afternoon, together with a piano, large portable screen, balopticon lantern-slide projector, public-address system, and spotlights for the leader and pianist. These arrangements have been an important factor in securing audience participation.

OPPORTUNITIES FOR LISTENING TO MUSIC

Participation is of primary importance, but opportunities for listening to good music are not neglected. The concerts regularly provided in many cities serve large audiences, and frequent opportunities for hearing good music are furnished by groups organized within the department. One department's music committee arranged fifty-four concerts in a single year for its music groups, and a total attendance of nearly 24,000 was reported at these concerts, many of which were held in outlying districts of the city. A Western city reports that a series of forty-eight Sunday-afternoon programs presented by orchestras, bands, chorus groups, string ensembles, readers, and lecturers was attended by more than 29,000. In the same city a successful series of twenty-four programs was given two evenings a week during the summer, with audiences totaling more than 35,500. .

Band concerts are common features of the program, especially during the summer months. Several large cities sponsor outdoor symphony concerts such as the Robin Hood Dell series in Fairmount Park, Philadelphia; the "pops" concerts on the Esplanade in Boston; and the Grant Park concerts in Chicago, which attract hundreds of thousands each season. Such concerts are not always sponsored by the recreation department but are given by a local music organization or by professional music groups paid by the city. St. Louis, with its Forest Park theatre, is one of the few cities in which the recreation authorities or a civic body sponsor outdoor opera programs in a public park. A two-week summer festival held annually in Portland, Oregon, under the sponsorship of the Bureau of Parks and Public Recreation, enables the people of that city to enjoy a variety of offerings. Programs include opera, band and orchestral concerts, barbershop-quartet singing, vocal concerts with the civic Mastersingers chorus, and dance presentations, performed by many local music groups. A Theater Arts Opera Association has been formed by the bureau to present opera during the fall, winter, and spring for the benefit of the amateur artists and the public.

In order that people may enjoy and better understand the programs which are presented, music-appreciation classes are sometimes organized to study the works to be presented by the local symphony orchestra. A lecturer describes the numbers, and recordings are played. Radio and television are being used more and more as means of carrying good music to a large audience. These media also demonstrate to the public the nature of the department's music program, as various music groups sponsored by local departments take part in regular broadcasts.

MUNICIPAL MUSIC PROGRAMS

Even though many recreation departments tend to leave to private groups the sponsorship of community music activities, several cities have demonstrated the value of municipal music programs. Los Angeles and Baltimore, for example, have a municipal bureau of music, and Denver and New Orleans have unusually comprehensive and effective music programs which point the way to similar developments in other cities.

The Denver Program. The objectives of the municipal music program in Denver, according to the coordinator of music for the city and county, are to supplement existing music opportunities and to provide more and better music for more people through both participation and listening for pleasure. Its activities are confined to adults and postschool youth, because the city schools provide an excellent music program. Membership in the Denver Municipal Musical Association is open to all local residents at a fee of $1. Its organizations consist of six choruses, a string orchestra, and a symphonic band, each of which rehearses weekly. All organizations make appearances at hospitals and church and civic groups, frequently during National Music Week, and take part in massed performances at Christmas, Easter, and Thanksgiving. Public concerts are taped and radio and television series are arranged. A municipal band performs six nights weekly in the summer at City Park. In cooperation with the public schools an eight-week recreational music program for beginning, intermediate, and advanced bands and orchestras is conducted during the vacation. As a public service a thirty- to forty-five-minute program called

The dance orchestra at the Danforth Center for senior citizens (Courtesy of the Danforth Center, Rochester, N. Y.).

"Music Can Be Fun," which includes audience participation, has been presented to several hundred groups. A comprehensive music library has been established for the use of the music groups. The influence of the music program may be judged by the findings in a 1954 survey, which indicated that at least one person in eight living in Denver was engaged in some form of music activity.

Activities in New Orleans. Music plays a major role in the New Orleans recreation department's cultural division, which embraces a wide variety of activities to suit the tastes and interests of practically all age groups. They include drama, dance, arts and crafts, movies, charm schools, a children's museum, and baton twirling, and so forth. The music program has been designed to offer a basic appreciation for music, with emphasis upon participation. Its opera group has presented several major productions besides *Bits from Hits*—capsule editions of Broadway successes. A community symphony consists of talented players who joined the group for the sheer enjoyment of playing good music. It presents a series of concerts in the municipal auditorium as well as neighborhood concerts and a youth symphony series under the sponsorship of the recreation department. A volunteer committee assists with this feature of the program, for which there is no admission charge.

COMMUNITY MUSIC SERVICES

The recreation department serves as a cooperative agency in planning local music activities and fostering music projects. Music festivals are an effective means for bringing together local music groups in a joint project. One traditional regional folk festival enlists the cooperation of such groups as the girls' municipal orchestra, synagogue choir, women's municipal chorus, college glee club, Negro choir, and dancers from several racial groups. Community-wide holiday celebrations are also promoted with the cooperation of local agencies. Typical examples are a Christmas "tree of light" program with several hundred participants, attracting thousands of spectators; and a caroling program, which brings Christmas cheer to hospitals, orphanages, hotels, railway stations, and even the local jails.

Several recreation departments have taken a prominent part in organizing local observances of National Music Week, which begins the first Sunday in May; others have been among the chief cooperating agencies. The observance of National Music Week affords an opportunity for the recreation authorities to let the public know what they are doing with music for children, young people, and adults and to call attention to unmet needs in this field. Many of the groups organized or sponsored by the recreation department arrange for public performances during the week.

Recreation departments also conduct institutes for the training of socially minded music leaders, who are so essential to the success of music groups. The Westchester County, New York, Recreation Commission operates a summer music center at which young people from many communities receive instruction on a variety of instruments and gain experience in playing in bands, orchestras, and ensembles. The Oglebay Institute in Wheeling, West Virginia, conducts a two-week opera workshop in Oglebay Park, where pupils study all phases of opera under noted artists and teachers and take part in workshop recitals and public performances.

Music groups organized by several recreation departments regularly sing or play for shut-ins or inmates of hospitals and children's institutions. Because the lack of music has hindered the success of music programs, several departments have established music libraries for the purpose of loaning suitable music to local groups. The Phoenix, Arizona, Parks and Recreation Department issues and distributes a bulletin listing the music activities and events scheduled by local organizations for the entire season; other recreation departments furnish song sheets and song leaders for conventions, banquets, and special occasions. A few departments help arrange programs for community groups; assist individuals or organizations in securing musical instruments, competent leaders, and appropriate music for particular occasions; organize conferences for a discussion of music problems; and conduct special music studies. Rooms in recreation buildings and indoor centers are generally made available for meetings and rehearsals of local music organizations.

In brief, the recreation department helps people find opportunities to make and enjoy good music. It cooperates with all agencies working toward this end and promotes music activities on all fronts, frequently coordinating music with other activities in the department's program.

24. NATURE, GARDENING, AND OUTING ACTIVITIES

LUTHER BURBANK once said: "Every child should have mud pies, grasshoppers, waterbugs, tadpoles, frogs, mud turtles, elderberries, wild strawberries, acorns, chestnuts, trees to climb, brooks to wade in, water lilies, woodchucks, bats, bees, butterflies, various animals to pet, hay fields, pine cones, rocks to roll, sand, snakes, huckleberries, and hornets, and any child who has been deprived of these has been deprived of the best part of his education."

Unfortunately large numbers of city children are deprived of these things, although natural science courses and nature projects in the schools acquaint many with the wonders and beauty of nature. Recreation departments are particularly well fitted to carry on an extensive nature program because the large parks and reservations under their control afford exceptional opportunities for studying forms of plant and animal life. Nature activities are receiving greater emphasis in the recreation program, and trained leaders are interpreting the wonders of the out-of-doors to growing numbers of children, youth, and adults.

NATURE ACTIVITIES FOR CHILDREN

Nature activities carried on as a part of the playground and day-camp programs foster in children a love of natural beauty and a respect for growing things. They furnish valuable training in observation, teach the importance of conservation, and arouse in children an interest in learning more about the world in which they live. Any playground director can initiate simple nature activities, but the most worthwhile results are accomplished in cities where at least one nature specialist is employed on the staff of the recreation department. Such a person trains the playground leaders, initiates nature projects, organizes nature clubs, and conducts activities on the playgrounds and at outlying areas.

Playground Nature Projects. To the alert leader the playground offers many opportunities for nature activities. The identification and labeling of playground trees and shrubs, observing and recording weather conditions, building and erecting birdbaths and feeding stations, planting shrubs and trees, and collecting, identifying, and mounting flowers, leaves, and insects are common playground projects. Activities on the playground are supplemented by hikes and outings in large city parks or outlying reservations. These enable children to observe nature in its many forms, secure specimens for the playground museum, gather information that can be used in nature-club programs, play nature games, and cook out of doors. Children attending a playground near the seashore in one city made a study of water birds.

A Summer Playground Program. The Junior League in Tacoma, Washington, has made possible the employment of a naturalist to introduce nature activities on the city playgrounds. The handcraft program was built around the nature theme; nature stories were told by leaders, and nature games were played daily. The naturalist helped train leaders at the preseason institute and visited the playgrounds with live specimens from the city zoo and aquarium. Summer activities included nature hikes, organizing nature clubs, and making nature posters and collections. The nature theme was further emphasized in scavenger hunts, flower shows, cookouts, visits to the zoo, pet shows, and activities involving sea life, animals, flowers, birds, trees, rocks, and insects.

Special Features. When playground directors in one large city reported that many children had never seen such farm animals as cows, goats, pigs, ducks, or turkeys, the department made a collection of these animals, constructed a barn on wheels with a runway, and conveyed the animals from one playground to another. A section of the playground was enclosed with portable fencing as a barnyard during the three-day visits. Many children saw farm animals for the first time and took a keen interest in them and in their care. A large number of adults, particularly those brought up in the country, also spent a great deal of time watching the animals.

Instead of bringing animals to the playgrounds, many cities take groups of children to the city zoo. These trips afford not only an enjoyable experience but also an opportunity to study the interesting behavior of animals. Other public facilities serving the city's nature interest, such as the natural-history museum or the planetarium, are also visited by playground groups. Special trips to these centers, as well as to the zoo, stimulate interesting playground discussions, activities, and projects.

The Junior Museum. The junior natural-history museum is one of the most interesting and valuable features of playground nature programs. Some museums are very simple, consisting merely of display cases and posters set up in a corner of the playground shelter. Living exhibits have a strong appeal, and aquariums are especially successful. Frogs, ants, mosquitoes, and other insects are reared through all life stages. Collections showing natural tree bark, wood color and grain, wild-flower seeds, flowers dried and mounted, and insect collections find a place in many of these museums. Where suitable space is available a miniature zoo may be established. Such a project has educational value but should be undertaken only if intelligent and continuous care of the specimens is assured.

An unusual playground visitor interests both children and adults (Courtesy of Recreation Department, South Haven, Mich.).

The establishment of a junior nature museum stimulates great interest in nature activities and furnishes a center where groups can pursue this interest throughout the year. Reference was made in Chapter 13 to the Junior Museum in San Francisco, where nature activities comprise a large part of its program. Under the heading of biology, groups study insects, reptiles, amphibia, and fish. The children also receive instruction in methods of collecting, mounting, and classifying biological material and in the care and feeding of the pets assembled by the children. Interest in geology is stimulated through a study of rocks, minerals, volcanoes, glaciers, and erosions; by instruction in collecting and classifying specimens; and by experience in polishing stones and gems. Museum members have the use of stories, charts, maps, pictures, and a laboratory for analyses. Regular field trips for observation and collecting are an important part of the program. A junior Audubon club holds meetings and bird hikes, and a garden club engages in a variety of activities. The study of botany is encouraged through instruction in collecting, pressing, mounting, and classifying flowers and leaves and casting them in wax. A monthly bulletin, the *Junior Naturalist*, prepared by the children, is a valuable educational medium.

The development of nature trails and outdoor gardens and the planting of shrubs and wild flowers on the building site make it unique and fascinating. The museum assists the city's playgrounds in their nature activities through the loan of terrariums, aquariums, and wall chart exhibits and makes available leadership for special projects on the individual grounds. The museum provides a meeting place for many local groups such as the Amateur Astronomers, Gem and Mineral Society, Cage Bird Society, Dog Trainers Club, and California Alpine Club.

Junior Rangers. A Junior Rangers Club has been formed in the East Bay (California) regional parks to teach children of the region about the out-of-doors. Meetings are held weekly in a natural wildlife preserve under the leadership of park rangers. The members are divided into three sections: peewee, junior, and senior rangers. The peewee learns to know all the trails in the nature area, to identify the common plants and animals along the trail, and to use and care for the trails. After passing an examination he becomes a junior. He must acquire a thorough acquaintance with the compass and with the ecology of the area before becoming a senior. Seniors undertake different projects each year, such as forestry, geology, or erosion, and learn to read and interpret the signs of animal life. Attendance records are kept, and children receive insignia as they advance from one group to another. Every spring and fall the juniors and seniors go on an overnight camping trip which includes a campfire program and flashlight hike and which further accustoms the children to life in the woods.

Junior Nature Clubs. Nature clubs for boys and girls aged eight and over meet weekly during the winter and spring months in several Minneapolis centers. Each month one meeting is devoted to a program relating to such subjects as the Eskimos and life in the Arctic, Minnesota's wild animals, Indian tribes, birds, plants, or a nature hobby show. At other meetings club members experiment with materials, make models of nature subjects, study types of flora and fauna, start seedlings, make dish gardens, or go on tree or bird hikes. Club members also enjoy the family-night film and slide programs dealing with nature subjects that are presented biweekly at the various centers.

NATURE ACTIVITIES FOR COMMUNITY GROUPS

Recreation departments are more and more providing nature activities which appeal to young people and adults and family groups. It has been truly said that nature study meets all the requirements of a good hobby because it deals with life itself and is therefore intensely interesting. It can be carried on practically without cost anywhere, at any age, alone

North Chagrin trailside explorers make tree exhibits (Courtesy of Cleveland Metropolitan Park District).

or with a group. Furthermore, it provides healthful activity out of doors and brings people in contact with the world of nature. Its growing popularity is indicated in a recreation department bulletin announcing its nature activities: "Plants and animals of the mountains, the fields and the seashore . . . birds and butterflies, snakes, insects, shellfish, seaweeds, wild flowers, and a host of other creations of prodigal nature are being collected and studied by people seeking constructive uses for their leisure." Bird clubs, marine-study groups, astronomy clubs, and other groups with nature interests meet in recreation centers in scores of cities.

Metropolitan Park Activities. Metropolitan parks are better adapted than most city parks for the development of a diversified nature program and the Cleveland, Ohio, Metropolitan Park District has been a leader in this field. For many years, in cooperation with the Cleveland Museum of Natural History, it has employed a park naturalist who has developed a program designed to interest people of the Cleveland region in the natural history of the district and to interpret nature to park visitors. Popular features of the program are the trailside museums, which contain exhibits and collections. Near each one are nature and wild-flower trails, which are labeled, and an area where outdoor lectures are given. Resident naturalists explain and interpret the exhibits, answer questions about the natural history of the park areas, give informal talks to visiting groups, and conduct guided trips during which talks are given on the trees, birds, geology, and other features. Bird walks are sponsored during the spring months. Valuable cooperation in the building and maintenance of the nature trails is received from the Cleveland Natural Science Club, which has constructed a lodge in one of the parks.

A comparable program in the Columbus, Ohio, metropolitan parks includes the showing of motion pictures on nature and wildlife subjects, a program of nature exploration for juniors, an adult natural-history club, and conducted park tours for grade school children. Park authorities furnish nature programs for day-camping groups, cooperate with local agencies in conducting leadership-training institutes, and issue field guides and interpretive bulletins on natural-history subjects.

Marine Museum. A marine museum, established in 1932 by the recreation department in Los Angeles, to capitalize on the natural curiosity of beachgoers about sea life, occupies a special building at one of the city beaches. All the 15,000 specimens in the collection have been donated. Exhibits include an extensive shell collection; a collection of crabs, marine turtles, starfish, aquatic birds, and fish; varieties of whales, marine fossils, and marine mammals, including porpoise and seals; an exhibition of shellcraft implements collected from the Channel Islands, made and used by ancient people; and a growing exhibit of ship models. Among the most attractive exhibits are a giant 1,100-pound turtle, curious fish which came from great depths of the ocean, and Eskimo kayaks made from driftwood and otter hides.

The attendance approximates 350,000 a year and includes hundreds of groups from schools, playgrounds, and recreation centers that come to see the exhibits and listen to lectures on the sea-life exhibit, specimens of which may be found on nature hunting trips along the shore nearby. Museum activities, in addition to lectures given to groups upon request, are classes in taxidermy and arrangement of shell collections, instruction in preserving fish for display, and identification of marine specimens brought to the museum.

Nature Outings in the Nation's Capital. One of the country's most diversified nature programs is provided by the National Capital Parks in and around Washington, D. C. A major feature is a series of trips conducted by park naturalists, as follows:

Explorations: leisurely one- and two-hour walks introduce participants to the plants, animals, and geology of the parks

Hikes: longer and more strenuous trips

"Level walker" hikes: conducted on the Chesapeake and Ohio Canal towpath

Caravans: half-day or all-day trips by private car or chartered bus to park areas otherwise not readily accessible

Bird observations: morning walks in cooperation with the Audubon Society; some of them for beginners

Evening adventures: family outings with nature walk followed by "Naturevan" program which makes possible projection of movies and slides, playing of recorded music and nature sounds, and exhibition of live animals

Barge trips on Chesapeake and Ohio Canal: mule-drawn barge trips on which history and natural features of the canal are interpreted.

The National Capital Parks maintains aquatic gardens where naturalists conduct interpretive walks; also Theodore Roosevelt Island, a nature sanctuary with trails and exhibits. Here a naturalist organizes bird observations and explorations, including evening walks followed by informal campfire programs. Other services include junior naturalist activities for children, a training course for summer-camp nature counselors, school assembly talks, and day-camp activities.

An Exceptional Nature Program. An outstanding nature program has been conducted for many years at Oglebay Park near Wheeling, West Virginia, under the sponsorship of Oglebay Institute and West Virginia University Agricultural Extension. The A. B. Brooks Nature Center, with library, auditorium, conference and exhibit rooms, laboratory, workshop, and office for the naturalist, houses the nature program. In addition to the trailside museum and zoo, nature walks, publications, and service to school and community groups, the program includes several unusual features. Frequent lectures and programs are arranged by an astronomy group which has two telescopes—a 4-inch refractor and an 8½-inch reflector. Nature camps—one for juniors and the other for advanced campers, nature hobbyists, and teachers—are conducted each summer. A winter lecture series presents authorities on natural history and travel, with colored motion pictures. Special events include Arbor Day observance, nature-night campfires, a winter bird-feeding party, and bird-counting days. Committees on nature education and conservation contribute to the effectiveness and success of the program.

Caddies on nature field trip in Oglebay Park (Courtesy of Wheeling, W. Va., Park Commission).

GARDENING

Garden activities are promoted by a number of recreation departments, frequently in cooperation with other interested groups such as schools, women's clubs, and garden clubs. Services include the provision of land for children's and adults' gardens; leadership for children's garden programs; the promotion of home gardens, indoor gardens, and terrariums; flower arranging and indoor gardening classes; and the furnishing of seeds. A Junior Gardeners Club, sponsored by the Santa Ana, California, Recreation and Parks Department with the cooperation of local garden clubs, has functioned for several years. Members study birds, wild flowers, and conservation as well as various aspects of gardening. A portion of each meeting is devoted to handcraft projects such as ornaments, favors, scrapbooks, and objects relating to gardening. Club members submit entries to the county fair and flower shows, clean and landscape vacant lots, plant trees, and furnish flowers for children in hospitals.

Special Services. Advice and information on horticultural problems are furnished to home gardeners by a number of park and recreation departments. In one city a garden-center institute in a park clubhouse helps garden clubs plan programs and furnishes home gardeners advice on everyday gardening activity. Particularly helpful to beginning gardeners are a landscape consultation service, a garden-maintenance service bureau, classes in gardening, and a series of horticultural lectures by outstanding authorities. A junior forestry program has been established in one city, where the city forester teaches grade school children and members of junior organizations to appreciate and care for trees.

The Metropolitan Dade County, Florida, Park and Recreation Department maintains a fruit and spice park which is a demonstration area for tropical fruits, nuts, and spice-producing plants. The park office is an information center on tropical-plant culture as well as a community garden center.

Park departments, in addition to their floral and horticultural exhibits, conduct educational activities including gardening lectures, assist in judging flower and garden contests, disseminate horticultural information, promote garden-club and neighborhood-improvement programs, and provide guide service in their conservatories for school classes, garden clubs, and other groups. A tendency of park authorities to consult garden clubs and other interested neighborhood groups with reference to the planning of park landscape features, particularly the gardens, yields valuable results in both park and neighborhood interest. The floral displays and plant exhibits at two park conservatories in Chicago have attracted more than 2,500,000 visitors during a single year.

OUTING ACTIVITIES

Some people go to the country to study nature; others do so primarily for exercise, relaxation, or simply to get away from the city environment. The recreation department serves the latter group by organizing hiking and outing clubs and providing areas and facilities for picnicking, camping, and other related activities. Equally important, however, are the informal enjoyment and use of the larger parks and reservations by individuals and small groups. As a matter of fact, the number of people who stroll along park paths or trails, lie on the grass or under the trees, or enjoy the beauty of the landscape while sitting on a park bench far exceeds the number participating in organized outing activities.

Hiking Clubs. Walking is one of the first activities of childhood and is enjoyed until old age. Many recreation departments sponsor hiking groups, most of which have a regular membership with nominal dues, a schedule extending throughout the year, and a definite plan for leadership, often furnished by members of the organization. Week-end hikes—usually to an outlying park, beach, reservation, or museum—commonly include a cookout and occasionally end at a park shelter or farm-house, where dancing or games are enjoyed by the group. Chapter 16 contains a brief description of the Minnehikers, a successful hiking group. Youth hostels and state-park facilities are sometimes used by municipal hiking groups for overnight and week-end outings. In one state park an old barn was remodeled to serve as the week-end objective for hikes and bicycle trips arranged by the recreation department in a nearby city.

Horseback Riding. Horseback riding is sponsored by many recreation departments, and bridle trails are a common feature in large parks and reservations. The Union County, New Jersey, Park Commission has long promoted riding by providing a modern stable, miles of improved bridle trails, two riding rings, several paddocks, and an outside jumping course in its 2,000-acre Watchung Reservation. It has organized the sport for beginners and advanced riders on an extensive scale, with spring, summer, and fall troops each year. Horses may be boarded at the stable, and mounts are also available for rental. Special events include a spring horse show promoted by a riding and driving club, a fall show for hunters and jumpers arranged by a special committee, several one-day troop shows, moonlight rides, paper chases, and gymkhanas. Pompano Beach, Florida, is a small community where the recreation department has organized a saddle club and provided a stable, show rings, and 8 miles of riding trails in its 1,200-acre park.

Bicycling. In response to the revival of public interest in bicycle riding, recreation departments have formed bicycle clubs, set aside and built paths for cyclists, and arranged outings for lovers of the sport. In Cincinnati, where a large area was set aside for bicycling, a quantity of bicycles was acquired by the recreation commission, and these are loaned to children who do not own any. Members of bicycle clubs for boys and girls are usually required to sign a safety pledge; weekly bicycle inspections are held to make sure that all equipment is in good condition; tests of riding skills are held; and lectures and moving pictures on highway safety are presented. In selecting routes for outings, care is taken to avoid roads with heavy traffic. An automobile equipped with a large sign, "Motorists please drive with care; bicycle club ahead," accompanies one club on all field trips. The car carries a complete first-aid kit, repair kit, and other tools, and is available for the transportation of any club member whose bicycle breaks down on the journey.

Camping. In Chapter 19 reference was made to the various types of camps conducted by recreation departments and to the variation in programs at the in-town day camp, the overnight or week-end camp, and the long-term vacation camp. Nature and outing interests play an important part in all camp programs, particularly in the camps where naturalists are employed, and the natural resources of the camp environment are utilized increasingly in the program.

All aboard for the annual hay ride and outing in Golden Gate Park (Courtesy of Recreation Center for the Handicapped, San Francisco).

Outings. Other types of day outings have been provided by communities that do not operate a day camp. Some of these take the form of trips to a lake for swimming, boating, and picnicking, or to a museum, industry, nearby city, historic site, or professional ball game. They have educational as well as recreational value, and are the highlights of many a summer program. A busload of boys from one city, equipped with pickaxes, shovels, packs, lunch, and a Geiger counter, enjoyed an unusual outing in the form of a uranium hunt. Over five hundred playground children in a New England city will long remember an eventful train trip to a state park, including the inspection of the diesel locomotive. Most extensive and significant are the trips of the Youth Ambassadors of

Friendship, sponsored by the Jefferson County, Kentucky, Playground and Recreation Board, under which groups of young people have visited Mexico and Cuba.

Fishing. Few outdoor activities engage the enthusiastic interest of children and adults more than fishing, and recreation authorities are increasingly rendering special services to anglers. Suitable water areas are stocked for the benefit of local fishermen, usually with the cooperation of state conservation departments, and fishing piers have been constructed. Hatcheries have been established to supply fish for some municipally owned and controlled waters and to supplement the supply obtained from the state. Only children are permitted to try their luck in some park streams and well-stocked lakes. Fishing derbies are widely popular spring events for boys and girls. In one city the recreation department, with the cooperation of an advisory council on junior fishing, conducted a fishing contest in a park lake each Saturday as a part of the summer playground program.

Anglers' clubs organized by the recreation department use the department's indoor and outdoor facilities, and fly-casting tournaments are conducted annually, in some instances at special casting pools. A Tackle Buster's Club, whose members are young fishing enthusiasts, goes on a fishing trip and meets weekly under an adviser in a Western city. Meetings are often addressed by state or county conservation officials or by deep-sea fishermen. The club receives much help from an adult Fly and Bait Casting Club, which is also sponsored by the recreation department. Fly-tying groups, like the casting clubs, are recruited largely from fishing enthusiasts. A few departments issue bulletins giving information on fishing waters in the region.

Local recreation agencies can seldom serve the interests of hunters in a comparable manner, but rifle or gun clubs have been organized, indoor or outdoor rifle ranges erected, and rifle tournaments conducted in a number of cities. Trapshooting ranges installed in a few parks help hunters prepare for the open season.

Picnics. Picnicking has become one of America's favorite outdoor recreation activities for families, informal groups, and organizations. Besides providing picnic sites, some recreation departments maintain a picnic bureau which helps groups select picnic sites, gives advice in organizing a program of games and entertainment, lends game equipment, reserves sports facilities adjoining the picnic grounds, and even assigns a worker to conduct the entire picnic program. A nominal fee is charged to cover the cost of leadership service, and usually a deposit is required for equipment; but most other picnic services are given without cost. The lighting of many picnic areas has greatly extended their periods of use.

25. OTHER PROGRAM FEATURES

Several of the most important aspects of the recreation department program have been described in the five preceding chapters, but other program features merit consideration. These include forums or discussion groups, which are less generally or extensively conducted than the ones previously mentioned; social recreation and dancing, which often supplement the activities of groups whose primary interest is in some other form of recreation; hobby groups, which represent a wide variety of activities; holiday celebrations, which include a cross section of several major groupings; service projects and many other types of activities. A separate division is rarely set up in the recreation department to administer these activities, although specialists are sometimes employed to conduct them.

SOCIAL RECREATION

One of the objectives of the recreation department is to encourage happier relationships among individuals by enabling them to take part in recreation activities with other people who have similar interests. Sociability and fellowship are promoted throughout the entire recreation program, but in several kinds of activity such as dinners, dances, parties, and play nights, the element of sociability is uppermost. These activities are sometimes conducted as distinct program features, but they often supplement the regular activities carried on by music, nature, drama, or craft groups. In fact, most groups include in their schedule functions intended to develop a better acquaintance and feeling of fellowship among the individual members.

Many a recreation department renders its greatest service in the field of social recreation to individuals and agencies not directly related to its program. It assists local organizations with their parties, picnics, and socials by furnishing suggestions, equipment, or leadership and by issuing and distributing party bulletins.

Holidays are occasions when social features receive special emphasis, particularly by groups meeting in recreation buildings and indoor centers.

Valentine's Day, Halloween, Thanksgiving, Christmas, and other holidays are celebrated by parties at which games, dramatic stunts, dancing, refreshments, and music are the chief attractions. Boys' and girls' club programs include occasional parties and dances and father-and-son or mother-and-daughter dinners. An "army bean feed," a sports night featuring outstanding athletic stars, and a talk by a noted traveler are typical events making for good fellowship in a boys' or men's club.

Table Games. The quiet game room where individuals can spend a social hour or an evening playing cards, chess, or checkers with their friends is one of the most popular and informal rooms in the recreation center. Interest in these games is fostered by classes for both beginners and advanced players. Checker, chess, canasta, and bridge clubs meet regularly for tournaments and informal play at many centers, and a municipal chess association has been organized in one city where enthusiasm for the game runs high. Players are classified according to ability, and a schedule of intercenter matches is carried on throughout the season. A room in one of the park centers has been set aside and attractively furnished as headquarters for the organization; here league, tournament, and social play takes place. The chess association is primarily for adults, but the game has caught the interest of the older boys in the evening centers and is also being taught to children of elementary school age on the playgrounds and in several afternoon centers.

Social Activities for Mixed Groups. The provision of co-recreational activities is a normal and growing tendency in recreation programs because young men and women need and seek opportunities for a wider acquaintance with persons of the opposite sex. One of the best functions for this purpose is the game party, which enables strangers to get acquainted without a formal introduction. The party can be the means of inducing young men and women to form their own social groups or to join organizations already participating in the program. Games such as table tennis, darts, and table shuffleboard are widely played by mixed groups. Interest in sociability and sightseeing is combined in a club of single young adults, which makes trips to local and out-of-city points of interest.

Training Courses. Leadership-training courses are one of the most widely used and effective means by which recreation departments enrich social-recreation programs. Leaders in schools, churches, clubs, and youth groups are offered instruction in game selection and leadership, party-planning methods, game supplies, and related subjects. Occasionally at the conclusion of a training course the group forms a social-recreation club for the purpose of continuing its training in leadership methods and materials and of assisting the department in meeting calls from local organizations for help in planning and conducting parties and other social functions. Institutes have sometimes resulted in the formation of party-a-month clubs, which meet monthly to enjoy a social evening, exchange ideas, and learn new activities.

Party Aids. Many departments have found it helpful to prepare game or party kits which, like the picnic kits, are lent to local organizations. These kits contain game supplies and materials such as Indian clubs, sets of alphabet cards, chalk, rubber balls, song sheets, hoops, wooden blocks, number cards, relay batons, tape measures, blindfolds, and one or more books with party-planning suggestions. The varying requirements of groups requesting assistance in planning their socials make it desirable to modify the standard kit in order to meet the needs of a particular group. Bulletins offering suggestions for games, stunts, refreshments, and party planning are issued by several departments.

DANCING

Dancing is one of the most popular teen-center activities. Its rhythm and beauty have a strong appeal for children and adults as well. Dance groups sponsored by the recreation department meet weekly in hundreds of cities.

A train trip between Danville and Lynchburg, Virginia, arranged by the recreation departments with the cooperation of city, railroad, and local radio-station officials, illustrates how a festive occasion can be centered around an activity like dancing. The widely heralded event attracted a large crowd to the Danville railroad station, where 500 merry-makers accompanied by two full orchestras enjoyed an hour of dancing before boarding the eleven-car train for Lynchburg. Loud-speakers brought music from the orchestras in the baggage car for community singing, and refreshments were served during the trip. More music, officials, and dancers greeted the group at Lynchburg, where dancing continued until the train departed for the trip home, rounding out a most successful outing.

Square dancing is competing successfully with social dancing for the interest of the young people in several cities, and it is well adapted to participation by the entire family. The number of square-dance groups is growing rapidly, and in many cities regularly scheduled square-dance nights are among the best attended events in the entire program. Square dances rank high in popularity among older adults and, in modified forms, among handicapped groups.

Dance Classes. To meet the need for instruction in dancing, classes for boys and girls and evening groups for adults have been organized by many departments. Members are helped to develop poise and social graces as well as acquire dance skills. Children's rhythms for preschoolers, modern dancing for teen-age girls, and ballet classes are increasing in popularity. The range of offerings is illustrated by the 1957 schedule in Arlington County, Virginia, where children's classes included modern, ballroom, tap, ballet, and square dancing, most of them at the beginning and intermediate levels; adults were offered instruction in ballroom, Latin American, square, and Hawaiian dancing.

In Oak Park, Illinois, as many as 700 children have been enrolled in the classes in ballet, ballroom, tap, old-fashioned square dancing, and acrobatic, folk, and character dancing in a single year. Preschool children are taught singing and dramatic games, in addition to folk dances and simple tap work. In some groups children have arranged their own dances, and the high school festival, circus, stunt day, and other occasions have furnished opportunities for demonstrating their ability. Social dances, barn dances, and old-fashioned square dances are also popular features of the program for both children and adults.

A junior civic ballet in San Diego, California, whose members are drawn from participants in ballet classes, has been formed for the study and development of appreciation of modern ballet. Besides taking part in lesser programs, the group has appeared with the symphony orchestra and presented numbers in various community-wide events.

Dancing Out of Doors. Social dancing is by no means limited to indoor centers, but has attained great popularity as an outdoor activity. As mentioned in Chapter 16, people dance in the open air on summer evenings on outdoor platforms, paved parking areas, or streets temporarily closed to traffic. Gaily colored lights suspended around the area used for dancing add a festive air to the street dances. If an orchestra is not available, music is broadcast over a public-address system. Square dancing out of doors has also proved exceedingly popular with people of all ages, as demonstrated in many cities such as Fort Wayne, Indiana, where dancing under the stars has been a regular family-night feature in two of the city's parks. Name bands have provided the music in a single season for more than fifty outdoor dances in the parks, which have been sponsored for many years by a public utility in New York City.

Folk Dancing. The varied and colorful folk dances, many of them introduced in this country from different nations of Europe, have a strong appeal and a conspicuous place in playground and center programs. They are commonly carried on throughout the playground season and have an important part in the pageant or festival. In Mobile, Alabama, for example, a spring music and folk-dance festival in which preschool, playground, and golden-age groups participate is an outstanding annual event. An annual Vermont country-dance festival, sponsored by the State Board of Recreation, has brought together, from communities throughout the state, dance groups representing schools, 4-H clubs, recreation departments, and dance clubs. The afternoon and evening programs comprise mass demonstrations, special demonstrations by dance teams, and general dancing.

It has been said that folk dancing contains the "very essence of social group play." In neighborhoods with a large foreign-born population who delight to take part in their familiar native dances, folk dancing has a conspicuous place in indoor-center programs. Twenty-five folk dance groups, authentically costumed, have been organized in a large Middle Western city, where the park authorities, in sponsoring folk-dance festivals, use every means to encourage a reviving interest in folk dancing among the different nationalities. An international dance group sponsored by another recreation department brings together people of many nationalities interested in folk dancing. Members attend the meetings dressed in national costumes, learn dances demonstrated and taught by national groups, and hold an annual festival.

HOBBIES

Hobbies can be divided into three fundamental types: those in which knowledge is acquired, those in which things are acquired, and those in which things are created. The term "hobby" is commonly applied to a wide range of activities, but some hold the opinion that a true hobby is a personal, intimate matter, capable of enjoyment by one's self, to be shared only with a few kindred souls. Because of the significance of hobbies in the leisure time of large numbers of individuals, the recreation department helps people acquire hobbies and find opportunities to enjoy them with others who have similar interests. Hobbies have a definite place in the playground program, and the long season and varied facilities of the indoor center favor the formation of hobby groups. Recreation departments foster hobbies among adults primarily by helping bring together persons with a common hobby interest and furnishing a place where the group can meet; in some cases, leadership and equipment are also provided. Special hobby centers have been established in several cities.

Photography. Photography is a hobby that appeals to old and young alike and enjoys wide popularity. One county camera club, started as an outgrowth of amateur photography contests sponsored by the recreation authorities, proved so successful that at least half a dozen other clubs were organized in the county during the following year. A juvenile camera club started in a park field house in one city met with such success that soon twenty-one similar clubs had been established in other centers, including adult as well as youth groups. Meetings were devoted to demonstration and experimentation on lighting, composition and picture taking, lectures by outside speakers, group instruction in developing, printing, enlarging, and toning, and criticism of the work of club members. A picture-of-the-month contest was carried on among the clubs to choose the picture for the frontispiece of the department's monthly report.

Photography can contribute greatly to the enjoyment of other recreation interests, such as travel or nature study. Related activities of camera clubs sponsored by recreation departments include a photographic holiday in the form of week-end outings at a municipal mountain camp,

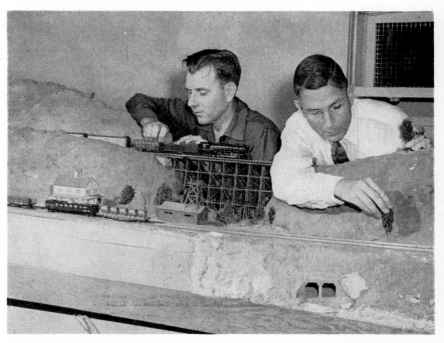

Model railroaders exhibit in annual craft and hobby show (Courtesy of San Diego, Calif., Park and Recreation Department).

managing the motion-picture shows at a recreation center, combining with a mountaineers' club in its annual pack trips, and taking pictures of the department's activities for use in its publicity.

Other Hobbies. Stamp collecting is another hobby, the cultivation of which is highly desirable since it embraces history, art, geography, civics, printing, design, and social relationships. An annual exhibit is an important part of many club programs.

Model railroading has a fascination for men and boys who have a mechanical bent, and clubs developed around this hobby have proved highly successful. Some clubs have adult members only, but model railroading is an excellent father-and-son activity. Model boat-building clubs, clown clubs, astronomy clubs, bird clubs, poetry clubs, and hot-rod clubs illustrate the great variety of groups that are developed by recreation departments around a hobby interest. Dog obedience-training classes have proved popular and successful in many cities.

Hobby Shows. Hobbies may be promoted by means of shows in which individuals and organizations throughout the city exhibit the articles they have made or collected. The shows afford enjoyment and satisfaction to exhibitors and visitors alike, and are a means of arousing interest in the various activities and of recruiting hobby-club members. Demonstrations of hobbies such as photography, art, model-railroad building, short-wave radio, and marionettes, which enable visitors to observe the hobbyists in action, arouse even greater interest than exhibits of the work accomplished by the various clubs.

STUDY GROUPS AND FORUMS

Current public interest in national and world problems has stimulated the formation of discussion groups, forums, and similar informal education activities at many indoor recreation centers. Study groups afford outlets for self-expression and personal development, and are a means of generating active interest in civic and world affairs. Typical of such groups is the Thursday Night Club which met in the library of a community house in a New England college town. Intended to stimulate interest in current events of local, state, national, and international importance, the club has been called a "place where everything is argued, debated, and discussed but where nothing is settled."

Some indoor-center programs include forums, lectures, debating clubs, parliamentary law and public-speaking classes, citizenship courses for the foreign-born, and foreign-language classes. Courses in personal care, or charm schools, have been popular with women and teen-age girls, and a few departments offer classes in real estate, insurance, investments, and family budgets. In general, however, these activities are associated with the adult education program, and few people participate in them primarily for recreation. Yet study and discussion play an important, though secondary, role in the activities of many groups sponsored by the recreation department. Arts and crafts groups, for example, make intensive studies of the history and development of forms, color, craft materials and their sources of production, the life of primitive peoples, and local arts and crafts resources. Music activities become more meaningful if the groups study the composers of the music used or trace the development of musical instruments or of music as a form of expression. Groups interested in a game or sport such as tennis or baseball welcome an opportunity to hear a lecture by an expert, see a technical sports film, or join a discussion of proposed changes in the rules governing play.

Interest in travel provides in some cities the basis for a series of meetings throughout the winter season at which persons who have visited foreign countries or taken unusually interesting trips report their experiences, usually illustrated with lantern slides or motion pictures. Films produced by travel agencies and industrial firms, or showing scenes in the national parks and forests, are shown in many indoor centers.

A hair-styling demonstration at a charm school for teen-agers (Courtesy of Leonia, N. J., Recreation Commission).

HOLIDAY CELEBRATIONS

Perhaps no project includes so many forms of recreation or involves so many community groups as the celebrations organized in connection with the more important holidays. Reference was made in Chapter 16 to the ways in which Halloween enthusiasm is directed into festive but wholesome channels. Independence Day is the occasion for parades, patriotic festivals, athletic events, and fireworks. Valentine's Day and St. Patrick's Day are celebrated by parties and other appropriate social activities in the indoor centers, but Christmas is the foremost holiday season.

Christmas. The activities promoted or conducted by recreation departments in celebration of Christmas are many and are acceptable to people of almost all faiths. Centers for repairing and distributing toys to needy children are conducted with the help of children or volunteer leaders. Scrapbooks, toys, and gifts for shut-ins and inmates of charitable institutions are made in recreation centers, and individuals make their Christmas gifts in craft classes. City-wide home decoration campaigns are organized, and cities erect a tree of light in their parks or decorate

The Christmas Ship brings light and music to the people of Seattle (Courtesy of Seattle, Wash., Park Department).

growing trees at which carols are sung and other services held. Carols are also sung in the centers and on a city-wide basis, on the streets and in hotels, radio stations, hospitals, and other institutions. Christmas parties are arranged for playground or center groups, sometimes for underprivileged children who receive toys made or repaired in the department's toy centers. Plays, tableaux, and operettas appropriate to the season or elaborate Christmas pageants are produced. Open-air reproductions of the Nativity scene or of Santa and his reindeer, effectively lighted, are erected in city parks. A Santa Clause house, a "Christmas-around-the-World" program series, and a letters-to-Santa service are other holiday features. A unique community project is the *Christmas Ship* in Seattle—a gaily decorated yacht that cruises slowly through the city's lakes and ship canal and along the Puget Sound shore line, carrying an orchestra and chorus that serenade the thousands thronging shoreside vantage points. No other project sponsored by the municipal recreation department enlists the cooperation of more individuals and organizations, or provides more opportunities for favorable public relations, than the city-wide community Christmas celebration.

COMMUNITY FESTIVALS

Festivals in which community groups participate have become annual events of major significance in several cities. Long popular in a number of communities are May Day festivals, municipal birthday anniversaries, international folk festivals, and similar events. One city sponsors an annual state-wide folk festival; another has a yearly Pan-American Day program. Joseph Lee Day is celebrated in cities across the country.

These community-wide events, which not only afford festive occasions for the cities conducting them but attract large numbers of visitors, play a major part in the recreational life of the people. They furnish opportunities for groups within the recreation department program to participate and also focus the attention of the citizens upon the city's recreation facilities and activities. To an exceptional degree they help to foster community pride and a consciousness of local resources and furnish an outlet for artistic, creative, and civic service.

SERVICE ACTIVITIES

No account of the services provided by and through the recreation department is complete that fails to mention the many opportunities it offers children, youth, and adults to render service to other individuals or to the community. Some of the projects undertaken involve much time and effort, but they are done in a spirit which gives them the quality of a recreation activity. In dozens of localities groups of men and boys, using donated materials and loaned equipment, have developed recreation areas and built equipment, facilities, and structures. The services rendered by volunteer recreation leaders have been mentioned repeatedly in this volume. Brief reference to projects in three localities suggest the variety of service activities.

Children attending the playgrounds conducted by the Essex County, New Jersey, Park Commission cooperated with the American Red Cross in making word-picture books, in which a carefully devised list of words is matched with pictures illustrating their meaning. Children brought magazines from home and selected appropriate pictures which were clipped, pasted, and labeled so as to give pictorial definitions. At first, the books were used by Hungarian refugees, but the project was continued to help foreign-born become acquainted with our language.

The motive of doing for others has been a primary factor in assuring over many years the continuity and success of the Youth Club of Algoma, Wisconsin. Among its service projects have been raising funds for CARE, collecting canned or packaged food items at a Christmas dance, adopting a needy youth through the Foster Parents' Plan for War Children, volunteering for assignment in the Ground Observer Corps, conducting a courteous-driver contest and essay contests on Americanization and the purpose of voting. These activities have in no way minimized interest and participation in the social, athletic, outing, and other programs typical of a youth group.

Five recreation areas in Los Angeles were improved through the efforts of 2,500 young people working over a three-year period. Five hundred University of California interfraternity members developed a 60-acre tract; teen-agers from youth organizations worked at the other areas. Picnic tables were put in place, a clubhouse was painted, 15,000 trees and 50,000 shrubs were planted, and lawn areas were seeded under the guidance of group leaders who had been instructed by park foremen. Every tree and shrub was suitably identified. Games and picnics interspersed with the work periods added the element of fun to the satisfaction the young people gained from their contribution to the city's recreation resources.

26. SERVICE TO SPECIAL GROUPS

H<small>OMES</small>, industries, churches, institutions, and many other community agencies offer channels through which the recreation department can serve the leisure-time interests of large numbers of people. The facilities and activities of the department are generally available for everyone, regardless of occupation, age, race, income, or any other factor. People participate in the program as members of the community, not as employees in a certain factory or members of a particular church or nationality group. Nevertheless, many recreation authorities realize that one of their most important functions is to assist existing agencies and groups with their own recreation activities and programs. They also provide special services for such groups as preschool children, the handicapped, and older adults, who are unable to participate in parts of the regular program. By furnishing leadership, facilities, and guidance to such groups, the recreation department supplements its normal program and greatly extends its influence and service.

HOME AND FAMILY RECREATION

Howard Braucher once said, "The first responsibility of recreation board, school board, church, with reference to play and recreation, is to create a play spirit that carries back to the home to make and keep family life vital." [1] Recreation departments have been criticized because they draw children, youth, and adults away from their homes and because their programs separate families rather than encourage them to play together. Many departments, however, promote home and family recreation. Games learned on the playground are later played in the back yard; social recreation activities enjoyed at the indoor centers are introduced at family and neighborhood gatherings. Mothers' clubs are taught games that can be played in the home, where the craft skills and hobby interests fostered in the department's program also occupy many leisure hours. Picnic facilities, camps, and beaches serve family groups, and increasingly recreation areas are developed as centers for the entire

[1] "Home and Leisure," *Recreation*, vol. 24, no. 12, p. 641, March, 1931.

family. Mother-and-daughter dinners induce better relations in the home; family nights at the playground or center inspire the family to play together; and special events and tournaments invite participation by married couples, fathers and sons, or other related groups.

Back-yard Playground Contests. The back-yard playground contest, which has been promoted successfully in both large and small cities, is a direct means by which recreation departments foster play in the home. The interest of parent-teacher and neighborhood groups is enlisted in the project of making attractive home playgrounds. Bulletins containing valuable hints on how to proceed, and working drawings and plans for the construction of simple apparatus are prepared and distributed. The improved back yards are rated by a committee of judges on their suitability for use by all members of the family and on the design and construction of the play facilities, with consideration given to workmanship, practical use, appearance, safety, cost, and originality.

Home-play Promotion. Publications containing suggestions for home-play activities and for the construction of back-yard playgrounds are issued in connection with intensive home-play campaigns and also as a special service to parents. Some of these publications are fairly comprehensive booklets, but more often they are simply bulletins relating to recreation activities adapted to home or family use. A distinctive feature of one recreation department's plan for the city-wide promotion of home play activities was the formation of a parents' home-play group. The fathers and mothers in the group agreed to try to play with their children at least three hours each week. A number of departments have organized home-play weeks, and the widespread celebration of National Recreation Month has afforded an excellent opportunity for promoting recreation in both home and community.

Because successful programs require a sympathetic attitude on the part of parents and an understanding of play-leadership methods and activities, courses in home recreation have been conducted in several cities. One such course consisted of crafts, stunts, simple dramatics, storytelling, singing games, music, story play, hobbies, magic suitable for use in the home, hiking, back-yard play, home-play equipment, sand modeling, active, quiet, and table games, and a series of demonstrations that included mixers with and without music.

Service to Shut-ins. The needs of individuals who are confined to their homes because of physical handicaps or illness and are unable to participate in the recreation program are being met through a service for shut-ins in a number of cities. Fresh flowers are delivered to each person regularly, magazines and games are provided, birthdays are remembered, and gifts are sent at Thanksgiving, Christmas, and Easter. Persons traveling are asked to send letters and post cards to the shut-ins. Leaders visit homes to tell stories, play games with the children, read to them, help them make scrapbooks, and teach them simple games and crafts.

Other Services. Several recreation departments have established toy loan centers which have proved a delight to children in homes where toys and other play materials are lacking. Appeals through the press and local organizations have brought in toys and games of all kinds, which are repaired, disinfected, and circulated through the centers in much the same way as library books. The radio is used more and more as a means of bringing to parents suggestions for home games, rainy-day activities, music, and dramatics. Plant-exchange days, home-beautification campaigns, lectures before neighborhood groups and garden clubs, and the publication of bulletins on flowers, shrubs, and lawns foster home gardens and the improvement of home grounds. By promoting attractive co-recreational activities, recreation departments are encouraging young men and women to play together and to develop common leisure-time interests which are considered so important in a happy, successful married life.

BUSINESS AND INDUSTRY

Many employers, as pointed out in Chapter 3, have established recreation facilities and promote recreation activities for their workers, usually in cooperation with employee groups. In some cases these services are available to members of workers' families; in one-industry towns they are essentially community programs, including children's playgrounds and indoor-center activities. Despite the development of employee recreation programs, a large majority of workers in most cities rely on other sources for their recreation. In industrial communities most participants in municipal recreation programs are industrial workers and their families, who engage in the activities without reference to their place of employment. A survey made in a Pacific Coast city showed that 60 per cent of all adult participants in the public recreation program were employed by local industries. A Middle Western city reports 50 per cent of the adult use of its indoor centers by workers in industry; still another that 75 per cent of all participation by women in its activities is by employed women. Nevertheless, many recreation departments are giving specialized service to industries and other employee groups.

Service to Employee Groups. Recreation departments in many cities organize leagues in baseball, softball, basketball, bowling, and other sports, composed of teams representing factories, banks, stores, and other business concerns. They assist in the organization and management of plant recreation programs, particularly activities such as dramatics, hikes, music festivals, hobby shows, gardening, and special celebrations. They make available to employee groups athletic fields, gymnasiums, parks, picnic grounds, beaches, swimming pools, auditoriums, and other indoor and outdoor facilities for their own recreation programs. Close cooperation and frequent communication between industrial and municipal recreation personnel can prove of mutual benefit to both programs.

Workers whose hours or conditions of employment do not enable them to take part in the regular recreation program have not been forgotten by recreation departments. Newsboy clubs and caddie clubs have been organized, and activities have been provided for bakers, milkmen, hotel employees, and policemen. A midnight baseball league was organized in one city for theatre workers who were employed during the late afternoon and evening. Gymnasium classes and other activities have been organized for nurses whose schedules make it difficult for them to join in the normal schedule of activities. Recreation departments strengthen their relations with the employees of other city departments by organizing outings, parties, and other special events for workers in the local city government.

The Industrial Division. Comprehensive programs involving direct service to industrial groups have been developed in several cities, where a special industrial division has been established in the recreation department.[2] The objectives of such a division, according to the constitution of the organization in San Francisco, are as follows:

1. To foster and promote athletic activities for employees of industrial firms in the city and county of San Francisco.
2. To encourage employees to participate in recreation activities.
3. To promote recreation within the firms.
4. To promote athletic meets and tournaments between member firms in all seasonal activities.
5. To further the social activities of those firms.

All industrial and business firms operating within the city are usually eligible for membership in the recreation association, and individuals employed by these member firms can participate in the activities. A board composed of representatives of the member firms administers the organization, and the program is conducted under the supervision of recreation personnel assigned to the division. Representative workers' committees have responsibility for the various sports and social activities comprising the program, which is usually financed by yearly company membership dues and individual or team entry fees.

[2] The program in Oakland, California, a pioneer in the industrial recreation field, is described in Chap. 27.

CHURCHES

Institutes to which churches send representatives for training in social recreation leadership are perhaps the most common form of special service rendered to churches by recreation departments. The interest in social recreation on the part of church groups in one city resulted in an annual training institute for leaders in young people's group activities. In a second city a demonstration of methods of leading community singing, conducting folk dancing and folk games, and planning stunt programs was arranged in cooperation with church leaders. A monthly social-recreation bulletin service to churches has been provided in more than one city. Leadership is sometimes furnished by the recreation department for church programs that are open to all the people of the neighborhood, and parks and other recreation facilities are made available to churches for Easter sunrise or special community services. Church facilities, on the other hand, are used by the recreation department for its programs in a number of cities. Churches avail themselves of the department's picnic and party kits and service, song sheets, costumes, and other materials, and are assisted in working out their own recreation programs.

INSTITUTIONS

Hospitals, orphanages, and similar institutions often lack recreation facilities or leadership, although their occupants are in special need of play opportunities. Comparatively few recreation departments provide regular service to institutions, but the results which have been accomplished fully justify the efforts expended in behalf of these unfortunate groups. Some ways in which recreation departments serve institutions are as follows: Service bureaus furnish leadership and equipment for picnics and parties; institution workers are enrolled in training courses; groups from institutions are transported to swimming pools or to unusual playground or community-wide events; roving storytellers make the rounds of institutions; and special programs such as Christmas plays, the playground circus, and folk-dance festivals are taken to homes, orphanages, and hospitals. A splendid example of combining a handcraft and service project occurred in one city where, before Christmas, children at nineteen playgrounds constructed miniature circuses which really functioned. After being displayed in the city hall they were distributed to orphanages and hospitals.

Hospital Services. Recreation departments cooperate with hospital recreation personnel by providing entertainment in the hospitals and by arranging transportation for ambulatory cases to special recreation events. Few recreation department services are more appreciated than the programs carried on in children's hospital wards, especially for long-term patients. Trained volunteers play games with the children and assist them with crafts projects. Motion pictures are shown for ambulatory patients, and a record-library service provides phonograph and records that can be played in the patients' rooms. Storytelling, stamp collecting, and other hobbies help the days to pass more quickly for the patients and in some cases contribute directly to recovery. "Sunshine baskets" for the hospital have been prepared by young people under a project sponsored by the recreation department in Jefferson County, Kentucky. The baskets contain seven packages—one to be opened each day of the week—and in each package is a different game. After a patient is through with the games he returns them for use by others. The Kansas City, Missouri, recreation department has developed a service termed "recreation counseling" designed to help individual patients continue their participation in recreation activities after discharge from the hospital.

NATIONAL AND RACIAL GROUPS

The community recreation program is a powerful agency for absorbing national and racial groups into American life. The groups are encouraged to participate in the program, not as members of a particular race or nationality but as neighbors and members of the community. Prejudices, ignorance, and timidity deter many persons from taking part, but such attitudes are gradually being eliminated through the efforts of competent leaders, often recruited from the racial groups themselves. The American principle that all residents of a community are entitled to a fair share of the services provided through tax funds is particularly applicable to recreation.

The special interests, skills, and customs of people from other nations influence the planning of facilities and programs. *Boccie* and pelota courts, bowling greens, and cricket fields are provided in neighborhoods with national groups among whom these games are traditional. Native festivals and holiday programs are built around the games, music, and dances of the various nations. Reference was previously made to foreign-born folk-dance and music groups. Widely publicized nationality nights have attracted large and enthusiastic audiences.

A special problem is presented in certain sections of the country, such as the Southern states, where a dual system of education and municipal services for white and nonwhite racial groups has long existed. Under such conditions, dual provision of recreation has been necessary; separate programs and facilities were therefore provided for whites and for Negroes or Mexicans. As stated in Chapter 5, recent court decisions affecting segregation have resulted in widely different attitudes and action with reference to the use of public recreation areas and facilities by the two races. No differentiation is made in most parts of the United States, however, where neighborhood facilities are provided irrespective of the race or ancestry of the residents and where city-wide facilities and services are available to the total population.

SPECIAL AGE GROUPS

In general, municipal recreation programs are available to all the people, regardless of age, but some activities are provided to meet th special needs of specific age groups. Programs designed to serve three age groups will be described briefly.

Preschool Children. For many years children of preschool age had little share in the recreation program, primarily because it was felt that the best place for them was in the home. Because of changing home conditions, and in response to rising demands, more and more recreation departments are providing activities for this group. In such widely different cities as Brunswick, Maine, Washington, D. C., Mobile, Alabama, and Miami, Florida, special preschool programs or play schools are conducted in recreation buildings of various types. These programs afford not only enjoyable activities for the children but group experiences which help them to adjust readily to school attendance. Most programs for preschool children are scheduled during the morning hours and thus utilize facilities that otherwise would be unused. Activities at preschool centers include singing and running games, rhythm bands, storytelling, simple crafts, rhythmics, block building, refreshments, and apparatus play. A nominal fee is charged for this service in most cities, and parents' groups have been formed to assist in various ways.

Increasingly a section of the neighborhood playground is set aside and equipped for the use of preschool children, as indicated in Chapter 11, and special activities are scheduled for this age group in the daily playground program.

Teen-age Youth. Youth have always constituted a large percentage of those using community recreation services and facilities, but in recent years their recreation needs have been greatly publicized, due in part to the widespread public concern over the rising tide of juvenile delinquency. During World War II hundreds of youth centers or canteens were established throughout the country, in small villages as well as in large urban centers. Although these centers were established under various auspices, many were started by recreation departments and are still operated by them. Financial and leadership assistance was given youth in furnishing their centers and in planning and conducting their programs. Responsibility for the success of the centers rested with the young people, but adult leadership was made available to help avoid the shortcomings of many centers. Teen-center members and groups were encouraged to make use of the department's other facilities and activities.

Even though the tendency to establish separate youth centers has largely disappeared, experience in the operation of teen centers caused many recreation departments to adjust their programs and methods in better to serve the changing interests and needs of youth. Youth participate more fully in the planning and conduct of activities; consideration is given to youth activities; and many youth clubs been organized. Special rooms have been set aside as centers for groups in recreation buildings, where gymnasiums, craft rooms, swimming pools, and other facilities are made available for their use during specified periods. Young people are more widely represented on recreation councils and planning committees.

Long Beach, California, affords an example of such cooperative service to young people through its canteen clubs, Friday Nighters, Youth Talent Showcase, and co-recreational fun nights in the high school gymnasiums. The canteen clubs are for the senior high school age group, including nonschool youth under twenty living in the district. An adult director attends the meetings of club officers who plan, organize, and administer the club activities and enforce its rules. Other youth committees handle specific club functions. The department's director of youth clubs serves as chairman of each club's advisory board, which consists of the club officers and adults representing the parent-teacher association and recreation and school departments. A somewhat similar group plans the program and conducts the social dances and parties of the Friday Nighters, composed of eighth and ninth graders. Through its Youth Talent Showcase, the recreation department affords youth opportunity to express their talents and abilities in a major production and in local programs open to the public, sponsored by parent-teacher associations, service clubs, and church groups.

In considering youth recreation services it is important to keep in mind that the youth center or club, popular as it is, represents only a part of the recreation service that youth want and are getting. The center merely supplements sports and athletics, camping, picnics and outings, family recreation, music, drama, arts and crafts, hobbies, winter and water sports, and other activities which constitute balanced, year-round youth recreation service.

The teen council of the Miami Beach Recreation Department assists the staff in planning, supervising, and coordinating a varied program of activities for boys and girls who are at least twelve years old and have completed the seventh grade. Teen-age headquarters are maintained at

two parks, and in order to qualify for special youth projects or to participate in city-wide tournaments, teen-agers must register at one of these
centers. Daytime activities for boys during the summer of 1958 included
softball, crafts, boxing, and baseball; for girls, baton twirling, charm
school, and crafts; for both, tennis, swimming, bowling, crafts, archery,
minor sports, and talent and water-show rehearsals. Evening summer
activities included junior and senior teen dances, volleyball, stamp clubs,
softball, and baseball. Tournaments and championships were he'
loop tennis, shuffleboard, archery, tennis, ping-pong, chess, and che
special events were a picnic, variety and water show, swimming
outings, and participation in the Florida Youth Workshop. Youth
course, take part in activities at all the city's recreation areas, bu
development of special programs for this age group with the cooperation
of the senior and junior divisions of the teen council provides an added
incentive for active participation.

Several departments have recognized the desire of young people to
earn money in return for useful service and have undertaken to help
them in various ways. For example, a work camp has been established
by the Essex County, New Jersey, Park Commission, at which teen-agers
under the guidance of competent leadership rehabilitated trails in a
reservation. In other localities a work program in the parks has been
combined with periods devoted to recreation. In Arlington County, Virginia, the recreation department has conducted a "work-earn-learn" program, under which teen-age boys are available for work in and around
the house and garden at a fixed hourly rate.

Older Adults. The adoption of the Federal social security program,
with its provisions for old-age insurance, compulsory retirement at a
comparatively early age, together with the lengthening span of life,
create a real need for recreation services to meet the increased leisure of
older adults. Such services are especially needed because older adults
grew up in a period when little consideration was given to recreation or
training for leisure; many of them are therefore at a loss to find ways of
spending their long periods of free time. Furnishing opportunities for
older people to enjoy the companionship of their own age group and
providing places where individuals can acquire or continue recreation
interests provide a challenge to recreation agencies. The fact that the
number of cities reporting special recreation services for older adults
more than doubled in the decade ending in 1956 indicates the striking
development of such programs during this period.

Many cities have set aside a portion of recreation areas, equipped with
bowling green, clock-golf course, courts for roque, shuffleboard, or horseshoes, tables and benches for chess, checkers, and card games, or other
facilities for the exclusive use of older adults. Clubrooms fitted out with

programs. Responsibility for the success of the centers rested with the young people, but adult leadership was made available to help avoid the shortcomings of many centers. Teen-center members and groups were encouraged to make use of the department's other facilities and activities.

Even though the tendency to establish separate youth centers has largely disappeared, experience in the operation of teen centers caused many recreation departments to adjust their programs and methods in order better to serve the changing interests and needs of youth. Youth now participate more fully in the planning and conduct of activities; greater consideration is given to youth activities; and many youth clubs have been organized. Special rooms have been set aside as centers for youth groups in recreation buildings, where gymnasiums, craft rooms, swimming pools, and other facilities are made available for their use during specified periods. Young people are more widely represented on recreation councils and planning committees.

Long Beach, California, affords an example of such cooperative service to young people through its canteen clubs, Friday Nighters, Youth Talent Showcase, and co-recreational fun nights in the high school gymnasiums. The canteen clubs are for the senior high school age group, including nonschool youth under twenty living in the district. An adult director attends the meetings of club officers who plan, organize, and administer the club activities and enforce its rules. Other youth committees handle specific club functions. The department's director of youth clubs serves as chairman of each club's advisory board, which consists of the club officers and adults representing the parent-teacher association and recreation and school departments. A somewhat similar group plans the program and conducts the social dances and parties of the Friday Nighters, composed of eighth and ninth graders. Through its Youth Talent Showcase, the recreation department affords youth opportunity to express their talents and abilities in a major production and in local programs open to the public, sponsored by parent-teacher associations, service clubs, and church groups.

In considering youth recreation services it is important to keep in mind that the youth center or club, popular as it is, represents only a part of the recreation service that youth want and are getting. The center merely supplements sports and athletics, camping, picnics and outings, family recreation, music, drama, arts and crafts, hobbies, winter and water sports, and other activities which constitute balanced, year-round youth recreation service.

The teen council of the Miami Beach Recreation Department assists the staff in planning, supervising, and coordinating a varied program of activities for boys and girls who are at least twelve years old and have completed the seventh grade. Teen-age headquarters are maintained at

two parks, and in order to qualify for special youth projects or to participate in city-wide tournaments, teen-agers must register at one of these centers. Daytime activities for boys during the summer of 1958 included softball, crafts, boxing, and baseball; for girls, baton twirling, charm school, and crafts; for both, tennis, swimming, bowling, crafts, archery, minor sports, and talent and water-show rehearsals. Evening summer activities included junior and senior teen dances, volleyball, stamp clubs, softball, and baseball. Tournaments and championships were held in loop tennis, shuffleboard, archery, tennis, ping-pong, chess, and checkers; special events were a picnic, variety and water show, swimming meet, outings, and participation in the Florida Youth Workshop. Youth can, of course, take part in activities at all the city's recreation areas, but the development of special programs for this age group with the cooperation of the senior and junior divisions of the teen council provides an added incentive for active participation.

Several departments have recognized the desire of young people to earn money in return for useful service and have undertaken to help them in various ways. For example, a work camp has been established by the Essex County, New Jersey, Park Commission, at which teen-agers under the guidance of competent leadership rehabilitated trails in a reservation. In other localities a work program in the parks has been combined with periods devoted to recreation. In Arlington County, Virginia, the recreation department has conducted a "work-earn-learn" program, under which teen-age boys are available for work in and around the house and garden at a fixed hourly rate.

Older Adults. The adoption of the Federal social security program, with its provisions for old-age insurance, compulsory retirement at a comparatively early age, together with the lengthening span of life, create a real need for recreation services to meet the increased leisure of older adults. Such services are especially needed because older adults grew up in a period when little consideration was given to recreation or training for leisure; many of them are therefore at a loss to find ways of spending their long periods of free time. Furnishing opportunities for older people to enjoy the companionship of their own age group and providing places where individuals can acquire or continue recreation interests provide a challenge to recreation agencies. The fact that the number of cities reporting special recreation services for older adults more than doubled in the decade ending in 1956 indicates the striking development of such programs during this period.

Many cities have set aside a portion of recreation areas, equipped with bowling green, clock-golf course, courts for roque, shuffleboard, or horseshoes, tables and benches for chess, checkers, and card games, or other facilities for the exclusive use of older adults. Clubrooms fitted out with

table games, reading matter, and hot plates for making coffee have been turned over to such groups in many recreation buildings. A few cities have developed areas especially for elderly men and women, and in 1956 special indoor centers for older adults were reported by recreation departments in ninety-three cities. Golden-age clubs meet regularly to engage in a variety of satisfying activities, planned by their own members with the help of recreation leaders. Older adults are also encouraged to

Golden-agers enjoy a social game in their own center (Courtesy of Senior Citizens Recreation Center, Columbus, Ohio).

participate with other age groups in other phases of the recreation program. A few examples of unusual services to older adults or of their activities follow.

A glee club in Mobile, Alabama, made several public appearances. Groups in several cities have taken bus trips to visit golden-age clubs in other localities. The New Orleans Recreation Department sponsored the first national senior-citizens convention, at which more than 1,000 persons registered. A monthly bulletin, *Senior Citizens Scribe*, prepared by editors representing centers in the county, is published by the Westchester County, New York, Recreation Commission, which has also provided a camping program for senior citizens at the county's camps and

conducted a training conference attended by representatives of twenty-eight local canteens. In San Francisco a creative writing class at the senior center spent two months preparing a dignified and inspiring ceremonial for use at the monthly birthday parties honoring members of the center. An over-sixty employment bureau in Arlington County, Virginia, serves talented and experienced retired men and women. Clubs in Montgomery, Alabama, have dressed dolls for the Salvation Army, collected magazines and radios and made quilts for mental hospitals, helped the Ground Observer Corps, made calls in the United Fund appeal, and served in other ways.

SPECIAL SERVICES

Space limitation permits only a brief mention of several other ways in which recreation departments render unusual service to restricted groups.

The Handicapped. Most public recreation programs have been planned for reasonably normal people, with the result that the mentally retarded and physically handicapped have had little opportunity to participate. Because of limited budget and staff, the recreation department has often looked to private agencies to provide needed services for such groups. An encouraging tendency on the part of recreation authorities to accept responsibility for providing recreation for all the people has resulted in an increasing number of programs for the handicapped. In some cases activities center around a particular group such as the blind. For example, swimming periods are arranged for them; in Wilmington, North Carolina, members of a club for the blind are transported to its monthly meeting for a widely varied program; and in several cities, fragrance gardens, filled with sweet-scented plants and pungent herbs, with Braille markers, are maintained as a service to the blind. More frequently, however, programs are established for groups that include individuals with many types of handicaps.

Underlying these programs is the conviction that retarded or physically handicapped individuals have the same right to participate in enjoyable recreation and to be happy as other people, and that they should be encouraged to take part in activities as normal people. Experience has demonstrated that while they become absorbed in recreation they forget about their infirmities and acquire confidence and satisfactions that were previously denied them.

The Detroit Department of Parks and Recreation has been a pioneer in serving less fortunate children. In 1949 it first established a day-camp program for crippled children, which has brought joy to thousands. A specially designed planting board, invented by the gardening supervisor, makes it possible for blind children to participate in the garden program.

The department's year-round program for retarded children, initiated with the help of the Detroit Association for Retarded Children, is conducted daily at three well-equipped centers with outdoor facilities in widely separate parts of the city. Activities include flag-raising ceremony, hikes, games, singing, and crafts, interspersed with lunch and rest periods and a weekly swim for the older children. The active participation of

Ready for a pony dance in the Handicapped Center circus (Courtesy of Recreation Center for the Handicapped, San Francisco).

parents is a significant factor in its success. Committees of mothers are assigned specific duties on certain days, such as looking after wardrobe needs, lunches and rest periods, and assisting the juniors in group play.

Active membership in the Able-Disabled Club in Lima, Ohio, is restricted to the physically handicapped who are sixteen years of age and older, and it includes people with a great variety of infirmities. The club meets in a school multipurpose room. It is a highly organized group, and its committee members in turn assist the recreation supervisor in planning the monthly meetings. Several members play musical instruments, and the group enjoys singing around the piano. Special programs

have included games nights, square dancing, picnics, birthday parties, and holiday celebrations. Prior to joining the club, many members rarely ventured outside their homes; now they have gained self-confidence and participate in community as well as club activities.

A pioneer cooperative and unusually successful program is carried on at the Recreation Center for the Handicapped in San Francisco. Opened in 1952 as the Cerebral Palsy Recreation Center, housed in a specially equipped building provided by the Recreation and Park Department, it has been operated through donated funds. The center has demonstrated the contribution in happiness and personal development that recreation can bring to people with serious physical handicaps. Puppetry, folk dancing, creative writing, parties, pottery, fishing, games, cookouts, and swimming have proved most popular. All activities have been especially adapted so that each individual, regardless of his handicap, has been able to participate by utilizing those parts of his body over which he has control. A day-camp program in a nearby park area has brought new and enjoyable experiences. Furthermore, the emphasis on creative self-expression has revealed hidden talents in several individuals; others have been helped to achieve better coordination. An advisory council composed of representatives from the various age groups, which include youth and adults, assists the trained staff in planning the special events at the center. Service on the council has given members the satisfaction of helping others and a recognition that they are useful members of society.

Tourists. Furnishing recreation for tourists and visitors is an important business in cities which thrive largely on the tourist trade. Recreation programs are looked upon primarily as a means of attracting and serving visitors rather than as a service to local residents. Special emphasis is therefore given to the provision of bowling on the green, shuffleboard, croquet, and other game courts; to facilities for aquatics and fishing; indoor centers for dining, dancing, cards, and other quiet games; picnic facilities; and opportunities for music, arts, and dramatics. Resort cities have frequent organ recitals, band and orchestra concerts, and community sings, and maintain reading rooms and library service. Recreation authorities organize social-recreation clubs for the visitors and conduct frequent dances, card parties, and socials for their benefit. Unfortunately, in some resort cities the needs of local residents tend to be neglected.

The Corpus Christi, Texas, Recreation Department operates a club for visitors winter and summer. Tours, dances, card parties, movies, pot-luck suppers, boat rides, barbecues, fishing events, and shuffleboard comprise the program. The Tourist and Newcomer Week in February offers a variety of free tours, boat rides, shows, fish fries, and sports events to each registered tourist. Summer activities at Exposition Hall overlooking the bay include a child-care service for parents while shopping.

Service Personnel. Large permanent military establishments have long provided recreation facilities for the personnel stationed in them, and local authorities and agencies have encouraged them and their families to take advantage of community recreation services. A few cities have operated clubhouses for servicemen. Since the end of World War II, however, many small Army and Air Force installations have been established with no recreation facilities; elsewhere large numbers of servicemen are living with their families outside military bases. The personnel of our Armed Forces are mostly civilians away from home, and they want for themselves, and especially for their wives and children, the same opportunities for recreation as prevail in their home communities.

Recreation departments have taken the lead in providing the opportunities in various ways. The departments have organized community committees to consider the needs of military personnel and their families and to develop a plan for serving them. The departments have also established a two-way communication between the post and the community to avoid duplication of effort. They have invited servicemen to participate in hobby groups, to make use of recreation facilities, and to enter teams in league or tournament play; have welcomed children and youth to the neighborhood playground or teen center; have issued bulletins describing recreation facilities and programs in the region. They have also furnished hostesses for on-base programs. Servicemen and their wives, in turn, have contributed leadership and other valuable services to many community recreation programs.

Emergency Service. In a number of instances, when disaster has befallen a community the city officials have turned to the recreation department for emergency service. Splendid assistance has been rendered the flood victims in several cities along the Ohio River. In Cincinnati, for example, when thousands of people were driven from their homes, recreation programs were carried on continuously from 8 A.M. into the evening hours at a number of centers. The services of orchestral, dramatic, and vaudeville units were enlisted, and in the larger centers entertainments were given three times a day. Volunteers presented or assisted with vaudeville shows, symphony concerts, band concerts, exhibitions of magic, motion-picture performances, and dance programs. Recreation leaders also helped the refugees provide their own entertainment by organizing athletic and tap-dancing contests, spelling bees, checker tournaments, and choruses. Similar service was rendered by recreation departments in several New England cities following the disastrous floods in 1955.

Following an earthquake at Long Beach, California, the staff of the recreation commission was similarly marshaled for emergency service. Refugee camps were established, and entertainment programs were arranged. Radio and newspaper requests for volunteers brought a splen-did response from amateur and professional music leaders, entertainers, orchestras, bands, and church choirs. During the two weeks following the earthquake, eighty-five community programs that were arranged and presented in the city parks were attended by approximately 200,000. As the period of excitement wore off, entertainment features were supplemented by organized programs, including activities in which people of all ages had an opportunity to participate. The program for children was especially appreciated by children and parents alike, because for a time the schools were closed.

Recreation departments have also come to the rescue in cases of serious epidemics when playgrounds, swimming pools, camps, and recreation programs have been closed to children. Newspapers, radio, and special bulletins are used to help parents provide for their children's play needs. Staff members tell stories, offer craft ideas, suggest games that can be played in the home, and initiate contests that help sustain interest during the emergency period.

The examples cited in the preceding pages demonstrate, among other things, the valuable contribution the recreation department is making to the enrichment of life in American communities.

27. TYPICAL COMMUNITY RECREATION PROGRAMS

$\mathbf{T}$HE PRECEDING chapters have dealt with the various types of personnel, areas, facilities, and activities that are important elements in community recreation service. An understanding of their relationship and application in a local setting is possible, however, only when they are studied in an actual situation. In order to illustrate how these elements are integrated in a progressive recreation department, a description of the facilities, programs, and services in six cities is presented in the following pages. The cities vary in population from 553,000 to 10,000. Different sections of the country are represented.

The programs described are outstanding among cities of comparable size but are not presented as necessarily representing the best examples. However, they typify the service carried on by well-administered departments of similar size, type, and management. Space does not permit a full account of all activities, but special mention is made of unusual projects and services. Sufficient detail is given for the reader to gain a fair appreciation of what each department is doing in furnishing opportunities for the enjoyable and constructive use of the people's leisure. The discussion describes the work carried on by park, recreation, and school authorities.

In the following pages are described the programs in Minneapolis, Minnesota; Oakland, California; Austin, Texas; Sheboygan, Wisconsin; Ma chester, Connecticut; and Statesboro, Georgia.

THE RECREATION PROGRAM IN MINNEAPOLIS, MINNESOTA

Minneapolis, a city of 553,000, has one of the outstanding park systems and park recreation programs of the country. Since its inception in 1883 the park department has been administered by a board of park commissioners. The park system, which includes some 5,900 acres (of which 609 acres are in the airport), is exceptionally well balanced as to the distribution, size, and development of its areas. Notable features are the parkways which connect major units in the system, the well-developed neighborhood recreation areas, and the acquisition and improvement for park use of the land surrounding its in-town lakes.

For operation and maintenance the board has a budget of approximately $2,500,000, in addition to funds for capital purposes. It employs some 1,000 workers, nearly one-half of them on a permanent basis. The recreation program is administered by a division of recreation under a director of recreation with a staff of more than two hundred leaders, plus twenty-four full-time supervisors. In addition, some four hundred attendants and officials are employed by the Minneapolis Municipal Athletic Association. Many university and college students, including recreation and physical education majors, serve as part-time leaders, and volunteers assist with various program features.

Facilities. Park facilities include sixty playgrounds (sixteen of which are operated the year round), fifty-one baseball diamonds, one hundred and fifty-nine softball diamonds, thirty picnic grounds, fifteen swimming beaches, one swimming pool, thirty-one wading pools, five 18-hole golf courses, eleven bandstands, twenty-two lighted hard-surface areas, and two hundred and five tennis courts. A lighted ski hill, two ski slides, sixty-two ice-skating rinks (forty-nine of them with warming shelters), sixteen lighted hockey rinks, and a speed skating track make the city an outstanding winter sports center. Boating centers, archery ranges, a stadium seating 17,000, and other game facilities contribute to the enjoyment of the parks. Field houses serve as warming shelters in winter; programs are carried on under leadership in sixteen of them the year round. Two golf-club houses are centers for social activities and headquarters for winter sports. Three principal public gardens are maintained, in addition to other floral displays. In spite of this extensive development, facilities are inadequate to meet the growing demand for recreation. Additional recreation buildings and personnel to supervise the new areas and facilities are particularly needed.

Activities. A broad program of informal and organized recreation activities is carried on at the indoor and outdoor centers. Playground programs include the usual activities, with such special events as puppet shows, playground circus, an aquacade night, and day camps. Competitive sports for boys and girls are organized on a district basis, with cub, midget, and junior divisions. Holiday programs and feature events supplement the regular indoor activities. City-wide sports are conducted under rules and regulations adopted by the Minneapolis Municipal Athletic Association, which acts as an agent for the board, serves as a committee of arbitration, and supervises collection and disbursement of funds received as entry fees. City-wide activities are conducted for women in golf, tennis, bowling, softball, basketball, ski instruction, and speed skating. Men's activities, city-wide, include softball, basketball, baseball, football, touch football, hockey, golf, ski jumping, and speed skating. Summer events include opera, orchestra and band concerts, and community dances on outdoor tennis courts. Day camping and nature activities are popular; boating and swimming are top-ranking activities. Clinics are conducted in various sports, and activities such as bait and fly casting, golf, hiking,

The Theodore Wirth Golf Course—one of Minneapolis' five golf centers—affords a variety of shots and scenery (Courtesy of Minneapolis Park Board).

and model-aircraft building are organized on a club basis. (The Minne-hikers' Club is described in Chapter 16.) The department participates actively in the annual Aquatennial celebration, which includes a variety of water, music, and sports events, extends for ten days, and attracts a million people.

Table 12 indicates the major types of activity promoted during the 1957–1958 season and the estimated participation in each. The number registered varies from 17 in the bait- and fly-casting club to 3,201 in nature activities and 4,756 in playground baseball.

Table 12. Participation in Recreation Activities, 1957–1958, Minneapolis, Minnesota

Activity	Total participation (estimated)
Swimming	1,870,646
Community and neighborhood centers (16)	1,645,514
Skating	1,300,680
Supervised playgrounds (60)	979,492
Picnics	364,361
Sliding	305,534
Golf	194,501
Tennis	177,753
Outdoor concerts (90)	165,940
After-school playgrounds (23)	137,042
Other activities	81,686
Softball	71,883
Baseball	37,079
Basketball	36,500
Football (including touch)	30,369
Archery	25,200
Bowling	20,347
Ice hockey	13,971
Hiking club	5,391
Trampoline	2,979
Speed-skating meets	2,562
Skiing	2,447
Bait and fly casting	2,030
Model-airplane club	1,950
Horseshoes	1,942
Volleyball	1,866
Day camping	1,853

In addition to the participant total of nearly seven million, some three-quarters of a million spectators were attracted by sports events, the chrysanthemum show, and other programs. The unorganized free use of park property has been estimated at around twenty-five million annually.

Cooperation with Other Agencies. Cooperative relationships are maintained with many public and private groups. The department's needs, for example, have been interpreted through frequent meetings with the city's Capital Long Range Improvements Committee. Proposals for state and interstate highways have been discussed with the state highway department with a view to preventing encroachments on the park system. Cooperation at all levels with school authorities has resulted in the joint development of park-school sites and some integration of programs, including a conservation project involving the use of students in planting materials on park property. Park areas and facilities are widely used by school, youth, and church groups. Coordination of planning on an over-all city basis requires frequent conferences with the staff of the City Planning Commission, the Minneapolis Housing and Redevelopment Authority, the city engineer's office, suburban villages, community-chest agencies, and the Citizens League of Minneapolis and Hennepin County.

THE RECREATION PROGRAM IN OAKLAND, CALIFORNIA

Oakland, a city of 400,000, was a pioneer in the field of public recreation, its first playground commission having been appointed in 1908. Since that time the city has been widely known for the quality and diversity of its program, which is under the jurisdiction of a recreation commission of five members. This board cooperates closely with the school authorities and, under a provision of the city charter, is responsible for the operation of all recreation areas and facilities in the city. The operating budget for the year ending June 30, 1958, was $1,485,000, of which some $280,000 represented revenue from service charges and specialized activities. An organization chart of the department is shown on page 487.

Among the facilities and areas operated by the department are:

18 municipal playgrounds	9 children's play lots (not located at
66 school grounds	playgrounds)
14 recreation buildings	1 model-car ring
2 family mountain camps	7 swimming pools
3 children's resident camps	1 tennis stadium
4 children's day camps	2 boathouses
30 tennis courts (26 lighted)	1 lake
1 18-hole golf course	16 clubhouses and 5 field houses
35 baseball and softball diamonds (not	44 school auditoriums
including school diamonds)	1 amphitheatre
15 school gymnasiums	3 outdoor children's theatres
16 special-activity rooms (school)	5 picnic areas
1 bowling-billiard court	2 arts and crafts studios

The statistics used in this statement are for the year ending June 30, 1958.

Playgrounds and Recreation Centers. The core of municipal recreation in Oakland is the program at its hundred playgrounds and recreation centers. Most of the municipal grounds are lighted for night use. In addition to games and sports, playground groups are organized for creative dramatics, crafts, rhythmic activities, music, dance, and storytelling. Clubs organized on the basis of common interests include social groups for both teen-agers and adults and hobby, drama, and sports groups. Doll shows, fishing derbies, bike days, junior Olympics, carnivals, treasure hunts, pet shows, kite-flying tournaments, and excursions away from the playground add variety to the program. Teen-agers and young adults are encouraged through center programs to take part in community affairs. Yearly workshops are organized to help teen-agers better understand the community in which they live, and they are also encouraged to take part in local and state-wide youth conferences.

Students in local colleges fulfill their field-work requirements at the playgrounds and centers, and each year approximately eight hundred volunteers help with the recreation programs.

Recreation for Adults. Adult activities constitute a large segment of the Oakland program. The eighteen-hole golf course, the clubhouses, art studios and neighborhood centers, school auditoriums and gymnasiums, the outdoor sports facilities, and Lake Merritt serve large numbers of men and women. The lighting of tennis courts, softball diamonds, and playgrounds has greatly increased the adult use of these facilities.

Clubs, classes, hobby groups, teams, service projects, trips, cultural activities, dances, banquets, special events, and activities of all kinds are organized in neighborhood recreation centers as a result of planning between the staff and patrons. City-wide programs, organized from the central office, are open to any interested adult. Adult classes in social, folk, square, and modern dance register over 3,000 each year, and thirty-five folk- and square-dance clubs have a total membership of 1,500. Nine groups of Senior Citizens, with some 2,500 members, have been organized.

A sports and recreation program for the employees of industrial plants and business establishments is provided through the Industrial Athletic Association of Metropolitan Oakland, which is directly sponsored by the department. Interplant activities include team games, athletic meets, tournaments in seasonal activities, and social functions. Similar programs are provided by the department staff for church groups, fraternal organizations, small businesses, and the general public.

The department operates an eighteen-hole golf course of spectacular beauty, where two golf clubs, one for men and one for women, promote the sport and encourage tournament play. Many tournaments and championships are held each year, and the clubhouse is the setting for social events, such as dinners, dances, and parties. A special effort is made to interest high school youth and other students in the game.

Cultural Activities. Creative and cultural activities are fostered through the development of exceptional facilities. Opportunities in arts and crafts, for example, are provided at two studios which register annually some 4,000 adults in 150 different classes. Informal instruction is provided in ceramics, oil painting, silk screening, drawing and design, jewelry making, enameling, art exploration, and mosaics. Art exhibits, art-in-action shows, and culturally and socially stimulating activities are arranged by the studio members and instructors. Creative workshops for children and teen-agers and experimental classes for talented children are a part of the creative-arts center program. Leadership is also provided for creative arts for some fifty children's groups at recreation centers and playgrounds.

Creative dramatic experiences and participation in children's plays are enjoyed by thousands of youngsters at the Oakland playgrounds. Pro-

This samba line in an Oakland center attests to the popularity of social dancing (Courtesy of Oakland, Calif., Recreation Commission).

grams are coordinated by a staff of specialists into weekly productions at two children's outdoor theatres, where some fifty plays are given each summer. A Teen Troupe and a Vagabond Puppet Trailer present shows at playgrounds and for handicapped groups. Music, dance, creative writing, stage design, costume design, and dramatic production are integrated in the end-of-the-summer performance by specially talented groups. Drama and pageantry reach their climax in Oakland in the annual Christmas pageant produced in cooperation with the public schools and with the help of hundreds of volunteers. Costumes used in the pageant, as well as in the department's other drama activities, are made in its costume room, which contains more than ten thousand costumes.

Community dance festivals are scheduled throughout the year under the sponsorship of the Oakland Folk Dance Council and the Square Dance Callers Association. An annual folk and square dance festival held at the mountain camps is preceded by a week of folk dancing and followed by a week of square dancing. Creative expression, through dance, is provided by a staff of instructors and accompanists for some forty-five modern-dance groups serving all ages. Social dances for youth and classes in dance etiquette are regularly conducted for young people throughout the city.

Aquatics. Lake Merritt, a 155-acre lake in the heart of the city, is a popular year-round recreation center. At the lake the department has a boathouse and a sailboat house from which a flotilla of rowboats, canoes, sailboats, and two large passenger launches operates. Boat landings and launching facilities, as well as storage for 140 privately owned sailboats, are provided. Activities include a year-round learn-to-sail program for children and fall and spring classes for adults. The Lake Merritt Sailing Club conducts many regattas during the year. Launches make around-the-lake trips on a regular schedule; crew rowing instruction is offered for all ages; rowboats, canoes, and boats for outboard-motor attachments can be rented. The boathouse and sailboat house also include clubroom facilities.

Opportunities for swimming are afforded by Oakland's six city pools, four of which are adjacent to city high schools. In addition to general swimming, there is a swim-to-live campaign, which attracts some eight thousand young children; regularly scheduled classes are held in life-saving, swimming, and synchronized swimming, and pageants and special events are conducted. During the school year the pools are used primarily by the public schools but are available for community use during the late afternoon and evening hours and on week ends. A seventh pool is at an in-town camp during the summer months, and four swimming areas are part of the mountain camps.

Vacation Camps. Oakland was a pioneer in providing vacation camps for its people on a cost-covering basis. Through the cooperation of the U.S. Forest Service, the department maintains two family camps in the Sierra Nevada, and in conjunction with each camp there is a second camp —one for boys and one for girls. Overnight trips, games, fishing, riding, hiking, swimming, evening campfires, and social-dance programs help to make camp life interesting. During the spring and fall fishing and hunting seasons, the camps are kept open for the convenience of people who wish to use the equipment and facilities. At the children's camps, leaders carry on a program in which nature activities, overnight trips, and camp-craft receive special emphasis. One of these camps, located in a wooded canyon on the golf course grounds, is available week ends to supervised groups of young people and adults. The department also operates children's day camps and a day camp for physically handicapped children.

Special Services. Services not previously mentioned include a program specifically designed for the handicapped, planned in cooperation with private agencies and the public schools. It includes semimonthly social nights for adults and teen-agers, a day camp, and a summer playground program. Charm classes, conducted by specialists, which culminate in impressive graduation programs, have proved highly popular. The department grants permits to groups wishing to use school gymnasiums, indoor centers, and picnic areas and also furnishes a recreation leader. It has issued instructions for party games, picnic suggestions, and social recreation in bulletin form. It assists local groups in planning and organizing programs and lends outing kits and social-recreation equipment. Its library of some five hundred volumes and files of resource material are available for reference, and its activities, on film, are shown on request.

Professional growth and increased leadership skills of the staff are fostered through training courses, demonstrations, conferences, and group discussions. Institutes are planned and conducted from time to time for leaders in parent-teacher associations, churches, clubs, and other community groups.

Cooperation. The recreation commission cooperates with, serves, and assists all public and private agencies which provide recreation services in the city. Its long cooperative relationship with the public schools enables the facilities of both types of agencies—playgrounds, sports facilities, swimming pools, and buildings—to be used to the greatest extent without duplication. A plan of cooperation in the acquisition of areas for school and community use has been adopted. The recreation department offers an accredited training course to selected high school seniors, who become eligible for positions as junior play leaders.

An outstanding example of cooperation is the joint financing and operation, with the Junior Center of Art and Science, of a building that offers a broad program of cultural and recreation activities. Another recently instituted project, dealing with problems attending the provision of recreation service to antisocial youth and arising from conflict between different ethnic groups, likewise involves the cooperation of many agencies.

Park Department. The people of Oakland also benefit from the services rendered by the city's park department, which, under the guidance of a park commission, operates and maintains a system of well-designed and -maintained properties. Among the special features in the parks are attractive picnic centers, an outdoor amphitheatre, and several play areas with colorful and creative playground equipment. Its Children's Fairyland, in which favorite characters from the fables of childhood come to life, has welcomed more than three million paid visitors. A Christmas decorations program, conducted with the cooperation of women's garden clubs in the area, has also proved popular.

THE RECREATION PROGRAM IN AUSTIN, TEXAS

The recreation department in this capital city of 190,000 was created in 1928 as a result of a survey conducted by the National Recreation Association. The director of recreation is responsible to the city manager, but the department is under the guidance of a parks and recreation board of nine members. The staff of 258 includes 75 full-time year-round workers, 22 of them full-time leadership personnel. The department's current budget of approximately $500,000 makes possible the recreation program and the operation and maintenance of twenty-nine playgrounds, eight school play centers, four recreation buildings, ten wading pools, twelve deep and seven shallow swimming pools, thirty-five tennis courts, thirty-five baseball and softball diamonds, one 9-hole and one 18-hole golf course, a metropolitan park, a bathing beach, a band shell and outdoor theatre, a nature trail and sanctuary, an art museum, and an O. Henry Memorial. A chart of the department's organization appears on page 493.

Playgrounds and Buildings. About one-third of the total annual attendance of 4 million participants and spectators is recorded at the playgrounds, buildings, and indoor centers. The limited outdoor winter program at several areas is expanded in the spring and is in full operation at thirty-two areas during the summer. Routine activities are interspersed with interplayground tournaments and special events. A specialist with a trampoline in a trailer visits playgrounds on schedule; other traveling leaders conduct classes in tumbling, arts and crafts, creative dramatics, nature activities, and tennis. An all-city playday and pageant climaxes the playground season. The nine playground swimming pools and seven junior pools make possible an unusually extensive children's aquatic program.

The indoor centers provide a highly organized program during the school year. Two of the recreation buildings operate on a membership basis, and fees are charged for activities. Morning programs include activities for preschool children and for women. Afternoon programs for school-age children and evening programs for adults comprise a wide variety of sports, social, and cultural activities. Social recreation and dancing for teen-agers are scheduled on Friday and Saturday nights.

At the Pan-American Center, on the other hand, more people make informal use of facilities such as table games, reading materials, or television than attend classes or regularly scheduled activities. Another indoor-outdoor center with swimming pool, gymnasium, clubhouse, outdoor theatre, and sports facilities serves the recreation needs of a Negro community. Approximately two hundred groups representing churches, schools, social clubs, scout troops, servicemen, etc., use the facilities each year.

Special Facilities. Austin rates high in its provision of swimming facilities, and its aquatic program includes swimming meets, playground water shows, and learn-to-swim, junior-lifesaving, and water-safety and first-aid classes. A tennis center with a battery of eight all-weather courts and a club building serves as a center for city-wide interest in this sport and for tournament play. A hillside theatre with band shell affords a setting for talent shows, movies, all-city playground events, special productions, and performances by a summer repertory theatre. A nature trail and bird sanctuary, maintained jointly with the Audubon Society, is used for nature study by school and playground groups.

Program Features. Social-, square-, and round-dance clubs organized by the department are represented on the Austin Square, Folk, and Round Dance Council, which with the department sponsors family-night square dances and dance workshops. The Municipal Art Guild, comprised of former members of women's art classes, holds informal meet-and-paint sessions. The department started and still helps finance the Austin Symphony Orchestra. It assists in conducting Golden Age Week, in operating a day center, and in arranging outings and activities for older adults.

Other program features are appropriate holiday celebrations, an annual kite tournament, a fish rodeo, and a small-arms firing school for teen-agers. An athletic program, including the widely popular sports, is conducted for men, women, and boys of all ages.

Cooperation. School officials for many years granted the recreation department the use of indoor and outdoor facilities; the department in turn provided services for school groups. In 1950 the city council and the board of education established a policy of joint action in the acquisition, planning, operation, and use of properties for school purposes and community recreation. Several areas have been acquired under this cooperative plan, and a major recreation building has been erected adjacent to a school. The building is used by the schools during school hours; both buildings serve for community recreation after school and at night. The active assistance of many local organizations similarly contributes to the success of Austin's recreation program.

A parks division in the public works department cares for the general maintenance of Austin's 2,500 acres of parks at an annual expenditure of approximately $180,000. However, maintenance of areas and facilities such as baseball diamonds, golf courses, and pools and the planning of park and recreation developments for the city are responsibilities of the recreation department.

THE RECREATION PROGRAM IN SHEBOYGAN, WISCONSIN

The Department of Public Recreation is responsible for the community recreation program in Sheboygan, Wisconsin, a city of 44,000. The department is under the supervision of the board of education and is administered by a director of public recreation. The city's park system, comprising 289 acres, is under the park division. Local recreation resources include a YMCA, several church youth recreation centers, and boy-scout and girl-scout programs.

The leadership staff of the Department of Public Recreation consists of the director, a full-time program supervisor, a little-theatre director employed on a ten-month basis, and part-time leaders and instructors, many of whom are teachers. Three maintenance workers and three secretaries are also employed on a full-time basis. Most activities are conducted on school property; thirteen schools are used for afterschool, evening, and summer programs. The school board also owns and operates a large lighted playfield. The department schedules or uses baseball and softball diamonds, tennis courts, football fields, and playgrounds on park property. Since the department is not required to pay rentals for the use of facilities, 85 per cent of its annual budget of about $98,000 is used for salaries.

The following list of activities organized and conducted by the department illustrates the wide range of recreation opportunities available to the people of Sheboygan:

Daytime Competitive Sports

Baseball
  Clinics
  Little League [1]
  Men
  Stars of Tomorrow
Basketball
  Adults (men and women)
  Clinics
  Junior (boys and girls)

Dart ball
Horseshoes
Soccer
Softball
  Junior (boys)
  Men and women
Summer tennis

Grade School Sports

Badminton
Basketball (public and parochial)
Flag football (public and parochial)

Softball (public and parochial)
Volleyball

Other Grade School Activities

Archery clinics
Ballet, tap dancing, and baton twirling
Creative dramatics
Handcraft
Knitting

Recreation clubs (physical activity)
Rifle range
Swimming
Tennis clinics

[1] Not nationally affiliated.

Adult Evening Activities

Archery	Photography
Art sketching and painting	Reupholstery and refinishing
Bridge (beginners and advanced)	Rifle and pistol range
Chess and checkers	Swimming
Chorus	Men
Clay modeling and sculpturing	Women
Family night	Textile painting
Gym (men)	TOPS [2] Club
Leathercraft	Adults
Metalcraft and jewelry making	Teen-agers
Pennsylvania Dutch art painting	Woodworking

Special services include informative talks, assistance in planning recreation programs and facilities, the provision of leadership for recreation activities by private organizations, and the loan of books, picnic kits, and game kits.

One of the most successful features of the department's program is the Community Players, a group composed of nearly 4,500 paid members. The Community Players present four major productions each year, using school facilities for practices and productions without charge. Closely affiliated with this group is the civic orchestra and choral group which presents two concerts each season and, with the little-theatre group, presents a Broadway musical every other year.

The outstanding summer program feature is Park and Recreation Day, a highly entertaining event. The program consists of a lantern parade, in which 1,200 youngsters participate, and a series of dramatic skits from each playground. The spectators are informed about the park resources at their disposal, which include facilities for archery, band concerts, basketball, horseback riding, football, hiking, picnics, shuffleboard, softball, baseball, skiing, supervised play, swimming, coasting, tobogganing, tennis, track and field events, wading, and ice skating. The park division supervises its four beaches and abandoned stone quarry, and is also responsible for the maintenance and supervision of eight skating rinks during the winter season. Its annual budget for operation and maintenance is approximately $150,000.

THE RECREATION PROGRAM IN MANCHESTER, CONNECTICUT

The recreation program in Manchester, a suburban residential town with small industrial establishments and some 40,000 people, is administered by a recreation department in charge of a superintendent of recreation. He has a close working relationship with the park department and

[2] Take off pounds sensibly.

the superintendent of parks; both officials meet with the park and recreation advisory board of five members. Assisting the superintendent of recreation are a program director and nearly a hundred part-time and seasonal leaders. Volunteers help with many parts of the program. The recreation budget, which covers both the recreation program and the operation and maintenance of three large recreation buildings, is approximately $97,000 annually. The park budget, which covers maintenance of 825 acres of parks and conduct of the ice-skating program, is $83,000.

Manchester has unusually ample indoor recreation facilities. Its recreation buildings contain five gymnasiums, ten bowling alleys, seven meeting rooms, one indoor swimming pool, five game rooms, one kitchen, one dining room, and five lounges, besides service facilities. In addition, four school gymnasiums and a high school indoor pool are used in the recreation program. Outdoor facilities include two baseball diamonds, six junior diamonds, three hard-surface basketball courts, six tennis courts, and two large ponds used for swimming. Programs are conducted at eleven playgrounds, morning, afternoon, and evening, in the summer.

The program in Manchester comprises many activities—sports, arts and crafts, clubs, tournaments, movies, and special events. Twelve unusual program features are described briefly:

Junior Marching Band. This group of thirty-six children rehearses weekly, plays at football games, and marches in all town celebrations. With its majorettes, it was uniformed by the Fire and Police Junior Athletic Association.

Roller Skating. Lessons in free style, dance, speed, and figure skating are held weekly for children. Skating periods for upper-grade children are scheduled Saturday afternoons and evenings. One hundred and fifty pairs of skates are available for rental.

Cooking Class. More than forty girls meet twice weekly for instruction in all phases of cooking.

Halloween. A window-painting contest in which children decorate merchants' windows is held in cooperation with the chamber of commerce. Dances for junior high school children are held at two centers; parties are also held, in cooperation with the parent-teacher associations and the American Legion.

Swimming. Indoor activities include weekly swimming and lifesaving lessons for boys and girls, a women's evening swim program, a weekly family swim night, Saturday evening swimming for teen-agers, and swim periods for young people and adults. Recreational swimming for the handicapped provides individual volunteer instruction for some two dozen physically and mentally handicapped youngsters.

Model-airplane Clubs. Each center has a club in which boys receive instruction in the building of model planes.

Children's Theatre. At weekly meetings the members learn the techniques of acting, scenery design and construction, and stage management.

Boys' Mechanics Club. This group meets weekly at a garage to receive instruction in auto mechanics. It has completely stripped and reassembled a car donated by the garage owner.

Senior Citizens' Club. The members, numbering over 140, meet one afternoon weekly for social recreation. A three-day camping program is a highlight of the club's summer season.

Christmas. Unusual events include Santa Claus's arrival by helicopter, followed by a parade up Main Street. A Santa Claus workshop, at which elves are on duty painting and remodeling old toys, is open for nine days before Christmas. Children come in and visit with Santa Claus. All letters to Santa dropped in gaily decorated mailboxes placed in the parks are answered by the department. With the junior chamber of commerce it sponsors a home-lighting contest.

Boys' Radio Club. At weekly meetings members, under the guidance of an electrical engineer, take apart old radios and learn how to construct new ones.

Fishing Derby. This event is held in a park each year the week before the opening of the fishing season. The pond is stocked the day before the derby.

THE RECREATION PROGRAM IN STATESBORO, GEORGIA

In 1948 the city of Statesboro, with a population of slightly more than 6,000, embarked on a plan to present a well-rounded program of recreation for all its citizens. A one-man recreation department, established under a recreation board of six members, started a program with $5,000 contributed for this purpose. Ten years later Statesboro, with a population of 10,000, boasted a recreation program with an operating budget of more than $40,000 and a staff of eight full-time workers.

Recreation resources in Statesboro, which could not be replaced for less than a quarter of a million dollars, include three recreation areas comprising some 20 acres which are being developed on a long-range basis. Among its facilities are five ball diamonds, an outdoor swimming pool, a children's swimming pool, two tennis courts, picnic areas, an athletic field, and facilities for organized games. Indoor activities are conducted in five recreation buildings and four school centers.

People of all ages are served through a year-round program of varied activities. Program planning is on a cooperative basis, and young people and adults sit in with the leaders in planning programs involving these groups. An unusual factor in securing community interest, understanding, and support is a community council composed of presidents of civic and business organizations in the community. This council meets monthly with the board of recreation, acts in an advisory capacity, and interprets the actions of the board to the member organizations.

The program at the three playgrounds includes games and sports, crafts, dancing, special events, and tournaments. Activities of unusual interest are a fishing rodeo, an annual birdhouse-building contest, picnics, fishing trips, day and overnight camping, and, for boys eight to twelve, a "knothole" club, which attends ball games on free passes. The swimming pool is the chief attraction at an area that is also used for picnicking, dancing, tennis, and other games and that has an annual attendance exceeding 50,000. The pool program includes swimming classes in which more than 600 are registered each year, water-safety demonstrations, and an annual water show and pageant. Adult square dances, dancing instruction for children, an *a cappella* Negro choir, a privately sponsored children's theatre, and a nursery school program on Saturdays show that sports and outing activities do not monopolize the program. Special emphasis is laid on events in which the whole family can participate.

Young people play an important part in the Statesboro program. A Drag-On Teen Club conducts dances, swimming parties, wiener roasts, and social events. The pre-teens in sixth and seventh grades have their own Happy Go Lucky Club. The objective of another group, YOPR, is indicated by its title, Youth Organization to Promote Recreation. The services of the Youth Council are recognized at an annual banquet when a community-service award is made to the boy and girl who have contributed most toward making their community a better place in which to live. Statesboro has had the honor of playing host to the annual statewide youth workshop.

A written agreement between the recreation department and the county school board calls for the joint use of all facilities, with each agency furnishing its own supervision regardless of the facility used. The department supervises and helps coordinate the program of girl scouting and makes its facilities available to 4-H clubs. It plays a large role in civil defense and the Red Cross, and helps in the planning of private recreation facilities, which include pools, a golf course, and several lake developments providing family and group camping, picnicking, and water sports. A splendid spirit of cooperation exists among all the recreation groups in the county. Civic, veterans', and fraternal organizations have constructed recreation facilities for the department and have loaned funds to teen-age clubs. Local business firms help the department, the recreation movement, and high school students by offering two $300 scholarships each year to students interested in making recreation a career. These students work part time in the local program, as do senior students in the local teachers college, where the superintendent of recreation assists in teaching a course in community recreation.

The success of the pilot program in Statesboro has been widely publicized throughout the state and has demonstrated that a small city can adequately finance a well-organized year-round program. The program has influenced many other Georgia communities of 10,000 or less to establish a similar program for their people.

PART SEVEN

ORGANIZATION AND
ADMINISTRATION PROBLEMS

Governmental organization for municipal recreation service is essential, and its form materially affects the extent and quality of the recreation program. The organization for recreation and the powers and duties of the authorities charged with responsibility for this function are based upon state and local legislative enactments. The internal organization of recreation departments, on the other hand, is determined largely by the recreation authorities themselves, who also adopt policies relating to such factors as records, reports, and public relations. Part Seven deals with these questions and with legislation, finance, types of governing authorities supervising recreation, and the organization of the recreation department. The final chapter deals with the subject of cooperation with other departments and organizations, which plays such an important part in the service of every recreation department.

28. THE LEGAL ASPECTS OF COMMUNITY RECREATION

A MUNICIPALITY or school board is a subdivision of the state and it must therefore have legal authorization from the state government under either general or special legislation in order to conduct recreation activities as a part of local municipal or school functions. Legal powers are needed for the acquisition, development, and maintenance of recreation areas, the construction and operation of buildings and facilities, the purchase of supplies, the employment of personnel for leadership and other services, and the levying of taxes or the expenditure of tax funds for recreation.

HOW RECREATION LEGISLATION DEVELOPED

The establishment of children's playgrounds in the larger cities, one of the first steps in the development of the municipal recreation movement, did not require enabling legislation by the state. Authority was based on the general welfare or police powers granted to municipalities in state constitutions and local home-rule charters and on broad interpretations of existing park and school legislation. Some cities, however, secured the enactment of special laws by the state legislature applicable to themselves alone.

As the necessity for local public action became increasingly evident, local authorities in some states were reluctant to act without having more specific legal powers. Consequently, park authorities made efforts to secure broader park legislation, and school authorities made similar efforts to enlarge the powers of school boards to include recreation. Other local officials and many recreation leaders worked for the passage of general recreation enabling acts. These acts permitted any locality in the state to conduct recreation programs under the type of administrative arrangement considered most effective or advantageous in the particular locality and to cooperate with other local political subdivisions in the conduct of a joint program.

Powers of Park Authorities. The broadening of park legislation in a number of states enabled park authorities to add—to the traditional park areas and services already being provided—the many facilities and activities essential to a comprehensive recreation program. The powers of park authorities under existing legislation in many states were enlarged through court decisions giving broad interpretations of the terms "park" and "park purposes." Minnesota and Kansas are two examples of states where outstanding liberal park decisions were handed down. These decisions, together with the broadening of park laws themselves, made possible the development of recreation service in many localities, but were ineffective in communities where local park leadership refused to take advantage of the power available to them.

School Legislation. For many years local school boards in a majority of the states have had the legal authority to conduct community-wide recreation activities for all ages. Indiana passed legislation authorizing the community use of school facilities as early as 1859; and by 1897, twenty-three states had laws permitting the use of school buildings as civic or social centers. Recreation was one of the approved uses in most of these states, but no expenditure of school funds was authorized for community purposes except in New York and Massachusetts. The intent of the laws was primarily to make school buildings available to community groups for meetings and to permit school authorities to provide heat, light, and janitor service and charge for them if advisable. Today most states have laws permitting the community use of school buildings and areas.

As the children's playground movement developed, some states passed laws permitting school authorities to operate children's playgrounds, but only a few states have special laws authorizing them to conduct and finance a broad recreation program for the whole community. In most cases where school boards are providing extensive recreation services, their authority for doing so is found either in general enabling acts which apply to school districts as well as to municipalities or in broad interpretations of their powers to provide civic centers, physical education, or adult education.

Special Laws. Many states have passed special laws covering specific forms of recreation and recreation facilities such as band concerts, municipal music and opera programs, public baths, auditoriums, community buildings, stadiums, swimming pools, golf courses, and Sunday recreation. Most of these laws were passed in the early 1900s, and in general they represent piecemeal approaches to the recreation problem rather than consideration of total local recreation needs. In many cases they resulted from the pressure of special-interest groups or the desire of local governing bodies to retain direct control of special revenue-producing facilities. Because the power to acquire, construct, and operate these facilities and to conduct activities is included in general enabling acts of the type described later in this chapter, the need for such special legislation no longer exists in most states.

State Services to Localities. State governments have become increasingly interested in helping local governmental units in the planning, organization, and conduct of recreation service. In many cases the services to communities rendered by state agencies, described in Chapter 3, are made available without special legislation. The three states in which special recreation departments or commissions have been established by law are North Carolina, Vermont, and California. The legislation in these states provides in some detail for the appointment of a state recreation commission and for its membership, duties, and powers; authorizes the appointment of an executive and other personnel; and appropriates funds to meet the expenses of the commission. The North Carolina law also provides for an advisory committee.

STATE RECREATION ENABLING ACTS

The multiplicity and variety of the laws designed to authorize local authorities to perform recreation functions indicate the desirability of general recreation enabling legislation. Most states have therefore passed laws which authorize every local governmental unit in the state to conduct a broad recreation program under any form of organization it considers most suitable or effective. In many cases the legislation was drafted and promoted with the cooperation of the National Recreation Association.

The enabling act provides for recreation home rule. It obviates the necessity for separate recreation laws applicable only to school, park, or separate recreation boards or to other city departments. It takes the place of special legislation authorizing joint or cooperative action on the part of different municipal departments or between local governmental units. It supplements the broad general powers relating to public welfare under which local recreation programs were established in some states.

Essential Features. Recreation enabling legislation in different states varies in certain respects. Some laws apply only to specific types of municipalities and are therefore essentially class legislation; others include school districts as well as municipalities, and several apply also to counties. Some acts briefly authorize the performance of the function; others list in detail the powers, structure, and procedures of the managing authority. Several include provision for a referendum and mill tax. Because of widely differing conditions in the various states no standard form of law is practicable. In general, however, it is desirable that recreation enabling laws include the following provisions, unless they are already contained in other legislation:

The legislation should apply to all cities, towns, villages, counties, school districts, and other local governmental units in the state.

Any two or more such political units should have the power to combine in the establishment, administration, and financing of recreation facilities and programs.

The governing bodies of any such political units (hereafter designated as municipalities) may dedicate and set aside for recreation use any lands, buildings or both, owned or leased by such municipality and not already dedicated or devoted to another public use.

Such municipalities should have the power to acquire and to spend money for lands or buildings for recreation use in the same manner as provided by law for the acquisition of lands and buildings or the spending of money for other public uses, making clear that such lands and buildings may be located and such expenditures made for services within or without the boundaries of the municipality.

Bonds may be voted for the acquisition of lands, buildings, and other recreation facilities by any municipality.

Any municipality may on the initiative of its governing body provide for the establishment, operation, and maintenance of playgrounds, recreation centers, and other recreation facilities and for the conduct of a program of recreation activities by appropriation from general or special funds or both, including general or special funds of school boards and park districts.

The governing body may vest the power to provide, maintain, and operate playgrounds, recreation centers, and other recreation facilities and to conduct a program of play and recreation activities in the school board, park board, or other existing body or in a separate recreation board or commission as the governing body may determine.

Any body or commission so designated should have the power to equip and maintain recreation areas, buildings, and facilities of all kinds; to conduct all kinds of recreation activities for all people of the community; to cooperate with other public and private agencies in the planning and conduct of recreation programs and services; and to employ such professional and other personnel for this purpose as it deems proper.

Where the governing body by resolution or ordinance establishes a recreation board or commission, it should provide for the manner of appointment of the board, the number of members, the terms of office, and the manner of filling vacancies.

The board in which is vested the power to conduct the recreation program should have the power to accept or reject any grant or devise of real estate or any gift or bequest of money or other personal properties or donation to be applied, principal or income, for either temporary or permanent use for recreation purposes; but where acceptance of such gifts would subject the municipality as a whole to additional expense for improvement, maintenance, or removal, the approval of the governing body should be required; any money so received should be deposited with the treasurer of the municipality to the credit of the board in which is vested the power to maintain and operate the recreation system and should be paid out in such manner as public money appropriated for recreation purposes.

The board in which is vested the power to conduct the recreation program should have the power to use the facilities of other municipal or county departments including school and park boards and districts, provided such use does not interfere with the primary purpose which such facilities are intended to serve and provided that the trusteeship and responsibility for such physical properties and lands should remain with the departments responsible for them when not used for recreation.

All laws or parts of laws in conflict with this legislation should be repealed.

In some states the opinion has prevailed that legislation would not prove adequate or effective unless it contained provisions for a local referendum and for the levying of an annual mill tax for recreation. Several state enabling acts therefore provide for local elections which permit the voters to express their desire for a recreation system and to authorize the levying of a tax to finance it. Such legislation specifies the conditions under which a referendum is to be held, the qualifications for voting, the amount or range of the mill tax, the procedure to be followed in case of a favorable vote, the method of collecting and administering the funds, and authorization for the governing body to appropriate supplementary funds for recreation if in its judgment this should be done. The advantages and disadvantages of the recreation mill tax are considered in Chapter 31.

States with Enabling Acts. Table 13 lists the states with general recreation enabling legislation and the year in which the legislation was passed. Other states have permissive laws, but because of their special nature or limited application they are not considered general enabling legislation. In some cases the dates in the table indicate the year in which existing laws were broadened so as to qualify as such legislation. New Jersey is generally considered to be the first state to pass a law of this type. By 1958, at least forty states had such laws.

Table 13. States with General Recreation Enabling Legislation

State	Year first passed	State	Year first passed
Alabama	1945	New Hampshire	1917
Arkansas	1941	New Jersey *	1915
California	1939	New Mexico *	1945
Colorado	1935	New York *	1917
Connecticut	1919	North Carolina *	1923
Florida *	1925	North Dakota *	1947
Georgia *	1923	Ohio *	1921
Illinois *	1923	Oklahoma *	1953
Indiana *	1925	Pennsylvania	1919
Iowa *	1923	Rhode Island	1924
Kansas *	1945	South Dakota *	1937
Kentucky	1924	Tennessee	1937
Louisiana	1924	Texas *	1955
Maryland	1937	Utah	1923
Massachusetts	1919	Vermont *	1925
Michigan	1917	Virginia *	1924
Minnesota	1937	Washington	1949
Mississippi *	1946	West Virginia *	1925
Montana	1939	Wisconsin *	1944
Nebraska *	1937	Wyoming	1951

* Enabling legislation contains referendum and/or special mill tax provisions.

Recreation Districts. Although many recreation enabling acts empower two or more political units to establish and operate a recreation program jointly, the problems encountered in such a joint operation have deterred use of this power. The rapid expansion of fringe communities, especially in unincorporated areas, has prompted the passage of legislation in several states authorizing the creation of recreation districts or park and recreation districts. These usually coincide with natural trade areas, include both the central city and the surrounding area, and disregard existing municipal political boundaries. The districts can be created by majority vote of the electorate of the area concerned at an election called by the county governing authorities. They have the power to maintain and operate recreation facilities and services and may levy taxes and issue bonds with the approval of the electors residing within their boundaries. In California, where many districts have been established, four separate acts were combined in 1957 under a single law authorizing the creation of recreation and/or park districts.

In sections of New York State where a complex pattern of local government has made it difficult to provide a community recreation service, such service is furnished by school districts under authority granted in enabling legislation. These districts comprise all or parts of two or more municipal jurisdictions and make possible a unified recreation program.

Granting county authorities the right to provide recreation, in some instances in cooperation with local departments, is another means of serving the recreation needs of people living outside the corporate limits of political units. An example of such action is the broadening of a Wisconsin law in 1957 to permit any county in the state to provide recreation service and employ full-time recreation directors.

LOCAL RECREATION LEGISLATION

In establishing a recreation department to administer a program with tax funds, a local governing body must act in accordance with the powers granted by state legislation. Any locality planning to establish a recreation program or to reorganize a recreation system should therefore consult the city attorney or some other competent legal advisor as to the nature and extent of its existing powers. In most states, as pointed out earlier in the chapter, such powers are specifically granted in enabling acts.

After analyzing the existing local powers to establish a recreation program, and determining the form of organization under which it may best be established, some kind of local legislation is necessary. This takes the form of a charter amendment in localities where general home-rule powers are used. Where action is based upon specific powers granted by state enabling legislation, an ordinance or resolution is passed by the local city council or other governing authority. An ordinance gives the recreation department greater stability than a resolution, since, once passed, it cannot be repealed except after a public hearing.

Local Charter Provisions. City-charter amendments vary in length, depending upon the extent to which they prescribe in detail the powers and procedures of recreation managing authorities. The following charter amendment, adopted by the city of Cincinnati in November, 1926, provides for the appointment of a public recreation commission. It is an example of a brief charter amendment which grants general authority and which needs to be supplemented by a city-council ordinance.

Article VII, Boards and Commissions
Section 14: Public Recreation Commission—Term—Appointments—Power—Funds, etc.
There shall be a Public Recreation Commission consisting of one member of the Board of Education appointed by said Board, one member of the Board of Park Commissioners appointed by said Board, and three citizens appointed by the Mayor, to serve without compensation. The term of office of said members and the powers and duties of said Commission shall be fixed by ordinance of

the Council, but all funds obtained from levies for recreational purposes, appropriated by other public bodies, or donated for such purposes to the City of Cincinnati or the Public Recreation Commission, shall be expended by said Commission.

Suggested Local Ordinance. The provisions of local ordinances differ according to the type of recreation managing authority they establish and the nature of the administrative responsibility delegated to it. They must conform to the conditions set forth in state laws and local charters. For example, in California general law cities and counties, as distinguished from chartered cities and counties, are not authorized to delegate administrative or policy-making functions to a recreation or park board or commission. Therefore they do not have the legal power to establish a board with policy-making or administrative authority; hence the many city ordinances in California creating an advisory recreation commission.

The suggested ordinance for the creation of a recreation commission which follows indicates the powers granted by most state enabling acts and which therefore are commonly incorporated in local ordinances. The allocation of powers is quite different in an ordinance creating an advisory commission.

An Ordinance Creating a Recreation Board
Prescribing Terms of Members, Organization,
Powers, and Duties
Be it Ordained by _____
    of the City of _____ :
1. Under the provisions of Section _____ of Chapter _____ of the General Laws of _____, there is hereby established a recreation commission. This commission shall consist of five (5) persons serving without pay who shall be appointed by the mayor.[1] The term of office shall be for five (5) years or until their successors are appointed and qualified, except that the members of such commission first appointed shall be appointed for such terms that the term of one member shall expire annually thereafter. Vacancies in such commission occurring otherwise than by expiration of term shall be filled by the mayor for the unexpired term.
2. Immediately after their appointment, they shall meet and organize by electing one of their members president and such other officers as may be necessary. The commission shall have the power to adopt bylaws, rules, and regulations for the proper conduct of public recreation for the city.
3. The recreation commission shall provide, conduct, and supervise public playgrounds, athletic fields, recreation centers, and other recreation facilities and activities on any of the properties owned or controlled by the city, or on other properties with the consent of the owners and authorities thereof. It shall

[1] It is often desirable that one member of the recreation commission be a member of the school board, and one a member of the park board or commission, if there is one.

have the power to conduct, or to cooperate with other agencies in conducting, any form of recreation that will employ the leisure time of the people in a constructive and wholesome manner.

4. The recreation commission shall have the power to appoint or designate someone to act as superintendent who is trained and properly qualified for the work and such other personnel as the commission deems proper.

5. Annually the recreation commission shall submit a budget to the city governing body for its approval. The commission may also solicit or receive any gifts or bequests of money or other personal property or any donation to be applied, principal or income, for either temporary or permanent use for playgrounds or other recreation purposes.

6. The recreation commission shall make full and complete monthly and annual reports to the governing body of the city and other reports from time to time as requested.

7. All ordinances, resolutions, or parts thereof, in conflict with the provisions and intent of this ordinance are hereby repealed.

Passed and Adopted this _____ day of _____ 19 _____

Attest:

_____

LEGAL LIABILITY OF MUNICIPALITIES

In establishing a new function such as recreation, local governing bodies are concerned with their financial liability for injuries sustained by individuals because of negligence in the exercise of the function. In general, the extent of liability is based upon the decision of the state's courts as to whether the conduct of recreation is a governmental or proprietary function.

Governmental versus Proprietary Functions. The following extract from a decision of the United States Supreme Court is frequently quoted in discussing the difference between a proprietary and a governmental function: [2]

The distinction between the municipality as an agent of the state for governmental purposes and as an organization to care for local needs in a private or proprietary capacity has been applied in various branches of the law of municipal corporations. The most numerous illustrations are found in cases involving the question of liability for negligent acts or omissions of its officers and agents. . . . It has been held that municipalities are not liable for such acts and omissions in the exercise of the police power, or in the performance of such municipal faculties as the erection and maintenance of a city hall and courthouse, the protection of the city's inhabitants against disease and insanitary conditions, the care of the sick, the operation of fire departments, the inspection of steam boilers, the promotion of education, and the administration of public charities. On the other hand, they have been held liable when such acts or omissions

[2] *City of Trenton v. State of New Jersey,* 262 U.S. 182 (1923).

occur in the exercise of the power to build and maintain bridges, streets and highways, and waterworks, construct sewers, collect refuse, and care for the dump where it is deposited. Recovery is denied where the act or omission occurs in the exercise of what are deemed to be governmental powers, and is permitted if it occurs in a proprietary capacity. The basis of the distinction is difficult to state, and there is no established rule for the determination of what belongs to the one or the other class. It originated with the courts.

A basic reason for relieving local governments of liability for those activities which are considered governmental is to remove a deterrent to the proper provision of such essential services. This is brought out in a decision of the Kentucky court as follows: [3]

The reason for exempting a municipality from damages for injuries inflicted in the performance of its governmental functions is one of public policy, to protect public funds and public property. Taxes are raised for certain specific governmental purposes; and, if they could be diverted to the payment of damage claims, the more important work of the government, which every municipality must perform regardless of its other relations, would be seriously impaired, if not totally destroyed.

Park Decisions. Many of the court decisions relating to this problem are generally considered "park" decisions, but they can reasonably be assumed to apply to all the more general types of park and recreation areas, structures, and activities. In Minnesota, for example, a playground is considered legally as a park area, the term "playground" being embraced in the term "park." [4] The Kansas Court outlined a broad definition of the term "park purposes" as follows: [5]

. . . to include, a race track, a tourist camp, bridle trails, boating, bathing, refreshment and lunch stands, providing bathing suits, towels, and rooms for bathers, dressing pavilion, waiting room for streetcars, refreshment room and shelter for the public, grandstand, baseball diamond, race meets, tennis courts, croquet grounds, children's playgrounds, hotels, restaurants, museums, art galleries, zoological and botanical gardens, conservatories, and many other recreational and educational facilities.

Nuisance Decisions. Court decisions in some states hold that even though recreation is accepted by the courts to be a governmental function, there is a liability for maintenance of an attractive nuisance. The Wisconsin court has stated: [6]

Negligence in the performance of a governmental function by the officers or agents of a municipality does not give a right of action, except that a munici-

[3] *O'Connell v. Merchants and Police District Telephone Company (Ky.)*, 180 S.W. 845, L.R.A. (1915) D. 508.

[4] *Horn v. Minneapolis*, 152 Minn. 175.

[5] *Wichita v. Clapp et al.*, 125 Kan. 100 (1928), 263 Pac. 12.

[6] *Bernstein v. City of Milwaukee (Wis.)*, 149 N.W. 362 (1914).

pality may not maintain a public nuisance even where it is performing a governmental duty.

Likewise, the Connecticut Supreme Court of Errors held: [7]

Where a municipal corporation creates and maintains a nuisance, it is liable for damages to any person suffering special injury therefrom, irrespective of whether the misfeasance or non-feasance causing the nuisance also constituted negligence. This liability cannot be avoided on the ground that the municipality was exercising governmental functions or powers, even in jurisdictions where, as here, immunity is afforded from liability for negligence in the performance of such functions.

These nuisance decisions have real significance to recreation authorities because they indicate that even in states where recreation is held to be a governmental function, reasonable precautions must be taken to protect the public. In the Connecticut case just cited, the authorities failed to do so in that they erected a diving board over shallow water at the municipal bathing beach without properly warning bathers of the danger.

RECREATION AS A GOVERNMENTAL FUNCTION

In 1932 a study of court decisions in thirty-six states revealed that in twenty-one of them park and recreation service was considered a governmental function; in fourteen it appeared to be proprietary, whereas in one it was doubtful.[8] Since that time several decisions of the higher courts have supported the claim of governmental status for parks and recreation. In one of these the United States Court of Appeals for the First Circuit, in an opinion handed down March 14, 1934, affirmed a decision of the board of tax appeals that a park employee was exempt from Federal income tax. It stated: [9]

Whatever may have been the early tendency of the courts in this respect, we think that the modern view, supported by the weight of authority, is that the creation and maintenance of public parks is a governmental function of the state and its exercise is essential to the health and general welfare of all the citizens of a state.

The decisions of state courts in recent years have not changed the picture substantially so far as type of function is concerned. However, there has been an increasing interest in the matter by courts, state legislatures, local government attorneys, and others; interest focuses on the

[7] *Hoffman v. City of Bristol* (*Conn.*), 155 Atl. 499.

[8] See *Is Park and Recreation Service a Governmental or Proprietary Function?* National Recreation Association, New York, 1932.

[9] *Commissioner of Internal Revenue v. Jessie P. Sherman, Executrix,* October Term (1933), no. 2863.

question of liability for personal or property damage due to negligence on the part of local governmental employees. There have been efforts to find some way of holding cities liable for negligence in the exercise of governmental functions where the injured party suffers an injustice because the municipality, as in most jurisdictions, is exempt from liability. In some cases the courts have attempted to meet such situations by invoking the nuisance doctrine and in others by attempting modifications of previous decisions.

This tendency of the courts to secure justice for injured parties has not changed the character of park and recreation activities to any extent. In fact, as Harold W. Kennedy, Los Angeles County counsel, stated at the 1957 National Recreation Congress, both statutorywise and as far as case law is concerned, the trend is toward the side of the governmental function. He added that some states which previously designated park and recreation service in its proprietary capacity have changed and given it governmental status, thus affording protection to the taxpayers of the unit and the individuals involved.

However, Mr. Kennedy also pointed out that some states,[10]

. . . historically holding that a public body is immune from liability for the negligence of its officers and employees in the performance of a governmental function, are sometimes found to draw a distinction between cases, on the one hand, of municipal nonliability for injury inflicted by public servants while negligently performing their governmental functions, and on the other, municipal liability for injury caused by dangerous conditions due to the municipality's own negligent failure to perform its delegated duty.

After citing many cases Mr. Kennedy added: [11]

It appears that the determination of what constitutes a dangerous or defective condition and under what circumstances liability will be imposed, is somewhat difficult to anticipate, but that the courts will not hesitate to impose liability on public entities where the injuries or damages can be reasonably considered to have been caused by a dangerous or defective condition of public property, providing that the public property is being used in its ordinary and customary manner.

In view of this lack of uniformity in decisions, it is important that recreation leaders keep in close touch with legislation and court decisions in their own states and also with the activities of state associations of local governmental attorneys, in order to be familiar with legislative programs that might affect recreation services. Regardless of the degree of liability that may be ascribed to municipalities by state legislation or

[10] *The Philosophy and Law of Recreation,* prepared for the 39th National Recreation Congress, Long Beach, Calif., October, 1957.
[11] *Ibid.*

court decisions, it is highly desirable that the status of local park and recreation service as a governmental function should be maintained.

How Fees and Charges Affect the Type of Function. Practically all the court decisions recognizing park and recreation service as a governmental function refer to its contribution to the public welfare, and some of them touch upon the public duty of the municipality to maintain such services. Many decisions refer to the free character of park services and to the assumption that no special benefit or pecuniary profit accrues to the municipal corporation or residents of the municipality. The growing tendency to charge for the use of park and recreation facilities therefore gives rise to the question as to the effect of such charges on the attitude of the courts in cases calling for a decision on the function of such services. The effects of charging have varied in different states. However, it would appear generally that, in the states where recreation is a governmental function, incidental charges do not affect the nature of the function; that charges which result in operating profits tend to change the function; and that charges imposed for the purpose of making a profit change the function in practically all states.

COURT DECISIONS ON SEGREGATION

Another group of court decisions that has influenced the provision and operation of public recreation areas and facilities in many cities is the series of verdicts in cases involving race segregation. Even before the decision of the United States Supreme Court in the historic case of Brown *v.* Board of Education of Topeka,[12] in 1954, several courts had decreed that segregation of the races on public golf courses and other facilities was unlawful. According to Charles S. Rhyne, "the Supreme Court, the Federal courts, and state courts have since (the Brown case) held that the 'separate but equal' doctrine may not be applied to the following state and municipal park and recreational facilities: municipal auditoriums, municipal golf courses, municipal parks, municipal swimming pools, state and municipal beaches, bathhouses and swimming pools, and state parks." [13] In the light of these pronouncements, as Harold W. Kennedy told the delegates to the National Recreation Congress in 1957, "the trend of the judicial decisions is definitely in support of integration. Legally there can be no distinction written or read into the case law as far as that problem is concerned." [14]

[12] 347 U.S. 483, 74 S.Ct. 686.
[13] *Municipal Law*, National Institute of Municipal Law Officers. Washington, 1957, pp. 471–472.
[14] *Op. cit.*

29. MUNICIPAL ORGANIZATION FOR RECREATION

There is no one pattern by which local government meets its responsibility for recreation service, nor should there necessarily be one. The governmental machinery for providing recreation service in any locality must conform to procedures authorized by state legislation and be worked out in the light of the local situation and of experience under similar conditions. The consideration of any plan for the organization of public recreation must take account of the following factors:

The existing legal powers of the municipality, county, school district, or other local governmental unit

The legal and extralegal relationships of the local school corporation to the local municipal corporation

The type and status of local governmental agencies

The ownership and control of properties available for recreation use

The attitude toward recreation of individuals in authoritative positions in local governmental agencies

The ability of local agencies to finance recreation service adequately

Local public opinion with reference to recreation and its place in the framework of local government

The legal authority and readiness of local agencies to cooperate in providing recreation service

However fine and idealistic a concept of local recreation administration might be developed, a recreation program can actually be achieved only if plans for its organization are worked out on a realistic basis, if they have the active cooperation and support of the agencies affected, and if they are acceptable to the people.

SUGGESTED ORGANIZATION METHODS

Educators, park authorities, recreation workers, and leaders in organizations promoting good government have from time to time advanced

460

"ideal" plans for the organization of municipal recreation. These plans, designed to provide a logical, simple, uniform procedure, usually reflect the major interest of the individuals or groups advancing them. Educators have proposed the organization of recreation from the point of view of the schools as the central controlling authority. Park officials have regarded the park department as the logical agency for providing and administering recreation service. Experts in municipal government have approached the problem with a view to the simplification of government and centralized control of all municipal services. There have been other proposals. However, the various suggestions have not been based on comprehensive studies of existing recreation services in cities throughout the country or on careful analyses of the factors which have resulted in success or failure in different communities.

Because the factors previously mentioned differ widely from state to state and city to city, no single specific plan of organization for recreation is advocated here for universal adoption. Examples of successful recreation administration may be found in cities where the program is under a board of education, a park department, a recreation commission, a separate recreation department without a commission, or other public authorities. Examples of mediocre and poor service may also be found under these various administrative agencies. Nevertheless, any locality considering the establishment of a recreation program will find it worthwhile to consider carefully the advantages and disadvantages commonly associated with the different forms of organization.

School Administration of Recreation. Educators and other advocates of the board of education as the proper administrative authority for community recreation have advanced the following arguments:

1. Recreation is largely educational and therefore should be provided by those who administer the city's public education system and are in daily contact with a majority of the children.

2. Parents and the public have confidence in the board of education and in its trained teaching staff and respect the work which they are doing for their children.

3. Large numbers of these teachers, with their knowledge of educational methods and experience in handling children, are available for recreation leadership.

4. School authorities control buildings and grounds suitable for community recreation use, near centers of population. Increasingly, school facilities are planned to render more recreation service for both school and community groups.

5. The school board already administers physical education, music, arts, nature, and other programs for school children in which recreation

is a motivating factor. The programs include many recreation activities and involve the development of leisure-time interests and the teaching of leisure-time skills. The board could coordinate these activities with the community recreation program.

6. Adult education programs offered by school systems include arts and crafts, music, discussion groups, dramatics, and other forms of recreation.

The following objections have been raised to the administration of the community recreation program by the school board:

1. The school board's first responsibility is to provide an educational program as prescribed by the state. Recreation at best would be a subordinate function. As such it would receive secondary consideration in personnel, program, and budget and could never achieve the status it needs for adequate development.

2. Because of their financial status, most school boards are not in a position to develop and support a community recreation program. They have a sufficient problem in financing needed school construction and in meeting demands for higher salaries for teachers without taking on the burden of financing the community recreation program.

3. School boards, although they have had the legal authority to provide community recreation programs in most states, have made only limited use of it over the years, primarily where state funds have helped subsidize the program. Experience has shown that recreation is one of the first items in the school budget to suffer in times of financial stress.

4. Because the nature of recreation requires that the program be based on local interests and needs, it is desirable that the agency responsible for it be free from outside control. In matters relating to community recreation, local school boards tend to be more subject to regulation and control from the state than are the local municipal agencies. For example, some state departments of education specify that only persons with teaching certificates can be employed by the schools for recreation leadership; others prescribe the ages that can be served or otherwise limit the scope of the program.

5. Few school boards that provide community recreation activities consider them of sufficient importance to assign a worker to recreation service on a full-time basis. In most cases recreation has been relegated to a subordinate position in the physical education department.

6. School authorities are primarily concerned with the children and youth attending the public schools. They have little or no responsibility for providing either the education or recreation of preschool-age children, children attending private or parochial schools, nonschool youth, and adults, who comprise a large majority of the population.

7. Although school boards control excellent indoor and outdoor facilities needed for community recreation and make them available for school use, municipal recreation properties in most cities are more extensive and include a greater variety of recreation facilities. These areas, some of which lie outside the city limits, could not well be administered by the school board, which is primarily concerned with its own properties.

Park Administration of Recreation. Advocates of the control of recreation by park boards or departments point out that:

1. Park departments control most publicly owned properties suitable for recreation use, and these contain many of the facilities essential for organized recreation service, such as playgrounds, playfields, ball diamonds, swimming pools, tennis courts, picnic areas, and golf courses.

2. The construction and maintenance of these properties are important functions in which park authorities have had special training and experience. Their operation can never be divorced successfully from these functions.

3. Recreation is the chief function of all park service. The enjoyment of beauty, motoring for pleasure on the parkways, and watching the animals at the zoo are as much forms of recreation as participation in organized activities.

4. Combining the administration of the community recreation program with the other functions of the park department results in more economical and effective service than when they are performed by two separate agencies.

5. The park department is experienced in serving large numbers of people and in maintaining relationships with the public.

Reasons why park authorities should not administer the municipal recreation program have been advanced as follows:

1. The work of the park department involves a wide variety of functions in which primary consideration is given to engineering and maintenance problems. Organization for the human use of facilities is considered of secondary importance by park authorities.

2. Because of the major emphasis upon construction and maintenance rather than program service, there is a tendency for park authorities to attach less importance to recreation leadership than to other types of personnel. Thus, in selecting an executive, park authorities generally seek a man trained in horticulture or engineering rather than in recreation and human relationships.

3. Park boards, like school boards, are primarily concerned with the operation of properties under their control, rather than with the develop-

ment of a program using all available facilities and serving the various recreation needs of all the people in the community.

4. In case of budget cuts, recreation leadership suffers to a greater extent than other park services.

ᵧ **Administration by a Recreation Department.** Many recreation leaders believe that recreation can best be administered as a distinct function of local government with a separate department, preferably under a citizens board or commission. Those who favor this plan of organization believe that:

1. Recreation is of sufficient importance to justify the establishment of a separate department, responsible for this function alone. Authorities already loaded with other primary responsibilities cannot adequately serve the recreation function.

2. A recreation department provides effective, unified, cooperative machinery for the harmonious use of all public recreation facilities and for the coordination of all local recreation services.

3. More money can be secured for recreation if it is not combined with some other service or subordinated to some other function.

4. A separate recreation department with a capable executive can best study the recreation needs and interests of the people, interpret recreation to the public, and conduct a program for everyone, using all available facilities, public and private.

5. Under a recreation department, the executive and staff are selected on the basis of their qualifications for recreation leadership.

Additional advantages when a board or commission is appointed to have responsibility for the policies and operations of the department are:

1. Since the municipality and school district are separate government corporations and neither has administrative control over the other, cooperation between the two can best be secured through a policy-making board on which both are represented, as well as the public at large.

2. A board composed of citizens chosen because of their ability and interest in recreation is in a better position to determine the recreation needs and interests of the people than the recreation executive and to develop policies for the recreation department.

3. Under a recreation board, the executive reports directly to a body that is primarily concerned with recreation, not to one that has responsibility for a wide variety of public functions. The executive has the continuous guidance of the board in dealing with the many problems that arise in the administration of the recreation department.

4. The recreation board can speak for recreation more effectively and

disinterestedly before the city authorities and the general public than a municipal employee.

Those who object to the creation of a separate recreation board or department say that:

1. Setting up another city department adds to the complexity of local governmental machinery and runs counter to current trends in city administration.

2. The creation of a recreation department results in duplication of work and unnecessary additional expense in a city with an existing park department.

3. It is inadvisable to create a department which controls little, if any, property, yet which conducts a program involving use of properties controlled and maintained by other departments.

4. All boards and commissions should be eliminated from local government in order to centralize responsibility and give the chief executive control of all city departments.

5. The appointment of a recreation commission, even though it includes representatives of the park and school boards, tends to minimize the place of these boards in the recreation movement.

Some who object to the recreation board favor a separate recreation department with an executive responsible directly to the mayor, city manager, or other city authority. They claim that under such a department an advisory recreation commission can perform the significant lay services which the advocates of the administrative board consider to be of great importance.

Administration by a Combined Recreation and Park Department. As mentioned in Chapter 5, the tendency to combine park and recreation functions in a single department has been gaining momentum in recent years. It will be recalled that the separate recreation department was established in many cities because the park authority was unwilling to develop recreation facilities and programs for the people; and that such a department was not created in cities where the park authority was willing to provide such service. As officials and the public have come to accept the principle that the primary function of the park department is to furnish recreation, the need for the separate park and recreation departments has lessened.

Consequently two trends in organization have been observed since World War II. First, in a number of cities with separate park and recreation departments, the department functions have been merged in a single agency. Second, in many cities that have established a year-round recreation program for the first time—especially smaller cities with no special park agency—park and recreation functions have been assigned to a new department. In some cases, it is known as a recreation department; in others, especially where consolidation has taken place, the agency title contains the names of both park and recreation departments. Administrating two services in a single agency provides many of the advantages of the separate park or recreation departments, listed earlier in the chapter, and eliminates some of their disadvantages.

In an editorial entitled "The Close Relationship of Parks and Recreation"[1] Charles E. Doell states: "Parks and recreation go together as completely as love and marriage. . . . It is the combination of both (facilities and program) in a single unified service, that constitutes the commodity which interests the public." Doell points out that the operation of parks and recreation as separate departments can be successful only when their services are under continual examination and their functions are allocated on a more or less logical basis.

The tendency noted above should not be interpreted as indicating that the separate recreation department has outlived its usefulness, for this is far from the case. In many communities no other public agency is willing or competent to take its place; in some cities the park authority is still concerned only with property acquisition, development, and maintenance. Many of the country's most successful programs are administered by a separate recreation department. Any city considering park and recreation consolidation would do well to study the experience in Santa Barbara, California, where repeated efforts were made to force the merger of the two departments, each of which functions under a commission. The last attempt was in 1954, when the departments appointed a joint committee to study the problem. Many California cities with different types of organization, some with merged departments, were visited, and special study was given to the results of consolidation. In its final report the joint committee stated that "in some of the merged cities, staff conflicts were sensed. No evidence was obtained indicating savings or staff elimination resulting from merger. None of the experiments being carried on in mergers have progressed far enough to indicate that a more efficient job was being done as a result."[2] Consequently it recommended that the departments continue as they were without change, except that some activities conducted by the park department be transferred to the recreation department.

Other Methods. Other proposals have been advanced from time to time but have received less widespread support. Some city managers have

[1] *Recreation*, vol. 51, no. 1, p. 4, January, 1958.

[2] Samuel Gerson, "Should Park and Recreation Departments Merge?" *Recreation*, vol. 49, no. 8, p. 397, October, 1956.

suggested that recreation should be under the local department of public welfare. Neither theory nor practice, however, justifies the opinion that the function of public recreation can be dealt with effectively along with public relief, unemployment insurance, old-age pensions, the operation of jails, and similar services. In fact, the 1956 *Recreation and Park Yearbook* [3] indicates that of a total of 2,660 authorities reporting, only 7 were departments of public welfare.

In 1931 a committee of the National Municipal League recommended that the schools should provide recreation for children of school age on a year-round basis and that the municipal government should be wholly responsible for providing recreation for the adult group. [4] Such a division of responsibility has proved utterly impracticable. Some have advocated establishing the recreation program under a youth board, but its very title indicates its limitations as the community recreation agency. Several variations in the common patterns of recreation organization have been adopted as cities have attempted to work out the most effective method of handling the recreation function; but in most cases these variations have been abandoned in favor of one of the widely used forms.

HOW MUNICIPAL RECREATION IS CONDUCTED

Political and financial considerations and local tradition play an important part in determining the form of organization under which recreation service is set up in a particular city. A study of present practice throughout the country and of organization trends over a period of years, however, reveals the extent to which the various forms of recreation authority have been adopted. Available statistics have therefore been analyzed to determine how widely cities are using the various major types of organization for recreation and the extent of certain services rendered under each.

The findings summarized in the following tables are based entirely upon yearbook reports submitted by local, including county, agencies and compiled by the National Recreation Association for the years 1928, 1937, 1946, and 1955. The figures used in preparing the tables in this chapter relate only to recreation programs financed in whole or primarily by local tax funds. Some of the authorities operate only a single playground for a short summer season; others conduct a diversified program of activities the year round. Since authorities employing at least one full-time, year-round recreation leader furnish the significant and comprehen-

[3] National Recreation Association, New York, 1956.
[4] Jay B. Nash, *Standards of Play and Recreation Administration,* National Municipal League, New York, 1931.

sive community recreation programs of the country and provide a large percentage of the total services, separate figures have been compiled for them.

It should be pointed out that data for 1928, 1937, and 1946 are comparable in that the same basis was used for accepting reports, and an attempt was made to secure reports from all qualifying agencies. Only agencies conducting programs under leadership or operating under supervision a facility such as a bathing beach, golf course, or swimming pool were included in the recreation yearbooks for these years. For 1955, on the other hand, reports were accepted from all authorities controlling parks regardless of the services rendered or the facilities operated, and the publication was therefore called the *1956 Recreation and Park Yearbook*.[5] Consequently reports were received from a much larger number of park authorities than in the earlier studies. In an attempt to give school boards an equal opportunity to report their community recreation service in 1955, a questionnaire was submitted to school authorities in every community of 2,500 and over.

Managing Authorities. Table 14 gives the total number of local public agencies of various types administering recreation in the continental United States in 1955, as well as the number providing full-time, year-round leadership, as reported to the yearbook.

Table 14. Types and Number of Local Public Recreation Authorities, 1955

Type of managing authority	Number of authorities	
	Total	With full-time, year-round leadership
Separate recreation authority	923	531
Park and recreation-park authority	920	282
School authority	343	45
Other municipal authority	474	55
Total	2,660	913

The table indicates that the separate recreation departments and park authorities are the most numerous, each representing about 35 per cent of the total number. Separate recreation authorities administer 58 per cent of all the programs under year-round leadership. More than one-half of the separate recreation authorities employ full-time, year-round leadership; less than one-third of the park authorities do; but relatively few of the school and other authorities employ such leadership.

[5] National Recreation Association, New York, 1956.

Trends in Organization. Important as it is to know how cities are conducting their municipal recreation services in any one year, it is of equal interest and significance to observe trends in the types of local recreation organization. In 1928 for the first time, agencies submitting yearbook reports were classified in a way that makes possible comparisons with later years. Table 15 indicates the number of authorities of the four major types administering recreation in 1928, 1937, 1946, and 1955, as well as the percentage of each type in the total increase.

Table 15. Types, Number, and Increase of Local Public Recreation Authorities, 1928, 1937, 1946, and 1955

Type of managing authority	Number				Percentage of total 1955	Increase 1928–1955	
	1928	1937	1946	1955		Number	Percentage of total *
Separate recreation authority	209	255	557	923	35	714	36
Park authority	231	282	300	920	34	689	35
School authority	158	179	251	343	13	185	9
Other municipal authority	99	211	246	474	18	375	19
Total	697	927	1,354	2,660	100	1,963	100

* Percentages rounded.

Table 15 indicates that between 1928 and 1955 the number of separate recreation departments increased by 342 per cent; the number of school authorities by 117 per cent. More than three times as many park departments reported in 1955 as in 1928, but the 1955 figures are not comparable to the others for the reasons previously stated. Nevertheless, the increase in park departments since 1946 reflects not only the creation of new park authorities but the tendency to merge park and recreation services under a single department.

Because cities providing programs the year round are the real backbone of the public recreation movement, trends in the administration of recreation agencies under full-time, year-round leadership are of primary significance. Table 16 gives, for 1928, 1937, 1946, and 1955, statistics comparable to those given in Table 15 for all administrative authorities.

The table reveals the remarkable increase in the year-round programs between 1928 and 1955, the number more than tripling during this period. It also indicates the major role played by the separate recreation department, which comprises 58 per cent of all the authorities employing full-time leadership and accounts for 62 per cent of the increase since 1928. The number of park authorities employing full-time leaders shows a striking gain in the decade since 1946, although park authorities are outnumbered nearly two to one by separate recreation departments. The school authorities, on the other hand, represent only 5 per cent of the total and show a relatively slight gain since 1928. Nearly one-half of the school departments with full-time leaders are in two states—New York and Wisconsin.

Table 16. Recreation Authorities Providing Full-time, Year-round Leadership, 1928, 1937, 1946, and 1955

Type of managing authority	Number				Percentage of total 1955	Increase 1928–1955	
	1928	1937	1946	1955		Number	Percentage of total
Separate recreation authority	116	151	356	531	58	415	62
Park authority	74	79	103	282	31	208	31
School authority	25	25	29	45	5	20	3
Other municipal authority	30	34	51	55	6	25	4
Total	245	289	539	913	100	668	100

The table shows that cities are increasingly considering year-round recreation service as a distinct municipal function, and for its administration are establishing separate recreation departments or departments combining park and recreation services.

COMPARISON OF SERVICES RENDERED BY DIFFERENT AUTHORITIES

Mere numbers do not afford a valid basis for judging the extent of the services rendered by managing authorities of different types. While the recreation service of some agencies consists merely of conducting a single playground or operating an outdoor swimming pool for a short summer season, others provide a diversified program for the entire community throughout the year. Some indication of the extent of the services rendered by the four types of managing authorities may be obtained from an analysis of the facilities they control and operate and of the leadership they employ. A study based upon *Recreation and Park Yearbook* [6] reports for 1955 provides some illuminating data.

[6] National Recreation Association, New York, 1956.

Table 17 indicates the number of facilities of several types reported by park, separate recreation, and school authorities. It does not record the facilities included in combined reports submitted by two or more agencies or by other public authorities. In studying the table it should be kept in mind that only three cities above 500,000 population—Philadelphia, Washington, D. C., and Cincinnati—have a separate recreation department. All cities in this population group have a park department which, in all but the three listed, furnishes the major municipal recreation service. In several of these cities the school authorities also provide community recreation programs. Another important factor is the considerable number of county park authorities, many of whom administer comprehensive properties with many recreation facilities.

Table 17. Facilities Reported by Selected Recreation Authorities, 1955

Facilities	Park authorities		Separate recreation authorities		School authorities	
	Number	Percentage	Number	Percentage	Number	Percentage
Playgrounds under leadership	6,046	40	5,786	39	3,157	21
Recreation buildings	2,064	62	1,007	32	215	6
Indoor recreation centers	2,380	29	3,037	37	2,863	34
Baseball diamonds	3,704	48	3,109	41	851	11
Golf courses	357	86	59	14	0	0
Swimming pools	1,094	59	590	32	157	9
Tennis courts	7,230	64	3,092	28	872	8

Park departments are shown to control most of the golf courses and a majority of the recreation buildings, swimming pools, and tennis courts. They operate fewer indoor recreation centers than the other authorities. Separate recreation departments report more than one-third of the playgrounds, indoor centers, and ball diamonds but very few golf courses. School authorities furnish the leadership for one-fifth of the playgrounds and one-third of the indoor centers but operate relatively few other facilities for community use.

It should be pointed out that full credit for furnishing recreation service does not always belong to the agency operating the facilities. In many instances the properties used are owned by another department, which may also furnish maintenance costs. Many indoor and outdoor school facilities are used for community recreation under the auspices of a recreation or park department; likewise many programs sponsored by separate recreation authorities take place on park properties.

Leadership. The extent to which paid and volunteer leaders were reported by the three types of authorities in 1955 is revealed by Table 18.

Table 18. Leadership Reported by Selected Recreation Authorities, 1955

Leadership	Park authorities		Separate recreation authorities		School authorities	
	Number	Percentage	Number	Percentage	Number	Percentage
Total paid leaders	23,426	36	24,234	38	16,505	26
Full-time, year-round paid leaders	3,730	57	2,169	33	616	9
Volunteers	71,488	53	63,153	45	5,132	4

Separate recreation departments employed the largest number of paid leaders, but owing to the greater employment of full-time workers in the large cities, more than one-half of all such leaders serve park agencies. A relatively large number of part-time and seasonal leaders—but comparatively few full-time workers—are employed by the school boards. Park and separate recreation authorities use volunteers to a much greater extent than do school authorities.

Services of Year-round Agencies. In this volume it has been emphasized repeatedly that year-round leadership is essential to an adequate recreation program. Any consideration of the organization of municipal recreation should therefore take into account the part which agencies employ-

Table 19. Accomplishments of Recreation Authorities, 1955

Facilities and leadership	Number in all agencies	Number in agencies with full-time, year-round workers	Full-time agency/ all-agency percentage
Playgrounds	18,224	14,034	77
Recreation buildings and indoor centers	14,029	10,814	77
Employed leaders	76,878	64,119	82
Amount spent for leadership *	$61,999,609	$56,742,368	92
Volunteers	164,714	144,496	88

* Expenditures for leadership alone are used because they are the only available expenditure figures reliable for comparative purposes.

ing full-time, year-round workers play in the total national picture. An indication of what year-round agencies accomplished in 1955 as compared with the total service reported by *all* agencies in 1955 is given in Table 19. The column headed "Number in all agencies" includes those figures appearing in the third column.

The figures show that the year-round recreation agencies operate a large percentage of the indoor and outdoor centers under leadership, employ a great majority of the leaders, and spend nine times as much money for leadership as the agencies employing only seasonal or part-time leaders. This being the case, it may be well to refer to Table 14, indicating the extent to which the four types of managing authorities employ full-time, year-round leadership. The willingness of authorities of different types to employ leaders on this basis is a factor to be considered in appraising forms of municipal recreation organization.

COOPERATION AMONG RECREATION AUTHORITIES

The assertion has sometimes been made that the lack of uniformity in methods of organizing local recreation service has resulted in confusion, conflicts over jurisdiction, overlapping programs, and duplication of areas and facilities. Unquestionably, in cities where recreation properties are owned and recreation programs are provided by two or more agencies, genuine cooperation between the authorities is essential for the best results. It is also true that, in general, recreation services have been developed most successfully in cities where recreation has been recognized as an essential function to be administered by a department or agency having this as its sole or primary function. It must be said, however, that no form of organization will work effectively unless there is a spirit of cooperation on the part of responsible public officials who have relationships with the recreation department. Furthermore, a successful recreation program can be developed even under an unsatisfactory administrative setup if there is a will to cooperate and to achieve this objective.

Duplication of effort has been eliminated in many cities through the coordination of programs or the consolidation of departments or bureaus. In a still greater number of cities, as pointed out elsewhere in this volume, a considerable degree of cooperation has been achieved by agreements among agencies concerned with some aspect of recreation. Although the possibilities of cooperative action are far from realized in most cities, there is much more cooperation than duplication or overlapping of services, and notable progress is being made in joint efforts to serve the recreation needs of the people. Examples of specific cooperation are given in Chapter 34.

GENERAL ORGANIZATION PRINCIPLES

Experience indicates that, regardless of the form of organization which a city adopts for handling its recreation service, the following principles should be adhered to:

1. All publicly owned property suitable for recreation should be made available for the use of the department responsible for conducting the program, under conditions worked out between the recreation authority and the departments controlling the property.

2. A commission, committee, or other organized group of citizens should be appointed to give continuous and collective thought to the leisure-time problems of the entire city and to work out effective means of solving them. It is usually advisable for the school board to have representation on this group, because the use of school property is so essential to a successful recreation program. Making the terms of office of the members overlap, so that not more than one or two expire each year, facilitates continuity of planning.

3. A full-time trained recreation executive should be employed to direct the program. This task requires all of his time and attention. Rarely can an executive do full justice to community recreation work if he must give part of his time to some other position.

4. A definite, separate recreation budget is desirable.

5. The program should serve all the recreation interests of the people; include games and sports, music, drama, arts and crafts, nature activities, hobbies, and social recreation; and provide for all groups without restriction as to race, religion, age, or sex.

6. Definite provision should be made for cooperative planning in the acquisition and development of new recreation areas and facilities, particularly between the city, school, and planning authorities.

7. Finally, vital, intelligent, efficient, progressive service of the public function, *recreation*, should be the primary consideration in determining the type of organization. The important factor in assuring the success of public recreation is not so much the exact form of organization—in the last analysis, local conditions must determine which is the best agency to administer the system—but the degree of cooperation which the recreation authority and the superintendent of recreation can secure from city departments and community agencies. Problems based on the joint use and control of facilities are bound to arise under any form of centralized administrative control yet devised. Wholehearted cooperation between the different departments is essential to success regardless of the form adopted; with such cooperation and under competent leadership, success is practically assured.

30. ORGANIZATION OF THE RECREATION DEPARTMENT

A RECREATION department can function effectively only if its staff and resources are organized in a way that enables it to accomplish its purpose—that of providing recreation service for the people. Just as communities have entrusted the recreation function to different forms of governmental agencies, so methods of departmental organization vary from city to city. Since the nature and scope of public recreation service likewise vary, no uniform pattern will fit every local situation. Furthermore, in view of the changing and expanding concept of the recreation function, any local plan of departmental organization is subject to revision from time to time.

In many respects the same organization principles apply equally to all types of recreation departments. However, since separate recreation, park, or combined recreation and park departments have recreation as their sole or primary function and provide a large percentage of the country's local recreation service, their organization will receive major consideration in this chapter. Special attention will also be given to the departments administered by policy-making boards or commissions, since more than one-half of the park and/or recreation departments with full-time leadership are operated under the control of such bodies.

As indicated in Chapter 28, the powers and functions of a recreation department depend upon state and local legislation. The type of organization needed to serve the purpose of the legislation depends largely upon the functions to be carried out. If the legislation merely provides for the conducting of school playgrounds or indoor centers or the furnishing of facilities for golf or swimming, a simple organization is adequate. On the other hand, the broad powers granted under a recreation enabling act call for a department with a more comprehensive plan. A still more complex organization is needed for a combined park and recreation department.

475

THE RECREATION BOARD OR COMMISSION

A recreation board or commission is the managing authority in the case of most separate recreation departments. Usually appointed by the mayor, in some instances with the city council's approval, the official recreation board has full responsibility for the operation of the department. Advisory boards have been appointed in a number of cities, in most instances where the recreation executive is directly responsible to a city manager, but they have no direct authority and must not be confused with the type of board discussed here. Boards of five members are most numerous, although others have from three to seven members; the terms generally overlap and run from three to five years—seldom for a longer period. In most cities one or more members are women; in many cases the school board, the park board, or city council is represented; in a few cities the park executive and superintendent of schools are ex officio members without a vote. Almost without exception, members receive no compensation for their services.

The preceding statements concerning the recreation board also apply in large measure to the park board or recreation and park board, especially where it is responsible for a municipal park department. However, in several states where separate park districts are created which are independent of the local governing authority, the members of the park board are elected, not appointed, and in every instance they are policy-making boards with authority, rather than advisory bodies.

Functions of the Board. In general the recreation board is responsible for determining every fundamental policy of the department not otherwise prescribed by the appointing authorities. Among the essential recognized functions of the recreation board, in the opinion of one chairman, are the following: [1]

The interpretation of the community recreation program to public officials and to the general citizenship in terms of adequate moral and financial support.
The maintenance of high standards in recreation leadership and in quality of program service.
The selection of the recreation executive or superintendent and the defining of the scope of his powers and duties.
The appointment, upon recommendation of the recreation executive, of all employees and the determination of their functions and duties.
The determination and establishment of the general policies to be followed in carrying out the purpose for which the department was established.
The consideration of and passing judgment upon the recommendations coming

[1] Clyde Doyle, "The Duties of a Recreation Board Member," *Recreation*, vol. 31, no. 1, p. 12, April, 1937.

from any source outside the department, especially if such suggestions involve matters of general policy.

Approval of the budget and the securing of the required funds.

The authorization of expenditures within the budget granted and the careful examination of expenditures.

A strict accounting to the people of the community through the proper fiscal authorities of the use of all funds.

A full report to the public of all the activities of the department during the year.

To this list might be added the responsibility for considering the future recreation needs of the city in terms of programs, areas, facilities, and services and for developing plans to meet these needs. Additional functions of a board also responsible for park services include:

Provision for a high standard in the development, preservation, care, and maintenance of park areas and facilities for the maximum enjoyment and use by the public.

The preparation, in cooperation with school and planning authorities, of a long-range plan for acquiring, developing, and maintaining areas designed for school and community recreation use.

The initiation, approval, and implementation of plans for the acquisition and improvement of other needed properties.

The function and value of boards were set forth at the 1957 National Recreation Congress as follows: [2]

Board members are the people's ambassadors to the higher authority. They transmit the will of the people . . . , provide a layman's view and advise in matters of broad public concern, provide continuity of policy and thinking despite changes in administration, develop long-range policy rather than acting by expediency, establish needed guide posts, and chart a broad course and direction for recreation as a service to the people of the community.

Board Organization. In order to function effectively, the board is formally organized and adopts rules and regulations governing its procedure. These specify the officers to be elected and their duties, the time and place of regular meetings, the order of business at meetings, and the committees to be appointed. Practices differ as to the appointment of committees, but many boards favor the use of committees because they give board members specific responsibilities and expedite the handling of board business. Typical of the standing committees are the following: finance, personnel, properties, and program. A member of the board may serve as secretary, although this duty is commonly assigned to the execu-

[2] *General Session Speeches and Section Meeting Summaries of the 39th National Recreation Congress,* National Recreation Association, New York, 1957, p. 136.

tive or another employee. It is of the utmost importance that a complete and accurate record be kept of all meetings and actions of the board.

The rules and regulations adopted by the board must conform with the provisions of the legislation creating it and with any other local regulations to which it is subject. The board adopts policies or procedures governing such matters as preparation of the budget, handling of funds, preparation of reports and publicity, personnel administration, fees and charges, and program development. They are in a sense the constitution and bylaws under which the department is operated, and determine the relationships and respective responsibilities of the board and the executive who is employed to administer the department.

In the well-organized department the board members recognize that their job is to determine policies, not to administer them. They do not assume the functions of the executive by attempting to dictate how details shall be carried out, by interfering with employment procedures, or by dealing directly in an executive capacity with subordinate workers. A sound principle in board-executive relationships is for the board to give the executive the authority, within the limits of the policies laid down by it, to organize and carry on the affairs of the department as long as his efforts produce the results desired and meet with the general approval of the public.

THE RECREATION EXECUTIVE

The executive officer of the department, usually called the superintendent of recreation, or of parks and recreation, has the duty of carrying out the policies of the board and administering the work of the department in accordance with these policies. He also serves as technical adviser to the board, in which capacity he conducts studies, develops plans, and recommends policies for its consideration and action. Within the limitations of these major functions his responsibilities and activities in the field of recreation are restricted only by his vision and resourcefulness.

Administrative Duties. The most important duties and responsibilities of the executive in his function of administrative officer, many of which are delegated to or shared with his assistants, may be grouped as follows:

Staff. To select, organize, train, and supervise the staff, including volunteers; to assign duties and to maintain good relationships between the workers.

Program. To select or approve the activities to be carried on, the special features to be presented, the services to be provided, and the new projects to be initiated, as well as to supervise the organization and conduct of the entire program.

Finance. To direct the expenditure of department funds in accordance with budget appropriations, to prepare annual estimates of the department's financial needs, and to supervise the keeping of complete records of receipts and expenditures.

Areas and Facilities. To arrange for proper development, maintenance, and operation of the areas and facilities under the control of the department, to determine the season during which they are to be open, and to recommend new improvements or extensions of the recreation system.

An attractive functional administration building, like the one in Seattle, facilitates departmental operations (Courtesy of Seattle, Wash., Park Department).

Records and Reports. To keep careful and complete records of department activities and services, personnel, and property and to prepare regular reports.

Research. To conduct studies of local conditions and needs affecting recreation, to check the effectiveness of the various department services, and to keep informed as to developments in the recreation field.

Public Relations. To interpret recreation to board members and the general public, to arrange for publicity, to keep in close touch with other officials and local agencies concerned with recreation, to participate in organizations and activities of particular interest to the department, and to organize neighborhood or city-wide recreation councils or other groups.

The relative time and attention which executives spend on these varied functions differ, depending upon the type of managing authority which they serve, the extent of the facilities controlled, the scope of the program, the number and ability of supervisors, and other factors. In a small city where the executive must perform many of the duties himself rather than delegate them to assistants, he usually spends much time on the supervision of workers and programs, whereas in a large city he is free to devote more attention to research, interpretation, and relationships. In a department combining park and recreation functions, the executive is likely to devote much of his time to problems relating to areas and facilities and finance.

The Executive and the Board. Perhaps the most important of all the executive's relationships are those with the members of his board, to whom he is directly responsible. Much of the success of the department depends upon his ability to take full advantage of their knowledge, ability, and interest in recreation. He keeps them informed as to the work of the department, invites them to inspect recreation facilities and to attend recreation programs, stimulates discussion of recreation problems, proposes plans for future action, furnishes them with literature on the recreation movement, and encourages them to attend recreation meetings and conferences. The wise executive welcomes fair and honest criticisms of his plans and recommendations because the board can often evaluate their strong and weak points and see them, sometimes better than the executive, as they will appear to the community. Where the relationship between the board and the executive is based upon mutual loyalty, respect, and cooperation, the work is certain to prosper.

OTHER MANAGING AUTHORITIES

The executive of a separate recreation department without a board has much the same duties as previously indicated, but he is responsible directly to a mayor, city council, city manager, or other official. The policies and procedures for the administration of the department are developed by the recreation executive but are subject to the approval of his superior. Advisory recreation boards have been appointed in many cities to assist the recreation executive in developing policies and programs.

In cases where the recreation executive is part of a school or park organization he is directly responsible to the superintendent of schools or of parks, and has little direct relationship with the school or park board. Major recommendations submitted by the recreation executive to his superior may be passed on for consideration to the board, who approve all policies relative to recreation as well as other activities of their department. In this way a school or park board provides some of the benefits of the recreation board, particularly where a committee of its members is appointed to pay special attention to recreation problems and to deal directly with the recreation executive.

DEPARTMENTAL ORGANIZATION

Organizing the recreation department staff and functions so as to secure the maximum results from available personnel, funds, and facilities is one of the major tasks of the recreation executive. A relatively simple problem in the small community, it increases in complexity and importance with the size of the city and the comprehensiveness of the recreation system. Organization is necessary in order to secure effective operation. The development of the desire and will to work together for a purpose is of primary importance. This is most easily attained when the department is so organized as to fix responsibility definitely, prevent overlapping of authority, and facilitate supervision and the smooth and effective operation of every part of the program.

There is no uniformity in the organization of recreation departments, even under the same type of managing authority, but all sound organization plans are designed to facilitate the performance of their common functions. Two principles underlying sound organization are to have each worker responsible to only one person and to relate each worker's authority to his degree of responsibility. Regardless of the specific arrangements adopted for handling the various functions, most plans are based on four major divisions of work: (1) recreation activities and program services, (2) special recreation facilities, (3) business and accounting, and (4) construction and maintenance.

The first two divisions furnish the primary, essential services for which the department is established. The other two serve secondary functions which are, however, necessary to its effective operation. In considering the specific forms of departmental organization, all four divisions will be discussed, but major emphasis will be given to the methods devised for conducting the work of the two primary divisions.

Division of Recreation Activities and Program Services. In smaller communities the superintendent supervises this division directly, often with the help of an assistant of the opposite sex. The worker in charge of the division, because of its importance, is given the title of assistant superintendent in some cities. The personnel assigned to it include general and special supervisors, directors, leaders, and specialists, whose duties were described in Chapter 7.

The work of this division may be divided roughly into three closely interrelated functions. One consists of the operation of playgrounds, buildings, and indoor centers, where diversified programs are carried on more or less continuously under leadership. Another involves the promotion of special program features, such as music, drama, athletics, nature, crafts, and hobbies, on a city-wide basis, including the organization of groups and the conduct of special events—community and holiday celebrations, for example—many of which necessitate the use of playgrounds and indoor centers. The third function of the division comprises special services to community agencies and groups, such as homes, industries, institutions, the aged, and the handicapped.

Organization of Playgrounds and Indoor Centers. A supervisor of playgrounds is commonly employed, at least during the summer months, to take charge of a community's playground program and its operation. In large cities, where a single general supervisor cannot keep in close touch with all playground and center operations, district organization proves effective. In each of the city districts there is a general supervisor who is assigned responsibility for all playgrounds and indoor centers in the area. In some cities this worker also acts for the superintendent in all matters relating to personnel, program, equipment, or interpretation of policies that may arise within the district, including the general promotion of recreation and the fostering of community relationships. A modification of this plan is in effect in a few cities, where the chief director of a major year-round center in each district is given general responsibility for the work at the other playgrounds and centers in the district.

Each playground or indoor-center unit is in the charge of one person, the director, who has full authority and responsibility for its operation. All other workers at the playground or center are responsible to the director for the work which they perform there.

Organization of Special Activities and Services. In a small city, the special supervisors or specialists—particularly if they are employed on a seasonal basis only—are directly responsible either to the recreation superintendent or supervisor of playgrounds. However, while working at a particular playground or center they are generally subject to the jurisdiction of the director. In several cities with a well-trained, year-round staff, on the other hand, the supervisors report to the head of the activities division. Each supervisor serves primarily as an adviser, teacher, and planner, and his suggestions relative to the program are put into effect chiefly by the "line" workers—the general supervisors, directors, and leaders, over whom he has no authority. Under this arrangement, much of the actual work in the fields of music, drama, nature, and other special fields is performed by the regular workers at the playgrounds and centers, who benefit from the technical advice and guidance of the supervisors of special activities but are not directly responsible to them.

In other cities the special supervisors have subordinate workers whom they assign to service at playgrounds and centers or to help with community-wide activities, and they initiate projects which call for the cooperation of playground directors. In such cases, directors must be protected from pressure by several special supervisors who may over-emphasize their particular activities. Regardless of the nature of the special supervisor's relationships with workers at playgrounds and indoor centers, he usually directs personally one or more program features, such as a municipal orchestra, drama tournament, crafts workshop, or munici-pal sports program, or supervises the workers who conduct them.

Some large departments employ one or more persons to take charge of a special program feature such as industrial recreation or service to institutions. These workers, like the supervisors of special activities, are usually responsible directly to the head of the activities division. They may call upon the special supervisors to help with their programs and may arrange with the general supervisors for the use of playgrounds and indoor-center facilities.

Special supervisors in most cities still have specific titles indicating responsibility for a field such as drama or athletics, but there is some indication of a tendency away from too much specialization in functions and titles. For example, workers give half of their time to some particular phase of the program such as music or crafts and the other half to general supervision. In this way the ability of the worker in a particular field is utilized; and by serving as a general supervisor, he gains an understand-ing of, and contact with, the entire program. Such plans make for flexi-bility and avoid a top-heavy overspecialized staff. In small cities it is common practice for a single supervisor to care for two or more phases of the program.

Division of Special Recreation Facilities. This division includes the personnel responsible for the operation of golf courses, stadiums, swim-ming pools, bathing beaches, boating centers, camps, and other special facilities. Its function of assuring the maximum satisfactory public use of these facilities calls for managerial as well as activity-leadership ability. Recreation departments under school auspices seldom have such a divi-sion because the aforementioned facilities are not generally provided. In many cities the managers of camps, golf courses, and swimming pools report directly to the superintendent; where there are several facilities of one kind, a special supervisor, such as a supervisor of camps, golf, or aquatics, may be employed.

Since these special operating units are becoming more varied and numerous, since there are many common problems of operation, and since most of these facilities involve the collection of fees, there is a tendency to set up a separate division for all of them, in charge of a supervisor responsible to the superintendent. In any case, each major facility should have a manager who is in complete charge of the personnel required for its operation and maintenance. Close cooperation is essential with both the maintenance division, if the maintenance division assigns caretaking personnel for work at the facilities, and with the accounting division, to which are submitted financial and service reports of the division's operations.

Division of Business and Accounting. This division has two primary functions: One is keeping the financial records and accounts; the other involves office management, handling the many business details, and keeping personnel, property, service, and other departmental records. In a small department the work of this division may be done by a book-keeper with the assistance of a stenographer-clerk who also answers the telephone and serves as secretary to the superintendent. In a large system, however, an accountant, auditor, chief clerk, typists, and clerical assistants are required. Employees of this division also include the telephone operator, receptionist, and in some instances the workers in charge of permits and the supply room. Where the size of the staff warrants, an office manager is employed. A worker whose duty is to keep the official records and handle the correspondence of the board is sometimes employed as secretary to the board.

Division of Construction and Maintenance. Recreation departments which own or control recreation areas and facilities require a group of workers to develop them and keep them in good condition. In some instances these workers maintain not only the department's own properties but also school areas and facilities on which it conducts activities. Separate recreation departments conducting a program involving the use of park and school areas only do not require a construction and maintenance division, the functions of which are performed by the park and school authorities. In cities where the recreation program is under park or school auspices, maintenance is usually provided by the regular park or school maintenance organization.

The composition of the staff of this division depends upon the nature and extent of the recreation system and also upon the degree to which it is expanding. A department that is acquiring new areas and developing new facilities requires a planning, engineering, and construction staff if it is to design and develop the properties with its own workers. On the other hand, if the system is comparatively adequate for the city's needs, maintenance is the division's primary function. In either case, a supervisor, engineer, or foreman is necessary, and his assistants include repair and maintenance mechanics, gardeners, caretakers, and laborers. Specialists, such as filter operators and greenskeepers, may be added as required. One or more clerical workers to keep the essential records of work projects, labor, and materials are needed where the volume of work demands such personnel.

Part of the employees of this division work at or out of the department's storehouse and workshops; others are assigned for regular duty at the various areas and facilities. At each major recreation area and at playgrounds and playfields with recreation buildings, the full-time service of at least one caretaker-janitor is required. Traveling maintenance crews, each under a foreman, have proved economical and satisfactory when assigned to a group of areas in a district. They either care for all upkeep and repairs or supplement the services of the maintenance workers regularly assigned to the areas. Caretakers and other maintenance workers, when assigned to a particular area or facility, report directly to the director or manager in charge.

PARK DEPARTMENT ORGANIZATION

Because of the growing tendency to combine recreation and traditional park functions under a single department, and because separate or combined park agencies render types of service not commonly included in the program of the separate recreation department, differences in their organization plans merit consideration. The *1956 Recreation and Park Yearbook* [3] contains a listing of the major divisions reported by park authorities in sixty-three cities over 100,000. It reveals a wide diversity in the number and types of divisions under which the work of park departments is carried on. A few departments reported little or no functional division; one or two indicated as many as ten bureaus or divisions, and most of them listed from three to six.

Recreation divisions, reported by fifty-three cities, outnumber all others. Nearly as many departments reported a division responsible for specific facilities such as golf courses, beaches and pools, or stadium, or a division of special facilities and/or services. The functions of these two groups are comparable to those of the recreation department's division of recreation activities and program services and division of special recreation facilities, respectively. Practically every park department reported either a maintenance or parks division; in some cases planning, construction, and engineering functions were combined in a single division. Business and accounting functions are commonly handled by an administrative division. Services rarely provided by separate recreation departments but administered under special divisions in a number of park departments are zoological parks, forestry and shade trees, horticulture, police, and airports.

Three of the charts in the pages that follow illustrate the plan of organization in departments providing recreation in conjunction with park service.

[3] National Recreation Association, New York, 1956.

DEPARTMENTAL ORGANIZATION IN SEVERAL CITIES

A study of the ways in which departments are actually organized illustrates various methods used in developing a plan for carrying on the work of a department. It is well to remember that if a department has not made changes in its organization plan for a period of years, in all probability it is not advancing or keeping abreast of the times. In progressive departments adjustments are made from year to year as experience reveals the strength or weakness of various units or relationships and as new activities and services are added to the program. In the following pages are presented charts illustrating organization methods used by six departments.

Departmental Organization in Oakland, California. Municipal recreation in Oakland is administered by a recreation commission, the five members of which are appointed by the city council upon nomination by the mayor, and serve for five-year terms without compensation. Broad powers are given the board under the city charter. A superintendent of recreation serves as department executive. (See Chapter 27 for a description of the work of the commission.)

As the accompanying chart indicates, four workers report directly to the superintendent and comprise his cabinet. These are an executive program director, who is responsible for the department's entire program as well as staff training and program evaluation; an administrative assistant, who is in charge of the department office and personnel procedures; an administrative analyst, whose division includes finance, budget control, purchasing, stores, and public relations; and a supervisor of construction and maintenance, whose duties include planning and design.

The entire leadership staff serves in the division of the executive director in charge of program. Reporting directly to him are three general supervisors—for community centers and playgrounds, special programs, and sports, aquatics, and industrial recreation—and a supervisor of recruitment and placement as well as community relations consultants. Under the general supervisor of centers and playgrounds, programs are administered on a district basis by five supervisors responsible for the work of the playground and indoor-center directors, leaders, and aides in their respective districts. Specialists in the cultural arts and in-town camp leaders report to the supervisor of special programs; staff at the pools and mountain camps and workers assigned to the industrial recreation and municipal sports programs report to the supervisor of sports, aquatics, and industrial recreation.

The relationships of other personnel in the other three divisions are indicated on the chart. The Oakland organization provides logical and

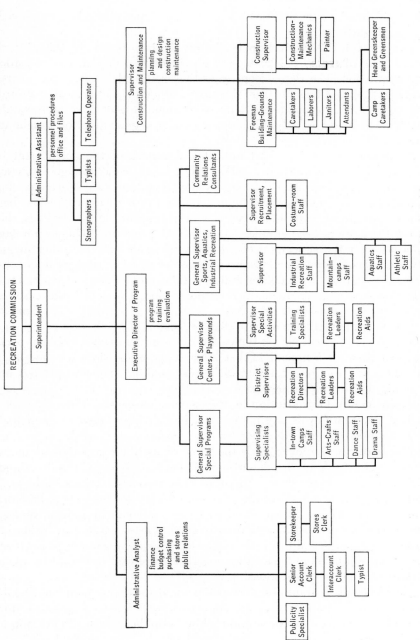

Fig. 1. Recreation department organization, Oakland, Calif.

clearly defined responsibilities for the various types of workers employed by the department.

Departmental Organization in Corpus Christi, Texas. In this city of nearly 175,000, recreation service is provided by a department of parks and recreation. The department executive is directly responsible to the city manager, but benefits from the advice of a park and recreation board of five members appointed by the city council for two-year terms. Although the board is only advisory, it carries a great deal of weight in the city.

As the accompanying chart indicates, the work of the department is performed by five divisions: parks, yacht basin, coliseum, golf course, and recreation. The head of each division reports to the director of the department. The recreation program, under the recreation division, has two sections, each with a supervisor. One is responsible for athletics, the other for centers, playgrounds, and special programs. The swimming pool is under the supervisor of athletics, but each of three other major facilities has a separate division. The parks division designs and constructs new areas and facilities and maintains all 694 acres of park property and buildings on them. Park maintenance, as is often the case, is provided on a zone or district basis. It is to be noted that each division has its own maintenance or custodial workers.

The Corpus Christi plan is typical of that used by many combined park and recreation departments in that it has separate divisions for these two functions and for the operation of special facilities. However, it has no separate division of business and accounting.

Departmental Organization in Milwaukee, Wisconsin. The major recreation program in this city is provided by the department of municipal recreation and adult education of the local school board, under the direction of an employee with the rank of assistant superintendent of schools. The work of the department is carried on largely under three divisions: (1) playgrounds and social centers, (2) municipal athletics, and (3) service and maintenance, each of which is in charge of a director. Unlike most park departments and some separate recreation departments, the Milwaukee school board does not administer large properties or special recreation facilities such as golf courses or swimming pools. The accompanying chart indicates the personnel employed by the Milwaukee department and their relationships.

The city is divided into four recreation areas for playground and social-center administration, and a staff supervisor is assigned as administrator in each area. Each of these supervisors also has responsibility for a special phase of the program: clubs, outdoor education, in-service education, or spring and fall playgrounds. The division of playgrounds and social centers has four additional supervisors, each of whom is responsible

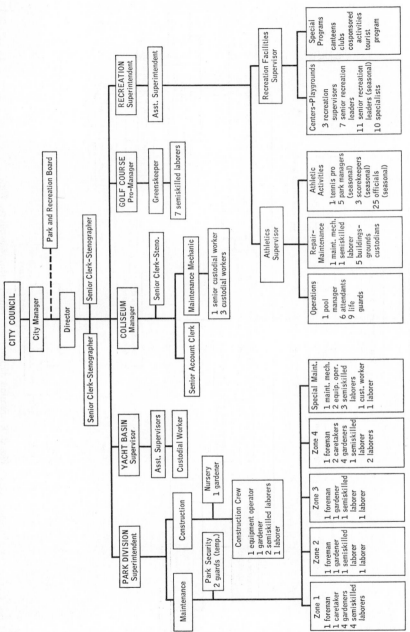

Fig. 2. Parks and recreation department organization, Corpus Christi, Tex.

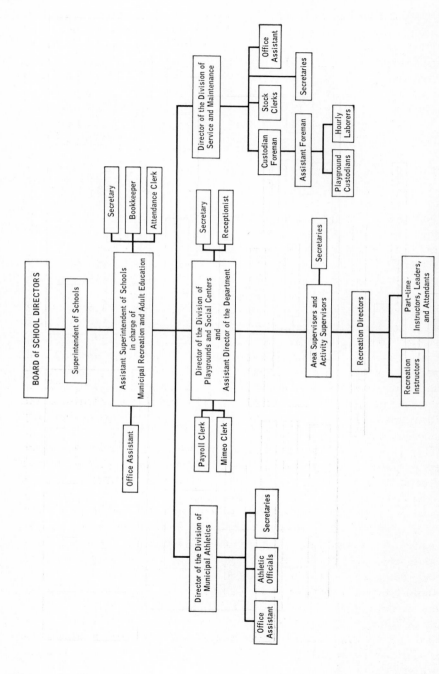

Fig. 3. Recreation department organization, Milwaukee, Wis.

for one of the following: (1) drama and music, (2) arts, crafts, and dance, (3) adult education, and (4) women's municipal athletics and leagues, tournaments, and meets sponsored by playgrounds and centers. Each of the four geographical areas in turn is divided into two or more recreation districts, in each of which one social center is designated as the district center. The full-time director of this center serves as district director and administrator, although most of his services are rendered at his own center. Each playground and center is in the charge of a director, who is assisted by full-time or part-time leadership personnel.

The division of athletics administers the comprehensive city-wide sports program for boys and men. Ice-skating rinks are one of the responsibilities of the division of service and maintenance.

Departmental Organization in Union County, New Jersey. The park system in Union County, comprising nearly 5,000 acres in twenty-five widely distributed areas, is under the control of a park commission of five members. The general superintendent also serves as secretary to the commission; the legal counsel, as is usually the case, is likewise directly responsible to the commission.

The work is divided among eight divisions—a somewhat larger number than usual. Because of the nature of the park system it requires the services of a special police division. Auditing-clerical and purchasing work are handled separately, although in some park departments they are combined in a single division. Construction-maintenance and engineering— land acquirement have separate divisions, although these functions are sometimes grouped together. Personnel-safety and public information and refectories receive a higher ranking than usual in the organization plan in Union County.

The recreation division has full responsibility not only for the organized programs and services but for the operation of all the county's recreation facilities. Each of the many diversified facilities is under a manager with assistants, all of whom are responsible to the superintendent of recreation and the assistant superintendent. Even in parks with two or more special recreation facilities, each has its own manager. Because the recreation division plays such an important role in the Union County park system, its organizational chart is presented in greater detail than that of the other divisions.

Departmental Organization in Austin, Texas. The recreation department in this city of 190,000 people is administered by a director who is directly responsible to the city manager. An advisory park and recreation board exerts a considerable influence in the development of policies for the operation of the department. (See Chapter 27 for a description of the work of the department.)

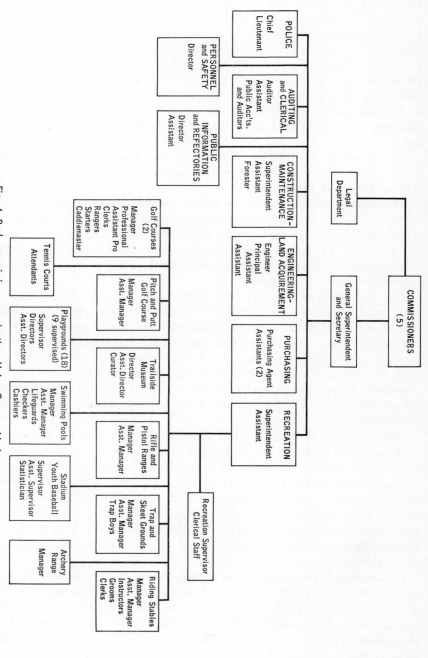

Fig. 4. Park commission organization, Union County, N. J.

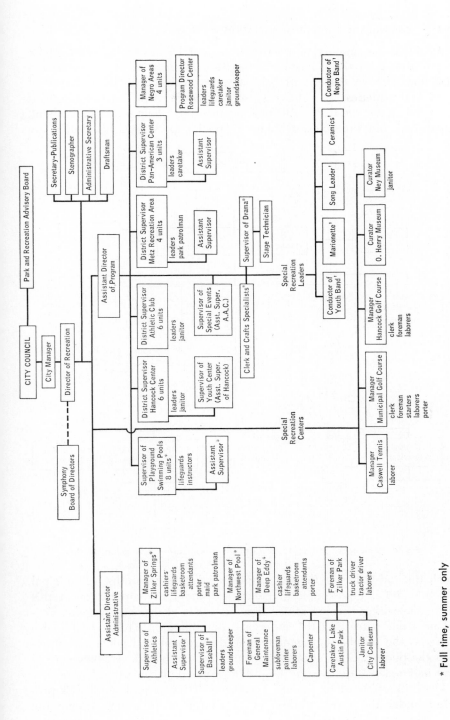

* Full time, summer only

† Part time

Fig. 5. Recreation department organization (summer), Austin, Tex.

As the accompanying summer organizational diagram indicates, major responsibility for the department's operations is carried by two assistant directors. One of these, with an "administrative"' title, is in charge of municipal athletics, three large swimming centers, the caretaker staff at several centers, and general maintenance of playground equipment, apparatus, and buildings. Except for pool supervision, his duties are

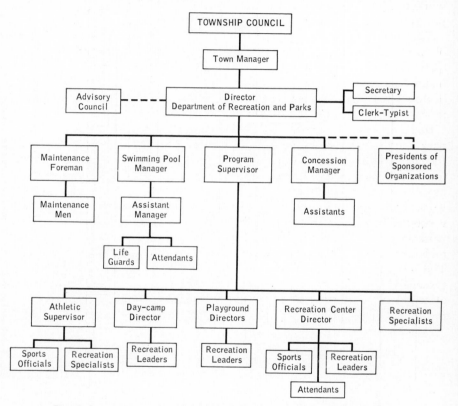

Fig. 6. Recreation and parks department organization, Livingston, N. J.

much the same during the fall, winter, and spring months. (Municipal athletics and large swimming centers are under the supervision of this particular worker because at one time he was in charge of a large municipal pool and later was the supervisor of athletics.) This assistant also serves as the purchasing agent for the department and generally supervises the budget. General maintenance of the city's parks is taken care of by a maintenance division in the public works department.

The bulk of the department's organized activities and services is provided under the assistant director in charge of program. Among the personnel who report to this worker during the summer are four district supervisors and a manager of Negro areas; supervisors of drama, special events, and playground swimming pools; and several special recreation leaders. Many of these people are employed on a full-time basis. During the fall, winter, and spring the district supervisors have direct responsibility for supervision of the major community recreation centers. More workers report directly to the assistant director in charge of the Austin program than are usually responsible to an executive or supervisor.

The managers of the tennis center and golf courses and the curators of two museums report to the director of recreation. He in turn delegates certain specific responsibilities to his assistants for supervision at these major facilities. The director of recreation has a relationship to the board of directors of the city symphony, since the recreation department shares in the financing and management of this organization.

Departmental Organization in Livingston, New Jersey. Recreation and park services are combined in a single department in Livingston, New Jersey, a suburban community of 20,000. The director is responsible to the town manager. Livingston has no official or policy-making board serving its recreation interests, but a recreation council. Most of the department's workers are employed on a seasonal or part-time basis. The organization is simple, as might be expected in a small city with limited facilities. Four workers report directly to the head of the department on their respective responsibilities: maintenance, swimming pool, program, and concessions. The program supervisor is in charge of all indoor and outdoor activities (except swimming) that are sponsored by the department. The importance attached to relationships with community organizations is illustrated by the fact that these are included in the department's organization chart.

31. FINANCING RECREATION

THE POWER which has been granted to municipal and school authorities to appropriate and expend tax funds for recreation is basic to the recreation movement, and the development of local recreation programs has been made possible in large measure by the laws authorizing the expenditure of public funds for recreation purposes. The financing of community recreation by taxation is commonly regarded as the only practicable method of furnishing these facilities and activities for all the people.

In Chapter 5 it was pointed out that private initiative made possible the beginning and early growth of the recreation movement by providing funds for conducting demonstration playgrounds and stimulating public interest in children's need for play. It soon became evident, however, that private philanthropy could not finance the purchase, equipment, and operation of the many areas that were needed and that public funds and credit would have to be made available. The prompt acceptance of this responsibility by public authorities is indicated by the first recreation survey conducted by the Playground Association of America for the year 1907. Only about 5 per cent of the money reported spent during the year by forty-four large cities came from private funds. Forty-eight years later, in 1955, private sources furnished only 2 per cent of the total expenditures reported in the *1956 Recreation and Park Yearbook*[1] by over 2,750 localities. Thus it is clear that since the early days of the movement, funds for community recreation leadership, facilities, and services have been derived almost entirely from public sources. Yet in dozens of communities private generosity alone makes recreation programs available, and in hundreds of others it finances activities and services which the city authorities are unwilling or unable to support fully from public funds.

SOURCES OF FUNDS FOR LAND AND IMPROVEMENTS

Municipal funds for recreation have come from the usual sources of local government revenue. Capital expenditures—for land purchase,

[1] National Recreation Association, New York, 1956.

buildings, facilities, and improvements—have been made largely from funds raised through bond issues. To a lesser degree land acquisition, construction, and improvements have been financed from special tax levies, appropriations from general city and school tax revenues, and special funds, such as a sales tax. In purchasing new areas a relatively small number of cities use the special-assessment method, by which owners of property benefited by the area are assessed part or all of the land and development cost. In one city the cost of constructing four swimming pools on municipally owned areas has been met by this method.

The extent to which bond issues have furnished the funds for financing the cost of land, buildings, and improvements is strikingly indicated by the fact that in 1930, when capital expenditures for parks and recreation in 721 cities exceeded $27,500,000, bond issues yielded $27,315,752. During the Depression years, however, few bonds were voted, and the cost of capital improvements in park and recreation areas was met largely from emergency or relief funds. Thus in 1935, bond issues for parks and recreation yielded only $1,000,000. Expenditures for land, buildings, and improvements were few during the war years except in critical military and war-industry areas, where much of the cost was met from Federal funds. Reserves accumulated during the war have since been used in some cities to acquire and develop properties for recreation, but in many cities bond issues have been authorized as a means of financing needed expansion of the cities' recreation resources. Issues of nearly $159,000,000 passed in 234 cities during the five-year period, 1951 to 1955, were reported to the *1956 Recreation and Park Yearbook*.[2] The number of cities voting bonds for parks and recreation attained a new high in 1956; as in 1957, they were predominantly for swimming pools, recreation buildings, acquisition of new parks, and the improvement of recreation areas and facilities. Los Angeles alone voted $39,500,000 for park and recreation purposes in 1957.

Some advocates of a pay-as-you-go policy for park and recreation projects oppose the borrowing of funds to finance them on the grounds that such procedure is more costly. According to a citizens' committee in San Jose, California, however, a pay-as-you-go policy in 1957 would cost about one-third more than deficit financing for two reasons: (1) anticipated increase of about 50 per cent in land values and the hazard that some land might not be available later, and (2) anticipated inflationary increases of as much as 25 per cent in six years in construction costs. In a period of rising land, labor, and material costs, bond issues seem the most advantageous method for raising funds for capital recreation ex-

[2] *Ibid.*

penditures, especially in localities where recreation land and facilities are far below standard.

Revenue bonds are not used widely in financing recreation facilities, but several cities have financed a golf course or swimming pool by this method. The construction of similar facilities on public property has been financed by membership organizations in a number of cities, with the understanding that after a certain period of private operation, the facility will be turned over to the municipality. In a few cities the governing authorities have appropriated funds to match voluntary contributions raised for a specific recreation purpose.

SOURCES OF FUNDS FOR CURRENT OPERATION

Current operating costs of recreation, unlike capital outlays, have been met largely through annual appropriations from general city, park, and school tax funds. Some cities, however, support their programs chiefly through special municipal, park, or school recreation mill tax levies.

City Appropriations. Municipal-government experts, among others, believe that recreation departments, like other city departments, should be financed by appropriations from the general city funds. They hold that the recreation budget should be subject to the review and approval of the appropriating body along with the budgets of the other departments; and that the amount made available for recreation in a given year should be determined in the light of the total funds available and in relation to recreation needs compared with the needs of other departments. This method of financing, which prevails in most cities, makes it necessary for recreation authorities to demonstrate to the city officials and to the public the value and effectiveness of their service. To the extent that they are successful in doing so, this method offers the possibility of increased appropriations as the need for them is demonstrated.

In cities where recreation is subordinated to the chief function of a park, school, public welfare, or other department, not only must budget requests for this work require the approval of the appropriating authorities, but also the recreation division must compete with other divisions for its share of the department's budget. This is one of the reasons why persons seeking the best interests of recreation feel that it should be administered by a separate recreation department.

The Recreation Mill Tax. In cities with a special mill tax for recreation, the amount is usually fixed at a certain number of mills on each dollar of assessed valuation, varying in most instances from 0.1 to 1 mill (equivalent to 1 to 10 cents per $100). The amount of the tax is sometimes indicated in terms of the number of cents on each hundred dollars of assessed valuation. Where a maximum and minimum levy are specified, the exact amount to be made available in a given year is determined by the local governing authorities. In some cities the tax is voted for a specified period of years and can be renewed only by a favorable referendum vote; in others, once voted, it remains in effect until repealed by a vote of the people.

The special recreation tax levy has been favored by many who believe that recreation requires assured financial support until it has established itself in the eyes of the governing authorities as an essential service. They feel that a new function like recreation is not likely to secure the funds it needs to meet the public demand for expanding service if it must compete with other larger and strongly entrenched departments which wield a greater influence with the appropriating body. The fact that a special mill tax can be put into effect and maintained only if a majority of the taxpayers are willing to support it justifies its use, in the opinion of its supporters. Such a tax also safeguards the recreation department against marked budget reductions, assuring a relatively steady annual income and an increase with a rise in assessed valuation.

The need and justification for the special recreation tax have diminished as recreation has gained wide acceptance as an essential governmental function. Furthermore, in many cities with a special tax, supplementary appropriations have been granted repeatedly in order to provide adequate services. Hence the tax may actually retard rather than assist the growth of the recreation department, where recreation needs increase at a greater rate than assessed valuations.

Fees and Charges. For many years certain recreation facilities and services have been financed in part from income received from fees and charges levied on persons benefiting directly from the facilities. Some authorities have considered such fees and charges an easy source of revenue and have advocated a rather general application of a policy of charging wherever possible. Others have felt that such a policy is neither sound nor justified. There is, however, general agreement that if the application of a fee appreciably reduces or restricts participation in an activity, there is something wrong with it.

Arguments Pro and Con. Several reasons advanced by advocates of a general application of charges and fees are:

1. People tend to appreciate things more if they are required to pay for them.
2. Charging simplifies control and discipline.
3. Charging makes it possible to expand facilities, programs, and services.

4. The public should not be asked to meet the entire cost of providing activities and facilities that involve considerable expense and serve relatively few.

5. The willingness of the public to pay for certain forms of recreation furnishes the authorities a guide in program planning.

Those who feel that there should be no fees and charges offer the following:

1. Recreation is a basic human need and, in the public interest, should be provided on the same basis of financial support as education and health service.

2. Charging tends to exclude from the program persons who need it most.

3. Charging stimulates the development of services and facilities which bring in revenue instead of programs which are of greater value and importance.

4. The tendency to charge fees and the attempt to make recreation self-supporting increase the difficulty of securing adequate tax support.

5. Where charging exists the city may become more liable to suit in case of personal injuries or property damage.

Local Practices. The extent to which charges are made, the objectives sought in making them, and the policies and practices followed with reference to fees and charges vary from city to city. However, in view of the recognized importance of play for children, it is generally agreed that children of elementary school age or younger should not be charged for recreation except for activities involving high leadership or equipment costs in relation to the number of children served. Because of the large initial investment in such facilities as golf courses, municipal camps, and artificial ice-skating rinks, and because of the limited numbers of people they accommodate, the practice of charging for the use of such facilities is almost universal. At swimming pools and beaches charges are also common, but with few exceptions children are permitted the free use of these facilities during certain periods. Local practices vary more widely in the case of tennis, dancing, membership in special-interest groups, the provision of handcraft materials, and instruction in various activities. Entry fees for adult teams enrolled in leagues or for individuals playing in tournaments conducted by the recreation department are common. Increasingly cities are charging fees, or higher fees, to nonresidents, either in order to secure more revenue or to discourage them from using the city's facilities and services, but such discrimination has been declared invalid by the courts in some states.

The objectives sought and the relationship of the charges to the people's ability to pay are major considerations in determining the results of any policy relating to fees. Reference was made in an earlier chapter to the remarkable impetus given to the playing of golf in one city by lowering the rates and furnishing facilities and equipment within the means of people who wished to play but previously had been unable to afford it. In other cities there is evidence that prevailing high rates restrict public use of the courses. Establishing a charge merely for income sometimes fails to accomplish this and also defeats the very purpose for which the facility was established. An excellent example is furnished by a large city where, after a fee for the use of tennis courts was instituted, play fell off 70 per cent, and the amount of money collected was just sufficient to pay the man who collected the fees. Very different was the experience in another city where week-end congestion on the courts was so great that the authorities held a referendum among the tennis players to determine whether they were willing to pay a nominal fee for installing a week-end reservation system. In this instance the object of the fee was to enable the department to furnish better service, and the suggestion met a hearty response.

Revenue from Fees and Charges. Since 1929 the recreation yearbooks have shown that in general income from fees and charges, like income from tax sources, fluctuates with changing economic conditions. The number of agencies reporting receipts from fees and charges has increased considerably, and there has been an appreciable increase in the ratio of receipts from these sources to the total amounts made available for recreation. In 1930, $3,836,686, or 11 per cent of all operating costs, came from fees and charges, 222 cities reporting income from this source. In 1937 the amount reported was $3,776,559, or 15 per cent of the total operating expenditures, with 430 cities reporting income from fees and charges. Comparable receipts in 575 cities in 1955 amounted to $30,473,-521, which, with $16,036,079 collected in 374 municipalities but turned over to city and county treasuries, represented 16 per cent of the current expenditures for the year, the source of which was reported.

Experience during the years of changing economic conditions since 1929 seems to indicate that, although charges and fees are desirable for some forms of municipal recreation service, in general they have not proved successful when applied on a money-raising basis. The attempt to carry the cost of some activities by using the profits from other activities is considered unsound in principle and has proved so in practice.

Other Sources of Funds. In a few states local recreation programs are financed in part with funds allocated by state agencies for extension education or recreation for special groups such as youth or the aged. Utility profits are used for recreation in a few localities, and in New

Mexico part of the proceeds from a cigarette tax passed in 1955 is earmarked for local recreation. Income from concessions, gifts, contributions from community chests or private recreation associations, and sale of materials supplements the amount received from municipal sources in many cities. The total amount of such income is comparatively small, and in some cases it must be used for specific purposes.

RECREATION EXPENDITURES

The recreation yearbooks issued since 1907 provide the best indication of the trend in expenditures for organized community recreation service. Prior to 1950 the yearbook recorded expenditures for areas, facilities, and buildings intended for community recreation use; for the operation of playgrounds, recreation buildings, indoor centers, and camps under leadership; for the promotion and conduct of community-wide programs and services; and for the operation and maintenance of such facilities as golf courses, playfields, swimming pools, and bathing beaches. However, the figures submitted by the agency which administered the program and operated the facilities did not always represent the entire capital and current expenditures for community recreation in the city. Items most often omitted were the cost of acquiring parks and other areas to be used at least in part for active recreation, expenditures for the construction of school buildings and other facilities which were utilized in the recreation program, and funds spent for maintaining areas and facilities. In the issues containing data for 1950 and 1955, on the other hand, park authorities reported their total expenditures, not merely the amount spent for organized recreation programs and special facilities, as in previous years. The expenditures data for 1950 and 1955 are therefore not comparable with the figures in preceding issues of the yearbook, except for the data on expenditures for recreation leadership.

A Summary of Expenditures. Table 20 shows the annual expenditures as reported in the recreation yearbook since 1917, by periods. The table gives a fair indication of trends, although if cities had reported the total amount spent for recreation each year, and if all cities providing recreation service had submitted a report, the figures for recreation expenditures would far exceed the amounts recorded.

Table 20 indicates the phenomenal rise in local recreation expenditures during the 1920s, the marked curtailment in the amount spent during the Depression, the gradual wartime rise, and the striking increase in expenditures following the end of World War II. Capital outlays throughout this period showed a similar trend, although they fell off much more sharply than total expenditures during the Depression and, owing primarily to the wartime shortage of labor and materials, did not rise appreciably until after the war ended. Expenditures for leadership were reduced proportionately less than other items during the Depression. The marked rise in expenditures in 1950 and 1955 is due in large measure to the fact that they included the total amount spent for all park services. Two significant trends since 1946 merit special mention. One is the increase in capital outlays, reflecting the marked expansion in recreation areas, facilities, and structures. The other is the mounting total spent for leadership, as a result of the growing recognition of the importance of employing qualified recreation leaders.

Table 20. Expenditures for Community Recreation, 1917 to 1955

| Year | Total expenditures | Expenditures for land, buildings, and permanent equipment | | Expenditures for leadership * | |
		Amount	Per cent of year's total expenditures	Amount	Per cent of year's current expenditures
1917	$ 6,659,600	$ 2,551,027	38.3		
1922	9,317,048	1,680,383	18.0		
1927	32,191,763	15,184,035	47.1		
1930	38,518,194	12,610,862	32.7	$ 8,135,656	31.4
1934	20,668,459	2,314,294	11.1	6,406,896	34.9
1937	25,794,537	3,403,191	13.1	7,469,427	33.4
1942	31,372,700	2,712,851	8.6	10,868,313	34.7
1946	51,785,090	8,012,517	15.4	19,862,869	45.4
1950	268,911,957	86,966,727	32.3	36,328,037	20.3
1955	378,422,214	92,995,363	24.5	61,999,609	21.8

* Not reported for 1917, 1922, and 1927.

Another source of information on municipal recreation expenditures is the publication issued annually by the Bureau of the Census, entitled *City Government Finances*. This report covers only cities of 25,000 and over and records the total amount spent during the year for recreation, including parks, organized recreation, cultural and scientific recreation, and other forms. In 1955 the average capital and current expenditure was $5.21 per capita, and this represented less than 4 per cent of the amount spent for all municipal purposes.

How Much Should a City Spend? No definite and universally applicable standard for recreation expenditures is practicable because communities differ in their public recreation needs and in their capacity to finance such a program. A well-to-do suburb with many private resources for individual, family, and group recreation may not need to spend so much per capita for community recreation as an industrial community of the same size; but on the other hand, it may be better able to meet the cost of needed services. Costs for the same facilities and services vary in different parts of the country. Easy and cheap access to facilities furnished by county, state, or Federal agencies may relieve a city of the expense of providing similar facilities. In the final analysis, as Charles E. Doell has stated: "A community should pay for community recreation as much as the citizens are willing to spend—and this depends upon how well informed they may be as to its values and how well satisfied they are with the amount and quality they have already purchased in competition with other values in the community budget." [3]

In spite of varying local factors, experience affords a basis for estimating the approximate amount a community needs to spend if it is to maintain and operate a system of recreation areas and facilities that meets generally accepted standards and if it is to employ the personnel that make possible a rich and varied program serving the entire population. On the basis of local and nationwide studies and after consultation with many experienced leaders, the National Recreation Association estimates that in order to operate and maintain a system of recreation areas and facilities and provide a well-balanced program of recreation activities and services that meet generally accepted standards, a city needs to spend at least $6 per capita annually. This amount would cover the types of service normally rendered by park and recreation departments. It relates to current expenditures only and does not include amounts spent for the expansion or improvement of areas and facilities. It is obvious that a community with limited recreation areas and substandard facilities cannot spend the proposed amount advantageously, but it should be making capital outlays in order to bring its properties up to standard. Some authorities have proposed that a city should spend more than $6 per capita; and if the inflationary tendency persists, a greater amount will certainly be needed.

The association further recommends that one-fourth of the $6 expenditure, or $1.50 per capita, should be spent for leadership salaries and wages, if the city is to employ the personnel required to make possible a well-balanced program. Every community can profitably spend $1.50 per capita for recreation leadership, regardless of the nature or adequacy of its existing indoor and outdoor facilities. It is not feasible to recommend the specific percentage of the total amount that should be spent for organized recreation as compared with traditional park services, but in many cities approximately one-half, or $3 per capita, might be allocated to each type of service.

There is reason to believe that the population of a city is a relatively

[3] "How Much Money Should Be Spent on Community Recreation?" *Recreation*, vol. 46, no. 3, p. 174, June, 1953.

unimportant factor in determining the per capita expenditure necessary to attain a given standard of recreation service. Except for very small communities, which may need to spend more per capita, cities of different population find, as they do in the case of education, that it costs approximately the same amount to provide a given recreation program.

Expenditures in most communities have fallen far short of these suggested amounts, although the number of cities that meet them is constantly increasing. An analysis of expenditures reported in the *1956 Recreation and Park Yearbook* [4] shows that of 908 cities with full-time, year-round recreation leadership, 46 (or 5 per cent) spent $6 or more, thus equaling or exceeding the proposed standard. Of 787 such cities reporting leadership expenditures, 112 (or 14 per cent of the total) met or exceeded the standard of $1.50 per capita. The rise in leadership expenditures is further illustrated by the fact that 36 per cent of the reporting cities spent $1 or more for leadership in 1955, as compared with only 17 per cent in 1950.

RECREATION BUDGETS

Responsibility for raising the funds needed to carry on the recreation program rests primarily with duly constituted officers in the local government and concerns directly the department of finance. Therefore the adoption and administration of the recreation budget are major concerns of the local governing authorities as well as of the recreation department. In general, budgetary procedure is prescribed by city charter, ordinance, or executive order, and applies uniformly to all departments.

The term "budget" in governmental practice is used to denote a plan prepared by an executive or board for financing the work of a department or other public enterprise for a given period. Until it has received the approval of the appropriating body, usually the city council, the budget is merely a proposal. After approval it becomes a controlling financial plan for carrying out a program of operations and services and for raising the necessary revenues for it.

In current practice the budget of the recreation department is set up according to an "object" classification based upon the form recommended by the National Municipal League for recording governmental expenditures. Under this classification the recreation department, like other departments, groups the similar "objects" such as personal services, purchase of supplies, contractual services, or equipment for which expenditures are to be made. This classification normally parallels the one used by the city auditor in classifying accounts; and if it is uniformly adopted by all city departments, it facilitates comparisons of expenditures for

[4] National Recreation Association, New York, 1956.

similar objects among departments. The following are the main headings for an object classification:

Services, personal	Current obligations
Services, contractual	Properties
Commodities	Debt payments
Current charges	

Important as it is for the city authorities to have the recreation department's expenditures recorded by objects, those charged with the operation of the department, as well as the taxpayers, are more interested in the cost of functions. Thus they want to know how much it costs to conduct playgrounds, to operate indoor centers, to maintain golf courses, or to provide a municipal athletic program. Consequently a growing number of recreation authorities are setting up their budgets on a community object-functional basis, known as a performance budget. A work plan is the fundamental basis for such a budget, in which the emphasis is placed upon the services to be rendered with the dollars requested rather than upon what is to be purchased with the dollars. A budget of this type not only provides the department with a definite financial plan, but it indicates to the appropriating authorities and the public the nature and scope of the department's program. A typical list of headings in a department's functional budget appears in the statement on page 508.

Preparing the Budget. Each year the recreation executive requests his supervisors or division heads to submit an estimate of their needs for the following year and the amounts necessary to meet them. He then prepares a tentative budget for the department, which is submitted to his superiors with an accompanying document describing in some detail the purposes for which the money is to be spent. If the department is under a board or commission, its members consider the budget request; and after changing it in any way they see fit, they give it official approval and forward it to the appropriating authorities with a request that the funds be granted. The board should have an opportunity to interpret and justify its request to the authorities before they take final action concerning it. If the executive is responsible directly to a city manager or other official, he submits the tentative budget to this official. In either case, the appropriating authorities consider it along with the estimates of other city departments, make any changes they deem essential or desirable, and determine the amount to be appropriated for recreation and the purposes for which it is to be used. The budget document setting forth these items then becomes the controlling financial plan of the department during the year or period which it covers. School and park districts, as a rule, are not required to submit their budgets to the city authorities for approval.

FINANCIAL RECORDS

Recreation authorities, like other public agencies, are required by law to give an accounting of the use they have made of the funds entrusted to them. Accurate records of all funds received and expended by the department are therefore necessary. Financial records have other important uses, however, for they enable recreation authorities to determine just what their services are costing; without such records it would be impossible to prepare or justify sound budget estimates or to interpret to city officials or to the public the cost of the department's services. Where uniform financial records are kept, the costs of units of service in different years can be compared and evaluated.

Methods of Recording Expenditures. The standard object classification recommended for use by municipal departments in budgeting and in recording current operating and maintenance costs is applicable to even the smallest recreation department.[5] However, records kept according to this classification, which includes personal services, contractual services, commodities, etc., do not furnish all the information essential to the intelligent preparation of a recreation budget. As previously stated, records of expenditures by functions or types of service are also desirable.

The three major types of records recommended under a functional classification relate to administration, facilities, and special services. Under "administration" are recorded all expenditures necessary to the proper running of the department *as a whole,* such as the recreation executive's salary and the expenses of the department office. Under "facilities," separate accounts are set up for each major type of facility operated, such as playgrounds, swimming pools, camps, or stadiums. The term "special services" refers to special phases of the program, such as music, drama, or athletics, which are largely conducted by specialists, are city-wide in scope, and are not confined to the department's facilities.

Owing to the lack of adequate office personnel in many recreation departments, the keeping of financial records and reports has been sadly neglected, and few cost records of this type are available. This situation will not be corrected until recreation and park boards, city managers, mayors, and school authorities insist upon complete financial information and support budget requests for funds to provide the necessary bookkeeping and clerical service. Financial transactions and records are handled by a central municipal fiscal department in many cities, but in gen-

[5] See *Recreation Cost Records,* a committee report issued by the National Recreation Association in 1938, for this classification and for a detailed discussion of financial record-keeping methods for recreation departments.

eral they are based on an object classification, and records of expenditures by functions must be kept in the office of the recreation department.

A Departmental Financial Summary. The accompanying financial statement covering the operations of the Cincinnati, Ohio, Recreation Commission for the year 1956 illustrates a number of factors described in this

Table 21. Cincinnati, Ohio, Recreation Commission, 1956 Financial Summary

Budget for 1956

1/10th mill from statute levy	$166,237.55
Council appropriation from city operating levy	806,031.01
Total 1956 Budget	$972,268.56

Budget Appropriations by Codes

1000 code—personal services	$677,439.00
2000 code—contractual services	65,178.00
3000 code—commodities	115,218.00
4000 code—fixed charges	55,890.56
5000 code—current obligations	56,408.00
6000 code—properties	2,135.00
Total 1956 Budget	$972,268.56

Division Budgets

	Receipts	Expenditures
Airport playfield	$ 58,961.46	$ 59,495.73
Athletics	5,864.50	31,119.23
Community activities	767.84	109,265.83
Correlated activities	3,878.47	68,145.67
General office	14,417.56	145,684.49
Golf	160,732.86	150,705.63
Maintenance	17,776.46	248,724.33
Music	131.19	2,985.25
Nature and camping	86.56	35,241.20
Playgrounds	1,143.67	73,446.13
Tennis and special activities	6,787.45	25,473.99
Engineering and design		7,248.13
Total 1956 receipts and expenditures	$270,548.02°	$957,535.61
Unexpended balance returned to General Fund		$ 14,732.95

Summary

Total appropriation	$972,268.56
Total expenditures	$957,535.61
Total receipts	$270,548.02
Net cost to taxpayers	$686,987.59
Population of Cincinnati	503,998
Net per capita cost	$1.363

° All receipts deposited in city's General Fund.

chapter. The listing of sources of funds indicates that the amount of supplementary appropriated funds is several times as large as the amount received from a special tax levy. The budgeted items are listed in two ways: (1) by an object classification and (2) by divisions of work or functions. The receipts from various recreation facilities and services are also recorded in relation to expenditures; they represent an unusually high percentage of total income and, unlike the practice in a majority of cities, they are deposited in the city's general funds.

FINANCIAL PLANNING

Recreation departments must share with other public agencies the funds that are raised annually to carry on the current functions of local government. Recreation departments' needs for funds to acquire and develop additional properties must be related to similar needs of other branches of the local government. In view of the growing demands for municipal economy and the resulting necessity to justify all requests for public funds for current or capital expenditures, recreation authorities are paying greater attention to fiscal planning. Existing service must be continually appraised in relation to relative needs, values, and numbers served, and plans for extensions of facilities and service must be supported by evidence that the resulting benefits fully justify the cost of putting them into effect. Heretofore recreation programs in many cities have been initiated and properties have been acquired and developed on a more or less opportunistic basis rather than according to a comprehensive plan for the entire city. Such procedure has been accepted largely because the need for facilities and services has been so apparent. There is reason to believe, however, that adequate recreation systems or programs will never be achieved in most cities until the recreation authorities have worked out sound long-range plans that are acceptable to the public and that include provisions for financing the cost. Some of the finest improvements in recent years have occurred in cities where a long-range program, based upon an expert study of local conditions and needs, has merited and secured public approval and financial support.

32. RECORDS, REPORTS, AND RESEARCH

THE FUNCTION of the recreation department is to help make available to all the people of the locality satisfying, constructive, leisure-time activities. The essential records of the department should therefore indicate in some way the enjoyment that has resulted from the program and its contribution to a fuller, richer life in the community. Obviously such intangible factors cannot be measured with accuracy, and it is necessary to rely upon various types of statistical information. Records of the number of people served by the department, the types of activities and facilities provided, and the comparative costs of the latter furnish the best basis now available for recording the extent and quality of the department's service.

Records are designed to serve various uses. A complete accounting of all department receipts and expenditures is generally required by law, but recreation authorities also owe it to the public to give a report of their stewardship over the funds entrusted to them. Only as a department demonstrates that it has rendered a worthwhile service can it merit or expect continued public support. Moreover, carefully kept records are essential to the preparation of departmental reports, without which recreation authorities cannot appraise or evaluate their activities, centers, or services. Intelligent planning for the future must be based upon an analysis of existing conditions and needs, which can be determined only as adequate data are available. Operation of a recreation department, like any other enterprise, requires current as well as accumulated records of personnel, facilities, programs, and business transactions. Because the records and reports of the recreation department are so numerous and important, a separate division is usually created to handle them.

RECORDS AND REPORTS

Financial Records. Major responsibility for departmental finances rests with the central office, but specific instructions for handling and recording funds must be given all employees whose work involves receiving or paying out money. This applies especially at facilities where charges are

510

made or fees are collected, such as golf courses or boathouses, or where refreshments are sold. Accurate daily reports are submitted to the department office on specially prepared forms. Types of financial records in recreation include budget work sheets, estimates, requests, appropriations, expenditures, and balances; accounting records including sources, amounts, and disposition of department funds and detailed statements of expenditures; records of income and operating costs of areas and facilities such as golf courses or swimming pools; records of capital expenditures; time sheets, payrolls, absences, workmen's liability cases, and funds; purchase orders, quotations, deliveries, contracts, concessions, bids, agreements, and reports; and insurance policies. The specific information recorded corresponds in general to financial data required in business establishments.

Recreation-service Records. Unlike financial records, which conform to usual business procedures, records of recreation service are directly related to the peculiar functions and objectives of the recreation department. For this reason and because of the special problems and difficulties encountered in adequately recording recreation services, special consideration is given to such records. Accurate reports are essential for two reasons: (1) They indicate the nature and scope of the activities provided by the department and the extent to which the people have taken advantage of the opportunities extended to them; (2) they enable authorities to evaluate the units in the recreation system and the various program features and to determine the relationship between their costs and the services rendered. Without such records it is impossible to budget funds intelligently or to plan wisely for the future. The records specifically include daily, weekly, monthly, seasonal, and annual reports of directors and managers of individual playgrounds, centers, and special facilities; reports of district and special supervisors; departmental reports of the superintendent; programs of special events, institutes, and other features; and registration and attendance at the department's activities and facilities. It is exceedingly important that the forms used for these reports be designed to facilitate the recording of all essential data. The periods covered by them vary, but the weekly report is perhaps the most common. It usually contains not only a record of service rendered but also information of administrative value to the department, such as reports of property damage, needed repairs, time records, or requisitions for supplies.[1]

Two questions commonly asked concerning the volume and extent of a recreation department's service are, How many different individuals

[1] For a suggested weekly playground report form and a detailed discussion of playground records see George D. Butler, *Playgrounds: Their Administration and Operation*, rev. ed., The Ronald Press Company, New York, 1950.

were served during the year? (the registration figure) and, What was the total attendance at all its activities and facilities? (the attendance figure). Whereas registration figures reveal the spread of the recreation department's service, attendance figures indicate its volume. A thoughtful questioner would also want to know how these figures were distributed among the various parts of the program and among the different age groups and neighborhoods. Ridley and Simon have pointed out: [2]

The record of attendance must be considered a measure both of performance and to a certain extent of results. For one of the objectives that recreation strives for is the very relaxation and enjoyment implied by participation. And the fact that adults prefer the municipal recreation program to alternative uses of leisure time is presumptive evidence that the recreational program is fulfilling its purposes.

Registration. Few recreation departments can estimate the number of different individuals served because the very nature of many recreation activities makes it difficult to obtain satisfactory attendance records. It is practically impossible to record the names of the individuals who use such facilities as a bathing beach, picnic center, athletic field, or handball court or who attend outdoor dances or band concerts. On the other hand, registration forms used at playgrounds and centers and for certain city-wide activities furnish authorities a definite record of the individuals regularly reached by these services. Since the registration forms give information as to age, sex, place of residence, and other factors, they furnish valuable data for use in studying and evaluating the services rendered different segments of the community.

Most recreation authorities believe the practical difficulties of keeping complete registration records outweigh their potential value. It is more important to know that a bathing beach is used to capacity and affords a certain number of swims (the attendance figure) than to know how many different persons use it during the season (the registration figure). Records of the total registration in drama groups, craft classes, and athletic leagues, on the other hand, which are relatively easy to obtain and indicate the degree of balance in the department's program, are kept by an increasing number of departments, and registration at playgrounds and indoor centers is fairly common.

Attendance. Unless they are broken down according to functions or activities, the significance of attendance figures is limited. Furthermore, participants and spectators should be recorded separately. Attendance data have little comparative value outside the department because the methods used to determine them vary widely. If determined according

[2] Clarence E. Ridley and Herbert A. Simon, *Measuring Municipal Activities,* International City Managers' Association, Chicago, 1938, chap. 7, p. 32.

to a sound, uniform basis over a period of years, however, they not only measure the service rendered but in case of a marked increase in attendance may serve to justify a request for additional funds or personnel.

The most feasible unit of playground attendance is the "visit." Test studies furnish a basis for estimating the average length of visit, if this information is desired. At the indoor center, where most activities are conducted on a highly organized basis and where many of the groups have a definite membership and meet regularly with the same leader, the problem of determining attendance is relatively simple. Attendance at pools, dance pavilions, picnic centers, toboggan slides, and other facilities can be determined with considerable accuracy, especially if a system of permits or fees is in effect.

Recording Summer Playground Attendance. In 1938 a committee of recreation executives sponsored a study conducted by the National Recreation Association for the purpose of developing a more accurate, uniform method of recording attendance at summer playgrounds. Based on its study of eighty-three playgrounds in forty-three cities, which involved an actual record of each person entering the grounds during a one-week period, and taking peak counts hourly, the committee recommended the following formula, which playground authorities have subsequently used in many cities: [3]

The Committee recommends that in determining playground attendance a careful count be taken at the peak of attendance during each morning, afternoon, or evening period during which the playground is open under leadership. (The afternoon session is considered as the period between the noon and evening meal, and the evening session the period between the evening meal and dark, or closing time.) This peak count furnishes the basis for recording attendance as follows: the morning count has an index value of 50; the afternoon count an index value of 40; and the evening count an index value of 66⅔. *In order to determine the actual attendance, the morning count is multiplied by 2, the afternoon count by 2.5, and the evening count by 1.5. The sum of these attendances represents the total for the day.* For example, if the peak count at a given playground is 50 in the morning, 100 in the afternoon, and 120 in the evening, the morning attendance will be 100, the afternoon attendance 250, and the evening attendance 180, making a total attendance for the day of 530.

Experience has proven the formula to be sound, and it is widely used in reporting summer playground attendance. Adaptations may be advisable at individual playgrounds with unusual conditions, but they should be based upon records secured by test counts. The formula is applicable only during the summer or vacation season and to participants in the playground program; it cannot be applied to a large spectator attendance.

[3] See *A New Formula for Determining Summer Playground Attendance,* National Recreation Association, New York, 1938.

A breakdown of total playground attendance figures by special activities—dramatics, nature, art, etc.—would be desirable but is not practical in most departments under present conditions. One of the values of such records, as of the other types previously mentioned, is to enable the authorities to estimate the unit costs of different types of service.

Other Departmental Records. The number and specific types of the following records, as well as those previously discussed, depend on the department's individual needs.

Legal Action, Policies, and Records. Legislation relating to the department, rules and regulations adopted, minutes of board meetings, official correspondence, department policies, legal actions and court decisions affecting the department, and the departmental organization plan.

Description of Properties. List of all departmental areas, their location, acreage, cost, assessed valuation, date and method of acquisition, facilities, and equipment; blueprints and drawings for all areas, buildings, facilities, and equipment; surveys and city maps; cost estimates and construction costs; specifications and inventories; and long-range plans for acquisitions and developments.

Personnel Records. Lists of all employees with their personnel and service records; volunteer activity leaders and their service records; members of advisory councils, committees, and neighborhood recreation groups; individuals with permits for golf, tennis, skating, and other activities; membership lists of all teams, clubs, associations, and groups affiliated with the department and their officers; playground and indoor-center registration lists; and winners in department activities, events, and tournaments.

Administrative Records. Permits and reservations for department properties; copies of publicity issued; instructions and suggestions for department workers; attendance reports; schedules of athletic leagues, interplayground programs, club activities, and city-wide projects; reports of complaints, property damage, and accidents resulting from department activities; and program forecasts.

Record Forms. In order to simplify record keeping, to secure uniform procedure throughout the department, and to reduce costs to a minimum, a variety of forms and blanks is used. Some of them have been mentioned. Certain forms, particularly those used for keeping financial, personnel, and other business data, have been highly standardized, and in some cities they are prescribed by the municipal authorities for use in all city departments. There is a wide diversity, however, in the types of forms used for recording recreation service and for administrative purposes. Special care must be taken in preparing the forms to make sure that they can be filled out easily and quickly, yield the essential data desired, and facilitate tabulation of the data in summary form. Careful instructions as to the methods and conditions of using the forms are also essential. Large cities with a comprehensive program use scores of such forms, but only a few types can be mentioned here:

Activity Report Forms. Daily, weekly, monthly, or seasonal. Separate forms are required for the playground, the recreation building or indoor center, golf course, camp, beach, and other facilities. Special forms are also needed for the supervisors, the specialists, and the executive.

Attendance Report Forms. Daily, weekly, monthly, or seasonal. These are sometimes combined with activity report forms.

Permits and Reservations. Applications for permits to use a building, facility, or area; individual registration cards; permit blanks for teams; etc.

Program Forms. Typical of the many forms used in conducting the program are the following athletic forms: team roster blanks, individual registration and entry forms, applications for affiliation, report forms for athletic officials, team reservation blanks, individual contracts and releases, receipt blanks for entry fees, financial reports, certificates of award, score sheets, schedule blanks, etc.

Administrative Forms. Accident and property damage reports including follow-up, requisitions, work plan, registration, achievement records, physicians' certification, parents' permission, and individual attendance record.

The Annual Department Report. The annual report of the recreation department, required by law in most cities, is based in large measure upon the records submitted by its workers throughout the year. The essential qualities of a good municipal report, as indicated by the International City Managers' Association, merit mention here: [4]

Specifically it explains the purpose and method of operation of the department; it describes major steps which have been taken to improve and modernize departmental operations; it attempts to measure the results attained, using the best statistical indices available, but not confining the evaluation to quantitative devices; it works the statistics into the text, relating them in proper perspective to the situation as a whole. Finally, it discusses the major problems of policy facing the department, attempting to give the reader information which will help him exercise intelligent citizenship.

Many recreation department reports are devoted largely to accounts of activities carried on during the year, and little ingenuity is used in presenting the facts graphically. Increasingly, however, departments use the annual report to interpret their objectives, to describe important progress in attaining them, or to stimulate desired action on major problems.

[4] "What Annual Municipal Reports Contain," *Public Management*, vol. 21, no. 1, p. 5, January, 1939.

Recreation executives have made considerable progress in recent years in making reports readable and effective as means of public education by the introduction of charts, graphs, and illustrative material.

Library and Information Files. In addition to the records relating specifically to its official procedures and program, the department needs a library and information file. These should contain general books on rec-

"It's More Fun to Live in Waterloo" is the title of this montage illustrating the activities in the city's recreation program (Courtesy of Waterloo, Iowa, Recreation Commission).

reation theory, philosophy, and administration; research reports and surveys; suggestions and rules for conducting all forms of recreation activities; descriptions and plans of recreation programs and facilities; and accounts of such services in other cities. Much of this information is mimeographed or printed in the form of books, bulletins, circulars, magazine articles, reports, charts, or blueprints. Data as to the city—its agencies, facilities, resources, finances, and programs—are kept in the information file, along with material on the values of recreation, developments throughout the nation, and other pertinent data relative to the movement. The information is available for use in in-service training, for study by the workers, and for use by the staff in planning activities and programs, in the preparation of speeches and publicity, and in serving the public in various ways. Copies of *Recreation,* professional journals, and other magazines dealing with recreation and related subjects should be available for current use as well as for reference and study.

Competent Office Workers Essential. No record system, however adequate it may be, will serve its purpose unless trained, competent personnel are employed for the department office. Many recreation departments are losing much in efficiency because their budgets do not provide needed clerical and accounting workers. Some highly trained recreation executives devote time to record keeping which might better be spent in developing or supervising the program. In order to do their work satisfactorily, office workers require carefully selected, properly arranged, and well-maintained office space and equipment. The ability to supply prompt and accurate information makes for effectiveness within the department and also gives city officials and the public a favorable impression of the department's efficiency and service.

A Work Schedule. A work schedule or calendar for each division greatly facilitates the carrying out of essential tasks on scheduled time. Many of the duties of the executive, for example, must be done each year at a given time; others are required regularly each month; some are seasonal responsibilities. The office manager must prepare reports of different types which are due at specified periods, and the supervisor of maintenance and construction must plan ahead in order to accomplish the many duties that otherwise would be crowded into the outdoor season and to make the best use of his workers. The preparation of a calendar for each month or season of the year listing the projects to be planned, started, or completed by the various workers during the period is a great aid to administration and operations.

RESEARCH IN THE RECREATION DEPARTMENT

Up to this point consideration has been limited to the current, continuous, routine records and reports. These furnish the necessary data for conducting the normal work of the department, but they do not afford all the information required by progressive authorities. Many problems and questions that arise in conducting the work of a recreation department cannot be answered satisfactorily without special study. The increasing complexity of the recreation field, the growing insistence that factual data support requests for funds for new or expanded facilities or programs, and the need for appraising and revising policies and procedures periodically have forced authorities to assemble facts on which to develop policies and programs and which will lend weight to their demands.

Because of the variable human factors underlying recreation service, it is easier to gather factual data than it is to draw definite conclusions from them. As Joseph Lee once said, "It is difficult, for instance, to know what games a thousand or so of these boys would really like if they had tried them and to find out the real reasons that cause them to come to the playgrounds or to stay away." [5] Nevertheless, studies of local conditions affecting recreation and of the leisure-time needs and interests of people have proved useful in program planning and in the development of recreation policies, and the number of local studies have increased greatly in recent years. The problems, methods, limitations, and values of research conducted by a recreation department were described in detail at the 1957 National Recreation Congress.[6]

Types of Research. Bigness is not an essential qualification for successful research. A single administrator seeking to supplement his personal judgment by gathering information based on observation, inquiry, or study can sometimes achieve more satisfactory results than a comprehensive survey. The careful analysis of playground and indoor-center reports for the purpose of determining unit costs, the relation of registration to attendance, and other factors is an essential and continuous type of research. Special studies of leisure-time interests, neighborhood conditions, future playground sites, street accidents, or juvenile delinquency in relation to playgrounds are required only from time to time. A type of study that is becoming fairly common is the appraisal of the recreation department in comparison with generally accepted criteria of service. A most ambitious form of local recreation research is the city-wide survey, which includes a study of many community agencies and factors affecting the services of the recreation department and the development of a long-range plan of action.

Studies of Recreation Interests. Attempts by authorities to ascertain recreation interests answer the criticism that recreation programs follow a standard pattern or are unrelated to the wishes of the individuals to be served. Occasional inquiries as to the recreation preferences of various segments of the population enable the recreation authorities to keep pace with changing interests and needs and to initiate new features for which a desire is indicated. Typical of such an inquiry is a study conducted in Long Beach, California, by the recreation department, which asked the

---

[5] "A Possible Justification of Research," *The Survey,* vol. 65, no. 12, p. 651, March, 1931.

[6] E. H. Thacker, "Research in Action," *Recreation,* vol. 51, no. 1, p. 12, January, 1958.

junior and senior high school boys and girls of the city to answer the following questions on a blank listing thirty-eight activities:

1. What activities do you frequently engage in?
2. What are your three favorite activities?
3. Indicate the activities concerning which you would like more information and greater opportunity.

The information obtained from an analysis of the blanks filled out by 3,340 students afforded a valuable guide for the modification of the program for young people.

Studies of the recreation interests of adults vary from the informal inquiry as to the desires of persons attending an individual center to community-wide surveys. It is rather common for persons enrolling at indoor centers to be asked in what activities they would care to participate. More extensive studies involve the widespread distribution of forms on which people are asked to indicate their present leisure-time activities, their group affiliations, unmet recreation interests, and other pertinent data. Studies of this type, especially if they contain questions designed to secure opinions as to local facilities, programs, or needs, prove exceedingly useful to local recreation authorities.

Playground Studies. Many studies have centered about the playground. Attempts have been made, for example, to determine the effect of playgrounds upon the valuation of property in the neighborhood. A careful analysis of the cost of playground supplies is reported to have reduced by one-half the amount spent for such supplies in one city. A three-year study of playground accidents, sponsored by a committee of recreation workers in Southern California cities, resulted in the elimination of apparatus presenting the greatest accident hazards and pointed out the need for protecting players in organized games through better supervision and more instruction. Attempts to trace the influence of playgrounds upon juvenile delinquency by comparing the number of arrests in neighborhoods without playgrounds and in the vicinity of play areas are numerous. Exceedingly valuable studies have been made of the relative drawing power of playgrounds of different sizes, leadership, and facilities. The study of playground attendance referred to earlier in this chapter yielded valuable data on the keeping of records. The relationship of leadership to the participants and activities at different portions of selected playgrounds in Los Angeles was one of the factors revealed in a recent study in that city.[7]

Area and Facility Studies. Most cities require additional areas, buildings, and facilities, but sound recommendations for acquiring and devel-

[7] Norman P. Miller and Irving S. Piliavin, *Public Recreation Service Units—Measuring Youth Services Needs*, Welfare Planning Council, Los Angeles, 1956.

oping them cannot be made except after a thorough study of neighborhood and city-wide conditions. Population trends, zoning, housing conditions, land uses and values, existing recreation resources, and other factors must be recorded and analyzed in relation to a system of recreation areas. All recreation planning must be done in the light of over-all neighborhood, city, and regional planning and must conform to basic master plans for the area. The high cost of land, especially in built-up sections, the difficulty in securing funds for the purchase of land in undeveloped areas, and the current high costs of labor and materials make it doubly important that all recommendations for new areas and facilities be based on studies that have demonstrated the wisdom of the projects. Long-range plans involving the acquisition of properties and the improvement of varied facilities have been developed and adopted in a large number of cities of all sizes. Preparation of these plans involves a recording of existing conditions and resources, their appraisal in the light of present standards and estimated future needs, and the formulation of specific recommendations for action. The thorough and intelligent research involved in the preparation of these long-range programs has been a factor in their approval by the local authorities and the public.

Other Research Problems. Other subjects that merit more thoughtful study are the basis for making fees and charges and the effects of such charges upon participation, the carry-over of recreation activities into the home, ways in which the recreation department may serve problem children, causes of failure and success in recreation programs, the comparative unit costs of providing different types of activities, the optimum size of different types of recreation groups, the relation of size and design to effectiveness of a playground or playfield, better methods of determining and serving recreation interests, methods of administering municipal sports activities, the possibilities of volunteer recreation leadership as a form of leisure-time activity, more accurate ways of recording recreation service, and sounder criteria for judging its effectiveness.

The Recreation Survey. Other studies, generally comprehensive in nature and commonly known as surveys, are concerned with such subjects as the leisure time of the people, an appraisal of the recreation department or of the recreation services of all agencies in a city, or the essential procedure for establishing a recreation department in the locality. These studies are seldom conducted by a recreation department; but since they involve an analysis and appraisal of its services, a consideration of its relationship to other community agencies, and specific recommendations affecting its work, the recreation department has a vital interest in them. Funds for conducting such community surveys are usually provided by local foundations, civic organizations, community chests, or committees of citizens concerned about recreation conditions in the city, although the surveys are sometimes financed from local tax funds.

Before a Survey. Because of the expense, time, and effort involved in conducting a recreation survey, it is of the highest importance that needs, objectives, and procedures be clearly defined and accepted by the parties involved in the project. Agreement should be reached as to the key problems to be faced and the best methods of tackling them. If a survey is considered necessary, it should be planned so as to secure facts that are essential for the formulation of sound conclusions and recommendations. There should be reasonable assurance that the group sponsoring the survey has sufficient influence to assure action deemed desirable on the basis of the findings. For this reason involvement of the local authorities is advisable. Appointment of a survey committee that is both influential and widely representative of community interests, and the active participation of this committee in the survey, help ensure the members' support of resulting recommendations. Selection of a competent director is a most important committee function.

In most comprehensive surveys the task of gathering the information desired involves the use of questionnaires, personal observation, personal interviews, special studies, and analysis of facts available from other local surveys and from the records of public and private agencies. The director requires the assistance of paid or volunteer workers, and in some cases committees have been organized to supervise the gathering of data on special subjects.

Tabulation and analysis of the findings afford the basis for preliminary conclusions and recommendations. These should be discussed thoroughly, especially with representatives of agencies involved, and should be officially approved by the committee before any proposals are publicized. Reports that are brief, concise, and written in simple, direct language are most effective. The official report should be accompanied by comprehensive supporting data, but a summary of the findings and recommendations is adequate for wide public distribution.

After the Survey—What? The purpose of the survey is to secure data upon which to develop a sound plan of action. Wide publicity interpreting the findings and the recommendations is essential to secure public understanding and support. Some particular group, usually the one responsible for initiating and conducting the study, is assigned responsibility for securing definite action on the recommendations in the report. Such action may involve the acquisition or improvement of areas, revision of the form of local recreation organization, appointment of an official or advisory citizen group, staff reorganization, coordination of recreation services, redistribution of recreation functions, or changes in financial support. Only as the desired results are attained—in whole or in part—does the recreation survey achieve the purpose for which it was carried on. A specific plan of action, intelligently and persistently promoted, is essential to success.

EVALUATING RECREATION SERVICE

Recreation authorities today recognize the need for evaluating the work which they are doing and for strengthening the shortcomings of their service. They have been stimulated in this self-analysis by an appraisal form for rating a community's recreation facilities and programs that has been prepared by the National Recreation Association and used in many cities.[8] Committees of recreation executives in more than one of the association's service districts have given painstaking study to evaluation methods.

Any city attempting to appraise or score its provisions for recreation is brought face to face with the need for two kinds of data. One consists of complete and accurate service records, without which a valid appraisal cannot be made. The other is a set of standards for areas, facilities, personnel, programs, participation, administration, finance, and other factors. Fairly acceptable standards have been adopted for some of these factors, as described earlier in this volume, but criteria for rating others are still inadequate. Periodic evaluations give evidence that the recreation department is willing to face criticism and desires to improve the quality of its service and adjust its program to changing needs.

Students majoring in recreation in colleges and universities have been used effectively in appraising the local recreation facilities and programs. In one city, for example, committees of graduate students were assigned to study such varied features as the municipal golf course, swimming pools, indoor recreation centers, and playgrounds. Besides observing the operation of the facilities, the students sought comments and opinions from the persons who used them. Recommendations presented in the reports prompted the recreation department to modify some of its policies and procedures. Recreation authorities have also joined with councils of social agencies in sponsoring studies designed to appraise and improve the operations and services of public and private agencies.

Securing Suggestions from Workers. Workers in the recreation department are particularly well fitted because of their training and intimate relationship to the people served to observe the shortcomings of its program and administration. Executives who realize this encourage their personnel to submit constructive criticism and from time to time attempt to secure specific suggestions from all of them. At the end of the summer

[8] *Schedule for the Appraisal of Community Recreation,* National Recreation Association, New York, 1951.

playground or indoor-center season, for example, the executives submit a questionnaire to all directors and supervisors asking for comments on the program and its operation. The information gathered in this way, while recollections of the past season are fresh in mind, presents a record of mistakes and successes and suggests desirable changes which may prove exceedingly useful in evaluating policies, procedures, and programs. Such a questionnaire yields results only if workers are convinced that their frank opinions are really desired, will receive consideration, and will be treated as confidential.

33. PUBLIC RELATIONS

Lᴀᴄᴋ ᴏF public understanding of the value and need of recreation, particularly of recreation leadership, has been one of the greatest obstacles to the growth and support of the recreation movement. The question, Why teach a child to play? typified the prevailing attitude for many years; even today many people fail to understand why recreation should be a matter of concern to local government. The demonstration of the worth of recreation during the Depression years of the 1930s and the two world wars helped to eliminate much public misunderstanding and apathy toward community recreation and to develop an appreciation of its positive values. Increasingly local recreation authorities and state and national agencies concerned with recreation are utilizing various media and methods of informing the public concerning the significance of recreation and its importance in the life of the people. A continuous program of public education is essential to assure not only adequate financial support for the recreation program but maximum participation and resulting benefits to the people it is designed to serve.

THE NATURE OF PUBLIC RELATIONS

According to *Fortune* magazine, public relations is good performance publicly appreciated because it is adequately communicated. This concise definition emphasizes several factors that are of primary importance to the public relations of a recreation department. It implies that unless the department functions on a high order, it is futile to publicize its service. Good performance alone is not sufficient for a recreation department, however, because public support requires that the people know about and appreciate its service. In order to achieve this result, adequate means of communication between the department and the public must be maintained continuously. The recreation department that performs effectively and keeps two-way communications open between itself and the public is assured of understanding and support.

The staff of the recreation department must understand that the public interest is of paramount importance and that every contact with the

524

public should be utilized to create good will for the program. Public relations is the implementation of a plan for creating and maintaining a favorable public opinion toward the work of the department. The plan involves the use of a variety of procedures and media. It consists of presenting and interpreting information and ideas to the public and at the same time of getting ideas and opinions from them. Some of the procedures and media used in a public relations program are described in this chapter.

PERSONAL CONTACTS

Public relations permeates the entire operation of a recreation department, but it is maintained primarily in two ways—through personal contacts and through publicity media. The Greensboro, North Carolina, Park and Recreation Department has offered some helpful suggestions to its workers in a manual entitled *Let's Take a Look at Our Public Relations*. It reminds its staff to:

Be courteous, friendly and thoughtful
Use all available information to help solve each problem
Not to be indifferent, impatient, inaccurate, or vague
Treat each problem with the sincere interest and respect which it is due.

It also offers tips on the right and wrong ways to act:

Right	*Wrong*
Courteous service	"We're doing you a favor" touch
Sincere attention	The "brush-off"
Prompt handling	The "run-around"
Patience and fortitude	The "let-them-wait" attitude
Specific referral	The temperamental touch

Influencing Factors. Each contact with an individual or group presents an opportunity to develop a favorable attitude toward and a confidence in the department. The courteous, efficient handling of inquiries or complaints in person or over the telephone, the expression of appreciation verbally or by letters for services rendered the department, the readiness to praise publicly individuals or groups that have done an unusually fine job and to give generous credit to cooperating agencies, the willingness to admit mistakes or failures when they occur—these are important elements in public relations. It goes without saying that a neat appearance and orderly conduct on the part of all employees tend to give the public a favorable impression of the department. The manner in which properties are maintained also influences the public attitude toward the department. People who do not participate in its program judge it in large measure by the extent to which its areas, buildings, and facilities are clean, well kept, and attractive.

Personal contacts with individuals and groups afford an excellent means of interpreting the objectives and services of the department, of influencing public opinion, and of securing valuable advice and suggestions for improving the service of the department. Much can be gained by talking with the man in the street, with parents of playground children, and with participants in the program. Opportunities are sought for the superintendent and other members of the recreation department staff to address meetings of neighborhood and community groups, such as parent-teacher associations, luncheon clubs, chambers of commerce, women's clubs, and labor unions, to name only a few. Talks are often supplemented by the use of display materials—motion pictures of local recreation activities, colored slides, slide films, objects made by recreation groups—or by question and discussion periods. These occasions are utilized to interpret the work of the department in a way that will appeal to the special interest of the group and in many instances to request some specific form of cooperation or action.

Satisfied Customers. No factor is more influential in gaining support for the recreation department than the good will of the people who benefit from its facilities and program. Their appreciation and their readiness to support the department are directly proportionate to the value and benefit which they attach to its services. Providing recreation areas and offering recreation activities do not necessarily produce "satisfied customers" unless there is a courteous, friendly, helpful attitude on the part of the recreation staff. This is a great asset to the department and a most significant aspect of its public relations program. In case the department requires evidence of public support, the mobilization of the people who have benefited from its services places at its disposal a force of inestimable influence and value.

Volunteers. No recreation department can expect to develop a satisfactory public relations program if it relies entirely upon the members of its paid staff. The more people involved in its operations, the more they will know what it is trying to accomplish, and the more public understanding and support the department will receive. Several recreation departments that have no budget item for a specially trained public relations worker have enlisted the help of such persons on a volunteer basis. As a service to the department, volunteers give advice in preparing the annual report, laying out the copy for a publicity booklet, framing a questionnaire and plan for conducting a research project, instructing the paid staff in methods of dealing with the public, producing radio or television programs, setting up a speakers' bureau, and countless other ways. Formation of a public relations advisory committee composed of a public relations executive, a newspaperman, artist, advertising layout man, and other skilled and experienced people can be of immeasurable value to a recreation department and give genuine satisfaction to the committee members.

Lay citizens are likewise effective in advising the recreation department as to the community's needs and interests as well as in interpreting its objectives and services. Reference was made in Chapter 10 to the ways in which members of groups such as recreation boards and commissions, advisory committees and councils formed on a neighborhood or city-wide basis, and playground mothers' clubs serve the recreation department. They are usually people with influence, civic interest, and wide contacts in the locality. By encouraging the formation of such groups and by working closely with them, the recreation executive and his staff assure a corps of volunteers in their public relations program.

PUBLICITY

Public opinion favorable to recreation must be systematically cultivated in order that the recreation department can attain its objectives. Furnishing recreation is the department's chief function, and efficient recreation service goes far in establishing good will; but it alone does not bring appropriations, votes, and widespread moral support. The recreation department needs an effective publicity program for the following reasons:

1. It must inform people in the city where its areas and facilities are, when they are open for use, and what activities are being carried on.
2. On the whole, its services involve human relationships, and participation in the program is on an individual basis. To a greater extent than is true of other city departments, the people must know about the services of the recreation department in order to benefit from them.
3. Since meagerness of recreation opportunities in many cities is primarily due to a lack of public understanding of the significance of recreation in the life of the individual and the community, a program of education as to the value and need of recreation is a responsibility of the department and is necessary in order to assure its continued financial support.
4. The widespread publicity, primarily from commercial agencies, designed to promote leisure-time activities makes it important that people should likewise be informed about publicly sponsored recreation services at their disposal.
5. Leadership, the cardinal element of municipal recreation, must be interpreted to be understood by the public.

Recreation publicity ranges in scope from intermittent newspaper notices on activities to a carefully planned year-round program of interpretation designed to create favorable public relations for the recreation department. Systematic publicity requires just as thorough advance planning as the budget and activity program. It is effective in so far as

A calendar of special playground events helps people plan their summer schedule (Courtesy of Butler, Pa., Recreation Department).

it has clearly visualized purposes, is directed toward definite groups, consists of wisely selected material, is timed appropriately, and utilizes all suitable media and available channels. The following pages contain a discussion of some of these planning factors, as applied to recreation department publicity.

Purposes. The objectives of such publicity may be summarized briefly as follows:

1. To give the public an accounting of the work accomplished.
2. To encourage people to participate in the activities and to use the facilities offered by the department.
3. To impress the public with the extent, variety, and accomplishments of the department's services.
4. To prepare the minds of citizens for proposed changes or expansion in the recreation system, such as the acquisition of needed areas, increased appropriations, or a new method of reserving tennis courts.
5. To interpret the significance of recreation and its importance in the life of the people.
6. To secure specific action in support of the department, such as signing a petition, speaking favorably of a measure, or voting in approval of a referendum.
7. To enlist individuals to give volunteer service in some specific form.
8. To give people information or suggestions on how to conduct recreation activities or construct facilities. Examples are radio talks on conducting picnics or newspaper articles on homemade play equipment.

The Various Publics. The community is not just one great public, identical in outlook, interests, and responsiveness, but a number of publics. Consequently, recreation publicity to be effective must be directed toward one or more of these groups. Often it is appropriately of the blunderbuss variety, directed to practically everybody at one time, but there are other occasions when the information is for particular groups and has a limited appeal, in which cases rifle-shot techniques must be used. Analysis of systematic publicity programs shows the attempt to focus on these different publics.

Summer playgrounds are of primary interest to children and their parents, so folders describing them are distributed through the schools and carried home by the children. Posters in places of employment, articles in company publications, and shop committees are effective means of informing workers of plans for an industrial recreation program. Addresses before civic and luncheon clubs afford opportunities for presenting special recreation needs to groups of influential citizens. To arouse interest in a neighborhood recreation center, posters in local stores and agencies, talks before neighborhood groups, the distribution of folders, and statements by local clergymen and other leaders have proved effective. Accounts of athletic activities, published on the sports page, reach the group most interested in them.

Content. The familiar formula for a news story may be applied to recreation publicity. That is, it should tell who, what, when, where, how, and why. Such information is required not simply for given events or projects but for the program of the department as a whole. In practice, since recreation is something people want and touches so many of them, it has proven easy for any live department to answer the fundamental questions except for the final one: Why? An analysis based on replies to a questionnaire sent to recreation departments in representative cities showed that only a minority paid much attention to this question.

Except during financial crises, publicity centers chiefly about past or projected activities rather than the plans and objectives of the department or the needs and social values of recreation. Nevertheless, an invitation to "come have a good time" is a common note in publicity announcing forthcoming events. Department reports increasingly contain quotations from local or national leaders on the value and philosophy of recreation, statements of local recreation needs, and recommendations for future expansion of facilities or programs.

Most departments take advantage of the appointment of new board members, staff changes, the construction of new facilities, the addition of areas, the inauguration of new activities, and special program features to secure publicity, especially in the daily press. They stress the numbers using their facilities or taking part in their programs and the variety of activities offered the public. The inexpensiveness of municipal recreation in terms of low per capita costs or small percentages of the tax dollar is often emphasized. The effect of this emphasis, however, unaccompanied by statements of unmet needs or of standard or desirable expenditures, has conditioned some communities to accept inadequate recreation budgets as normal.

Many people recognize recreation as essential to normal living and having sufficient value in itself to require no further justification. Communities as a whole, however, are more ready to support a recreation program if they are convinced that it contributes to health, safety, and character, particularly if it can be shown that it also results in financial savings. Consequently, the values frequently advanced for spending public funds for recreation are crime prevention, safety to children, health building, and character growth. In many a city during a referendum campaign on the establishment of a recreation department, fliers, posters, and news stories have declared that it would keep the children off the streets, save their lives, build their health, guard their character, and prevent juvenile delinquency. These same values were stressed in a campaign in Milwaukee to increase the tax levy for recreation. The publicity included a table showing the city's good crime record and appealed to citizens to interest themselves in boys and their future. An exhibit in a

Decatur, Illinois, campaign displayed a miniature baseball diamond and beside it, for contrast, a miniature jail.

The overemphasis on by-products of a recreation program can be overcome by stressing its positive values, such as greater joy to the individual and a richer community life. Recreation's contribution to training for citizenship, its relationship to successful family living and to the prevention of mental illness, and the opportunity which the recreation

Lighted outdoor displays are an appropriate feature of a community Christmas observance and attract wide attention (Courtesy of Dearborn, Mich., Department of Parks and Recreation).

program offers for applying the methods and principles of democracy have not been stressed adequately in many cities.

Timing. The most appropriate timing of publicity depends on the nature of its objectives. Statesmanlike executives begin to educate their boards, advisory committees, and the public as to needed major improvements involving large sums of money months or even years before they hope to have them put into effect. Sudden attempts to secure favorable action on such projects are likely to end in defeat. The foundations of referendum campaigns are usually laid three to six months before Election Day, with a gradual intensification of effort on all fronts, reaching a climax one or two days before the vote. Advance publicity and planning for special events, institutes, and other projects involving the recruiting of personnel start weeks or months prior to the event.

A continuous program of public education the year round is much more valuable than splurges of copious publicity at infrequent intervals. Local happenings of wide public interest, such as the opening of a public housing project or the announcement of a new city plan, furnish an opportunity for publicity concerning some phase of the recreation department's work. A drowning in an unprotected stream may serve as the basis for a campaign for a swimming pool. A report on street accidents can be interpreted as evidence of the effectiveness of playgrounds as a safety measure or of the need for more such service.

Media of Publicity. The familiar media and devices for publicity generally employed in American communities have been used to a greater or lesser extent by all recreation departments.

Newspapers. The newspaper has been the principal stand-by of the recreation department. A good recreation program directly affects and interests so many newspaper readers that the press readily gives it good coverage. In large cities this extends to regular calls at the recreation department office by reporters. The preparation of live news copy requires reasonable skill in news writing on the part of the recreation executive or some member of his staff. There is a great deal of truth in the statement that although playing, like eating and sleeping, is a fundamental instinct, in print it is likely to sound dull unless treated with skill. The recreation program affords much material in the form of dramatic human-interest stories and illustrations which are welcomed by the papers if presented effectively. The importance of utilizing the neighborhood and foreign-language newspapers must not be overlooked. Whenever possible in a news story, the significance of the particular aspect of recreation should be pointed out.

Alert leaders secure an interpretation of recreation needs and values in the local newspapers by arranging for feature articles, furnishing material periodically as a basis for editorials, making suggestions to the cartoonist, writing letters to the editor, or submitting photographs with appropriate titles and comments. Recreation leaders also create news of the interpretive sort through interviews with educators, clergymen, jurists, police officials, and others whose opinions carry weight with the press and the public. The preponderance of sports news in the scrapbooks of some departments reflects wide public interest in sports but usually also indicates overemphasis on this phase of the program. Recreation workers who cultivate the acquaintance of editors, explain their objectives and activities, and cooperate with reporters are usually rewarded by the assignment of able reporters, generous news space, favorable editorials, and other evidences of newspaper good will.

Radio. The radio, like the newspaper, is a means of addressing the public at large and is being used effectively by many recreation departments. Little difficulty has been experienced in securing free radio time from local stations, but the time and effort involved in preparing good programs have deterred some departments from using this publicity medium. Because the public is accustomed to hearing professional-caliber productions over the networks, it will not listen to dull, ineffectively presented programs. The department therefore needs to enlist the advice of persons experienced in the preparation of scripts and the presentation of programs on the air. Regular broadcasts, once or twice weekly, have been found effective. In order to secure a large number of listeners to regular broadcasts, it is usually necessary to use spot radio announcements, newspaper notices, circulars, and announcements at meetings and on bulletin boards. Recreation department news is welcomed by radio commentators conducting programs featuring local happenings. Experience has shown that a regular, well-developed series of broadcasts creates good will for the department and affords people an insight into its objectives and program.

Types of broadcasts found successful by recreation departments are:

Announcements of forthcoming activities
Descriptions of special events such as playground opening days, pageants, festivals, holiday celebrations, and city-wide athletic contests
Imaginary or actual trips through playgrounds and indoor centers
Talks or interviews by influential persons on recreation objectives, values, or local needs
Musical programs
Informative talks on such subjects as hobbies, holidays, or home and family play
Dramatizations by players' groups
Variety programs, in some cases conducted as an amateur hour
Suggestions or directions for games, crafts, or social-recreation activities
Stories about the history of the recreation department and its activities
Round-table or forum discussions of subjects of local interest
Human-interest stories of participants in the program

Television. Through the use of television, recreation departments have an unparalleled opportunity not only for reaching a mass audience with the story of their activities, facilities, problems, and needs but also for carrying their recreation programs into the homes of many more people than could possibly be reached or served in any other way. Increasingly recreation authorities are making use of this exceptional public relations medium. In most cases local stations donate public service time for these telecasts, although a few programs, such as the Chicago Park District's

Zoo Parade, have found a commercial sponsor. The technical difficulties encountered in planning and producing successful television programs have deterred some departments from attempting to use them, but other departments have hired special personnel or enlisted the advice of qualified volunteers. Mrs. Ruth E. Pike, of the Northwest at Play Committee, after considerable experience with cooperative television programs offers the following advice: "Plan carefully; get the show on the road; then,

Demonstrating craft activities to the television audience (Courtesy of Washington State Parks and Recreation Commission).

while learning, enjoy yourself. No one person should carry the load; the framework should provide a team. Station personnel, performers, agency staff members will be helpful allies." [1]

Television programs, which in most cases are presented weekly, vary widely. Activities predominate—sports events, folk and square dancing, instrumental and vocal numbers, craft demonstrations, playground contests and festivals, family play, marionette shows, and nature projects. Tours of recreation areas, previews of indoor-center or playground programs, visits to a zoo or floral displays, and programs designed to show

[1] "Television, A Year Later," *Recreation,* vol. 48, no. 10, p. 469, December, 1955.

various groups in action have been shown effectively. Available films dealing with playground safety, how-to-do-it instructions, and recreation organization can be used to advantage with a speaker, panel, or demonstration. A series title such as *Your City at Play, Family Fun, Just Kids, Your Leisure Time,* or *Playground Reporter* helps to attract attention and sustain interest in the program.

Exhibits and Demonstrations. Exhibits of crafts, photographs, models, charts, and other display materials are another common publicity medium. Models of playgrounds or recreation facilities and city maps showing graphically the drawing power of the individual playgrounds or the unserved neighborhoods are especially effective. One city used a spot map to secure night lighting in a neighborhood with a high delinquency rate. Handcraft displays in department-store windows or at playgrounds are customary near the end of the season. Traveling exhibits of the work of the recreation department are sometimes sent from one section of the community to another. Silent lecturers displaying illuminated scenes of department activities with appropriate titles have been used effectively at conventions and in public buildings.

No publicity medium interprets the work of the department more strikingly or effectively than a demonstration of recreation activities. The playground circus, pageant, or festival, the community Halloween or Christmas celebration, the aquatic or sports carnival—presenting as they do various recreation activities—reach large numbers of people, some of whom gain their chief impression of the department from watching such demonstrations. Programs in the form of a recreation review at recreation centers acquaint the general public with the indoor activities conducted by the department. Group demonstrations add interest to exhibits and hobby shows. Much of the publicity value of such events lies in the effectiveness with which they are conducted and in the joy and enthusiasm exhibited by the persons taking part in them.

Model-home exhibits, county and state fairs, and other functions attracting large numbers of people are used by recreation departments to display and demonstrate their activities and services. The recreation department has had an important place in municipal and industrial expositions held in Pasadena's Civic Auditorium. Features of the department's exhibit include marionettes arranged to depict recreation activities graphically, periodic showing of motion pictures of Pasadena playground and park scenes, and demonstrations of craft, make-up, costume making, and hobbies. Signs and pictures tell of the department's service, folders are distributed, and paid and volunteer leaders in costume, stationed at the various booths, furnish special information as requested.

Motion Pictures. Films recording recreation activities, if made of carefully selected subjects and accompanied by appropriate titles, are useful in interpreting the work of the department to neighborhood audiences and community groups. The successful use of color film in depicting recreation scenes and activities has awakened added interest among recreation executives in the educational values of motion pictures and 35-mm slides. A number of recreation departments have made excellent films portraying features of their programs. Films showing activities in other communities are also used to arouse interest in starting a program

An annual exhibit is an effective means of informing the public about the recreation department's services (Courtesy of New Orleans, La., Recreation Department).

or to point out the possibility of expanding existing local programs. Trailers in motion-picture houses are an effective and inexpensive medium of flash news from the screen.

Publications. Every recreation department uses printed or mimeographed material to tell its story. The most common publication is the annual report, the characteristics of which were mentioned in Chapter 32. Directories listing the outdoor areas and indoor centers and giving their location, the facilities in each, the hours during which they are open, charges for their use, and other similar data are published in many cities. Bulletins announcing seasonal programs, with schedules for classes, groups, and special events are sometimes combined with the directory. Announcements of institute courses or of the opening of playgrounds or centers, booklets on home-play or picnic activities, folders on the municipal athletic organization, or programs of special productions by the music or drama groups are typical. Yearbooks are issued by affiliated organizations such as a hiking or outing club, and some playgrounds and centers issue a bulletin either regularly or on special occasions. In many of its publications the recreation department includes material interpreting the significance of the work it is performing. Attractive posters placed in schools, store windows, and other appropriate centers have been used effectively. Before a referendum on a recreation issue, leaflets describing the proposals and pointing out the reasons for supporting them are commonly printed and distributed.

Publicity materials should be attractive and tell their story simply and effectively. An attention-getting title, suitable color, and plenty of open space on the page help in securing reader interest. Typical folders announcing summer programs bear such titles as *Summer Is for Fun and Growth, Detroit's Playgrounds Are Your Big Back Yard,* or *Playtime Varieties.* Slogans and appropriate quotations can be used to advantage in interpreting the importance of recreation. Publications are more effective when they are addressed and appeal directly to the individual citizen.

National Recreation Month. The events taking place during National Recreation Month have helped focus public attention on recreation in hundreds of localities. Sponsored by the National Recreation Association and celebrated in June, it affords an opportunity for national and local publicity, for the promotion of special recreation events, and for cooperative action with many groups. Governors and mayors have issued proclamations announcing National Recreation Month, city-wide committees have been organized to plan local celebrations, and slogans such as "Live *All* Your Life," and "It's Your Leisure—Make the Most of It" have received nationwide use. Recreation Sabbath and Recreation Sunday have been widely observed, and special "weeks" during the month, such as Youth Fitness Week, Family Recreation Week, National Flag Week, Recreation-and-the-Arts Week, Recreation through Service Week, and National Swim-for-Health Week, among others, have been suitably celebrated. Music, drama, and sports festivals, radio and television shows, photography, poster, and essay contests, and the presentation of national awards for outstanding contributions to recreation are among the month's featured activities. All of these, under competent leadership, can serve to develop a better understanding of the importance of recreation and the service rendered by local recreation agencies.

Tours. "Come and see" tours of the parks and playgrounds, usually by automobile, have proved effective in giving city officials, parents, and other selected groups of citizens a firsthand view of recreation service in operation. Open nights at the indoor centers have shown the people what is being done during the indoor season. A sense of reality as to conditions and services is thus obtained by people who might not be impressed by speeches or the printed word. The saying "Seeing is believing" has been borne out by the results of a number of these trips, for those participating not only were convinced of the value of the program but also translated their convictions into favorable action. Some tours are conducted for the purpose of demonstrating unmet recreation needs or to show the advantages of acquiring a particular area for recreation use.

Other Publicity Media. Parades of children to announce the opening of playgrounds or a special event, the constant use of bulletin boards at playgrounds and indoor centers, public-address systems, discussion groups, and conferences on problems such as safety and delinquency in relation to recreation are other familiar media of publicity. The celebration of Joseph Lee Day each summer gives recreation departments an opportunity to use many media for securing helpful publicity. These celebrations and, to an even greater extent, referendum campaigns and other general efforts calling for action by the voters call into play all major publicity methods. Instances of cooperation by commercial groups in publicizing recreation are the enclosure of printed matter in pay envelopes, in store packages, on milk bottles, and in monthly bills, as well as the display of posters or slogans on trucks and buses. In one city a company furnished 4,000 caps labeled "National Recreation Month" to be worn during the local celebration. Attempts to reach the entire electorate for favorable action on recreation measures involve as much intensive planning and effort as political campaigns or community-chest drives. In such campaigns no method or medium of reaching the public effectively and favorably is overlooked.

34. COOPERATION AND RELATIONSHIPS WITH PUBLIC AND PRIVATE GROUPS

Teamwork by agreement has been called the greatest invention since the wheel. Certainly the recreation department, affecting as it does the lives of people of all ages, types, and interests and rendering such a variety of services, cannot achieve its objectives unless it establishes cooperative relationships with many public and private groups. The preceding chapters, especially Chapter 27, describing municipal recreation programs in several cities, contain numerous accounts of cooperation in conducting recreation activities and of recreation projects jointly sponsored by recreation departments and other authorities. Resourceful recreation leaders seek opportunities to extend the influence and service of the department and make possible a wider and more effective service by utilizing community resources that may contribute to the recreation life of the people. There are few community agencies and groups with which the recreation department cannot establish and maintain cooperative relationships to mutual advantage.

COOPERATION WITH PUBLIC DEPARTMENTS

The recreation department, as a local governmental unit, is brought into close touch with many city departments and other public agencies. It must rely on them for assistance in carrying on many of its services, and in turn it helps them in various ways. Some of these relationships are described in the pages that follow.

School Relationships. Education and recreation are closely interrelated; school properties include many facilities suited to community recreation use; the same children are served by school and recreation leaders; training for leisure by the schools affects participation in community recreation programs; there are many common activities in the programs carried on in the schools and on the playgrounds. For these reasons it is essential that there be the closest understanding and cooperation between the two authorities. Fortunately, much progress has been made in achieving this objective. The following are specific ways in which school and recreation authorities are working together:

School-board Representation on the Recreation Board. As suggested in a previous chapter, it is usually advisable for the recreation board to include a member of the school board. Such representation enables the school officials to be fully informed as to recreation plans and programs, keeps the recreation board in touch with the opinion of the school author-

These high school pools are open under the supervision of the recreation commission for public use during evenings, Saturdays, holidays, and vacation periods (Courtesy of Long Beach, Calif., Recreation Commission).

ities on recreation matters, and facilitates cooperation in the planning and use of school properties and joint action on problems of common interest and concern.

Cooperation in Acquisition and Development of Areas. School authorities need increasingly large sites for use in the regular school program, and recreation departments also require recreation areas for serving children, youth, and adults, chiefly during nonschool hours. Since school and recreation areas require a location near the center of a neighborhood or community, economy and efficiency result when there is joint planning in their acquisition. In some cities a portion of the site is acquired as a neighborhood park, thus making possible a school-park playground. For an account of developments in eighteen cities see *School-City Cooperation in the Planning of Recreation Areas and Facilities.*[1] Outstanding examples of cooperative action between school and city authorities in acquiring recreation areas were cited in Chapter 11; the instances of such cooperation are increasing.

Joint Use of School and City Recreation Properties. The agreements between school and recreation authorities in many cities include the provision that the playgrounds jointly developed will be used by the schools during the school day under school auspices and during other hours for community use under recreation department leadership. The use of city-owned properties by school groups and of school properties by community groups is common. During school hours the school authorities have full use of the city-owned outdoor areas and facilities; after school the recreation department uses the gymnasiums, pools, and other recreation facilities in the school buildings. Maintenance costs resulting from such use are generally met by the authorities controlling the properties.

Joint Financing of Recreation Programs. Municipal and school authorities together provide the funds for the community recreation program, especially in states where the enabling legislation provides that the school board designate one or more of its members to serve on the local recreation commission. In some instances, the appropriations are placed in a common fund; in others, each agency agrees to meet the cost of specific items, such as executive or activity leadership, supplies, maintenance of grounds, heat, light, and janitor service.

Joint Employment of Recreation Executive. Under this arrangement a person is employed by the recreation department for part-time service as superintendent of recreation and also by the school board to perform some other service such as supervisor of a special subject, like physical education. With notable exceptions—for example, Long Beach, California —this plan has not worked out successfully because the demands on the worker's time and attention are likely to be such that one aspect of his work is neglected.

Program Planning. Because the two departments serve the same children and because the recreation authorities provide activities for young people after they leave school, a mutual understanding concerning program methods, objectives, and standards is highly desirable. Successful results have been achieved in this respect, especially in cities where recreation is administered under school auspices or under a coordinated plan. For example, schedules of leagues and special events are worked

[1] National Recreation Association, New York, 1953.

out to minimize conflicts and duplication. Playing rules and standards of competition are adopted on a uniform basis, where practicable. Parent-teacher groups co-sponsor activities with school and recreation authorities in some cities. Attempts to enlist high school graduates in music and drama groups formed to meet their special needs, the employment of school music leaders to assist with the recreation music program, and the furnishing of instruction in golf, tennis, and other sports to classes formed among school pupils with the help of school authorities are other examples of coordination in school and recreation department programs.

Voluntary Coordination of Recreation Services. In Baltimore County, Maryland, where the recreation board utilizes primarily the buildings and grounds of the board of education for its program, cooperation is greatly facilitated by the creation of five joint committees which meet monthly. The committees are concerned with finance, site selection, planning of buildings and grounds, operation and maintenance of buildings and grounds, and program, respectively. Each committee has at least one member from each board and a member of the staff of each board, in addition to representatives of other interested county agencies. In some localities the school and recreation-board members meet from time to time, and in others the executives meet regularly for a discussion of common problems.

Many of the working relationships and agreements reached between city and school authorities relating to recreation do not require legislative action or special organization. They are informal in nature and represent the desire of the two authorities to cooperate in achieving a maximum recreation service. As G. Robert Koopman stated at the 1957 Conference on Education for Leisure, "A strong feeling of mutual concern, much cooperative planning, and abstention from agency empire building are the real conditions for progress in the decade ahead." [2]

Park Relationships. In a department combining the so-called park and recreation functions, cooperation is achieved by the allocation of duties and authority. Where these functions are administered by separate authorities, formal or informal agreements between the two departments are essential. This is true because most separate recreation departments operate playgrounds in parks and supervise other recreation facilities on park property, even though maintenance of such areas and facilities is provided by the park authorities. In such cases definite understanding must be reached between the two departments as to their respective responsibilities and the conditions under which the properties are to be maintained and operated.

[2] *The Community Approach to the Leisure Problem,* American Association for Health, Physical Education, and Recreation, Washington, 1957, p. 11.

Library Cooperation. Library and recreation officials are both interested in the promotion of reading as a popular and enjoyable leisure-time activity. In furthering this objective, many forms of cooperation have been developed. Branch libraries in field houses and recreation buildings are serving many people who do not use library buildings. On the other hand, clubrooms and auditoriums in libraries are used by recreation departments for music, drama, crafts, and other activities. Some city libraries have a music division which maintains a collection of opera and orchestral scores and choral works, which are loaned to recreation department groups and the public. Children's librarians advise playground workers in the selection of stories to tell children and in some instances serve as storytellers. One librarian prepared a special container with ten suitable books of stories for each of the local playgrounds. In several cities library trucks make weekly trips to the summer playgrounds, taking books to the children.

Special displays of books on seasonal recreation activities have helped recruit participants for department programs, and literature on recreation subjects has been set aside in a number of libraries for use by persons attending recreation institutes. Recreation departments extend their cooperation to librarians in the promotion of National Book Week and in posting on their bulletin boards announcements of activities sponsored by the library.

Housing Authorities. The construction of large-scale public housing developments has presented to housing and recreation authorities alike the problem of furnishing recreation service to the people occupying the new dwellings. Cooperation by the recreation department has been primarily of two types: (1) providing leadership at indoor and outdoor facilities within the housing development and (2) establishing recreation areas in close proximity to the housing units. The first type of cooperation has been fairly common; and since, with the exception of play lots, recreation areas in public housing projects are open to persons in the surrounding neighborhood, housing authorities look to the recreation department to provide leadership at these areas, as at other properties open to public use.

The development of a large-scale housing project gives rise to many problems, the solution of which is a matter of direct concern not only to the housing and recreation authorities but also to planning, school, and other agencies. Some recreation authorities have succeeded in working out a cooperative plan with the housing agency whereby suitable outdoor recreation space and indoor recreation facilities have been provided through joint action, but in other cities a satisfactory solution has not been achieved. The provision of recreation areas and facilities in some housing developments is carried out in cooperation with the school and planning authorities.

Courts and Probation Officials. In view of the close relationships between the lack of suitable recreation opportunities and delinquency, it is only natural that court and probation officials should turn to the recreation department for aid in preventing delinquency and in dealing with first offenders. This form of cooperation varies. In some cities the juvenile court or probation department turns the young offender over to the recreation executive or to the director of the playground in the neighborhood in which he lives. The boy or girl is required to report regularly to the recreation worker, who encourages the child to participate in the recreation program. In one city juvenile protective committees composed of persons living in the vicinity of each playground assist the directors in dealing with children whose names are submitted each month to the recreation department by the juvenile court. On the other hand, recreation workers notify the authorities of problem children who seem headed for trouble and who need special observation or treatment.

Coordinating councils in which public and private groups are represented and in which the recreation department plays an active part have made studies of neighborhood conditions and leisure-time activities and have cooperated with police and court officials in bringing troublesome children into contact with facilities and programs provided by the department. The head of a juvenile division of one police department cooperates with the recreation executive by helping boys who have committed misdemeanors and minor offenses adjust themselves to the playground program and organize activities for their own group. Through information submitted by the juvenile court and officials of municipal welfare agencies, the recreation authorities in another city sought out problem boys who were induced to come to the playgrounds and who were subsequently enrolled in a playground boys' club.

City Planning. The relation of recreation areas to the city plan and the necessity of cooperation between recreation and city-planning authorities were clearly indicated in Chapter 11. Cooperation is needed not only for the purpose of relating proposed recreation developments to other types of proposed improvements but also to correlate programs of area acquisition and development of the various recreation agencies in the city. An outstanding example of such cooperative planning is the Washington, D. C., Coordinating Committee on Recreation Plans. It is, generally speaking, a technicians' committee, including representatives from the public school officers, the municipal architect's office, the National Capital Parks office, the National Capital Park and Planning Commission, and the recreation department. The committee has enlarged its membership to include the executive secretary of the recreation division of the council of social agencies, a step which provides effective correlation and coordination of private- and public-agency plans and programs. Representatives of the housing agency and of other groups are invited to meet with the committee when problems affecting these agencies are being discussed.

Cooperation with Other Departments. The following references to cooperation extended by other departments to the recreation authorities briefly suggest the nature and scope of such relationships:

Police. This department provides safe coasting places at city streets, sets aside play streets, assigns police for special events, assists junior safety clubs and playground police organizations, furnishes meeting places for boys' recreation activities, and cooperates in dealing with problem children.

Water. The water department furnishes water for recreation areas, pools, buildings, and areas to be flooded for skating. It also permits use of its properties for fishing, picnicking, and other suitable activities.

Fire. The department permits use of fire hydrants for street showers and, in some instances, operates them. It floods skating rinks, loans ladders and equipment, permits its buildings to be used for recreation activities, and cooperates in Fire-prevention Week.

Lighting. Lights and other electrical equipment are furnished for festivals, pageants, and special functions. Equipment is installed and repaired at outdoor and indoor centers.

Health. This department provides regulations for sanitation at pools and beaches and makes periodic water analyses. It holds physical examinations for participants in strenuous activities, conducts health activities on playgrounds, and cooperates in disease prevention.

Public Works. The department furnishes topsoil, sand, stone, or other materials, removes rubbish, transports equipment used at special events, and loans equipment such as a steam roller. In some cities the department does construction, such as grading or paving, and prepares or approves plans, specifications, and contract documents for construction and major maintenance projects.

Welfare. This department selects children to attend municipal camp, assists with Christmas toy campaigns, and calls attention to children with special play needs.

Museums. These organizations prepare exhibits for recreation department groups, make arrangements for visits by playground children to museums, assist with art, craft, or nature programs, provide meeting places, and conduct classes, lectures, and demonstrations.

Miscellaneous. The recreation department needs to maintain an especially close working relationship with the auxiliary or staff service agencies of the city government such as the finance department, the central purchasing and personnel agencies, the city attorney, and the planning department, all of which may directly control certain of its policies and procedures.

Cooperation with Other Communities. The overflow of population from the central cities into the surrounding region, frequently into unincorporated areas, and the increasing mobility of city residents have made it necessary for recreation departments to be concerned about developments outside their city limits. Policies adopted by recreation departments in a central city may affect the residents of suburban communities, and the lack of adequate recreation services in fringe areas creates difficult problems in many cities. To face this situation, recreation authorities are meeting with officials in nearby communities, and amicable agreements have been worked out whereby recreation service is furnished to residents of fringe areas on a shared-cost basis. In several instances two adjacent communities have jointly financed and are operating a recreation facility, or have organized a program feature that serves the residents of both areas to their mutual advantage.

Many recreation departments share their knowledge, resources, and experience with smaller nearby communities. Assistance takes various forms, such as helping with the organization of sports and athletics, giving advice in the development of recreation areas, training leaders and sports officials, interpreting recreation to officials and community groups, helping establish recreation committees or departments, and leading recreation activities. Several recreation departments have arranged one-day conferences which local officials and recreation leaders in towns and cities in the surrounding region have been invited to attend and which have afforded an opportunity for an exchange of experiences and a consideration of common problems. The smaller community usually gains most from these services rendered by the larger city, with its staff and organized program, but definite values accrue to the city from its missionary effort. Participation by recreation personnel in activities and projects sponsored by state and district recreation organizations affords a valuable means of cooperative action that can benefit the organization, the individual, and the local program.

County, State, and Federal Authorities. Local recreation authorities are increasingly cooperating with county, state, and Federal agencies to the end that their people may fully benefit from the use of extra-urban properties suitable for recreation use or from services provided by these agencies. City recreation departments, for example, lease Federal forest or reclamation properties as sites for municipal camps, picnic grounds, or boating centers. In other instances state or county properties have been transferred to local authorities that were prepared to develop them for recreation use. The city of Worcester, Massachusetts, on the other hand, deeded to the state for one dollar four lake-front properties totaling

220 acres, for the initial development of which the legislature has authorized a $1,500,000 bond issue. The importance of consultation with state highway authorities concerning their plans for highways affecting the city has been demonstrated by experiences in Minneapolis and other cities. Cooperative plans have been worked out by several county and local authorities for a jointly sponsored recreation program.

COOPERATION WITH VOLUNTARY AGENCIES

Inadequacy of the total available facilities and services is a more serious problem than duplication of facilities and overlapping of services in most localities. The solution of this problem calls for cooperative planning and administration, with a view to making existing facilities and services most effective and extending them where needed. Much cooperation of this sort exists today between public and voluntary agencies, and it is increasing. Voluntary agencies use public areas for camping and day camping and indoor facilities for appropriate activities; some public agencies use private facilities. Widespread cooperation in planning and administration between public and voluntary agencies is facilitated through local councils of social agencies, in most of which recreation departments are cooperating members. Many recreation executives serve as members of the recreation, leisure, youth, or camping committees of local councils; some participate actively in the work of individual youth-serving agencies. Typical of projects jointly sponsored with voluntary agencies are institutes for training paid and volunteer workers, camping programs, studies of special problems such as the recreation needs of preschool children, youth, or the aged, campaigns to secure needed facilities or services, more effective interpretation methods, additional funds for the recreation program, or the publication of leaflets describing recreation resources and programs in the locality.

COOPERATION WITH COMMUNITY ORGANIZATIONS

The chapters describing various features of the recreation department's service indicated many ways in which the department assists local organizations in carrying on their recreation projects. Similarly, recreation departments receive valuable aid from many local groups. For example, parent-teacher associations have been loyal allies on frequent occasions by sponsoring referendum campaigns, furnishing volunteer playground leaders, "rescuing" recreation budgets, and cooperating in the promotion of home play. Junior Leagues have furnished funds for conducting indoor centers and have organized and financed junior garden clubs, children's drama and radio programs, and library service at community buildings. Colleges and universities have permitted recreation departments to use their athletic facilities during the summer months, admitted playground boys and girls to football and baseball games, assisted in music and drama programs, cooperated in recreation training institutes, and furnished student leaders to help with the department's program. Automobile clubs, junior chambers of commerce, the American Legion, and other groups have furnished awards for safety patrols, organized boys' baseball leagues, provided officials for sports events, and sponsored community dances and holiday celebrations. Service clubs, especially

The outdoor theatre in Oglebay Park is made available for vesper services (Courtesy of Oglebay Institute, Wheeling, W. Va.).

Lions clubs, have been helpful in furnishing funds, leadership, and support for playgrounds and other specific projects. Private golf clubs have made their facilities and personnel available to boys and girls for instruction, and owners of professional baseball parks have admitted members of "knothole" clubs to games without charge.

The American National Red Cross gives advice regarding the development and operation of aquatic facilities, assists with learn-to-swim campaigns, and furnishes instructors for first-aid and lifesaving classes. Athletic, music, drama, garden, art, and other clubs furnish volunteer leaders and assist in planning programs and in organizing city-wide tournaments and special events. Perhaps no group of organizations has been more helpful than the playground mothers' clubs, the playground and recreation center councils, dads' clubs, and playground federations, which have raised money for equipment, furnished transportation, and actively supported the department's program. Industries, churches, newspapers, women's clubs, labor organizations, all help; in fact, there is probably no type of organization which is not serving the recreation department in one or more cities.

Cooperation in Mobile, Alabama. The annual report of the recreation department probably affords the best indication of the extent to which it has served community groups and benefited from the assistance of public and private agencies and individuals. The extent and variety of such cooperation are indicated by a report of the Mobile, Alabama, Recreation Department. It records service to and cooperation with some thirty-five groups and organizations during the year, including parent-teacher associations, social, civic, and veterans organizations, and school groups. It furthermore extends appreciation to forty-six organizations, not including city departments, that provided assistance and cooperation. Examples are:

A newspaper furnished awards for winning boys' and girls' teams, and its children's editor conducted monthly birthday parties.

The Lions Club sponsored Halloween parties; the Kiwanis Club, a kite contest.

Radio stations furnished time and help with regular radio and television programs.

The American National Red Cross conducted learn-to-swim campaigns and lifesaving classes.

The Touchdown Club promoted baseball, basketball, and football for boys.

The Opera Guild Auxiliary, Symphony Guild, and Civic Ballet Association helped with the children's Fun With Music Club.

A sorority sponsored and presented awards in a boys' and girls' table-tennis tournament.

The United Daughters of the Confederacy sponsored girls' volleyball; the Business and Professional Business Women's Club, girls' softball.

The Baseball Association admitted members of the Knothole Club to home games; the Softball Association furnished awards for boys' teams.

The Tennis Club conducted the junior boys' and girls' tennis tournament.

The stadium officials granted free admission to high school games to boys participating in the department's football program.

A department store displayed the winners in a city-wide doll-show series.

This impressive list of cooperating organizations could be duplicated in many cities.

SECURING AND CONTROLLING COOPERATION

The diversity and range of cooperative relationships and activities that can be utilized by recreation authorities present a tremendous challenge to the alert, resourceful recreation executive or commission. It is clear that in most cities recreation resources adequate to serve the needs of the people will not be made available unless all agencies concerned with recreation join hands in a concerted effort to secure those resources. The readiness of the local authorities to appropriate tax funds depends upon evidence of wholehearted public approval, and large contributors to chests and voluntary agencies increasingly insist upon cooperative long-range planning, especially for capital programs. The universal appeal of recreation and the readiness with which all types of organizations respond to requests for assistance make it imperative that recreation departments give the securing and maintaining of cooperation a high priority among their objectives and functions. If members of a recreation commission have been chosen because of their integrity and standing in the locality, they can be extremely useful to the executive in enlisting the interest and cooperation of local groups.

Obviously, in dealing with many individuals and groups and in developing cooperative projects, problems are bound to arise, and it is highly important that definite policies and rules be adopted for the guidance of the recreation department staff in dealing with them. It is desirable, for example, that all offers of equipment, such as playground apparatus, game tables, or a kiln, be officially approved before they are accepted. Employees should be required to secure permission before they agree to cooperate with any individual or organization in promoting a recreation activity or project. Such rules are not intended to discourage cooperation but rather to prevent difficulties and misunderstandings and to make sure that cooperative action is carried on according to the department's standards and policies.

How to Secure Cooperation. There is no patent formula for securing cooperation. Repeatedly reference has been made to the formation of various groups designed to achieve planning and action on a cooperative basis. Informal dinner conferences between executives of the park, school, and recreation departments sometimes achieve effective results; in other cases a highly organized recreation council has proven successful. It is axiomatic, however, that cooperation cannot be secured unless there is a desire to cooperate coupled with a degree of initiative and resourcefulness in utilizing the resources available in the community.

Since, in the final analysis, the recreation department can achieve the maximum success by not serving alone, however effectively, but by enlisting the cooperation of individuals and community agencies—homes, churches, industries, clubs, social-welfare groups, and others—it is perhaps fitting to end this volume with a word on how to secure that cooperation. The paragraph which follows is taken from the summary of a National Recreation Congress discussion on "How to Secure the Cooperation of All Agencies Concerned in a Community Recreation Program." Though the statement was made in 1938, it is still highly pertinent.

Reports from many parts of the country convince one that variety in recreation programs can best be preserved through cooperation. Moreover, each community evolves its own ways of securing it. The kind and degree of cooperation attained are related to the history of the established institutions in this and in related fields. The answer to the question of how to secure cooperation must be found in the communities themselves and in the neighborhood groupings. It cannot be made categorically. The reply of each recreation leader reveals his comprehension of the genius of the people of his community, his appreciation of the ideals and of the commitments of all the agencies concerned. Cooperation among agencies is a process being substituted for the unsatisfactory competition which prevailed when, as separate units, they aspired to unrealizable community-wide dominance in the control of people's leisure. Achievement in the securing of cooperation is proportional to the length of time over which it has been sought by those directly interested in the matter. No community yields a report of sudden success, but a story of community-minded men and women discussing their problems and undertaking to assist each other in solving them. Cooperation results from vision and the supremacy of the community over the agency.

IN CONCLUSION

In the minds of many people, the recreation department is primarily a part of the machinery of local government. They think of it chiefly in terms of areas and facilities, supervisors and caretakers, playground schedules and athletic leagues, budgets and reports, or as a means of keeping children and young people out of mischief during their leisure hours. As the preceding chapters have shown, the recreation department is all these things. Most of them are merely means for achieving its larger objectives—to develop personality, to build a finer community spirit, and to contribute fully to the enrichment of life for the people of the city. Recreation authorities increasingly recognize their larger responsibility and are adjusting their programs to meet more fully the growing demands for richer, more satisfying service. The evidence presented in this chapter reaffirms that the recreation department is not an isolated unit of the local government but is vitally related to all other community forces and that its work is closely integrated with that of all other agencies serving the leisure-time interests of the people.

The harnessing of the atom and the new dimensions in space, power, time, and speed make necessary new dimensions in recreation planning. They present a challenge to all who believe that recreation can contribute richly to the welfare of all the people. As Joseph Prendergast has said, "This is a time of great hope for all mankind. It is a time when the recreation forces of the nation and the world are destined to play an even greater role in man's continuing search for peace and happiness." [3]

[3] "The Past Is a Prologue to the Future," *Recreation,* vol. 49, no. 1, p. 5, January, 1956.

BIBLIOGRAPHY

The following bibliography of books and other published material dealing with the subjects considered in this volume affords a guide to supplementary reading and a list of valuable reference sources. Most of these publications have been issued since 1950. For a more complete list of reference materials, readers are referred to the bibliographies in earlier editions of this text.

Titles are grouped under seven headings, which correspond with the seven major divisions of the book. Each publication has been listed under the heading that is most applicable, although many reference sources deal with subjects treated in two or more parts of this volume. The bibliography does not include publications describing specific recreation activities; however, information and bibliographies on such activities are available from the National Recreation Association.

In addition to the titles listed in the following pages, publications issued by community recreation agencies, such as annual reports, information folders, staff guides, directories, and program materials, furnish data of great value to teachers, students, and recreation workers. Bulletins and newsletters issued by state recreation and park associations, societies, and agencies are a valuable source of information on current developments in the community recreation movement.

Several magazines and periodicals regularly carry articles dealing with various aspects of community recreation. Files of *Recreation* and its predecessors *Playground and Recreation* and *The Playground,* issued by the National Recreation Association, afford the most comprehensive available source of information on the beginnings of community recreation and its growth over more than half a century. Of the many other journals that contain articles on recreation, the following merit special mention: *American Recreation Society Bulletin,* Washington, *Journal of Health–Physical Education–Recreation,* Washington, *Park Maintenance,* Appleton, Wisconsin, *Parks and Recreation,* Wheeling, West Virginia, *Planning and Civic Comment,* Washington.

Sources of information on motion-picture films relating to recreation and other visual aids include the Film Council of America, Evanston, Illinois; Association Films, New York; The Athletic Institute, Chicago; and the National Citizens Committee for Educational Television, Washington.

I. Recreation—Its Nature, Extent, and Significance

Books

Braucher, Howard: *A Treasury of Living,* National Recreation Association, New York, 1950.

Brightbill, Charles K., and Harold D. Meyer: *Recreation: Text and Readings,* Prentice-Hall, Inc., Englewood Cliffs, N. J., 1953.

Cabot, Richard C.: *What Men Live By,* Houghton Mifflin Company, Boston, 1914.

Cozens, Frederick W., and Florence S. Stumpf: *Sports in American Life,* University of Chicago Press, Chicago, 1953.

Danford, Howard G.: *Recreation in the American Community,* Harper & Brothers, New York, 1953.

Dewhurst, J. Frederic, et al.: "Recreation," *America's Needs and Resources: A New Survey,* The Twentieth Century Fund, Inc., New York, 1955, chap. 11.

Doell, Charles E., and Gerald B. Fitzgerald: *A Brief History of Parks and Recreation in the United States,* The Athletic Institute, Chicago, 1954.

Huizinga, Johan: *Homo Ludens: A Study of the Play Element in Culture,* The Beacon Press, Boston, 1955.

Hutchinson, John L.: *Principles of Recreation,* The Ronald Press Company, New York, 1951.

Jacks, L. P.: *Education through Recreation,* Harper & Brothers, New York, 1932.

Jenny, John H.: *Introduction to Recreation Education,* W. B. Saunders Company, Philadelphia, 1955.

Lee, Joseph: *Play in Education,* National Recreation Association, New York, 1942.

Meyer, Harold D., and Charles K. Brightbill: *Community Recreation,* rev. ed., Prentice-Hall, Inc., Englewood Cliffs, N. J., 1956.

Mitchell, Elmer D., and Bernard S. Mason: *Theory of Play,* The Ronald Press Company, New York, 1948.

Municipal Year Book, International City Managers' Association, Chicago. Issued annually since 1934. Contains section on park and recreation developments.

Nash, Jay B.: *Philosophy of Recreation and Leisure,* The C. V. Mosby Company, St. Louis, 1953.

Neumeyer, M. H., and E. S. Neumeyer: *Leisure and Recreation,* rev. ed., The Ronald Press Company, New York, 1958.

Social Work Year Book, Russell Sage Foundation, New York. Each issue of this biennial publication contains articles on the current status of recreation and of related subjects such as camping, adult education, boys' and girls' work organizations, and youth services.

Other Publications

Clawson, Marion: *Statistics on Outdoor Recreation,* Resources for the Future, Washington, 1958.

Denney, Ruel, and Mary Lea Meyersohn: "A Preliminary Bibliography on Leisure," *American Journal of Sociology,* vol. 62, no. 6, pp. 602–615, Chicago, May, 1957.

Douglass, Paul F. (ed.): "Recreation in the Age of Automation," *Annals of the American Academy of Political and Social Science,* vol. 313, pp. 1–147, Philadelphia, September, 1957. A symposium.

Education for Leisure, American Association for Health, Physical Education, and Recreation, Washington, 1957. A conference report.

Fitness for American Youth, President's Council on Youth Fitness, Washington, 1956.

Karter, Thomas: "The Development of Organized Recreation in the United States," reprinted from the *Social Security Bulletin,* vol. 20, no. 5, p. 8, U.S. Department of Health, Education and Welfare, May, 1957.

Martin, Alexander Reid: *A Philosophy of Recreation,* National Recreation Association, New York, 1955.

Menninger, William C.: *Recreation and Mental Health,* National Recreation Association, New York, 1948.

Meyerson, Martin (ed.): "Metropolis in Ferment," *Annals of the American Academy of Political and Social Science,* vol. 314, p. 144, November, 1957. A symposium.

National Recreation Association: *Agencies of the Federal Government Concerned with Recreation: Trends, Inadequacies, Needs,* New York, 1954.

———: *1956 Recreation and Park Yearbook,* New York, 1956. An inventory of public recreation and park services of local, county, state, and Federal agencies.

———: *Proceedings of the National Recreation Congress.* Issued annually.

———: *Recreation.* A magazine. Special issues: May, 1931, twenty-fifth anniversary number containing articles on the beginnings and development of the community recreation movement in the United States; December, 1937, Joseph Lee memorial issue; June, 1956, National Recreation Association golden-anniversary issue.

———: *The Recreational Resources of the United States: Their Conservation, Development and Wise Use,* New York, 1953.

———: *The Role of the Federal Government in the Field of Public Recreation,* New York, 1953.

Our Heritage: A Plan for Its Protection and Use: "Mission 66," U.S. Department of the Interior, National Park Service, undated.

Park and Recreation Progress Yearbook, National Conference on State Parks, Washington. Issued periodically.

Publications and annual reports of Federal, state, and municipal recreation agencies.

Recreation for Community Living, The Athletic Institute, Chicago, 1952. A workshop report.

Solomon, Ben (ed.): "Definitions of Recreation," *Youth Leaders Digest,* May, 1951, vol. 13, no. 8, pp. 284–305. A symposium.

State Park Statistics, U.S. Department of the Interior, National Park Service. Issued annually.

"The Uses of Leisure," *American Journal of Sociology,* vol. 62, no. 6, pp. 541–601, Chicago, May, 1957. A symposium on the popular arts.

II. Leadership

Books

Beckard, Richard: *How to Plan and Conduct Workshops and Conferences,* Leadership Library Series, Association Press, New York, 1956.

Blumenthal, Louis B.: *How to Work with Boards and Committees,* Leadership Library Series, Association Press, New York, 1954.

Fitzgerald, Gerald B.: *Leadership in Recreation,* The Ronald Press Company, New York, 1951.

Frank, Lawrence K.: *How to Be a Modern Leader,* Leadership Library Series, Association Press, New York, 1954.

Knowles, Malcolm, and Hulda Knowles: *How to Develop Better Leaders,* Leadership Library Series, Association Press, New York, 1955.

Recreation as a Profession in the Southern Region, National Recreation Association, New York, 1955.

Roberts, Dorothy: *Leadership of Teen-age Groups,* Association Press, New York, 1950.

Slavson, S. R.: *Creative Group Education,* Association Press, New York, 1937.

Sorenson, Roy: *How to Be a Board or Committee Member,* Leadership Library Series, Association Press, New York, 1953.

Stone, Walter L., and Charles G. Stone: *Recreation Leadership,* The William-Frederick Press, New York, 1952.

Trecker, Audrey, and Harleigh Trecker: *How to Work with Groups,* Association Press, New York, 1952.

Williamson, Margaret: *Supervision: Principles and Methods,* William Morrow & Company, Inc., New York, 1950.

Other Publications

The Athletic Institute: *Graduate Study in Health Education, Physical Education, and Recreation,* Chicago, 1950. A conference report.

————: *National Conference on Undergraduate Professional Preparation in Physical Education, Health Education, and Recreation,* Chicago, 1948.

Ball, Edith L.: *Developing Volunteers for Service in Recreation Programs,* National Recreation Association, New York, 1958.

Byers, Kenneth, M. Robert Montilla, and Elmer V. Williams: *Elements of Position Classification in Local Government,* Civil Service Assembly, Chicago, 1955.

Dyer, Donald B.: *In-service Education for Community Center Leadership,* National Recreation Association, New York, 1955.

Forsberg, Raymond T.: *Playground Leaders—Their Selection and Training,* National Recreation Association, New York, 1955.

Johnson, George E.: *Why Teach a Child to Play?* National Recreation Association, New York, 1909.

Musselman, Virginia: *The Playground Leader—His Place in the Program,* National Recreation Association, New York, 1952.

National Recreation Association: *Leadership Evaluation: A Checklist,* undated.

————: *Personnel Standards in Community Recreation Leadership,* rev. ed., New York, 1957. A committee report.

Procedures that Improve Personnel Administration, Civil Service Assembly, Chicago, 1955. Twelve papers.

Professional Preparation of Recreation Personnel, American Association for Health, Physical Education, and Recreation, Washington, 1957. A conference report.

Romilly, E. P.: *In-service Training for Park Employees,* National Recreation Association, New York, 1950.

Sutherland, W. C.: *Recreation Leadership,* Bellman Publishing Company, Cambridge, Mass., 1957.

III. Areas and Facilities

Books

Butler, George D.: *Recreation Areas: Their Design and Equipment,* rev. ed., The Ronald Press Company, New York, 1958. Profusely illustrated.

Cliffer, Harold J.: *Planning the Golf Clubhouse,* National Golf Foundation, Inc., Chicago, 1956. Profusely illustrated.

Colborn, Fern M.: *Buildings of Tomorrow,* William Morrow & Company, Inc., New York, 1955.

Engelhardt, N. L., N. L. Engelhardt, Jr., and S. Leggett: *Planning Elementary School Buildings,* F. W. Dodge Corporation, New York, 1953. Profusely illustrated.

Gabrielsen, M. A., and Caswell M. Miles (eds.): *Sports and Recreation Facilities for School and Community,* Prentice-Hall, Inc., Englewood Cliffs, N. J., 1958. Illustrated.

Hawkins, Reginald R.: *Easy-to-make Outdoor Play Equipment*, The Macmillan Company, New York, 1957.

Salamon, Julian H.: *Camp Site Development*, Girl Scouts of the United States of America, New York, 1948.

Schools for the New Needs—Educational, Social, Economic, F. W. Dodge Corporation, New York, 1956. Profusely illustrated.

Stein, Clarence S.: *Toward New Towns for America*, Reinhold Publishing Corporation, New York, 1957. Illustrated.

Williams, Wayne R.: *Recreation Places*, Reinhold Publishing Corporation, New York, 1958. Profusely illustrated.

Other Publications

American Institute of Park Executives: *A Zoological Park*, Wheeling, W. Va. undated. A workshop report. Profusely illustrated.

Architecture for Adult Education, Commission on Architecture, Adult Education Association of the U.S.A., Chicago, 1956. Illustrated.

Butler, George D.: *Outdoor Swimming Pools*, National Recreation Association, New York, 1955.

————: *School-City Cooperation in the Planning of Recreation Areas and Facilities*, National Recreation Association, New York, 1953.

Chlevin, Ben (ed.): *Golf Operators Handbook*, National Golf Foundation, Inc., Chicago, 1956. Driving ranges and miniature and par-3 courses. Illustrated.

Construction and Maintenance of Tennis Courts, United States Lawn Tennis Association, New York, undated.

Cornacchia, H. J., and John E. Nixon: *Playground Facilities for Rural and Small Elementary Schools*, School Planning Laboratory, Stanford University Press, Stanford, Calif., 1955.

Hake, Herbert V.: *Here's How: A Basic Stagecraft Book*, rev. ed., Row, Peterson & Company, Evanston, Ill., 1958.

"Land for Recreation," *Recreation*, vol. 50, no. 6, pp. 197–209, June, 1957. A special issue.

Meadows, C. A.: *Ice Rinks*, C. A. Meadows & Associates, Toronto, undated. Artificial rinks.

Means, Louis E., and Charles D. Gibson: *Planning School-Community Swimming Pools*, California State Department of Education, Sacramento, Calif., 1955. Illustrated.

The Modern Marina, National Association of Engine and Boat Manufacturers, Inc., New York, 1953. Illustrated.

National Golf Foundation: *Planning and Building the Golf Course*, Chicago, undated.

National Recreation Association: *Planning a Community Recreation Building*, New York, 1955.

————: *School Grounds Designed for Community Use*, New York, 1949.

————: *Surfacing Playground Areas*, New York, 1952.

Neilson, Donald W., and John S. Nixon: *Swimming Pools for Schools*, School Planning Laboratory, Stanford University Press, Stanford, Calif., 1954. Illustrated.

Outboard Marinas, Outboard Boating Club of America, Chicago, undated. Illustrated.

Planning Facilities for Health, Physical Education, and Recreation, rev. ed., The Athletic Institute, Chicago, 1956. A workshop report. Illustrated.

Planning for Recreation Parks in California: A Guide, California Recreation Commission, Sacramento, Calif., 1956. A committee report. Illustrated.

Recommended Practice for Design, Equipment, and Operation of Swimming Pools and Other Public Bathing Places, rev. ed., American Public Health Association, 1957. A committee report.

Reid, Leslie M. (ed.): *Interpretive Programs,* American Institute of Park Executives, Wheeling, W. Va., 1957.

Scholastic Coach, New York. Each January issue features sports facilities and equipment.

School Planning Laboratory: *Creative Planning for Parks and Play Areas,* Stanford University Press, Stanford, Calif., 1957. A conference report. Illustrated.

Sleeper, Harold R.: *Modern Gymnasium Seating,* rev. ed., Gymnasium Seating Council, New York, 1949.

Standard Floodlight Layouts for Floodlighting Sports Areas, National Electrical Manufacturers Association, New York, undated.

Swimming Pool Age. A monthly magazine published by Hoffman-Harris, Inc., New York.

Swimming Pool Data and Reference Annual, Hoffman-Harris, Inc., New York. Issued annually.

Take the Guesswork Out of Pool Planning, rev. ed., Hoffman-Harris, Inc., New York, 1957. Illustrated.

Wickham, Verne (ed.): *Municipal Golf Course Organizing and Operating Guide,* National Golf Foundation, Inc., Chicago, 1955. Illustrated.

IV. Activities and Program Planning

Books

Anderson, Jackson M.: *Industrial Recreation,* McGraw-Hill Book Company, Inc., New York, 1955.

Bucher, Charles A. (ed.): *Methods and Materials in Physical Education and Recreation,* The C. V. Mosby Company, St. Louis, 1954.

Clemens, Frances, et al. (ed.): *Recreation and the Local Church,* Brethren Publishing House, Elgin, Ill., 1956. A workshop report.

Corbin, H. Dan: *Recreation Leadership,* Prentice-Hall, Inc., Englewood Cliffs, N. J., 1953.

Gulick, Luther H.: *A Philosophy of Play,* Charles Scribner's Sons, New York, 1920.

Hartley, Ruth E., Lawrence K. Frank, and Robert M. Goldenson: *Understanding Children's Play,* Columbia University Press, New York, 1952.

————, and Robert M. Goldenson: *The Complete Book of Children's Play,* Thomas Y. Crowell Company, New York, 1957.

Hunt, Valerie V.: *Recreation for the Handicapped,* Prentice-Hall, Inc., Englewood Cliffs, N. J., 1955.

Johnson, George E.: *Education by Plays and Games,* Ginn & Company, Boston, 1907.

Kraus, Richard: *Recreation Leader's Handbook,* McGraw-Hill Book Company, Inc., New York, 1955.

The Recreation Program, The Athletic Institute, Chicago, 1954. A workshop report.

Simmons, Harry: *How to Run a Club,* Harper & Brothers, New York, 1955.

Vannier, Maryhelen: *Methods and Materials in Recreation Leadership,* W. B. Saunders Company, Philadelphia, 1956.

Vettiner, Charles J.: *The New Horizon of Recreation,* published by the author, Louisville, Ky., 1956. A guide to small communities and counties.

Williams, Arthur M.: *Recreation for the Aging,* Association Press, New York, 1953.

Wilson, Gertrude, and Gladys Ryland: *Social Group Work Practice,* Houghton Mifflin Company, Boston, 1949.

Other Publications

The Athletic Institute: *Essentials for Developing Community Recreation,* Chicago, 1946.

——: *Physical Education for Children of Elementary School Age,* Chicago, 1951. A conference report.

Bowen, Georgene: *Summer Is Ageless: Recreation Programs for Older Adults,* National Recreation Association, New York, 1958.

A *Guide for Community Recreation in Indiana,* Indiana State Board of Health, Indianapolis, 1958.

Hill, Beatrice: *Starting a Recreation Program in a Civilian Hospital,* National Recreation Association, New York, 1952.

Lee, Joseph: *Play and Playgrounds,* National Recreation Association, New York, 1908.

National Recreation Association: *Clubs in the Recreation Program,* New York, 1947.

——: *11% Plus—Recreation for Older People,* New York, 1947.

——: *Planning for Girls in the Community Recreation Program,* New York, 1953.

——: *Recreation and the Church,* New York, 1951.

——: *Recreation for the Ill and Handicapped Homebound,* Proceedings of Hospital Recreation Institute, New York, 1958.

——: *What Can We Do in Our Town?,* New York, 1932.

Niederfrank, E. J., and Virginia Musselman: *Planning Recreation for the Rural Home and Community,* U.S. Department of Agriculture, Extension Division, 1950.

The North Carolina Recreation Commission: *Community Recreation in North Carolina,* Raleigh, N. C., 1949.

——: *Recreation and Community Groups in North Carolina,* Raleigh, N. C., undated.

——: *Recreation for Later Maturity,* Raleigh, N. C., undated.

Phillips, B. E. (ed.): *Recreation for the Mentally Ill,* American Association for Health, Physical Education, and Recreation, Washington, 1957. A conference report.

Planning for Recreation: A Guide for Tennessee Communities, Tennessee State Planning Commission, Nashville, Tenn., 1953.

Program Evaluation in a Boys' Club, Boys' Clubs of America, New York, undated. A committee report.

Reaching Teen-agers through Group Work and Recreation, New York City Youth Board, New York, 1954.

Recreation for Older People in California, California Recreation Commission, Sacramento, Calif., 1951.

Robbins, Florence G.: *Sociology of Play, Recreation and Leisure Time,* William C. Brown Company, Dubuque, Iowa, 1955.

School Athletics: Problems and Policies, National Education Association, Educational Policies Commission, Washington, 1954.

V. The Operation of Areas and Facilities

Books

Butler, George D.: *Playgrounds: Their Administration and Operation,* rev. ed., The Ronald Press Company, New York, 1950.

Dimock, Hedley S. (ed.): *Administration of the Modern Camp,* rev. ed., Association Press, New York, 1952.

Franklin, Adele, and Agnes E. Benedict: *Play Centers for School Children: A Guide to Their Establishment and Operation,* William Morrow & Company, Inc., New York, 1943.

Manual of Boys' Club Operation, rev. ed., Boys' Clubs of America, Dodd, Mead & Company, Inc., New York, 1956.

Reimann, Lewis C.: *The Successful Camp,* University of Michigan Press, Ann Arbor, Mich., 1958.

Other Publications

Calkins, E. E.: *Care and Feeding of Hobby Horses,* Leisure League of America, New York, 1934.

Elkow, J. Duke (ed.): *Safety for Recreation Areas and Playgrounds,* Center for Safety Education, New York University Press, New York, 1955.

Joy, Barbara E.: *Camping,* Burgess Publishing Company, Minneapolis, 1957.

Lutzin, Sidney G.: *Making Playgrounds Succeed,* New York State Youth Commission, Albany, N. Y., 1956.

————: *Making Teen Centers Succeed,* New York State Youth Commission, Albany, N. Y., 1952.

National Recreation Association: *Community Center Recreation Quiz,* New York, 1945.

————: *Conduct of Playgrounds,* rev. ed., New York, 1954.

————: *Conduct of School Community Centers,* New York, 1946.

————: *Playground Summer Notebook,* New York. Issued annually, twelve bulletins.

————: *Summer Playground Evaluation—A Checklist,* New York, 1951.

————: *Teen-age Centers—A Bird's Eye View,* New York, 1944.

————: *The Use of School Buildings for Recreation,* New York, 1950. A study report.

Recommended Standards for the Group Care of Children of Elementary School Age, Play Schools Association, New York, 1953.

Summer Programs on California Playgrounds—A Guide, California Recreation Commission, Sacramento, Calif., 1953.

VI. Program Features and Services

Books

Benson, Kenneth R.: *Creative Crafts for Children,* Prentice-Hall, Inc., Englewood Cliffs, N. J., 1958.

Butler, George D.: *Community Sports and Athletics: Organization, Administration, Program,* The Ronald Press Company, New York, 1949.

Coffey, Ernestine S., and Dorothy F. Minton: *A Leader's Guide to Nature and Garden Fun,* Hearthside Press, New York, 1957.

Duran, Clement A.: *The Program Encyclopedia,* Association Press, New York, 1955.

Eisenberg, Helen, and Larry Eisenberg: *Omnibus of Fun,* Association Press, New York, 1956.

Hammett, Catherine T., and Virginia Musselman: *The Camp Program Book,* Association Press, New York, 1951.

Kaplan, Max: *Music in Recreation: Social Foundations and Practices,* Stipes Publishing Company, Champaign, Ill., 1955.

Kraus, Richard: *Play Activities for Boys and Girls,* McGraw-Hill Book Company, Inc., New York, 1957.

Lease, Ruth G., and Geraldine B. Siks: *Creative Dramatics in Home, School and Community,* Harper & Brothers, New York, 1952.

Leonhard, Charles: *Recreation through Music,* The Ronald Press Company, New York, 1952.

Tilden, Freeman: *Interpreting Our Heritage,* The University of North Carolina Press, Chapel Hill, N. C., 1957. Principles and practices for visitor services.
Vinal, William G.: *Nature Recreation,* American Humane Education Society, Boston, 1954.
Wright, Sally: *Gardening: A New World for Children,* The Macmillan Company, New York, 1957.

Other Publications

Buell, Charles E.: *Recreation for the Blind,* American Foundation for the Blind, New York, 1951.
Musselman, Virginia: *Informal Dramatics,* National Recreation Association, New York, 1952.
————: *Storytelling,* National Recreation Association, New York, 1952.
National Recreation Association: *88 Successful Play Activities,* New York, 1951.
————: *Home Play,* New York, 1945.
————: *Planning for Patriotic Holidays,* New York, 1955.
Outdoor Education for Better Living, American Institute of Park Executives, Wheeling, W. Va., 1956. A workshop report. Illustrated.
Price, Betty: *Adventuring in Nature,* National Recreation Association, New York, 1939.
Six Years of Growth in a Community Program, Rural Research Institute, Inc., New York, undated.
Smith, Julian W.: *Outdoor Education,* American Association for Health, Physical Education, and Recreation, Washington, 1956.
Staples, Frank A.: *Arts and Crafts Program Manual,* National Recreation Association, New York, 1954.
Zanzig, Augustus D.: *Community and Assembly Singing,* National Recreation Association, New York, 1933.

VII. Organization and Administration Problems

Books

American Association for Health, Physical Education, and Recreation: *Developing Democratic Human Relations through Health, Physical Education, and Recreation,* Washington, 1951.
————: *Research Methods Applied to Health, Physical Education, and Recreation,* rev. ed., Washington, 1952.
Bachman, John W.: *How to Use Audio-Visual Materials,* Association Press, New York, 1956.
Baus, Herbert M.: *Publicity in Action,* Harper & Brothers, New York, 1954.
Johns, Ray: *Executive Responsibility,* Association Press, New York, 1954.
Levy, Harold P.: *Public Relations for Social Agencies,* Harper & Brothers, New York, 1956.
Meyer, Harold D., and Charles K. Brightbill: *Recreation Administration: A Guide to Its Practices,* Prentice-Hall, Inc., Englewood Cliffs, N. J., 1956.
Municipal Recreation Administration, rev. ed., International City Managers' Association, Chicago, 1948.
Punke, Harold H.: *Community Uses of Public School Facilities,* King's Crown Press, New York, 1951.
Rhyne, Charles S.: *Municipal Law,* National Institute of Municipal Law Officers, Washington, 1957.

Other Publications

Arnold, Serena: *Desirable Practice for the Administration of Consolidated Park and Recreation Departments,* American Institute of Park Executives, Wheeling, W. Va., 1957.

Bright, Sallie E.: *Public Relations Programs,* National Publicity Council for Health and Welfare, New York, 1950.

California Recreation Commission: *Public Recreation and Parks in California: Principles and Current Practices,* State Printing Office, Sacramento, Calif., 1957.

Checklist on How to Improve Municipal Services, International City Managers' Association, Chicago, 1958.

Church, David: *The Public Relations Committee,* National Publicity Council for Health and Welfare, New York, 1949.

Evaluation of a Boys' Club, Boys' Clubs of America, New York, undated. A committee report.

First on the Agenda: A Guide for Boards of Voluntary Agencies, Community Chests and Councils of America and the National Social Welfare Assembly, New York, 1954.

Leibee, Howard C.: *Liability for Accidents in Physical Education, Athletics, Recreation,* Ann Arbor Publishers, Ann Arbor, Mich., 1952.

McCune, Ellis: "Recreation and Parks," *Metropolitan Los Angeles: A Study in Integration,* The Haynes Foundation, Los Angeles, 1954.

National Recreation Association: *The ABC's of Public Relations for Recreation,* New York, 1946.

————: *Checklist for Recreation and Park Boards,* New York, undated.

————: *Financial Record Keeping,* New York, 1938. A committee report.

————: *A Guide to Books on Recreation,* New York. Issued annually.

————: *How to Conduct a Referendum Campaign,* New York, 1947.

————: *Know Your Community,* New York, 1955.

————: *Manual on Recording Services of Public Recreation Departments,* New York, 1954. A committee report.

————: *Recreation Topics Meriting Study or Research,* New York, 1957.

————: *Research in Recreation—Completed,* New York. Issued annually since 1954.

————: *Schedule for the Appraisal of Community Recreation,* rev. ed., New York, 1951.

Putting PR into HPER, American Association for Health, Physical Education, and Recreation, Washington, 1953.

Simpson, Gertrude: *Meeting the Press,* National Publicity Council for Health and Welfare, New York, 1955.

Stein, Herman D.: *Measuring Your Public Relations,* National Publicity Council for Health and Welfare, New York, 1952.

Van der Smissen, Betty: *State Laws for Parks and Recreation,* American Institute of Park Executives, Wheeling, W. Va., 1956.

INDEX